ELEANOR
OF AQUITAINE

AND THE FOUR KINGS

ELEANOR AND HENRY II · *The Cloisters, The Metropolitan Museum of Art*

ELEANOR
OF AQUITAINE

AND THE FOUR KINGS

BY AMY KELLY

PUBLISHED BY HARVARD UNIVERSITY PRESS

CAMBRIDGE · MASSACHUSETTS
LONDON · ENGLAND

LIBRARY OF CONGRESS CATALOG CARD NUMBER 50-6545

ISBN 0-674-24254-8

PRINTED IN THE UNITED STATES OF AMERICA

Preface

THIS ACCOUNT OF QUEEN ELEANOR and her century is offered as a study of individuals who set their stamp upon the events of their time, rather than as a study of developing systems of politics, economics, or jurisprudence. While it is hoped that it is conformable to what is known of institutions, it explores a different area, using many materials that the historian of institutions must perforce, for reasons of brevity and clarity, leave aside, yet which are a part of the tradition that is history in a wide sense.

The materials used are in general "contemporary" sources (those of the twelfth century, expanded by a decade or two at either end), and they include chronicles, biographies, literature — secular and ecclesiastic — epistles, and commentaries, in which the reader may see brought together in one account what the century says about itself. Occasionally incidents about the century recorded in later eras, but not found in the documents of the time, are included as tradition. I am, of course, greatly indebted to secondary sources, particularly for guidance to primary materials. Students who have worked with primary sources know that these records vary greatly in trustworthiness; it is beyond the scope of this book, however, to offer even a summary of the considerable critical work that has been done about twelfth-century writings. Suffice it to say that in that early period large borrowings without acknowledgment were common; some chroniclers were tempted, through the influence of patronage, self-interest, egotism, rancor, to select or distort facts; others were able, through favorable location or employment, to have firsthand knowledge of what they report, and scholarly evaluation has judged these latter writers generally reliable.

In the use of primary materials considerable effort has been made to discriminate between probable hearsay and probable fact, between gossip and authentic report, and frequent reference is made to sources so that the curious reader may set forth at any point upon critical excursions of his own. As much inference is required in a study of this kind as in a study of selected aspects of the time, but where inference is required to bridge gaps in the sources or to explain situations, it is indicated, with the sources on which it is based.

The twelfth century affords especially rich materials for such study. Persons representing important aspects of experience flourished in numbers —

Capets and Plantagenets, Becket, Saint Bernard, Abélard, troubadour poets, Guillaume le Maréchal, Héloïse — to cite a varied few. The time is marked by many stirrings — the intellectual revolt, the turn from Romanesque to Gothic, the impulse to crusade, the struggle between church and state, the rise of vernacular literature, and others. The urban culture of the great cities is distinctive.

Queen Eleanor knew all the personages; she was concerned with all the movements, to many of which she contributed notably; and she knew every city from London and Paris to Byzantium, Jerusalem, Rome, besides all those of her own provinces in western Europe. Her story, which runs through the last three quarters of the century, provides a "plot" almost as compact as that of a novel, for she was the center of the feud between the Capets and the Plantagenets that agitated the whole period and culminated in the collapse of the Angevin empire. Without historical distortion or any attempt to fictionize, her history brings the diverse elements together and into relation.

This work has been finished only with valuable assistance. First, I should like to thank certain scholars who on many matters have given me generously the benefit of their special knowledge: Professor Roger Sherman Loomis, Laura Hibbard Loomis, Professor Urban Tigner Holmes, Elizabeth McCracken, Professor Andrée Bruel, and the late Professor W. L. Bullock of the University of Manchester.

For research assistance I am indebted to reference librarians and archivists in many places, and to the libraries they represent for special privileges: the Library of Congress; the Peabody Library in Baltimore; the New York Public Library; the libraries of Princeton University and the General Theological Seminary, New York; the Boston Public Library; and especially the libraries of Harvard University — the collections of Houghton, Widener, and the Fogg Museum — and of Wellesley College. To Miss Margaret Boyce of the Wellesley College Library, my debt is beyond acknowledgment. Abroad I have enjoyed special courtesies at the Rylands Library, the Manchester Central Library, and the British Museum; and I have had assistance in the libraries and archives of Tours, Poitiers, Bordeaux, in the library of the University of Beirut, and in certain numismatic collections in Jerusalem.

I owe special gratitude to Mrs. W. S. Tower for her gift to the Wellesley Library of the twenty-four folio volumes of the *Recueil des historiens des Gaules et de la France*, which made it possible to work at home in fragments of leisure over several years; and to many others who have made rare books accessible to me; to friends who have traveled with me over most of the queen's itineraries in England and on the Continent and on her journeyings during the Second Crusade; to Helene B. Bullock, Vera Nabokov, Professor Elizabeth Hodder, Antoinette P. Metcalf, and Elizabeth Kelly, who, with others previously mentioned, have read the manuscript from various points of view; to Professor Helen Sard Hughes and Margaret Malcolm for practical assistance that has been a gift of time and energy.

Here I should like to acknowledge gratefully the permission of the Mediaeval Academy of America to use the substance of an article published in *Speculum*, January, 1937, entitled "Eleanor of Aquitaine and her Courts of Love"; and to Houghton Mifflin Company for permission to quote (pages 307–308 above) some lines from Henry Adams' translation of Coeur-de-Lion's *sirventés*. Unless otherwise indicated, translations in the text are mine. The end-paper map was drawn by Dr. Erwin Raisz of the Institute of Geographical Exploration at Harvard University, and I wish to thank him for his care and interest in preparing this chart.

AMY KELLY

Wellesley
1950

CONTENTS

1 The Rich Dower   1

2 O Paris!   10

3 Via Crucis   29

4 Fear the Greeks   40

5 Antioch the Glorious   52

6 Jerusalem   64

7 The Queen and the Duke   73

8 The Countess and the Poet   82

9 The Second Crown   91

10 Forging the Empire   104

11 King and Archbishop   113

12 Becket in Exile   124

13 Montmirail and Canterbury   134

14 The Flower of the World   150

15 The Court of Poitiers   157

16 Henry and His Sons   168

17 Sedition   179

18 Poor Prisoner   189

19 The Christmas Court   203

20 War Was in His Heart   213

21 Henry Revokes His Lands   224

22 The Fallen Elm of Gisors   236

23 The Lion Heart Is King   247

24 The Sicilian Interlude   257

25 Things Done Overseas   266

26 Shipwreck and Disguise   283

27 Eleanor Queen of England   288

28 The Ransom   300

29 Captive and Betrayer   319

30 The Treasure of Châlus   333

31 Lackland's Portion   345

32 Blanche and Isabella   356

33 Mirebeau   365

34 The Hope of Brittany   374

35 The Queen Goes Home   384

NOTES   389

BIBLIOGRAPHY   407

INDEX   417

ILLUSTRATIONS

ELEANOR AND HENRY II. *By permission of The Cloisters, The Metropolitan Museum of Art, New York.* FRONTISPIECE

Whether the fine commemorative sculptures of the twelfth century have the value of portraiture is a matter of differing opinion. But the tomb effigies of Fontevrault, like the sculptures of Chartres, have each an individuality that precludes the possibility of their being conventional or merely stylized figures. The representation of Eleanor most likely to be contemporary and authentic is that shown here from the Romanesque chapel in The Cloisters in New York. It is on a capital that came from the church of Langon near Bordeaux and is believed to be one of a number made to celebrate the progress which Eleanor and Henry made after their marriage in 1152 to efface from her domain the memory of Louis's overlordship. The head of Henry is paired with hers. Other such pairs can be found: one, for instance, in Saint André of Bordeaux, and one in the tiny church of Chaniers near Saintes; one also in England at the castle of Oakham in Rutlandshire. The one in The Cloisters is the finest of these. It shows the queen in the flower of her age and warrants all the chroniclers have recorded of her. The face is nobly intelligent, richly expressive, and distinctly pleasant. Gazing at it, one understands the descriptive words of poet and annalist: "welcoming," "charming" (*avenante*), "gallant" (*vaillante*), "of remarkable sagacity" (*admirabilis astuciae*).

MARRIAGE VASE. *Gift of Eleanor to Louis VII. The Louvre, Paris. Photograph, A. D. Braun and Company, Paris.* 20

The marriage vase of rock crystal ornamented with pearls and other stones is now preserved in the Louvre. It is the only object surviving that can be confidently associated with Eleanor. The Latin inscription on its base bears her name and declares that as a bride she gave it to Louis VII, and that (probably after the divorce) he gave it to the Abbé Suger, who dedicated it to service on the altar of Saint Denis.

KING AND QUEEN. *Chartres Cathedral, west portal jamb figures. Photograph, Les Archives photographiques d'art et d'histoire, Paris.* 21

The magnificent sculptures of Chartres went up on the west façade about the middle of the twelfth century. These highly individualized figures are said to represent the kings and queens of Judah. They are superbly regal. It has been suggested that, to the people of the century, these appeared as contemporary nobles returned from crusade, serving as models for Biblical prototypes. If this is true, one pair may well be assigned as representing Eleanor and Louis Capet. The "queen" here, as in the portrait of The Cloisters, looks out upon the world welcoming, gallant, admirably sagacious, mistress of herself; and the "king," gaunt, solemn, self-accusing, bends his gaze inward upon the appalling confusions of his own soul.

TOMB EFFIGIES OF HENRY II, ELEANOR, RICHARD, AND JOHN. 244

Henry, Eleanor, and Richard are buried at Fontevrault. John is entombed at Worcester Cathedral. Drawings reproduced from C. A. Stothard, *The Monumental Effigies of Great Britain,* J. Hewitt, ed. (new ed.; London, 1876).

APSE OF A TWELFTH-CENTURY CHURCH IN TALMONT. *Photograph by the author.* 245

This little church is near the site of the ancient ducal castle whose ruins are now washed by the tide.

ENTRANCE TO CASTLE OF ANGERS. *Photograph, Levy and Neurdein Reunis, Paris.* 245

NOTRE-DAME LA GRANDE IN POITIERS. 276

This church was begun in the twelfth century under the auspices of Eleanor.

NUNS' KITCHEN, ABBEY OF FONTEVRAULT. *Photograph, R. Dorange, Tours.* 276

This kitchen was built by Eleanor and endowed by Joanna Plantagenet.

SAINT PIERRE DE MONS. *Photograph by the author.* 276

This small church in Mons near Belin is said to have been built by Eleanor. In Belin the Dukes of Aquitaine maintained a château, which is locally claimed to be the birthplace of Eleanor, marking the route from Bordeaux to Saint James of Compostella. In this region the queen's reputation has suffered at the hands of clerical annalists, who relate the legend that she buried her "numerous bastards" in the churchyard at Mons.

MURAL IN THE TEMPLE CHURCH, LONDON. *Photograph, Fleming, London.* 277

The twelfth-century Temple Church was heavily damaged, and this mural certainly destroyed, in the bombings of London during the Second World War. The painting shows Stephen, Henry II, Henry the young king, Richard, and John. It was not contemporary, but made use of nearly contemporary materials. The figure of the young king, for instance, is from illuminations illustrating the life of Thomas Becket. Those Plantagenets dedicated to crusade hold models of the Holy Sepulcher.

TOMB EFFIGIES OF ELEANOR AND RICHARD AT FONTEVRAULT. *From Marcel Aubert,* La Sculpture française au moyen-âge *(Paris, 1946). Photograph, Les Archives photographiques d'art et d'histoire.* 277

Map by Dr. Erwin Raisz, Curator of Maps at the Institute of Geographical Exploration, Harvard University.

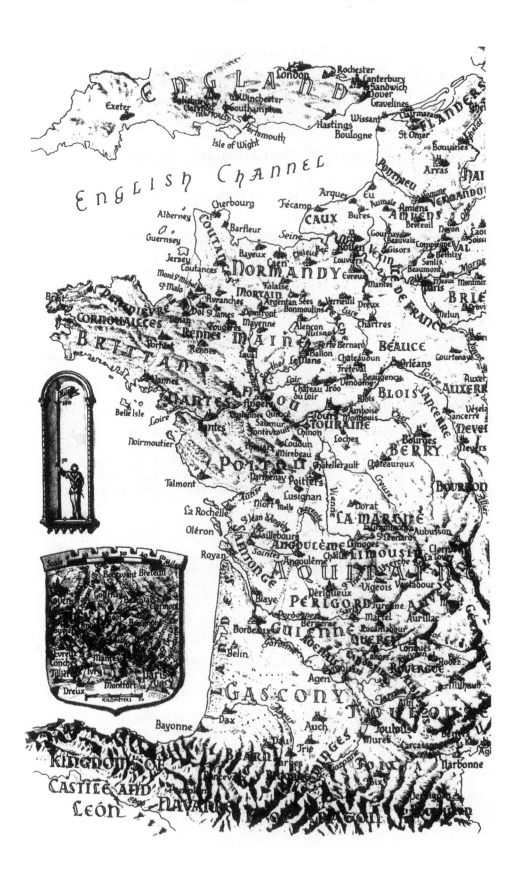

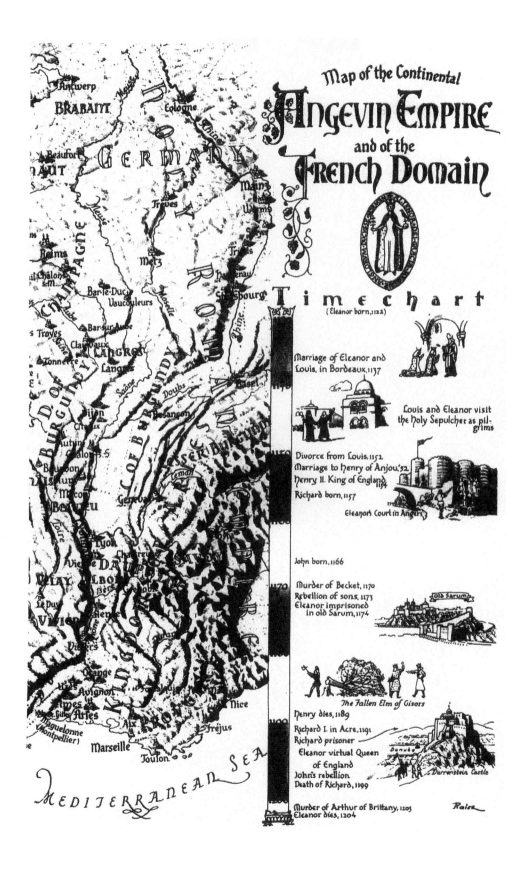

Map of the Continental

Angevin Empire

and of the

French Domain

Timechart
(Eleanor born, 1122)

Marriage of Eleanor and
Louis, in Bordeaux, 1137

Louis and Eleanor visit
the holy Sepulcher as pilgrims

Divorce from Louis, 1152
Marriage to henry of Anjou, '52
henry II. King of England
Richard born, 1157

Eleanor's Court in Angers

John born, 1166

Murder of Becket, 1170
Rebellion of sons, 1173
Eleanor imprisoned
in old Sarum, 1174

Old Sarum

The Fallen Elm of Gisors

henry dies, 1189

Richard I. in Acre, 1191
Richard prisoner
Eleanor virtual Queen
of England
John's rebellion
Death of Richard, 1199

Danube
Durrenstein Castle

Murder of Arthur of Brittany, 1203
Eleanor dies, 1204

Raisz

I ✚

The Rich Dower

LOUIS THE SIXTH OF FRANCE, Louis the Fat, lay sick in his hunting lodge at Béthizy, whither his bearers had brought him from the unprecedented heat and the fetid odors of the summer in Paris. He was not old — verging on sixty — but he was failing perceptibly. The chalky pallor, the bleared vision, the occasional palsy that had long marked him, were attributed to an abortive attempt of his stepmother, Queen Bertrade, to dispose of him by poison in his early years. Latterly he had grown so ponderous that he could no longer mount a horse or stoop to lace a shoe. About him in the sultry room were gathered some of his prelates and barons palatine, chief among them his lifelong friend and counselor, Abbé Suger. A confessor stood by prepared to administer the sacrament *in extremis*.[1]

It was an ill-chosen time to assail the king with matters of the utmost urgency. Yet in the antechamber certain knights who had posted over the burning leagues of western Europe from Bordeaux were impatiently awaiting royal deliberations on business they had brought from the greatest fief dependent upon the crown. Briefly this was their affair.

Louis's most difficult feudatory, Guillaume, Count of Poitou and Duke of Aquitaine, had, by a culmination of disasters, come to an untimely end in the course of an Easter pilgrimage to the shrine of Saint James of Compostella, and had already for some weeks lain buried at the foot of the saint's altar in far-off Galicia.[2] The fact of his death had been discreetly concealed. It was not yet widely known even in his own provinces. Guillaume, who was distinguished by a special intransigence, had in his last hours been at swords' points with certain of his own vassals. It was even said that he had gone as a pilgrim to Spain for no other reason than to bespeak the puissant aid of Saint James against his enemies at home, and that his sudden death had providentially saved the Limousin from a drenching with blood.[3] Guillaume was only thirty-eight and might have been expected to worry along in his very perfunctory allegiance to the King of France for many years to come, while Louis busied himself with other pressing matters. But his early death in 1137 brought the king face to face with problems that could not be postponed.

Guillaume's only heirs were two daughters. Eleanor, the elder, was a girl (*jeune pucelle*) scarcely fifteen. This young duchess, with her legacy of violent and unfinished quarrels, was King Louis's vassal, his lawful marriage prize to bestow as best suited his interests. But she was, in the circumstances, a prize to be quickly gathered in, for by reason of the anarchy that reigned in her provinces, she was more than likely to be·rapt away by some rebel baron of her own vassalage, who might thus make himself a formidable rival of the king.[4]

It was of the inestimable treasure of Poitou and Aquitaine in its material sense that Louis and the barons of France discoursed in Béthizy. The great Capetian was a sober and practical king. His physical handicaps might seem to reveal a weakling; yet steadily for long years he had advanced the interests of his people, pressed outward the boundaries of his domain, curbed a presumptuous vassalage, and made his court a bulwark of Christendom, a bar of feudal justice, a seat of philosophy. For the twenty-nine years of his reign his central policy had been to build up from adjoining fiefs a solid royal domain. He was at the moment watching with apprehensive eye the growing Angevin pretensions in Normandy, which lay athwart both his own lands and those of the late Count Guillaume. What could be more propitious than the peaceful acquisition of Poitou and Aquitaine, which would more than double his lands and enable him to close, like a pair of gigantic scissors, on the provinces of Geoffrey the Fair, Count of Anjou?

Who could gainsay the plain duty of the king in the crisis to attach the Duchy of Aquitaine, the County of Poitou, by the strongest possible feudal ties to the royal domain? And when were ever duty and interest more consonant? Having taken counsel with the wise men gathered about his couch, the King of the Franks summoned his namesake heir. He described to the prince the excellence of the duchess' dowry, the reputed merits of her person, and unfolded to the youth his manifest destiny.

Louis Capet, the Young, had not originally been designated for the brilliant fortune that now awaited him. As second son of Louis the Fat, he had been bred in the cloister of Notre Dame for one of those ecclesiastical preferments reserved for younger brothers.[5] His senior, Philip, had been anointed as the future King of France. But these arrangements had been inscrutably changed in the twinkling of an eye, and by a very humble agency. Philip, riding in Paris with an escort on an autumn day in the neighborhood of the Grève, had aroused from the ooze of the Seine a vagrant sow, which, floundering between the legs of his horse, had caused it to stumble and fall. The precious prince had been carried, broken and senseless, to a burger's house along the quay, and had there died without recovering consciousness for confession or viaticum. Thereupon Louis, a boy of ten, was brought blinking from the cloister and anointed by the Pope himself as successor of the Capets in the royal cathedral of Reims. The youth had been thus suddenly in a single night translated from the highest spiritual to the highest temporal prospects.[6]

The prince who had thus been retrieved from the cloister, although the rigors of monastic disciplines had already laid hold of him, appears to have been wholly docile toward the plan to provide him with a dowry and a wife. An accident had designated him as king, and another chance as strange now six years later more than doubled his realm and offered him a duchess in whom, from all he could learn, he would be fortunate in every way. The conviction that he had been summoned by heaven from the renunciations of the cloister to some august service in the world bore in upon him. Everything gave him to think himself a dedicated instrument. By some strange moving of destiny he had been called to be a king; but he would never forget that he had first made his vows to champion the church and renounce the world.

✣

In view of the disorders in Aquitaine and the crisis certain to ensue if Count Guillaume's death became known among his enemies, Louis the Fat perceived that haste was of the essence of his enterprise. Such an escort as should put the fear of the Capets into the brigandly vassals of Poitou and Aquitaine was speedily made ready for the prince. Five hundred of the *preux chevaliers* of the French domain were summoned, the most imposing, the richest, the best. None was spared by reason of age or dignity from going down to Bordeaux in the insufferable heat to fetch the duchess to Paris — not the great Thibault of Champagne himself, nor Abbé Suger, nor the king's cousin, Raoul de Vermandois, nor the Count of Nevers, nor any other knight of importance.[7]

While the escort was assembling, the sick king took the prince in hand, preparing him as best he might for the role thrust prematurely upon him. In looks Louis the Young was comely and well set, tall, with a slender boy's figure and courteous mien. Blond locks fell upon his shoulders, and he looked out upon the world with mild azure eyes. The youth was every way a credit to Abbé Suger, who had directed his education, for he felt the compulsion of nobility to be virtuous.[8] He had some of the humility of the oblate still clinging about him, which his more recent knightly disciplines had failed to eradicate. However, he was well endowed and personable as befitted his fortunes. The king counseled his son to comport himself on the journey at all times with dignity and justice, to pay his way liberally, to offer no offense by billeting his troops, as he might have claimed a feudal right to do, in the territories of the duchess. He warned him against putting his precious life in jeopardy by any show of violence against the turbulent vassals of Poitou and Aquitaine. He provided rich coffers in the hands of Thibault of Champagne and Abbé Suger, who were designated as the prince's special mentors. And at last he gave his son, with his blessing, a royal gift of jewels for the Duchess Eleanor.

Setting out from Paris in mid-June, the prince and his escort took a route midway between Toulouse and Angoulême, avoiding the scenes of Count Guillaume's recent encounters with his enemies. It was said that the heat obliged the cortege to travel by night, and this is perhaps why they arrived in Limoges, apparently without heralding, in time for the feast of Saint Martial, the patron of that province. They had made the expedition from Paris in less than a month. It seems to have been from Limoges, still more than a week's journey from Bordeaux, that the rumor of Count Guillaume's death and the advent of the French king's cavalcade spread far and wide. But if there had been barons bold enough at the moment of Guillaume's death to seize the duchess, none dared to stir with the Capetian's men-at-arms on the road southward from Limoges.[9]

In the burning heat the French cavaliers pressed on, though suffering horse and man. Their supplies melted, says the chronicler, like wax. They passed through Périgueux and arrived at length on the east bank of the Garonne, opposite the ducal city. Before the middle of July they debouched from the low wooded hills of Larmont and pitched their colored pavilions on the level stretches by the river. From his royal tent, sown with the lilies of France, the prince could look westward when the sun went low upon the moon-shaped bend of the Garonne where Bordeaux sat enthroned, moated among rivers and girdled with towers. Above the crenelated walls loomed the domes of Saint André and the square towers and bastions of the palace of the Ombrière, from some one of which he could not doubt the duchess looked out upon the stir of his encampment. The next day the prince and his escort crossed the river.

⚜

The Poitevins are full of life, able as soldiers, brave, nimble in the chase, elegant in dress, handsome, sprightly of mind, liberal, hospitable.

Twelfth-century Pilgrim's Guide

The Duchess Eleanor was a prize to draw the covetous attention of ambitious nobles, for the patrimony she inherited from her forebears was one of the goodliest of the feudal world.[10] It spread from the river Loire to the foothills of the Pyrenees, from the central heights of Auvergne to the western ocean. It was wider and fairer than that of her overlord, the King of France himself; ampler and more gracious than the counties which the Dukes of Normandy held north of the Loire; richer and more genial than the island of Britain, where Stephen of Blois wore the crown of the Norman conquerors. The fief of the duchess was rich and desirable in itself; but its special importance was that its addition, through the marriage of its heiress to any other domain in western Europe, would raise that domain to preëminence over all the others.

The contours of the land itself gave scope for the florescence of a feudal aristocracy. It is sharply accented especially in the south, marked by ridges and buttes, towering, sudden, sheer, where the seigneurs of the regime withdrew themselves and there, islanded aloft in pride and security, overlooked the river courses, the crossroads, and the tangle of lesser thoroughfares cutting the woodlands and the arable plains they held in fee. Aquitaine is said to have its name from the abundance of its waters. On a map the Garonne looks like a great fern graven in the earth, the stalk its course, the leaflets its numerous tributaries, all offering easy routes of intercourse. Farther north the Loire is stem to a more straggling system watering a wide, inviting land. The river networks, the striking tors, interspersed with fertile plains, both suggest and emphasize the character of feudal society. In the day of the Duchess Eleanor this society was, as a way of life, passing its brilliant prime.

Some fragrance of the ancient Roman culture that had been extinguished or absorbed in other European centers still lingered in Bordeaux. In its schools and the riverain villas of the deep south, where its scholars and philosophers took their leisure, there still bloomed some late roses of that summer. The ducal court itself was a center of diffusion for an art and a civility that spread among the great fiefs of the river valleys and along the busy thoroughfare from Tours to the Pyrenees. For the Counts of Poitou were not merely soldiers and administrators. The duchess's forebear, Guillaume V, the Grand, in the midst of heavy campaigns, gave his nights to reading. Alone throughout long evenings, he conned the treasury of books he had acquired by exchange with other potentates, or by loan from the great monastic libraries of Limoges and Cluny.[11] Eleanor's grandfather, Guillaume IX, composed and gave vogue to the new vernacular poetry of the troubadours, and his verse itself gives evidence of his roving mind and foot and the widest liberality of view. Through it shine glints of Ovidian sophistry and the rich romantic colors of Moorish Spain. It is a poetry highly organized in form, intellectually subtle, lusty, piquant, cynical, the pastime of a worldling, who lived each day with gusto, dined well, slept heartily, and recked little of the awful day of judgment. These and other forebears as illustrious were heroes of those rhymed tales, the *chansons de geste*, recited not only in the high places of Poitou and the Limousin, but in all the courts of Europe. The family had founded Cluny, that "pleasance of the angels,"[12] and they had seated popes in Rome; but more often the dukes were found supporting antipopes, scourging their local bishops, and abetting the schisms that sprang up abundantly on the soil of Aquitaine. Altogether the mind of the young duchess had been freely exposed to a great variety of ideas and made hospitable to novelty.

The duchess herself was no liability to her rich dower. She was no simple marriage prize to be gathered in by the Capets for her weight in gold. She claimed descent from Charlemagne, whose effigy was still borne on the coins of Poitou, and knew herself the heiress of a great tradition, who could acquire no incomparable luster from the marriage decreed for her by circumstance.

When her grandfather, the famous troubadour, returned from his disastrous crusade early in the century in a very cynical mood, he found his countess, Philippa of Toulouse, taken up with one of those religious movements perennially arising on the soil of Aquitaine. Being at the time less than usually inclined to spiritual restoratives, he abandoned his lady with her innocent nose in a breviary and rapt away the Countess of Châtellerault to enliven his middle years.[13] The new countess was the mother of a daughter Anor by her previous marriage; and this demoiselle the troubadour married to his own heir, born of Philippa. It was a marriage designed to canalize the ducal fortunes, sadly diminished by the disasters *outre-mer*. Of this union the Duchess Eleanor was born in 1122 in some high place of the far south (Bordeaux and Belin both claim her birth site), and she was named after her mother, as the legend says, Alia-Anor, or as history has chosen to call her, Eleanor.[14] There was a sister Petronilla, and a brother Agret; but the boy and his mother Anor died in the Talmont while Eleanor was still a child.

That the young heiress was fair enough to content any king appears from subsequent accounts. "Charming," "welcoming" and "lively" (*avenante, vaillante, courtoise*) are the words used by the chroniclers to portray her.[15] While the Prince of France had been indentured to canons and abbés to learn his destined role as archbishop, Eleanor had made another use of time. What the magnates of the prince's escort noted especially when they met her in Bordeaux was her maturity of mind. She had grown in the enlightened traditions of her family. Her education had not of course furnished her with the orderly intellectual baggage fit for an abbess. Though doubtless, like all the heirs of her race, she had had her tutors, her real school had been a varied experience. Movement with the itinerant ducal family from castle to castle had afforded that training in taste and judgment that comes from frequent contrast of persons, places, things. Though but fifteen, and therefore the prince's junior by two years, in practical experience, in that decisiveness gained from instant appraisals, she far outdistanced him. Her education had taught her especially to be intolerant of ennui.

As a girl she must have traveled much with the peripatetic household from the foothills of the Pyrenees to the Loire on those long *chevauchées* made necessary by the ducal business of overlooking intriguing vassals and presumptuous clergy, and carrying law and justice to the remoter corners of creation. She knew a land of mellow harvests, where grain shocks bent like humble homagers; of forests dark at noon; of scarped heights where the baronial strongholds loomed with their clustering mud hamlets; the vast agglomerations of the abbeys, their mills, salt marshes, vineyards, wine and olive presses, their fantastic dovecotes and apiaries spread along garden walls.

She knew the aspect of the red-roofed towns, and the traffic of each one, here a fair, there a market; here a lazar house, there a hostel thronging with pilgrims returning from Saint James or the shrines of the pious Limousin. Familiar were the domes of Saint Jean d'Angély showing from afar as the road wound in; familiar the church of Saint Eutrope of Saintes, its dark Romanesque nave cut across with swords of sunlight, the great collegials of Limoges. Melle she knew where there was a mint, and Blaye, where, in the glow of forges, armorers repaired their traveling gear; and Maillezais, where her aunt, the Abbess Agnes, never failed to halt the ducal progress for a largess. At the end of *chevauchée* she found herself in motley assemblies of castellans, bishops, abbots, merchant princes, poets, travelers, and all the entertainers and hangers-on that gave an outward air of careless wealth and gaiety to a solid program of feudal business.

⚜

Of course, the emotions of the prince and the duchess were of no concern to the chroniclers. Later events suggest that Louis was somewhat more transported by his fortunes than Eleanor; but even she would not have thought of questioning manifest destiny. Like all feudal marriages, the union of the young pair was a purely rational matter. The duchess simply went with her fiefs, and she went, as befitted her rich patrimony, to the proudest station in Europe. Louis's cloistral disciplines had not aptly equipped him for the functions thrust upon him in the ducal court. In those days of his awakening, he dismayed his mentors by unpredictable conduct, now headlong, now uneasy and diffident, as if already, in the secret citadel of his being, the king did violence to the archbishop, and the archbishop accused the king.

Two weeks elapsed before the vassals of the south could be gathered from the corners of Gascony and Poitou to do homage to their new overlord.[16] Even then some of the most powerful, through fear or umbrage, stayed away. In spite of the heat and their fatigues, we are told that the barons of France enjoyed such feasts as Seneca and Terence could hardly have described.[17] They tasted the fish, salt meadow mutton, and planked meats for which the land was famous, and quaffed the red, white, and amber vintages of Poitou and the Limousin. They viewed Bordeaux, that polished cornerstone of Europe, its abundant churches, its rich relics of Charlemagne and his paladins, its semitropical gardens, embellished with tiles and fountains, the flotillas of its maritime trade moving on the bosom of the Garonne, the gay and rich disorder of the palace of the Ombrière.

At last, on a Sunday of midsummer, the nuptials were celebrated in the church of Saint André.[18] Through streets where housefronts were hung with tapestries and banners and green boughs went processions with tabor and flute. The decorous chant of choristers mingled with the gross epithalamia of the people, who stamped out the rhythms with their sabots in the cobbled squares and shouted "Plentë, plentë," as if their duchess were a common bride. In the dimness of the church, its rounded apse blazing with tapers, its vaults clouded with incense, its domes gathering the chant of choirs, the prince and the duchess, having fasted and confessed, were married in the presence of their vassals by Geoffrey, Archbishop of Bordeaux. After the sacrament Louis put on the coronet of the Dukes of Aquitaine.

From the tables spread with the wedding feast the royal escort rose hastily, leaving the populace drowsed with satiety in the midday heat. The *mesnies* of the duke and the duchess were already assembled on the far side of the Garonne on the road for Poitiers. Eleanor's withdrawal from her southern city with a troop armed cap-a-pie was very like a flight. Avoiding the roads overlooked by the fortresses of Duke Guillaume's enemy vassals, the cavalcade pressed on until they had put the river Charente between themselves and ambush. Two leagues above Saintes the huge castle of Taillebourg, the stronghold of the loyal Geoffroi de Rançon, loomed reassuringly. Here aloft above the valley, whence the land stretched away in the burning distance, Louis and Eleanor were first left alone to explore each other's thoughts and talk of the high destiny to which they had been so abruptly summoned.[19]

At the beginning of August the cortege reached Poitiers, and the duchess and her bridegroom lodged in the ancestral palace of the Counts of Poitou, in the beautiful tower of Maubergeonne, which Eleanor's grandfather, Guillaume the troubadour poet, had built for the Countess of Châtellerault. In Poitiers, says Abbé Suger, the duke and duchess were received by clergy and populace with transports of joy. Here Louis put on the coronet of the Counts of Poitou, and the pair and their escort lingered for some days to receive the homage of certain laggard vassals not eager to give allegiance to their new overlord.[20]

While the reluctant homagers delayed the cavalcade in Poitiers, the King of the Franks, laboring in extremity, "ended his life-days in the world." Messengers posting over the bridge of Moutierneuf brought the news from Béthizy. Louis the Fat, the astute king who never slept, was dead. There had been no time to realize his wish to die in the guise of a monk. But in his last hour he had called for a carpet strewn with ashes. On this rude bed, after confession and viaticum, he had stretched out his arms to simulate a cross, and so had made his end. He had not stayed to greet his dear son, nor to turn his dim eyes upon the Duchess Eleanor, nor to confirm the rich accession to his fiefs.[21]

It thus befell that when the Duchess of Aquitaine came to Paris in the late summer of 1137, she arrived as Queen of the Franks. Her escort led her amongst tall houses thrusting their narrow fronts upon the crooked streets. She came at last to royal gates thrown open to admit her to a precinct in which uprose the dim old palace that had lodged the Merovingian kings. A long flight of marble steps, worn hollow by all the vassalage of France, ascended to the tower of the Capets. Beside an ancient olive tree, where the Kings of France were wont to dismount from their horses, the weary duchess at last alighted and went up the stairs to take her place in history.

2 ✠

O Paris!

To know is more than to believe.
> Clement of Alexandria

O queen among cities, O island of royal palaces, whereon Philosophy hath set her ancient seat, Philosophy who alone, with study her sole companion, holds the city of light and immortality, and sets her victorious foot on the withering flower of the fast-aging world.
> Guy de Bazoches, *Éloge de Paris*, translated by Helen Waddell

THE YOUNG QUEEN OF FRANCE was familiar with archaic cities built from Roman ruins and worn with the immemorial uses of long vanished generations. But her new capital crowded on its little island in the Seine had the appearance of very long survival. It had not yet shaken off its Merovingian decay nor felt the refashioning stir of the Renaissance in its ancient fabric.

The city on the Île gathered about two quarters, that of the archbishop and that of the king.[1] The domain of the archbishop in the eastern end centered about the old basilica of Notre Dame that then still stood near the site where the modern cathedral now lifts its towers. Louis the Fat had lately expended treasure to repair its sagging roof. Around it, in the episcopal purlieus and on the margin of the parvis, lodged the prelates and the canons. In the royal quarter in the western end, the Capets still held their court in the ancient tower and precincts of the Merovingian kings. There rose the fortress pile that "shouldered above the roofs of the whole city,"[2] tunneled with dim passages and hollow stairs giving access to somber rooms and glowering chambers that seemed quarried from the solid stone. From deep embrasures admitting shafts of sunlight or little areas of stars, the solar looked down upon the embankment of the Seine, whence ascended by day the cries of boatmen and by night the songs of students turning in from their pothouse congregations to the hostels provided in the quarter by the bounty of the king. Beyond the palace a little garden plot set with figs and cypresses, trellised vines and shrubbery, extended to the tip of the Île, where the divided currents of the Seine rejoined and moved onward in a broad stream toward Rouen and the sea.

Outside the walled citadels of the archbishop and the king the Île was crowded with churches great and small, their façades storied with the epic of salvation wrought in shining mosaics or dim carvings; with sprawling cloisters; with the huddled *fenestrae* of the Jewry; with taverns and lodgings and the eating places of swarming students; with the dwellings of burghers thrusting their nodding upper stories over streets no wider than a corridor and crooked as a maze. Above the lively traffic of the thoroughfares, among the steep gables and tiled roofs where pigeons wheeled, there was a frequent clamor of bells overlying each other in a kind of round or descant, in which the denizens of the Île and the *faubourgs* discerned the brazen voices, big or thin, calling the roster of their parish saints: Saint Peter and Saint John; Saint Stephen and Saint Bartholomew; Saint Denis and Saint Christopher; Saint Croix and Saint Marine; Saint Martial and Saint Eloi; and discoursing amidst them all, they heard the mistress voice of Notre Dame. The portals of the sanctuaries moved to and fro for the worshipers, letting out to the world drafts of incense and the fading murmurs of plain song: *Et nunc, et semper, et in saecula saeculorum, amen.*

The corners of the streets were angles of surprise, where a bread or a fish cart ran plump into the equipage of a baron or a bishop; where a pot-boy or a poor scholar collided with some famous doctor of the schools. Everywhere passengers avoided milch goats and roving swine. The old Roman paving stones, worn and askew, made beds for mud and household bilge, for dust and refuse, and scavengers with great rakes and besoms were forever raising stench and shifting filth from hole to hole. Never were the proud affirmation of man's immortality and the moldy evidences of his transiency so closely juxtaposed.

An old Roman wall had once encircled the Île and the segments that remained were here and there cut away to give landings; and in these places, near bridges, even under their very arches, mill wheels churned the waters of the Seine. On the river the noisy traffic came and went, fish wherries and ferryboats and the slow barges from Mantes or Rouen laden with merchandise — millet and cattle, hides, faggots, turf, rushes, wattle-osiers, salt, wax, and wine.

Two stone bridges moored the Île to the farther banks of the Seine, where the expanding new city spread on either side amidst spacious orchards and vineyards. On the north, near the royal palace, the Grand Pont linked the island with the commercial area from whose concessions the king drew rich revenues. Here the corporations, the butchers, the bakers, tanners and clothiers, ironmongers and carpenters, bellfounders, hemp-dressers and potters — those craftsmen wise in their work without whom cities can neither be builded nor inhabited — plied their arts and sold their wares. In the little stalls on the bridge itself the licensed money-changers jangled their coins to hawk their trade and weighed the money of Paris against the coinage of London and Anjou, Venice and Cologne.

On the southern side, debouching from the parvis of Notre Dame and the episcopal domain, the Petit Pont joined the Île with the more rustic left bank of the Seine; and here the schools, outgrowing the narrow space and doctrinal authority of Notre Dame, had found a refuge for philosophy. This smaller bridge, says one of the scholars, was given over to strollers and disputers in logic. Along the quays the doctors walked, and in little exedrae open to the sun, students feeling themselves poised on the ripe end of time and heirs of all the ages discussed the latest heresies or weighed Plato against the doctors of the church. In the shallow houses on the bridge itself lodged the apothecaries, and in the rooms overhead the doctors discoursed of "universals" to audiences that overflowed upon the entries and the stairs.

In Paris these "nations" of scholars were distinguished from each other by legible marks of provincial dress and accent. There were scores of hard-drinking English in fur-lined coats and leather hose; brawling Germans in toploftical fur hats; Burgundians brutal and thick-headed; Bretons impudent, frivolous, full of song; the native Franks, foppish and arrogant; men of Béarn, challenging all and sundry with their dry quips; Italians richly dressed in oriental stuffs; Champagnois, men of Flanders and Normandy — the yeast and ferment of the world.[3] Master Abélard, it was said, had emptied the episcopal schools of Chartres and Reims and Laon, and drawn the flower of creation to Paris. And these flocked there, declares the chronicler,[4] not only because of the delightsomeness of the place and the abundance of good things to be found there, but because of the air of freedom that prevailed and because all manner of instruction was there provided, the seven liberal arts, civil and canon law, medicine and theology.

All these young men, merging the dialects of distant provinces in a muddy Latin, swarmed together in noisy independence under no common discipline, in unsupervised places where they were free to think, drink, love, and fight, according to their humor. In the lecture rooms on the Petit Pont and on the left bank in the leafy groves of academe, the masters and scholars of Paris ransacked the lore of the ancient world, defined the "universals," and clinched their dialectic with the syllogism. To have no knowledge of Aristotle and the fathers of the church, no dogma, to have no art in framing syllogisms was to live the darkling life of a mole in Paris. The prime concerns of the city were intellectual. The breath of its life was controversy.

"When we speak," said the doctors, "in universal terms of class and category, do these terms correspond to realities existing outside the mind? When we speak of the species *man* and the species *animal*, do these terms awaken ideas of *collection*? But does the idea of *collection* correspond to a reality outside the mind, or is it a mere concept of the mind? And if these terms, or 'universals,' are not mere concepts, but do correspond to realities, what is their nature? Are they corporeal entities? And further, what is their mode of existing? Do they have their being outside the sensual domain, that is, outside the individual, or do they lodge within?"[5]

Young men with the lust of life in them went without their suppers and consumed their last inch of candle wax to snare universals, corporeal or incorporeal. They devised syllogisms fortified with citations, chapter and verse, from Aristotle or Plato or fathers of the church.

Thomas Becket and John of Salisbury were giving their young minds to philosophy in Paris in those days. To John one of the masters wrote reminiscently long after, of the city on the Seine: "How apt art thou, O Paris, to bewitch and seduce! There was an affluence of men suave and agreeable, an abundance of all good things, gay streets, rare food, incomparable wine."[6] John, dwelling in one of his letters to Becket on his student days, recalls that in Paris he saw abundance of life, popular joy, a crowd of philosophers absorbed in studies. As he listened to the celestial discourse of the doctors, he was moved with admiration and bethought him of Jacob's ladder whereon angels mounted and descended.[7] Men who were in Paris in the mid-century were stirred with a kind of ecstasy by the vision that opened to the mind.

❧

Les Francs à la bataille, les Provençaux aux vivres.
Raoul of Caen

The young king and queen, arriving in 1137 to rule over the city of light, at first made little impression beyond the precincts of the palace. Because of his youth, Louis was put back, after his marriage, to his studies and his cloistral disciplines. He returned to his masters and to the steadying routine of Notre Dame and learned to improve his natural gifts by industry. On Fridays he fasted with the monks on bread and water; he kept the vigils; he sang in choir and was never so much himself as when he stood to read the canticles. The youth was so pious, so kind, so mild, that a person, unless he knew him, would not guess from the simplicity of his dress and his demeanor that he was king, but might suppose him some monk. He loved justice above all things, and his conversation and behavior would have done credit to a priest. Louis was often seen in the church of Notre Dame, following after the bishop and looking about to make sure that he was displacing no clerk or scholar, or even any insignificant worshiper. There was about him a dovelike sweetness and humility. He was so meek that any monk might precede him to his stall.[8] For the young king pursuing his studies there were few interruptions; only now and then some crisis called for a sporadic exercise of royal authority.

We do not know expressly that Queen Eleanor shared in counterpart her lord's monastic disciplines. However, to fit her for her high pretensions in the court of the Franks, there would have been need to improve her use of the *langue d'oïl* spoken in the Île, her knowledge of local hagiography and of the Capetian dynasty, about which she was sure to have entertained many erroneous notions acquired in random ways in the rival courts of her forebears. It seems certain that she mastered the rudiments of dialectic and examined the structure of the syllogism, for she was able later in her own behalf to cite Scripture, chapter and verse, even to popes and cardinals, and to employ the syllogism with good effect in Rome and Tusculum.

At the time of her debut, beguiling specimens of Aristotelian logic were going the rounds in Paris, perhaps designed, some of them, for the exercise of nuns. There were formulae applicable to the unresolved question as to whether the Blessed Virgin had mastered the trivium and the quadrivium; whether the *langue d'oïl* was the language of paradise; and there were tricky little contrivances to prove that even logic can lie, such as that poser, popular in garrets where starveling students met, which proved that six breakfast eggs were twelve. Dialectic settled the puzzle as to whether the pig that is being taken to market is held by the driver or the rope, as to whether goat's hair may be called wool. A shield is white on one side, black on the other. What color does it boast? Exercises like these made learning lovable and accessible to the wayfaring intelligence of women. Anyone desiring enlightenment, said Peter of Blois, ought to resort to Paris, where the most inextricable knots were unsnarled. In those days the queen was surely not vainly losing her time.

On certain days the king's gardens were thrown open to the schools, and there in the sweet open air, in the shade of the cypresses, with the Seine sparkling on either side, the masters held their disputations. That the kingdom of the mind was open to women in Paris we know from Abélard, who at that very time had been giving fresh charm to study. He himself boasted that noble ladies flocked to his lectures,[9] and Héloïse tells how they twitched aside their wimples or pressed to windows but to see him passing in the street.[10] If the queen developed no such erudition in Paris as had betrayed Héloïse to the Paraclete in this world and to perdition in the next, she at least dipped into the refreshing currents of her time.

But if in the Île as a whole the new monarchs at first made themselves little felt, there were presently agitations in the limited palace precincts that troubled the clerical mentors of the dynasty. The young queen, as a matter of course, brought a household with her. The Poitevins, says the Frankish chronicler, "were better feeders than fighters." The ménage was expensive, and the ecclesiastical entourage of the Capets found much of it superfluous. However, it was not the Poitevins who presently retired in order to simplify the establishment. It was the dowager queen, Agnes of Maurienne, who, relieved of much of her marriage portion, withdrew with her retinue to one of her dower castles in Champagne. Thereupon the Poitevins stretched their legs more comfortably in the palace, and such of the monastic entourage as weathered the change were introduced willy-nilly to aspects of secular life that had found no place in the sober court of Louis the Fat.[11]

It is noteworthy as suggesting the young queen's influence in Paris, that Louis's first essays in his kingly role were in vindication of the titles he had assumed as Duke of Aquitaine and Count of Poitou. In these matters he seems to have swung surprisingly free from those clerical controls that kept him generally in the straight and narrow way, and to have acted with a kind of Poitevin simplicity of purpose. There appeared no question of his valor. The stripling king in person led an army to the County of Toulouse, which Eleanor never ceased to claim as heir of her grandmother, Philippa of Toulouse, and he brought back a temporary settlement of her claims; he quenched an uprising to establish a commune in her capital of Poitiers; and with his own arm he hacked off the hands of some of Eleanor's recreant vassals in the Talmont.[12]

The affair in Poitiers developed such fury under Louis's unchecked initiative that Abbé Suger himself was forced to post from Saint Denis in all haste to mitigate the king's severity. Before he reached the outskirts of the city, the abbé was met by delegations from the populace, who prostrated themselves before him with groans and supplications. In the square before the ducal palace, Louis had obliged the burghers to assemble their heirs, each with a cartload of baggage, for exile from Poitou. Their lamentations, which rose to heaven day and night, seemed not to reach the chamber of the obdurate king. It was as if Louis and Eleanor, in the course of their studies in Paris, had lifted ideas from the dreadful story of the Minotaur. Only with difficulty the abbé persuaded his ward to renounce his desperate scheme.[13]

In all these enterprises the king displayed the stubborn and reckless valor that sometimes masks profound indecision. But these secular acts, though straws in the wind, failed at first to arouse the custodians of the Île. Paris was shaken by larger issues, and it was only when the young sovereigns emerged upon their theater that the guardians of authority took alarm. But at last the king and queen broke upon the spiritual stillness of the Abbé of Clairvaux.

⚜

Abbé Bernard was hot in burning love, humble in conversation, a well of flowing doctrine, a pit in deepness of science, and well-smelling in sweetness of fame.

Golden Legend

On the threshold of his theology he [Abélard] defines faith as private judgment, as though in these mysteries, everyone is allowed to think and speak as he pleases; as though the mysteries of our faith were to hang uncertainly in the midst of shifting and varying opinion. Is not our hope baseless if our faith is subject to inquiry?

Abbé Bernard to Pope Innocent

In the diocese of Sens, of which Paris was a part, the most exciting diversions of the mid-century were the tournaments in diálectic in which the masters of disputation met each other in public combat over some proposition bequeathed to posterity by a Greek philosopher or a father of the church. If the proposition involved a possible heresy challenged by some famous doctor of the schools, not even the cathedrals could contain the crowds of every sort that drew to the arena. The triumph of champions spread to the verge of the Continent, and even dabblers in logic sharpened their wits on the minor syllogisms that flew off the main argument like sparks from the forge. The issues of public debate were discussed in Chartres and Laon and Bologna, and wherever the seven liberal arts and the canon law held sway. The occasions, moreover, drew the feudal orders to places of common resort, enabled boors to stare without hindrance upon bishops and nobles, and these to survey the motley objects of their ministries. Even if the syllogism flew above the ceiling of some men's intellect, the stress of combat could be felt by anyone with eyes and ears as plainly as if the disputants wielded the weapons of tournament.

It was in 1136 that the church was mortally assailed by the heresies of Master Peter Abélard, who had suddenly returned to his old haunts in Paris from his exile in Brittany and the obscure wanderings to which his calamities had condemned him. Abélard's *Discourse on the Trinity*, which had been burned fifteen years before by the authority of the church in Soissons, had risen from its ashes revamped but not amended, and Abélard himself, without metropolitan authority, was preaching his false doctrine. When he was rebuked by the bishops for not planting his discourse on authority, he answered defiantly that reason, as well as faith, was the gift of God, and that a text itself was sufficient for its own explanation with reason for a guide.[14] He marshaled scores of instances in which the apostles and the fathers of the church contradicted each other in stating the very foundations of our faith, and he held that these contradictions ought to be examined and resolved in the light of reason. His bringing of the disturbing passages into juxtaposition where they could readily be compared proclaimed that even beginners in dialectic could, by selecting the right passages from the doctrinists, bolster either side of fundamental arguments. His display was as good as a boast that he could, by merely citing authorities, prove that God was one or that God was three; that God is the author of evil or contrariwise; that God has free will or contrariwise.[15] He did thus subject, as Abbé Bernard declared, the mysteries of our faith to private judgment.

Consternation invaded the cloisters when Abélard said that no one ought to teach what he did not himself rightly understand, and that to challenge doctors with questions was a method of uncovering truth — or error. At the same time that he uttered these impious audacities, he professed to adore God and to cherish the scheme of salvation. The custodians of the Île were deeply perturbed, and, as always, youth found it beautiful to see them in confusion before the onset of new modes of thought and usage. Students leaving the safety of Notre Dame swarmed to the left bank of the Seine and drank his poison.

It was with the utmost reluctance that Bernard, the Abbé of Clairvaux, took up Abélard's challenge to authority. He was no master of disputation; and he knew it was not his business to keep discipline in the schools of Paris. He had long since withdrawn from the tumult of the world to the cloisters of his abbey, whence only some threat to the fabric of the church could lure him. He had attained such inwardness that the world of sense no longer intruded upon his calm or penetrated the depths of his meditations. He had once, it was said, ridden away from his chapter, not on his own gaunt little donkey, but upon the nicely caparisoned horse of a relative, and had never known the difference.[16] He skirted the shores of Lake Geneva without lifting his eyes to the waters or the mountains. He drank any sop with indifference as wine.[17]

But when he learned that pernicious doctrines ran like sparks among the stubble on the left bank where the students gathered, and that the Metropolitan of Paris, the doctrinaires of Reims, the masters of Laon all forbore to meet in public disputation the "Goliath of heretics"; that the young men of the schools, scarcely weaned from dialectic, were being enticed from the security of Notre Dame to their perdition, he issued from the blessed seclusion of Clairvaux. He had asked himself where were the pastors whose flocks had gone so astray, the Archbishop of Sens and his suffragans, the Archbishop of Reims and his? Where were the abbés and priors of the Île dé France? How had they allowed learning in one generation to wander thus from the cloister into the street? He saw that Satan in the deceptive guise of reason had again seduced mankind. Through Lent in 1140 the fiery evangel of Abbé Bernard in the slums and schools of Paris recovered scores of young souls floundering in dialectic into the safety of the cloister.[18]

The abbé never prepared public discourse, propped with citations after the fashion of the schools, for he suspected the guile of the devil in the slipperiness of logic.[19] His methods were more intuitive. He waited to see what words of divine inspiration would be found in his mouth when occasion called upon him to speak. But when he rode out of Paris after each day's work, he led off to some rural solitude the remnant he had that morning rescued from the dangers of damnation. His predications at length aroused the supine masters of the schools and drove Abélard to appeal for a competent examination of the charges that his doctrines were really heretical. It became known that the "Socrates of Gaul," whose dialectic all men feared, would defend an inquiry into his "heresies" before an ecclesiastical consistory in the metropolitan city of Sens; and that Abbé Bernard, "the hawk of Rome," would sit with the doctors of the church in judgment of the case.

Spring was the time for universal pilgrimage. Winter was the hated season, not merely because of the dullness of the world under gray skies, with the uncivil wind and rain prying at latches and casements, but even more because of the cramped inactivity of men in the narrow solars of their houses; the crowding of burghers' families about the hearth where the pot seethed over the glow of turf; the shivering of students in dim garrets overhead, cupping tapers with their frozen fingers; the living under the eye, ear, and tongue of household shrews, too many at the hearth, too many at the trestle. The palmers who set out from the Tabard Inn for Canterbury were not the first pilgrims that spring set loose from their winter's imprisonment. The road from Paris to Sens, hardly longer than that to Canterbury from Southwark, thronged in May of 1140 with multitudes, and Thomas Becket may have been of their number, for he was in those days a poor student in Paris, his august destiny still unguessed. The crowd went down to Sens to witness a great display of relics, to have a look at the rising metropolitan cathedral with its novelties of structure, and to get a place if possible in the enclosure of nave or choir where Abbé Bernard and the bishops and the papal legate were going to argue with Master Abélard on the essence of the Trinity. It was good to leave the stench of Paris behind and be abroad where the roadsides bloomed with wild hyacinths and yellow cuckooflowers.

On the octave of Pentecost, after the mass, Abbé Bernard preached a sermon to the crowds on the foundations of faith, and offered a prayer for a nameless unbeliever. On the next day the cathedral filled to the last cranny for the trial. On one side of the choir was ranged the tribunal of ten bishops in gorgeous panoply, encompassed by a cloud of abbés in their jeweled miters, in their midst the Bishop of Chartres, who was the papal legate, and Abbé Bernard in his white Cistercian wool, his eyes cast down to shut out the glitter of the world. On the opposite side, in unrestrained spring finery, gathered the barons temporal, King Louis in the center, embellished by the presence of Thibault of Champagne, the Count of Nevers, and other magnates. A little lower down sat certain black-robed Benedictines, some of whom were to pay dearly for their heresies — Arnold of Brescia, Gilbert de la Porrée, Berenger of Poitiers, and the young Roman, Hyacinthus Bobo, who would one day be cardinal and Pope.

The inquiry began briskly with Abbé Bernard in charge, and all bent to hear what he who put no trust in dialectic would do with the beautiful rhetoric of Master Abélard. The abbé simply did nothing with beautiful rhetoric. He read off straightly the damnable passages in the works of Master Abélard, one after another, without pausing anywhere to call for the great logician's defensive eloquence. Those who had ears to hear, let them hear.

When Master Peter saw that there would be no disputation, that the trial would be over in no time, and that he was already condemned by his tribunal, he stood forth and the voice that had enthralled the schools filled the choir.

"I refuse to be thus judged like a guilty clerk," he cried. "I appeal to Rome."

A confusion as of a sudden commotion of leaves in a forest passed through the enclosure. A rumor flew about that the affair had been rehearsed in the chapter house the night before, and that Master Abélard had been prejudged by the bishops. In the midst of murmurings and expostulations, the defendant beckoned a few of his followers and strode down the aisle, leaving the judges to whom he had appealed gaping at a sea of astonished faces. Abbé Bernard of all that hierarchy stood unperturbed. There had been no need of dialectic. Holy church had uttered her efficacious words and error had fled from the sanctuary.[20]

But the occasion marked as well as any the turn from the dead end of Romanesque certainties to the new Gothic spirit of inquiry that marked the mid-century; for the eclipse of Abélard stirred the schools from the bishop's palace to the dingiest pothouse where any student found his "garlic and his dice"; and the defeat of the great master, like many other triumphs, furnished the fuel for new fires of controversy.

✢

It was at about this time, when his fame was at its height, that Abbé Bernard came in contact with Queen Eleanor. Since he avoided palaces and the gaudy spectacles that royalty present, he must have encountered her at some public event, very possibly at Sens. Louis was there, and it is not likely that Eleanor, stirred always by the movement and color of life, denied herself that pilgrimage, or that she was unconcerned over the fate of Abélard, whose lectures had made learning so delightsome for women in Paris. She would not easily have foregone a tribune seat on the edge of that arena. But wherever she and the abbé met in the early days of the new regime, there must have been for both a sudden leap back in memory. The spectral figure of the queen's father, Count Guillaume X, rose between them, and his huge shadow beckoned them back to one of the early miracles of the abbé's ministrations in the west. For the house of Poitou was not unknown to Bernard of Clairvaux. In one of his letters he speaks of himself as kinsman of the ducal family.[21]

It is a matter of record that the forebears of the queen were seldom at peace with their clergy. It was not in the nature of the Counts of Poitou to tolerate in their provinces prelates who seemed likely to wander from their diocesan concerns into secular affairs, or offer correction to the ducal house. Count Guillaume, whose talent for broilsomeness was unsurpassed by that of any of his predecessors, had opposed with violence the election of certain

bishops in his domains whom he suspected of obstructing his own freehearted
enterprise. When even excommunication failed to make him yield and church
bells had been silenced in important sees, the clergy in extremity had summoned Bernard from Clairvaux to bring the culprit to submission. For a
time Guillaume thought he could defend himself from the abbé by keeping
warily out of the reach of direct admonition. But Bernard, circling about him
like a hawk, at length closed in upon him; and finally Guillaume, worn down
by the inconveniences of excommunication, determined, since he was afraid
of no one, to himself accost the man of God boldly with threats of reprisal.

On a Sunday, while Bernard was celebrating mass at the church of Par-
thenay, which lay in the ducal domains, Guillaume drew up with his escort
to the narthex, beyond which he could not pass by reason of his ban, and
waited for the exit of the abbé in order to assail him. Bernard, while at the
altar, learned of Guillaume's assault upon the sanctuary. With one of the sudden miraculous inspirations for which he was famous, he seized the pyx
and, brandishing it aloft, hastened down the aisle amidst the astonished worshipers and brought it swiftly before Guillaume's towering forehead, adjuring
him meantime to abhor his sins, confess, restore the bishops. Guillaume, who
had counted upon surprising the abbé with the first word, fell back in confusion. He suffered something like a stroke and measured his gigantic length
upon the pavement at the feet of the frail little abbé, where he lay groaning
and foaming at the mouth. Frightened witnesses pressed about to get a sight
of this miraculous performance. Not a word or gesture of resistance remained
in the prostrate count. The bishops were forthwith restored to their high
seats, bells rang again in their dioceses. The miracle of regeneration by which
the fear of the Lord was put into the stiff-necked house of Poitou greatly
enhanced the abbé's already high renown, not only in Poitou but in remote
corners of Christendom. But his triumph planted a thorn in the flesh of the
Poitevins.[22]

Of course, queens were as grass to the abbé. But when he first had sight
of Eleanor there must have been a special secular magnificence about her to
draw his reluctant eye and his burning words. To whom if not to the queen
and her suite does the abbé allude in that epistle in which he describes the
practices of noble ladies to his nuns as an example of all they must take pains
to avoid? The passage in some points takes substance from Isaiah's strictures
on the harlots of Israel.

> The garments of court ladies are fashioned from the finest tissues of wool or silk.
> A costly fur between two layers of rich stuffs forms the lining and border of their
> cloaks. Their arms are loaded with bracelets; from their ears hang pendants enshrin-
> ing precious stones. For head dress they have a kerchief of fine linen which they
> drape about their neck and shoulders, allowing one corner to fall over the left arm.
> This is their wimple, ordinarily fastened to their brows by a chaplet, a fillet, or a

MARRIAGE VASE · Eleanor's gift to Louis VII
The Latin inscription at the base reads:
*Hoc vas Sponsa dedit Aanor Regi Ludovico,
Mitadolus avo, mihi Rex, sanctisque Sugerus.*

KING AND QUEEN (LOUIS VII AND ELEANOR?)
Chartres Cathedral

circle of wrought gold. Gotten up in this way, they walk with mincing steps, their necks thrust forward; and furnished and adorned as only temples should be, they drag after them a tail of precious stuff that raises a cloud of dust. . . Some you see who are not so much adorned as loaded down with gold, silver, and precious stones, and indeed with everything that pertains to queenly splendor.[23]

This, it must be admitted, is a fairly circumstantial description for the introspective abbé, so little accustomed as he was to give eye to the false colors of the world. He cannot understand, he goes on, referring to the same ladies, how Christian women can borrow the skins of squirrels and the labor of worms to lend them a purely meretricious beauty. Silk and purple and rouge have a beauty of their own, no doubt, but he feels sure they cannot confer it elsewhere. Fie on a beauty that is put on in the morning and laid aside at night![24]

This makes the abbé's convictions clear, but does not define the temper of the queen. However, her state of mind was presently disclosed upon the plane of action.

✤

A clash between royal and ecclesiastical authorities in 1141 brought matters to a head and marshaled all the forces of the church against the young dynasts. It was not merely that Abbé Bernard and the bishops were called out. Even the Pope took up the glaive of Saint Peter to rebuke the intransigence of the pious king, who so strangely emerged from his schooling in the cloister to flout the church that had bred and nourished him.

In that year the bishopric of Bourges fell vacant. Bourges as a palatine city near the borders of Poitou and the French domain was a favorite royal seat in which to assemble for ceremonious courts not only the vassals of the king, but those as well from the provinces of the queen. It is said that it was here that Eleanor was formally crowned Queen of France and Louis was recrowned with her. In the matter of the bishopric, Louis resolved, under some obscure influence that none of his mentors seemed able to fathom, to secure the election of his own chancellor to this important see. The chapter, however, proceeded to elect a Cluniac, Pierre de la Châtre, who was at the time of his election in Rome; and the Pope, following the nomination of the chapter, consecrated Pierre and sent him to Bourges without concern for Louis's nominee.

Upon Pierre's arrival from Rome to assume his administration, he found to his unmeasured surprise that the gates of the see to which he had been elevated were closed against him. The king, who held obstinately to his own candidate, had raised his sceptered arm against the advance of Pierre's episcopal *mesnie*. Full of chagrin, the bishop-elect fell back upon the hospitality of Champagne, and thence communicated with Rome. Innocent thereupon sent him a second time to Bourges. At the same time His Holiness addressed a letter to the king's ministers in which he remarked that the King of France was "behaving like a foolish schoolboy," and that the masters who had him in hand would better look to it that he got no bad habit of meddling with what was not his royal business. These words reached the king and had the effect of hardening his heart. The gates of the see remained closed to the papal candidate. Inside the city walls, Louis, placing his hands on the holiest relics, so that he could not be tempted to recant, vowed publicly that not while he breathed should Pierre de la Châtre set foot in the royal episcopal city of Bourges.[25]

Pierre withdrew again to Champagne. In due time the rumble of anathema was heard on the far side of the Alps. In the face of this alarm, Louis, "the foolish schoolboy," maintained that he could not, even under papal mandate, jeopardize his soul by renouncing the vows he had made directly to heaven with his hands upon the relics. The Pope for his part, as vicegerent of God, could not relinquish to the stripling king the sovereign instrument heaven had granted him of binding and loosing upon earth. Did not the king receive his glaive from the church before he could rule? Innocent found himself obliged to launch upon the household of the king the edict of excommunication and interdict. The mentors of the "schoolboy" were appalled. How could it be that, in spite of the auspicious beginning of his reign, the pious Louis, the oblate of Notre Dame, the sworn protector of the church, should find himself excommunicate, excluded by office of book, bell, and candle, from all the sacraments upon which his soul's health depended?

While the affair at Bourges was at impasse, a scandal in another quarter spread alarm and drove the king's mentors to seek out the influences moving their sovereign to unnatural acts in defiance of Holy Church and to the jeopardy of his soul. In the queen's Poitevin household was her younger sister Petronilla, who, by virtue of her relation to the royal house and her dower properties in Burgundy, was an enviable marriage prize. The king's elder cousin, Count Raoul of Vermandois, with rich fiefs between Flanders and the Vexin, sought alliance with Petronilla, and the proposal, though in some respects astonishing, commended itself to the royal household as having advantages. The only difficulty was that Raoul, who was middle-aged, had some years before, with the very same object of attaching himself to the crown, married the niece of Louis the Fat's chief vassal, Thibault of Champagne. To the queen, who was eager for the marriage of her sister, Raoul's unfortunate ties with the house of Champagne were merely knots to be cut. For Louis, however, canonical sanctions had to be invoked. Legalists were shortly found who discovered a degree of consanguinity between Raoul and the heiress of Champagne prohibited by the church. On this safe ecclesiastical ground, Louis allied himself with the queen's party, eager to repair his cousin's conjugal "irregularity." When, late in the summer of 1142, the court returned from a *chevauchée* in Poitou and Aquitaine, during which Petronilla and the Count of Vermandois were part of the retinue, the sovereigns found three bishops to the north of Paris, well out of the narrowly authoritative diocese of Sens, who annulled the count's marriage and almost at once united him to the Lady Petronilla.[26]

When in consequence of these operations, Thibault of Champagne was summoned to receive into his own estates his niece, the late Countess of Vermandois, and her children, he was considerably taken aback. In his troubles Thibault very naturally had recourse to his friend, Abbé Bernard. And Abbé Bernard very naturally felt a just sympathy for Thibault in the circumstances, and of course he was scandalized that whom God had joined together, the Capets had put asunder. In behalf of Thibault and the sacraments, the abbé addressed himself to Rome. With incredible swiftness there came through the Alpine passes the thunder of anathema. It smote the bishops who had executed the royal plans, widowed the newly wed sister of the queen, and adjured the Count of Vermandois to return to his lawful wife on pain of excommunication and interdict on all his lands.[27]

So far Louis's exploits in ecclesiastical diplomacy had brought him a miserable malaise. Yet he accepted no one of the occasions offered for retreat. Some demon of pride or obstinacy, as it was thought, drove him to extremity. At last he drew his sword. For all his spiritual humiliations he cast the blame on Thibault. The Count of Champagne had sheltered the exiled bishop-elect whom Louis had vowed on the relics never to receive in Bourges. And Thibault, interfering in the marriage of Raoul and Petronilla, which bishops of the church had been found to bless, had brought upon the noble house of Vermandois the consuming blight of anathema.

Leading the royal army himself, Louis invaded Champagne, the territory of his proudest vassal. He attacked the ill-defended town of Vitry on the Marne and set torches to its wooden houses and thatched roofs. In flight from their flaming dwellings, the people sought sanctuary in their church. But this too caught fire. The roof collapsed and Louis with horror viewed the scene where the populace of the defenseless town had been trapped and burned before the altar in a ghastly holocaust. More than a thousand souls, innocent burghers, with their women and children, were smothered in the ruins.[28] The king was sickened by a sudden sense of guilt, a conviction that heaven in this catastrophe had declared its displeasure with him. Yet in spite of his compunction over the tragedy of Vitry, the royal armies continued to ravage the domain of Thibault.

Abbé Bernard, roused again from the quiet of Clairvaux to witness Louis's harrowing of Champagne, was confounded. How was it that this boy king, who had given every promise of sobriety, had so deceived the hopes of his poor people and the church his mother? And how was it that Abbé Suger and the Bishop of Soissons, who should have guided the young king's courses, had failed so signally? He wrote letters to discover and admonish. During this period of the king's rebelliousness, he wrote to Louis himself.

"You are evidently kicking," he said, "with too much haste and inconstancy against the wholesome advice you have received, and you are hurrying, under I know not what counsel of the devil, to your former evil courses. . . For from whom except the devil can I say that this counsel proceeds that adds fire to fire and slaughter to slaughter; which lifts the cry of the poor, the groanings of captives, the blood of the slain to the ears of the Father of the fatherless and the Judge of widows? . . . Do not, my King, with rash audacity lift your hand against the terrible Lord who takes away the breath of kings. I speak sharply, because I fear sharp things for you." [29]

Presently Louis, who could not banish from his ears the horrible cries of the people of Vitry, the roar and crackling of the roof, the toppling of the altars, fell into a spiritual panic and depression from which nothing could raise him. He saw ever more plainly in that disaster the unmistakable wrath of heaven and the peril into which he had put his soul. He lost all interest in his military triumphs in Champagne and fell so ill that his spiritual physicians despaired of his life. He who had been so froward and impassioned lapsed into being the most desperate of creatures. Cut off from the consolations of religion by interdict, he suffered horribly.[30] Though he continued to cherish the queen "with an almost foolish fondness," not even she could longer support his morale. Not even the lifting of the ban revived his spirits.

❧

It is only through symbols of beauty that our poor spirits can raise themselves from things temporal to things eternal.
Abbé Suger, *De Administratione*

Abbé Bernard during all those woeful months had asked himself why Abbé Suger, who should have stayed the disastrous courses of his sovereign, had held himself aloof from the affairs that convulsed Champagne. The fact was that Abbé Suger was leaving affairs in Champagne to Abbé Bernard. He was himself engrossed in an experience so compelling that he could be insensible to the rash behavior of his ward and the ravages of the civil war at his very gates. Since his rebuke by Abbé Bernard some years before, he too had attained an inwardness. He had put off the worldly splendor of his dress, his retinue, his table. He had restored sobriety to his abbey and vied with his monkish brethren in the simplicity of his life. He had swept out of his precincts the war office and the chancellery and the secular luxuries and disorders that Louis the Fat had brought to Saint Denis. For himself he had taken one little room in the cloister, less severe certainly than Abbé Bernard's crooked nook in the angle of the stairs at Clairvaux, but modest, homely, serviceable.[31]

He had not, however, like Abbé Bernard, succeeded in closing his senses to the alluring beauty of the world. He still felt the sensuous qualities of things, the preciousness of gems and embroidered stuffs, the veinings of marble, the gleam of gold and mosaic, the radiance of glass, the touching narrative of sculpture and fresco, the ecstasy of plain song. If to possess beauty were corrupting, then it might be dedicated to God the giver, and thus purified, become a means to lift the soul to grace. There were, he believed, diversities in the soul's progress suited to the several degrees of men's needs. In Saint Denis resplendent symbols of redemption lured sinners to salvation; in Clairvaux the absence of these, like the putting off of mortality itself, freed the spirits of the nearly ransomed to foretaste of heaven.[32]

During the civil war that desolated France from Reims to Troyes, Abbé Suger was at the climax of his reconstruction of the royal abbey of Saint Denis. He had made his abbey a vast atelier for the study and fabrication of every kind of beauty that devotion could sanctify. He searched the world for the richest materials and the most skillful craftsmen. He saw the shrine of the patron saint of France as the object of a vast pilgrimage, and he had studied all that architectural stir in the Île de France responsive to new need for ampler spaces and more light and a more passionate votive worship for the thousands that swarmed to holy places upon days of fete. He had studied the abbey of Cluny and the rising cathedrals in the diocese of Sens, among them the growing splendors of Chartres. In his atelier, under compulsion of needs arising from urban development and pilgrimage, he and his builders half designed and half divined the nascent forms of Gothic.

In 1144 the abbey church, with the stonecutter's dust white as frost upon it, was ready for dedication. Bronze doors on the west front exhibited the Passion and the Resurrection; in the tympanum above the majestic figure of Christ in Judgment sat enthroned above the elders of Israel, and in a humble corner, as if by way of signature to his good work of restoration, showed the small figure of Abbé Suger himself. Inside it seemed that the dim frowning walls and squat arches of the old Romanesque basilica had been beaten into a vast and airy shell blazing with light, gleaming with gold and color. Here tall windows, retelling in brilliant glaze the epic of salvation, dissolved the walls to radiance and shed upon the pavement pools of light that shone here and there as red as martyrs' blood.

It seemed to Abbé Suger that the dedication of the royal abbey, the shrine of the patron saint of France, the necropolis of the Capetian house, might lift the king from the prostration that now so utterly depressed his spirits. He planned a program in which the king, by bearing a noble part, should recover his confidence. The feast of Saint Barnabas, the 11th of June, was chosen for the translation of the relics of Dionysius the Areopagite from the crypt where they had rested for so many years to the new reliquary tomb in the choir. Not since the dedication of Cluny by Pope Innocent in 1132 had there been a like event of such significance.

Louis, Eleanor, and the queen mother arrived at Saint Denis on the 10th, so that Louis might share the vigils of the monks and be present for the services at dawn. At daybreak the bishops not only of the Île, but of Bordeaux and Rouen and Canterbury, with many others, assembled to asperge the edifice with lustral water. A late biographer of Suger adds some details. There were processions in which the king, carrying the most precious of the reliquaries, led queues of monks and prelates through the cloister to the sound of chanting choirs and instruments; and all the lesser chasses dipped before his reliquary, like the sheaves of Joseph's brethren before the master sheaf. "No one would have taken the king," says the chronicler, "for that scourge of war who had lately destroyed so many towns, burned so many churches, shed so much blood. The spirit of penitence shone in his whole aspect." [33]

At the translation of the relics, the king, the bishops, and Abbé Suger, overcome with holy awe, saw the bones of Saint Denis placed in the choir. Where the relics reposed, marble and porphyry, gold and blue, gleamed on every side. Above the tomb Suger had placed a retable of gold encrusted with precious stones; and at the passage of the transept towered the majestic cross blazing with gold and filagree, jewels and cabochons, which was the central glory of the shrine. The throng was so vast that it was said one could have walked upon the shoulders of the crowd. The day was so hot and the press so great that Eleanor and the queen mother were all but suffocated.

The occasion did the king much good. In the course of it he met Abbé Bernard with whom he had been in such long and painful collision. Though the Abbé of Clairvaux was oppressed by crowds and spectacles, and though he deplored the ostentation of the royal abbey church, he was induced to quit the solitude of Champagne for the dedication of this famous shrine in the hope of serving there the interests of peace. He had expected to be stern with Louis, but he was impressed with the king's dovelike humility and his wretchedness. It was obvious that he had not deliberately plotted his evil courses, but that he had been the victim of rash advice. Although the abbé had declared that many tears would be required to extinguish the fires of Vitry, he was now put to it to find a means of raising Louis's spirits. He explained that the king was increasing his sins by giving way to despair; that he must be sad, not disconsolate; fearful, but not desperate; contrite without weakness; ashamed, but holding the hope of forgiveness. He then said such touching things of the goodness of God and the largeness of His mercy, that the king recovered a faint hope.[34]

The abbé then, whether upon his own initiative or upon some urgency from Louis, had a talk with the queen. He had seen her before, but he now perhaps for the first time opened his eyes upon her fully, taking the measure of her stature from top to toe. He exhorted her to use her wife's influence over the erring king to bring him to a better mind, and he was prepared, when she was chastened, to offer her spiritual consolations for the woeful tragedies that had befallen the royal house.

But he was amazed to find that she was not sharing in the same degree the king's agony over Vitry, nor seeking counsel about a suitable penance for that catastrophe. She seems to have had uppermost in her mind a bargain, and she had apparently concluded that a compact negotiated with Abbé Bernard would hold in Rome. What she desired was that the abbé should use his influence with the Pope to lift the ban from the Count of Vermandois and recognize his marriage with the Lady Petronilla. She seems to have employed dialectic and proffered some exchange of benefits in the parley, for the abbé was presently obliged to wave her out of the arena of debate.

That the queen should venture on discussion of the issues at stake was very surprising to the abbé. In a sudden illumination he recognized the evil genius of the king, that "counsel of the devil" that had plunged Louis into abysses of sin and remorse. Why had he, so wary of the snares of the flesh, been blind to this primordial ruse, Satan in the guise of a fair-seeming woman? The Abbé of Clairvaux realized that he should in all conscience have been more prescient, and reproached himself for having been so slow in resolving the mystery of the pious king's godless behavior. He was forced to rebuke the queen sternly for meddling in what were certainly not her concerns. "Put an end," he said, "to your interference with affairs of state."

Thibault also shared in the dedication of Saint Denis. He made a rich gift of rubies and jacinths to Abbé Suger for the fabric in gratitude for the latter's good offices in helping to extricate him from the impasse with Louis and the Pope.

Suger had reason to feel that the consecration of his abbey church was pleasing to heaven. The ceremony was rich in itself, but richer in the fruits of peace. A treaty ended the long confusions. It shows the marks of compromise and was certainly not the untrammeled device of Abbé Bernard, nor of Louis, nor of Thibault of Champagne. It recited, among other things, that Louis should restore to Thibault his ravaged provinces; and that he should renounce the rash oath he had sworn on the relics and admit Pierre de la Châtre to Bourges. Thibault made his concessions too. Of course, the treaty does not broach the matter of the interdict on the house of Vermandois, which burdened the queen's mind at the conference. It seems that here the irresistible force encountered the impenetrable obstacle and the effect of the collision could not be written down, since none eventuated from the argument. It was visible only in subsequent events. The interdict remained in force; but the royal house rendered its operation null and void by the simple expedient of ignoring the bans that it imposed. This result offers a singular instance in which Abbé Bernard was obliged to skirt a moral obstacle and content himself with less than a loaf in a contention with transgressors.

When peace had been restored and enmities allayed, the queen confided in the abbé in his character as thaumaturge. She had another urgent matter on her mind, in which, in a more subdued mood, she sought his help and advice. She had been Queen of France for seven years and she was now twenty-two, but she had not yet presented to her people the heir so earnestly desired. Could the man of God who had healed the halt, the blind, the deaf, move heaven to bestow on her the grace of motherhood? [35] The Abbé, rejoicing in what seemed a favorable alteration of the queen's purposes, and judging this at least a pious aspiration, promised to support the royal novenas to the Virgin. Whereupon, in the course of 1145, Eleanor gave birth, not to the son so fondly desired by Louis, but to a daughter whom she named Marie in honor of the Queen of Heaven.

3 ✠

Via Crucis

AFTER THE CONCORD AT SAINT DENIS there still remained the question of Louis's penance. The concern of the bishops for his spiritual state and the deference to his royal person exhibited at the dedication of the abbey church had restored a measure of his confidence and self-esteem. He had been led to see that there was hope in expiation. But how expiate? The hair shirt and other mortifications of the flesh yielded only a moderate relief. Sin so deadly in one in whom virtue was so great an obligation called for no ordinary propitiation. Nothing could be suggested sufficient to demonstrate the extent of the king's remorse. He did what he could to redress the grievances of his people; he lifted his wrath from the provinces he had ravaged with fire and sword; he admitted bishops to the sees of Reims, Paris, and Châlons, which his long obstinacy and blindness had held vacant; but these were mere acts of justice, righting wrongs; they had no virtue as propitiations.

Naturally he considered the salutary effects of pilgrimage.[1] From his days as oblate of Notre Dame, when the vision of a miter swam before him, he had harbored a project of going as a palmer to Jerusalem and of being in the church of the Holy Sepulcher for the Easter miracle of the sacred fire by which the resurrection of our Lord was annually commemorated. And when his destiny was suddenly confounded, he hoped at some time to fulfill by proxy the vow his brother Philip had made to carry the oriflamme of France to the tomb of Christ.[2] Presently, amidst the groanings of his spirit, it was revealed to Louis what he should do to wipe out his guilt, and these old dreams merged suddenly into a plan of scope and grandeur befitting a king who had put his soul in jeopardy and brought anathema upon his people. It was as if Divine Wrath and Clemency had summoned him with a trumpet to an ordeal signal, impressive, adequate.

Early in 1145 official messengers arrived in Europe from the Latin Kingdom of Jerusalem with accounts of the disasters that threatened that Christian state as a result of the fall of Edessa in the closing days of 1144. The fact of the catastrophe had long since shed gloom in Europe. It was known that while Count Joscelin of Edessa had been celebrating the season of the Nativity at one of his estates upon the upper reaches of the Euphrates, Moslem hordes had fallen upon his principal city on the northern outposts of the Latin Kingdom, breached its walls, laid low its altars, and taken its burghers into captivity. But what had at first accounts appeared a distressing incident in the history of those eastern fiefs was now revealed by the messengers as a threat to the very existence of the Christian state of which Edessa was a part. The whole Kingdom of Jerusalem lay exposed by its downfall to the onsets of the infidel. The heroic conquests of the first crusaders were in peril. The patrimony of Christ, the highways of His pilgrimage upon the earth, His Holy Sepulcher, were again laid open to the wanton despite of the Saracens. It seemed that the paynim, revived after two generations, were in the way of digesting the first crusade. If the Latin Kingdom, beleaguered by fresh foes and enfeebled by the dwindling of its own princely houses, was to maintain custody of the holy places, the West must rise to a great occasion.[3]

These tidings, urgent and authentic, produced widespread consternation in Europe, though not all people reacted to them spontaneously in the same way. As a practical matter, the loss of Edessa exposed first and especially the Fief of Antioch; and the Prince of Antioch, Raymond of Toulouse, was the uncle of Queen Eleanor, son of her grandfather the crusading troubadour, and her nearest male relative. The Bishop of Djebail, who was one of the harbingers of disaster, was Raymond's friend and vassal. Naturally, the Prince of Antioch hoped that the danger to which his fief was exposed would move especially the house of Capet to which his house of Poitou and Aquitaine was now related.

Of all the freebooters in the Latin Kingdom of Jerusalem, Raymond had been, through both chance and enterprise, one of the most successful. He was a gentleman adventurer whom no obstacles could daunt and no misfortunes could depress. Queen Eleanor remembered him as a youth but eight years her senior in the courts of Poitou, a landless and fatherless kinsman, a younger brother casting about for his place in the sun. He had no relish for the younger brother's portion in the church, preferring a sword to a crosier and the lively *chansons de geste* to the Latin litanies. Henry I of England, after the calamity of the White Ship had bereft his house of so many princes, had adopted the foot-loose Raymond into his household, bred him to a knight's service, and given him the accolade. Even so, he was but an errant knight, a cavalier without a fief, a prince without a prince's state, and at the death of his patron he was again set wholly adrift.

But while Raymond in the flower of his youth was casting about for a career, fortune was seeking him with both land and titles. Bohemund, the overlord of the great Fief of Antioch, died in the Latin Kingdom overseas, leaving among the dwindling nobility of the East only women to defend his county, which was encompassed by enemies on every hand. The barons of Antioch, not wishing to fall subject to the Fief of Jerusalem, scanned the West for an untrammeled knight of high lineage, bred to the exercise of true chivalry, but not too closely related to any crown, to marry their heiress, the widow of their late Count Bohemund, and defend their feudal state. Their eyes lighted upon Raymond. For the overlordship of this rich fief there were rivals of course, but Raymond, who was, as the chronicle says, *sages et apercevanz*, outwitted them. To avoid arrest by his enemies on the way out from Poitou to take possession, he divided his followers into little companies, who, adopting various disguises, journeyed at intervals of a day or two along the Mediterranean littoral. He himself, garbed now as a pilgrim, now as a merchant's colporteur, made the journey unassumingly and arrived in his new provinces without being recognized. In adroit collaboration with the Patriarch of Antioch, who, in the interregnum, held the reins of government, he was able also to outwit the widow and presumptive heir of the late Bohemund, who had expected to share the government with him. He succeeded in banishing her from her provinces and espousing in her stead her nine-year-old daughter Constance, thus forming an alliance which left him with a much freer hand in pursuing his policies. Since Constance was cousin of the King of Jerusalem, Raymond at once found himself in an enviable station. For ten years before the call to rescue Edessa had alarmed the western world, he had prospered in Antioch and had become so thoroughly expatriate that he no longer coveted any part of the heritage of the house of Poitou. But when Joscelin, by the loss of Edessa, exposed his own Fief of Antioch to the ravages of Turks and Arabs, Raymond's thoughts turned back to that reservoir of superfluous men and inactive treasure in the old Limousin and to his niece, the Queen of the Franks, who could command those resources.[4]

It is very probable that the Capets had early and direct communication from Raymond of Antioch, presenting his own views with regard to the calamity of Edessa. William of Tyre relates that Raymond plied his Capetian relatives in Paris with rich gifts from the bazaars of the Levant.[5] But the sovereigns of the Franks, as it happened, needed no seduction. Boredom (*accidia*) was one of the seven deadly sins, and the queen had need of absolution. In the eight years since she had come up from the lively courts of the south, she had exhausted the Île de France as a theater of interest. Paris offered no proper arena for women, for duchesses, for queens. She was bored with dialectic, bored with universals, with discourse upon the unfathomable nature of the Trinity, bored with bishops and with abbés and the ecclesiastical conclaves over which they presided, bored with dedications and with pious pilgrimages. She was not a little bored by her overlord, by his naïveté, his scruple over trifles, his slavery to ritual, his lingering immaturity. She longed for the ease and freedom of the road that she had known in Aquitaine, its random contacts, its accidents, its laughter. Antioch, where she was certain to be of the greatest consideration in her uncle's court, offered a purge for the evil that threatened her. As for Louis, his heart burned at the thought of leading his people to the succor of Jerusalem. His mission had been made manifest.[6] Without hesitation — and also without the unanimous consent of his counselors — he expressed the warmth and depth of his feeling to the new Pope, and Eugenius replied commending his valor and bestowing his papal blessing upon the enterprise.

Perhaps the uncertainties of his own situation at the time may have influenced Pope Eugenius' theories in regard to the propitiousness of a crusade in the mid-century. The messengers from the Orient found him in exile in Viterbo, unable to occupy Rome and distraught by factions that menaced, on both sides of the Alps, his universal see. What might a common ardor, kindled by the loftiest motives, do to exorcise the heresy and schism and restore Christendom to concord and unity? And since Eugenius relied, in the crises of his career, upon Abbé Bernard, he turned the development of his plans over to the Abbé of Clairvaux, and the abbé, much as he detested war, suppressed his own sentiments and early gave his sanction to the cause. It thus happened that, long before the people of Europe had sensed their destiny, they had been committed to crusade.

In 1145 the king and queen assembled their barons for their Christmas court again in Bourges.[7] On the crossroad between France and Poitou, the court was the grand gathering of the year, an assembly in which to grasp and direct the driving currents of the feudal will. When the Capets had received the homage of their vassals in the palatine city, Louis addressed the concourse gathered from the far corners of Gaul on the matter he had so much at heart. The fall of Edessa had stirred the West; but there was obvious consternation at the king's proposal of a new holy war to redress that grievance. The barons of France, and especially those of the queen's provinces, had been made circumspect by the costly and inconclusive character of former expeditions to the Orient. They remembered the seventy thousand Provençaux who had accompanied the troubadour Count of Poitou upon his ill-starred pilgrimage and whose bones now lay whitening in a far-off Cappadocian wadi many leagues from Jerusalem. Perhaps Louis leaned too much upon the penitential idea in his address, and the barons were not inclined to undertake so much merely to relieve the king from the danger of damnation. The militant Bishop of Langres alone among his vassals rose to the occasion in a striking burst of eloquence. But there was no popular demand to set forth. There was on the contrary a disposition to let those who had fattened in the Orient draw upon their own resources in fallow times.

Abbé Suger surveyed with distinct alarm his sovereigns and his wards in the high mood that possessed them in Bourges.[8] He perceived somewhat belatedly that Louis's education, his indoctrination first with the ideology of a bishop and then with that of a king, had produced a strange confusion in his brain. Louis's ideas of himself were mixed, his decisions clouded with conflict. The issue seemed likely to be folly. It was certain that the queen meant to accompany the expedition. Whether her going were to be preferred to her abiding at home was an important question; but it was a vain one. Who could detain her or circumvent her resolution? Could the king, or the Pope, or Abbé Bernard? She could muster more soldiers for the succor of Jerusalem than her lord, and the revenues of her duchy were indispensable. Her spirit fanned the king's aspirations. With *élan* she moved among the barons of Aquitaine who remembered Raymond of Antioch — the sieurs of Rancon and Lusignan, of Limoges and Angoulême, of Thouars and Poitiers. Speaking as one of them in the amiable *langue d'oc*, she exhorted the hesitant, jibed at poltroons, fired the ambitious, called upon the ardors of the old Limousin, invoked its saints. Who could say that her motives were less pure than the king's? While the momentous decision was still in the balance, Abbé Suger gave his support to the hesitation of the vassalage. With the courage that challenges martyrdom, he raised his solitary voice against the royal plans, urging reflection and delay. But how could even the Abbé of Saint Denis oppose the Pope, the Abbé of Clairvaux, his king and queen?

From Bourges the ferment spread over the three quarters of Gaul. It crossed the Rhine, the Alps, the Channel, the Pyrenees. In Paris the universals were neglected. Heresies died down even in Aquitaine. The armorer's industry throve from Cologne to Blaye. Barons mortgaged their lands for the wherewithal to go to Palestine. Common men, peering into the matter from the outside, got their minds off the famine that had raged for the past five years and forgot the desolations of the recent civil wars.[9]

At the end of Lent in 1146 the barons of Gaul met in council in Burgundy at Vézelay.[10] But the vast new pilgrim church of Saint Mary Magdalene could by no means shelter the throngs that gathered to hear the papal bull, the predication of Abbé Bernard, to learn what barons were certainly mustering their vassals for overseas, what the tithes would be. From a tribune built on the hillside beyond the walls of the town, Abbé Bernard spoke to the people of his century under the wide roof of the sky, which alone could cover them.

Behind him, enthroned among their barons and their bishops, sat the king and queen, lately shriven, apotheosized by the solemnity of their Easter vows. The abbé was frail and ill, already spent with his wrestlings and his fastings, a mere specter. But setting his lips, as he said, "to the apostolic trumpet," he called with a loud voice upon his generation, and his potent words were "carried alive into their hearts." He unfurled the bull and read the call to arms, the proffered indulgence for all who, for the remission of their sins, should hasten to rescue the patrimony of Christ from the swelling pride of the infidel. All saw that the king wore upon his shoulder the cross which the Pope had sent for his dedication. Bernard could hardly finish his discourse. Louis, his heart dissolved within him, gave way abundantly to tears, of which he had the gift. He prostrated himself before the abbé in the presence of all his people and received the holy accolade. The barons of Gaul fell in ranks before the Abbé of Clairvaux, eager to have from the man of God their sign and seal. The redoubtable Bishops of Langres and Lisieux pledged their hosts. Every noble house offered its lord, or at least its heir. The common enthusiasm was a purge for private enmities. Old foes closed their ranks. Alphonse-Jourdain of Toulouse placed his banners beside those of the king. Thibault of Champagne enrolled Henry, his eldest son, under the lilies of France.

When Louis had taken his cross, Eleanor knelt before the abbé and offered her thousands of vassals from Poitou and Aquitaine. It was a wonder to see the young dynasts, who less than a year before had been so rash and arrogant, upon their knees receiving the symbol of their dedication from the humblest of all their subjects, the poor little brother of Clairvaux. With the queen came "many other ladies of quality," Sybille, Countess of Flanders, whose half brother was King of Jerusalem, Mamille of Roucy, Florine of Bourgogne, Torqueri of Bouillon, Faydide of Toulouse, and scores of others whom the chroniclers could not afford the parchment to enumerate.[11]

Whatever may have been said secretly behind the palm of the hand, no one appears to have asked publicly what these female warriors were to inflict upon the Saracens. The historians do not well explain why hordes of women took the cross. However, the chronicler Newburgh suspects that in the case of Queen Eleanor, Louis was overborne; she had doubtless, he says, so bedazzled her young spouse with her excellent beauty that, fearing out of jealousy to leave her behind, he decided to take her with him to the wars. The annalist deplores the fact that the queen's example made other ladies intractable, and the policy led in the end to the infiltration of a good many women who had no business to be included in the army.[12] It is perhaps more profitable to search the secular poetry upspringing in the time for explanations. Chivalry, we learn from many a troubadour, could not endure the winter-long isolation of the feudal castle. It must move upon the road, drink the sunshine and the racy humors of the mob. Poetry was made upon the pilgrim trail in the springtime of the year. Pilgrimage to the Holy Land had passed the pioneering stage. By the middle of the century it had become the grand tour, a civilizing part of the education of persons of consequence, and a sovereign remedy for ennui. There were facilities — routes as worn as the bed of a river, hostels by the way, money-changers at the frontiers, markets for forage. And there beyond the floods of the Danube rose glorious Byzantium on the Bosporus and beyond Byzantium the fabulous bazaars of Antioch and Tripoli, the incomparable shrines of Jerusalem.

At Vézelay the crosses gave out and still the crowd bore down upon the saintly abbé. The token! The token! A legend tells us that the queen and her ladies disappeared and presently reappeared on white horses in the guise of Amazons, in gilded buskins, plumed, and with banners: that like Penthesilea and her warriors, the queen and her cavalcade galloped over the hillside of Vézelay, rallying laggard knights, tossing distaffs to faint-hearted cavaliers. The tale is in character, and later allusions to Amazons en route, found in Greek historians, give some substance to it.[13] This dazzling dramatization of the story of the Amazons, popular in every castle, must have made a sensation and stimulated the recruiting notably. Even the foot soldiers called for the sign that should keep them safe. Other supplies failing, the abbé's white wool cassock was snipped into little crosses, and these he sowed rather than distributed with his blessing among the crowd. As at Clermont fifty years before, the cry rose to heaven in all the dialects of Gaul, "It is God's will."

⚜

Yet in spite of the enthusiasm at Vézelay, Edessa was obliged to languish a full year more before the forces of Europe could be launched against the Saracens. The crusade could be of advantage to the Pope, harried as he was by the "tyranny of the Romans" and the disaffection of the Holy Roman Emperor, only if his formidable enemies could be involved in the war with the Moslems. But to engage Conrad of Hohenstaufen, the Holy Roman Emperor, in an expedition under papal auspices and under the leadership of the King of the Franks, was to accomplish a prodigy. Only one person alive, and certainly not Pope Eugenius himself, could bring about such a Christian concord. All looked to the Abbé of Clairvaux to bring the miracle to pass. Those who saw Bernard at Vézelay — his flush and pallor, the febrile brilliance of his eye, his wasted frame — believed that death had already laid a finger on him. Indeed, Bernard longed inexpressibly to seal his thoughts forever from the world in the blessed retreat of Clairvaux. But he was summoned again to sound the apostolic trumpet, to carry the call to arms to the remote, the hesitant, the slumbering. Using the daughter houses of his abbey, the "hives" that had swarmed from his parent house, he sent the summons far and wide. Within a few months he visited the Low Countries, the Rhine cities, the Alpine provinces, besides all the regions nearer home. Presently he wrote to Eugenius that towns and villages were deserted by those who had taken the cross, so that there hardly remained in all his territory one man for seven women.

It was, however, no easy matter to bring Conrad of Hohenstaufen into the general plan. The abbé circled anxiously about him several times. Bernard's ardor fired the German populace, even though he addressed them through interpreters. When words failed, miracles spoke for him. The deaf heard, the halt walked, the blind saw. But when he approached the emperor, Conrad made self-interested excuses for staying at home. His obstinacy became a heavy burden to Bernard, for a crusade that should steady the See of Saint Peter dared not leave the emperor behind. The Christmas of 1146 passed at Speyer and still Conrad demurred. On the 27th of December Bernard celebrated mass in the imperial presence. At a certain moment he felt himself moved, and suddenly, as if with the trump of doom, he called upon the emperor publicly to account before heaven for his stewardship. Taken thus unawares, Conrad withered under the heat of Bernard's spiritual fervor. In the midst of a vast enthusiasm he pledged his person and his men, among them the youthful Barbarossa. Speyer became another Vézelay. Bells rang; the people sang hymns and the *Via Crucis*. Conrad, fearing the abbé would be smothered in the press, wrapped him in his own cloak and carried him from the basilica. The crusade was assured.[14]

All over Europe the taxes fell heavily. Neither sex nor rank nor order was spared. The churches poured out their treasure and the Jews were forced to disgorge the fruits of usury. The queen's provinces of Poitou and Aquitaine groaned especially under the oppression. Arguments about routes to the East and the leadership of the various contingents, some marshaled by barons and some by bishops, were roughly adjusted in conclave. There would be time to discuss military strategy on the long journey, for not all were agreed upon the precise objectives of the campaign.

The king did not forget, in the midst of vast operations, to make the most anxious personal preparation for his pilgrimage. He visited monasteries and lazar houses, distributing alms and bespeaking the intercessory prayers of the most humble and wretched of his subjects. For the journey he put himself under the advice of his wise men and these, in order to hedge him about with the soundest influence, selected his entourage. Odo of Duilio, a monk of Saint Denis, who wrote a chronicle of the expedition, became the king's chaplain and secretary and undertook, as a part of his duty, to lodge by night near the royal tent.[15] And Thierry Galeran, a eunuch of the order of the Temple who appears to have opened and closed the coffers of the Franks, engaged to defend the king from sycophants and hangers on.[16]

The lateness of Easter and Pentecost in 1147 determined the Franks to postpone their departure until the fete of Saint Denis on June 11, so that they might leave their homes under the special auspices of their patron saint. Pope Eugenius crossed the Alps to give his blessing to the banners and to

bestow upon Louis with his own hands the staff and wallet for his pilgrimage and the martyr-red oriflamme of France, which reposed between
wars upon the altars of the abbey. After the ceremonies the queen and her
company were sent ahead so that their baggage wains might not encumber
the road for the foot soldiers. Louis dined for the last time sparely with the
monks in their refectory and had from each the kiss of peace. The bull of
Vézelay had proscribed ermine and vair.[17] With the cross alone gleaming upon his pilgrim's tunic, the King of the Franks set his face toward
Jerusalem.

✤

> Anyone seeing these cohorts with their helmets and bucklers shining in the sun,
> with their banners streaming in the breeze, would have been certain that they were
> about to triumph over all the enemies of the cross and reduce to submission all the
> countries of the Orient. And this they would doubtless have done if the pilgrimage
> had been pleasing to God.
>
> *Gestes de Louis VII*

The final concentration of the hordes that Abbé Bernard had marshaled
in the west of Europe for the rescue of the Holy Land took place at Metz.
The German forces of Conrad, one hundred thousand strong, were already
in the valley of the Danube. Having finally cast the die, the emperor moved
his hosts without dalliance. The division of the French and German forces
was said to have been determined by the impossibility of provisioning the
united armies on the journey. But in any case, Conrad had no idea of trailing
the King of the Franks into Jerusalem, nor even into Byzantium. He had
only a moderate confidence in the Truce of God enjoined by the Pope; he
had been overimpressed by Abbé Bernard to set forth; and he despised the
military genius of the royal pilgrim from France. He judged it best to be
early on the scene to make his own terms with the Emperor of Byzantium,
whom he also mistrusted, and with the barons of the Latin Kingdom, whom
he suspected of self-interest.

But the host that remained under the banners of France on the banks of
the Moselle and the Rhine were legion and as motley as the muster of the
Last Judgment. Besides the Franks and the Burgundians with their knights
bannerets, and vast contingents from the queen's provinces of Poitou and
Aquitaine, there were Normans under the Bishop of Lisieux, Bretons, men
from the Low Countries, and belated stragglers from the Rhine and Alpine
provinces. The lower ranks dependent upon the king's bounty were abundant, many having been driven by famine to take up their arms. In his
recruiting Abbé Bernard had opened the spiritual benefits of crusade to the
meanest sinners. "Marvel," he said, "at the fathomless mercy of God. Is it
not a heavenly intention and worthy of Him to admit to his service mur-

derers and ravishers, adulterers, the perjured, and other malefactors, and offer them thus a hope of redemption?"[18] And later, when he had to raise the spirits of Abbé Suger, he called upon him to admire the operations of a Providence that by one stroke furnished the hope of rescue to Jerusalem, ridded Europe of the burden of its criminals and paupers, and offered these the reward of paradise for their labor or their lives. "There were in the army," says a commentator, "plenty of gallows birds recalled for this enterprise from the gates of hell."

The bull of Vézelay expressly forbade falcons, hounds, and rich habiliments, and it proscribed concubines, troubadours, and other camp followers. Nevertheless, a good many luxuries got across the Rhine after the confusions at Metz,[19] and Louis, occupied with the vast operations of departure, had no force left to scourge out the wastrels. We do not learn how Penthesilea and her warriors got themselves and their baggage wains over the river, but they were certainly not reduced to nondescript in the cavalcade, for we hear later of their smart appearance in Byzantium.

The vast movement of the pilgrim soldiers over central Europe was a prodigy. They kept a pace of ten to twenty miles a day by river and by road, for they were but three summer months from Metz to the Bosporus, and they found their forage by the way. The great barons, turn by turn, led the van, and Louis, like a good shepherd, brought up the rear. Having been taught that the crusade of the troubadour Count of Poitou fifty years before had been rejected by heaven and come to nought by reason of the godlessness of the rabble that followed in his train, Louis maintained a rigorous discipline among the malefactors in his host. He put down pillagers and ravishers with severity and made an example of recreants by cutting off their noses and their ears. But to the needy he showed a liberal compassion. Even in the utmost stress, he began every day with mass and undertook no movement without the guidance of his bodyguard. Odo of Duilio, who slept beside the royal tent, vouches for the blameless purity of all the king's designs.

Eleanor was by some oversight less carefully protected from the impact of the world. The very arrangements for keeping Louis safe were in their nature destined to deprive the queen of the soundest influence and leave her somewhat to the devices of her own heart. Though she doubtless had her chaplain and said her prayers, her entourage was on the whole distinctly secular. She appears to have kept en route to her role of Penthesilea, which, as it is said, had been such a success and inspiration at Vézelay. The Greek historian Nicetas, who writes of the crusade, remarks that "there were in the army women dressed as men, mounted on horses and armed with lance and battle axe. They kept a martial mien, bold as Amazons. At the head of these was one in particular, richly dressed, that went by the name of the 'lady of the golden boot.' The elegance of her bearing and the freedom of her movements recalled the celebrated leader of the Amazons." [20]

In the course of the expedition Penthesilea, as mistress of the forces of Poitou and Aquitaine, was of necessity thrown much among the barons of her own provinces, old friends and relatives, who naturally made much of her. There were Geoffrey de Rancon the Poitevin, Hugues of Lusignan, and Geoffrey of Thouars, and many another, friends and kinsmen of Raymond of Antioch, all dreaming of glorious and profitable careers in the Orient. These knights were not sustained by the ideology that kept Louis upright. They were "younger sons of younger brothers," emigrating from the unemployment and the profitless ennui of the old counties south of the Loire, with whom Eleanor could express herself in her native dialect. It is said that, in spite of the bull of Vézelay, there were troubadours among them who, singing of love and beauty, accustomed the queen to moods of grandeur and elation, as the crusaders traversed the plains of Hungary or floated on the bosom of the Danube in the soft summer weather and the moonlit nights, on their way to the holy city of Jerusalem.

4 ✠

Fear the Greeks

THE HETEROGENEOUS ARMY OF THE FRANKS made a surprisingly rapid passage to Ratisbon, where a part at least of the forces embarked upon the Danube. It was in Ratisbon that the French high command made its first contact with the imperial Comneni, their Greek allies, with whom, as with the famous Ulysses, war was an affair of the intellect, though greatly refined since the days of the crude Trojan horse. To Ratisbon the envoys of the ineffable Manuel Comnenus, Porphyrogenitus, the lofty, sublime, august, Emperor of Byzantium, etc., came to meet the King of the Franks.[1]

Manuel's sentiments in regard to crusades from western Europe were strangely mixed. As a Christian emperor, he was concerned over the possible loss of Jerusalem to the Saracens; but he had no great confidence in the Latins as instruments of his own welfare in the Levant. He was torn between the temptation to employ them in the destruction of his enemies, the Turks in Asia Minor, and the fear that they might, if too successful, rob him of the fruits of their enterprise. The ideal thing would be to feed the Turks and the crusaders into each others' jaws until no remnant of either remained, but this was exceedingly difficult and dangerous to arrange. Manuel could not forget the defiance of the late Bohemund of Antioch to the emperor his father, nor the unspeakable treachery and violence of Prince Raymond of Antioch to the emperor, his brother John, when these relatives of his had asserted their rights as overlords of Antioch. He was not without anxiety about the intentions of the hordes from Poitou and Aquitaine, those old compatriots of Raymond, in the army of the Franks. But Manuel did not betray his uneasiness to the French. Through his envoys dispatched far up the Danube he renewed the cordial and flattering sentiments with which he had long before greeted Louis's overtures from Paris.

However, as the French approached the Bosporus, they were perplexed by the difficulty of according their actual experiences with the civility of the envoys. The courtesy and punctilio of these emissaries had been utterly refined, the sentiments they conveyed most cordial. Yet, although the Greeks indeed lent their altars to the crusaders for mass, they purged them afterwards, as if they had been profaned. Although the Franks had been promised markets for forage, they were obliged, in order to buy necessities, to exchange their silver oboles and their deniers, weight by weight, for large

bronze coins struck with effigies of the King of Kings, but having no great
purchasing value. Presently there were no longer open markets for victuals
and fodder. The Greeks through whose lands they passed were huddled in
well-garrisoned citadels as if expecting a siege, and the Franks paid well for
whatever the guards chose to let down in baskets from their armed towers.
In Adrianople the French crusaders were sorely puzzled to interpret two
prodigious facts that there emerged: one, that Conrad, who was to have
awaited them near Byzantium, had already crossed the Bosporus and was
on his prosperous way toward Cappadocia; and two, that Manuel had lately
concluded a twelve-year truce with his mortal enemies the Turks, which left
them free for any enterprises of their own in Asia Minor which were not
directly menacing to the Byzantine dynasty.

On hearing of these matters a suspicion of treachery entered the minds
of the high command. At this point it was recalled in the councils of the
French king that every previous crusade passing by this route had seriously
considered destroying Byzantium as a stone in its way. So had the great
Bohemund; so had the queen's grandfather, the crusading troubadour
Count of Poitou. Louis's best military strategist, the Bishop of Langres, out-
lined a plan for diverting all the sweet waters from the city and taking it
by siege. All regretted that Conrad's army had already proceeded too far
to add its forces to this enterprise. But Louis, remembering the admonitions
of Abbé Bernard not to be diverted by any counsels whatsoever from the
clear-cut objective of the crusade to save Jerusalem, determined to press on.[2]
He remembered the injunction of Abbé Bernard: "Like a sparrow with careful watchfulness, avoid the snares of the fowler."

It was in September that the weary pilgrim from France with the cross
and seal of the Latin Pope of Rome gleaming upon his tunic drew up his
hosts before the double walls of Byzantium — his barons, his wise men, his
bishops, his foot soldiers, the impious rabble described by Abbé Bernard,
the Amazons, the camp followers, the wagons and sumpter trains bearing
the heavy armor and the business equipment for warfare and the baggage
of the women. The queen city of Christendom with her blazing domes
shone among her waters like a crown of carbuncles. And beyond the
Bosporus, where the shores of Asia, as blue as grapes, came down to greet
the shores of Europe, lay, still far away, beleaguered Jerusalem, the precious
shrines, the foe! On the ramparts encircling the domes and minarets, the
populace of the city and the emperor's men-at-arms thronged to have sight
of this second horde of barbarians from the West, swarming like locusts
from the plains of Thrace.

The French, who did not yet understand the sublime elevation that
separated the Greek emperors born in the purple from all other earthly
potentates, were at first surprised that Manuel did not, according to the

custom of the West, come out of his city processionally with shawms and viols to welcome the most Christian King of the Franks and his baronage, but sent them only emissaries who with salaams directed them to pitch their tents outside the walls at the tip of the Golden Horn. However, there came presently a delegation of satraps bringing gifts of a splendid luster to persons of consequence in Louis's suite and an invitation to the king and a few of his nearest to wait upon the emperor in his imperial palace, the Boukoleon,[3] on the Bosporus.[4]

Louis's chaplain describes the interview of the two Christian monarchs. They met, with the customary feudal precaution against treachery, in the open, and, each flanked by his bodyguard, exchanged the kiss of peace. The king and the emperor, says Odo, were nearly of an age and of almost equal stature, and from the amiability of their intercourse might have seemed brothers. After the greeting, they went inside the palace to an ante-chamber, sat upon two seats which had been prepared, and conversed through an interpreter in the idiom of diplomacy. The emperor inquired, for instance, about the king's health and his desires and called upon heaven to prosper his purposes. Louis, in his penitential garb with his obvious simplicity and his candid mien, seemed not so very frightening after all. Manuel did not invite the French to lodge fraternally in the Boukoleon with the imperial household, but offered the king and his suite his second palace, the Blaquernae, overlooking the Golden Horn, and assigned a cohort of satraps to escort him thither.[5]

There, while the common soldiers of the cross rested from their fatigues in the meadows outside the walls and exhausted the resources for which Abbé Suger groaned at home, Louis and his high command and the royal ladies were entertained with the wonders of Byzantium. As soon as he was lodged, Louis sent off a letter to Abbé Suger: "Following with divine help the laborious journey of our pilgrimage, we have passed through intolerable hardships and infinite dangers, and we have come safe and joyful to Constantinople." He then urged Suger to use every available means to send him, as quickly as possible, as much money as he could raise.

If the sojourn among the shrines of Byzantium was a nine days' wonder to the king, it was an awakening experience for the queen, whose education had progressed just far enough to make her travels profitable. It opened her eyes to vast, lofty, undreamed-of possibilities for majesty, and all the *accidia* from which she had suffered at home was purged from her soul. The magnificent entertainment of the crusaders in Manuel's capital was of a nature to fire the imagination of the young Queen of France. The reality was far above the rumor, and every way extravagant. She learned that Paris was not, as she had been taught by her clerks, the highest of all high places in Christendom. Byzantium, set in its pomp of water and of light, was not only incredibly vaster; it was infinitely more refined. The famous city had inherited much of the outward grandeur of ancient Rome, but it was as well a treasury of artistic marvels that had drifted down to the Bosporus from Persia and Cathay, from Baghdad and Mosul.[6]

The vast imperial palaces, surrounded by their parks sloping to the waters of the Bosporus and the Golden Horn, were as brilliant and as well tended as shrines, and more intricate than hives. These establishments housed not only the domestic but the official activities of the Comneni, and they were administered by hierarchies of functionaries that moved with the supernal majesty and order of the heavenly constellations.

In the palace of the Blaquernae which Manuel vacated for the noblest of the Franks, there were two or three hundred chambers and at least a score of chapels gleaming with gold and mosaic, the whole set in the midst of gardens and groves and shaded alleys giving on the Horn. The rooms were immense, the floors brilliantly paved, the columns gilded, the walls hung with tapestries depicting the triumphs of the Comneni over their barbarian foes. Chandeliers twinkled with the fire of precious stones. Pavilions in the shade offered invitation to enjoy marine vistas framed by cypresses; and from the balconies of upper windows the pilgrims could look back over the plains of Thrace, whence they had lately come.[7] Within the confines of the palace grounds were parks stocked with game for the imperial hunt. The crusaders, as one of their chroniclers observes, knew not whether to admire more the rich materials used in the arts of the East, or the remarkable skill with which these were employed.

From the Boukoleon a long arcaded street opened westward, broken at intervals by wide forums adorned with monuments and fountains and flanked by churches crowned with domes and the graceful inflorescence of minarets. These open squares, embellished with obelisks and triumphal arches, diffused an air of grandeur, as if some magic had arrested the fleeting beauty of the world and endued it with permanence; and the magic seemed to lie not merely in the unique virtue of the separate objects of admiration, but in the arrangement, in which each responded to the other. Nothing came to view haphazardly. In the bazaars that lined the shady passages of the arcades, goldwork and gems from the Orient, the brocades of Tripoli and Baghdad, the glass of Hebron and Antioch, carved ivories, perfumes, embroideries, the linens of Alexandria, illuminated books, were offered in abundance to the purse of royalty.[8]

An imposing hippodrome adjacent to the palace of the Boukoleon was consecrated to races and tournaments and public games, with which the citizens were constantly amused. The amphitheater with its thirty or forty ranks of seats was enclosed by a wall truncated at a height of fifteen feet to make a platform for the display of heroic bronze figures of men and women, horses, oxen, camels, lions, bears, of such marvelous execution that there were no longer craftsmen in Christendom or pagandom who could produce such noble works; and some of these by a magical ingenuity of contrivance could be made to roar, or sing, or move, to the unmeasured delight of the populace. The imperial party entered the hippodrome by private passages and occupied a loge "very dainty and very noble," whence, without suffering contact with their baser human fellows, they could at the same time view the contests and contribute to the spectacle.[9]

In Byzantium the Franks visited church after church rich with marble and mosaic, enshrining the most precious relics; and crowning them all Sancta Sophia, with its heaped-up domes, fantasies caught out of the September sunshine of the Bosporus and the Golden Horn and resting "lightly as cloud upon pillars of porphyry." In the dazzling glimmer of that vast sanctuary the crusaders attended masses intoned with impeccable felicity; and they heard the three-rhymed chant of the eunuchs and the celestial polyphony of the Greek church sung by choirs disciplined to perfection. Upon the sustained vibrant bass drone, the tenor pattern rose and fell in finely graduated notes that seemed to get their perfect contour by traversing the exquisite curves of the domes; and when the sound ceased, the silence was solid and palpable. At the recent dedication of Saint Denis, Louis himself had wielded a rod to keep the rabble from thronging the passages of the abbey church.[10] Here such a prostitution of the purple would have been unthinkable. There were orders upon orders of functionaries to preserve the imperturbable dignity of the Comneni and their guests.

Where half a century before the Emperor Alexius had entertained Godfrey of Bouillon in the triclinium of the Grand Palace, Manuel now entertained Louis and his suite, who doubtless saw behind the imperial throne that already fabled golden tree upon which, when the emperor listed, little golden birds sang with harmonious chirrupings. Here the Franks were bedazzled with such exhibitions of imperial splendor that some of the westerners found them overdone in view of the pious object of their expedition. Reclining upon couches in the Roman fashion, the pilgrims from Gaul were served with farfetched delicacies subtly compounded and wines cooled with snows from the Caucasus; entertained with dancing women and acrobats; refreshed by fountains jetting perfume, and by music blending many instruments in strange harmonies.[11]

In the Boukoleon the French noted that the emperor and empress dwelt apart in seclusion, withdrawn from profane eyes in chambers with rich carpets and hangings of gorgeous stuffs and in gardens and pavilions provided with unimaginable luxury of tile and fountain, and there they were served by slaves whose perfect discipline made the French menials seem altogether loutish. For Louis's feast of his patron saint, Dionysius the

Areopagite, the emperor, graciously recalling the Greek origin of this saint, sent a chorus of Greek priests, and the Franks were entranced not merely by their vestments and painted tapers, but by their dramatic genuflections and the ensemble of bass and treble voices.

In all these refining experiences the queen was certainly impressed not merely by the artistic splendors of Byzantium, from church, palace, and hippodrome to brocade and reliquary, but especially by the court ritual, the high ceremoniousness of all procedures, the ineffable punctilio of all functionaries, and the flawless discipline of menials. Vulgarity came not near the purple tent of majesty; even the mighty prostrated themselves before the royal presence; satraps awaited the imperial nod before seating themselves within the eyesweep of the emperor. The mass movements of whole choruses of slaves, their salaams and genuflections, the fine precision of their oncomings and withdrawals, had all the perfection of a ritual. It was superb, and the effect of it was to enhance incalculably the sublimity of majesty. It was a shame for the queen to think of the chill and dilapidation of her Merovingian tower in Paris, the disorderly simplicity of the royal ménage, the careless freedom of vassals in the royal presence, the disgusting familiarity of servants, the distressing *laissez faire* of authority. Louis (Abbé Bernard's "watchful sparrow"), whose entourage did not permit him to forget in the midst of all this splendor the penitential character of his pilgrimage, did little to increase the prestige of the Capets in Byzantium. He edified the clergy by his tireless pursuit of relics, his fastings, and his alms. But he made no regalian display to offset the pride of the Comneni, nor to arrest their condescensions.

The higher orders of the Franks might willingly have taken more time to explore the glories of Manuel's capital; but they had already, in order to embrace their saint's fete, lingered well into October, while Jerusalem still cried out for succor. The Frankish rabble outside the walls was consuming the royal treasure alarmingly, and Louis was eager to be off lest the November snows should overtake his army in the mountain passes of Asia Minor that still separated him from the Holy Land. Before embarking on the Bosporus he prepared a letter to Abbé Suger setting forth in sanguine terms the progress of the crusade; reporting his momentary uneasiness about the Emperor Conrad's departure ahead of him and about Manuel's curious truce with the Turks; giving good news of his health; and begging his regent to dispatch abundant supplies of tax money for his needs, since the accounts for expenses were not balancing in accordance with estimates.[12]

✤

While Louis, in the brilliant weather of October, was skirting the peninsula of Asia Minor and passing by the famous ecclesiastical cities of Chalcedon and Nicaea, both so full of interest to his bishops, the Holy Roman Emperor was pressing forward into Cappadocia. Conrad was in a hurry to fulfill the vows that Abbé Bernard had wrung from him in Speyer against his better judgment, and to be home again to resume his interrupted warfare with the Pope. He had shaken the dust of Byzantium from his feet because Manuel Porphyrogenitus, who was not only his ally but his brother-in-law as well, had not accorded him a dignity equal to his own, and had even, so far as Asia was concerned, insisted that Conrad was his vassal. In order to proceed as directly as possible to the scene of operations with the Saracens, the Holy Roman Emperor had chosen, under counsel of the guides supplied to him by Manuel, the ancient caravan route from Byzantium to Tarsus, Aleppo, and Edessa, the general route centuries later of the Berlin to Baghdad railway. It had always been the thoroughfare of conquest, the same over which Tancred and Bohemund had passed triumphantly; in some one of its wadies bleached the bones of Guillaume the troubadour's seventy thousand Provençaux. It had always been a trying route for military maneuvers of a grand sort, because of the difficulty of providing sufficient food and water for large companies of men and beasts.

As the Greek guides brought the Germans farther into the camel trails, they assured the high command that abundant supplies lay beyond the next desolate ridge, the next day's march. Put under heavy pressure at last to produce food and water in place of promises, these dragomans absconded in the night "before prime" and made their way back toward Byzantium, leaving the Germans greatly perplexed without a Moses in the wilderness. While consternation spread and the barons took counsel whether to press on or to retreat, and saw their men and beasts too famished for either course, the Turks, with whom Manuel had lately made his truce, swarmed out of the hills from all directions. Lightly armed and crouched on their tough little ponies, they advanced in whirlwinds, yelping like dogs and making an infernal din with tomtoms and tambourines, showering the Germans with slings and arrows, and then wheeling to covert before the heavy arms of the West could be brought to bear upon them. Conrad's foot soldiers, already reduced by thirst and famine, fell into a panic before this sudden onset, scattered, fled, fell into ambush, were lost in the desolate terrain, died of exhaustion, drought, and fear. The royal treasure was captured and Conrad, like the troubadour Count of Poitou before him, narrowly escaped "with a few of his own," a little company of armored knights, who turned back, greatly shaken, toward the Bosporus.[13]

It was while Louis and his host were pressing on, engaged incidentally in that improvement of the mind that rewards the thoughtful traveler in ancient sites, that the dragomans who had abandoned Conrad under cover of darkness arrived in the king's camps. These capable liars reported with an artful semblance of enthusiasm that Conrad had arrived safely in Iconium, having hacked to pieces en route an incredible host of Turks. The Frankish high command was in the course of considering how to take advantage of this cheerful news when a handful of Conrad's knights bore in with ghastly tidings. Then came the emperor's nephew Barbarossa all distraught. He begged Louis to proceed to a rendezvous with the stricken emperor. The circumstances put the Frankish barons in a position to recall the unseemly haste of Conrad in getting into Asia; but Louis waived all malice and bent his whole mind to the succor of his ally. He sent a corps out into the desert to rescue survivors and bury the dead, and he himself pressed forward to comfort the emperor. He found Conrad utterly depressed and very cynical about his Greek allies. The emperor vowed he would go home, and by way of Byzantium, so as to have a colloquy with Manuel, his brother-in-law. He was eager to proceed to Speyer. But the papal interdicts that fell upon crusaders returning from unaccomplished pilgrimage made it humiliating to the emperor to return to Europe. Louis offered his brother-in-arms a liberal bounty to make up for the lost German treasure and did what he could to restore his confidence in Manuel; and at last Conrad was persuaded to travel with the remnant of his army in company with the Franks to Antioch. However, many German barons, who had lost to the Turks the wherewithal they had garnered for their pilgrimage, now renounced their vows and turned back to Europe. It was probably by the agency of these nobles that so much disquieting news regarding the progress of the crusade reached Abbé Suger and Abbé Bernard in the course of the autumn.

The joint councils of the Germans and the Franks now definitely renounced the route through Cappadocia which had proved so disastrous to Conrad, and determined to cling to the littoral where they could remain in the territory of their Greek allies and near ports of issue. The route was, to be sure, much longer and more mountainous, both disadvantages as the season of rain and snow approached; but it was safer and, without being planned to that end, offered incidental opportunity of visiting the ancient apostolic cities of the coast with their uniquely precious shrines.

The crusaders turned westward toward Demetria. In the brilliant October and November days they skirted the archipelago where the isles of Greece rose Venus-like from the foam of the Aegean. In Pergamos and Smyrna they trod the footsteps of the apostles. In Ephesus they saw where "Messire sainz Johann l'evangelistes" had preached the redemption of mankind, and Saint Paul had scourged out of the temples and the colonnades the hoary pagan rites of Diana.

The army moved under a regime democratic to the point of casualness. The great barons turn by turn forged ahead with the van; the Amazons with their baggage moved well guarded in the midst; and Louis, with a cohort of elect knights and his sanhedrin, brought up the rear. There were fatigues and hardships, of course, but these were mainly felt by the rank and file. When the queen and her ladies were weary of *chevauchée*, they were borne in litters for a time, or rode in wains, and at night their painted beds were laid in pavilions where the air was free and open.

By Christmas the pilgrims had reached the valley of a stream which issued directly to the sea. The Nativity of 1147 marked the third anniversary of the fall of Edessa; the crusaders were now seven months out from Metz and two months behind their schedule. But Louis was tempted by the beauty of the site to linger for the fete. The army encamped on the slopes of the river, making of their tents a streeted city gay with banners, and disposed their heavy gear on the level meadows along the shore. Horses were scattered to pasture and the foot soldiers stretched their legs in a sweet repose. The day before Christmas a little cloud drifted over the encampment bearing a flurry of rain. The next morning, while the clerks were singing lauds, a violent wind arose that overset most of the tents and swept them away in a downpour. The river, fed suddenly from the mountains, flooded all the lower ground. In a wild effort to rescue their gear, men and their horses were borne away by the current, crushed upon rocks, or swallowed by the waves. Animals, engines, equipment were carried to the sea. Otto of Freising set down in his chronicle a melancholy line: "The aspect of our tents, which the day before had been so gay, offered a desolating spectacle, showing how great is the divine power, how transitory the delights of men." This episode, crowning their former miseries and losses, utterly discouraged the Teutons, who turned back with the new year to Byzantium, Conrad ill with tertian fever and chagrin, his barons lean with the meager bounty of the Franks.[14]

By this time the Franks as well had had enough of the Levantine riviera. The belated rainy season had broken with wintry gales upon those shores. Closing their ranks upon their losses, they determined to strike inland along the valley of the Maeander to the apostolic city of Laodicea, perched among the Phrygian mountains, and thus avoid the flood-swollen rivers and shorten the distance, as the crow flies, to Antioch, where all were now impatient to arrive. "The way had by this time grown so rough," Odo remarks, "that now the knights' helmets brushed the sky, now their steeds footed the floor of hell." They made the ascent in three difficult stages, only to find Laodicea fallen upon evil days. They were surprised to discover that the Greek governor, in obvious collusion with the Turks, had alienated all supplies likely to prove useful; and this obliged the high command to take hasty counsels on some plan of getting down again from the roof of Asia Minor to the more hospitable coast. They lacked guides, and the lofty mountain ranges strewn higgledy-piggledy in the land made navigation by dead reckoning more difficult than on the littoral. Since no plan seemed superior, they took their bearings from the sun and bore southward toward summer and the sea. Here and there in the course of reconnoitering, they came upon the bodies of Germans lately slain, hapless remnants from Conrad's debacle in the wilderness.[15]

In January they were still floundering among mountain passes too narrow and steep for their sumpter trains, difficult even for the cavalry, in a desolate region offering little invitation to encampment. On a day, the queen's vassal, Geoffrey de Rancon, a Poitevin noble, and the king's uncle, the Count of Maurienne, were directing the van. They had orders to set up their tents for the night on a bare tableland looming ahead that seemed to offer sufficient area. This elevation the leaders reached long before sundown. But the place, viewed at close range, seemed inhospitable, barren, and exposed. Beyond, as the crest was passed, spread an alluring valley with promise of shelter, water, pasturage. In this situation Geoffrey de Rancon presumed upon his mandate from the high command. He unfixed the royal standard from the bleak tableland which he had been ordered to occupy, and proceeded with the forward contingent of the army into the pleasant valley that lay beyond. The official chronicler does not implicate the queen in this treasonous breach of discipline, but the French subsequently blamed her for the result. Since she appears not to have suffered in the melee that ensued, she and her Poitevins were probably in the van, whose leaders would hardly have altered the royal command without her consent.

Geoffrey's ill-starred maneuver left a wide gap between the van and the rear, of which the rear, whose vision was obscured by the mountains, was unaware. Louis in the meantime labored at his post, prodding the last baggage wains up the ascent and urging his cavalry to pass through the abysmal gorges before the fall of night. Arrived within view of the tableland, he was amazed to see no sign of the encampment. While scouts investigated this strange circumstance, there burst from the ravines on every hand between the rear and van a swarm of Turks. Crouched on their tough little ponies, they advanced as before in whirlwinds, yelping like dogs and making an infernal din with tomtoms and tambourines, repeating the tactics that had thrown Conrad's army into panic and flight.

Bewildered by the disappearance of the van and confused by the falling dark, the Franks were driven into a rout. The day had been unseasonably warm, and the Frankish knights had laid aside the encumbrance of their armor for the difficult ascent. Like Conrad's Teutons, they fled to shelter from the Turkish hail of arrows, and, like the Teutons, fell thus into Turkish ambush. Baggage wains, horses and riders, with loosened boulders, tumbled into the gorges of the mountain pass. The sun went down wildly on carnage and outcry. At last the blessed dark concealed the remnant of the Franks dispersed in thicket and ravine. Under cover of the night Louis took refuge in a tree, from which, according to the chronicle, he laid about valiantly with his sword and slew an incredible number of Turks. His little company stood guard about his arboreal retreat, and in the obscurity, in his inconspicuous pilgrim's garb, he passed unrecognized.

Late in the night Odo of Duilio, having captured an errant mount, made his way through scrub and underbrush toward the flare of campfires in the distant valley where the queen's vassals were encamped. But other outriders had already thrown this vanguard into a panic. Her scouts returning toward the summit of the tableland had stumbled upon heaps of dead. What horror had befallen? Where were the lords of Dreux and Courtenay, of Flanders and Champagne? Where was the king? The night gave neither sight nor sound. As the hours wore on, stragglers came in to the Poitevin camp torn with thorns, bruised, wounded, fainting with thirst, unable to speak for weakness and anguish. Toward prime a monk led the dazed King of the Franks into the queen's camp on a stray horse that majesty had never owned. When the roster was taken at daybreak, the survivors wrote off many an armored knight and hundreds of men-at-arms that Abbé Bernard had signed with the cross at Vézelay.[16]

This fortuitous tragedy in the mountains of Paphlagonia so far from the Holy Land cost Eleanor much prestige and marked the final eclipse of the Amazons. Her vassal Geoffrey, on whom fell the brunt of public censure, was in a desperate plight. There was a widespread demand that he be swung from a gibbet there in the wilderness. However, the awkward fact that the king's uncle, the Count of Maurienne, had shared his treason served to save his life.[17] Eleanor suffered the rebuke of her high vassal's dismissal from the pilgrimage, and Geoffrey made his way home to Poitou without getting sight of the glories of Jerusalem. Just what passed between the queen and the king must have been known to Odo of Duilio, but he passes over the royal interview with a silence more eloquent than words.

The army, decimated by the loss of the Teutons, the flood of the river the massacre in Paphlagonia, again closed its ranks and took its reckonings for the Greek port of Satalia (modern Adalia). Here the pilgrims had hope, through the agency of their Greek allies, to repair their equipage, woefully reduced by their misfortunes and the wear and tear of the long journey from Metz. Cold, rain, and famine now assailed the hosts beleaguered in the mountains. Late in January they emerged, mostly on foot, famished and tattered, on the southern coast of Asia Minor. In those desolate and wintry peaks that lay behind, they had been obliged to eat the horses and mules that died of starvation.[18]

Satalia proved a sordid town. Here, however, the Franks were detained above a month by the strategic dilemma now confronting them. According to the best geographical information available, the land route to Antioch was a forty days' journey over a wilderness of mountains. Since even bishops at this stage lacked shoes, the prospect of a February march over that itinerary filled them with dismay. By sea, assuming enough boats procurable, Antioch was reported but a few days distant; but the Greek price for passage, four marks of silver for every man, was out of the reach of any save the barons and the higher orders of the clergy. Though every day's sojourn in Satalia, owing to the prices for commodities, was ruinous, the rank and file lacked the sums and the equipment essential to proceed by either route.

In these days of dire distress Louis shone conspicuously. He sought to share the miseries of his foot soldiers and desired to lead them in person, all bedraggled as they were and impoverished even beyond the reach of his bounty, into the Holy Land. He was driven only under the compulsion of those whose advice he had agreed to take, to leave them behind and to embark with his nobles and his bishops and the remnant of the women in the few seaworthy vessels obtainable. Two seasoned veterans, Thierry, Count of Flanders, and Archimbaud de Bourbon, remained behind in Satalia to wrestle with the problem of forwarding the infantry. These leaders, having made an ineffectual attempt to penetrate the land route, returned to Satalia and, convinced that they could accomplish nothing by lingering, also took ship and followed in the wake of the king.[19]

According to the chaplain, some seven thousand or more foot soldiers were thus left stranded between the inner and the outer walls of Satalia, where they were restrained from pillage for their necessities by Greeks from within and Turks from without. At length a plague broke out among them. Since the menace of the infidel Turks seemed less to the prisoners than that of their Christian allies, they fled from their charnel into the open. Here the infidels, attacking those whom the plague had spared, were mercifully overwhelmed by their wretched condition, opened an alliance with them against the common enemy, the Greeks, and procured for them an alms. It thus befell that the Frankish infantry, the remnant of that rabble Abbé Bernard had gathered in the provinces of Gaul for the rescue of Jerusalem and the redemption of their own souls, was received charitably, under the walls of Satalia, into the bosom of Islam, and so lost to the history of Christendom.[20]

5 ✠

Antioch the Glorious

IT WAS PROBABLY FROM SATALIA that Raymond of Antioch learned with immense relief of the fortunes and whereabouts of the Franks, including his niece the queen, about whose fate everything had conspired to make him very anxious. He had the most personal reasons to doubt that the Emperor Manuel would lend his protection unfeignedly to a host destined for the relief of Antioch and Edessa. He had learned with grave concern of Conrad's losses in Cappadocia, and he knew that the Turks that had inflicted them were still at large in pursuit of crusaders in the mountains of Phrygia and Paphlagonia. He was worried about the quality of the galleys and the mariners supplied by the Greeks for the transport of the pilgrims.

When the sails of the Franks were sighted at last upon the sea, Raymond did not, like Manuel, hold himself aloof in his palaces. The Prince of Antioch went down ten miles from his city to the port of Saint Simeon to lift the broken and bedraggled Franks from the little vessels in which they had been herded for three weeks and set them upon the shores of Syria to the music of instruments and the hymning of choirs. The warmth of the welcome was like nothing the pilgrims had experienced since crossing the Rhine. Processions with banners and escorts, lay and clerical, brought them with a tumult of music and cheers up the valley of the Orontes. The hill slopes were purple and scarlet with anemones, those lilies of the field. The sun stood high after the "latter rains." The barren defiles of Asia Minor lay like a map of nightmare behind them.[1]

For two generations the Franks had thrilled to the story of the first crusade and visioned the herioc figures of Godfrey, Tancred, and Bohemund scaling the battlements of Antioch. To the travel-worn remnant of the Franks, after all their unutterable fatigues and losses, the city with its ramparts, with the flood of the Orontes at its feet and the bulwark of Mount Silpius at its back, spread in a celestial vision bespeaking shelter, repose, succor, plenty, a triumphant hope. To the queen after the weariness of the journey from Metz that now stretched back illimitably in her memory, and especially after the stage from Laodicea under the lamentable eyes of the Franks, her uncle's city had the comforting aspect of home. According to their rank, Raymond disposed the pilgrims in his villas and palaces.

Soon after the arrival of the Franks, Odo the Chaplain wrote to his master in Paris:

> O my father Suger, the king has reached Antioch only at the end of immense danger. We now know that he can take care of himself and meet reverses with firmness and courage. He thinks only of the misfortunes of others and he has done his utmost to relieve them, for he knows that a king exists only to procure the common welfare. He is in good health . . . and keeps up his religious observances. He has never gone against the enemy without having received the Sacrament, and at his return he recites vespers and compline. God is the Alpha and Omega of his enterprise.[2]

The situation of Antioch had made it, by reason of its hinterland and its waterways, a chief commercial center of the world from ancient times.[3] The city lay just where the stream of north and south traffic from Asia Minor and Egypt was crossed by one of the most practicable caravan routes from the vast interior of Asia to the western sea. Tide after tide of civilization had washed over its site and left characteristic deposits on the soil. The famous cities of antiquity that had succeeded each other had been convulsed with earthquake and ravaged by fire and conquest, yet always on the ruins of their ancient grandeurs new life had sprung, appropriating to itself the vestiges of an immemorial past. In the twelfth century Antioch was an indecipherable palimpsest recording, layer on layer, the passage of empire — Hellenic, Roman, Persian, Sassanian, Byzantine. Through it for unnumbered centuries had streamed the arts and industries of the Tigris and the Euphrates and the remoter East. In its days of utmost grandeur the city had climbed from the wide plateau by the river up the slope of Mount Silpius, and thus lay exposed magnificently to view, a maze, terrace on terrace, of domes and colonnades, stadia and minarets, embosoming garden and harim, the whole framed by the many-towered wall that, climbing the Mount and striding across its heights, girdled the miles of streets. From the palaces where Raymond lodged the baronage of France, they looked eastward upon the fertile river valley; southward to that gap between the Lebanon and the Anti-Lebanon through which the caravans crossed from Alexandria and Trebizond; northward toward mountain ranges and the blue lake of Antioch. From the towers of the prince's citadel upon the Mount, the royal guests looked down on the curves of a rocky coast embracing the dye-blue sea. The sweetness of sojourn there, like a lotus eater's dream, was an anodyne for the sorrows the pilgrims had endured and a magic to drench away those valorous plans for crusade and martyrdom with which they had departed from Saint Denis.

In the spring of 1147 Raymond of Antioch was in his early thirties and such a man as the queen could recognize proudly as one of her race and blood. He was, like the other members of her ducal house, tall, handsome, and well knit; in war brave as a lion; in feats of skill and endurance un-surpassed. For strength he was a very Hercules. It was said he could drive his war horse under an arch, grasp the ring of its keystone, and with the strength of his thighs alone, prevent his beast from moving forward. He delighted not only in the hunt, but in games of draughts and dice. Un-learned himself, the prince sought the company of learned men and gladly heard heroic tales and chronicles of history. He observed the Christian rites and attended mass willingly, but liked to have his chapel splendid as a bishop's. Raymond displayed not only the Poitevin physical traits and their tastes for gaiety and splendor, but he shared their yeasty temperament. Though an intensely practical man and no romancer, he often acted in-stinctively; like his father and his grandfather, he occasionally fell into sud-den rages that for a time bereft him of his reason; in negotiations he recked little of breaches of good faith if some advantage could be gained thereby; in crises he was hampered by no narrow view of consistency. William of Tyre, who gives us these facts, takes pains to add that the prince was abstemious in his habits — no glutton, no winebibber, no *débauché*.[4]

Since Raymond of Antioch had been deeply responsible for the second crusade, he naturally had definite military plans to offer to the French high command. When they came in contact with him in his capital, the back-ground of the affair leading to the crusade became much clearer. It now appeared that Joscelin, Count of Edessa, for whose rescue all Europe had stirred at Vézelay, had more than a little merited the catastrophe which had been visited upon him by the infidel. The Capets, whose relative he was, were amazed to hear him described in Antioch as an unsavory knight, an indolent and avaricious lord, a trafficker with paynim, unworthy of the hard-won heritage of Baldwin of Boulogne. Having pretty thoroughly mulcted his Armenian burghers and failed for above a year to pay his garrison, he had quitted his post of duty in Edessa at a critical time for a salubrious country seat on the Euphrates; and the Moslems, taking advantage of his absence, had compounded with the spiritless defenders of the place, breached the walls, and gone in on Christmas day with only the semblance of a siege. The crux of the matter as it now appeared was that the ineffectual Joscelin had thus laid open the frontiers of Raymond's principality, and the latter was inex-pressibly relieved that his nephew, the King of France, and his old com-patriots from Poitou and the Limousin in the vassalage of his niece, the queen, had at last arrived to repair the situation and elevate the house of Poitou to that preëminence it might now easily acquire in the Latin Kingdom of Jerusalem. The prince's plan of campaign for the crusaders was clear, con-vincing, well coördinated. According to it, the Franks, uniting with the barons of Antioch and its fiefs, abetted by certain Knights Templars and whatever forces could be recruited in Tripoli and Jerusalem, would go against

Islam in the east and north, rescue Edessa, and repair the bulwarks of Antioch against the danger of invasion. Raymond with his practical sense felt confident that plans so favorable to the house of Poitou could not fail to engage the Capetian monarch with whom that house was now united.[5]

But in spite of Raymond's reasonable conjectures, the plan thus succinctly disclosed proved very surprising to Louis Capet and his barons from the Île de France, from Flanders, and from Burgundy. It was of course the fall of Edessa that had roused Europe to crusade. But Louis had not taken down the oriflamme from the altars of Saint Denis nor had the barons put their fiefs in gage at Vézelay with any idea of elevating and securing the house of Poitou. The barons almost immediately detected a taint of self-interest in the plans of Raymond, and being already out of sorts with Poitevins, they fell at once into a state of suspicion and alarm. The prince's representations betrayed ambitions out of accord with the high ideals of Abbé Bernard and bade fair to drag the crusade, undertaken with such lofty purposes at Vézelay, into the semblance of a common secular war of conquest. Thierry of Flanders, having learned that Edessa, if rescued, and Aleppo and Caesarea, if taken, would merely be absorbed among the fiefs of Antioch, had no zest for the enterprise, since it would obviously secure no settlement for his sons Henry and Theodoric, who had accompanied him and his countess overseas, and who, as own cousins of the King of Jerusalem, had a right to expect some reward for their labors.

Louis realized that it was not by the practical business of repairing Edessa that he should wipe away the guilt that lay on his soul for the burning of Vitry. Not for this had Eugenius blessed the banners of France. Furthermore, it was observed that the Poitevins who, by the accident of traveling in the van on that fatal day in Paphlagonia, had suffered considerably less than the Franks from their joint disaster, were privy to Raymond's counsels. There were among them many of his compatriots, the comrades of his youth, men of the noble houses of Lusignan, Thouars, Melle, Châtellerault, bound to him by ancient ties of kinship and affection. These vassals of the queen's were so comparatively well lodged and so feted in Antioch that they somewhat lost sight of the fact that it was to the French king and his nobles that Pope Eugenius had committed the direction of the holy war. When all angles of the situation had been considered, the Franks decided to take counsel of the barons of Jerusalem, beyond the Poitevin influences of Antioch, before committing themselves to action. However, they did not for the moment utterly discourage Raymond, for they had it in mind to await in his city the arrival of the infantry they had left behind in Satalia.

The queen, upon her arrival in the prince's capital, was weary after the three-weeks' confinement in the foul little sailing bark from Satalia and vexed by the melancholy allusions of her fellow passengers to that horrible February night in Asia Minor. She was moreover certainly tired of movement, of mountain scenery, of ruined apostolic cities, of stinking boats and drafty tents, of snow and rain, roast mutton, sour cheese, and reveille. She was infinitely relieved to find in the palace of the Prince of Antioch shelter from the censure of the Franks, from the surveillance of the king's chaplain with his recording eye, and from the aggrieved stares of those remnants of the Amazons who had lost too many relatives near Laodicea to be any longer boon traveling companions. But when in the delicious sunshine of the East her native vitality returned, she showed herself to her relatives and the expatriates from her provinces a loyal Poitevin and a radiant Queen of France. She was of so much consequence in Antioch that Louis, who continued, in spite of all his trials, to cherish her with an unreasoning love, appears to have felt almost repaid for the hardship and expense of bringing her out three thousand miles from Paris.

A sympathy at once sprang up between the Prince of Antioch and his niece the queen. Raymond's clear Poitevin eye at once divined that the fortunes of Antioch rested not with Louis, his diminished forces and his monkish counselors, but with Eleanor and her Provençaux. The queen and the prince, who had now to compensate for their ten years' separation, conversed long hours together in their native dialect, whose racy idiom was perhaps not quite intelligible to the Franks. After having caught up with each other on the vital history of that decade, so full of incident to them both, it is probable that they found themselves in accord not only on the proper objectives of the crusade, but also on the character of the idealists who had come from the West for the rescue of Jerusalem. Since these visionaries from Gaul lacked a clear-cut policy, the Poitevin genius aspired to maneuver them one by one into action on behalf of Antioch. This strategy was tried. Raymond ransacked his bazaars and his princely treasure for the spoils of the East; he called ceremoniously upon the most noble of the Frankish barons where they lodged in his villas and palaces, and plied them with strange and splendid gifts.[6] He was a liberal and a persuasive man, and he employed all the seductions of his riches and his eloquence to prevail upon his guests. At his expense they tasted wines cooled with mountain snows, the fruits and spices of the Orient; they were enriched with jewels, amulets, and the most precious relics of the Holy Land. But these costly overtures evoked from the Franks no evidence of gratitude of a strictly practical quality.

While Louis awaited the arrival of his infantry and considered what course of action would most commend itself to heaven as a propitiation for his sins, he visited the shrines of Antioch, that cradle of evangelists. As he got about Raymond's capital, the conviction grew upon him that to preserve the integrity of Antioch was not his primal mission. He had the traveler's common experience of finding the famous city other than he had dreamed it. He had expected to find the city of Luke and Peter, Barnabas and Paul, crying from its desecrated shrines for the puissant vindication of Christendom. As a result of earthquake, conquest, and fire, Antioch was indeed a rich archaeological heap, but not altogether composed, as he had figured it, of ruined Christian altars. Superficially, it had the aspect of a thriving caravansary. At its very core was not the basilica of Saint Paul but a forum presided over by an image of Apollo, where the caravans poured in, where the wares of three continents were sifted for transport and exchange, where turbaned Saracen merchants without hindrance weighed the paynim moneys of Baghdad and Isfahan against the coinage of Venice, Pisa, Alexandria, Bordeaux. There was a babel of language, an easy commingling of races, a bewildering strangeness of costume.[7] Raymond had not even banished the ancient Greek and Roman gods from Antioch. In fact, the Christian civilization seemed to flourish only in certain razed areas of its lingering pagan and Saracenic past. If Apollo and Diana had taken a fancy to lend their fanes to Saint Paul and the Virgin for a time, they had not forsworn their dedicated sites. With an air of knowing that gods have forever, they still peered out from many a fountainhead and from oddments quaintly revamped in church and palace walls. If their pagan whim tolerated Christian basilicas in the precincts of their ancient temples, it permitted mosque, harim, and mihrab equally. Minarets bloomed thickly among the cypresses, and the call of the muezzin fell musically upon the dawn and evening air.

The second generation of those first crusaders, forgetting the mystical transport of their sires and the cradle of their nurture in the West, had intermarried, not only with the Greeks, but even with the Saracens, and their progeny, the "Pullani," were often men of substance and consequence who went arrogantly in the Christian city of Antioch. They wore flowing eastern dress, spoke the language of the infidel with native ease, fraternized in eating-houses with the enemies of Christ, and were unashamed. These mongrels, some of them bearing names famous in the West for valor and piety, amused and enriched themselves by despoiling innocent pilgrims of their substance.[8] Was it for the defense of this degenerate race that the Franks had mortgaged their fiefs and suffered their hardships and their losses?

It was otherwise with the queen, whose childhood in Bordeaux made not only turbaned Moslems but Roman temples and stadia and playful bacchanalian figures more companionable. To her Antioch was the essence of poetry, the "trite touched with the strange." Here in the market of Pisan and Amalfitan, she stood in the gateway of that merchant route which, beginning beyond the harems of Scheherazade in the East, ended in the West beyond the Pillars of Hercules. Some of the red and brown sails of Moor and Jew and Sicilian would be shaken down at last in the river moats of Bordeaux below the towers of her own castle of the Ombrière. Paris was no longer to her the summit of the world. Byzantium was infinitely more glorious; Antioch was more intellectually quickening, more stirring to the heart, than the Île with all its schools. As for the prayer call of the Saracens, it evoked memories of her own land. She had seen the Moors of Spain upon the highways of the Limousin and understood that Moslem traders will not come where they have no muezzin, no harim where they can wash the desert sand from their feet, no mihrab where they can set their faces toward Mecca.

It was embarrassing in the circumstances that the king was obliged to accept so long the hospitality of the Prince of Antioch while awaiting the arrival of the troops from Satalia. But in this interval Raymond's hospitality knew no bounds. The Frankish lords hunted on the shaggy slopes of Baghras, chased gazelles beyond the lake of Antioch, loosed their falcons on the banks of the Orontes. In the full tide of spring the queen doubtless made *chevauchée* to that very grove where Apollo, pursuing Daphne among the cypresses and the waterfalls, found himself at last embracing a pink laurel bush.

In spite of all this splendid entertainment, Louis temporized. He would not commit himself to the strategies proposed in Antioch. And the more the queen declared for Raymond's military plans, the more certain he became that he must not support them. He hardly needed the wakefulness of the chaplain in his bedchamber to remind him that the queen's counsels in war had always been regrettable. He had only to bethink him of the ineffaceable tragedies of Laodicea and of Vitry. Hosts of unshriven dead cried out to him from purgatory to beware. Louis and his *mesnie* were frozen into distrust of the queen, and what they saw in Antioch did not serve to reassure them. Let the Poitevin plan seem never so expedient, the Franks could not have followed Eleanor or Raymond over the safest of bridges to the new Jerusalem.

During those brilliant spring days in which military plans were under discussion, Louis and his counselors had been disquieted by certain long and animated conversations in the *langue d'oc* that went on between the Prince of Antioch and the queen in the gardens of the Orontes and on the terraces of Mount Silpius. There was both eagerness and vivacity in these colloquies, and certain Poitevins, who were not excluded by the barrier of dialect, appeared to find the talk not only significant, but richly amusing. The prince and his friends seemed to waken latent gifts of speech and manner in the queen. She was twenty-five and conscious of her moment. In Antioch she held life in her hand like a goblet of untasted wine. Louis had never seen her shine with such colors nor maneuver such followings. Was it merely the return to familiar speech and custom in her uncle's palaces, or something in the sharp chiaroscuro of Syria that, reminding her of her own provinces, restored her to herself? It seemed that the clear black shadows of the cypresses, the crisp break of water in fountains, the definite scent of lemons in gardens and spice in the bazaar, cleared her senses and purged the humors from her brain.

It was in the course of these intimacies that Raymond learned about the queen's attacks of *accidia*, which, beginning with moderate onsets in Paris, had swollen to a first-rate malady between Metz and Antioch. He was not surprised to find she was discontented with her role as Queen of France and that her mind had strayed to alternatives. The bishops and abbés and chaplains assigned to hedge Louis from dangerous influences in the course of his pilgrimage had thwarted her native gifts for creating a milieu of her own that might have given a little luster to the enterprise of kings and nobles even on the dusty way to Palestine. The vigils of Odo of Duilio outside the king's chamber, and the grip of Thierry Galeran upon the coffers of the expedition, had deprived her of her lawful influence in the counsels of her lord, an influence to which not only her station as queen, but her contribution to the resources of crusade, seemed to entitle her.

There was a touch of chagrin too in her malaise. Louis's counsel of wise men found some fault with her and armed him and themselves against her with concerted disapproval. Abbé Bernard had discovered in her the evil genius of the king in his wretched wars with Thibault of Champagne; in ten years of marriage she had given the Franks no prince; and to cap the climax of their censure the high command blamed her liege vassal, Geoffrey de Rancon, for the disaster in the mountains of Paphlagonia.

Raymond and the Poitevins in Eleanor's vassalage were the last people in the world to admire the austerities of the Franks, and the sequestration of the king in the custody of the eunuch and the monk moved them to sardonic mirth. Thierry Galeran was the special butt of the queen's derision. She played him up amusingly in Antioch with touches of irony.[9] If Louis suspected the pantomime upon the terraces of the palace in which he and his mentors were involved, he behaved with singular magnanimity.

In the midst of these doings in Antioch the apostasy of the infantry left behind in Satalia became known. The prestige of the Franks, now deprived of the valuable hope vested in the foot soldiers for the holy war, fell sharply. At the same time, envoys from Jerusalem with plans to utilize the Frankish hosts in the interests of that city were reported at the gates. Raymond in sudden alarm demanded a plenary council of the barons of France and Antioch on the question of military plans. Again the Prince of Antioch recapitulated his strategy. His was the capable plan of an experienced man, a plan better calculated than others to stay the disastrous course of affairs in the East and shore up the Latin Kingdom of Jerusalem for another century. When the prince had made his last point clear, the king was called upon to subscribe. It was a terrible moment. Louis was no such orator as the Prince of Antioch, but he met the challenge with a noble courage. He rose with the

Pope's silver cross gleaming on his shoulder and spoke with measure and discretion.

"I have made my vows to go to the Holy Sepulcher, and for this purpose expressly I took the cross. I have come from my country hardly, having endured many calamities. I have no disposition to undertake any wars until I shall have fulfilled my pilgrimage. Afterward I will hear the Prince of Antioch and the other barons of Syria, and following a general council, I will, according to my power, offer myself for the needs of our Lord." [10]

The barons of Antioch, who had been to a terrific expense, were thus undone by the humble pilgrim from France. Raymond entered straightway into one of the rages for which his house was famous. He swore by all the effectual saints of the old Limousin that he would be speedily avenged upon the Franks and the Flemings, who had deceived his reasonable hope and laid the Latin Kingdom open to the despite of the Saracens. It was a fearful transport which appears to have been quoted and misquoted for a long time afterward. William of Tyre, writing forty years after the event, contents himself with saying that, whereas Raymond had surpassed himself in showering benefits upon the Franks, he now flew to the other extreme of doing all he could to injure them.[11]

When the die had been cast in the council of war, there was no longer occasion for amenities. Raymond's fury was undisguised. There was no question of lingering in his villas and palaces. The necessity was obvious of getting out of Antioch with all speed and repairing to the shelter and the counsel of the barons of Jerusalem. Louis, alive now to the snares of Satan, was in the midst of the intricate and perplexing business of marshaling his hosts and getting his harness together when the queen demanded and obtained an audience. At this critical moment she brought him face to face with what proved in the long run the major incident of the holy war. In short, she let him know that she had taken a resolution to separate herself then and there from the Capetian dynasty, to go with him no further on crusade, to lay aside her crown adorned with the lilies of France, to resume her status as Duchess of Aquitaine, to fix her pilgrim staff in Antioch and remain with Raymond in his high place on Mount Silpius.[12]

Significant as it was, the chroniclers give few details of the episode. However, John of Salisbury relates that Louis, who had not ceased to cherish the queen with an almost boyish ardor, was surprised, chagrined, and terribly upset by the outpouring of her grievances, and at once took measures to resist her purposes. If he asked her for the grounds of her discontent, she made no such saucy rejoinder as that ascribed to her by the Minstrel of Reims: "Why do I renounce you? Because of your fecklessness. You are not worth a rotten pear." [13] To attribute these words to her is a slander on the polished manners of the queen. It would have been easier to deal with her if she had been moved by mere caprice. But not for nothing had she been bred in dialectic among the scholars of the Île. What she offered was no madcap impulse secure from reason, but a syllogism that not even the wisest doctors of Paris could refute. She reminded Louis, on no less an authority than that of Abbé Bernard himself, that she was related to him in a degree forbidden by the church, and that by holding her to a sinful marriage, he was putting his soul and hers in jeopardy.[14]

It was true that in the day when Thibault of Champagne had sought to strengthen himself against the king by the marriage of two of his heirs to Louis's vassals, Louis had forbidden the bans on grounds of consanguinity; and Abbé Bernard had written with more than a tone of asperity to the Bishop of Préneste, "How is it that the king is so scrupulous about consanguinity in the case of Thibault's heirs, when everyone knows that he himself has married his cousin in the fourth degree?"[15] The words had then sounded like a tocsin in Louis's ears, but he had tried to shut them out as part of the clamor of war. Now on the lips of the queen, they rang with new and portentous import.

The council, to which Louis repaired in this crisis, was more alive to Raymond's role in the affair than to the novel and capricious ideas of the queen. Queen or no queen, syllogism or no syllogism, Eleanor was Louis's vassal and his lawful marriage prize, the most valuable piece on the chessboard of feudal Europe. In case of her separation from the king, she could not long remain at large as Duchess of Aquitaine. On whom then did the treasonous Raymond intend to bestow the king's ward in order to buttress his own estates? On himself? On a vassal? On one of the Pullani? On some merchant prince of Amalfi or Genoa? On some emir of the Saracens, with whom he seemed to be so privy? The council fell into a panic. How was Louis, the Pope's emissary, the most Christian King of the Franks, to appear in Jerusalem for conference on the holy war with King Baldwin and his barons, with the Templars, the Patriarch, the Holy Roman Emperor, if, after all his losses from Metz to Antioch, he were to lose besides, within the very limits of the Latin Kingdom, his queen and all her provinces? What story would this be for Abbé Bernard, for Abbé Suger, for the Pope?

The sound vigorous counsels of Thierry Galeran to keep the queen in custody at any cost prevailed. A signal was given to the French army in the night. The queen was seized and fetched, in what state of woe and anguish or downright Poitevin rage we can only guess, to Saint Paul's gate. Before the prayer call sounded from the minarets or Raymond's sleepy watch awoke upon the towers of Mount Silpius, the Frankish hosts for the rescue of *Dame-Dieu outre-mer* had shaken the dust of the city from their feet and taken the road past the fortress of Margab for Tripoli. The midnight exit of the King of the Franks from Antioch with his captive queen, observes William of Tyre, was by no means suitable to the dignity of the foremost king of Christendom, nor by any means comparable to his entrance a few weeks before with flying banners, the pomp of instruments, and the psalmody of choirs.

Over the "Pilgrim's Ladder," that narrow defile above the sea, Louis bore southward with a terrible agitation in his breast. His brain swam in dialectic, but the universals helped him not at all. He might, he reflected, let the queen go in peace, whereupon he might marry another princess: but he would have to restore her provinces, and she might bestow them elsewhere. Or he might incarcerate the queen and keep her provinces as the price of treason; but he would then be unable to marry another princess, and he had no son. Or he might temporize and cocker the queen, and bring her to a better mind: but, even if this were possible, what about the sin of consanguinity?

As soon as he could, Louis unbosomed himself to Abbé Suger on the affair in Antioch. It is a great pity that his letter, like many other documents which fell into the hands of the discreet abbé, has been lost; but the reply, which came into more careless fingers, still remains. "If the queen has given you offense," wrote the abbé, "conceal your resentment as best you may until such time as you both shall have returned to your own estates, when this grievance and other matters may be attended to." [16] In view of their desperate procedure in Antioch, this letter was probably a solace not only to the king but to those mentors by whose advice he had been guided.

However, in spite of the discretions of the high council, the "resentment" of which the abbé wrote could not be "concealed" from the profane ranks of the crusading pilgrims. The custody of Eleanor made it very apparent that something dreadful had occurred in Antioch to warrant such proceedings. Only some shocking misbehavior on her part seemed adequate to account for the breach between the Franks and the Poitevins that threatened once more to dissipate the forces for crusade. In consequence, a variety of stories arose among the Franks to explain the anomaly and to preserve Louis and the high command from blame for the situation. William of Tyre charges the queen with indiscretions and with conduct both in Antioch and later unworthy of her royal dignity and disregardful of her marriage bond; [17] but his sources were certainly the French high command. John of Salisbury accuses her of too great familiarity with the Prince of Antioch. [18] The Minstrel of Reims, most of whose other yarns are preposterous, details the queen's effort to escape with her jewels from Tyre in a galley supplied by Saladin (a potentate at the time about ten or twelve years of age), and he relates that Louis himself frustrated her flight by setting his foot on the landing stage, just as the craft was ready to slip its moorings, and convoying her back under the shelter of midnight to the palace where she had been lodged. The stories are all suspect in view of their Frankish source and of the Frankish interest in giving a proper color to the grievous incident. Gervase of Canterbury recommends silence for rumors current in regard to Eleanor's conduct in the Orient.[19] But whether or not there was in any of them an element of fact, they became, in spite of efforts to stifle them, a stock in trade, revived from time to time, of scandalmongers and balladeers, and so pursued the Duchess of Aquitaine to the end of her days and farther down the corridors of history.

6 ✠

Jerusalem

Urbs Sion inclyta, turris et edita littore tuto,
To peto, te colo, te flagro, te volo, canto, saluto.
Bernard of Cluny

HOW SHALL AN AGE CONCERNED WITH MATERIAL THINGS comprehend the fervor
that engaged whole generations of men in the Middle Ages with the theme of
immortality? The vast perspective of that theme alters all the values of existence. In its immensity, life has but a feeble transiency; not here, but in the
timeless sweep of eternity lies its meaning and man's true destiny. Thus
mortality gets no enhancement from its brevity; wealth is perplexity; status
but a vassal's tenure; joy a bubble; beauty a withering flower. So kings leave
their governing in their brief mortal hour, make their crowns a votive offering, and go upon crusade. Merchants and hinds leave kindred, shop, and
plow, eager for that labor whose wages are incorruptible. He who sees life
as but

> *a little strip of light*
> *'Twixt night and night* [1]

can by no means sense the ardor that burned in the breasts of those pilgrims
who, having put all their substance in pawn, traversed strange lands, and lost
many of their fellows by the way, came at last, shoeless and destitute,
in view of Jerusalem. "When the crusaders came near the city of Jesus Christ,"
says one of them, "they wept tears of joy. They could not sleep that night,
they burned with such desire to see that city that marked the goal of their
labors and the accomplishment of their vows. The night seemed longer than
other nights; they felt the day would never dawn." [2]

✠

Led by the standard of the Holy Sepulcher, the *gonfanon baucent* of the
Templars, and the oriflamme, the remnant of the grand crusade made its
way over the stony highways of Palestine to the immemorial city. Winding
among the brilliant arid hills, they came in sight of the Roman walls buttressed by the Tower of David, once fallen to Saracens, and now briefly recovered for a Christian dynasty. There it stood, the high place of Israel, not
cloudy in a vision, but compact, succinct, its gathered domes and towers

burning in the radiant air under the intense blue dome of sky, symbol in transient colors of the eternal city, the term of pilgrimage, and the end of man's desire.[3]

Foulques, the Patriach of Jerusalem, and a company of Templars had gone out to meet the Franks and bring them in triumph to the holy city. This escort had traveled almost to the gates of Antioch for fear Louis might be persuaded to make up his quarrel with Raymond, or that he might be diverted en route by the Count of Tripoli for the defense of that principality. This going forth of the patriarch had been wise, because all along the way Louis had received envoys with letters and gifts and suggestions as to which of the cities of pagandom it would be profitable for the crusaders to take.[4]

The chroniclers agree that Louis's arrival in Jerusalem "animated all hearts." "He was received," says William of Tyre, "as an angel of the Lord." For nearly three years since the fall of Edessa the Christians of the Holy Land had watched from their housetops for the dust of this host rising from the road. It was almost so long ago that the widowed Queen Melisende had written to Abbé Bernard about the hapless state of Jerusalem and had sent the abbé a fragment of the true cross; it was many months since Bernard had replied, raising hope in her heart.

The whole population came out to the Jaffa Gate to welcome the deliverer of the Holy Land with music and processions: the court, the religious orders, and a multitude of palmers from all the corners of Christendom, fanning the air with olive branches and the fronds of palms — such an indiscriminate company as only Pentecostal gifts and the wide charity of heaven itself could embrace in one Christian family. Queen Melisende was there, that valiant half-Oriental woman with the sap of the first crusaders in her veins, and her son, the boy king Baldwin, scion of the late Angevin King Foulques. There, too, was Conrad of Hohenstaufen, who, all refreshed and refurbished during his winter with Manuel in Byzantium, had achieved his original plan of anticipating the King of the Franks in Jerusalem.[5]

Louis, like King Baldwin I before him, repudiated all royal acclaim in that city where Christ had worn the crown of thorns, and refused to break his fast or to take any rest until he should have been brought to the Holy Sepulcher. The Franks went processionally, the patriarch at their head, to the tomb; and there, in a transport of joy, Louis cast down the burden of his sins, reposed the oriflamme which the Pope had taken from Saint Denis, and laid his offering upon the holiest altar in the world. He then made a tour of other precious shrines and, thanks to the Templars, was able to scatter alms along the pilgrims' thoroughfare. It was only after this circuit of the city that the king and his *mesnie* were lodged at last in the ancient Tower of David, where the patriarch had provided richly for their entertainment.

We are at a loss to account for the captive queen in the midst of this demonstration. The silence of the chroniclers at this point is universal. We do not know whether Eleanor was borne sullenly into Jerusalem in her painted wain with the curtains drawn, or whether she rode proud as Penthesilea under the Jaffa Gate on her own hackney, or came on foot in palmer's weeds bearing the cross which Abbé Bernard had given her at Vézelay. In any case, she was of less consequence in Jerusalem than she had been in Antioch and Byzantium. She may have been under a certain surveillance after the incident in Antioch, but not under an actual restraint since that would have outraged her vassals. Even the king's council seem to have agreed after they had rescued her from her uncle's citadel that their best course was to improve her spirits. It is interesting in this connection that not much is heard in the chronicles about Odo of Duilio after the exodus from Antioch; but Thierry Galeran seems to have passed the year overseas, since he is found as one of the advance guard announcing Louis's return to France.[6]

In Jerusalem the king and his barons found themselves in a new milieu, with new counsels for the holy war. Here they were free from the factious colonies of the south of Europe that flourished in Antioch and Tripoli and in company with reasonable men of their own provinces, akin in speech and race, men with profounder ideas about the significance of crusade.

There was already a special bond between the Capets and the reigning Latin dynasty. The late King Foulques of Jerusalem, in his original incarnation as Count of Anjou, had been a vassal of Louis the Fat. Foulques had been translated, as it were, in the midst of high emprise in Europe to a new existence overseas. At the age of about forty, after a successful career in his own provinces, he had folded his tents in Anjou, distributed his estates among his heirs, and gone out upon invitation from King Baldwin II to marry his daughter, the half-Armenian Princess Melisende, and bolster up the declining Kingdom of Jerusalem. He had hewed out a new destiny as king of the Christian colonies. For years he had steadied the fortunes of the little state, fought its wars, strengthened its frontiers with fortress castles, rebuilt much of the holy city, repaired its shrines, and begotten sons for the dwindling Latin dynasty. It was his untimely death in 1144 that had emboldened the Saracens to assault Edessa. The Countess of Flanders, who had accompanied her husband and her sons, Henry and Theodoric, upon Louis's crusade, was Foulques's daughter in his European incarnation, and so a half sister of the reigning King of Jerusalem. With this reliable world, shepherded by the patriarch, Louis found himself more thoroughly *en rapport*. He soon saw how providential it had been that he had not yielded to the pressures of Raymond of Antioch. Though the fall of Edessa had provoked the crusade, the rescue of Edessa seemed, according to advices in Jerusalem, by no means the proper objective of campaigns in Palestine. In fact, anything profiting Raymond seemed, in the clearer light of Jerusalem, a kind of sacrilege.

On the very day after their arrival, Louis and his barons went into conclave with the *haute cour* and with the German bishops and barons whom Conrad had recruited in imposing numbers. All agreed that they ought to assemble a plenary council in Acre to survey in a large way the destinies of the Latin Kingdom and the measures to be taken for the recovery and defense of the holy places. According to William of Tyre's account of the session in Acre, there was a strong ecclesiastical preponderance, with the Patriarch of Jerusalem as the guiding genius of the counsels. The kings and their barons, even the Holy Roman Emperor, appear to have waited to learn from the patriarch how they and their hosts were to be employed for the succor of Jerusalem. The Count of Tripoli and the Prince of Antioch were not there; nor was there any representation from Edessa. Queen Melisende and other noble ladies shared the counsel, but the Queen of France is not mentioned. In her case, it is impossible to say whether she was not summoned or whether she refused to go.[7]

A great many projects were discussed. It proved very hard to find an objective upon which all could agree. At length it was decided that an offensive against Damascus offered the best likelihood of safeguarding the Latin Kingdom, without overadvancing the interests of any single Christian prince. To take Damascus would stop up that route which united the Moslems of the two caliphates of Egypt and Baghdad, and destroy that center from which they might coöperate to attack the Christian fiefs. The high command therefore "let cry" the summons for a muster on the Sea of Galilee on the 25th of May. In the town of Tiberias the King of the Franks, the King of Jerusalem, and the Holy Roman Emperor marshaled their hosts. They spread their tents, newly revamped by the Templars in Jerusalem, and planted their banners above the lake. At dawn they could look down upon the little boats where fishermen, as in the day of the apostles, were drawing their nets and dropping their sails, and, as the mist lifted from the water, upon that Gadarene desert country that brooded beyond the narrow green rim of the lake. Resuming their march, they passed through Caesarea Philippi and there received from its shrine the true cross, which most venerable relic they bore with them as sovereign token of their enterprise. Thence they set out briskly over the Anti-Lebanon in the first glowing days of the Syrian summer. Arriving in sight of Damascus without obstacle, they encamped among the vineyards, orchards, and cucumber gardens of the Damascene oasis.

The late King Foulques, lacking the soldiers to take the city, had pursued a policy of reciprocal toleration with the Emir of Damascus. The Moslems were therefore somewhat unprepared and thoroughly terrified by the advent of the "Christian dogs." However, they diverted all the water they could from their irrigation streams, plundered their own gardens, drew in their provisions, and prayed in all their mosques to Allah to smite the enemy with the desert sun.

The Christian army, led by the more experienced knights of Jerusalem, dashed valiantly against the walls. Louis led his barons in person and flung himself with ardor into the thick of the onslaught. They were making hopeful progress when some unofficial opinion got abroad among the various contingents that an attack from another quarter would be more certain of success. William of Tyre describes this mysterious counsel that insinuated itself at the very moment of triumph as "malice of the devil." However this may be, it went into the ear of the high command and the siege was diverted to another angle of the wall. Here the Christians found themselves cut off from water, and the heat, dust, and thirst brought them, horse and man, to extremity. A confusion arose among the council. The blame for the evil advice could not be fixed upon a guilty man who could be hanged for it; but a suspicion spread abroad that there was treachery afoot. Some said Raymond of Antioch, out of enmity to the French king, had betrayed the Christians to the infidels; some that Thierry of Flanders had bargained for the fief, when it should fall, as a settlement for Henry and Theodoric, who had never profited by the status of their grandfather, King Foulques of Jerusalem; some talked of venality among the barons of Jerusalem. Conrad of Hohenstaufen, who was unaccustomed to such loose organization and ineffectual work in warfare, declared himself quit of his vows and eager to go home. With all his courage and fervor, the King of the Franks, who was certainly disinterested, could not persuade these veterans of other wars to persevere. The Damascenes gave thanks in all their mosques when the King of Jerusalem and his allies folded their tents and struck off from the trampled gardens and vineyards across the desert for the valley of the Jordan.[8]

Since it subsequently seemed impossible to rally for any special project the various forces that Abbé Bernard had recruited in Europe, the second crusade, as a military operation, crumbled to its final ruin. The long journey and the many delays had depleted the coffers as well as the man power for the expedition, and the sedition of Antioch and Tripoli hopelessly divided the forces overseas. The King of Jerusalem, even the Templars, lacked the means to carry on the war. Louis turned over the remnant of his homesick barons and prelates to his brother, the Count of Dreux, and they returned by sea to their own lands. As for the king himself, he could not make up his mind to depart from Palestine.

Abbé Suger besought him to return to his own estates, where the seeds of sedition were being sown by his recent brothers-in-arms. "Why, my dear Lord and King," wrote the abbé, "are you still in flight from us? Have we not hated those who hate you, have we not burned against your enemies?

Why do you persist in enduring so many desperate ills overseas after your barons and nobles have returned? By reason of what harshness of ours, or what theory of your own, do you delay your return?"[9] But in spite of these importunities, Louis resolved to stay over the winter for the season of Easter in 1149. The long delays in Antioch had obliged him to forego the Easter celebrations of 1148.

Perhaps Louis had other than religious motives for his long delay in Palestine. At least he took respite for a time from the heavy and thankless task of being King of the Franks. If only Providence had so disposed the principalities of this world, the role of being King of Jerusalem might have suited him. Under guidance of the better minds of the East, he studied the possibility of leading out another crusade from Europe which should profit by all the hard-earned experience of the first. It is probable that he made a careful tour of the Holy Land, which then had its guidebooks and its guides from Dan to Beersheba. And especially he turned over in his mind the perplexing problem of the queen, whom he could neither leave behind nor persuade to accompany him home in amity.[10] A note in the annals of Monte Cassino, where the sovereigns lodged on their return from overseas, states that, after the siege of Damascus, Louis went back to Antioch — a statement which provokes speculation without supplying anything to give color to it.

Having lingered all around the calendar and celebrated the whole year's cycle of feasts and fasts, the king and queen passed Easter, that climax of the Christian's experience, in the holy city. Sometime after that fervor of vigil and rejoicing, they went down finally to Acre to take ship for home. There they embarked separately, each with a small *mesnie*, in two of those high-pooped, two-masted sailing vessels with supplementary oars (*galea*) that plied the Mediterranean for the pilgrim traffic.

They had safely passed the glistening isles of the Aegean and were skirting the Peloponnesus off Cape Melaea when they encountered a Sicilian vessel with men-at-arms. Louis went aboard this buss, after the manner of mariners, probably to get the news. On board he was astonished to learn that his ally, Roger of Sicily, was engaged by the agency of this very ship in a war against his other ally and friend, the Emperor Manuel of Byzantium. He was just considering the fact that his presence in Roger's ship might be gravely misunderstood by the Emperor of Byzantium when some of Manuel's vessels actually came down like pirates in the wind, captured the queen's galley, and bore her and her women off toward the shores of Greece. Louis himself escaped capture by running up on the Sicilian ship the flag of a Greek ally; but his escort and his baggage were borne off in the wake of Eleanor. The Sicilian fleet, drawing up in hot pursuit, overhauled the Greeks, rescued the queen, and subsequently recovered the king's effects. But the sovereigns, still in separate vessels, were carried apart out of each other's sight and borne in widely sundered routes upon the sea. The incidents of their Odyssey, which consumed a full two months, are lost to history.[11]

On the 29th of July, after alarums and excursions, Louis was brought up like a wraith of himself on the shores of Calabria, perhaps at Brindisi. He had in the course of his experiences developed such a prejudice against the sea that nothing but extremity induced him in later years to set his foot again upon a landing stage. He was without his *mesnie*; he had lost all his baggage; and he was sick with anxiety about the queen, of whose fate he was altogether ignorant.

On the shores of Calabria, Roger of Sicily received him as the "anointed of the Lord," comforted him for his calamities, provided for his necessities, which were of every sort, and best of all, gave him news of Eleanor. She had been driven by adverse winds off the "coast of Barbary" and had lately "by the mercy of God" come safely to the port of Palermo in Sicily. Her hardships had left her for the moment incapable of further journeyings. She gave promise of gratifying the Franks at last with an heir, and was hence an object of more than usual solicitude. In spite of his haste to get forward to his own estates, Louis waited three weeks for her crossing to the mainland. Together they made a brief visit in Potenza to Roger of Sicily, whose ships had rescued them, and then pressed on to meet the Pope in Tusculum.

Eugenius found himself still an exile from Rome by reason of the aggressions of Conrad of Hohenstaufen, which had been promptly renewed upon the latter's return from the crusade. The Pope received the young sovereigns of the Franks, whom he had dedicated more than two years before at Saint Denis, as he might have welcomed angels, and comforted them spiritually for all the calamities they had endured. There was a great deal for Eugenius to talk over with the king who had suffered so much as an instrument of the church, who had studied the lamentable condition of the Latin Kingdom long and thoroughly, and who cherished the hope of going out a second time to Palestine. At last they came to the grievous incident of Antioch.

The queen, the Pope discovered, was by no means appeased for her abduction from her uncle's citadel. Even after a year in the Holy Land, she clung to the idea of separation and harped capably upon the theme of consanguinity and the unquestionable authority of Abbé Bernard. This insistence was now especially painful to Louis, since it added to his other afflictions anxiety about the legitimacy of the heir that heaven at last promised him. John of Salisbury, who was at this time papal secretary, relates the known details of the interviews. He remarks with an accent of wonder that Louis, in spite of his qualms about consanquinity, still seemed to cherish the queen immoderately with a kind of boyish ardor. Consanguinity! The thought had stuck like a barb in Louis's conscience through all the pilgrimage. To the royal astonishment, Eugenius with skillful leech-craft at once drew out that painful thing. Never again, he declared, should that fatal word be uttered by either of the spouses. He confirmed and blessed their marriage and their unborn heir. He declared that he would smite with anathema anyone so rash as to mention consanguinity as an obstacle to their union. This remedial dispensation, says John, proved very pleasing to the king. But to the queen, the apostolic gesture by which Eugenius swept aside her dialectic and voided both reason and the canons was disconcerting. The monks, she saw, had reached the Pope's ear before her. She perceived with sudden insight how inapt is logic, how much too specialized the syllogism, for dealing with matters of general policy. Following this perception, Eleanor appears to have shifted from purely logical grounds and spilled out rather freely her real grievances, her hatred of that ascetic Thierry Galeran, her resentment at being carried away ignominiously from Antioch, her restraints in the court of France.

Before this new outpouring Eugenius was incredulous and kind. He saw that these sovereigns were young, worn with their hardships, weary with the reiteration of their wrongs. He caused a couch to be prepared for them and spread it with some of his own most precious brocades against the autumn chill of Tusculum. There he bade them take their rest, trusting to nature and to sleep to finish the good work he had begun. For another day he sought with gifts, diversions, and familiar talks to beguile them to good will. Somehow Eugenius persuaded himself from these interviews that he had at least revived a hope of reconciliation. Though, as his secretary tells us, he was a reserved man, he gave way to tears when at last he turned these dear children of his over to an escort of cardinals and set them on their way to Rome.[12]

The royal pilgrims and their company lodged a day and a night in Saint Benedict's famous monastery of Monte Cassino and the next day were met by a delegation of Roman senators and nobles come to offer them the freedom of the Imperial City. Rome, scarred with the grim marks of her long anarchy and the unhallowed depredations of the crusading Hohenstaufen, was no such glittering throne of religion as Byzantium. But there were the apostolic shrines. While Louis and Eleanor made a brief tour of these, citizens followed them in the streets chanting, *Sanctus, sanctus, qui venit in nomine Domini.* Thence again they were conducted by their ecclesiastical escort to the frontiers of papal territory. From Aqua Pendente, the sovereigns made their way over the Jural Alpine pass, were joined at Auxerre for secret conclave by Abbé Suger, and finally arrived in Paris in November 1149, in time for the fete of Saint Martin.

Paris, we are told, received Louis with rejoicing. The grateful citizens are said to have had a medal struck commemorating the king's exploits and his prosperous return from exile and peril of his life. On the face, the leader of the crusade was seen seated in a triumphal chariot with Victory soaring above, bearing him a palm and crown. The legend recited: *Regi invicto ab Oriente reduci, Frementes Laetitia cives. 1149* (To the king returning victorious from the Orient the citizens give joyful welcome. 1149). Then, lest this expression of enthusiasm seem too general, a second medal was struck to record an actual circumstance in Asia Minor. On this the river Maeander was represented naturally, and on its shores appeared a trophy with the inscription: *Turcis ad ripas Meandri caesis fugatis* (Turks killed and in flight on the shores of the Maeander). No medal is found celebrating the share of the Amazons in these exploits.[13]

In view of the majesty of the departure from Metz thirty months before, there was no concealing the fact that the accomplishment of the second crusade was disappointing, and this fact perplexed the best philosophers of the age. It was easy enough for slackers to dispose of the question by pointing to the godlessness of the army mustered for the holy war, and this many did. Others complained of the treachery of the allies both in Byzantium and in Palestine. More worthy of study are the reflections of those who bore the heat and burden of the day. The Bishop of Freising, who was Conrad's brother and the official German chronicler, divines that the crusade, if not precisely happy in its issue, was nevertheless a boon to those who thereby procured a martyr's crown.[14]

"It is of the nature of terrestrial things," declared the Pope, "to change and perish. Prosperity should not swell the heart of man, nor misfortune overwhelm his courage. He must learn to bless heaven when it sends him woes and calamities in order that it may teach him to despise the things of this world."

The failure of the crusade, which heaven had seemed to authorize and sanctify, descended, an inscrutable visitation, upon Abbé Bernard. "We have fallen on evil times," he says; "it seemed as though . . . the Lord, provoked by our sins, were almost judging the world before the time, with equity indeed, but forgetful of His mercy . . . We all know that the judgments of the Lord are true. But this judgment is such a great deep that I could almost justify myself for calling him blessed who is not offended thereat."[15]

But the disposal of heaven in this affair remained for the ordinary man one of the impenetrable mysteries of Divine Grace. The general bewilderment is perhaps best summed up in the query of William of Tyre in his reflection upon the disaster in Paphlagonia: "No one may question the acts of God, for all His works are just and right. But it remains a mystery to the feeble judgment of mankind why our Lord should suffer the French, who of all the people in the world have the deepest faith and most honor Him, to be destroyed by the enemies of religion."[16]

7 ✢

The Queen and the Duke

THE WINTER OF 1149–50 was one of unusual severity in northern Europe.[1] Frosts stilled the rivers and drove travelers from the roads. Fortunately Abbé Suger, in the absence of the king, had repaired somewhat the dilapidation of the royal palaces and made all as cheerful as possible for the dejected pilgrims from Jerusalem. But the Capets were exposed on their arrival in Paris to a chill not due to the rigors of the winter. The barons and the wise men of the king's council overseas, who had preceded him home, had by no means awaited their sovereigns' return from Palestine to explain in detail the catastrophic finale of the holy war. In the unofficial chronicles that flourished in the Île long before the royal advent, the Poitevin lese majesty in Paphlagonia, the Poitevin treason in Antioch, the Capetian delay in Jerusalem, were the rubrics of the piece.

Those failures that mystics were intent upon interpreting in terms of theology, the more extrovert among mankind were explaining in far simpler ways. While the ecclesiastical authorities were expounding the moral defects of certain of the allies and searching the heavens for signs, many barons and burghers, both those who had been pilgrims and those who had stayed at home, were already considering plans for deposing the king who, in spite of the blessings of the Pope and the Abbé of Clairvaux, and their own outpouring of treasure, had failed not only to relieve the Christians in the Holy Land, but had lost his hosts far from the scene of battle and had then held aloof for a year from his royal responsibilities at home.[2]

Abbé Suger had with difficulty quenched seditious plots among the barons, including one to set Louis aside in favor of his brother Robert, Count of Dreux, with whom he had quarreled in Syria. It was not the least of the great statesman's services to the monarchy that he preserved the feudal law against the king's arrival. Louis's final return from shipwreck and disaster hardly served to lift the tone of popular sentiment. In spite of the commemorative medals, the only trophy of his long excursion overseas to which the king could point with pride was the sullen queen herself, offering the ambiguous promise of an heir for France.

It cannot be supposed that Eleanor made efforts to dispel the gloom. To her who had for months experienced the delicious stir and novelty of the road in the companionship of her Poitevins, the Île must have seemed more than ever a ship bound as by incantations to the left and right banks of the Seine, unable to move against the currents of the stream; a ship in which she sat embarked, but as a mere voyager without the power to lift a sail. About her again, as in the early days, the cowled figures came and went, as if all the world were a cloister and this life but a precarious bridge to heaven or hell. Thierry Galeran, with his sour visage and censorious eye, held his place in the counsels of the king. Abbé Bernard "croaked" again from the frog-mires of Champagne. Louis, beset by a variety of melancholy reflections to which she had contributed, was not in a state to raise her spirits. The old sin of *accidia* laid hold of her. After the vernal brilliance and agitation of Jerusalem, life seemed stifled in Paris, quenched in winter desolation. The plunge of mill wheels on the river was stilled. The criers of fish and wine, the goliards and their songs were gone from the streets. Troops of students, slithering on the muddy paving stones, made now and then a moment's gaiety, but these were mainly gathered in pothouses where the fires of a spit made a corner of warmth. Master Abélard was dead. Abbé Bernard had stilled the intellectual revolt. The peerless Héloïse was grown a gray cenobite in the Paraclete. Eleanor saw her proper heritage foregone, her years of grace fleeing away, while she remained a king's hostage in the dim Merovingian dungeon on the Seine. The hope of rescue from this world grown cold and senile had receded as the queen journeyed from Tusculum to Paris. Her case had certainly not fared well with Eugenius. The apostolic gesture with which he had passed over the matter of consanguinity had thrown her back upon caprice in wishing to be free, and against caprice in women the feudal system was more than adequate.

At some time in this interval of cold and malaise, Eleanor gave birth to her second child. If she had borne a son to give joy to the Franks after all their miserable mischances, history might have taken a different turn by reason of that fortuity alone. Not only would a male child have gone far to attach the Franks to their unhappy queen, but a son might have bound her by stern necessity to the destinies of France. As it was, the disastrous Poitevin presented to her anxious world a second daughter.[3] Whatever the king's council may have made of her perversity, Eleanor herself was not perhaps inconsolable. Her dynastic incompetence at least left her freer to demand release and more certain to be heard. Even those clerics who had been so lenient about consanguinity now saw no reason for patience with a queen who, in addition to all the other catastrophes she had brought upon her people, failed to provide, in a span of fifteen years, a male heir for the house of Capet.

For a time the practical sagacity of Abbé Suger prevented a widening of the breach between Louis and Eleanor after the birth of the Princess Alix.[4] But the abbé approached his threescore years and ten, and the effort, in the face of popular sentiment, to provide men and treasure for a new crusade, brought him to his end. Early in 1151, without seeing the consummation of his hope to redeem Jerusalem, Suger "passed from the world," rich in years and honors, leaving a fame that shines with good luster to this day. He had been a familiar figure in the palace throughout two generations, seasoning all counsels with his moderation and common talk with his mellow wisdom — a little, humble man, who wore his honors with simplicity and bore his burdens without complaint. It was one of Louis's happy phrases to name him "Father of his country." Deprived of the abbé's counsels, Louis no longer struggled against the queen's discontent.

✤

In August of 1151 two of Louis's chief vassals outside the French domain arrived in the court to pay their belated homage to their overlord for the lands they held of him. As a matter of fact, Louis had been obliged to send the Bishop of Lisieux to remind Count Geoffrey of Anjou and Henry, Duke of Normandy, of the devoirs they owed their liege lord upon his return from overseas, and even then they had shown only a feeble alacrity.[5] It had been for the purpose of bringing Geoffrey's domains into the jaws of a vast pair of pincers, the Île on one hand and Poitou on the other, that Louis the Fat had been so eager fifteen years before to marry his heir to the Duchess Eleanor.

The Count of Anjou, Geoffrey the Fair, or Geoffrey Plantagenet, as he was called from his custom of pluming his helmet with golden sprays of broom,[6] was son and heir of that Foulques who had transmigrated to be King of Jerusalem; he was half brother to the boy king Baldwin, and lord in his own right of those central counties of Maine and Anjou without which neither the King of France nor the Duke of Normandy could be secure. In his late thirties, he was a striking figure, one of the handsomest, most lettered, and most courtly men of his generation, and he was a very hardy knight.[7] In spite of his close connections with the *haute cour* of Jerusalem, he had not deemed it best, in view of the uncertainty of his own affairs, to go upon crusade.[8] The Angevins were intensely practical men. For them crusades, with their distant fields of battle and their merely transcendental triumphs, seemed nothing to exchange for the solid advantages of local warfare. Geoffrey was no stranger to the court of France; nor was he stranger to the queen. With her father, Count Guillaume of Poitou, he had fought more than one campaign in Normandy, sometimes as his enemy, sometimes as his ally, but always with ferocity.

With Geoffrey came his son Henry Fitz-Empress, Duke of Normandy, a personage of prime consideration in himself. He was less important as Geoffrey's son and heir than as the heir of his mother, Matilda Empress, to

Normandy, and through her, as pretender to the throne of England. Henry was eighteen, recently knighted by his uncle, the King of Scotland, and lately invested with the Duchy of Normandy.[9] He had been bred to be a king. His schooling, both in books and experience, had brought him to an early maturity. He appeared now striking, if not handsome, robust, capable, courteous, and resplendent as befitted a great prince. He too was not for the first time in the Île de France, where his prospects made him an object of respect and lively interest. There had been among the Franks a hope of attaching him to the crown by offering him as a marriage prize the elder daughter of Louis and Eleanor; but this alliance had been forbidden by Abbé Bernard on grounds of consanguinity.[10] The abbé distrusted the Angevins. It was said that he had long before studied Henry's physiognomy and appeared to find something legible in his childish lineaments. After scanning him searchingly, the Abbé had thrust the infant Angevin away with a melancholy air, predicting that he would come to an evil end.[11]

When Geoffrey the Fair came up to Paris from his provinces in 1151, it was not merely to pay his homage to the royal pilgrim returned from overseas. His principal business was to get Louis's formal assent to young Henry's investiture as Duke of Normandy, and the matter had a special urgency in view of Louis's natural sympathy with Eustace of Blois, who was Henry's rival pretender to the throne of England. But Geoffrey had also brought an acute grievance to his overlord for which he was determined to have redress before he made any proffers of homage. With him he dragged a prisoner, no less a personage than Louis's seneschal for Poitou, one Geraud Berlai, whom he charged Louis with abetting in depredations against him on the marches of Anjou. Nothing but the Truce of God during Louis's absence on pilgrimage had restrained him from taking his own vengeance on his captive. He had this high official of the Franks hauled ignominiously into the king's presence to answer the charges against him. For Geoffrey's summary treatment of his prisoner, Abbé Bernard had contrived to have him excommunicated, and it was the Abbé's idea that Geoffrey should be heartily glad to exchange his captive for a lifting of the ban. But Count Geoffrey stubbornly refused to give up his man or to ask for absolution, and prayed publicly that, if holding his prisoner were a sin, God would not forgive him for it. This astounding blasphemy led Bernard to predict for the count an early and sudden death.[12] Unwilling to yield, Geoffrey withdrew from parley, as was the custom of the Angevins when negotiations failed to please them, tormented, as says the chronicler, "by a black and bitter bile." [13]

The Count of Anjou's stouthearted way of dealing with anathema must have stirred the blood of the queen, for she cannot have failed to remember it was the way of her forebears in Poitou, who had supported antipopes and plucked the beards of bishops when they came into collision with secular affairs. It would have been easy for Eleanor in her isolation and despair in the French court to disclose to her father's admirable friend the heaviness that weighed upon her in Paris. And it is certain that Geoffrey would have seized at once upon the political implications of her case. It was perhaps to Geoffrey that she said what has been so often quoted: "I thought to have married a king, but find I have wed a monk." [14] Giraldus Cambrensis suggests baldly that Geoffrey the Fair offered more than homage and friendship to Louis's queen, and found her willing to betray her overlord. But Giraldus dipped his quill in venom when he wrote of Eleanor, and he wrote long after the events he chronicles, when calumny was rife; and Map, repeating the story, admits he is reporting gossip.[15] William of Newburgh, who was better placed to know, declares that Eleanor was enchanted by that rich and rising young Duke of Normandy and desired a marriage with him on mere grounds of compatibility.[16] What seems clear is that Eleanor at this time grasped at some tangible prospect the Angevins offered her of freedom from the Capetian yoke.

Henry, already a belted knight, who had entered upon a vast and goodly portion of his heritage, was for his part casting about for a solid alliance and one that should offer him every possible advantage in dealing with his overlord, the King of France, with whom he was certain to have conclusions to try. Of course, whatever the theories of women might be, the property value of great heiresses made it impractical for feudal lords to be carried away by regard for temperament in choosing wives. But in this case, though Henry was a born and bred feudal bargainer, he could see the queen was no liability to her dower. Newburgh, writing of this time, speaks of Eleanor's charms of person and her lively mind. As arbiter of the *haut monde* in the Île, she was mistress of her queen's role, and Henry expected to have uses for a proper queen. She had seen the world at its very best, its notables in all the citadels of Christendom. Her knowledge of places and personages, of affairs, of gossip and intrigue, made her a helpmate nonpareil for an ascendant king. That she was the proud victim of calumny, enkindled by unmastered emotions, merely enhanced her with an air of melancholy sophistication. Youth, "the fast-withering flower," still bloomed triumphant in her mien. The queen was nearly thirty, Henry but eighteen; but such disparate marriages were not uncommon where great fiefs were at stake. Henry's own mother, the Empress Matilda, was fifteen years older than Geoffrey the Fair. Eleanor was unquestionably a prize with a dower meet for any king. With the acquisition of her fiefs, there would be new stores of men and treasure for the vindication of Henry's claim to England, and England the Angevins were determined shortly to wrest from the house of Blois.

Whatever may actually have passed between the Angevins and the queen was so secret that no syllable remains to betray the intrigue. But perhaps their understanding explains the otherwise curious change of front that Geoffrey suddenly displayed in his quarrel with Abbé Bernard and the king. He not only dismissed his captive Berlai without insisting on the fullness of his demands, but he gave up to his overlord the perennial bone of contention between the Capetians and the Normans, that frontier area between them, known as the Vexin,[17] with its castles; and he stood by while the Duke of Normandy did homage for his duchy (shorn of the Vexin), placed his hands in Louis's palms, and swore to defend his liege lord faithfully and to protect him from all his enemies; and he looked on while Louis gave Henry the kiss of peace.[18] What had dissolved Geoffrey's "black and bitter bile"? Was he perhaps intimidated by his overlord, or alarmed by Abbé Bernard's predictions? Or could he, in view of understandings with the queen, afford to be generous?

As the Count of Anjou and the Duke of Normandy went down from Paris toward Angers, they may have been in some dudgeon over the concessions they had made in the matter of the Vexin, but the ultimate prospect solaced them. As they rode through the heather of Maine in the early September days, they rehearsed their plans and uttered treason against their overlord. The riders came at last to the river Loir, which lay across their way at no great distance from their city of Le Mans. The days were hot and clouds of dust rose from their stallions' heels. They stepped aside to swim in the stream which near Château-du-Loir offers tempting wayside pools, and then lodged nearby for the night, perhaps in the castle of Le Lude. There Geoffrey was seized with chills and fever, and three days later, as if to vindicate the predictions of Abbé Bernard, he "paid the debt to nature" without time to see the culmination of his designs. Henry, upon whom, by reason of this calamity, the gravest responsibility now sat, accompanied the count's body to Saint Julian in Le Mans, and having given him hasty burial there, pressed on to Angers, where he was at once received as heir of his father's provinces of Maine and Anjou.[19]

✦

It is significant as evidence that some understanding reassuring to the queen had been reached in Paris between her and the Angevins, that the first decisive steps were taken for the royal separation almost immediately after the departure of the Count of Anjou and the Duke of Normandy from the Île. In September 1151, the King and Queen of the Franks made their last progress together through Aquitaine. Their escort was so important as to indicate that this was no occasional *chevauchée* upon the routine of administration. The king was accompanied by Thierry Galeran and other business advisers, by Hugues de Champfleury, who had succeeded to the ministerial office of Abbé Suger, and by various other magnates. The queen had in her train the Archbishop of Bordeaux, into whose grasp the critical affairs of Aquitaine had largely come, and many bishops of her southern provinces, along with several of her chief vassals and sundry relatives. This retinue spent the whole season of the vintage in the queen's estates. The sovereigns held their Christmas assembly in Limoges, and for Candlemas convened a plenary court in Saint Jean d'Angély, over which the Archbishop of Bordeaux presided. In the course of this progress Eleanor's domain was undoubtedly set in order for the withdrawal of Louis's administration and his garrisons.[20] At the end of the *chevauchée* the king and the queen seem to have taken final leave of one another in northern Poitou. On his return to his own lands Louis avoided Poitiers, where as the bridegroom of the duchess he had put on the coronet of the Counts of Poitou. It was therefore doubtless to Poitiers that Eleanor retired in the early spring of 1152.

No step so critical to the destinies of France as the divorce of the king and queen could be considered without the sanction of the Pope, and Eugenius would not have failed to be advised in this matter by Abbé Bernard, who had first pointed out the flaw in the royal marriage. The abbé's apologists have sought to relieve him in the matter of responsibility for the step to which Louis now consented. But this is to belittle the abbé. For Bernard the political interests of France did not transcend the sanctity of the moral order. His was no Hellenic mind seeking to harmonize reason and the will of God. In fact, the abbé had little regard for the pure works of intellect, so prone, as he had seen in his century, to lead the noblest minds to heresy and schism. It was the singleness of Bernard's inward eye that was the instrument of his power; it saved him from confusions with secular concerns. With this eye he could see no ultimate good springing from the Poitevin root. He knew the queen's stock: Guillaume the troubadour, living his irreverent life under anathema, corrupting his bishops to gain his will, supporting monsters of ungodliness in Rome; Guillaume the Toulousain, dragged from his persistent heresies only by a miracle from heaven. He knew them root and branch; ungodly, stiff-necked, puffed up with pride and arrogance, broilsome, self-willed, garnering the worthless treasure of this world, and always impenitent. As for the conversion of the queen herself at Saint Denis, he could not count it one of the triumphs of his predication. Her past accused her. She had provoked Louis's wars with Thibault of Champagne to procure her sister's infamous marriage. Her levity overseas had cost the Franks incalculable losses. And there was the certainty of consanguinity. His mandate was clear. "If thine eye offend thee, pluck it out." It would have been lax of the abbé to tolerate the queen.

On the Friday before Palm Sunday (March 21, 1152), the Archbishop of Sens, who had presided at the condemnation of Abélard, convened a synod for the sanction of the separation in the king's castle of Beaugency near

Orléans, whence the queen might, upon her liberation, proceed without hindrance to her own domain. The conclave was august. Present were the Archbishops of Reims, of Bordeaux, and of Rouen, with certain of their suffragans, and a large gathering of barons and of nobles. The details were prearranged. If Louis had reason to discredit the queen, he forbore to injure her. On the other hand, his own sovereign dignity was preserved. It was the king's party that bore witness to the consanguinity of the royal spouses. The Princesses of France were declared legitimate and awarded to the king. The Archbishop of Bordeaux, as cautioner for the queen, made no protest against the charges, but received assurance of the restoration of her domains as she possessed them before her marriage, and the assurance that either party might marry again without hindrance, so long as the duchess preserved her vassal's allegiance to the king. Thereupon the decree of separation was announced.[21]

For an event of such consequence, the termination of the royal marriage passed with significantly meager comment in the chronicles. The French historians, overlooking John of Salisbury's account of Eleanor's initiative in the affair, relate the event as Louis's "repudiation" of his consanguineous queen. It is Bouchet in his seventeenth-century narrative who invents the circumstantial account of the proceeding.[22] According to his engaging chronicle, the King of the Franks cast off his brokenhearted queen. Eleanor in fearful trepidation awaited the decree of the bishops outside the assembly. The two prelates and the two barons assigned to break the decision to her went softly, fearing their tidings might unhinge her mind. Bouchet represents her as so overcome with anguish and desperation at the verdict that she fell in a swoon from her chair, and so remained above two hours with her teeth firmly locked, beyond the relief of speech or tears, too far gone for restoratives. At last, when she had recovered her senses, she bent her clear green eyes upon her accusers and exhausted the rhetoric of helpless innocence and despair in defense of her honor and her crown. The plain facts do not, however, accord with this sensitive account. The Duchess of Aquitaine and Countess of Poitou, restored now to her own titles, was able, in spite of her ordeal, to mount her palfrey and make a hasty departure from Beaugency. With an escort of her own vassals, she took at once the familiar road by way of Blois for Tours.

The rumor of her release flew before her. Not far from Blois her train fell into the ambush of Geoffrey of Anjou (aged sixteen), the enterprising younger brother of Henry, Duke of Normandy, who, without leave from his overlord or invitation from the duchess, plotted brigand-wise to possess himself of her person and her fiefs. Protected by her escort from this rude sally, she hastened toward the crossing of the Loire near Tours, which would bring her almost at once into her own estates. But then, as the chronicle of Tours relates, "her good angel" warned her that Thibault of Blois, second son of Louis's vassal, the Count of Champagne, lay in wait to capture her at the crossing of the river. Though lacking for the moment an elect champion, Eleanor was not yet reduced to younger brothers. Avoiding the usual ford, she outmaneuvered him, and so passed quickly "by another way" to her own high place in Poitiers, where her Poitevin garrisons made her safe for the time from brigandly young counts.[23]

While Eleanor was drawing her first draughts of freedom in her own ancestral city, assembling her household, and settling her effects in the long unused tower of Maubergeonne, the Duke of Normandy kept discreetly in his own estates observing the penitential rites of Lent. He must have heard with sardonic humor of the abortive plots of King Stephen's nephew Thibault and his own younger brother Geoffrey to capture the whilom queen. Not without challenge, he observed, did the richest dower in Europe pass over the highways of that troubled border region. On April 6 Henry took council with his barons in Normandy. He had need of their advice, for he had it in mind to affront his overlord, the King of France.

Near the middle of May, whether in pursuance of his own plans or on summons of the duchess, Henry came to Poitiers, Eleanor had never seen Louis until he came to Bordeaux to marry her. But she had already had a view of this bridegroom and was prepared for the bold, stocky, deep-chested, high-hearted, rufous young duke who came riding his stallion over the bridge of Moutierneuf to her high place, his falcon on his wrist and a sprig of plantagenesta in his bonnet. On the 18th of May, scarcely eight weeks after the decree of Beaugency, the erstwhile queen became Duchess of Normandy.[24] Some canonists must have been required to enable the spouses to avoid the sin of consanguinity about which the queen had been so scrupulous in Antioch and Tusculum. But this was somehow managed. The marriage was concluded without fanfare but not without responsible witnesses, lest some impediment should be discovered in the contract. The Duchess of Aquitaine was thus in a single hour swept into the orbit and encompassed by the destiny of her former lord's hereditary enemy. Because of this, says the chronicler, a mighty feud arose between the two kings.[25]

8 ✠

The Countess and the Poet

TIDINGS OF THE EVENT IN POITIERS broke like a mighty thunderclap in the Île. Even if the court of Paris had suspected the queen of seeking the security of a new alliance, there was, from the Capetian point of view, no disconcerting potentate at large to whom she might attach herself. Certainly the wise men of the king's council, buttressed by the law and the canons, would not have regarded Henry Plantagenet with suspicious eye. Had not Abbé Bernard forbidden as consanguineous a marriage between this very Henry and the queen's daughter, the Princess Marie of France? Had not the queen harried the king and the court all the way from Antioch to Tusculum and from Tusculum to Beaugency with her scruples about consanguinity? Had she not, on this issue, been more precise than Rome itself? Was not Eleanor, as Countess of Poitou, the ward and vassal of the king, and did she not therefore require his sanction to marry anyone whomsoever? Had not the Duke of Normandy lately paid his vassal's vow of fealty to his overlord and received from him the kiss of peace?

It was merely the practical advantages of the alliance to the high contracting parties that the cautious Franks somehow overlooked. The late queen's marriage with the Duke of Normandy, incredible from a legalistic view, was precisely the only one that could raise Eleanor to a status from which she could survey her former role without humiliation and regret; and the capture of her provinces without the cost of an Angevin mark or a single man-at-arms was the one stroke that could certainly make Henry Plantagenet the more than peer of his overlord on the Continent, and in England the invincible rival of the reigning house of Blois.

In his palace Louis took counsel of the new advisers that surrounded him after the deaths of his nearest mentors, Abbé Suger, Thibault of Champagne, and Raoul of Vermandois. In the face of the fact accomplished in the west, the new council was perplexed as to whether to employ ecclesiastical or secular weapons in dealing with it. Too speedily the fears of Abbé Suger had been realized, but the ghostly weapons of Abbé Bernard offered little prospect of reaching the recreant Duke and Duchess of Normandy, safely ensconced within their own frontiers. The air was sultry, but no bolt of anathema from Clairvaux or Rome touched the consanguineous spouses in Poitou. The council, which considered some notion of revoking the conditions of the royal separation,[1] cited Henry to the French court to answer for his double treason; but this summons produced no sound or movement in the west.

When at last the king's advisers realized that it would be necessary to shift from the plane of concepts to the plane of action in dealing with the troth-breachers, it required a month to organize the French allies and to launch them on the borders of Anjou and Normandy: Louis's brother, the Count of Dreux, the friends of King Stephen and his nephew Eustace, Henry of Champagne, and Thibault of Blois, and Geoffrey Plantagenet, the two latter the recent suitors for the hand of Eleanor, all uniting against the Duke and Duchess of Normandy, who suddenly through perfidy had become their universal foes. Torigny says these five had formed an alliance to recover Poitou and Aquitaine and divide it among themselves.[2] Louis himself charged into Normandy. At this invasion Henry appeared like a whirlwind out of the west, leaving foundered horses and exhausted followers in his wake. Louis, who sensed heaven's displeasure in all his calamities, gave way at Henry's onset. All his experience as a warrior had taught him to distrust battle as a means of ending confusions. The military valor that had distinguished his early days ebbed away. He fell sick of a fever, retired to his own borders, and quickly succumbed to the church's cry for truce.

✤

Louis's demonstrations had the effect, however, of delaying Henry's projected visit to England to vindicate his claim to the crown, and the duchess persuaded him instead to make an autumn progress through her southern provinces. Together they passed the vintage in Poitou and the Limousin, reviewing the strongholds from which Louis had recently removed his garrisons, and surveying Eleanor's rich dower — fiefs gathering their harvests of olives and wine, the salt marshes covered with grazing sheep. The best horses throve in Landes and the Saintonge. The ducal pleasure grounds in the Talmont were well stocked with game, and the best falcons in the world were bred in the region. While Eleanor took the sunshine of old towns, old friends, old vintages, and her native Provençal, Henry took stock of Gascon ships and men for the coming struggle beyond the Channel. In January 1153, leaving his duchess behind, he set forth with twenty-six vessels he had recruited in various harbors to try his conclusions with destiny.[3]

From some castle in the confines of her lord's estates, the Duchess of Normandy and Poitou, the Countess of Anjou, kept her eye during Henry's absence on the marches of their new domain. Doubtless she was sometimes in Poitiers; but it has been surmised that Eleanor took up her chief residence in Angers, and this is probable.[4] Angers was a fitting residence for the feudal chatelaine whose most significant title for the moment was Countess of

Anjou. The place was safe in the heart of Henry's undisputed inheritance, and it was far removed from the machinations of the Franks.

The citadel which Henry's grandfather Foulques, when he went to be King of Jerusalem, had abandoned to Geoffrey the Fair, was no obscure retreat;[5] it stood full in the currents of the day and cast its beam of enlightenment along the valleys of the Loire and the Mayenne, and the roads that there converged from Brittany, Poitou, and Normandy. No city, says the chronicler, could boast a more venerable religious tradition than this foyer of the Angevins, more churches, more monastic orders, more schools. Geoffrey the Fair had made his court the resort of scholars for his own solace and for the education of his sons. It was here that Henry first went to school to Pierre of Saintes and Matthew of Loudun.[6] The abbey of Ronceray across the river had nurtured its Héloïse in the Abbess Tetburge, and still offered a solid discipline for women, not unmingled with secular delights. The high place had produced its bishops and its philosophers, but dialectic was set in Angers to sweet pastoral airs, the lusty flow of the Mayenne amidst its green isles, and the drone of country bees. "The city," said one of her sons, "puts a man out of the way of knowing himself."[7] Persons of consequence withdrew to river villas at Quincé and Chalonnes for a Virgilian recollection of themselves. The white wine, the country fare, were excellent. In the spaciousness of the valley, out of the reach of Rome and Clairvaux, there was something left of man's singularity. But Geoffrey the Fair had not sought in Angers, nor in any of his cities, to rival the babel and the bedlam of a royal court.

Now that Geoffrey had "passed from his generation" and Henry was away and Matilda Empress kept her own establishments in Rouen, it devolved upon the Duchess Eleanor to set up centers of civility in the West befitting the new Angevin dynasty whose prospects at this time rose so fair as to cast a shadow over the Île itself. General conditions in 1153 favored her necessity. The world was unsettled by the late crusade, the calamities of the Franks, and that recurrence of famine and distress that haunts the trail of military enterprise. Poets, artists, annalists, and other foot-loose professionals who require a measure of bread and tranquillity for the flowering of their gifts, found hardly a patron in the western world. In Paris, after the queen's withdrawal, Louis scourged to exile the remnant of wastrels and gallants that had demoralized his court and settled down to a monastic quiet in which the trivium and the quadrivium resumed their proper ascendancy over romance and gasconnade.[8] Henry Beauclerc and Thibault of Champagne, those rich and bountiful scions of the Conqueror, had ended their days. Stephen in England was harried with war. The times were hard.

Harbingers of the dawning era of the Angevins beat their way over the rivers and the roads to the drawbridge of the castle where the Countess of

Anjou presided, young, rich, liberal, eager to be sung as the lodestar of the dynasty rising in the West. At this juncture Eleanor enjoyed a large new freedom from surveillance and restraint in which to create her own milieu and infuse it with all she had learned of *savoir-faire*, not only in the palaces of the Capets but in the brilliant cities of the East. No woman of her day was so fitted by talent or experience to diffuse the benefits of the enlightenment she had absorbed in the highest citadels of Christendom. To her bounty flocked not only her own Poitevins, vassals and relatives, upon whom she bestowed her largess with a free hand,[9] but a generation of poets and chroniclers eager to merit her praise and her reward.

※

And he [the poet Ventadour] went away and came to the Duchess of Normandy, who was young and of great worth, and she had understanding in matters of valor and honor, and cared for a song of praise; and the songs of Bernard pleased her; she received and welcomed him cordially. He was a long time in her court and he fell in love with her and she with him. He made many good songs. And while he was with her the King Henry of England married her and took her from Normandy and led her away.

Raynouard, *Choix des poésies originales des troubadours*, V, 70

It was perhaps during the *chevauchée* of Henry and Eleanor through the Limousin, when the ducal household was taking shape, that the troubadour Bernard,[10] exiled at the moment from his native Fief of Ventadour, joined the duchess' *mesnie*, followed her to her residence, and began those relations with her, Platonic or otherwise, which he celebrates in some of the most exquisite lyrics surviving from the century. Bernard, though humble in origin, had been trained from his youth in the troubadour's art of poetry and courtesy (*trobar*). He was of about the countess' age, her vassal, a young man goodly in aspect, ardent, poor, touched especially by the lamentable transiency of things. He had been banished from his native fief for employing his amorous skills too successfully in praise of the Countess of Ventadour. The nature of the relationship of Bernard and Eleanor and the duration of it are not clear from the chroniclers; but the poems remain as evidence of some reality, and from these we gather glimpses of the Countess of Anjou and the court she developed for her own milieu in that first heyday of freedom when she consulted only her own desire.

Bernard praises his lady in the framework of the *gai savoir*, that ritual of the troubadour that had its roots in the Limousin. It is impossible to unriddle from songs fashioned under the exacting rhetoric of that poetry the secrets of personal feeling, but there are accents in his verse more genuine than those of fashion or servility. The poet responds as a lyre should to the touch of his mistress. All is *de règle*. The lover, who is marked for favor not by birth or status, but only by his art of *trobar*, looks up humbly to the eyes of his chosen lady, who is, by the rule, the wife of some great lord. Secrecy is of the essence of the liaison. With the utmost caution, lest she betray herself to the world, the lady whets the lover's ardor first with enticing advances, then with cruel retreats. At one moment she encourages him with gifts; at the next she puts him off with frowns and dearth of favors. Her caprice disturbs his wakeful hours and agitates his dreams. Now she is intimate, now mysteriously aloof. The lover lives in an alternation of hope and despair, a sweet torment not to be exchanged, however, for the state of any "king, duke, or admiral." With a dawnlike freshness, as if he were the first lyrical poet of all time, Bernard opens his heart and weaves the story of his adoration in harmonies that can be brought from the *langue d'oc* into no other tongue.

No chronicler gives us so many glimpses of the duchess as she appeared to her own day as does her vassal poet: "noble and sweet," "faithful and loyal," "one meet to crown the state of any king," "gracious, lovely, the embodiment of charm." When she bent upon him her eyes, full of fire and eloquence, he felt the joy of a Christmas fete. She was the most beautiful of women. For her gifts he would not give the rich city of Pisa in exchange. He rejoiced that she could read and interpret his secret messages for herself. He addresses her as "my Comfort." Tristram, he swore, never suffered such woes for Ysolt the Fair as he suffered for his lady. In her presence he trembled like an aspen, was witless as a child.

Perhaps Henry, who was said to have ears everywhere, thought it best, in view of the episode in Ventadour, not to let these matters proceed in Angers. At any rate, he cut off in its glory this lyrical affair between his duchess and the poet, and summoned Bernard to bring his lyre to England for service to more martial themes. There in the midst of fog and chill, the troubadour warmed himself with the embers of his passion. The snow by the Thames appeared to bloom with April flowers, crimson, yellow, white. In exile from his mistress, he begged to return from Henry's heavy service to her court, where "ladies and chevaliers, fair and courteous," moved in a world composed.

When the sweet breeze
Blows hither from your dwelling
Methinks I feel
A breath of paradise.[11]

Somehow he found his way back to the duchess' castle and sought, on some pretext of incompetence, to elude a second summons from his lady's side. But this time it was Eleanor who moved, leaving Bernard to pine in desolation with the remnant of her temporary court. The duchess, swept off in Henry's wake to new scenes and new activities, seems to have found no further place in her life for dalliance with her humble vassal of the Limousin. Two years later, as Bernard scuffs the autumn leaves in the "deserted flat country" far from her presence, he comforts himself with the rumor that she still hears his songs. But he fears the "fair disdain," and offers himself as her bedside slave to draw off her boots when she retires. And so he passes from the scene. However, the outpourings of the poet in this interlude, such as it was, might have gone far to assuage the jealousy of any woman of the century for the famous love songs (now lost) of Abélard for Héloïse.

Down some one of the highways leading to Eleanor's court there came, as the poetry of Ventadour suggests, the story of Tristram and Ysolt, not as the poet Thomas told it later in the court of England, but in some earlier form. And who can guess what other tales lost amidst the violent commotions of the Plantagenets were heard in the duchess' halls, where "matter of Britain" and "matter of Byzantium" and the substance of ancient hero tales were all wrought together into something new and strange? All the factors for the creation of a new literature were there in a favoring atmosphere: the bountiful duchess herself, bent upon fashioning with befitting elegance her new milieu, a patron whom the biographer of the troubadours describes as given to liberality, to chivalry, and to poetry, together with her gay young household; returned crusaders like herself filled with eastern themes; story-tellers out of Brittany purveying Arthurian romance; travelers upon the pilgrim routes; starveling poets, unemployed canons, chroniclers of the Normans and the Angevins — all commingling in an ancient tradition of learning, and all vying with each other to please a fair young world and earn the duchess' largess. In view of the circumstances, it is impossible to escape wondering whether the Tristram story was not dressed at this time by some necessitous *conteur* to have a pleasing, if veiled, topical significance for the duchess who had renounced a dull king for a bold young knight.

It was in the lyrical interval between her two roles as queen, and in the midst of her dalliance with the poet, that Eleanor, as if executing a final affront to her past and a salvo to the future, gave birth to her first son, whom, with a felicitous regard for both his Norman and Poitevin forebears, she christened with the name of Guillaume and hastened to designate as her own heir, the future Count of Poitou.[12]

The Angevin star was in the ascendant in those years of the mid-century. The chroniclers report that the constellations in their courses were seen to conspire in Henry's favor.[13] In the summer of 1153 Stephen's son Eustace, in the midst of impious depredations on the properties of Bury Saint Edmunds, strangled on a dish of eels, and that fortuity, which removed Henry's most formidable rival for the crown, was seen by partisans of the Angevins as a judgment on the house of Blois.[14] When in the spring of 1154 the Duke of Normandy appeared upon the threshold of his ancestral high place, it was to greet his duchess and his heir with fortune and the fairest hopes. He came not merely as Duke of Normandy and Count of Anjou, but as the acknowledged successor of Stephen, the lineal heir of William the Conqueror, Henry Beauclerc, Matilda Empress. The success of his campaign in England enabled him to promise to his duchess such royal wealth and prestige as placed her quite beyond the reach of regret or the envying of any princess reigning in Christendom.

It was probably when Henry rejoined Eleanor after his campaign in England that she had opportunity to try her role as Duchess of Normandy in the seat of the Norman dukes in Rouen, of appraising the members of the dynasty to which she had attached herself, and of bringing her mind to bear upon the sudden political and territorial adjustments to which her divorce and remarriage had exposed the Kings of France and England. If her withdrawal from the court of France had reduced the ambitions of the Capets, it was plain that it had by somewhat more than the same measure expanded those of the Plantagenets.

In Rouen Eleanor was brought vis-à-vis her mother-in-law, that *maîtresse femme*, Matilda Empress, at whose knee Henry had learned the first principles of statecraft. Under her tutelage Eleanor conned the hornbook of that science and learned something of the "hungry falcon" politics by which the empress managed to impose her will and keep her vassals and her prelates docile and compliant. The substance was strictly feudal, yet distinctly tougher in fiber than the Capetian precepts Eleanor had learned in Paris, and so far as that distinction went, more like the philosophy to which she had been bred in Poitou. "Dangle the prize before their eyes," the astute empress taught her son, "but be sure to withdraw it again before they taste it. Then you will keep them eager and find them devoted when you need them." [15] A Scotch rigor, a Norman energy, the grave habits of a German chatelaine, merged in Matilda in a temper which had been uncertain and tenacious, but which, now that her destiny was fulfilled, reflected some of Henry Beauclerc's qualities of measure and benignity. Her court was solemnly reminiscent of her early days in Aachen as Empress of Saxony and the Holy Roman Empire, which her reluctant second marriage to Geoffrey the Fair had not enabled her to forget. It was seemly and decorous but not in the least flamboyant. Patron of arts and letters though she was, her favors went not to poets and mimes, but to men of substance and condition. It was she who taught Henry to avoid triflers and hangers-on and to closet himself in his little leisure with men of wisdom and with books. She was the one woman to whose ideas Henry listened with attention, the only one whose advice he sought; and to her precepts were attributed the more flinty elements of his policy.

Henry himself had developed perceptibly during the strenuous months of trying conclusions with Stephen in England. As his fortunes brightened, his horizon widened and new prospects expanded before him. He who had been born to inherit certainly only the Counties of Maine and Anjou had already at twenty-one seen Normandy and England retrieved from the house of Blois, and he had alienated from his overlord the wide and splendid provinces of Poitou and Aquitaine. A magnificent, an unforeseen destiny now engrossed him, a destiny owed not wholly to his own merit nor to Angevin contrivance, but also to some happy conjunction of the planets. These fortunate accessions, in their totality so vastly larger than his early hopes envisioned, opened before him a boundless space. He saw his star rising over an empire that stretched from the Scottish border to the Pyrenees. It had been a lucky stroke determining the future fatefully — his unexpected capture of the Countess of Poitou. No one, not even the Holy Roman Emperor, certainly not his overlord in Paris, stood in so favorable a position to become the king of feudal kings in Europe.

In these arduous days he was driven by a prodigious energy that he applied fitfully to a great variety of undertakings. In exertions he wore out his hardiest associates. When not actually upon some foray or following his hounds or birds in chase until the light failed, he was riding fast and far to surprise in untoward moments his stewards and the keepers of his castles. He dismounted only to stand interminably in colloquy with men of pith and action, the burden of whose minds he unloaded into his own with a mental activity that matched his physical exertion. Men marveled at his information about every sort of thing. His senses were all alert at once, seizing a manifold experience. While he talked or listened, his fingers moved, touching things of use or beauty. He examined everything — armor, gems, stuffs, instruments, birds, or dogs — with eye, ear, and hand. When not in the saddle, he seldom sat except to eat or play a game of chess. When he at last retired, varlets rubbed his swollen feet, and entertainers with viol or book relieved the tension of his mind. Even at mass his glance roved, he plucked his neighbor's sleeve, shifted, scribbled, whispered, or paced about impatiently. His dress was rich and seemly, but carelessly worn. In manner and talk he was free and accessible, for one who could engage his interest, a genial companion. Yet no one mistook his restlessness for uneasiness, nor his geniality for want of sovereign authority.[16]

Life in Rouen, as Eleanor saw it in 1154, was earnest, infused with vigor, edged with danger and anxiety. Epic events were plainly shaping just ahead. Into the capital of the Norman dukes, as emissaries came and went, flowed news from Rome and Britain, Paris and Bordeaux, from Flanders and the waning Kingdom of Jerusalem. For the duchess, time, mortal time, that had been wont in Paris to pour so slowly from the unstinted abundance of eternity, came, in Henry's company, to have a precious value for itself, as it raced over the sun clocks on the walls of Notre-Dame des Prés, or drained through the hourglass irrecoverably. If there was little practice of the *gai savoir* in Rouen, there was also no *accidia*.

✤

As the Angevin star rose in the mid-century, Louis's star declined. The last prop he had inherited from Louis the Fat fell away. A few days after the birth of Eleanor's son, the Angevin Prince Guillaume, Abbé Bernard followed Abbé Suger and Thibault of Champagne in their "migration from the world." The sins of his generation, the collapse of the crusade, the disastrous consequences of his efforts to square politics with the moral law, combined with the austerities of his monastic life to reduce the abbé to a frail ghost of himself. However, the adversities that beset his earthly pilgrimage could not becloud the virtue of his miracles. The movement for his canonization began in 1155, and in 1174 he was heralded throughout Christendom as Saint Bernard.

The birth of an heir to the Angevins drove Louis to bend his mind again to his own deficiency in that regard. In this time of eclipse he determined to solace himself with a pilgrimage to Saint James of Compostella, which he had long promised himself to add to his record as the most famous palmer of Europe. He did not ask for safe-conduct to pass through the territories of the Duchess of Aquitaine, but in company with the Count of Toulouse he traversed Languedoc, passed through Maguelonne (Montpellier), stopped off in Castres to venerate the relics of Saint Vincent, and thence made his way to Spain without trespassing on Gascony.[17] A Spanish annalist remarks that his pilgrimage veiled another object, that is, an investigation of the fitness of the King of Spain's daughter to be his queen.[18] Louis was richly entertained in Spain. When his scruples were satisfied, the Princess Constance (otherwise Marguerite) came to France a young maid of good countenance, and the French king was, as the chronicler declares, "better married than he had been."

9 ✠

The Second Crown

ELEANOR'S SUMMONS TO TAKE HER SECOND CROWN came sooner than any signs foretold. Stephen did not long survive his son's violent death and his own military reverses. On October 26, six months after Henry's return to Normandy, messengers from Thibault, Archbishop of Canterbury, brought news to Rouen of the king's death. After years of anxious delay, the call of the Angevins came like a thief in the night.

The brusque and urgent summons to grasp the crown of England found Henry on a campaign in the Vexin. He had lately risen from an all but mortal illness. However, scarcely a fortnight sufficed for him to muster such an escort of archbishops, bishops, and nobles as should signalize to anarchy in England the powerful ecclesiastical and secular auspices under which he assumed the crown of the conquerors.[1] Eleanor, so far as records show, had no time to assemble a suitable Poitevin *mesnie*, but she found herself not altogether strange in the sudden company that gathered in Barfleur for the crossing. Here were certain Norman and Flemish bishops and barons who, in her previous dispensation as Queen of France, had shared with her and Louis the vicissitudes of their crusade, men who had seen her shine with the colors of France in the most glorious cities of Christendom, in Byzantium, Antioch, Jerusalem, and who now, as her liege lord's men, supported her pretensions to another crown. Matilda Empress stayed behind to maintain the peace in Normandy; but Henry's brother Geoffrey, whose ambush Eleanor had escaped on her way from Beaugency to Poitiers, was of the company. It was a man's world in which the Duchess of Normandy found herself engaged in the harbor town.

For a month in Barfleur the court looked out upon the Channel chopped with gales and driven sleet. Though the delay was intolerable to Henry, the time cannot, in that company, have sped altogether dully for Eleanor in the hostels of the port. Hourly the duke and his mariners scanned the November sky for a turn of weather favorable for the passage. Across the narrow gray stretch of sea, beyond a barrier of storm more effectual than stone, England waited kingless, and no news came through from thence to proclaim the loyalty of the castled Normans and the keepers of the treasure, all left in confusion and uncertainty by the untimely death of Stephen.

At length, determined to hold his Christmas court in London, Henry on

December 7, 1154, gave orders to embark in defiance of the storm. If he heard warnings of the fate of the White Ship lost in those very waters with all its royal freight, he did not heed them. Demurs were silenced. The bishops and the barons were stowed in the rocking smacks. The duchess and the infant Guillaume were hurried aboard with the rest, and sail was set for England. For more than twenty-four hours the ships, their lanterns and trumpets lost to each other in the tempest, toiled in their separate courses. On the second day they made their way into various havens. The royal smack, which had set out for Southampton, drew up in some harbor below New Forest. From Mont-Saint-Michel-in-Peril-of-the-Sea, the archangel had stretched forth his mighty arm and brought that precious company up living from the deep.[2]

From their scattered landings the duke's escort emerged upon the highway from Southampton to Winchester. The rumor that Henry had ridden the storm flew with the gale, starting incredulous men from their hearthsides in castle and town. Stephen's barons quaked, says Henry of Huntingdon, "like a bed of reeds in the wind for fear and anxiety," but no man stirred against the new authority. Along his route he marshaled an army of nobles and prelates of Britain to swell his continental following. The cortege stopped briefly in Winchester, where part of the royal treasure lay, and then pressed on to London.

Thibault of Canterbury, to whose offices Henry owed the tranquillity of the interregnum, had assembled the bishops of Britain in readiness for the royal advent. The coronation that restored the line of Henry I to the throne of England was marked by strange contrasts of dinginess and magnificence. The ceremonies were richly but hastily contrived in a setting that bore witness to the long struggles of Stephen and Matilda Empress for the crown. Westminster Abbey, already the traditional place for the consecration of the kings of England, was dilapidated from long neglect. Yet within its sanctuary on the Sunday before Christmas in 1154, Henry and Eleanor assumed their crowns in the presence of an august assembly offering by every token of affluence and splendor the general support of the new regime.[3] On such occasions Henry, who knew the virtue of symbols, bore himself with magnificence and cut a royal figure. His robust youth, his build and bearing, his lively countenance, his prowess in war and strategy, his arrival in defiance of season and tide, proclaimed to that eager and anxious assembly a king with courage and energy worthy of his conquering forebears. "In London," says Gervase of Canterbury, "the young king was received with transports of joy." Shouts of "vivat rex" from the Normans and "waes hael" from the Saxon burghers resounded the length of the Strand, welcoming the Duke of Normandy and the rich and famous Countess of Poitou to their noble city on the Thames.

The palace of Westminster, rebuilt upon its ancient Saxon site by William Rufus and further enriched for the court of Henry Beauclerc, had been so despoiled by the followers of Stephen that it could not be occupied. The Plantagenets were obliged to take residence in Bermondsey.[4] But the situation at the busy east end of the city, below the old bridge and nearly opposite the Tower, commanded a wider view of London's spread and activity than the newer palace. What was this vaunted city by the Thames which Eleanor had exchanged for the citadel of philosophy upon the Seine?

"London," says the contemporary tale of Tristram, "is a right rich city, a better not in Christendom, nor a worthier, nor a better esteemed, nor a better garnished of rich folk. Much they love largess and honor, and lead their life in great pleasance."[5] London from the quarter of Bermondsey, as it spread to view westward from the Tower, can have been like nothing Eleanor had seen before in all her many journeyings among the feudal aeries of the world. It was not a lofty seat at all, but a vast crowded area in which the domes and belfries of innumerable churches with their abbeys and schools thrust up among the tiles and thatch of sharp house roofs. Whereas in Paris the Seine was the encircling moat of the Île, in London, Thames was the city's central thoroughfare. Across the river from the royal quarters London wall framed three sides of an old town, but crumbled away before the traffic of the river, where streets ended in docks and wharves, cook shops and wine shops along the Strand. A hearty smell of fish, wool, and beer rose from the water side, and the calls of boatmen and eel-wives filled the air with babel. The ancient bridge, with its jumble of narrow houses, gathered swarms of smacks and wherries about its landing stairs. Along the wharves the shipping of the north countries, of Flanders and Rouen, of Nantes and La Rochelle, even of Syria, lay in haven, their oars banked, their colored sails furled against the wintry fury of the sea. Opposite Bermondsey the tower of the conquerors, its mortar drenched, as legend said, with the blood of beasts, its dungeons already rich with the harvest of history, stood grimly fortified against the times that were to unfold before her. Beyond the walls the newer city spread in unconfined suburbs set among wintry orchards and stockaded gardens.

Whereas Paris swarmed with students and resounded with their irresponsible levity, London thronged with burghers — merchants, shippers, changers, masters of guilds — who went soberly, but with a cheerful and prosperous air, from their rich homes to their profitable stalls and warehouses upon the Strand. The town houses of bishops and nobles were of princely elegance and wide hospitality. "Nowhere," writes a contemporary, "are faces more joyous at the board, or hosts more eager to please, or entertainments more sumptuous." Not only beside roaring chimneys was there a conviviality that dispelled the fog and chill; even in the open there was ado and gaiety. In times of bitter cold, the queen saw a novel sight upon the marshy fields toward Clerkenwell — burghers' sons of London, the shin bones of animals thonged to their shoes, careening in lusty play upon the ice.[6]

London was a right rich city garnished of rich folk that led their life in great pleasance. But it seemed to be a man's city. The parish bells of London cut through the fog with a frosty sound. Where in the rime by Thames bloomed those April flowers of Ventadour, red, yellow, white? The women of London, says her chronicler, were paragons of virtue, "very Sabines." But they were unlearned in the *gai savoir*. However, for her first weeks in Britain the queen, peering at London from the residence that marooned her in a rural seclusion, had diversions of her own. In February, two months after her stormy passage and her coronation, Eleanor gave birth in Bermondsey to her second son, a prince born in the purple. The Bishop of London christened him with the king's name, and he was designated as the future Count of Anjou.[7]

⚜

In the first lively years of their reign, Henry Plantagenet and the Countess of Poitou were the hammer and the anvil of a single enterprise — to weld the widespread and individual provinces that were theirs by conquest and inheritance into a massive domain, and to plant thereon a dynasty owing subservience to no temporal potentate, and least of all to their feudal overlord in Paris. To round out the edges and compact the core of this domain became the controlling object of their desire. In this enterprise they saw eye to eye.

Necessarily, its first phase was to quench the anarchy bequeathed to them by Stephen; to recover into their own hands the license gained by bishops and barons during his unsteady reign; to restore order and security; and to exact the royal revenues. For such labors the young Angevin had not only the ability of his race, but he had had an unusually varied experience and the most astute of teachers. To impose order, to ferret out disloyalty and incompetence, to secure the administration of a common justice, the sovereigns at once undertook wide peregrinations in which they visited the most important castles and cities of their realm.[8] The queen's experience as an Amazon in the wilds of Paphlagonia had prepared her to accompany Henry on the bedlam and unseasonable *chevauchées* that became the despair of his hardiest followers.

Sudden as a pestilence, Henry was wont to appear, here, there, and everywhere, when he was least expected. Even his own clerks bringing him news of importance could not find him or catch up with him. He moved, says Map, in stages intolerable, like a common carrier.[9] It pleased his humor to vex his stewards with the pandemonium and uncertainty of his plans. The royal household, from chamberlain to scullion, often numbered at least two hundred souls,[10] equipped with chapel, bed furnishings, kitchen utensils, plate, treasure, garments, vestments, documents, and all the services thereunto pertaining. If Henry announced his departure for sunrise and kept his courtiers and servants all night in a turmoil of preparation, he was almost, but not quite certain, upon some shallow pretext, to delay his departure until ten o'clock or noon. When his orders came at last, the cortege made off with an infernal clamor and commotion. The abbots of monasteries where the king was privileged to billet his horses and his men would rather have welcomed a swarm of locusts than the royal company. The queen, when not riding herself, made these journeys with her household and the royal children in litters or in barrel-topped wains, safe from rain, but not from the abysses of roads often hardly wider than a bridle path. Says Map, who often shared the stress of Henry's progresses, "We wear out our garments, break our bodies and our beasts, and never find a moment for the cure of our sick souls." [11]

Henry already knew his island; but in the course of these early journeyings, Eleanor had her first sight of the realm for which she had forsworn the more settled domain of her overlord in Paris. England was deeply scarred by the recent civil wars. The queen saw once busy towns half emptied of their folk, grazing lands gone to bramble, deep forests infested with dispossessed men turned poachers and robbers, on every tor a ruined citadel or one marked for doom. With her household and with her gear trussed up in leather sacks or stowed in chests, she drew up for the king's Christmas and Easter courts and his provincial assizes in the great fortress castles of Winchester and Wallingford, Nottingham, Oxford, Lincoln, Marlborough. Now and again she presided over those more privy gatherings in the forestal palaces of Clarendon or Woodstock, that favorite retreat of the Norman kings, and made a part of Henry's hunting parties at Brill and the Peak, and along the windings of the Glyme. In these progresses, as high symbol of the king's wealth and consequence, as the mother of princes, she shone like a sunstone among the lesser things of his treasury.

However, from the beginning of Henry's reign it was clear, in spite of the long struggle for England, that the focus of Plantagenet interest and ambition was still beyond the Channel. England gave Henry his status with kings; it should become the fertile source of revenues for the establishment of peace and security among the disparate parts of his continental empire. But his desire burned for the old familiar cities of Rouen and Angers, Tours, Le Mans, and Poitiers. The king made haste to set his island realm in order, so that he might be secure and free to pursue his courses overseas.

The wide dispersal of the Plantagenet provinces and their partition by the Channel gave Henry urgent need for a man of high endowment and of character to whom he could delegate affairs of first importance. In the circumstances, what the Angevin required was a man of large ability whom he could trust as another self, a chancellor — and something more, an intimate whose loyalty and intelligence should enlarge his own administration, yet who should, in the last resort, be subject to the royal will. Henry looked as a matter of course to Thibault of Canterbury to supply the needed paragon. Thibault had labored for the settlement between Stephen and Henry that had brought the Angevin to the throne; and his household was the best school of the day for preparing young men for careers whether in church or state. The forethoughtful archbishop, who felt grave concern for the prosperity of the church under the new regime, had already trained this public servant for the king.[12]

His election had fallen upon Thomas Becket, a rising young Londoner in his middle thirties who had been in his court for a dozen years and shown himself, under important employments, of subtle understanding, steadfast purpose, incorruptible integrity. He was tall and personable, this burgher's son, well-knit, dark haired, pallid, with wide clear brow, candid eyes, a courtly bearing, ingratiating manner, deliberate speech. Though intelligent and well-schooled, he had not the born scholar's zest for learning, but rather the courtier's interest in men and activity.[13] A boyhood in a prosperous and up-right burgher's house with a pious mother's teaching, a period with the canons of Merton in Surrey, were followed by two years in the schools of Paris in the days of Abélard's return to Saint Genevieve — years which brought him to acquaintanceship with the great teachers of his time and with the stirring issues of the intellectual revolt against Clairvaux. Journeys as a young man with Thibault to Rome, and other missions on the affairs of Canterbury, had given him contact with men influential in court and *curia*. His early adoption into the archbishop's household associated him with the rising generation of statesmen and ecclesiastics in England and abroad. Thomas' rise in Thibault's court had been rapid and brilliant and had occasioned some envy among his companions there. As Archdeacon of Canterbury the young man already held rich benefices; and, as with many wealthy clerks, his bent was toward the world and not the cloister. He would be acceptable to the king for his practical sagacity and his forthrightness; to the See of Canterbury for that substratum in his character of rectitude and tenacity.

The chancellor was thus assigned to Henry by that authority from which, according to prevailing theories, kings themselves derived their sanction, to be not merely the Angevin's civil servant, but his privy counselor and guide in the tangled affairs awaiting him in England. Thomas as chancellor was given a mandate by Canterbury to conciliate the king, to direct his judgments, curb his youthful violence, and steer him in the paths of peace and justice. Becket was Henry's senior by fifteen years, old enough to admonish, young enough to companion the young sovereign. Henry, burning to bring the island to order and be off to those capital affairs he had to conclude abroad, welcomed the man of good fame, sobriety, and experience, commended to him so warmly by Archbishop Thibault. In the circumstances, he knew himself fortunate to find at hand the very man designed by nature and prepared by nurture for his needs.

In all the early enterprises of the Plantagenets, Becket was the king's intimate, and Henry found his zeal and energy drive hard upon his own in all the royal interests. In pleasure and in toil the king and his chancellor kept company.[14] Together they followed hounds and hawks, vied in chess and tilt, dined at the same board. When Henry went on *chevauchée*, Thomas traveled with him.[15]

*

> To recognize his house
> Is not an arduous task; the beaten path
> Is plain to all without the need of guide.
> The house is known to all; unknown to vice
> Alone it sheds its beams on poor as well
> As rich. Its door stands open for the wretched
> And the blest alike; and here each stranger
> Finds a father to fill his heart with joy.
>> John of Salisbury, *Entheticus*, translated by J. B. Pike

The chancellor's establishment in London became the talk of European courts. It buzzed with the activities of half a hundred clerks attendant upon official business. His household, as offering a forum of experience and an exemplar of courtly custom, became, rather than the king's residence, the school of young nobles, the rendezvous of ambitious men. The highest courtiers envied him for the favors he enjoyed.[16] His tables, hospitably furnished for guests and pensioners of every rank, were adorned with the most precious vessels and spread with sumptuous foods and costly wines. But though elegance and affluence distinguished the chancellery of the king, profligacy and insobriety were shut from the gates of Thomas' house in London.

The queen appears to have been not insensitive to the fact that the rise of the chancellor involved some decline of her own ascendancy in the royal counsels. The deflection of business to Thomas' house and Henry's sojourns abroad produced a change in the feudal custom she had known, calculated to diminish the status of queens and to cut her off from that large intercourse with persons of consequence which had been her prime means of keeping herself abreast in the racing currents of her time. To the chancellery, rather than to the king's outlying residence, went those equipages that signalized the grandees of Christendom, lay and clerical, for whose approach outriders cleared the streets of London. There, and not to Bermondsey, went emissaries from far places with the secrets of Pope and king, the gossip of court and fief, market, school, shrine, and cloister. There men sought the king's patronage and found it dispensed by the king's chancellor.

In Henry's absences the queen and the royal children were left under the guardianship of Thibault of Canterbury and John of Salisbury. It is possible that the See of Canterbury, in view of her lamentable career among the Franks and the canonical flaw in her marriage to the king of the English, had not regretted the separation of the palace and the chancellery and the confinement of the queen in Henry's absences to a merely accessory role in Bermondsey. There, in spite of her sumptuous household, her personal corodies, and her regal trappings, she who had been accustomed in Paris and Antioch, Angers and Rouen, to be at the heart of enterprise, in the thick of rumor and discussion, found herself at times sequestered, companioned by women, visited not by the authors of significant events, but by sycophants and triflers who found no vocation in the chancellery. Henry himself complained that Becket's house emptied his own. Peter of Blois comments upon the relative shabbiness of Henry's provision for his own household, upon the "half-baked bread, sour wine, stale fish and meat" with which guests and pensioners were regaled at the royal board.[17] He had doubtless dined at Becket's better furnished table.[18] Eleanor at this stage of her career, when the future seemed so full of promise, can have felt no inclination for a semi-seclusion with the infant princes and the king's female relatives while the homage of the court was received in the house of the chancellor, and the royal gifts, upon which the feudal prestige so much depended, were dispensed by his hand.

It was not long before Becket received from his king a summary commission to restore the dilapidated palace of Westminster as the proper royal residence in London.[19] Fitz-Stephen relates that the vast work, undertaken suddenly, was accomplished between Easter and Whitsuntide with such a babel of activity that upon the scene men could not hear each other speak.[20] Thereupon this palace, restored and refurbished, became the ampler theater of Plantagenet enterprise.

❧

The sweet young queen
Draws the thoughts of all upon her
As sirens lure the witless mariners
Upon the reefs.

Minnesinger's song, reputedly in praise of Eleanor

If we may believe the critics of the second half of the century, new influences exerted in this period brought the society of London almost abruptly out of its insular backwardness and its gravity into the full currents of continental gaiety and enlightenment. It seems that there grew up at that time in which the famous Countess of Poitou presided in the courts of the Plantagenets, a notable change in social patterns, to which not only expatriated Normans and Poitevins, but the barons of Britain and the Sabines of London, learned in some measure and in the course of time to respond. Reflective persons on the spot observed those innovations not without dismay. Whereas, said one of these, it is the manifest function of the arts to divert men's thoughts from profane things, these very agencies were now employed to arouse his passions and engage his mortal senses.

Much has been said about Henry's patronage of the arts, but the influences that now especially prevailed can hardly have been conceived by the king himself, however much his tastes inclined to the literature and learning of his day. He liked to surround himself with able and well-furnished men and whet his mind upon their talents and their erudition. Like all the Plantagenets, he enjoyed the enrichment art lends to life, and certainly his tastes were not austere. But he was too preoccupied, at least in those early years of his reign, to have elaborated the artistic milieu of which the critics complain. This milieu was not in any case the kind of thing to which his special genius turned. With the king, says Peter of Blois, there is school every day, constant conversation of the best scholars, and discussion of questions.[21] His instincts were conservative. Nor can the innovations of which we hear have grown up in the unexceptionable atmosphere of the chancellor's house.

Within the reach of the Plantagenet influence the courtly literature of Europe underwent a remarkable change which infused it with new significances, profoundly altered its centers of interest, and sent it upon the romantic course that it has followed, in spite of the outcries of scientists, philosophers, and other cynics, to this day. It represents strains of influence the queen was uniquely prepared to bring together. The new romances that displaced the heroic *chansons de geste* for the delight of the court were aristocratic, the work of men trained in the schools, familiar with the classic authors comprised in the trivium and the quadrivium. But the earlier tales of antiquity were now infused with something not indigenous to them. New themes and new materials drew not only from the "matter of Rome" and that of "Byzantium," but especially from the courtly tradition of the troubadours of the Limousin and from that "matter of Britain" which had for two generations been filtering into Poitou,[22] and which had lately come to the duchess' castles on the marches of Anjou over the easy highway of the Loire. If her clerks at first went back to Virgil and Ovid and Statius to steep their work in elect tradition and to find that otherness of time and place essential to romance, it is not antiquity nor the heroic age of the *chansons de geste* that we find in their fabrications, but that courtly life, present and palpable, of the twelfth century, appropriating to itself all the luxury which crusade and pilgrimage had taught the West to desire; through it was diffused the ideology of that feminized leisure class to which the Angevin wealth and peace were giving rise.

The enthralling story of Tristram, with its triumph of fateful love over feudal loyalties, enchanted this court as it had charmed that of the Countess of Anjou.[23] "Matter of Britain" gained such a vogue in this period that the fame of Arthur and his knights spread over all the pilgrim routes of Christendom and pagandom, and was heard with wonder and delight in Byzantium, Antioch, Alexandria, Rome. It has been suggested that the scarcely fledged Plantagenet dynasty, in order to offset Capetian and imperial exploitation of Charlemagne as forebear, appropriated Arthur as their genealogical hero — Arthur the renowned paladin who had brought ancient and sovereign Rome to despite. The legendary character appeared, however, a figure dressed cap-a-pie in all the chivalric virtues of the current mode. In this noble guise he presently eclipsed the valiants of the *chansons de geste* and ultimately took his place with Godfrey of Bouillon and Charlemagne as one of the three great worthies of Christendom. Said Geoffrey of Monmouth, "There was neither king nor powerful lord who did not try to school himself according to the modes and manners of the men of Arthur." In the course of time, just as earlier travelers had turned aside to muse on Roland in the passes of Roncevaux, young aristocrats like Giraldus Cambrensis turned aside to note among the ruins of Caerleon on Usk the spot where Arthur received the Roman envoys.[24] The legend became so extravagant and developed such political inconveniences for Henry that he is said to have been obliged to purge it of the notion that Arthur would return one day to reclaim his glory; and to this end he launched a successful archaeological research to discover and expose his hopeless dust along with that of Guinevere.[25]

The queen was to poets, as one of her apologists has said, "what dawn is to birds." [26] They sang for her. It would require a textbook to catalogue the dedications and rededications and other literary salutations addressed to Eleanor herself. Wace had offered his redaction of Geoffrey of Monmouth's *History of the Kings of Britain* — that bubbling spring of Arthurian lore — to her while she was still only Duchess of Normandy; and she is commonly identified as the "riche dame de riche rei" of Benoît de Sainte-Maure in his romance of *Troie*.

> *For my presumption shall I be chid*
> *By her whose kindness knows no bounds?*
> *Highborn lady, excellent and valiant,*
> *True, understanding, noble,*
> *Ruled by right and justice,*
> *Queen of beauty and largess,*

By whose example many ladies
Are upheld in emulous right-doing;
In whom all learning lodges,
Whose equal in no peer is found,
Rich lady of the wealthy king
No ill, no ire, no sadness
Mars thy goodly reign.
May all thy days be joy.[27]

Even old things were brought from the closet and refurbished with an eye to Plantagenet munificence. Philippe de Thaün revived interest in the bestiary which he had formerly dedicated to Henry I's queen, Adelaide of Louvain, with a few offertory words to the Countess of Poitou.[28]

God save lady Alianor,
Queen who art the arbiter
Of honor, wit, and beauty,
Of largess and loyalty.
Lady, born wert thou in a happy hour
And wed to Henry King.

The queen's fame was spread far beyond the precincts of the court along the pilgrim routes by minnesingers and balladeers.

Were the lands all mine
From the Elbe to the Rhine,
I'd count them little case
If the Queen of England
Lay in my embrace.[29]

The new literature brought with it a cult of manners. Under court discipline the careless male learned that to present himself before the queen's assize with hair unkempt, "like an ill-dressed shock of barley," was to be effaced from the presence of majesty. John of Salisbury and Walter Map, who must often have seen what they describe, report that the aesthetic movement of their time was producing an effeminate effect upon the ways of hearty England. From the civilizing influence of dress, it was only a step to the ritual of flattery which these critics found so depressing. Barons renounced their native dignity and addressed each other in meaching phrases as "best of men, mirror of wisdom, my refuge, my sun, my life." [30] John declared that the foolish dawdling and love-making of rustics, once reckoned depraved by serious men, was affected by gallants of the court, a statement that suggests that the mortifying ritual of the courts of love was somewhat understood in London, even as it had been in Poitou and the Limousin. This particular branch of art, dramatized so especially by Ventadour and other troubadours in the queen's provinces, seems never to have had the thoroughgoing success in England that it enjoyed on the Continent; yet something it must have accomplished, for, when the innovations were well under way, the cynical Map exclaims, "There is now in London no Lucretia, no Penelope, no Sabine woman. Fear all the sex."[31]

If the popular romance and *lai* turned men's thoughts from the robust elder literature into profane channels, the case with dramatic spectacles was even worse. John of Salisbury could find no words equal to expressing the measure of his censure for the forms of entertainment that came into vogue under his very eyes. He could only recommend excommunication for the mimes and histrions who were corrupting the public taste. Fabliaux, flouting virtue and making a comedy of vice, were the diversion of those who should have offered loftier example to their kind. Mimes, dancers, acrobats, prestidigitators, found their way into the most famous houses and delivered such business as even cynics blushed to see. Actors sought, said John, to provoke outbursts of gross laughter by their unrestrained gestures and loose buffoonery. They rolled their eyes, shrugged their shoulders, waved their arms. An infinitude of vain diversions engaged the idle, who would better have been merely idle than so employed. The whole situation reminded John, coming as he did from the sobriety of Thomas' house, of ancient Babylon, and the worst of it was that he laid the responsibility for the state of things he describes on the entertainers employed to amuse the wanton leisure of Henry's court.

The impulse to the secularization of the arts invaded even the special province of the church. Abbé Bernard, bred on the serene raptures of plain song,[32] had long since explained that the charm of pure melody should never render the ear more attentive to the vocal inflections of the singer than to the thoughts those inflections were meant to insinuate into the soul. But what was the impious cacophony that John heard in the chapels of London? The soul was teased from its devotion, he declared, by the ludicrous pantomime with which choirs accompanied the swelling harmony of organs. Performers trilled, he says, and overlaid one cadence with another, and jangled their words until listeners were bereft of their senses and could not examine the merits of the substance.

William Fitz-Stephen, who, like John of Salisbury, belonged to the Archbishop's household, ascribes a decent sobriety to the city which the queen found on her advent.[33] It was one of the distinctions of London among cities, he says, that instead of theatrical sights and scenic spectacles, the people had diversions of a sacred sort, miracles depicting the constancy of the holy confessors, the sufferings of the martyrs. But court tastes seem to have declined from these bourgeois standards, and one is constrained to see, in the whole aesthetic movement that so dismayed the chancellor's associates, the liberating and fashioning hand of the queen releasing her treasure of art and civility in London, introducing the scenic splendors of Antioch and

Byzantium, to say nothing of continental cities, to her insular court and her
Norman lords in exile. "The arts," says Map, "are swords of the mighty."
These various diversions appear to have corrected in some measure the dis-
proportionate traffic to Becket's gates of which the king himself complained.
If we may judge from the works of Giraldus Cambrensis, as well as those
of Map and John of Salisbury, the royal court at Westminster must presently
have set up a lively competition with the chancellery as a place of resort in
London, and drawn off from it, at least occasionally, all the notables the
queen cared to welcome. Men of the world, perfectly *au courant*, men with
careers to make and acquaintances to forge, could not afford to be unfamiliar
with the wit and the novelty, the spectacles, the fashions, and the social rigors
of the king's palace in Westminster.

In the intervals of her cultural activities, Eleanor, crossing and recrossing
the Channel at any season of the year, and making the rounds from castle
to castle in England and abroad, shared Henry's confidence and the labors
of his government. Sometimes in his absence, herself holding a royal court,
she sat with the king's justiciars on matters of importance and set her own
seal to writs of royal exigence.[34] She drew her own revenues and kept oversight of a lively domestic household, as is shown by her expenditures for
rushes, plate, and linen. And in the meantime, with a perversity to confound
the Franks, she secured the future of the Angevin empire and supplied the
instruments of a diplomacy which, no less than force of arms, was to solidify
the whole.

Her first son, Guillaume, born on the Continent before Henry's accession,
died in 1156;[35] but in the meantime she had given birth to Prince Henry
(February 1155) and to a princess named for the Empress Matilda (June
1156). In September 1157 the future Coeur-de-Lion was born in the palace
of Oxford and designated in Guillaume's stead as the queen's special heir to
the County of Poitou and Duchy of Aquitaine. In 1158 a fourth son, born
at the moment of Henry's absorption of lower Brittany, was named for the
king's brother Geoffrey, and subsequently designated as the Count of Brittany. In September 1161 the queen gave birth in Domfront in Normandy to
a second daughter, who was baptized by the cardinal legate with her own
name; in October 1165 the Princess Joanna was born in Angers; and in
Oxford in December 1166, John "Lackland," the last of the "eaglets." The
names make a roster of famous kings and queens.

10 ✥

Forging the Empire

WHILE THE QUEEN AND HER COURTIERS, left somewhat to their own devices, were teaching London to emulate the most famous centers of civility in Christendom, Henry, chiefly abroad, was occupied with Angevin problems of another sort. In Normandy he found himself near the mid-point of an elongated empire that stretched from the borders of Scotland over a vast latitude to the foothills of the Pyrenees. He knew his lands, for he had measured them from the saddle, rood by rood, with his own eye. He knew the diverse aspects of them and their diverse worth, from the vineyards and olive groves of Aquitaine to the sheepfolds of the English midlands and the fens and forests of Northumberland. He knew their populous towns, each cast in its archaic mold and busy with its local crafts, their fairs and markets, their fortressed tors looming over the junction of roads and the crossings of rivers, their abbeys and granges, salt marshes and fisheries, their malt and dye houses, forges, tanneries, wine presses, their mill and water wheels, their fields brought to tillage by the immemorial toil of ox and colon, the vast hunting ranges where his hounds bayed and his falcons soared. He regarded the small husbandry by the wayside — osier beds, dovecots, apiaries. And he took for overplus the careless largess of earth and sky — heather and broom, the magpie scouring the turned furrow, English lark and nightingale of the Limousin. He was rich beyond the dreams of Angevin counts. Time too unrolled before him, time enough for enterprise.

Henry set himself to the colossal tasks imposed by his fortunes, first among them the fusing of the diverse provinces that spread from Gascony to Scotland into one solid realm, and the girding of them with impregnable frontiers. A month's journey measured the length of his empire; but only a short day's journey from Tours to the edges of Brittany, through the heart of his ancestral province of Anjou, marked its narrowest breadth and therewith its weakest point. At his father's deathbed Henry had agreed that, upon his accession to Normandy, he would cede to his brother Geoffrey that part of Anjou lying south of the Loire and including the castles of Chinon, Loudun, and Mirebeau. But after his marriage with Eleanor this triangle sharply indented Henry's borders, thrusting like a wedge between his lands and the queen's County of Poitou. The King of the English therefore repented of his promise to his brother, and by siege recovered this portion of his patrimony, with the southern marches of Anjou. Then taking advantage of a local strife over the inheritance of Brittany, he secured the election of his brother Geoffrey as count of that province; but when Geoffrey shortly died, he claimed this land as his own inheritance, and so gained control of Nantes and the outer reaches of the Loire.[1]

In this time of accumulating treasure and rising fortune, Henry bent his energy and his substance to strengthening his hold upon the uneasy domains he had consolidated and his access to all parts of them. He stormed and took the castles of rebellious vassals and overhauled their garrisons; put docile prelates, when he could, in vacant sees; descended like the judgment upon drowsy stewards and crooked seneschals. Everywhere he razed the strongholds of presumptuous barons, but strengthened and rebuilt his own capital fortresses. Upon the sovereign heights of his river valleys he marked the craggy bulwarks set there by his forebears, who had built grandly in every generation. The strategic castles of his realm underwent vast extension and repair: the seat of the Norman dukes in Rouen; the castle of the Norman exchequer in Caen; the fortress that guarded the passage of the Loire in Tours; Argentan on the marches of Anjou; the treasure castle of Chinon looking down from Anjou into Poitou and Aquitaine. He dyked the floods of the Mayenne and the Loire near Angers, reconstructed bridges over the Loire and the Vienne, restored roads and fords and barbicans.[2]

�֍

These bold Plantagenet operations in the West had as one of their effects that of driving Louis Capet within the confines of his own proper domain centering about the Île de France. It remained a fact, to be sure, that the Count of Brittany owed a vassal allegiance to Louis which was disturbed by Henry's sudden occupation of that province; but this hardly more than nominal dependence mattered little to Henry, so long as he was in actual possession of the land. More important still to the Angevin's security were two other segments which jutted from the domain of the Capets into his eastern frontier: the indispensable Vexin with its border fortresses controlling the Seine between Paris and Rouen, which Geoffrey the Fair had bartered away to Louis for value received in the year of the queen's divorce; and Berry, which with the force of the hostile house of Blois behind it, drove sharply into the edges of Poitou. The logic of Henry's plans required the recovery of the Vexin and the addition of Berry, which could only be had at the expense of his overlord. But bold and sudden as he was where projects were clearly realizable, he forbore to make war upon Louis to obtain these precious morsels.

It was the Capets themselves who presently offered the Plantagenets an opportunity to expand in the direction of the Vexin. Early in 1158, Louis's amiable Spanish Queen Constance, in whom no defect had hitherto been found, presented her lord and her expectant people with a disappointing female child. It was at about this time that Louis began to murmur about the "frightening superfluity of his daughters."[3] It had become clear, on the other hand, that the Angevin dynasty would not collapse for want of lineal heirs of "the better sex." There were already three young Plantagenets not counting the eldest Prince Guillaume, who had died in infancy, and two of these were sons (Henry and Richard). The plain, if second-rate, remedy to balance matters for the Franks, was to warm up the feudal allegiance the Angevins owed the Capets by strengthening feudal ties, before Henry Fitz-Empress should affiance his very desirable scions to some other noble house. Thus, if worse came to worst, in another generation at least a grandchild of Capets and Plantagenets might own sovereignty over all of western Europe; yet if heaven should in the course of time vouchsafe a male heir to the Capets, the alliance with the Angevins could not prejudice his claims to the Frankish domain, but would on the contrary buttress it. The church favored the employment of the "meaner sex" (Louis's words) as instruments of destiny to quiet uneasy borders and forestall bloodshed over property. Eleanor's two elder daughters, whom at the time of her divorce she had abandoned in the court of France, had already been employed to bolster the Capetian dynasty. They were now, in childhood, betrothed to brothers of the house of Champagne: Marie to Henry, Count of Champagne; Alix to Thibault, Count of Blois. And this house, after the long struggle between Stephen of Blois and Henry Fitz-Empress for the succession in England, were no friends of the Angevins.

The political theories of the Franks were very clear to Henry. He too foresaw his grandson — if the Angevin star did not fail him — wearing the double crown of France and England. In the spring of 1158 Henry met Louis on the marches of Normandy and came away with a most advantageous bargain.[4] By its terms not only was the disappointing infant Marguerite affianced to the three-year-old heir of England, but for her dower it was agreed that she should, at the time of her marriage, receive the precious Vexin and its castles, which Geoffrey the Fair had bartered away to Louis just before his death.

The Franks had not, however, as yet subdued their rancor over the Angevin's treachery in detaching Poitou and Aquitaine from the French domain. This alliance of Henry's son and Louis's daughter required some preparation in the public mind. In the face of Frankish fear and hatred of the Plantagenets, the coup could not be managed with sheer Angevin bluntness nor Capetian naïveté. The case seemed to the Plantagenets one to employ the brilliant talents of the king's chancellor. In spite of Becket's experience in negotiation, it can hardly be doubted that in the matter of this strategic alliance, which set her forth with renewed luster in Paris, Eleanor advised him about the manner of his assault upon the citadel of her overlord. Certainly the equipage with which Thomas set out from the Norman capital in the summer of 1158 exceeded the bounds of Henry's artistic imagination and of his wonted expenditure for mere display, and it outdid in sumptuary effects anything Becket otherwise devised in the whole course of his gorgeous career as chancellor.

The gaping crowds that witnessed Thomas' journey to Paris to confirm the alliance beheld a nine days' wonder on the road, such as the later pageants of Benozzo Gozzoli scarcely rival. First they beheld eight wagons bearing the chancellor's personal gear, besides wains carrying his chapel marked by its gilded cross, the furnishings of his bedchamber, his kitchen hung underneath with pots and buckets. Carts followed with loads of English beer with which to treat the Franks, cargoes of food and drink for the journey. Then came barrel-topped wagons covered with hides and weighted with bags and coffers containing vestments, carpets, and bedcoverings for the chancellor's lodgings. Twelve sumpter horses bore Thomas' table plate, his books and rolls. Armed guards accompanied by fierce and terrible dogs escorted the cortege. On the back of each lead horse rode with gravity a long-tailed ape. Next came grooms and hawkers leading pairs of hounds and carrying upon their gloved wrists those highly bred falcons and gyrfalcons in which the King of England took special pride. Then followed a jovial English exhibition: two hundred and fifty stalwarts, in companies of five and ten, passed through the towns singing in turn their native songs in native dialect. Squires bearing their knights' shields, pack-trains, servants of the household, then mounted knights and clerks, two and two, drew on, and finally as climax of the spectacle, the magnificent chancellor himself accompanied by the dignitaries of his office. The pageant offered a notable contrast to Louis's unpretentious progresses from shrine to shrine. No one failed to get the correct impression. "If this," said the burghers and the yokels, "be but the chancellor of the English, grant us sight of the king himself." It occurred to the Franks that the Countess of Poitou had forsaken the court of the Capets for a higher high place; but the grievances they had suffered seemed now in the way of amendment.[5]

The new halls of the Templars outside the old walls offered the only lodging in Paris that could be proposed for such a host, and even here it spilled into adjoining streets. Louis closed the markets of Paris to prevent his guests from providing for their own needs while in his capital. But the chancellor's stewards circumvented him. Scouring the bazaars of suburban towns, they gathered provision for a thousand men. In this jubilee for vendors a dish of eels for Thomas' table is said to have sold for one hundred shillings sterling. With unexampled liberality the chancellor bestowed gifts of clothing and vestments, plate, horses, dogs, falcons, and English beer in appropriate quarters of Paris. In the city in whose streets he had wandered as an obscure student in the days of Abbé Bernard and Master Abélard, he now rode resplendent, dispensing a royal largess to all poor scholars of English blood. It became plain to every soul in Paris that the princess bestowed on the Franks by Constance of Spain was destined one day to retrieve the disastrous fortunes brought upon their king by the Countess of Poitou. There are no details of the chancellor's interviews with the Capets and the barons palatine, by which the miraculous effects of his grace and his dialectic could be judged; but the mission must be reckoned as not the least of his diplomatic triumphs.

It only remained for Henry to collect the guarantees. In September the King of the English went less ostentatiously to Paris, where he earned the praise not only of the Capets but of the citizens of the Île, who had dreaded some catastrophe from the meeting of the two monarchs upon this business. If the chancellor had offered some display of Plantagenet wealth and power, the king bore himself with modesty and restraint. He eschewed the royal escort proffered by his overlord, and went about Paris with simple elegance, making more of good works than of himself. He took pains to visit all the shrines, to deal liberally with churches, with lepers and the poor. He dined in the old Merovingian palace with the Capets, but did not tarry overlong.[6]

On the Sunday that ended the visit, Queen Constance delivered her firstborn into the hands of Henry's *mesnie* to be reared, according to feudal custom, in the domain of her destiny. Louis accompanied the cortege bearing away his daughter as far as the royal city of Mantes, where the six-months-old infant was consigned to the keeping of Robert of Newburgh, the dapifer and justice of Normandy, a man of unexceptionable rank and piety. A few understandable stipulations the Capets seem to have made: first, that the princess should not be bred, as feudal custom might have dictated, in the household of Queen Eleanor, but in certain Norman castles near the marches of the French domain; and second, that the priceless castles of her dowry should not be at once surrendered to Henry, but should be held in custody by three Knights Templars against the day of her marriage.

Later in the autumn, as if afflicted with a vague malaise, Louis made a pretext for a progress through the whole breadth of Normandy.[7] He had long desired to make a pilgrimage to the shrine of the archangel, Michael-in-Peril-of-the-Sea. Incidentally he looked in upon the arrangements for his daughter Marguerite in Newburgh and inspected the city of Avranches, which Henry had designated as one of her honors, and he cast this eye upon the events developing under Henry's heavy hand in Brittany. The castles and abbeys of Henry's provinces opened hospitably before him as he proceeded toward the shrine. From his ancestral city of Le Mans, Henry convoyed his overlord with an escort of bishops and abbés to the mount of the archangel. Together, to the rush and roar of the tide, the two kings heard mass in the abbey above the sea, and then dined austerely in the refectory with the monks, as Louis loved to do.[8] This communion upon the pinnacle of Mont-Saint-Michel, above the clamor of the world and the tides that wash its shores, was one of the happiest and most fraternal incidents in the whole intercourse of the two kings. On the homeward way Louis rested at the abbey of Bec near Rouen and admired that scholars' citadel, which the sanctity of Lanfranc and Anselm had rendered famous. Here Henry vacated his own chamber for the use of his overlord, and Louis exclaimed — to somewhat astonished bystanders — that he had hardly found any man he could, on near acquaintance, so thoroughly love as the King of the English. He returned to Paris laden with gifts and the most agreeable impression of the Angevin good will and generosity.

The arrangements for assuaging the rancors between Capets and Plantagenets, to which anxious march vassals looked for peace, suffered an unexpected check in the late summer of 1159. The Countess of Poitou had never ceased to claim inheritance to the splendid Mediterranean province of Toulouse. It had belonged to her grandmother the Countess Philippa, the wife of the troubadour Count of Poitou. The troubadour appears to have mortgaged Philippa's patrimony for means to go upon his famous but ill-starred crusade, and finding himself in financial ruin on his return, he had probably done little to redeem it; and his subsequent abandonment of Philippa for the Countess of Châtellerault had further attenuated his claims. The county had passed to other heirs and it lay, unfortunately for Henry, in the vassalage of the Capets. But Eleanor never ceased to regard as part of her rightful inheritance the great red city with its castle of the Narbonnais, where Philippa had reigned as countess, and where her own father Guillaume le Toulousain and her uncle Raymond of Antioch had been born. The demand was now revived by a quarrel between the reigning Count of Toulouse and the Count of Barcelona, in which the succession of Philippa's inheritance ran in danger of slipping away from the Counts of Toulouse without slipping into the hands of the Plantagenets.

The moment at which the problem presented itself was not an auspicious time for Henry to sully his immaculate relations with his overlord, but this crisis of the queen's, involving the rich domain lying on the borders of Aquitaine, could not be subdued to his convenience. He had no choice but to strike while the iron was hot. Becket, who threw himself with zeal into the project of the Plantagenets, equipped and brought a force to the support of Barcelona, which gave Henry's expedition the appearance not precisely of a thrust at his overlord, but as one of Barcelona against the house of Toulouse.

But when Barcelona and his allies, the King of the English and his chancellor, drew up their troops and their engines before the high red walls of Toulouse, they learned that Louis was within, and that, with just such reckless gallantry as he had displayed at the siege of Damascus, he had thrown himself into the defense. There was a limit, it seemed, to his "dovelike simplicity." It was one thing for him to concede the Vexin and its castles as a domain to enhance the portion of his future son-in-law; quite another to yield up Toulouse to the Countess of Poitou. Henry hesitated before the dilemma that confronted him as Eleanor's husband and Louis's vassal. To the chagrin of his following, and especially of his chancellor, he folded his tents and withdrew. He had been uneasily aware of a legal flaw in the proceeding from the start. He would not, he declared, set the bad example of an attack upon the person of his overlord.[9]

The affair dragged out through the autumn in inconclusive forays and reprisals on other fronts until winter ended operations in the field. The Plantagenets lingered through the vintage in Poitou and held their Christmas court in Falaise in Normandy. Shortly after Advent Eleanor returned to her delegated sovereignty in Britain and to the supervision of her court and household. The Pipe Rolls show her acting responsibly in matters of government, making progresses of her own from one royal seat to another, and drawing handsomely upon the revenues for the expenses of herself and her growing family.[10] But Henry remained for the fourth year abroad near the heart of his domain, where rumor of all the stirrings in Europe came swiftly to his ear.

In the fall of 1160 someone brought to him a disturbing bit of news from the Île. As soon as it reached his ears, Henry summoned the queen from a six-months' sojourn in Britain to join him forthwith in Rouen, and ordered her to bring with her the heir of England and the little Princess Matilda.[11] The Pipe Rolls show that Eleanor at once put out in the royal smack at a cost of seven pounds, and succeeded in arriving in Normandy in plenty of time. In October of this year one of the inscrutable visitations on the just overtook Louis in Paris. On the fourth of the month his Queen Constance gave birth to a second daughter, and then, having brought this calamity on the Capets, closed her eyes and "passed from the world." In this double disaster Louis cast about almost wildly for solace and redress. He was now forty, for the second time without a queen, the father of four daughters, and not a single son. He considered with his barons whether he should now cast his lot with those vassals of the house of Champagne whose influence the Capets had dreaded for two generations as rivaling their own. A daughter of Champagne long ago, before the Poitevin alliance, had been denied Louis's brother Philip on grounds of consanguinity. But perhaps the Capets had suffered enough for consanguinity.[12] Without waiting to lay aside his weeds, he offered the queen's coronet to a daughter of that house. In less than a month from the death of Constance, Louis married, as his third queen, Adele of Champagne, who was a sister of his future sons-in-law, the Counts of Champagne and of Blois.[13]

In the meantime the Plantagenets had been well prepared for most of the contingencies in Paris. Before the birth of the unfortunate Frankish princess, Henry had at once taken the precaution to present his own namesake heir to Louis on the marches of the French domain and witnessed the lad's homage to his overlord for Normandy. The Angevin's own struggle for the crown had made him a believer in the frequent renewal of pledges, and he wished now to make sure that Louis had no intention of qualifying the investiture of the little duke, in case heaven should vouchsafe the Capets an heir of their own. The subsequent birth of a second princess had rendered this precaution less significant, as it had also rendered superfluous the fetching over of the little Princess Matilda for betrothal to a possible male Capet. But prescient as the Plantagenets were, they had not gone so far as to imagine the death of Queen Constance. This incalculable event, followed by Louis's sudden remarriage with the house of Champagne and Blois — those hereditary enemies of the Angevins — roused them to fresh anxieties, and they took their own impromptu measures to safeguard their interests. While Louis was preoccupied with his hurried nuptials, and without giving notice to any of the Franks, the Plantagenets took it upon themselves to celebrate with an unseemly haste the marriage of their five-year-old heir to the three-year-old Princess Marguerite of France in Newburgh in Normandy.[14] They did not distract Louis, pre-engaged as he was at the moment, with their intentions, nor summon the Capets to the affair, but they were careful to have everything done in strict accordance with the canons as Louis would have wished. Fortunately, they had the offices of two legates of the Holy See who were at hand and eager to gratify Henry in order to procure his recognition of their papal candidate.[15] Upon the conclusion of the marriage, Henry, without waiting for Louis's assent nor any other formalities, took over from the Templars the castles of the Vexin, which had been left in their keeping as the bride's dower against the day of her marriage; and he also took into his custody his infant daughter-in-law as hostage for Louis's faithful adherence to all the articles of agreement between them.[16]

These proceedings over the borders of Normandy, coming as a climax to other calamities, appear to have stunned Louis. In reprisal he scourged the perfidious Templars out of Paris.[17] The house of Champagne interpreted Henry's enterprise as an unmitigated feudal affront and determined to redress it by recourse to arms. But the foresight of the Plantagenets rendered their demonstrations innocuous. At their first feint Henry seized Thibault of Blois's castle of Chaumont, which he had long coveted anyway to round out an angle of his territory on the Loire. Then, as the season of winter put a term to war, the King and Queen of the English withdrew well within their own frontiers with the heir of England and the Princess of France and a goodly company of nobles to keep the time of Advent in the seat of the Angevin counts in Le Mans.

For the Plantagenets the decade from 1155 to 1165 had been lively and prosperous. They had founded a dynasty, established an empire, fortified its frontiers with strong castles, made it proof against arms, filled it with treasure, enlivened it with learning and the arts. Abruptly, invincibly, they had altered the map, the balance of power, the destiny of peoples.

11 ✣

King and Archbishop

Princes receive their glaive from the Church, to which it properly belongs. To the prince the Church gives authority over the bodies of men, but reserves to herself the cure of souls. Hence the prince is minister to the priest, from whom he derives his less worthy part.

John of Salisbury, *Polycraticus*, IV, 3

IN 1161 HENRY'S ATTENTION HAD BEEN DRAWN from the labor of solidifying his empire on the Continent by events in England. Early in the spring a long decline brought Thibault of Canterbury "to the end of his life days." In most of the annals this important event is recorded merely by the chronicler's stock line, *In hoc anno obiit Theobaldus*. He died an anxious and unrequited soul.[1] Neither Thomas nor Henry came at his summons to console his last days. It was he who, by his policies of forbearance and conciliation, had brought about the peaceful transition to the new regime. He had faithfully supported Matilda Empress and her heir and produced the compromise resulting in Henry's succession; and in all the period following he had so dealt with the difficult issues between the church and the king as to keep the peace and soothe the rancors of the civil war. He had given Henry his devoted chancellor and put his household of disciplined clerks at the services of the new order. Thibault had hoped that Becket would incline a grateful king to protection of the church; but Henry seemed, on the contrary, to have indentured Becket to the world. It was Thomas himself, the son of Canterbury, who had laid upon the bishoprics the arbitrary tax for the queen's campaign against Toulouse. In his last days Thibault turned his face to the wall. His household had been the school for episcopal careers; yet churchmen found among his suffragans no obvious successor to his see.

But even if the church had had a conspicuous candidate upon whom all factions could unite, Henry had no idea of leaving initiative in selection of a primate to the church alone. Issues which could not much longer be postponed had for years been accumulating between the See of Canterbury and the king. Both had grievances. Canterbury could well complain that Henry held vacant important bishoprics while their revenues poured into his secular enterprise, that church properties alienated in the days of Stephen were not yet restored. Henry, on the other hand, was resolved to end the situation by which a large portion of his subjects were able to find in the ecclesiastical courts means of avoiding the civil justice of the king. He resolved that these courts, with their special protection of clerks and their appeals to Rome, should offer no immunities from the universal operation of his law. The Angevin, who above all things liked to count and consolidate his gains in conflict, foresaw a long train of inconclusive aggressions and reprisals between church and state in which his arm, however powerful, could not effectively come at the ghostly armor of his antagonist. In the critical state of affairs, it was of the essence of statesmanship to secure as successor to Thibault a prelate with a not too ecclesiastical view of things.

During the archbishop's months of failing health, Henry turned over his problem in his mind, to light upon the fit man for the primacy, to make him acceptable to the electors of Canterbury, and his thoughts turned irresistibly to the chancellor, Thomas, who was of the archbishop's household, yet had shown himself more zealous than the king in all the royal interest; Thomas, whose training in the law schools of Bologna and Auxerre had made him so conveniently apt in argument, so skillful to foreclose; Thomas, whom custom had made familiar with the royal purpose and intent. If the church had given the king his chancellor, the king would now give the church its primate.[2] If the Archbishop of Canterbury and the king's confidential servant were one and the same man, and that man Becket, then Becket, the king's chancellor, would speak privily to Becket, the archbishop, and persuade him to be reasonable with the king. The idea of uniting in Thomas the complementary functions of primate and chancellor seemed to Matilda Empress, who had seen such operations in Germany, impolitic and she opposed it. But Henry, feeling the sap of prescience running in him, took bolder counsel.

At the very core of Henry's imperial thoughts was the matter of establishing beyond any possible breach of faith the succession of his heirs to the empire he was building. The years of struggle for his own crown made him keenly aware of the dangers besetting the royal pretensions of a child. A stickler for oaths and their frequent renewal, Henry sought occasions to invoke these feudal sanctions in favor of his dynasty. He had presented his first two sons with the queen to his barons at Wallingford in the year after his coronation and secured recognition of the two infants in succession as his heirs.[3] The king and queen had worn their crowns in London and Winchester and at the Christmas and Easter courts of their chief provincial seats, and Henry had been careful to give authority to the feudal oath by tendering his own homage and witnessing that of his eldest son to the King of France. He now foresaw that there might be some demur among the bishops of England at accepting as their primate a worldly clerk who had not even taken priest's orders, and he wanted to make sure that the interim between Thibault's death and the elevation of his successor should give no occasion for a lapse of allegiance to the little Prince Henry.

Accordingly, in the spring of 1162, he summoned the chancellor to the castle of Falaise, where he and the queen had held their Easter court. He charged Thomas to take the lad at once to Britain, convene the barons and the bishops in Winchester, and require a renewal of their recognition of the prince as heir of England. The child was glad to go with his dear master Thomas,[4] who was authorized to procure a little golden crown and sumptuous regalia for the presentation. The farewells were done and Becket and his ward were about to set forth with their cortege for Barfleur when Henry, as if moved by some sudden impulse, drew Becket aside and broke to him his resolution touching the primacy. But the chancellor was not taken unawares: the idea was already in his mind, and Henry was dashed that Thomas betrayed no elation at this, his second elevation to power and dignity. Jocosely, as the king's intimate, Becket twitched his own brocaded sleeve and asked how such trappings befitted the shepherd of Canterbury.[5] Then looking down with gravity upon his lord the king, he spoke courteously and with emotion. Their friendship, he said, so happy and unconstrained, their common enterprise, could not survive the change. There were other men he would rather see in the primacy. The king found himself obliged to argue away Thomas' reluctance. In that hour the two men scanned each other with a deep surmise, each seeking to divine a sudden strangeness in the other's thought. Then, as time sped for departure, they clasped hands and separated with the kiss of peace. Over the Channel, by the same wind that drove Becket and the prince to Southampton, went messengers, both bishops and barons, to Canterbury summoning the monks to present Archdeacon Thomas to the suffragans of the see for election to the primacy.

While these brethren murmured together in their chapter house over the peremptory mandate of the king, Becket betrayed no concern with their affairs. He busied himself with the king's orders to convene the barons and the bishops in Winchester at Whitsuntide, procured the crownlet, and himself, with a most unusual courtesy and grace, gave example to that august convocation by first offering his own homage to the little prince, his ward. Neither Henry nor Eleanor was present at the scene to diminish the splendors of their heir. The child Henry, who then presided in the hall of Winchester with the golden circlet on his brow and saw his master Becket on his knee before him, and then received the oaths of fealty of the lords temporal and spiritual of the realm, was seven years of age. The chroniclers do not say whether the Princess of France shared in the pledges made to her wedded lord.[6]

A month later Thomas was ordained priest, and three days later still (June 3, 1162) he was consecrated and enthroned as Archbishop of Canterbury by Henry, Bishop of Winchester.[7] Not without some protest among his peers did Thomas the Chancellor, "who nourished himself with meat

and wine," mount to the highest churchly dignity, the highest place in
Britain save only the status of the king.

It was only in January 1163 that Henry and Eleanor, having been long
delayed by winter storms, crossed from Normandy to England. A cortege of
nobles and prelates went down to Southampton to meet the royal smack,
to welcome with cries of "vivat rex" the king who had been four years absent
from the island. On the levee Thomas and the little heir of England waited
hand in hand for the push of the tide, the lowering of the sail.[8] It was
from the archbishop's sheltering cloak the prince leapt forward to embrace
the king and queen whom he had quitted in Falaise nine months before.
One chronicler observes that when Thomas, clad now more with dignity
than splendor,[9] advanced to meet the king, Henry's manner was "blithe";
another that Henry cast a dark look upon his old friend and gave him but
a perfunctory salute. Whatever the greeting may have been, they rode together up to London.

It was true that furious barons had already sought the king in Normandy
with their grievances against Canterbury. Without ceremony, the archbishop
had dispossessed them of properties alienated from the see in Stephen's reign,
properties to which long tenure seemed to convey to them a right.[10] In the
episcopal courts clerks were finding immunity from the penalties meted to
laics for similar crimes in secular courts, those shire tribunals that Henry,
with the aid of his admirable chancellor, had been at such labor to establish
at the outset of his rule as the indispensable foundation of order in his
realm.[11]

In the six months since his elevation, Becket had become a sedulous archbishop. He had put off grandeur and put on simplicity. He had subdued his
days to the austere regimen of the priest. His sermons, his vigils, the abundance of his penitential tears, marked him as one changed by a miracle
of grace.[12] He had, to Henry's deep chagrin, resigned the chancellorship and
been formally discharged from all secular liabilities.[13] More than all, he had
begun to employ in the service of his see those talents once so useful to the
king.

All these sudden changes in Thomas accused Henry of some grave error
of judgment in the character of the man who had for eight years of his reign
been most intimately associated with him in privy matters of state.[14] Henry
was cynical about miracles of grace. He who had seen Thomas in ribald
company with soldiers on the road, and known him as the promoter of
devious royal schemes, had shared his gaiety, his eloquence, his lavishness,
his wit, saw in the austere figure now clothed in the black *cappa* of the
Augustinian canons a plain hypocrite, a betrayer of the very hand that had
raised him up. He was galled too by the fact that, although Becket had withdrawn to the privacy of a new role, the secrets of his own mind and polity

were as familiar to his once-friend Thomas as an old mass book. He reflected that he had himself raised this ingrate from clerk to chancellor, from chancellor to archbishop; and he resolved that he would bring him down by the same stairs by which he had gone up. If, in his agitation, Henry remembered Rome, he was perhaps not very much alarmed by the specter of Pope Alexander, who had lately besought Angevin support to gain the throne of Saint Peter, and who had only just ventured back to his temporalities from his long exile in Provence.

With the intention of bringing the issues raised by Thomas before his liege men, Henry convened an assembly of bishops and barons at Westminster in October 1163.[15] In the first six months after his return to Britain, the king had found occasions for breaches with the archbishop, and angry words had flown between them. It was in London that his wrath broke in torrents on his old favorite. The interval had given time for both Henry and Thomas to measure the ground that lay between them, and for the bishops and barons to take counsel with each other as to where their interest and safety lay in the schism that now plainly threatened.

At Westminster Henry complained before the bishops of the lenience and venality of the ecclesiastical courts, and of the character of the judges. He declared that evil men pushed themselves into ordination only to turn the "dignity and liberty" of the church into contempt. He demanded to know why he, as his ancestors had never done, should wear a tottering crown, why he should forego those prerogatives belonging to his forebears of maintaining an even justice in his lands. He demanded the obedience owed to the crown, and especially the delivery of guilty clerks into his courts, and he required from Thomas' suffragans a "clear answer" on the articles of his complaint. The issue raised thus suddenly was too formidable for settlement on the hour. Thomas replied cautiously for his fearful bishops that the lords spiritual desired to obey the king's will in all things save only if it should show itself menacingly against the will of God and the laws and dignities of the church. Henry could not make of this the "clear answer" he required. The assembly broke up in confusion and dismay. The king strode out of the hall without inviting the customary blessing of the bishops.

The next day Henry summoned Becket to a personal humiliation. He called upon him to surrender the chief sources of his wealth, the rich manors of Berkhampstead and Eye;[16] and as a special biting mark of his disfavor, he recalled Prince Henry and the Princess of France from Becket's house, where for most of the time since their marriage these children had grown together as playmates in the dear custody and tutelage of Canterbury. To make these insults signal and notorious, Henry summoned his own Christmas court, his queen and children, to keep the season of Advent in the castle of Berkhampstead.

In January 1164 Henry convened a new council at Clarendon [17] to bring Becket, chastened perhaps by his recent misfortunes, to public submission on the issues of Westminster. The king was confident of a triumph over his troublesome archbishop. Since Westminster the Pope (again in exile) had enjoined Becket to modify his promise to obey the king "saving the dignity of his order" to a more conciliatory promise "to obey in good faith." Besides, in the meantime, Henry had alienated from Becket's cause some of his suffragans. The king's own mind was single and his course was clear. At Clarendon Henry called on Thomas to assent to the old "customs" of rendering justice as these prevailed "aforetime in the realm." But Becket was every way divided: he owed allegiance to the Pope, for whom conflict with Henry meant the loss of indispensable support; yet more truly than the Pope, he realized that Henry would now reach beyond the "customs" to abridge ancient ecclesiastical rights, such as the appeal to Rome. He hesitated, ill at ease, and uncertain to what extent Henry had suborned the bishops, among whom were some who had opposed his elevation to the primacy. Pressed in the course of several days of argument by those bishops and nobles who dreaded above all a conflict that would oblige every man to make the dangerous choice between allegiance to the archbishop or to the king, Becket at last yielded "in good faith" to the "customs."

It thereupon appeared that his general concession was but the prelude to something more significant. Thomas found himself confronted with a weighty document, which he had had no opportunity to peruse with the care it deserved. A scroll was unfurled whereon Henry's legists had set down, chapter and verse, their definition of the "ancient customs," so describing the relations of church and state as to place the power and authorities in question under control of the king. If Becket, bred in Bologna on the canon law, had interested himself in codices, here were the decretals of the king, ordering the secular customs of Britain as the canons gave order to the usage of the church. Here was the "clear answer" Henry required of Thomas. Let him in "good faith," in the presence of bishops and barons, set the seal of Canterbury to the "customs," as put down in writing by Thomas' old associates in the king's court. Yes, or no?

In the Constitutions of Clarendon Becket scanned not merely the issue of the guilty clerks, but the whole area of conflicting jurisdiction between the church and the state. He read the articles with dismay. There he read that the king checked appeals to Rome, made excommunication conditional, exercised control over vacant sees and ecclesiastical preferments. Thomas had assented in "good faith" to the "customs." But he withdrew his seal from this strange document. "Never," he found voice to say, "never, while the breath of life is in me, will I assent to these articles." [18] Grasping his copy of the Constitutions, he himself ended the conclave. Drawing off his following, he left the astonished council to bewilderment and awe. From that day the salvos of the king and the archbishop, "saving the customs" and "saving the dignity of our order," were on the lips of every liege man of the Angevin; and presently they resounded from Clarendon in all the centers of Christendom. The quarrel between the king and the primate had grown big.

Nine months later, in October, the Archbishop of Canterbury was given an experience of the king's justice. Thomas was summoned to appear in the court of Northampton to answer a charge of contempt.[19] Since Clarendon he had done penance for his faltering assent to the "customs." Fortified in the spirit, as men said, by the sacraments, the comfort of the poor, and the counsel of a few intimates of the old household of Thibault, he had renounced his assent to the "customs" and revived his salvo. The bishops of his see were divided; but even those who clung to the suffrage of Canterbury besought him to avoid a breach that must tear the fabric of the church itself; those of Normandy clove to the king. Mediation between Thomas and Henry had failed; appeals to Rome had failed. Alexander, who could not sustain his own throne, could much less protect his archbishop from the very king whose support he himself could not forfeit. The disorder of the Pope's mind was seen in his correspondence. In successive letters to Henry and to the adherents of Becket, he alternately explained away his previous concessions to the other. In the interval between the assemblies of Clarendon and Northampton, Becket had attempted an unsuccessful flight to France from the intolerable thunderbolts of the king. He who, as chancellor, had commanded six vessels of his own for crossing the Channel now, as primate, was denied passage in a common smack. And after this chagrin Henry had taunted him with a question that defined its own answer: "Has the island grown too narrow to contain us both?"

Thomas was summoned to Northampton to answer for his nonappearance a short time before in a case in which a baron complained to the king that he had not obtained justice in Becket's court. When in response to his citation Becket reached Northampton on the appointed day, the principals had not yet arrived. John Marshall, who had proffered the charge against Thomas, had lingered in London to finish a certain business of his own. Henry had found the hawking fine on a watercourse along his route. The lodgings reserved for some of the primate's suite were found occupied by the careless retinue of one of Henry's courtiers. The people of the town peered out of chinks to see the following of great Thomas pausing in the streets, moving backward, casting about. Plainly the "dignity of his order" was in despite.

Late on the morning of the delayed hearing, Henry slept off the fatigues of his exercise with his dogs and falcons on the day before. He was not yet abroad when Becket, having already said mass and observed the hours, arrived at the castle. In the course of time, while he waited, Henry crossed the antechamber on his way to his own chapel. Becket rose, but the king passed him by without the customary greeting. Thomas sat outside while Henry heard mass and broke his fast.[20]

When the cause came up for trial the question was found to be not justice for John Marshall, but Becket's contempt for a previous summons to hear John's complaint. Becket offered the plea that he had been ill. He had sent messengers. He had not in any case been under compulsion to answer such a summons. But the judgment went against him, and he was, as the "customs" provided for guilty clerks, turned over to the "mercy of the king." A fine of three hundred pounds was set;[21] but, although the bishops gave surety for the fine, not one was found among the judges to serve the sentence upon Thomas, who awaited the verdict in the outer room. In the end, Henry, the aged Bishop of Winchester, who had consecrated Becket sixteen months before, went out and broke the sentence to his spiritual overlord.

The archbishop was calm in the midst of his anxious following. Here, he remarked, were seen the operations of the "customs" of Clarendon; yet never in the days of Henry's forebears had it been the "custom" for the Archbishop of Canterbury, the spiritual father of the king and all his people, to be thus tried in the king's court. However, he would not have it said that, for his own sake, he had thwarted the king's justice. He passed into the audience chamber to face the Angevin whom his predecessor Thibault had given him to curb and admonish. Henry was truculent. He now required the restitution of an additional three hundred pounds of revenues Becket had sometime received from the surrendered manors of Berkhampstead and Eye. Still proud Thomas found surety for the heavy sums. He had now been sentenced and fined, but he had not yielded *in bono* to the king's will.

Overnight Henry considered how he might come at those reservations with which Thomas invariably retired from the field. Perhaps he got a suggestion from some of those churchmen who had not forgotten the chancellor's levy on the bishoprics for the recovery of the queen's province of Toulouse six years before. At any rate, in the morning, Henry bethought him to require the return of one thousand marks which Thomas had taken on the king's surety for that costly and unfortunate affair, and certain lay folk gave pledge for this sum. Then the king demanded an accounting for the revenues that Becket, during his office as chancellor, had taken from vacant sees and abbacies, an amount reckoned by several chroniclers as 30,000 marks of silver.[22] At these extraordinary demands, reaching back into his secular career, Thomas' sureties fled away. No one dared to offer himself as pledge for such redemptions. There might be more to follow. At this point the exactions of the king became too immense. Thomas, and some of his bishops with him, threw themselves at the king's feet, beseeching a limit to the royal anger, a mitigation of the claims. Henry, like the Conqueror before him, swore "by the splendors of God." He would not abate a penny. Again the assembly broke up in consternation. The night passed in fearful talk. Some declared Thomas should resign his primacy to save the church from the king's fury; some that he should hold fast to defend the church from the king's tyranny; some that Henry had sworn "by the eyes of God" to proceed to Becket's limbs, to tear out his tongue, his eyes.

The next day Thomas was sick, but on the following day he had recovered possession of himself. He rose early and was clothed in his archepiscopal miter and the pallium which his friend John of Salisbury had fetched for him from the Pope. He celebrated the mass of Saint Stephen with its introit, "Princes sat and spake against me." He was dissuaded by certain Templars from going to the castle barefoot in penitential garb. Though clothed as usual, he rode from his lodgings with his primate's silver cross borne before him, and this, with his own hands, he carried into the antechamber. Several tried, but vainly, to dissuade him from thus impressing his authority upon the king. When the trumpet sounded for the assembly, Becket saw the Archbishop of York proceed to the inner hall, his cross borne before him in defiance of the cross of Canterbury.[23] This presumption Thomas let pass. No longer a party to deliberations, he waited outside with the little company of his household for the conclusion of his trial. Bystanders saw that he had withdrawn to "inwardness."

Becket, who had mastered the articles of Clarendon, and knew Henry, as he said, "only too well," cannot have been surprised at the comprehensiveness of the verdict. He was to make no appeals to Rome, issue no commands to his suffragans; and he would presently submit to a review of his accounts as chancellor, although it was a matter of record that he had been discharged from the liabilities of this office before his consecration. Becket did not rise to meet the officer sent to pronounce these terms upon him. He was no longer Thomas, the king's proud chancellor, brought low; but Canterbury, clothed in the ghostly panoply of his see, fortified against the world by his primatial cross. Measuring his words, he spoke without the stuttering that sometimes checked his utterance.

"I came hither to the king's court for one cause only, that brought by John Marshall. For none other will I answer. I was given to Canterbury free of all reckonings. I will bring no other sureties. I appeal, I appeal for myself and the church of Canterbury, to God and the Pope." [24]

These words, uttered in direct defiance of the king's sentence and at the moment when Henry's party believed his triumph complete, threw the conclave again into turmoil. In the face of Becket's appeal to Rome, those who had ranged themselves under the crosier of York could not drive away a ghostly fear. Again men searched their conscience, their reason, their interest.

Some appealed to Becket, some to the king to yield a jot. Becket heard that the Archbishop of York had already protested to Rome against his "perjury" at Clarendon — his first assenting to the "customs" and then withholding his seal from the written scroll.

In the inner chamber Henry and his liege men devised some further thing. The Earl of Leicester, the king's chief justiciar, returned with a new decree. But this was not uttered.[25] Becket rose to his full stature to meet this high and venerable authority of the king's council. Between them he planted the cross of Canterbury and forbade the earl to speak. The habit of awe and reverence stayed the words upon Leicester's lips. It was Becket who spoke. Even by the "customs" there had been no trial. Canterbury was not amenable to the king's summons on the matters that had been dragged forth. He would hear no sentence from those who were of his spiritual family, his own suffragans. "Now," he said, "I will depart, for the hour is past." As if shaking the dust of Sodom from their feet, Thomas and his company turned to the outer door.[26]

Some who had been in the king's hall crowded out to see the end of the drama in the antechamber. The substance of York's appeal to Rome was hurled after the archbishop's following: "Traitor, traitor."[27] One of the bystanders pelted Thomas with trodden rushes from the floor. Some say Becket gave back to his tormentors better words for good; others that he passed with a stern mien amongst them to the door. This was found locked, and a fearful surmise went about that Canterbury was the king's prisoner in the castle.[28] But the key was presently found hanging on its nail, and Thomas passed into the afternoon streets of Northampton. Here crowds of the populace waited for news of the monstrous conflict between the lord of their bodies and the shepherd of their souls. Perhaps Henry, looking out from the chamber of his justice, saw Thomas ride away from the castle preceded by his cross and followed by the rabble of burghers and villeins, that still undisciplined army of the third estate.[29]

No one knew better than Becket the tenacity and suddenness of Henry's tactics in war. He spent the first hours of the night in sanctuary beside the altar of Saint Stephen, rose early, said mass,[30] and before cockcrow departed in disguise by secret ways from the king's court in Northampton. Under another name he moved darkly from one monastic shelter to another; at the end of a week he found passage from Sandwich in a common smack manned with two pairs of oars to help its speed; landed at Oye; floundered for leagues upon the sodden roads of Flanders; obtained refuge for a few days from cold and hunger with the monks of Saint Omer near Clairmarais. Here he was joined by several of his clerks and servants who had pressed after him from Canterbury with horses, raiment, and some treasure for his needs.[31]

Alexander was in Sens, and it was to the *curia* that Thomas made all haste in order to lay his case before the Pope. Louis chanced to be in Compiègne along the shortest route to Sens.[32] On his passage Thomas was cordially received by the Capetian, who gave him safe-conduct and ministered to his necessities. Canterbury found respite and relief at last from the fury of the Angevin in the citadels of the pious King of the Franks.

12 ✠

Becket in Exile

The most persistent hate is that which doth degenerate from love.
                                                Map, *De Nugis Curialium*, 245

WHEN HENRY HEARD, on the morning after the council, that Becket had left Northampton in the night without his safe-conduct, he let it be known that "he had not done with" his archbishop.[1] He closed the ports against his taking refuge with the Pope in France, as he had no doubt that Thomas meant to do; and, lest the thunder of anathema should overleap the Channel, he forbade any person, on pain of the direst penalties, to fetch or carry letters, and charged his officers to search all travelers to or from the Continent. He at once dispatched his own embassy, made up of the chief bishops and barons who had sat in judgment at Northampton, to seek an audience with the Pope in Sens, to anticipate there any appeal of the renegade archbishop. It was therefore with some dismay that he presently learned that Thomas had eluded the wardens of the ports, had escaped to Flanders, and was bearing his appeal in person to the papal *curia*. As it happened, Henry's embassy crossed the Channel on the same stormy day, All Saints,[2] on which Becket and his companions toiled from Sandwich to Oye.

The king's envoys were absent a month.[3] Henry received them on their return at Marlborough where he had convened his Christmas court in 1164. There was nothing to lend festivity to the season in their account of the proceedings in the Île de France. They related that, while traversing the shortest routes toward Sens, they had learned that the archbishop, as he passed ever a little ahead of them, was making merit of his beggared state, rousing the prelates of Gaul to pious indignation. The envoys learned that the King of the Franks was in Compiègne, and they had turned aside to seek an audience and passport through his lands, and especially to deliver Henry's letter asking Louis not to harbor Thomas. Louis had been courteous, but sanctimonious too. When they had urged that he remand the errant archbishop to his own diocese of Canterbury, which he had quitted without the king's leave, Louis had lifted incredulous eyebrows.

"What do I hear," he said, "a prelate subject to the judgment and condemnation of his king? How could this be? I myself am a king no doubt, yet I am bound to state that it would be beyond my royal power to degrade the humblest clerk of my realm."

Thereupon the embassy from England had changed the tenor of the conversation and reminded Louis of Becket's campaign against him in Toulouse; but the Capetian had replied with admirable justice that he could not condemn Becket, as chancellor of the English king, for serving his master as best he might. He remarked that the King of the English would do well to keep in mind the versicle for the office of Saint Martin's vigil, which he himself had just been keeping: "Stand in awe and sin not" (*Irascamini et nolite peccare*).

"Perhaps," he added with a quaint smile, "if your king kept the vigils as often as his clerks do, he might be more familiar with it." [4]

Hastening from this unsatisfactory delay, the envoys had pressed on toward Sens and just outside that city had passed a cavalcade assembling for the crossing of the Yonne. This, they had discovered, was nothing less than the cortege of the Archbishop of Canterbury, converging, like themselves, upon the metropolitan city in which Alexander sat. They had overtaken Thomas in the full panoply of his office with retinue of clerks, servants, horses, chapel, vestments — all supplied, it seemed, by the munificence of the pious King of the Franks and the indignant prelates of Gaul.

Henry's embassy had, however, contrived to arrive before Becket in the presence of Alexander and his cardinals. They had addressed his Holiness, one after another, bishops and barons in turn, on the intransigency of Thomas since his elevation to the primacy. But the envoys had found themselves stiffly received, sharply cross-examined, greeted with incredulity, even with sarcastic twitterings when the Bishop of Chichester had stumbled a little, not in the mazes of his dialectic, but of his Latin. [5] Certain of the envoys had taken pains to remind Alexander of the indispensable support of Henry in his struggle for the papacy and to recall the occasion of his acclamation only two years before, when King Henry and King Louis, rivaling each other in filial piety, had walked abreast leading forth Alexander upon his mule as successor of Saint Peter amidst the plaudits of the universal church. [6]

When even this circumstance had failed of the generous response that it deserved, they had veered from the dreary effects of dialectic and history to a fiscal argument. They had offered to revive a more careful levy of the Peter-penny in Britain, which had somewhat lapsed under the Angevin — an English penny every year for Rome from every chimney that gave forth smoke in England. But, in spite of everything, the envoys had at last been put off more with threats than with promise of appeasement. The sultry odor of anathema was in the air. They had been forestalled. Thomas had sold his grievance at a good price in Sens and Compiègne. The insular affair of the king and the archbishop had gone mischievously abroad and into the arbitrament of the king's enemies.

Various chroniclers relate that the Angevins were subject on occasion to rages that gave warrant for the legend, current in their day, of a demon ancestress in the house of Anjou. One of these demonic seizures overcame Henry in Marlborough when he heard the report of the envoys. On the day after Christmas, as if to defy anathema, he himself fulminated a fearful decree of banishment against all the kith and kin of Becket, male and female, old and young.[7] Some four hundred victims were routed from their firesides and their labors, stripped of resource, laden on smacks, and shipped to the wintry shores of Flanders. There were enough of them to tax not only the private purses of Thomas' friends, but even the monastic foundations and the unbounded charity of Louis Capet. At the same time Henry committed the properties of Canterbury to Ranulf de Broc, the castellan of Dover, a very secular knight with an exact sense of his duty to the king.

⚜

In two prosperous decades the great Plantagenet had risen triumphant as the sun. By his marriage with the Countess of Poitou, Henry had doubled his lands with spoils slipped from the grasp of Louis Capet. He had won England from the related house of Blois. He had subdued disorders in Wales. On the Continent he had conquered Brittany, thrust out his ancestral borders here and there, and fortified a solid domain vastly superior to that of his overlord and chiefly at his overlord's expense. But he had ringed himself with enemies, each smarting with his own particular humiliation. His uneasy gains were not fully mastered when the quarrel with Becket forced him into the opprobrious role of outlaw against the church and encouraged his scattered foes to look in high places for asylum and redress. These they found with the King of the Franks, the Archbishop of Canterbury, the Pope, the dispossessed barons of Henry's enlarged living space.

The role thrust upon Louis by the Becket affair was the most superb that a grudging fortune had ever cast for him. In his long traffic with the Angevin he had never known such sweet commerce between his conscience and his will as that which enabled him to earn merit with heaven by harrying his mortal enemy. He was encouraged by the rising tide of his fortunes to make decisions he had long held in cautious reserve. He presently threw in his lot wholly with the house of Champagne, whose power he had long dreaded in his vassalage. He had married as his third queen the daughter of that house. He now married the two daughters of Queen Eleanor, whom she had been obliged to leave in the court of France at the time of her divorce, to two brothers of the reigning Queen of France: Marie to Henry, Count of Champagne, and Alix to Thibault of Blois. Guillaume, another brother of the same house, became Archbishop of Sens, metropolitan of the see to which Paris belonged.

Louis's general truculence toward the Angevins was greatly increased by an event in 1165, which signalized for him, after his long afflictions, the returning favor of heaven. During the first year of Becket's exile, when the whole outlook so greatly improved for the Capetians, the royal house had renewed with particular ardor its petitions for an heir, and had, with propitiatory intent, increased its alms and engaged the prayers of the clergy and the people.[8] Louis had prostrated himself before the chapter of Clairvaux and refused to get up until assured that his supplications for "an heir of the better sex" should be borne aloft upon that holy order's intercessions. "Give it not to my enemies to say," he implored, "that my hopes are deceived, my alms and prayers rejected."[9]

The answer to the prayers of the Capetians is recorded by the famous Giraldus Cambrensis, who chanced to be toiling over his studies in the schools of Paris in the summer of 1165.[10] Giraldus relates that the August days were suffocating in the Île and he had profited by the coolness of the night to pursue the universals in his chamber, which overlooked one of the public squares of the Cité. He had just after midnight pillowed his head, all brimming with dialectic, when a sudden clamor of bells broke like a tocsin upon his ear. His first thought was that a conflagration must have started in some quarter of the Île. He plunged into his shirt and leaned from the window. The city was alight with bonfires in the squares. The bells rose to bedlam, chiming over the roofs, among the towers, far abroad over the Seine. Burghers and students flocked in the streets, tending westward toward the king's domain, swinging torches and lanterns, shouting and gesticulating after the Gallic manner. Giraldus was amazed. He called down from his window to a pair of poor women racing along with faggot brands. By his accent they knew him for a subject of Henry Plantagenet, and one of them stopped long enough to brandish her torch at the window.

"By the grace of heaven," she cried, "there is born in Paris tonight a king who shall be a hammer to the King of the English."[11]

At last the intercessions of the Franks had been regarded. The moment of Louis's triumph had come. The noble house of Champagne had brought to the Franks a king, to Louis a son. The tidings flew over the Seine to the burghers' city on the right bank, to the schools on the left. It was Saturday night, the octave of the Assumption of the Virgin, and the messengers announced the event at Saint-Germain-des-Prés just before matins, as the monks were beginning the canticle, "Blessed be the Lord God of Israel, for he has visited us and ransomed his people." Paris hailed Philip Augustus, Dieu-Donné, heir of the Capets. To the queen's servant Olger, who brought him the joyful news, Louis granted in perpetuity three *muids* of cheese to be taken annually from his grange of Gonesse, and to that grant he affixed the royal seal.[12]

✣

The Pope, though eager to support the "most Christian King of France" and defend the Primate of England and the universal authority of the church, was often placed in strained attitudes by Becket's intransigence. Alexander III owed his papal throne in no small measure to Henry's recognition of his election against the candidate of the Holy Roman Emperor, and Henry's support was indispensable to him in the schism that had, before Becket's flight, driven him from Rome to the protection of the French king in Sens; yet in the struggle of Henry with his primate, it was Becket who championed the interests of the universal church. Alexander, in spite of acts that make up a tissue of contradictions, upheld his irreconcilable archbishop as much as his own situation enabled him to do. His policies with both Henry and Becket were alternately stern and conciliatory. If he authorized Becket to threaten Henry with the dread censures of the church, he cautiously annulled for Henry the effect of his suspension from grace; if he made promises to Henry, he countermanded them to Becket. But these fluctuations of policy simply register the tides in his own affairs.[13]

Becket, after his first successes in the *curia* and the French court, was persuaded by his friends to give up his episcopal retinue and bide the issue of a struggle that must be protracted, in some retirement, where maintenance of his dignities would be less expensive to those who were supporting not only his exile, but the banishment of all his kin.[14] These friends hinted that a cloistral seclusion might, in the circumstances, do more for the stakes at issue than any insistence on those temporal grandeurs to which Thomas was accustomed. Becket willingly submitted his person to the hair shirt and cowl, the regimen of fasts and vigils; but when he put on the white wool cassock of the Cistercians blessed for his use by Alexander and retired to the simplicity of the abbey of Pontigny,[15] it was not to a mystical retreat. He busied himself collecting works on the canon law and worked up his case, item by item. He beset his suffragans, the chapters of the orders, the courts and chancelleries of Europe, and the *curia* with a tide of correspondence, brief upon brief, arguing his position, insisting upon his salvos, inveighing against the "constitutions," pressing for the redress of his grievances, which were the grievances of Rome.

Early in 1166 Alexander's own prospects against the antipope and the Holy Roman Emperor brightened for a season, and he was able to return for an interval to Rome. In this auspicious moment he raised Becket's fortunes with his own. At Easter he made the exiled archbishop legate for all England save the diocese of York, which had anciently been excluded from the governance of Canterbury. Thus, even though Henry's malice thwarted Thomas from the exercise of his authority as primate, he might use his legatine authority from abroad to control his rebellious bishops in England

and to threaten the king. Armed with these extraordinary powers, Becket sought to force from Henry the surrender of his sequestered see.

Henry and Eleanor were holding their Easter court in Angers when this alarming edict went forth from Rome. Very expeditiously, on the Sunday following, three of Becket's closest friends arrived at Angers with demands for the restoration of the properties of Canterbury and the repatriation of the exiles. Henry received them superciliously and sent them back to Pontigny with dry evasive answers and the veiled threat that, if he were pressed by papal legates in his affairs with his primate, he would seek his safety with the schismatic German emperor. He had already been dangling this sword above the papal conclaves by threatening to affiance his eldest daughter Matilda to the nephew of the emperor.[16]

When his envoys returned to Pontigny empty handed, Becket addressed three successive letters to the king, which were marked by a sharp crescendo.[17] They passed swiftly from pastoral admonition to condign threats. First, he reminded Henry that, as his spiritual father, he was above all mindful of his spiritual weal, and that, after Henry had submitted himself to correction, he would find Thomas' grace to him unbounded; next, he reminded the king that sovereigns receive their glaive from the church and warned him lest his arrogance lead him to error and perdition; and finally, having had no answer to these admonitions, he served notice that, if the king did not shortly change his evil courses, something a good deal more dire than warnings would swiftly follow. He concluded this correspondence by giving Henry the term until Pentecost for penance and reflection.

Nothing was more ineffectual with Henry than unction. The warning letters did not produce the expected collapse in Angers. Henry remarked to his entourage that in his previous experience with Becket he had often known the archbishop to mistake his own will for that of Providence. The king did, however, take measures to defend himself. Although he had decreed in the Constitutions of Clarendon that appeals to Rome should be unlawful, he himself sent off an embassy to Alexander demanding restraint of the intolerable Thomas; and in the meantime, as a practical rejoinder to Becket, he dispatched to the abbé of the Cistercians, then in chapter, a threat to confiscate all the Cistercian properties in England unless the order ceased at once to harbor Becket and his fellow exiles in their house of Pontigny.[18]

Henry's bold gestures could not, however, conceal the fact that anathema, possibly interdict, was again in the air. The Plantagenets would, as a practical matter, dread the effects of fulmination, but more as a political inconvenience than as an actual instrument of damnation. They were less sensitive in this regard than the Capets. The Angevins throughout their generations had now and then been exposed to the censures of the church; and Eleanor, both as heiress of Poitou and as Queen of France, had more than once weathered anathema.

However, anathema and interdict imposed considerable affliction on feudal magnates and alienated the pious common folk from their overlords. Simple souls abhorred as the plague the awful withholding of the sacraments, the darkening of altars, the silencing of the parish bells, the sudden extinction of those communal rites that marked with solemnity and grandeur the narrow round of their existence. The people could not, like powerful nobles, avoid the effect of anathema and interdict. Kings could, of course, as a last resort, protect themselves by threats of schism. They could support antipopes, who could also fulminate, bind and unbind, loose and unloose. But the people had no such resource.

Though the Plantagenets could not be intimidated by any personal dread of interdict, they had at this time a very special reason for not courting a breach with Rome that might make them unpopular throughout their provinces. This reason was the fact that Henry, the heir of England, though now in his twelfth year, had not yet been ceremoniously crowned, consecrated, and recognized by the assembled barons and prelates of Britain as the successor of the conquerors. The custom of anointing the heirs of kings in the lifetime of their sires had been established in Europe. Louis Capet had been consecrated by the Pope himself in the royal cathedral of Reims before the death of Louis the Fat. The birth of the heir of the Capets, diminishing as it did the status of Henry's son in the French court, gave added urgency to the Plantagenet's desire to see the youth firmly established in his English heritage. He had always taken every precaution to secure the recognition of his heir in England; but that actual anointing of the prince had not taken place, and the only person authorized by custom and tradition to consecrate the heir of England was the Archbishop of Canterbury. With his legatine commission from the Pope, Becket was now in a position to prevent any other bishop's serving under an arbitrary mandate from Henry to officiate in his place. It was thus important for the Plantagenets to avoid proceeding to extremity with Rome until the prince should have been established with the indispensable sanctions of the church.

Having flouted Becket's legatine mission in Angers, Henry shut himself up from the world in his fortress castle of Chinon to gain a respite of time. Sick kings were not subject to excommunication, and the chronicle says that Henry was sick in his stronghold above the Vienne. While the king wrestled with his malady, Becket was not idle. He came forth from his Lenten retreat and fortified himself at the shrine of Saint Drausius, the crusader's champion.[19] The spring season for pilgrimage was on, and the people of Champagne and Burgundy, the burghers and scholars of Paris, were on the road. It had gone abroad that Thomas, armed with papal authority, had threatened the King of the English, and that, exiled now from his poor monk's portion in Pontigny by the malice of that king, he was on his way to the great shrine of Saint Mary Magdalene in Vézelay for the day of Pentecost. The time assigned for Henry's penance had expired. As in the spring of Saint Bernard's condemnation of Abélard at Sens, the people now thronged to a great shrine of Burgundy anticipating another thunderous episode in that everlasting magnificent drama between the powers of light and the powers of darkness.

The vast Cluniac church of Vézelay was that which Abbé Bernard (now named for sainthood) had found too small for his call to the second crusade. It was the center of convocation from whose portals news took wing over the thoroughfares of pilgrimage to the farthest corners of Gaul. On a Sunday of May, before a concourse of "divers nations" and certain distinguished prelates of France, the exiled archbishop, *miser et miserabilis*, but mighty with authority, preached the sermon of Pentecost.

The ritual of excommunication was by custom performed in the narthex, beyond the holy bounds of sanctuary. After the offices, the throngs moved from the nave into the open with a solemn procession of the clergy. There in the entry of the church, the candles were lighted, one for each impenitent; then as the formula was recited, these were extinguished one by one and trampled underfoot; the book was closed; the doors to the sanctuary were barred to those cut off from the church's grace; and bells announced to the whole believing world the expulsion of the excommunicates; their names were affixed to the portals to warn all men, as they loved their own salvation, to shun them. So it was at Vézelay.

After the sermon, Thomas recited the wrongs of the church, reviewed his citation of all the malefactors in service of the king to acknowledgment of their crimes and to repentance, described their stubborn disobedience. When he spoke of his old friend the king, his voice broke and his words were dissolved in tears. But the burden of duty and conscience lay upon him. Denouncing each in turn, and specifying again the sin of each, he did with book, bell, and candle excommunicate Henry's clerks, Richard of Ilchester and John of Oxford for their damnable traffic with schismatics in Germany; Henry's legists, Richard of Lucy and John of Balliol, for setting up the subversive Constitutions of Clarendon; Henry's officers, Ranulf de Broc, Hugh of Saint Clare and Thomas Fitz-Stephen, for their unlawful seizure and holding of the properties of Canterbury. No bolt of anathema touched the king directly, but the finger of the archbishop pointed straight at his forehead with a dreadful warning. The Primate of England, armed by the Pope with legatine power, outlawed all the noxious acts of the king's agents and rendered them null and void. Like a ripple widening in a pool, the tidings spread in every direction from Vézelay.[20]

"Rumor does in truth fly on wings to kings and princes," says Hoveden.

It was presently said that Henry received the news in Chinon with tears of rage. But when he at last emerged from seclusion he had recovered both health and composure. "As with the voice of a crier" he announced to an astonished world that he had not only the Archbishop of Canterbury but the Pope and the Roman cardinals "in his purse." [21] He related to his familiars how much this business of his had cost in the *curia*. He displayed documents certifying that Alexander, waiving the legateship of Thomas, had given a dispensation to the Archbishop of York to crown the heir of England. He declared that the Pope considered relieving him of his insufferable archbishop by translating Becket to some distant see, perhaps to Sicily. It was rumored that he had offered his infant daughter Joanna to the Prince of Sicily to prosper this arrangement.[22] He gave it out that the censures pronounced by Becket at Vézelay were suspended pending the arrival of papal envoys. Alexander, he proclaimed, was sending two cardinal legates to Gaul to put an end to the intolerable *démarches* of the archbishop against the dignity of the king. These cardinals were William of Pavia and Otto of Ostia, and they were already getting over the Alps. The person who brought these heartening tidings to Chinon was no other than John of Oxford, whom Becket had recently excommunicated at Vézelay, now absolved by agency of the Pope himself.

No one was more dumfounded by this surprising turn of affairs than the Archbishop of Canterbury. William of Pavia was one of his dearest enemies and was now rumored to be Henry's candidate for his see. Otto of Ostia was one to blow neither hot nor cold upon his grievances. Becket's friend, John of Salisbury, familiar with the *curia*, dreaded them both merely as Romans and cardinals. Becket at once surmised that Rome had "smelled of English sterling." He had a vision in which he was offered a cup of poisoned wine from the edges of which two spiders crawled.[23]

The fact was that Alexander was again "in shipwreck," this time in the very trough of the wave. The Holy Roman Emperor's army, abetted, as some suspected, by English subsidy, was at the gates of Rome. In this crisis of his affairs, the Pope wrote to Becket obscurely. "If," he said, "matters do not come off for the moment to your satisfaction, wait for a more favorable time." But patience was not Thomas' most conspicuous virtue. He dipped his pen in gall and composed letters to Alexander and expostulations to the legates, some of which his tactful friend edited and re-edited before they could be dispatched to the Holy See. John observes that in some instances Becket's original language was "not fit to be addressed to the Pope's postilion." [24]

The legates, arrived in Gaul after unexpected delays, found it more difficult than they had imagined to bring the wounded Becket before a tribunal procured in Rome by his adversary. He demurred; he made legal difficulties;

he begged the question, declaring he would come to the parley only after the restoration of his see. At last, late in the fall of 1168 (Saint Martin's) he was induced to meet the cardinals at Gisors. Though the legates engaged him cautiously and forbore to press him, they could not bring him to negotiate, nor could they contrive any formula to which he would assent. William and Otto were obliged to retire empty handed to Henry in Argentan. Henry, who had been willing to spend liberally to gain his ends, suffered an attack of Angevin fury at the failure of his mission. The legates were dismissed so promptly, says Diceto, that they did not wait for their own equipage to be assembled, but rode hurriedly away on such horses as they could find, their ears burning with Henry's parting shout, "I hope I may never lay eyes on a cardinal again." [25]

13 ✠

Montmirail and Canterbury

The wrath of a woman is much to dread.
                                        Tristram and Ysolt

IN THE SPRING OF 1168 HENRY, by threat of joining the German schismatics,[1] to one of the most powerful of whom he had already married his daughter Matilda, had procured two valuable concessions from Alexander: one, a renewal of the papal authority to the Archbishop of York to crown the young king; the other, a letter forbidding Becket to proceed forthwith with the excommunication of the king or nobles in England. These boons were offset, however, by a new delegation summoning Becket and the king again to arbitrament of their grievances, and setting Ascension Day as the term of papal leniency.

Neither Henry nor Becket displayed any eagerness for further parleyings, and it was not until early in 1169 that the legation found any contrivance for bringing them together. In January the papal commission took advantage of an occasion arranged by Louis Capet to bring Henry with his sons to the frontiers of the Île de France to do homage, in presence of a cloud of noble and ecclesiastical witnesses, for Angevin provinces held of the French king as overlord. The time appeared to the Capets ripe and propitious for an inviolable definition of boundaries and a limitation of the presumptions of the Angevin who, for twenty years, had been thrusting out his fortresses in ever-widening encroachment upon Louis and his vassals.

The total circumstances in which the assembly was convened gave it much more than usual significance to an anxious feudal world. There was not only the customary periodic renewal of homage by vassals to their overlords, and especially by the King of England to the King of France; but these relations were complicated by the Becket affair which had penetrated the whole area of ecclesiastical relationships. And just at this crisis in the affairs of the Angevin, when straws might tip the balance of his fortunes, the Countess of Poitou had interjected a new and most disturbing issue.

The chroniclers are, as usual in matters touching the privy concerns of kings, discreet. But the news had already spread that a breach had occurred between the King of the English and the Countess of Poitou; and that the Queen of England, taking with her her own dedicated heir, the young Prince

Richard, had set sail from Britain with seven ships carrying her retinue and her belongings; [2] and that, after sharing Henry's Christmas court in Argentan, she had retired to her own ducal city of Poitiers. There she had set up her own court and assumed the administration of her own provinces. She was under a certain protective surveillance, to be sure; but her status as vassal of the King of the Franks for her own domains gave to her initiative, to say nothing of its piquancy, an ominous tinge.

Henry and Louis met, with considerable display on both sides, at Montmirail, a castled town on the borders of Maine and the Chartrain, on the day of Epiphany, January 6, 1169.[3] It was not precisely with the air of a simple homager that Henry arrived at the conclave. He was accompanied by an imposing retinue, in which his three sons appeared, each resplendent with his own *mesnie*, the rival barons of the rival counties to which the young princes had been assigned. Henry's words to Louis were carefully composed and full of grace.

"My lord King," he said, "on this day of Epiphany, on which the three kings brought their gifts to the King of Kings, I commend my three sons and my lands to your keeping." [4]

This speech did not discompose Louis, who was often admired in his day for his gift of rejoinder. Bending his dovelike eyes upon Henry and the sons of Eleanor, he replied,

"Since the King who received those gifts from the Magi appears to have inspired your words, may your sons, as they take possession of their lands by the title of our grace, do so as in the presence of our Lord."

This hint to the Angevins to weigh their homage honestly, which the witnesses assembled at Montmirail could well appreciate, Henry allowed to pass. He brought forward for presentation to his overlord the apple of his eye, his namesake, the heir of England, a handsome stripling of fourteen, with the distinguished grace of the Poitevins, fine stature, proud expressive mien, and bright clustering locks. Upon him the King of England confirmed his ancestral inheritance of Maine and Anjou, and the young count, still unknighted and uncrowned, then placed his hands in the palm of his father-in-law, the King of France, and did homage for his provinces. He had already done homage as Duke of Normandy. The Abbé of Mont-Saint-Michel reports that Louis now, as a special mark of his favor, restored to Prince Henry the seneschalship of France, which he had previously bestowed upon his other son-in-law, the Count of Blois.[5]

The magnates then saw the queen's favorite stand forth, Richard the tawny lion cub, his sturdy Angevin frame well grown, a youth with bold darting eyes and long arms apt for sword and strong bow. Henry confirmed to him the title to the inheritance assigned to him at birth, the magnificent provinces of the queen extending southward from the Loire, that rich portion which, added to the feudal domain of either king, made him, in spite of gestures of homage, the virtual master of the other. To this prince, the special scion of the queen, Louis now gave striking evidence of his paternal grace. As he had formerly attached the Angevin dynasty by offering the Princess Marguerite to Henry's heir, he now attached the house of Poitou by presenting one of his superfluity of daughters to Prince Richard, and with her he gave as her dowry the County of Berry, which Henry had long required to widen his frontier. Alais Capet, a child of nine,[6] sister of the elder prince's consort Marguerite, orphaned now from her own kin, was given over to the Plantagenets to be reared among them as the future Countess of Poitou. The feudal world, blinking at this scene, remarked that Louis, by hook and by crook, seemed likely to bring back into his domain that rich duchy which he had lost with Eleanor.

For Geoffrey, the third son, now but nine, Henry had made the conquest of Brittany, which owed nominal feudal homage to Louis, and the French king now gave consent to that *fait accompli* and assented to the marriage of the Count of Brittany to the Countess Constance, the hereditary heiress of the province, who was already, in any case, a hostage of the Plantagenets.[7] The marriage was definitely consanguineous, but Henry had been careful to appeal for a papal dispensation to circumvent that difficulty. It was arranged at Montmirail that Geoffrey should do homage for Brittany to his brother Henry, Duke of Normandy, by which subinfeudation Louis would still retain a nominal homage for those western lands.

The chroniclers of the Angevin dynasty, accustomed as they were to see Henry sign charters with the point of his sword, were sorely confused by this business at Montmirail. They offer various explanations as to why the King of England, who had been so energetic and successful in seizing and welding together a solid domain upon the Continent, should now, in his mighty prime, divide that structure that had cost him so much stress, among sons not yet grown to knighthood. Some said that a recent presentiment of death while in a fever had made the king foresee what fratricidal strife might ensue if he were carried off before his testament was certified. Some said the Becket affair threatened the succession of Prince Henry, wherefore the king was eager to see the rights of all his sons acknowledged before the bishops and nobles of both realms. Some held that Henry had set his house in order because he had been moved by the peril of the Angevin dynasty in Palestine, and expected to take the cross and go to the succor of King Baldwin of Jerusalem. Others subsequently conjectured that Henry had secretly been offered the Kingdom of Lombardy, even the Holy Roman Empire, and that the Count of Maurienne had opened to him the mountain passes to Italy whereby he might connect a Gallic with a Roman domain of Carolingian scope.[8] These chroniclers recalled that Henry had once lightly remarked that the whole world might be better off under the rule of one just and able man. All were perplexed. But if the queen, because of some breach with the king, had insisted upon withdrawing to her own continental domains and setting up her second son there in an estate almost equal to Henry's own possessions, it was high time for Henry to make some such offsetting provision for the first son of the Plantagenets as was actually made at Montmirail.[9]

✥

It was with the greatest difficulty that Alexander's legates had brought Becket to the place of conclave. He had grown weary of inconclusive bargainings with the king. His awful weapon of anathema gained impressiveness when thundered over a vast intervening heaven. Henry's malice in routing him from Pontigny had reduced him to such poverty that he lacked the means of appearing with befitting dignity before kings and bishops. It was Louis who overcame his objections. The French king provided him with a modest equipage of horses for himself and a decent escort of clerks, lent his castle for Becket's entertainment, and summoned some of the prelates of Gaul, especially his brother-in-law, the newly consecrated Bishop of Sens, to conduct the Archbishop of Canterbury into the presence.

Prelates and clerks from many provinces of Gaul pressed about as Becket, accompanied by his escort, traversed the field to the place where the kings and their suites awaited him. The king and the archbishop, who had once been as close as David and Jonathan, had not for four years laid eyes upon each other, and they now lifted their gaze above a vast abyss. Both were deeply moved. It was whispered that Becket had been urged by his best friends to withhold his salvo, and that Henry, though he still stood his ground, was eager for the sake of his son's coronation to keep the peace. Overlooking all others, Becket cast himself before the king and let his tears flow. Henry sprang forward and raised him to his feet. The archbishop had been greatly changed by the austerities of his life and the stress of his sufferings. His tall figure was gaunt, his native pallor had become transparent, his brilliant eyes subdued. Bystanders were touched by the visible signs of his spiritual combat. With a humility he had learned in exile, he pleaded the cause of the church, vowed his loyalty to the king, explained with apology his flight from his see. The assistants hung upon his words, finding them agreeable to reason, sweet and good. As he drew to a close, he appealed to the king for clemency for the church in England.[10]

"In presence of the King of France, the nuncios of the Pope, and the Princes, your sons," he said, "I commit the whole case and the issues that have arisen between us to your royal arbitrament . . . saving the honor of God!"

The king, who to this moment had followed the archbishop's words with evident approbation, now started forward with gestures of rage and a burst of opprobrious language.[11] When his reproaches at length died down, Thomas replied quietly and without rancor, and Henry was quickly aware that his own violence had turned the sympathies of the bystanders to the archbishop. Changing his tone, but ignoring the nuncios, he turned to the King of France and said,

"My lord King, attend me, if you please. Whatever displeases him he will declare contrary to the honor of God, and thus he will ever have the last word with me. But lest I seem in any way not to honor God, I offer this proposal. There have been before me many kings of England, some with more, some with less, authority than mine; and there have been many archbishops of Canterbury, great and holy men. Let him yield to me what the greatest and most saintly of his predecessors conceded to the least of mine, and I shall be satisfied." [12]

Thereupon the bystanders cried out, "Hear, hear! This is fair. The King makes a just offer."

But Thomas, who heard in the king's words a reaffirmation of the Constitutions of Clarendon, remained silent. Louis spoke instead.

"My lord Archbishop, do you desire to be higher than the saints, more strict than Peter's self? Why do you hesitate? Behold, the peace you desire is offered you."

Then the bishops drew Thomas aside, all trying to be heard at once. They besought him not to let the peace fail, implored him to be silent for the time about "the honor of God."

Only at length Thomas spoke.

"Shall I," said he, "when our fathers have suffered so much in the name of Christ, forswear the reverence I owe to God in order to regain my temporal state? Heaven forbid. (*Absit, absit.*)"

Hereupon the bishops, the nobles, the exiles for Becket's sake, who longed to go home after this day's business, drew off in groups condemning the obstinacy of Thomas. One of the archbishop's kinsmen, when his horse stumbled in the twilight as he rode off, rallied the steed ruefully. "Come up, come up, Dobbin," he said, "saving the honor of God, of Holy Church, and the dignity of our order." [13] Henry, riding away with Louis, berated Thomas in the most richly flavored language, and for once his abuse fell without hindrance upon the French king's ears.

If Becket was dismayed by the outcome of the day, Henry can hardly have given himself to sleep after the conclave of Montmirail with a sense of profitable Angevin work accomplished. The course of the business with Louis and Becket had not left in his hands the tangible gains with which he was accustomed to retire from parleys. He seemed to have stepped over some boundary of adversity. He had always avoided committing himself; yet now he had done so. He had certainly not meant to deliver to his unfledged sons more than prospective rights and titles; yet the ambitious vassals of the princes, if not the striplings themselves, and the queen, and Louis Capet, would presume upon the feudal pledges to which he had borne witness. The queen especially.

As for the Becket affair, it was no more satisfactory. Henry could now expect the full blast of fulmination, for Becket had been authorized, if the peace failed, to launch his thunder on Ascension Day, now only a few weeks distant. Thomas would use his favorable moment to prevent the coronation of the young king by any bishop other than himself, and he would use his prohibition to procure the restoration of his see. It was without doubt to give himself an excuse for such proceedings that he had revived his salvo. After Montmirail it became more than ever urgent to invest the prince with his title to the throne of England.

❧

The failure of the peace at Montmirail brought Alexander under a fresh hailstorm of appeals. Louis's brother-in-law, Guillaume de Sens, hurried to Rome on Becket's behalf to urge papal severity with a king whom, as Thomas wrote, only severe chastisement could amend. The Bishops of London and Salisbury appealed to the Pope for absolution from the excommunication visited upon them from Clairvaux on the previous Palm Sunday. Henry sought guarantees against interdict upon his lands. Always, when in confusion, Alexander sent legatine missions. He now sent two legists, Vivian and Gratian, who were deemed incorruptible and capable of standing up to Henry.[14]

The king met these astute bargainers with counter demands. Becket might reclaim his see and lead his exiles home, if, when, and after the bishops of England were freed from excommunication and his lands from the menaces of interdict. When the nuncios tried to preface their demands with if, when, and after, Henry again brandished his threat of schism and shouted the legates out of court.

"I care not an egg for nuncios," he cried, "and if I am threatened, I will seek elsewhere than in Rome my safety and honor."[15]

But as the time for the return of Guillaume de Sens from Rome drew near, Henry began those sudden flittings from place to place that betrayed some uneasiness. He angled for another interview with Becket on the pretext of getting the precise schedule of the latter's claims for the restoration of the properties of Canterbury. He judged that he might circumvent the Archbishop of Sens if he could surprise the world with a pact reached without the mediation of Rome. It proved not so very difficult for Henry to draw Louis into a scheme for maneuvering an interview with Thomas. He had only to profess a pious desire to perform his devotions at the shrine of the martyrdom of Saint Denis at Montmartre;[16] and to take the occasion of his nearness to Paris to offer his blessing to little Philip Augustus, who would one day, by the grace of God, be his overlord; and lastly to deliver his son, the young Count of Poitou, affianced since the treaty of Montmirail to one of Louis's daughters, into the hands of the Capets, for a period of education in the court of France. As if incidentally, Louis engaged to see to it that the Archbishop of Canterbury came also to the chapel of the martyr- dom at Montmartre.

All was arranged. Henry performed his devotions. He then paid a visit to Queen Adele and the little prince, who had come out some distance from the city to receive him. The heir of the Capets was now a fine, upstanding child nearly four years old. Becket, describing the interview to the Pope, relates that Henry drew the boy, whom he now saw for the first time, to his knee and scanned his countenance with keenest scrutiny. Presently, how- ever, he thrust him aside with a melancholy air, as if he there read some dreadful portent.[17] But we are told the infant scion of the Capets stood manfully over against the King of the English and gave vent to an unfalter- ing rhetoric. He admonished Henry to love the French, their king, and Holy Church with a right devotion and to earn thus the favor of God and man.[18]

Becket arrived at Montmartre in company with Guillaume de Sens and the legate Vivian, not willingly, but out of scruple lest he should frustrate some destined miracle of reconciliation.[19] The recent return of Guillaume from Rome had heartened him with promises of severity against the king and his followers and with a strict limitation of papal leniency. Thomas brought a whacking account for all the sequestered properties and the usurped revenues of Canterbury. Not a farthing lost in the five years of his exile had been remitted nor forgotten. Henry appeared in edifying mood. He accepted the account and even submitted to reproof and correction. He promised restoration and amendment. No one could find any fault with his consent. The bargain seemed to Becket's party almost too good to be true. Would the king be pleased to give some contractual guarantee? Let him, for instance, give Becket, in the presence of assistants, the kiss of peace.[20]

Hereupon Henry drew off. He recalled that he had once, in a fit of anger, vowed never again to kiss Thomas in all his life, and he supposed that churchmen could hardly expect him to disregard his solemn vow. A dispensation to relieve him of his inconvenient oath was proffered. But Henry was scrupulous. In England, after the archbishop should have returned to his see, the king would willingly kiss him a thousand times — his cheek, his hand, his foot. But here and now the kiss seemed to be exacted and would therefore have no significance.[21]

The conclave broke up in gloom. Vivian publicly declared that he had never in all his rich experience with the *curia* seen or heard so crafty and slippery a prevaricator as the King of England.[22] Louis warned Becket that he should not for his weight in gold return to England under such loose arrangements, and offered him the highest ecclesiastical honors to remain abroad. Thomas returned to Paris and the two kings rode off to Passy, where Louis expected to take Richard, the young Count of Poitou, into his custody. But when they arrived, the count, by some casual mischance as it seemed, was not there.

Presently rumblings from Rome revealed the impact of the appeals and counterappeals that had been lodged there — first a blast in favor of Becket, then one for Henry. On the 19th of January the Pope commissioned the Archbishop of Rouen and the Bishop of Nevers to exact the kiss from Henry, and only if this were obtained within forty days (that is, by the first of March), to absolve the Bishops of London and Salisbury from the excommunication that Thomas had launched on the Palm Sunday of the previous year. Then prematurely and unaccountably, on the 12th of February, the Archbishop of Rouen, acting alone, absolved the bishops without having first chastened Henry. This act of Rotrou of Rouen was presently seen as a prelude to Henry's urgent movements to stave off Thomas' interference with the crowning of the young king by the Archbishop of York.

In the third week of February, Henry with a considerable following put to sea from Barfleur for Portsmouth. With the first of March set as the term to papal lenience, he could not wait for weather. His fleet set out at midnight in the teeth of a gale. His ships labored all night and the next day, when his sundered vessels, with broken masts and tattered sails, were driven into various English harbors. One of the newest and best of the ships with four hundred passengers, men and women, was lost in the crossing. But the king's ship, by the grace of Saint-Michael-in-Peril-of-the-Sea, landed in Portsmouth before the ninth hour.[23]

Arrived prodigiously on the wings of the storm, Henry put his coercive hand upon reluctant prelates and nobles of his realm, steadying with threats and importunities those who suffered qualms and scruples at the prospect of defying Canterbury in the matter of the coronation. He closed the Channel ports strictly, lest Becket's emissaries should launch unseasonable thunderbolts to restrain him from his purpose. He imposed the penalties of confiscation, mutilation, exile, for informers, and warned all his subjects against receiving or respecting proclamations from abroad.

Prince Henry had been left for the time in the custody of the queen in Caen, out of the reach of interdict on English lands. In Normandy remained the loyal Bishops of Sées and Bayeux, also immune from censures that might be visited on the suffragans of Canterbury. At last, when his plans were ready, Henry dispatched Richard of Ilchester to escort the prince and these bishops to London.[24] There was some question in the minds of the Plantagenets about what should be done with the prince's consort Marguerite in the matter of the coronation. No course seemed free of difficulty. If Marguerite were ignored in the coronation of her husband, the Capets would of course be outraged; but would that be more serious in the eyes of Louis than having her crowned in defiance of Thomas and Pope Alexander by bishops subject to censure? The cautious Plantagenets had very suitable and expensive garments made ready for the princess both in Caen and in London in anticipation of emergency,[25] but they finally decided that leaving her in Normandy with the queen would be the more remediable of the evils that confronted them.[26]

Eleanor remained in charge of the court abroad and acted with the constable of Normandy in keeping the Channel ports closed against Becket's threat to outlaw the project of the king.[27] Becket was known to have charged the Bishop of Nevers, as well as his own suffragan and the king's cousin, the Bishop of Worcester, to get passage to England in time to visit proscription and excommunication upon all the ecclesiastics upon whom Henry depended for the coronation. The Bishop of Nevers, out of respect for the torments Henry had prepared for informers, sought passage very languidly. The Bishop of Worcester, who was in the dilemma of having been likewise summoned by Henry to lend his episcopal splendor to the coronation, as an English bishop and as a relative of the king, found no means of crossing. The queen relieved both voyagers of their perplexity. Not a sail left the ports of Normandy.

It is to be wondered whether some miscarriage in his plans delayed Henry's proceeding at once with the crowning. Ascension Day, at which time Becket was free to renew his censures on the English prelates, occurred on May 29, whereas the coronation was set for the 14th of June. A throng of Londoners filled Saint Paul's on Ascension Day. Restrained perhaps by some foreboding, neither the Bishop of London nor the dean was present in the cathedral on that fateful morning. A minor priest, one Vitalis, celebrated mass. As he began to chant the *offertorium* and the wine and bread were being made ready, a stranger, who appeared to be a clerk, drew near, and falling devoutly on his knees, presented his offering. When the priest, somewhat surprised at this approach to the altar, reached out his hand to receive the gift, the stranger seized and detained him long enough to utter these words:

"In the absence of the bishop and dean of this diocese, I here present to you this letter from the Archbishop of Canterbury conveying the sentence he has pronounced on the Bishop of London and enjoining him and his clergy to observe this sentence. I bid you, by God's authority, to celebrate mass no more in this church until you shall have delivered this letter."[28]

Thereupon the stranger disappeared in the crowd, which was already dispersing, and not even the king's officers, who scoured the whole city and posted guards at all the crossroads, found any trace of him. The bystanders in Saint Paul's, who saw rather than heard the incident, asked fearfully if mass had been prohibited in the cathedral; but when reassured they went out quietly. A day later the same mysterious person delivered in York a prohibition forbidding the archbishop to crown the young king in despite of the primatial rights of Canterbury. Precisely on the day of wrath, and in defiance of the king's defensive measures, Thomas' thunderbolt struck awe in the heart of England. The prelates of Britain were now obliged to choose unequivocally between the authority of Rome and Canterbury and that of the king.

In the face of these august menaces, Henry assembled his nobles and his bishops for the feast of Saint Barnabas[29] and went forward with his plans. He himself hastily dubbed the prince, whose knighting by the King of the Franks had been inconveniently postponed. The coronation, though carried through without the blessing of Rome or Canterbury, was no clandestine or niggardly affair. It lacked no traditional feature that could give it sanction except the presence of the primate and a few of his suffragans. The setting, as custom decreed, was Westminster Abbey. Roger of York, relying on the mandate conferred upon him long before, but now twice outlawed by Becket's prohibitions, performed the offices in the anointing of the prince. The assistants, if confused and uneasy about the auspices of the occasion, took comfort in the number of their fellows. The royal accounts show that no expense was spared for the regalia of the prince, nor for the feasts that entertained the king's magnates in the palace of Westminster.

At the banquet following the ceremonies in the Abbey, the "young king" as the prince was now to be called, is said to have dined in hall with Roger of York, and the sewer who brought in the boar's head was no other than Henry Plantagenet himself, signalizing in this fashion the incomparable estate of his first-born son. At this gorgeous spectacle, the archbishop brought forth a neat epigram.

"Not every prince," he remarked, "can be served at table by a king."

The prince, who since Montmirail had been encouraged to nurse delusions of grandeur, capped this with another even wittier.

"Certainly," he said, "it can be no condescension for the son of a count to serve the son of a king."[30]

The astonishment of the company is unrecorded. The prince was not, however, presented with a scepter after the feast. He was kept safely in

England and remanded to his tutors, sound legists and loyal subjects of the Angevin.

After the summary and successful business of establishing the most important of his sons in his heritage, Henry returned at once to Normandy to forestall whatever Gaul and Rome might do about the *fait accompli*. As he went from his port to Falaise to rejoin the queen, he chanced to fall in with his cousin, the Bishop of Worcester. At sight of him Henry burst into a fury of abuse because the bishop had not presented himself at the coronation. Worcester explained that, when he had sought passage, he had been intercepted by royal mandate in the port.

"What!" exclaimed Henry. "The queen at this moment is in Falaise, and the constable is either with her or will shortly be. You cannot mean that either of them intercepted you in contravention of my summons."

"I do not cite the queen," replied the bishop, "for either her respect or fear of you will make her conceal the truth, so that your anger against me will be increased; or if she states the truth, your indignation will fall upon that noble lady. Better that I should lose a leg than that she should hear one harsh word from you." [31]

Thus Henry was reminded that in his situation with the queen, Worcester, not only as bishop but as his kinsman, sought to shield the Countess of Poitou.

✦

All the incidents of the coronation were at once known to Becket and his party. Louis promptly answered the insult to his dynasty by making incursions in Normandy. That Louis should raise outcries about the offense to his daughter was inevitable, but he was never beyond the reach of appeasement. The case of Becket would be more difficult. Henry had the best of reasons to fear that Thomas would now procure some invalidation of the coronation, and that he would certainly launch the interdict upon England. He therefore resolved that, having gained his principal point, he would propitiate the archbishop on other counts at any price. Since his visit to Britain he had come to recognize advantages in getting Thomas back to his see, where his onsets could be more effectually contained. He opened his mind again hospitably to overtures for Thomas' return to Canterbury.

The Angevin appeased Louis for the indignity to his daughter by promising that, when Thomas should presently be restored to his see, there should be a second final crowning in which Marguerite should share with the young king the blessings of the primate. The King of the Franks, as a sign of his restored good will, brought Becket to Fréteval in the Chartrain for the feast of Saint Mary Magdalene on July 20 and for a conference with Henry. Becket's faithful Herbert Bosham reports the interview. Thomas found Henry softened as if by some stirring of his conscience. He was docile under rebuke, admitted he had wronged the church and injured Canterbury, and promised to make amends. As for the coronation, he cited historical precedent for the procedure. Becket, he promised again, should recrown his foster son. The king again assented to the terms of Montmartre and even hinted that, if this were demanded of him for the sake of removing all suspicion of lingering enmity, he would yield that kiss of peace he had formerly refused.

Those who stood apart from the colloquy beheld the king and Becket in such intimacy as they had kept in the days of Thomas' chancellorship, except that now the king showed a befitting deference to Thomas as to a spiritual father. He was seen to spring from his horse and hold the archbishop's stirrup, so that the latter could mount. Henry, who possessed the valued gift of tears, now shed them abundantly for Thomas. All was well at last after the terrible misunderstandings, the excommunications, the kiss denied.

"Come, my Archbishop," said the king, "let us renew our ancient love for one another; let us show each other all the good we can and forget our old quarrel. . . But, I beseech you, show me honor in the sight of those who watch us from afar." [32]

Later they went over the terms for the restoration more particularly, and struck a difficulty when one of the Norman bishops demanded absolution of the English bishops as a precondition, and satisfaction of this demand in turn was made conditional upon amendment of the bishops. The tinder did not quite break into blaze. Henry and Thomas retired from Fréteval in outward amity; but each carried away his reservation: Thomas kept a free hand with his suffragans, and Henry withheld the indispensable kiss of peace. [33]

The King of the English had no sooner left Fréteval than he came to his senses. He saw, in the course of a fever that presently overtook him, that he had conceded too much. As in other times of indecision, he took to restless journeyings. He wore out his following bustling from place to place, so that Thomas could not surprise him with demands for the kiss. Twice Thomas, who had been warned not to return to Britain without that guarantee, caught up with him. When other expedients failed, the archbishop sought to obtain the token by the ruse of standing next to the king at mass and offering him the pax. But Henry managed to have a requiem sung that day, so that no kiss should be required of the communicants.

The king and the archbishop who had quarreled so long, who had been the nearest of friends, the bitterest of foes, whose salvos had embroiled the century, met for the last time at Chaumont, between Amboise and Blois. The old terms were again confirmed. Becket, escorted by the king himself in token of their reconciliation, was to go home. Afterwards, in England, the kiss should be accorded him. Neither dared any longer to stir up the fiery embers of their old enmity.

"My heart tells me," said Becket, "that I shall see you no more in this life."

Henry read his thought. "Dost take me for a traitor?"

"That be far from me, my lord." (*Absit, absit.*)[34]

When Becket came to Rouen where Henry was to join him for the crossing, the king was not there. Instead, there was a letter [35] explaining that Henry had been obliged to go to Auvergne to quench disturbances in that province. But he had sent a deputy to escort Thomas to Canterbury. This guarantor proved to be John of Oxford, whom Becket had excommunicated four years before at Vézelay for his "damnable traffic with the schismatics of Cologne." The archbishop, who had hoped to go back to England in a kind of triumph accompanied by the king and distinguished by marks of honor, saw himself in the custody of one of his most relentless foes. There was no fleet ready, nor the promised sterling for the passage. The Archbishop of Rouen gave Becket a sum to make his crossing with a solitary ship. In these dismal circumstances, Becket, before putting forth upon the Channel, took the precaution of disarming those rebellious suffragans of his who might be contriving in England only God knew what connivance with the king to enslave Canterbury. He suspended the Archbishop of York and renewed the excommunication of the Bishops of London and Salisbury, who had been relieved of his censures all out of season by the Archbishop of Rouen to make way for the coronation.[36]

It was late November, six years almost to a day from the time of Thomas' flight from Henry's wrath in Northampton, that he embarked for home. When he set sail from Wissant with his little company, he planted his primatial cross in the prow of his vessel,[37] and under this protection alone he came at length into the haven of Sandwich in his own see, the port from which he had fled to exile. The nobles, not knowing certainly under what terms the peace had been made, held aloof. But the common folk of the diocese made festival of his return. They drew up his boat upon the pebbly beach, spread their coats upon the road, and scattered autumn branches in his path, hymning and rejoicing as if for the return of Israel from captivity. The young king, who had been instructed to confirm all the elder king's promises to Becket, took no part in the welcome, but kept his court at a distance in Winchester, surrounded by the most reliable of Henry's justiciars. As for the Archbishop of York and the Bishops of London and Salisbury, they did not go to greet the primate. They were in Dover seeking passage to Normandy when Thomas' letters renewing their suspension were delivered into their hands.[38]

✤

As Henry came northward from his campaign in Auvergne, he bore toward Bures where the queen, his sons, and his vassals were convening for his Christmas court. As he approached his castle he encountered those outlawed prelates of Britain recently arrived from Dover, and these gave him their own account of the incidents of Becket's return to his see. They reported the extravagant rejoicing of the common people of the diocese, where whole towns and villages had emptied themselves of folk to join the archbishop's cavalcade.[39] They described Thomas' entry barefoot into his city of Canterbury amidst the joyful tears of the monks and his old retainers. They related a progress Thomas had made toward Winchester, gathering a rabble as he went, on the pretext of taking a gift of Flemish horses to the young king who had formerly been his dear foster son — a progress promptly held up in London by young Henry's wardens, who suspected an armed uprising to deprive the prince of his crown.[40] They told of the clashes in divers places between the lieges of the king and those of Thomas. Then the bishops rehearsed the insolent, the unmerited affront, all in violation of the peace, to York, London, and Salisbury, now again interdicted from the use of fire and water!

"By God's eyes," exclaimed the king, "if all who shared the coronation of my son are to be excommunicated, I will be counted one of their number."[41]

"Have patience, my lord," said the Archbishop of York. "By proper management we may yet turn the case to some advantage."

"How will you so?" asked the king.

"It is not our business to counsel your Majesty," replied the Archbishop of York, "but. . ."

"But," interrupted one of the barons, "so long as Thomas lives, you will never know an hour of peace."[42]

Thereupon a fit of passion seized the king. His choleric eyes flashed fire. His whole countenance was disordered.

"A curse," he cried, "a curse on all the false varlets I have nursed in my household, who leave me thus exposed to the insolence of a fellow that came to my court on a lame sumpter mule, and now sits without hindrance upon the throne itself."[43]

The brilliant Christmas entertainments in which the young Counts of Poitou and Brittany were to shine amidst their followings were forgotten. In counsel with his barons, Henry rehearsed his wrongs. There was a great deal of talk, interspersed with anecdotes, that would have shocked the Pope and the King of the Franks. As for Thomas, the barons' advice was well summed up in the suggestion of a relative of the Bishop of Salisbury, himself under the ban.

"The only way to deal with such a traitor is to plait a few withes into a rope and hoist him therewith upon a gallows."[44]

Before the counsel had arrived at any plan other than that of arresting the mischievous archbishop, it was noted with consternation that four courtiers, "hotheaded and in the flower of their age," had rushed from the chamber and taken leave of the court. Two nobles and the constable of Normandy were at once dispatched to overtake them, but they scoured the Channel ports in vain. For two days an atmosphere heavy with foreboding hung over the festivities in Bures. At length in an evil and apprehensive humor, Henry dismissed his court and withdrew to Argentan.

Presently, on the last day of December, riders came foaming to the bridge of that bare fortress castle and were admitted to the king. Breathless they told their story. Thomas, the man of God, in the dim hour of vespers and on the very steps of the altar of Canterbury, had shed the red blood of the martyrs. Those who had slain him were the henchmen flying from the king's furious words in Bures. Thomas, finding the world too small a place for both himself and the king, had stood up to death for his salvo.

They told of the consternation among the monks of Canterbury, of the dumb awe of the populace. A violent storm, all out of season, had seemed to transport the soul of Thomas away in a whirl of thunder and fire. A strange succession of miracles instantly following the event attested God's certain favor. It was remembered that Thomas had foretold his martyrdom in his Christmas sermon, his discourse on Saint Stephen's day, and lo! under his sacerdotal robes the murdered prelate was found marked with scourgings and clothed in sackcloth from head to foot. His blood, spilled upon the pavement of the sanctuary, was already gathered in reliquaries by the faithful. The episcopal palace was sacked. The vandals and the assassins had fled. Even the young king, whose wardens had spurned Becket on his way to Winchester with the gift of horses, had cried out in anger at the elder king's implacable harshness to his dear foster father. "Alas!" said he, raising his hands and eyes to heaven, "but thank God it was done secretly and that no liege of mine had share in it."[45] A consuming excitement, moved by something more than mortal, was spreading from the altars of Canterbury to the corners of the world.

Divining the heart of the message before it was uttered, the king burst into loud lamentations. He threw off his royal robes and called for sackcloth strewn with ashes. He dismissed even his own intimates. For days, eschewing all company and consolation, refusing food and rest, the king alternated outcries of grief with periods of fixity and silence from which no comforter could lure him.[46] Before the familiar choir of Canterbury in the solemnity of twilight, the tall lean shade of Becket rose before the vision of the king, and as he looked, that somber figure was multiplied to serried ranks of other figures, clothed like Thomas in pallium and cope — the whole hierarchy of the church — all bending their gaze upon him; and the eyes of all that company were the accusing eyes of Becket. Canterbury, as he merged into "the dignity of his order," lost his familiar stamp of human singularity and became one of a cloud of witnesses, the quick and the dead. Thomas' vindication of his salvo with his life was seen as something more than the final episode in conflict to be swallowed up without memorial in time. Already the people, testifying to miracles, and attentive Rome invested the event with supernatural significance.

Now and again Henry called God to witness that he was in no way responsible for the death of Thomas, unless he had perhaps loved him too little and denied him the kiss of peace. Thus for days the king lay fasting and groaning, until his household feared for his very life.[47] The aged Archbishop of Rouen was summoned from his see to comfort him spiritually, but his ministrations were of no avail. Another of his Norman bishops, Arnulf of Lisieux, wrote to the Pope and begged his Holiness to offer some healing consolation to the king for the loss of one who, though for a time estranged, had long before been his dearest, his most trusted friend. In Rome Alexander saw in a vision the chasuble of Thomas changed to the color of blood.

14 ✣

The Flower of the World

When as king Henry rulde this land,
The second of that name,
Besides the queene, he dearly lovde
A faire and comely dame.

Most peerlesse was her beautye founde,
Her favour, and her face;
A sweeter creature in this worlde
Could never prince embrace.

Her crisped lockes like threads of golde
Appeard to each mans sight;
Her sparkling eyes, like Orient pearles,
Did cast a heavenlye light.

The blood within her crystal cheekes
Did such a colour drive,
As though the lillye and the rose
For mastership did strive.

Yea Rosamonde, fair Rosamonde,
Her name was called so,
To whom our queene, dame Ellinor,
Was known a deadlye foe.

The king therefore, for her defence
Against the furious queene,
At Woodstocke builded such a bower,
The like was never seene.

Most curiously that bower was built
Of stone and timber strong,
An hundered and fifty doors
Did to this bower belong.

And they so cunninglye contriv'd,
With turnings round about,
That none but with a clue of thread
Could enter in or out.
        The Ballad of Fair Rosamond [1]

THE ESTRANGEMENT BETWEEN HENRY AND ELEANOR, disclosed to the more observing in the feudal world by the treaty of Montmirail, had been growing for some time. It is Giraldus Cambrensis who relates that it was in the late sixties and the early seventies that Henry's relations with Rosamond Clifford were an open scandal in the English court. "He [Henry]," says Giraldus, "who had long been a secret adulterer, now flaunted his paramour for all to see, not that Rose of the World (*Rosa-mundi*) as some vain and foolish people called her, but that Rose of Unchastity (*Rosa-immundi*)." [2]

There was something very special about the famous case of Rosamond Clifford that deeply roused the Plantagenet queen. Her rancor could not have been due to the mere fact of the king's infidelities. To make the best of their lords' philanderings was the common lot of highborn ladies when nobles married fiefs and errant spouses took their pleasures as they could on *chevauchée*. It was not a paltry amour that affronted the queen. She knew as well as the rest of the world that vassals retired their comely wives and daughters from the king's lust,[3] and that no hostage of high or low degree was secure in Henry's strongholds. Eleanor had averted her eyes from many other episodes. What so stirred the queen must have been that public flaunting of the favorite, of which Giraldus speaks, in those palaces where she herself had reigned, by virtue of her lineage, as undisputed mistress, and by virtue of her own exploits, as the most brilliant queen of Christendom. It is significant of the special flagrancy of the Clifford episode that the scandal whereby the queen was affronted aroused for her not only the support of her sons, but the indignation of both Henry's relatives and her own.

The idyll of Henry's love for Rosamond, which has given rise to such abundant legend, is circumscribed by but little time and space.[4] It is associated with a small locality — Oxford, the palace of Woodstock, and the nunnery of Godstow, all threaded together by the pastoral windings of the Glyme and the noisy churning of the upper Thames. The girl whose beauty drew upon her the eyes of her king was the daughter of Walter de Clifford of Bredelais on the Welsh border, a Norman knight who paid feudal service to Henry in his war in Wales.[5] It was possibly in the course of his Welsh campaign in 1165, while Eleanor was still serving as the king's vicegerent in distant Angers, that Henry encountered that "masterpiece of nature"[6] at Bredelais or at Godstow, where legend affirms that she was educated. The period of the affair was between 1166 and 1177, so its earlier phase ran concurrently with Becket's primacy and then somewhat beyond his martyrdom.[7] Rosamond died in 1177, and during the decade Henry was at various times abroad.

Everyone knows the legend of the tower and maze at Woodstock, "wunderliche ywrought of Daedalus werke," which Henry is said to have built in the park of his forestal palace to sequester Rosamond from jealous eyes; of Rosamond's well gushing from its beechen slope into the Glyme, where wild conies, peering from the thorn and holly, came to drink; of the needlework chest, carved with birds and other creatures, which the king gave Rosamond for her embroidery; of the fatal silken clue that fell from it, whereby the queen at last threaded her way to the sylvan retreat by the river. Everyone has heard it said and sung that the queen here offered the beauteous leman of the king her choice between the dagger and the poison bowl as an escape from the royal fury. Some tell of the sons the "flower of the world" bore to the king.

Rosamond died young in pious retirement at Godstow. Hoveden, writing in the century, relates that the pitiful nuns, condoning her fault, placed her tomb in the midst of their choir, and that Bishop Hugh of Lincoln, making his pastoral rounds in Oxfordshire as late as 1191 or 1192, was shocked to find it there, draped with a costly pall and bright with candles. The nuns, brought to account, explained that for the sake of Rosamond, a royal alms had greatly enriched their poor little house. The bishop was scandalized. He banished her dust from the sanctuary lest virtuous women, beholding her burial place decked like a shrine, should be led to fear not at all the consequence of sin.[8] She was removed then to the nuns' chapter house beside the Thames, which here makes a loud noise as it runs toward Oxford. But soon a miraculous token rebuked Hugh's episcopal severity. In the garth of Godstow an old nut tree was presently found bearing hollow shells instead of proper fruit, and the nuns remembered that Rosamond herself foretold that the end of her penance in purgatory and her entry into paradise would be marked by this very sign.[9]

Later we hear that her dust was distinguished from that of the Godstow nuns by that jingling couplet in which the poet, as Giraldus had done in his chronicle, plays upon the Latin of her name.

> Hic jacet in tumba Rosa mundi, non Rosa munda:
> Non redolet, sed olet, quae redolere solet.[10]

Whatever germ of truth may lurk in certain of these tales, the legend that Rosamond was the mother of Henry's two eldest illegitimate sons, Geoffrey the Chancellor and William, Earl of Salisbury, is rendered impossible by Giraldus' fixing of the period of Henry's relations with her, and affirming her youth at the time of them. These sons were old enough to have been Rosamond's grown brothers, and must therefore have been the fruit of some liaison of the king's early manhood. The story of the queen's proffer of the dagger and the poison bowl must likewise be discarded, because at the time of Rosamond's death in the late seventies, Eleanor was certainly in a very safe place where she could not strike at the king's favorite.

The legend of the little park at Woodstock with the tower and the maze "of Daedalus werke" persisted long in popular imagination, but if that retreat comprised, as the story says, the spring still known as "Rosamond's well," it was somewhat too near the palace to be overlooked by the mistress of Woodstock and too much in the way of the queen's country *chevauchées* beside the Glyme to remain long a secret bower. It may be that Henry, intensely preoccupied with his campaign in Wales and knowing Eleanor then at a safe distance in Angers, had grown careless and admitted the lovely Clifford to Woodstock itself.

In 1165, during the king's Welsh campaign, Eleanor had been his vicegerent on the marches of Anjou. In 1166 Henry joined her for the Easter court in Angers, and then in October of that year she crossed to Britain while Henry remained abroad. In England the queen made peregrinations in Oxfordshire and then retired to the castle of Oxford, where on the day after Christmas she gave birth to her youngest son, whom she named John in honor of the saint of his natal day. It may be that in the course of her autumn journeyings, and perhaps alerted by informers, she closed in on Woodstock without harbingers and found her rival lodged in that most intimate, domestic, and beloved of all the Plantagenet residences in England.

✤

Whatever the final incidents may have been, they led Eleanor to remember that, before ever she had been the Queen of France or of England, she had been the Countess of Poitou, and that, as scion of those Poitevins, Guillaume le Grand and Guillaume le Troubadour, she held in her own right a province beyond the Loire as sovereign as any king's, and a resolution to grasp into her own hands its wealth and freedom possessed her. She made up her mind to cut off with the bright sword of the river her portion of the world from Henry's, set up her second son as heir to her patrimony, and leave the king to make whatever division he could among his other heirs of what was left of his empire, a division in which her son Richard would hold enough to offset any rival among the other sons. Her vengeance for the Clifford affair was aimed not at the flaxen beauty of the king's folly, but at Henry himself, his mounting ambition, his nearly realized dreams of empire. And her decisions presently, as says Devizes, "troubled" the Angevin house "like that of Oedipus."

Such feudal dereliction in a woman was so ·xtraordinary as to escape the apprehension of the average man, as witness the mystification of the assistants at Montmirail. The queen, no longer an apprentice at statesmanship, surveyed a situation favorable to the course on which she had determined. In the first place, she was Louis Capet's vassal for Poitou and Aquitaine, and could, in spite of the circumstances that had estranged her from the King of the Franks, depend upon his faithful support of any measures calculated to harry the King of the English. The Bretons were in the habit of breaking into scattered uprisings whenever Henry's attention was turned to other provinces, and to these malcontents certain dispossessed castellans of Maine and Anjou were drawn by an irresistible attraction. Moreover, the Becket affair, consolidating many of Henry's foes and bringing him into collision with the church, weakened his prestige with Rome. But more than all, her own vassals, who had for thirty years borne with recurrent mutiny the "oppression" of her two royal consorts, were eager to see the time ripening when they could throw off altogether the shackles of alien kings fastened upon them secretly at the death of their last native duke; and they were certain to welcome the revival of the splendid ducal court.

Henry was not, of course, among the merely curious observers of the queen's movements. He promptly took what measures he could to protect his interests. While Eleanor spent the season of Advent in 1166 in Oxford, preoccupied with the birth of her youngest son, Henry on the other side of the Channel convened his Christmas court in her newly rebuilt palace of Poitiers; and there he presented to the queen's vassals his eldest son, not as being heir of Poitou, to be sure, but as destined to be the future overlord of that heir.[11]

Throughout 1167, though beset in his own provinces, Henry wrestled with the queen's rebellious homagers in Auvergne, Poitou, and the Limousin. The Lusignans, the most powerful of the duchess' liege men, that feudal house that "yielded to no yoke, or ever kept faith with any overlord," led the rebellion. But the furious barons of the south could not submerge their rivalries in a common cause, and Henry scotched them one by one. He scaled the impossible steeps of the fortress of Lusignan that loomed over the road from Poitiers to Niort, razed its redoubtable walls, burned its ruins, and ravaged its fruitful lands.[12] The scions of the most famous houses were reduced to brigandage, and in their distress those bitter vassals of the queen found refuge in the unbounded hospitality of Louis Capet.

Early in 1168, after the Christmas court in Argentan, victorious Henry escorted the Countess of Poitou through her own domain as Louis had done before him, and left her at last in the deep south with a household purely Poitevin. She was not, however, abandoned to the seditious counsel of her own *mesnie*. Perhaps with her consent, in view of the violence and anarchy in the provinces; perhaps also by way of reminding the Poitevins to whom they owed allegiance, she was placed under the protective custody of Henry's distinguished vassal, Patrick, Earl of Salisbury, with a body of soldiers. But the king had no sooner returned to his own affairs north of the Loire than a signal event bore witness to the insecurity of the Angevin peace he had enforced.

As the countess journeyed northward toward Poitiers about Easter time under escort of Earl Patrick and his bodyguard, the dispossessed Lusignans burst from ambush upon her convoy and tried to capture her, as it was said, for ransom to recoup their recent losses. Eleanor, who knew how to manage herself in the saddle, and who had moreover fended off brigands in these regions several times before, rode to the safety of a nearby castle; but Earl Patrick, who protected her flight in person, was murdered by a fell blow from behind and his *mesnie* was captured, wounded, or put to flight.

The surviving hero of the incident was Earl Patrick's nephew, the recently knighted Guillaume le Maréchal. The youth found in this combat the golden opportunity to flesh his sword, find his patron, and open his way to fame and fortune. The episode offered the first steppingstone to Guillaume in his brilliant rise in the courts of the Plantagenets from simple knight to the highest dignities in the gift of kings. Eleanor, "valiant and courteous lady that she was," says the account, "bestowed upon him horses, arms, gold, and rich garments, and more than all opened her palace gates and fostered his ambition." In her behalf he had fought "like a wild boar against dogs."[13]

✤

Eleanor's proceedings from the time she resumed her residence in Poitou indicate a resolution to cut herself away from feudal kings and to establish a Poitevin domain subject to a distinctively Poitevin regime. Though continuing now and then to coöperate with Henry outside her provinces in the interests of her other sons, she at once took measures to establish her own heir in Poitou and Aquitaine under such auspices as ratified the coronation of princes royal in the realms of kings; and to restore throughout her provinces the ancient glories of the native dukes and counts. She invoked every feudal sanction to draw her rival vassals together, to allay their internecine strife, to focus their common allegiance in the ducal centers. Leading out Richard, the stripling figurehead of the new regime, she went on royal progresses from the Loire to the foothills of the Pyrenees, receiving the homage of her vassals in Niort, Limoges, Bayonne, presenting her heir with a pomp all but forgotten in the far corners of her duchy, associating him with acts of grace, undoing right and left the oppressive works of Henry's seneschals. Exiled barons came home and were restored to their dignities. The church was refreshed by her leniency and the plenteousness of her largess. She hastened to renew in her towns the agreeable customs of the native dukes, and wherever she went, old fetes and fairs revived and there was concourse of the people.

The recognition of Richard as Eleanor's inviolable heir was accomplished with as much traditional ceremony as marked the anointing of the heirs of France and England during the lifetime of their sires. Aquitaine had its own venerable ceremonial for the induction of its dukes, distinguished by such pageantry as delighted the provinces of the duchess. This ritual centered on an ancient legend of the Limousin which related that a noble virgin Valerie had, in the very dawn of the Christian dispensation, and in the city of Limoges, spilled her blood for the sake of her faith. But the tradition had lapsed for a generation and Eleanor was obliged to recreate its pomp and rekindle the imagination of her vassals. Limoges had never regarded the city of Poitiers as its spiritual fountainhead, and this bit of local history had the important value in the south country of maintaining the superior antiquity of Limoges as a center of Christian diffusion in Gaul.[14] Furthermore, the city had suffered especially under the oppressions of Henry, and it was a matter of concern to divert the homagers of the Limousin from those bitter memories.

A miraculous occurrence assisted the duchess' plans. It chanced that, just at the opportune moment, the monks of Saint Martial dredged up from the ancient archives of their abbey, where it had apparently lain hidden for generations from foraging clerks, a new and circumstantial life of Saint Valerie that greatly stirred the pious ardors of the Limousin. Eleanor and her ecclesiastical advisers made brilliant use of this discovery to revive old-time custom. A great procession escorted Richard to the church of Saint Étienne, where he contracted a symbolic marriage with Saint Valerie, whose ring was put upon his finger, thus signifying allegorically his indissoluble bond with the provinces and vassals of his Aquitainian forebears. Henceforth neither Westminster Abbey nor the cathedral of Reims were to be more authentic sacring places; and the bishop, like the Archbishop of Canterbury, held his privileged rank as officiant. While in the city the duke and the duchess presided at the laying of the cornerstone for the church of Saint Augustine. Richard had already been invested in Poitiers with his title as Abbé of Saint Hilaire, the most venerable dignity, apart from that of the bishopric in that ancient city, and something comparable to King Louis's dignity as Abbé of Notre Dame.[15]

15 ✠

The Court of Poitiers

We gather rosebuds from the sharp thorns amid which they bloom.
Andreas, *De Amore*

WHEN THE COUNTESS OF POITOU settled down to rule her own heritage, she took her residence in Poitiers, which offered a wide eye-sweep on the world of still operative kings. In the recent Plantagenet building program her ancestral city, the seat and necropolis of her forebears, had been magnificently enlarged and rebuilt, and it stood at her coming thoroughly renewed, a gleaming exemplar of urban elegance.[1] The site rose superbly amidst encircling rivers. Its narrow Merovingian area had lately been extended to include with new and ampler walls parishes that had previously straggled over its outer slopes; ancient quarters had been cleared of immemorial decay; new churches and collegials had sprung up; the cathedral of Saint Pierre was enriched; markets and shops of tradesmen and artisans bore witness to renewed life among the *bourgeoisie*; bridges fanned out to suburbs and monastic establishments lying beyond the streams that moated the city. Brimming with sunshine, the valleys ebbed far away below — hamlet and croft, mill and vineyard — to a haze as blue as the vintage.

In the center of the restored capital rose the elegant tower that Guillaume le Troubadour had built for the pleasure of the Countess of Châtellerault. To this builders had lately made additions, and on these one is tempted to discern the stamp of Eleanor, for they were domestic chambers unlike those in Henry's cheerless strongholds, affording space and privacy for women who made an art, not a circumstance, of being queens. These chambers clustered about a noble hall for the plenary ducal court. This vast room, meet for unsurpassable fetes, still stands, with one of its lovely arcaded walls intact as in Eleanor's day, a hall whose windows once gave out upon a pleasance with vistas of river valley and sea-blue ridges bearing planes, poplars, and umbrella pines. Here was no disordered bivouac like the bleak castles of sheer Angevin contrivance in Normandy and Anjou, strewn with the straw bedding of feudal soldiery; no depot for the forage of *routiers*; no drafty harborage with unglazed mullions and flapping hangings lighted with the slant beams of flares and murky with wind-driven smoke; no armory for shield and helmet, trophies of the chase, the litter of hounds and falcons. Here was a proper setting for majesty, refined in its way like the decorous palaces of Byzantium, a woman's place in the sun, a fit stage for the social arts, a foil for beauty, a comfortable house in which to "fix one's buttoned staff and stay." Most of the Plantagenet building was secular, but from the windows of the renovated palace one might have looked out upon the rising walls of that jewel box of a church, Notre-Dame-la-Grande. It may still be seen. An Oriental quality has been remarked in it. It is not large, but ornate as a reliquary; its façade, threefold, like an open triptych, is crowded with a confusion of sculptured episodes in stone.[2]

When Eleanor came in about 1170 to take full possession of her newly restored city of Poitiers and to install her favorite son there as ruling count and duke in her own patrimony, she was no mere game piece as were most feudal women, to be moved like a queen in chess. She had learned her role as *domina* in Paris, Byzantium, Antioch, London, and Rouen, and knew her value in the feudal world. She was prepared of her own unguided wisdom to reject the imperfect destinies to which she had been, as it were, assigned. In this, her third important role in history, she was the pawn of neither prince nor prelate, the victim of no dynastic scheme. She came as her own mistress, the most sophisticated of women, equipped with plans to establish her own assize, to inaugurate a regime dedicated neither to Mars nor to the Pope, nor to any king, but to Minerva, Venus, and the Virgin. She was resolved to escape from secondary roles, to assert her independent sovereignty in her own citadel, to dispense her own justice, her own patronage, and when at leisure, to survey, like the Empress of Byzantium, a vast decorum in her precincts.

It is easy to see that the problems of disunion and anarchy that engaged Eleanor in the governance of her dominions were such as to tax the energies of the most vigilant and experienced overlord; yet they were by no means her only responsibility. In the intervals of her administrative journeyings to rectify Capetian and Angevin misrule in the far corners of her provinces, she was obliged to give a certain supervision to the ducal household in Poitiers. This household, by a feudal process of accretion, had become a nursery and academy of prospective kings and queens, dukes and princesses. It was the irony of fate that gave into Eleanor's keeping the pawns of the rival dynastic schemes of the Capets and the Plantagenets, the children of the two royal husbands from whom she was estranged. Certainly neither Louis Capet nor Henry Plantagenet would in cool deliberation have sought out Eleanor as the guardian and mentor of their dynastic hopes. It so befell, however, that the very woman most unlikely to have been recommended for the responsibility was entrusted with the education and safekeeping of most of the children of mark west of the Rhine and north of the Pyrenees. In her Poitevin palace at various times were Marguerite, the elder daughter of Louis Capet's second marriage, who was the seventeen-year-old wife of young Henry Plantagenet, heir of England and Normandy; and Alais, the younger sister of Marguerite, affianced at Montmirail to Richard Plantagenet; Constance, Countess of Brittany, betrothed to Geoffrey; Alix, the child heiress of Maurienne, pledged in infancy to John. There were besides the queen's own daughters, Eleanor, the future Queen of Castile, and Joanna, the future Queen of Sicily; also from time to time the queen's sons, Henry, Richard, Geoffrey. The young Plantagenets of the group — they were all under twenty — mingled with their Poitevin cousins of Faye and Châtellerault, with their relatives of Flanders and Champagne, in the foyer of their common ancestors, Guillaume le Grand and Guillaume le Troubadour. And since the queen's household included as many as sixty ladies upon occasion, it may be presumed that the revival of the ducal court brought to Poitiers the negotiable heirs and heiresses of the great fiefs of the south.[3]

The queen's court was astir at all times with the passage of guests and travelers; but the height of the social season was the spring, the post-Lenten period from Pentecost to the feast of Saint John in June, at which date truces frequently ended and barons mustered their vassals for war. It was the season par excellence for tournament and pilgrimage, and chatelaines made the most of the affluence of *preux chevaliers* occasioned by these events and by the challenge of the *nouvel saison* so very sweet and flowery in the south of France, for their annual fetes and assemblies. Since no vassal might bestow his heir in marriage without the consent of his overlord, the Easter court served, for one thing, as a fair for the negotiable marriage prizes, young knights and squires and demoiselles. The assemblies of the barons, which coincided in the south with ancient popular fetes in Maytime praise of Venus, offered apt occasions for the vernal entertainments of the chatelaines.

The heirs of Poitou and Aquitaine who came to the queen's high place for their vassals' homage, their squires' training, and their courtiers' service, were truculent youths, boisterous young men from the baronial strongholds of the south without the Norman or Frankish sense of nationality, bred on feuds and violence, some of them with rich fiefs and proud lineage, but with little solidarity and no business but local warfare and daredevil escapade. The custom of lateral rather than vertical inheritance of fiefs in vogue in some parts of Poitou and Aquitaine — the system by which lands passed through a whole generation before descending to the next generation[4] — produced a vast number of landless but expectant younger men, foot-loose, unemployed, ambitious, yet dependent upon the reluctant bounty of uncles and brothers, or their own violent exploits. These wild young men were a deep anxiety not only to the heads of their houses, but to the Kings of France and England and to the Pope in Rome. They were the stuff of which rebellion and schism are made. For two generations the church had done what it could with the problem of their unemployment, marching hordes out of Europe on crusade and rounding other hordes into the cloister.

It was with this spirited world of princes and princesses, of apprentice knights and chatelaines, at once the school and the court of young Richard, that the duchess, busy as she was with the multifarious business of a feudal suzerain, had to deal in her palace in Poitiers. It must be remembered that for nearly forty years the ducal court had been in abeyance as a center of social influence in Poitou and Aquitaine. It was necessary for the duchess to reassemble the exiled remnants of the Poitevin entourage and subdue to civility a generation that had lacked the disciplines of a somewhat fixed and authentic court. The duchess really needed some dependable deputy in her royal household. The pious King of the Franks, who had valuable hostages in that court in the persons of his two younger daughters, must have felt the urgency of some provision for orthodoxy in Poitiers quite as much as the harried queen. It was therefore an inspiration to hit upon the Countess of Champagne as the *maitresse d'école* for the royal academy in Poitiers.

Marie, Countess of Champagne,[5] was the elder daughter of Louis Capet and Eleanor of Aquitaine, and herself a person of first consequence. She was that disappointing female child born to the Capets in 1145, heaven's ambiguous answer to the supplications of Eleanor and Abbé Bernard for a royal heir. Whether, when she journeyed down from Troyes or Paris to assume her place in the court of Poitiers, she confronted her mother as a dear familiar child or as an apparition from a previous existence cannot with certainty be said. For long years, in default of male heirs, she had been the hope of the Capet dynasty, and hence the cynosure of courtly eyes. Henry Plantagenet had once sought union with her before marrying her mother, but Abbé Bernard had forbidden that alliance as consanguineous.[6] Following the divorce of the king and queen, her parents, she had been left at the age of six or so in the court of France. One may guess that, under the supervision of Louis and the two excellent stepmothers who had succeeded Eleanor in Paris, her education had been of the very best and strictly orthodox. Louis had bestowed Marie, after careful reflection, at what was, in the twelfth century, the spinsterly age of nineteen, upon one of his most powerful vassals, Henry the Liberal of Champagne, a *preux chevalier* nearly twice her age and a brother of his own Queen Adele. At the time of Marie's ascendancy in the court of Poitiers, she was just under thirty, the mother of a son who was later to be the King of Jerusalem, and of a daughter whose pretty name was Scholastique. No woman of the *beau monde* had more prestige; none was more correct. Marie shed the aura of Paris and Troyes upon the renaissance in Poitiers.

The condition which the Countess of Champagne found in the court of the queen her mother must have been very disquieting to one fresh from the courts of the Capets and more or less unfamiliar with Plantagenet heartiness and informality. She must have seen that the demoiselles, the undubbed squires, and the superfluous clerks would have to be engaged in something profitable. Indeed, to leave that young world unemployed was to invite disaster and confusion. However, the character of the milieu which Marie appears to have set up in Poitiers suggests a genuine sympathy between the queen and her daughter who had so long been sundered by the bleak fortuities of life. Old relationships were knit up. Something native blossomed in the countess, who shone with a special luster in her mother's court. The young Count of Poitou learned to love particularly his half sister Marie and forever to regard the Poitiers of her dispensation as the world's citadel of valor, the seat of courtesy, and the fountainhead of poetic inspiration. Long after, in his darkest hours, it was to her good graces he appealed. The countess, having carte blanche to proceed with the very necessary business of getting control of her academy, must have striven first for order. Since the miscellaneous and high-spirited young persons in her charge had not learned order from the liturgy nor yet from hagiography, the countess bethought her, like many an astute pedagogue, to deduce her principles from something more germane to their interests. She did not precisely invent her regime; rather she appropriated it from the abundant resources at her hand.

The liberal court of Eleanor had again drawn a company of those gifted persons who thrive by talent or by art. Poets, *conteurs* purveying romance, ecclesiastics with Latin literature at their tongues' end and mere clerks with smatterings of Ovid learned from quotation books, chroniclers engaged upon the sober epic of the Plantagenets, came to their haven in Poitiers. The queen and the countess, with their native poetic tradition, were the natural patrons of the troubadours. It will be seen that the Countess Marie's resources were rich and abundant, but not so formalized as to afford the disciplines for a royal academy nor give substance to a social ritual. The great hall was ready for her grand assize; the expectant court already thronged to gape at its suggestive splendors. But neither the pious ritual of the French court, nor the disorderly bustlings of Henry's chancelleries, nor the thrifty regime of Matilda Empress in Rouen, nor even the somewhat slumberous decorum of Troyes, offered any valid precedents for the great court of Poitiers with its burgeoning young world and its boundless possibilities. The countess had to improvise; and it is one of the miraculous conjunctions of destiny that she possessed in high degree not only the rich patron's resource, but also the chatelaine's supreme talent for contrivance. The means, the time, the place, the occasion — all were hers. Singularly in the feudal world women confident of prestige and the authority it brings, possessing royal wealth to execute, possessed also the freedom to devise their own milieu.

Amongst the throng of gifted persons, literati, journeymen artists, and philosophers that jostled each other in the countess's foyer, was one André, a clerk known as the Chaplain. He had once served his calling in the court of Louis Capet, so perhaps he went down to Poitiers as one of Marie's spiritual counselors. If so, he came under the disturbing necessity, in her employ, of sacrificing his high principles for the sake of his stipend. What the countess obviously needed for her royal academy was not advice for penitents, but a code of manners to transform the anarchy and confusion that confronted her into something refined, serious, and decorous, a code to give currency to her own ideals for an elect society to be impelled not by the brute force that generally prevailed, nor by casual impulse, but by an inner disciplined sense of propriety. What progress could be made in dialectic by untutored squires who rode hacks into mess halls, or by hoydens who diverted eyes from psalters in the very midst of mass? And upon what could one ground a code of chivalry save on the classic and universal theme of love? "Oh what a wonderful thing is love," the chaplain presently exclaims, "which makes a man shine with so many virtues, and teaches everyone . . . so many good traits of character." [7] Marie set André at work. Perhaps she suggested his model, though any clerk of his day with access to a monastic library would have hit upon it easily. Abélard had quoted it in Paris, and so had Abbé Bernard. It was Ovid's treatises on the Art of Loving and the Remedy for Love, the *Ars Amatoria* and the *Remedia Amoris*.

Ovid's *Ars Amatoria*, as the poet himself contrived it, is a bit of foolery for a sophisticated audience that well appreciates the author's transparent intention to make fun of the young Roman's illicit love affairs by pretending to take them seriously. It is a screed on the fine art of seduction done with all the delicate analysis of a disputation. In it the art of loving is reduced to rule. How to proceed and succeed with the business of seduction: how to dress, how to scrape an acquaintance, how to get on in conversation, how to humor the mood of the fair one, how to give and withhold, to please and torment — the gamut of the little comedy — furnish the themes of his discourse. The *Ars* is elegantly embellished with allusions to classical instances, which enhance its air of make-believe solemnity.

This work, which provides an admirable framework for Marie's doctrines of civility, underwent, however, a most remarkable change in André's redaction, which offers itself to the court as a guide to a young man seeking to equip himself for admission to elect society. André's work,[8] like Ovid's, is frankly erotic. It would not have occurred to Marie to be squeamish about the seduction and adultery in her original. Both works discourse with all the precision of dialectic on the science of loving in all its branches, define the principles of love, its disciplines, its code, its etiquette. But whereas in the work of Ovid, man is the master, employing his arts to seduce women for his pleasure, in André's work, woman is the mistress, man her pupil in homage, her vassal in service.

There are internal evidences of the strain this redaction imposed upon André. He was unable to make either the free doctrines of the classical poet or the fantastic notions of the countess rest comfortably in his clerical mind. Sensing the doubly subversive nature of the document upon which he was engaged, he seems to have made good Latin of it only under a certain compulsion from his sovereign lady. The chaplain's discourse is so full of the conflict between pagan naturalism and Christian restraint that the reader perceives through his mind's eye the shadow of Marie at his elbow, correcting, refining, interpolating, and deleting, with the high-handed disregard for sources that made composition a pleasure of self-expression in her day. It is therefore not surprising to find that André at some time added to his work a final section, *De Remedio*, in which he repudiates the essential philosophy of the major portion, and warns the social neophyte to be wary. Chrétien de Troyes, another of Marie's literary vassals, also revolts from the too liberal implications of her scheme. In his *Cligès* he gainsays the doctrine he had expressed in *Lancelot*, which latter he wrote upon urgency of Marie and on themes supplied by her.

Besides taking liberties with her classic original, the editorial Marie infused André's gentleman's guide with the very breath of the prevailing mode. To support the rather threadbare dicta of Ovid, who was after all in that court the passion of the elder generation, Marie's code professed to derive authority for good form from the authentic practice of chivalry in the court of King Arthur in Caerleon on Usk, than which nothing could afford a more unexceptionable pattern for society. It elucidated for aspiring knights the true inwardness of Gawain, the sustaining principles of Arthur himself.

At least one other important source Marie employed. She levied upon the social traditions of her Poitevin forebears. Nostredame relates that in Provence chatelaines were accustomed to entertain their seasonal assemblies with so-called "courts of love," in which, just as feudal vassals brought their grievances to the assizes of their overlords for regulation, litigants in love's thrall brought their problems for the judgment of the ladies.[9] André in his famous work makes reference to antecedent decisions in questions of an amatory nature by "les dames de Gascogne," [10] and the poetry of the troubadours presupposes a milieu in which their doctrines of homage and deference could be exploited. Thus we have in André's *Tractatus* the framework of Ovid with the central emphasis reversed, the Arthurian code of manners, the southern ritual of the "courts of love," all burnished with a golden wash of troubadour poetry learned by the queen's forebears and their vassals in the deep Midi, probably beyond the barrier of the Pyrenees.[11] Marie made these familiar materials the vehicle for her woman's doctrine of civility, and in so doing, she transformed the gross and cynical pagan doctrines of Ovid into something more ideal, the woman's canon, the chivalric code of manners. Manners, she plainly saw, were after all the fine residuum of philosophies, the very flower of ethics.

There is something ghoulish in exposing André's book, which is also Marie's, to the callous scrutiny of an age hostile to sentiment. A faint odor of cloistral mold and feudal decay clings to it. But the ideal of *l'amour courtois* which grew up in Poitiers had, as has been well said, more than a little to do with freeing woman from the millstone which the church in the first millennium hung about her neck as the author of man's fall and the facile instrument of the devil in the world. The court of Poitiers gave its high sanction to ideals which spread so rapidly throughout Europe that the "doctrine of the inferiority of woman has never had the same standing since."[12] The code of André gives glimpses of a woman's notions of society different in essential respects from the prevailing feudal scheme, which was certainly man-made. In the Poitevin code, man is the property, the very thing of woman; whereas a precisely contrary state of things existed in the adjacent realms of the two kings from whom the reigning Duchess of Aquitaine was estranged. The sheer originality of Marie's scheme can be grasped by trying to imagine Henry Fitz-Empress (or Louis Capet for that matter) transformed by its agency into the beau ideal. As critics we may make what we please of this upside-down philosophy of women. There it is in the first two books of André the Chaplain. There have always been two schools of thought about it.

With this anatomy of the whole corpus of love in hand, Marie organized the rabble of soldiers, fighting cocks, jousters, springers, riding masters, troubadours, Poitevin nobles and debutantes, young chatelaines, adolescent princes, and infant princesses in the great hall of Poitiers. Of this pandemonium the countess fashioned a seemly and elegant society, the fame of which spread to the world. Here was a woman's assize to draw men from the excitements of the tilt and the hunt, from dice and games to feminine society, an assize to outlaw boorishness and compel the tribute of adulation to female majesty.

The book, together with the poetry of the troubadours, enables us to catch a glimpse of those famous assemblies in the queen's new hall to which lovers brought their complaints for the judgment of the ladies. The female portion of the academy, disciplined by the fashionable example of the countess and the queen to a noble grace of bearing, a flattering condescension, mount the dais, an areopagus sometimes sixty strong.[13] They gather about the queen,[14] and among them shine, besides Marie, Isabel, Countess of Flanders,[15] who is the queen's niece; Ermengarde, Countess of Narbonne, doubtless familiar with some such proceedings in the south;[16] probably also

Henry Plantagenet's sister, the lovely Emma of Anjou; perhaps also, if she was another sister of the king, Marie de France [17] — all except Ermengarde, who was more nearly the queen's contemporary, women from twenty-five to thirty, the notable high priestesses of art and beauty in the day.

The chronicle of Geoffroi de Vigeois leads us to conclude that the standards of the court impressed themselves upon Poitou and the Limousin. "Time was," he says, "when the Bishop of Limoges and the Viscount of Comborn were content to go in sheep and fox skins. But today [the queen's day] the humblest would blush to be seen in such poor things. Now they have clothes fashioned of rich and precious stuffs, in colors to suit their humor. They snip out the cloth in rings and longish slashes to show the lining through, so they look like the devils that we see in paintings. They slash their mantles, and their sleeves flow like those of hermits. Youths affect long hair and shoes with pointed toes." "As for women," he goes on, "you might think them adders, if you judged by the tails they drag after them." (This last is precisely the extravagance of which Abbé Bernard had complained in the Île de France.) The price of fur and cloth had doubled in the Limousin during the period of Geoffroi's observation.[18] As for minor luxuries, the *Tractatus*, in listing gifts a lover might make to his mistress, reveals what might have been seen in the smart new *fenestrae* of the Rue Saint Porchaire: "a handkerchief, a fillet, a wreath of gold or silver, a brooch, a mirror, a purse, a girdle, a tassel, a comb, sleeves, gloves, a ring, a powder box, little dishes, or any small object useful for the toilet or serving to remind of the lover, if it be certain that, in receiving the token, the lady is without touch of avarice."[19] The grants made by the queen in this period to a local merchant prince suggest that Eleanor herself invested heavily in the goods mentioned by the chronicler.[20]

While the ladies, well-accoutered, sit above upon the dais, the sterner portion of society purged, according to the code, from the odors of the kennels and the highway and free for a time from spurs and falcons, range themselves about the stone benches that line the walls, stirring the fragrant rushes with neatly pointed shoe. There are doubtless preludes of music luring the last reluctant knight from the gaming table, *tensons* or *pastourelles*, the plucking of rotes, the "voicing of a fair song and sweet," perhaps even some of the more complicated musical harmonies so ill-received by the clerical critics in London; a Breton *lai* adding an episode to Arthurian romance, or a chapter in the tale of "sad-man" Tristram, bringing a gush of tears from the tender audience clustered about the queen and the Countess of Champagne.

After the romance of the evening in the queen's court, the jury comes to attention upon petition of a young knight in the hall. He bespeaks the judgment of the queen and her ladies upon a point of conduct, through an advocate, of course, so he may remain anonymous. A certain knight, the advocate deposes, has sworn to his lady, as the hard condition of obtaining her love, that he will upon no provocation boast of her merits in company. But one day he overhears detractors heaping his mistress with calumnies. Forgetting his vow in the heat of his passion, he warms to eloquence in defense of his lady. This coming to her ears, she repudiates her champion. Does the lover, who admits he has broken his pledge to his mistress, deserve in this instance to be driven from her presence? [21]

The Countess of Champagne, subduing suggestions from the floor and the buzz of conference upon the dais, renders the judgment of the areopagus. The lady in the case, anonymous of course, is at fault, declares the Countess Marie. She has laid upon her lover a vow too impossibly difficult. The lover has been remiss, no doubt, in breaking his vow to his mistress, no matter what cruel hardship it involves; but he deserves leniency for the merit of his ardor and his constancy. The jury recommends that the stern lady reinstate the plaintiff. The court takes down the judgment. It constitutes a precedent. Does anyone guess the identity of the young pair whose estrangement is thus delicately knit up by the countess? As a bit of suspense it is delicious. As a theme for talk, how loosening to the tongue!

A disappointed petitioner brings forward a case, through an advocate, involving the question whether love survives marriage. The countess, applying her mind to the code, which says that marriage is no proper obstacle to lovers (*Causa coniugii ab amore non est excusatio recta*),[22] and after grave deliberation with her ladies, creates a sensation in the court by expressing doubt whether love in the ideal sense can exist between spouses.[23] This is so arresting a proposition that the observations of the countess are referred to the queen for corroboration, and all wait upon the opinion of this deeply experienced judge. The queen with dignity affirms that she cannot gainsay the Countess of Champagne, though she finds it admirable that a wife should find love and marriage consonant. Eleanor, Queen of France and then of England, had learned at fifty-two that, as another medieval lady put it, "Mortal love is but the licking of honey from thorns." [24]

Of course, they rationalize a conduct that has outburst the rigid feudal scheme for women; but disillusion speaks also in those noble ladies, who, though they divine some unattainable ideal value in life, know that actually they remain feudal property, mere part and parcel of their fiefs. It is plain that each and every one of the judgments in the queen's court is an arrant feudal heresy. Taken together they undermine all the primary sanctions and are subversive of the social order. No proper king or baron, even at the risk of being reckoned a boor, ought to subscribe to a single one of them. And indeed, among the artists and innovators in the audience, a few of the higher clergy and certain barons survey the whole scene in order to report to absent kings what goes on in the queen's palace in Poitiers.

At the culmination of the queen's significant remarks, the court adjourns to the pleasance for a breath of air. Lent is over, though the chestnut trees are still decked like paschal altars with their white wax lights. Laburnum pours a flood of gold along the wall and nightingales weave melody through a neighboring copse; frogs ply their bassoons in the oozy river bed that makes the city's outer moat. On the terrace the courtiers of the queen and the countess, pacing in the moonlight, discourse not at all of the *Tractatus* but of many other things: of the prompt canonization of Thomas Becket; of the recent confession of Henry for his share in the martyrdom, his absolution, his reconciliation with Rome; of his folly at Montmirail in parceling his dominion among his heirs, which is already accumulating a harvest of revolt against the king in Normandy, Anjou, and Brittany; of the young king, who, urged by his vassals to require for himself a status as fair as that of his brother Richard, is getting out of hand. They whisper of conspiracies and counterconspiracies in Paris, even in Poitiers. Here is the very center of rumor and surmise, and pitchers with big ears gather information to distill elsewhere.

The queen moves among her guests — bishops and clerks, *conteurs* and troubadours, the vassals of great fiefs, the Princesses of France, the Poitevin ladies of the courts of love, her daughters, nieces, cousins, her *fideles*; but, if she overhears omens of brewing disasters, they are to her like summer thunder bellowing on the distant plains of Normandy. Snatches of melody float on the air, fine and pure as plain song. She hears a tenor like that of Ventadour singing that poet's song in praise of her:[25]

Lan-can vei la fo-lha Jos dels al-bres cha-zer,

Cui que pes ni do - lha, A me deu bo sa - ber.

Laughter comes from a group perched with the young Count of Poitou on the parapet. He is repeating with anecdote those famous words of Abbé Bernard (soon to be Saint Bernard), "From the devil they came, to the devil they will go."[26]

But the April moon sets at last upon the grand assize of the ladies, and cocks call for the sun from a distant croft in the valley. Quiet falls upon the palace and the little streets of the high place where the carven saints and angels dream in the portals of the Romanesque façades; and in the stillness lauds sound faintly from the precincts of Saint Porchaire.

16 ✛

Henry and His Sons

A man's enemies are the men of his own house.
Micah 7:6

WHILE THESE GAY REUNIONS were engrossing the younger generation in Poitiers, where were the feudal kings? Louis's role was only that of waiting with shuttered eyes for the dropping of those fruits of justice and patience that had long been ripening on the bough. With the Countess Marie and her coterie so valued in Poitiers, he doubtless felt less cut off from his former homagers in Poitou and more privy to the counsels of that brilliant court. The neatness of his coöperation with it was presently revealed.

Time added only benignity to Louis. In his later years he renounced temporal aspirations and the vain shows of this world. Giraldus admired his simplicity when the great Capetian said without a touch of envy,

"The King of the Indies is rich with gems, with lions, leopards, and elephants; the Emperor of Byzantium and the King of Sicily boast gold and silken garments . . . Thy master, however, the King of England, lacks nothing. To him belong men, horses, gold, silk, gems, fruits, wild beasts, and all things else. As for us in France, we have only our bread, our wine, and simple gaieties." [1]

When his daily duties and offices were done, Louis played a quiet game of chess, but when prelates like Bishop Hugh of Lincoln were announced, he hid his board away, lest he suffer rebuke for hours lost to good works.[2] As he felt age stealing on him, he fell back more and more on his role as Abbé of Notre Dame. He gave himself increasingly to fast and meditation, when possible observed the hours and lunched frugally with his monks in their refectory. He dozed innocently wherever he happened to find himself in need of rest. In his ordered background he mellowed like autumn fruit on an espalier. His brother-in-law, the Count of Champagne, was once alarmed to find him on a summer's day alone and asleep in the green alley of a garden near a grove with only two guards on watch nearby, and reproached him for so exposing himself to villainy. A serene smile overspread the king's face.

"Although alone," he said, "I sleep free from danger, for no one wishes me ill." [3]

Sometimes he woke from a dream of carrying the oriflamme again to Jerusalem; but this vision faded in the sober light of day in the realization that younger arms would carry that banner to the Holy Land. Probably with a new crusade in view, he sent his youngest daughter Agnes, born of the noble house of Champagne, with a distinguished escort of bishops and barons to Byzantium to be wedded to the son of Manuel Comnenus,[4] who had entertained him and his counselors and the Amazons so brilliantly in his palaces on the Bosporus. At home he could look forward to laying down the heavy burden of his crown, since his prayers for an "heir of the better sex" had been requited.

King Henry Plantagenet was not slumbering in shady groves nor dreaming of crusades nor praying for release from the burden of his crown. In the twenty years of his reign, Henry had withstood formidable foes — popes, kings, archbishops, and barons — but never had he been confronted with such a confederation of enemies, nor enemies with unpredictable courses and subtle instruments of malignity that sheer force could not restrain. The whole malevolent world, it seemed, had seized upon the negotiations of Montmirail to menace his security.

Becket's martyrdom in 1170 had cost Henry much prestige. The instant fame of Canterbury as the scene of miracles, the vast popular pilgrimage to Becket's shrine, the prompt movement for his canonization, gave ever wider currency and significance to the incidents of his exile, his return in the face of death, his murder in the very sanctuary at the hour of evensong. Thomas among the saints in heaven became more difficult to circumvent than Thomas on the parley fields of France and Normandy. His blood cried out to the Christian world from the stones of Canterbury.[5] As veneration for Saint Thomas grew, the Angevin lost some of his honor among men. Who could tell what share the king bore in the terrible sacrilege? Henry had not pursued nor punished the assassins. Was this because, although he may not have ordered the act, he nevertheless condoned it? Or because, if he brought them to justice, he would seem to have been doubly wicked in punishing them for doing his will? [6]

The apportionment of their prospective inheritances among his sons at Montmirail had bred rancor among the brothers Plantagenet and encouraged their rival vassalages to nurse the princes' grievances. Meantime the queen and her eldest daughter, that flower of the court of France, were maintaining in Poitiers, under cover of their brilliant entertainments, heaven only knew what commerce with his other enemies, and, worst of all, were filling the minds of his own sons not only with folly but with sedition.[7] Henry Fitz-Empress took stock of his situation and with Angevin energy and thoroughness set about a program of threats and appeasements to recover control of his household and retrieve his waning prestige.

✤

Henry . . . had that goodly household, valiant, wise, and prudent; father of the
young king who jousted with such ardor; father of Richard the cunning, who was so
wise and so shrewd; father of Geoffrey of Brittany, who likewise was a man of
great deeds; and father of John Lackland, because of whom he suffered much strife
and warfare.

Ambrose, *L'Estoire de la guerre sainte*

Louis Capet and the young king were appeased in 1172 by a second
coronation in Winchester in which Marguerite shared her husband's dignities.[8] It was perhaps for this occasion that Henry went to considerable
expense for the repair of the palace of Winchester and the painting of new
frescoes on its walls. In one chamber he for some time reserved a bare space
to be filled ultimately with a conceit of his own. When the fresco was at
length executed, it depicted a great eagle with spread wings set upon by
four eaglets. Two of the fledglings, with furious beak and claws, wounded
the pinions of the parent bird; a third dug at his vitals; and a fourth, perched
upon his neck, clawed at his eyes. Asked what this grim figment meant,
Henry explained that the great eagle was himself, and the eaglets were his
four sons. "Thus will they pursue me till I die," he said, "and that least one,
whom I now cherish with so much affection, will be the most malignant of
them all."

Giraldus, who relates the story as if Henry himself had displayed the
painting to him and interpreted its meaning, was impressed with the fierce
irony of the piece. It is he who cites the words of the prophet: a man's
enemies are the men of his own house.[9]

The scions of the Plantagenets in 1172 were no longer the passive boys
of Montmirail, and their diverse characters had become apparent in the years
following the occasion on which the elder king had designated for each his
inheritance. Among their intimates the brothers were wont to repeat jocosely
the legend that the Angevin line had descended through a few generations
from the demon countess of Foulques the Black.[10] They bandied the words
Abbé Bernard was said to have uttered years before when he had scanned
the infant face of Henry Fitz-Empress: "From the devil he came; to the devil
he will go."

If the Plantagenets bore the legend of demonic ancestry as part of their
Angevin inheritance, the Countess of Poitou had, in the view of the times,
brought little to redeem it. The Franks — probably as ex post facto explanations for her withdrawal from their court — reproached her for her levity,
her flouting of authority, her impenitence. *Instabilis* (fickle, unsteady) is
the word the chroniclers use to characterize the Poitevin line. "A giddy
unstable kind of man," says Malmesbury of the queen's troubadour grand-

father. "A very intelligent woman, sprung from a noble race, but unsteady" (*Prudens femina valde, sed instabilis*), says Gervase of Eleanor herself.[11]

The young king was a Poitevin.[12] He was tall, beautifully formed of body, of most agreeable countenance, so full of golden words that few could resist his blandishments. He had a native warmth and grace that drew his own generation to him irresistibly. He was grandly munificent. Guillaume le Maréchal describes him as the "beauty and flower of all Christian princes, and the fountain of largess." The prince had a regal taste for splendor and for military pageantry that gave some semblance of reality to the titles he bore. The Abbé of Mont-Saint-Michel tells that once, when a gay impulse was on him, the prince bade his heralds summon all the knights in Normandy who bore the name of Guillaume to dine with him, and one hundred and ten guests hastened to the royal board.[13] Salimbene relates that once the young king and his followers came to a spring to drink after a strenuous hunt; there it was discovered that the servants had brought only one bottle of wine for the prince and none for the company.[14] Observing this, the young king emptied the bottle into the spring that all might share the little he had. Whether true or false, the story is in character. Yet it must be said that the largess he distributed with so free a hand was the rich substance from his father's treasure chests, or plunder taken on the jousting fields by his valiant knight-at-arms, Guillaume le Maréchal, or the promissory notes of Philip of Flanders. "He was less generous than prodigal," says the monk, Geoffroi de Vigeois; [15] "foolishly liberal and spendthrift," adds the Abbé of Mont-Saint-Michel.[16]

Though lauded as the prince of chivalry and the rewarder of champions in the list, he possessed, if we may credit the biographer of the marshal, no extraordinary skill at arms. His was rather the talent of the patron and the courtier. Inconstancy was his very name. "He was," says the chronicler, "like wax." He had the sudden inspirations and made the imprudent plans of a man unsure of himself, driven now by this, now by that flickering vision of his destiny, by this or that evil counsel, this or that compunction. At various times he fell under the spell of stronger men — Philip of Flanders, Guillaume le Maréchal, the trouvère rebel Bertran de Born. His interests were diffused and without permanence. Often in crises, when his whole attention should have been engaged with affairs, he would be found solitary, deep in a book. He flew easily from rage to tears, from bold defiance to abject submission, from high hope to desperation. "He was," says Newburgh, "a restless youth born for many men's undoing." [17]

Of all his sons Henry loved this eldest one with special predilection. In him were fixed his hopes and his ambitions. The prince was to become the first potentate in Europe, allied to the most noble houses, heir to all the king's own striving and contriving. The beauty and brilliance of the boy promised well, and the king planned to bend the twig to the tree of his desire. Peter of Blois urged Henry to look to the education of the prince. A king without learning, he said, was a ship without a rudder, a bird without wings. But Henry, taught himself by the best masters in Angers and Le Mans, and in the household of his uncle the Earl of Gloucester, did not need the admonition. He placed his heir, as a young child, with the infant Princess of France, in the household of Becket, to be taught, bred to courtesy and to familiarity with men of substance and with the affairs of the king's chancellery. Between the prince and Becket, says the chronicler, there was such love as exists between noble kinsmen whether they happen to be together or apart. They walked abroad hand in hand. Henry himself had often presented the little prince in court to receive the homage of the nobles. He trained him from childhood to sit in his company in the royal assize and at the Christmas and Easter courts of the Plantagenets. He accustomed him early to *chevauchée*, and himself taught him all the arts of the huntsman and the falconer. For tutors he gave him the most famous scholars and the best legists of the day. He tried as far as he could to center the prince in England, to indenture him to English law and custom, and for this purpose maintained for him separate households, apart from the itinerant royal ménage.

But the prince had known no settled residence, no continuity of experience, no steady discipline. His precocious induction into the role reserved for him made him witness of the violent conflicts of the mid-century and subject to the tensions of irreconcilable loyalties. As a child of nine he had been snatched from the well-ordered household of Becket to attend the stormy assize of Clarendon, and had been moved now with indignation, now with ruth, in the bitter quarrels that ensued between the king his father and the archbishop who claimed him as his "fond foster son." He saw his father first in terrible triumph over Becket and later enduring his penitential stripes for his confessed share in the martyrdom. As son-in-law of Louis Capet, he was subjected in the French court to a view of Angevin history and Angevin aspirations quite inconsistent with that which prevailed in Rouen and Le Mans. He was party to the domestic strife that had driven the Countess of Poitou to her own domain, and there, in her lively continental court, he had learned to prefer the glamor of chivalry and romance to the hardier business of synod and assize in Britain.

The Plantagenet princes could not but feel that the foyer of the culture to which they were heir was on the Continent in those ancient capitals of Normandy, Maine, Anjou, and Poitou, with their venerable establishments, their mellower atmosphere, their greater luxury and more elegant diversions. The young king was ill content to accompany his father on his laborious inspection of garrisons and law courts, of tax and tithe in Britain, while his junior in Poitou enjoyed ampler freedom in the more brilliant environment of the queen.

Richard, the queen's favorite son, was the best Angevin among the brothers.[18] Though taller than his father, he probably bore most resemblance to him. He had the ruddy color of the Angevins, their bold expression and furious eyes. His build was stocky but not ungraceful, his fiber sinewy, his stance that of the soldier and the horseman. In physical strength and in boldness of action, he greatly surpassed his brother. He was a born strategist and warrior and in all this a worthy descendant of the Angevins, Foulques the Black, Foulques, King of Jerusalem, and of his own father. His mind was quick and his interests were more concentrated and persistent than the young king's. Nothing more completely engaged his attention than military engines, the design of fortresses, the craft of siege and assault. He displayed likewise the Angevin suddenness and violence. He was quick to take offense and to accept a challenge and more ruthless to conquered foes than the king his father. This prince figured at tournaments less often than the young king. He had plenty of real warfare to divert him in Poitou and Aquitaine and needed no mimic outlet for his genius on the jousting fields. But when he did appear, the hardiest made way for him. Though born in Oxford, he early abandoned interest in England as having no special significance for him. He never learned Saxon nor adapted himself to insular ways of life. He cared "not an egg" that Henry should wear the crown of England so long as Poitou was his portion and Poitiers his capital.

No *preux chevalier* bred in the queen's court could remain a mere martial hero. His was also the legacy of the troubadours, and his nurture was theirs too. The Countess of Champagne taught him to love poetry and romance. Under her tutelage he composed verse quite worthy of his Poitevin lineage. A little survives to give substance to the fame he enjoyed as a poet and musician bred in the tradition of his mother's race. It is said that it sometimes pleased him to appear in choir where he sang with gusto, encouraging his fellow choristers to give more breath to their psalmody.[19] At mass he was punctilious.

Richard was less affable in crowds than Henry, more selective in his friendships, and less accessible to general company. He lacked the charm that attracted a large personal following to the young king. He often ruffled his peers with an overweening brusqueness. His reputed popularity was, like that of the elder king, especially among small folk, whom he won by acts of condescension and generosity.[20] Though he knew how to reward service and gain favor with largess, his giving was less indiscriminate than his senior's and his avarice was much more marked. In comparing the brothers Giraldus says, "Henry was a shield, but Richard was a hammer."

Geoffrey and John, Giraldus goes on to remark, were "corn in the ear and corn in the blade" — very like in some respects.[21] Both were smaller in stature than their elder brothers and darker in coloring. Geoffrey was thought to have perhaps the best mind in the family, if ability meant an extraordinary ingenuity in intrigue and a persuasiveness that few could resist even when they knew they could not rely upon his plans or his promises. He had below the surface, says Giraldus, more aloes than honey in his constitution; but with ingratiating air, shedding oil in his speech, he succeeded with suavity in turning reason upside down and making black seem white with remarkable contrivance. Benedict of Peterborough names him "that son of iniquity and perdition." He was of reckless daring, bold, decisive, swift as lightning. When confronted with his own crookedness, he was shameless, crafty, full of excuses. John in the early seventies was still a child. He had been too young to share in the partitions of Montmirail.

It was upon these sons who had known nothing constant or permanent in life, who had been bred in the most different milieus, assigned to empty and vainglorious titles, dandled, according to the "hungry falcon" politics, with great expectations constantly deferred, placed in positions of inevitable rivalry, made witness to violent feudal conflicts and domestic scenes, that Henry was obliged to depend as the instruments of his policy. They were apter tools for the ripening schemes of Louis Capet and the injured queen.

The young Plantagenets, whose prospects were so magnificent, naturally drew a great following among their own generation, a swarming horde that gave deep uneasiness not only to Henry Fitz-Empress, but to the heads of noble families everywhere. The biographer of Guillaume le Maréchal gives an idea of how this rabble of courtly *routiers* amused itself upon the jousting fields of western Europe.[22] To the tournaments, occurring in a brisk season about twice a month from Pentecost to the feast of Saint John, flocked the young bloods, sometimes three thousand strong, taking possession of the nearest town. Thither also flocked horse dealers from Lombardy and Spain, from Brittany and the Low Countries, as well as armorers, haberdashers for man and beast, usurers, mimes and storytellers, acrobats, necromancers, and other gentlemen of the lists, the field, the road. Entertainers of every stripe found liberal patronage; troubadours singing of love and war and the *bel saison* in the south country, storytellers out of Brittany, goliards from the Paris streets. For the elect there were feasts in upper chambers. We hear from the romance of *Joufrois* that for lesser dignitaries tables were laid in the streets, where candles set in blossoming pear trees assisted the moon to light the scene.[23] The gossip of palace and fief and school, of shrine and cloister, of synod and assize, flew through the town. Forges rang in the smithies all night long to repair the jousters' gear. Brawls with grizzly incidents — a cracked skull, a gouged eye — occurred as the betting progressed and the dice flew. To cry up their champions in the field came ladies of fair name and others of no name at all. There was dancing below the pavilions on the greensward, with heralds and knights clapping the measures and calling out the changes.

The hazards, the concourse, the prizes of the tourney keyed men to the pitch of war. The stakes were magnificent, for the victor held his prize, horse and man, for ransom. And for these ransoms fiefs went in gage or the hapless victim fell into the hands of usurers, giving his men, and in extremity himself, as hostages. Fortunes were made and lost on the point of a lance, and many a mother's son failed to ride home.

The freehanded young king became the idol of his following. His household had gathered moss in rolling about and came to comprise a fine company of knights and squires dependent on the royal treasury when the loot from tournaments was not forthcoming.[24] Guillaume le Maréchal, to whom his biographer says Henry committed the oversight of his heir, was a fortune seeker in the lists, like many another impecunious knight, but he was honest too, and it is easy to see that his service to both the elder and the younger kings at the same time strained to the utmost his chivalric virtuosity. He is seen laboring in his dual and inconsistent role. As master of the young king's household, he looks to the entertainment of the knights who gather before their tents on the day of combat, and of the *dames choisies* who ride down from the neighboring castles to the margins of the lists. He himself rallies the heralds, sings topical songs for the company after the manner of a good jongleur, claps the measures for the dances. In those flagging moments while the spectators wait for the jousting to begin, he brings off spontaneously the most brilliant and generous little exploits. Amidst bursts of laughter and applause, he unhorses a parading coxcomb knight and turns over his beautifully caparisoned mount to some eager young squire, who is thus made a prince for a day. But when the trumpets sound, Guillaume leads the young king's knights to victory in the field, and takes good care to bring in enough ransoms to keep the expenses of his lord's household somewhere near the inadequate allowances of the elder king for the maintenance of his heir. Even with his best efforts, the marshal could not contrive to make ends meet. "God," he said in this connection, "is kind and courteous, and comes to the aid of those that trust in Him." [25] "As for the young king's personal exploits," says Guillaume, "neither Alexander the Great nor King Arthur himself accomplished so much in so little time." [26] Ultimately King Henry and King Louis and the Pope were obliged to outlaw this pastime of the younger generation.[27] The giving of hostages, the taxing of vassals for their lords' debts, contributed its bit to that movement which subsequently became known as the rise of the third estate.

It was not merely the young king's extravagance that bore down on the Angevin. His heir was restless and foot-loose and went about acquiring grievances. He was bored with the dull role of king's apprentice. Every argument with his father led to the same end. He wanted independence. He demanded England, or at least Normandy, or even Anjou, for his own domain. Had not his brothers the freedom of their own provinces? Then why not the principal heir of his? He railed at the meagerness of his subsidies, yet he was expensive too. He wanted to get away from guidance and surveillance on visits to Paris, Rouen, Arras, Poitiers, where the fresh breath of life stirred in the century. Reproached for vagrancy, he flew into Angevin rages. Though named king, he possessed no furrow in England nor in Gaul on which to set his foot. Stay where? He was only a pensioner on the king's bounty, generous or niggardly, as the case might be. Neither present cockerings nor future prospects soothed his spleen.

For a time Henry sought with gifts and promises and a slackening of his tether to assuage the young king. But before he could get his son in hand, the menacing aftermath of the Becket affair obliged him to turn his attention to his relation with the church. The Franks had overlooked no device for fixing responsibility for the lamentable tragedy in Canterbury on the King of the English.[28] They besieged Alexander with demands for an interdict upon his lands, so that Henry was forced to send capable agents hurrying to pursue the Frankish envoys to the *curia*.[29] These legists managed to get over the Alps in the dead of winter just in time to stay the censure. When the returning Frankish envoys reached Paris armed with the menace of interdict, they were astonished to hear that the Pope had already dispatched two special legates to Normandy to examine Henry's case and hear his appeal for clemency.

However, while these movements of doubtful issue went forward, the climate of the Continent seemed likely to prove unwholesome for Henry, especially if the envoys for the Franks should get him under censure before the arrival of the legates for whom he had himself appealed. The king therefore resolved to give his attention at this juncture to affairs in Ireland. He had, since the early seventies, had the conquest of that island in progress as a domain for John Lackland, and he had long since received papal assent to his avowed plan to bring its outlandish ecclesiastical practices into line with the usages of Rome.[30] This was a mission certain not to provoke the *curia*.

It was while getting things in hand over there that disquieting rumors of sedition in his own household reached his ears. In those barbarous parts he learned that the great hall in Poitiers with its brilliant assemblies of *preux chevaliers*, his vassals and the queen's, had become a hotbed of sedition, a rendezvous for traitors. He heard the queen herself was the center of an unnatural confederation which included not only the disaffected barons of Brittany, Aquitaine, and Anjou, whom his oppressive measures had moved to revolt, but his own sons, Richard, Count of Poitou, and Geoffrey, Count of Brittany, those beardless youths with whom he had dealt so liberally at Montmirail; his own cousin, Philip of Flanders, whose countess sat in the courts of love; his heir, the young king, whom he had crowned with honors. He heard an incredible thing: that all these beneficiaries of his bounty were moving toward a coalition with his inveterate enemy, the King of France.

These tidings may have somewhat softened Henry's conscience in the Becket matter. At any rate, he hastened to return to Normandy to meet the legates and make his peace, not at any price, but at a good price if necessary, for whatever unwitting share he might have had in the martyrdom of Canterbury. He arrived unostentatiously from England, but so suddenly that Louis gave him credit for some supernatural means of locomotion. "Now in Ireland, now in England, now in Anjou, the King of the English seems rather to come on wings than by horse or boat." [31] He met the legates sent to him in Savigny. He found them more stern than he had hoped in their terms for absolution and undertook to whittle these down. Henry let the cardinals know how far he would go in reconciliation. At length in dudgeon, he reined in his horse as if to leave the parley.

"I will go back to Ireland," he said, "where I have plenty of business to engage me." [32]

Some of the king's Norman bishops followed him to Avranches on the western marches of Normandy and persuaded him to a second conference. There for some days they awaited the arrival of the young king so that he might witness and confirm the agreement.

Presently a gathering at the cathedral of Saint Andrew, which still marks the site, witnessed a signal event.[33] The king, in the presence of a concourse of prelates and nobles, submitted to an examination of his reported crimes against Thomas, in which he showed himself spiritually humble, contrite, and very reasonable. With his hands on the Gospels and certain holy relics, he swore publicly that he had neither ordered nor desired the death of the archbishop, and that the news of it had been a terrible shock to him. Of his own free will he added that the death of his own father had scarcely affected him more grievously. He admitted, however, that his conscience troubled him for fear he might have had something to do indirectly with the martyrdom. He confessed that he had been exceedingly angry upon hearing of the excommunication of his bishops, and that it was possible that the discomposure of his face, the flashing of his eyes, and certain choleric words that had slipped from his lips in that moment of passion, had put it into the heads of the assassins to avenge his indignation. He would, therefore, he said, not pretend to escape from Christian discipline. He was prepared to accept whatever the cardinals might decree for penance in the circumstances. He was ready to go on pilgrimage to Rome, to Compostella, or even to Jerusalem, if they thought best.[34] The cardinals were convinced that he had "purged his conscience" in the most salutary manner. They must have been puzzled over the stories of his stiff-necked impiety that had circulated through the agency of the Franks in Tusculum and Rome.

At the end of the confession, the cardinals conducted the king to the porch of the cathedral where sinners beyond the pale were customarily dealt with. There Henry knelt upon the pavement and attendants stripped off his outer garment disclosing to astonished spectators a hair shirt, which he was wearing underneath. This too was taken off to expose his bare back to scourgings. A delegation of monks then told off each one his prescribed number of stripes. Everyone was profoundly moved.[35] There was hardly a dry eye among the assistants. Even the cardinals wept. No one records the effect of the scene upon the young king who witnessed the penitential flagellation of his father for a confessed share in the crime against his dear master Becket.

17 ✤

Sedition

FOLLOWING THE PENANCE IN AVRANCHES, Henry undertook to get the young king in hand. Fearing to allow this furious malcontent out of his sight, he dragged him from the spectacle in Saint Andrew's to the province of Auvergne. There the young man found himself, to his surprise, witness to his father's prearrangement of a marriage of John Plantagenet with the heiress of the vast estates of Maurienne.[1] What did this portend — this aggrandizement of the infant John with a great province spreading southward and eastward from the region of Lake Geneva and about the base of the Alps to the frontiers of Italy and the edges of Provence, controlling all the mountain passes and blocking the land routes from Toulouse to Rome? And what, besides the five thousand marks of silver covenanted on the spot, was the *quid pro quo*? When the Count of Maurienne inquired what dower the king meant to set aside for John in his own estates, Henry mentioned the three master castles of Chinon, Loudun, and Mirebeau, marking the triangle where the domains of the three elder Plantagenets converged on the marches of Anjou, Poitou, and Brittany, a region cut from the young king's inheritance.[2] Henry had likewise recently designated for John central estates in England taken also from the portion of the young king.

The family conclave summoned to Limoges to confirm the pact, at which Richard and the queen were present, fell into alarm.[3] What was the meaning of this negotiation? The king was reserving for John strategic strongholds at the very heart of his English and continental domains, carving out an inheritance for this belated scion of the house from portions already assigned to his elders. Was it a scheme for the surveillance of frontiers, and did it presage other whittlings in other provinces? Ireland, Maurienne, and now these castles? At this rate, would John outtop them all? The elder Plantagenets viewed their cadet with bitter hostility and stoutly refused to ratify the pact. However, pledges were exchanged; the Count of Maurienne carried home the marks of silver and Henry took the infant princess into his custody.

While this conclave was in progress, the Count of Toulouse came privily to Henry and warned him of seditions brewing in Poitiers and of the evil influences besetting the young king among his intimates.[4] Henry when perplexed was wont to thrust mongers away and take counsel with himself. He decided to examine the subjects of these rumors. Accordingly, he took young Henry and some of his roistering cavaliers on a hunting expedition in the valley of the Aveyron, and there in the windings of the forest and by the cascading streams where they let their falcons fly, he studied the native qualities of these young men and made his own observations on the pernicious doctrines of Poitiers and the joyous freedom of the jousting fields. What he learned alarmed him; wherefore, when he returned to Limoges, without warning or if-you-please, he banished several *preux chevaliers* from the munificence of the young king's household to their own estates or to whatever brigandage their calling laid in their way. These scurrying fugitives carried their own rancors and the young king's to distant quarters of Gaul. Having purged some of his son's intimates from his following, Henry hastened to provide his heir with more reliable associates.[5]

He furthermore decided to withdraw the youth from the noxious influences of Poitiers and with that intent dragged the prince, hot with resentment and chagrin, a virtual prisoner to Chinon.[6] But while the elder king was in a forty-fathom sleep after a hard day, that light-footed young man escaped from his father's very bedchamber, passed the fortress drawbridge, which only treachery could have opened, and made off before cockcrow for Paris to lay his case before the just tribunal of his father-in-law and overlord, Louis Capet.[7] Unable in two days of posting with relays to overtake the renegade, Henry sought to get his younger sons in custody, only to learn that the queen had already dispatched them also to Paris, where Louis had knighted Richard and was giving the brothers all the help and comfort that he could.

The Easter court in Paris was a signal for a general uprising, which had waited only for the escape of young Henry from his father's surveillance. All of a sudden a hundred helpless individual grievances, some of them reaching far back in time, flowed into a common river bed, whose streams rushed to the city of the Capets. Dispossessed barons, heirs mulcted of their inheritance, vassals impressed for service, adventurers looking for a new disposition of feudal prizes, liege men of the princes, fugitives from the young king's *mesnie*, partisans of the rebellious queen, the watchful houses of Capet, Champagne, and Flanders — all found that their hour had struck.

When Henry's headlong pursuit of his son from Chinon to the French frontier had left him empty-handed, he sent messengers to Paris demanding his father's right to have his heir sent back to Normandy.[8] The bishops who carried his demand to Louis were mild and courteous. Let the young king return to his father, they said, and if he were found to have suffered a grievance, it would be amended. The French king's response was lofty.

"Who is this," he asked, "that makes these demands of me?"

"Sire, the King of the English," came the reply.

"That cannot be," said Louis, "for the King of the English is here with me, and he makes no demands of me by your agency. But if perchance he who was formerly King of the English makes these demands, know that he is king no more. If he is eager to 'amend' anything, the best thing he can do is to cease playing the part of king, since everyone knows that he resigned the kingship to his son." [9]

The bishops returning to Henry to report these things warned him to look not only to the safety of his castles but to the security of his person.

From Rouen, after the flight, the keeper of the young king's seal, whom Henry had placed in office, restored that instrument to the elder king, and with it he sent some of the reliable associates that Henry had added to his son's household, together with their sumpter horses and trappings and such treasure as lay at hand. But, except for the seal, Henry refused to accept these reversions and sent the retainers back with conciliatory gifts of plate and fabrics and injunctions to serve their young lord faithfully.[10]

As for the seal with which the young king had been provided at his coronation, who cared for that trumpery thing? Louis had a new one made for him in Paris. When this was ready, the King of the Franks convened a brilliant assemblage in his city. The foremost bishops and barons of the realm were summoned to confer with the brothers Plantagenet: the house of Champagne, the Counts of Flanders and Boulogne, besides all the conspirators from Henry's domains. Oaths were exchanged. Louis's liege men swore to make no peace with the "former King of the English" without Louis's consent. The new seal then came into use to testify to young Henry's matchless liberality. In return for their homage, Philip of Flanders received Kent and the castle of Dover; his brother, the Count of Boulogne, the County of Mortaine and other appurtenances; William of Scotland, who had already begun incursions in the north of England, received Northumbria to the Tyne; and his brother David the Counties of Huntingdon and Cambridgeshire. Others shared handsomely in the possessions of the elder king. The new seal made in Paris impressed a vast quantity of wax that day, signifying that "he who had formerly been King of the English was king no more." [11] Except for concessions to the Count of Blois in Touraine, where Henry had dispossessed him, and the County of Mortaine, England offered the grand prizes for revolt. For himself the young king preferred to keep the continental domains, those rich and ancient seats of his forebears in Rouen, Le Mans, Tours, Angers.

Both weather and the church calendar made midsummer the most agreeable time for military operations on the Continent.[12] The barons of France, who detested the cold, went to war by the almanac, awaiting, as Rigord explains, that season "when the grain began to head and the fields were fair with flowers." On June 29, 1173, Philip of Flanders laid siege to Aumale north of Rouen; and only a little later Louis and the young king attacked

Verneuil to the south;[13] later still the barons of Brittany seized and held the strong fortress of Dol on their frontier. From England came news of rapine on the Scottish border, of castles far and wide falling into the hands of traitors. The English dispatched everything, says Diceto, except the Tower of London to implore Henry to come to the rescue of his kingdom.[14]

The correctly scheduled maneuvers of the Franks gave the Angevin a brief respite to organize defense. The defection of his sons and the dread of treachery among his barons deprived him of his normal levies. He dipped deeply into his treasure and put his jeweled coronation sword in gage to hire twenty thousand mercenaries. Employing these with the energy, dispatch, and that Angevin good luck that seemed to his enemies to prosper all his enterprise, he put out one by one the fires of sedition that had broken out on all the borders of his domains. By accident the Count of Boulogne met his death before the castle of Drincourt in Normandy,[15] whereupon Philip of Flanders withdrew from the campaign directed against Rouen. At the collapse of these allies, Louis prudently withdrew from Verneuil. The forty days' military service owed by his vassals was expiring, and he had no idea of going so far as to invest his royal treasure to buttress the young Plantagenets. Some of Henry's mercenaries, having reduced ancillary castles, presently captured Dol. Arriving with incredible speed hard upon that event, the king took a host of captives, including some of the banished remnants of the young king's household.[16]

By September the leaders of the revolt were sufficiently depressed to seek a truce with Henry. The conspirators fronted the king at the ancient trysting place under the Gisors elm.[17] But Henry's victories were not yet decisive enough to bring them to complete surrender. The revolt was gaining headway in England and they hoped to haggle for handsome gains. Though Henry tried to buy his sons out of the rebellion with unexpectedly generous terms, the brothers and their adherents withdrew to await further decisions in the field.

⚜

While the confederates in Paris through the unseasonable months gathered resources for new campaigns, Henry, resisting the appeals from Britain, turned his own operations southward toward the queen's provinces. There, he made sure, was the cradle of conspiracy, the wellspring of all his miseries.[18] Through the Archbishop of Rouen he made an appeal to Eleanor to end the suicidal strife by restoring her sons to amity with him, and warned her that she would be the author of a general ruin if she persisted in inciting them. The archbishop, addressing her as "pious Queen, most illustrious Queen," wrote that Henry was prepared to forget his past wrongs and receive her again into the plenitude of his grace; but that if she disowned her wifely duty and continued to embitter her sons against their father, he himself would, "albeit with grief and tears," feel obliged, as her ghostly father, to visit her with extreme penalties. The archbishop buttressed his exhortation elaborately with scriptural references.[19] Since this warning had produced no visible effect, Henry proceeded in another way. He began by clearing a wide swath north of her capital. He stormed and took the castles of rebel vassals between Tours and Poitiers, razing their walls and burning their ruins, uprooting orchards and vineyards, leaving terror in his wake, and filling the dungeons of Normandy with the captives that he seized. Where, if not with that archconspirator, Raoul de Faye, her kinsman, her confidant, the keeper of her soldiers and her revenues, would the queen be found? He stormed and took Faye-la-Vineuse, but found there neither Raoul nor the queen.

Meanwhile, somewhere in the smoking wilderness north of Poitiers, Henry's reconnoiterers descried a small band of Poitevin knights fleeing over the map of desolation he had made, toward the frontiers of the French domain. Overhauling this remnant, they found not Raoul de Faye, for he had crossed the boundary of the Chartrain on his way to Paris, but Eleanor the queen, disguised in man's attire, astride her mount.[20] Had she also decided at the last moment, but too late, to betake herself to the refuge of her overlord in Paris? With her rode a fear-stricken and bedraggled remnant of her noble household, jousters and troubadours forsooth. Among her captors she faced some who had lately been of her household: Poitevin barons rich with her bounty, chevaliers who had paced the terrace of her palace under the recent Easter moon, which had hardly waned.[21] The time and place of her betrayal are obscure. The torch of the rebellion was extinguished in silence. It was perhaps the portcullis of Chinon that rasped down on the queen's little train. The chroniclers say not a word.

Subsequently, at Pentecost in 1174, Henry arrived in Poitiers on the threshold of that elegant hall which had lately been the scene of such glittering spectacles. Since the Countess of Champagne's last recorded judgment in the courts of love dates from this spring, it may perhaps be assumed that she stood by her mother's citadel until the last moment. Certain it is that Henry swept out that hall and extinguished the fires that had flared up briefly on the hearthstones of Guillaume le Grand and Guillaume le Troubadour, in their ancient high place of Poitiers. Later we find Marie carrying on in Champagne, patroness of Chrétien and André and others who may perhaps have wrought together in the queen's court. It seems also that the Countess of Flanders reached her goodly city of Arras, for one of the chroniclers reports that her husband Philip in the next year had one of his vassals beaten half dead and then suspended head downward in a sewer for sighing Poitiers-fashion in the presence of his countess.[22]

Henry took valuable prizes in the queen's famous palace. He ordered the royal smacks to put into the port of Barfleur and on them in the early summer of 1174 he assembled the remnant of the royal academy of Poitiers: Eleanor, the mistress of them all; his son John and his daughter Joanna; Marguerite and Alais, the French king's two daughters; Constance of Brittany, Emma of Anjou, the infant of Maurienne, and other highborn ladies. And if Marie de France was, as some now suppose, the king's sister, she too may have been of that company.[23]

The Channel was, as the chroniclers say, "big" that day, and mariners reminded the king of the calamity of the White Ship in the waters off Barfleur. But Henry could not wait for weather, for the young king and the Count of Flanders were in Flemish ports awaiting a favorable wind for an invasion of England. With more than his customary pandemonium, Henry embarked his mercenaries and his captives in some forty ships. Then, spreading his hands to the stormy sky and uttering one of those challenges that served him for prayer, he called upon heaven to let the sea overwhelm his boats with all their freight unless God meant to vindicate his wrongs.[24] With difficulty and after many buffetings, the smacks rode into Southampton on an evening tide. Thence the king distributed his captives in strong places out of the reach of Poitevin treachery. Marguerite was sent to the castle of Devizes and Eleanor was immured in Salisbury Tower, there to reflect upon that code of chivalry which was the masterpiece of all the arts that flourished under her patronage.[25]

For the moment the feudal system triumphed. Sedition looked out from barred windows upon a world of havoc. The poets were dispersed, some to sing no more. The Poitevin knights who escaped went back to their native anarchy. Without regard for the *Tractatus*, the heiresses of Poitou and Aquitaine were henceforth given to those barons to whom they were due. The code of Marie and André the Chaplain fell for a time in abeyance. But ideas had gone forth from the palace in Poitiers, and these remained to shed a brightness in the world when rods had fallen from the hands of feudal kings and bolts had rusted in the tower of Salisbury.

Having looked to the security of his captives, Henry went at once, not to the succor of his hard-pressed liege men, but to the shrine of Saint Thomas to conclude his penance in the place hallowed by the martyrdom.[26] When, at the edge of Canterbury, he came within sight of the cathedral crowned with its golden cherubim, he put off his soldier's habit and shoes, donned simple pilgrim's wool, and made his way barefoot over the rough cobbles of the streets. The rumor of his coming had drawn a crowd, but permitting no pomp of royal welcome, he went directly to the crypt, where, without food or sleep, he passed the night kneeling before the tomb shedding abundant tears. At matins he rose and made a tour of the ambulatory and heard early mass. Then, as at Avranches, he offered his bare back to scourgings, and the monks of Canterbury, some of whom had witnessed the martyrdom, each laid on three stripes.[27] Henry was then raised from the pavement, refreshed, and supplied with relics. He had come to peace at last with Thomas without the interjection of the salvos.

As he hastened back to London he was beset with alarming tidings. The King of Scotland and his confederates were laying waste the marches of the north; a troop of five hundred mercenaries dispatched from the Continent by the Count of Flanders was harrying East Anglia;[28] strong castles had fallen into the hands of his enemies. However, the troops of the young king, expected to sustain the rebels in Britain, had not yet found favorable weather for sailing from Flanders for Dover.

In spite of the reassurances of loyal Londoners who met him with pledges and gifts outside the walls, Henry was weary and disheartened by the harbingers of disaster and the heavy odds against him. As soon as he reached his palace of Westminster, he dismissed his retainers and went at once to his closet. No harp or viol, says the chronicler, upon this night broke the stillness of his chamber. Overcome with the fatigues of his pilgrimage and his three-day fast, he took to his couch, called his physician for a blood letting, and then, leaning on his elbow, dozed while a varlet chafed his feet bruised from the rough stones of Canterbury. Suddenly someone beat loudly on the door. The keeper rushed to quiet the disturbing noise.

"Who's there?" he called. "Begone. Come in the morning. The king is asleep."

But Henry, with one ear still open to the world, started up and shouted, "Open the door."

Without ceremony a young man whom the king had seen in the service of his faithful De Glanville burst, all sweating from the saddle, into the room and approached his couch. In spite of the joyful aspect of the youth, Henry braced himself for evil news. To his astonishment, the messenger in a tumult of words poured out the tidings of signal victories for Henry's forces in the north. The King of Scotland, his legs tied under his horse's belly, a captive of De Glanville in Richmond Castle; his barons routed, taken. The rebellion in the north, surprised by Henry's men and lacking the expected support of the young king's diversionary attack in the south, collapsed in a single day. Henry, never a careless optimist, could hardly credit his senses, even when shown letters with De Glanville's seal.

"By my faith," cried the young man, "may I be nailed to a cross, or hanged by a rope, or burnt at the stake, if all this be not confirmed by noon tomorrow."

Throwing off his coverlet, Henry leapt from his bed.

"Now," cried the king, "God be thanked for it, and Saint Thomas the martyr, and all the saints of God."

He then went about the palace rousing his sleep-drunk retainers from their midnight rest. In the morning he ordered the bells in all the churches of London to ring out the tidings to the loyal burghers and the garrisons in the Tower.[29]

Three weeks had sufficed for the control of the revolt in England and the capture of the principal rebels. But across the Channel the young king and Philip of Flanders were still stalking abroad. Louis had recalled them from their scheme of invading England when he had learned of Henry's departure from Barfleur on the wings of a gale with his mercenaries and his precious hostages, two of whom were Capetian flesh and blood. The Franks as usual were just too late. But the forces that had been assembled in the Channel ports of Flanders could be turned to other uses. About the first of August, under Louis's personal direction, they attacked the capital of Normandy.

Rouen, from its position on a loop of the Seine and under the shelter of background heights, was highly defensible, and the Franks could come at it only in a narrow quarter. Here for more than two weeks they battered at its walls day and night, but were held off by the burghers and the garrison.[30] Then came the tenth of August. This was Saint Lawrence's day, and Louis held Saint Lawrence in special veneration. He proposed a truce so that he and all good Christians could observe the feast.

The burghers of Rouen gave their assent without reluctance, but they used the respite unchivalrously for other purposes than that for which it was designed. They took the saint's day to thumb their noses at the Franks. Young men and maidens, says the chronicler, poured from the gates of Rouen, disported themselves with song and dance along the river in plain view of the armies encamped before them, practicing feats of derring-do, tossing their lances under the very eyes of their assailants. Philip of Flanders, who in two ventures had been unable to take the city, saw derisive gestures in these maneuvers and desired to take vengeance for the effrontery. He tried to poison Louis's mind with a perfidious scheme.

"Behold," he said, "the city for which we have sweat so long is now ripe for attack. Engrossed now with singing and sports, it offers itself an easy prize. Let us take arms quietly, set ladders to the walls, and overwhelm those who flaunt us."

"Heaven forbid," said Louis, "that I should stain my honor with such a blot. I have granted a truce this day for the veneration of the most blessed Lawrence."

But Philip's suggestion found general favor and Louis was overruled. Heralds went about secretly among the tents of the Franks giving orders for an attack without warning. However, as Newburgh relates, it happened that some monks of Rouen were celebrating the feast of the saint in more reverent ways in the lofty tower of a church overlooking the countryside. From their height they observed suspicious movements in the camps of the Franks and so, without waiting for consultation with their garrisons, they pulled the rope of that mighty bell, "old Rouvel," and sounded a warning to the burghers still amusing themselves far and wide. The people poured into the gates and, taking their places upon the walls, they gave the Franks such a reception that "the perfidy was turned against those who devised it."

Henry, on learning in England that his enemies were knocking at the gates of Normandy, roused himself again. Taking some of his more important captives seized in Britain, to whose number he added the King of Scotland, and embarking a contingent of Welsh soldiers with his *routiers,* he crossed to Barfleur. He stowed his hostages in Caen and Falaise and then hastened to Rouen to find the city stoutly besieged, though the crisis had been held off by the vigilance of the monks and the valor of the burghers. Henry was received into the gates on the day after the treachery to such a ringing of bells as had never been heard before — old Rouvel joined by the clamor of all the many belfries in the capital of the Norman dukes and the blare of trumpets from all its towers. The report circulated that he was prepared to cross the frontiers of Normandy with an army of redoubtable Welsh to lay siege to Paris itself.[31]

Louis was stupefied by the suddenness of Henry's arrival and alarmed by the accounts he had heard of the army of barbarous outlanders the English king had brought with him.[32] He took counsel with Philip of Flanders and the young king. Thereupon these allies folded their tents, destroyed their shelters for the siege, set fire to their engines, and withdrew, not, remarks the chronicler, without loss of honor.

The siege of Rouen had lasted just over three weeks. At the end of it, no foe of consequence was left in the field. Henry's victory was signal and complete from Scotland to the Loire, from the Seine to Finisterre. Nothing remained but to gather in his renegade sons. Pursuing these fugitives from place to place with threats and promises, he brought them together at Montlouis between Tours and Amboise at the end of September. Though the king displayed no thirst for vengeance, the rebels who had been offered good terms at Gisors the year before now contented themselves with less; yet never before had Henry conceded so much to give substance to the promises of Montmirail.[33]

The young king, instead of one half the revenues of England with four castles there, or if he preferred, one half the revenues of Normandy with three castles there, now received an annual stipend of £15,000 Angevin, with two castles of Henry's designation. Richard, instead of one half the revenues of Aquitaine and three castles there, was allowed one half the revenues, but only two castles suitable for residence, and these without garrisons. Geoffrey received, as before, the inheritance of Constance of Brittany. But it was now stipulated that Henry's provisions for John were to stand. Castles on both sides were restored to ante-bellum status and Henry liberated nearly one thousand hostages, almost ten times as many as the young king was able to free. Having triumphed, Henry was magnanimous. He placed the blame for the execrable strife on interested troublemakers — Louis, the queen, ambitious barons — and excused his sons' perfidy because of their youth. However, he took the occasion to document the treaty of Montmirail. Like William the Conqueror, he made it clear that, although all his strivings were for his sons' sakes alone, he had no intention of casting off all his clothes until he was ready to take to his bed. Richard and Geoffrey renewed homage to their father; but the young king was courteously excused because of his royal title.[34]

18 ✦

Poor Prisoner

You have been snatched from your own lands and carried away to an alien country. Reared with abundance of all delights, you enjoyed a royal liberty. You lived richly on your own inheritance; you took pleasure in the pastimes of your women, in their songs, in the music of lute and drum. And now you grieve, you weep, you are consumed with sorrow. But come back to your own towns, poor prisoner. Where is your court? Where are the young men of your household? Where are your counselors? Some, dragged far from their own soil, have suffered a shameful death; others have been deprived of sight; and still others wander exiled in far places. You cry out and no one heeds you, for the King of the North holds you in captivity. But cry out and cease not to cry; lift your voice like a trumpet and it shall reach the ears of your sons. The day will come when they shall deliver you, and you shall come again to dwell in your own lands.

Richard le Poitevin, Lament for Eleanor

HENRY HAD NO NEED OF TRUMPETS to tell him that sedition in Poitou had not been quenched by the imprisonment of Eleanor. He had suppressed the rebellion that had threatened the Angevin empire with a success so signal that it was popularly attributed to the miraculous intervention of Saint Thomas. But to the prescient Angevin the conclusion had less the character of finale than of ominous prelude. The whole uprising had revealed, not only to him, but to his enemies, the extent of a many-sided discontent that needed only coherence to be overwhelming. The queen, though in his hands, remained the object of intrigue, the inspiration of her rival foot-loose sons and of the turbulent fortune seekers who found their profit in war and rapine. The king turned over in his mind the problem of what to do with his captive.

Some of the considerations that had boggled Louis's counsels when he had taken the Countess of Poitou in custody in Antioch in the mid-century now, twenty-five years later, perplexed Henry in Winchester. To divorce her might be tempting; the grounds were excellent — treason and two more degrees of consanguinity than had been sufficient in Louis's case — but he could not set her free in her own estates to make some new alliance of her own. Capable as he was of reading the lessons of history, he had no mind to repeat Louis's fatal blunder. He needed no legates to suggest to him how scrupulous the King of France would be in the interests of his vassal, if once she were at liberty. To keep her in custody (forever?) might hinder new intrigues; but this course would prevent him from fortifying himself with a new alliance. His choice was between unsatisfactory alternatives; to divorce her and then imprison her offered the surest prospect of ending her treasons. This remedy, which Louis had not ventured to apply, Henry tried.

About All Saints in 1175 Cardinal Huguezon arrived in England ostensibly to quiet a controversy between York and Canterbury. But more than one chronicler relates that Henry had bespoken the cardinal on an affair of his own and that he poured much sterling into Huguezon's coffers to expedite his business.[1] He expected the legate to rid him of the disastrous Poitevin.[2] What he proposed was that, after a divorce that would leave him free for a possible new alliance, the Countess of Poitou should renounce the pomps of this world and exchange the coronet of her forebears for the abbatial cross and other insignia of the Abbess of Fontevrault.[3]

The important establishment of Fontevrault, that rich community of monks and nuns ruled always by a noble abbess, seemed a suitable sanctuary for the queen. It was in the countryside of her predilection, yet safe in Angevin territory.[4] It was par excellence the asylum where ladies of rank whose worldly destinies were at an end, or the turbulent or merely inconvenient relicts of kings and princes and high barons, or the superfluity of princesses that embarrassed noble houses, were given an interval to put off vaingloriousness before putting on immortality.[5] The hierarchies of the world were there respected, the commitment dowries regal, the dignities high, the preferments honorable. A cell in Fontevrault and ultimately an enrollment in its necrology should have satisfied a captive queen of fifty-three, whose path in life had led her in any case to seclusion from the world.

But the queen was not reasonable. She refused to forget her sovereign inheritance, her loyal sons, her liege men, or the fact that her provinces were in the vassalage of France, or that her favorite son had been invested with their titles. Even at fifty-three, she felt no vocation for the monastic life. She would entertain no idea of going back to the region of Poitiers in the weeds of an abbess. She had the support of her eldest three sons, who had been summoned to the Easter court in Winchester in 1176 for this matter and probably also to discuss the projected marriage of Joanna Plantagenet to William, King of Sicily. It is said that Eleanor appealed to the Archbishop of Rouen as her ghostly father against closing the cloistral doors upon her, and that he, in spite of the fact that she had the year before ignored his exhortations to be reconciled with Henry, refused his consent to her commitment to the abbey. However, domestic fury notwithstanding, Henry appealed to Alexander for license to repudiate the queen.

Even though in durance Eleanor seems not to have been strictly confined to a solitary tower nor deprived of the light of heaven. If one may judge by the centers from which her allowances for maintenance were paid, she appears to have moved about, sojourning at times in Salisbury, Winchester, or Ludgershall, in Berkshire or Buckinghamshire, but always under the surveillance of De Glanville or Fitz-Stephen or some other high public servant — watched, restrained, denied her sovereign liberty, her ancestral revenues, the use of her years of prime.[6] The king, says Gervase, ordered her kept in custody in the most strongly fortified towns.[7] Her resources in this seclusion dwindled to mere pittance, if the Pipe Rolls show their totality. Upon a few occasions in the years of her confinement, she emerged, probably on the demand of her children, to preside at some family conclave or plenary seasonal court. Thus at the time of her daughter Matilda's visit to Britain with her children, Eleanor appeared at Winchester and in something more than penitential garb.[8] The Pipe Rolls record a royal expense of more than £28 for scarlet robes, gray fur, and embroidered cushions for her, together with perquisites for her maid Amaria; and upon another occasion a payment for a gilt saddle for the queen with fur and raiment. Twice during her surveillance she was taken under custody to the Continent to justify Henry's claims for lands she held in fee.[9] But, except for brief journeys, she who had been the observed of all observers was held back from the currents of life and obliged to survey from the windows of her prison events to which she had given impulse. For news from that world she became dependent upon her keepers and the chaplains who ministered to her spiritual needs. "It is in solitude," wrote Pierre de la Celle, "that merits accumulate." Some of the queen's purveyors learned in time to admire her insight and her fortitude.

❖

Just what plans Henry revolved after the rebellion of 1173 for the reordering of his whole dynastic system is matter for conjecture. But his project for divorce gave rise to various speculations, which may have been bred from fear and suspicion in the minds of the young Plantagenets and spread from thence. A theory circulated that Henry, having lost confidence in the beneficiaries of Montmirail, who had proved ungrateful for his paternal liberality, weighed the possibility of repudiating that Poitevin brood of eaglets, retrieving his misprized gifts, and setting up the child John, who had shared neither the dispositions of Montmirail nor the unfilial upbringing of his elder brothers, as the chief heir and object of his bounty. For John the king had made a conquest of Ireland, the lordship of which he now, in the presence of his barons and bishops, conferred on his youngest son;[10] for John he had cut strategic portions both in England and Anjou from the young king's inheritance; and now, the infant of Maurienne having died, he arranged a marriage between John and his own (the king's) cousin, Isabelle (otherwise Hawisa or Avise) of Gloucester, the heiress of the most powerful earl in England who had defended the hereditary claims of Matilda Empress. These enrichments were viewed as something more than the mere providing for John Lackland his due place in the sun.[11] Furthermore, in spite of pressures from the Île de France and the importunities of Richard, Henry continued to put obstacles in the way of the marriage of the Count of Poitou to Alais Capet, which had been arranged at Montmirail. Why? Why did Henry withhold the Frankish princess, who was of marriageable age, from her betrothed, whereas Marguerite had been wedded to the young king in infancy? Alais's dowry, Bourges and its appurtenances in Berry, was as essential to rounding out the Angevin frontiers as Marguerite's dowry, the Norman Vexin. Why did Henry hesitate? For what destiny was Alais waiting?

It would be interesting to know who presided in the Plantagenet courts in Britain after the stormy Channel passage of the royal ladies in the summer of 1174. In that year Henry gave his sister, Emma of Anjou, to a Welsh prince who had supported his wars upon the marches.[12] If she who styled herself Marie de France was another sister, she emerges later as Abbess of Shaftesbury. Among the ladies of mark there was that seventeen-year-old matron, the young Queen Marguerite, who doubtless often served in place of the imprisoned queen, for her allowances, as the Pipe Rolls show, now greatly exceeded Eleanor's. But Marguerite followed the young king's fortunes and spent long intervals in Angevin domains abroad, or in Paris with the Capets. Henry was often at Woodstock in 1176 and 1177, and possibly Rosamond Clifford sometimes kept him company there; but she died in 1177 after a pious retreat in Godstow nunnery.

In the court there remained alone of the famous coterie of the Plantagenets the Capetian princess Alais. In 1176 she was sixteen. No fault was found with her person. She was comely, gifted, nobly dowered, and she too had been polished for her role in the school of Marie of Champagne. Why was the Frankish princess alone of all that noble company of *dames choisies* left unwed in the palaces of the Plantagenet king? Why had other marriages been proposed for the Count of Poitou? The world made these inquiries and the Capets pressed them home. In 1177, in extreme agitation, Louis appealed to Rome to enforce the marriage of Alais to the Count of Poitou on pain of interdict on all the lands of Henry Fitz-Empress on both sides of the Channel.[13]

The chroniclers are discreetly reserved about the facts; but mischievous rumors got abroad and found their way to the court of France. They traveled quite possibly by the agency of the young king and queen, who had been at Winchester at the time of Cardinal Huguezon's visit and had gone from there to Paris. Giraldus relates that Henry, confident of his prospect of getting rid of the queen through his appeal to the Pope, intended to take the Capetian princess for himself, disinherit the fierce eaglets of Poitou as the bastards of a consanguineous marriage, and rear a new progeny to possess the Angevin empire. Giraldus, never more piously enthusiastic than when exposing Henry's vices, declares that after his separation from the queen, the king turned openly to the evil courses he had long secretly pursued. Briefly he flaunted the beautiful Clifford, and when she had vanished from the scene, he made a mistress of his precious hostage, the daughter of his over-lord, the bride affianced to his son.[14] Did the Angevin mean to erase from his life story the chapter of his union with the disastrous Poitevin and go back to his earlier plan for a primary alliance with his overlord? It was re-called that before he had sold his birthright for Poitou and Aquitaine, he had sought a marriage with Louis's eldest daughter, the Countess of Cham-pagne.

❧

Inactivity is shameful for a young man.
(*Long repos pour un jeune homme, c'est la honte.*)
Guillaume le Maréchal, III, 35.

When, after the peace of Montlouis which had ended the rebellion, Henry proposed to take his recreant eldest son with him to England, that young man eluded him. The prince fled to Paris, where he was warned that in Britain he would surely be a captive. Had he not already been his father's prisoner in Argentan? Was not Queen Eleanor held in Salisbury Tower? Had not even the young queen Marguerite been detained in Devizes? Had not the whole Poitevin court been taken into custody? Not for his weight in gold should the young king risk his liberty. However, the Capets did little to relieve their son-in-law from the intolerable debts that oppressed him. With his stipend cut off, the patron of champions cut hardly more figure than a starveling troubadour. At last, by dint of promised indulgence and cajolery and engagements to set his affairs aright, Henry induced the prince to join him. Then, as always, the young king found himself unable to resist the placating grace, the patient overtures of affection that sought, no matter what his derelictions, to bring him home.[15] Before solemn witnesses the young man threw himself at his father's feet, implored his forgiveness, and begged to be received into his homage.[16] Presently, as says Diceto, the two kings whom recently the whole realm could not contain because of their rancor crossed to Britain in the same ship, slept in the same chamber, ate at the same board.

While Henry repaired the havoc in Britain and made it safe after the rebellion, he tried to root the young king there and give him a share in the onerous business of government. Together they made a pilgrimage to Canter-bury and at the shrine purged away some of the bitterness over Thomas that had so long divided them.[17] Then they made a wide circuit of the island.

Their journeys included no tournaments, no courts of love, no lavish banquets, none of those pomps that had brightened civilization in Normandy, Poitou, and the Île de France. Henry apprenticed his son to the somber royal business of putting England in order after the anarchy.[18] He supervised the destruction or sequestration of the fortresses that had withstood him; he saw to the filling of long vacant sees and the election of abbots, and made sure there were no Beckets among the new incumbents; he regularized and concentrated the courts of justice, and dealt severely with those who had taken advantage of the rebellion to trespass on his forests. He received the envoys of foreign states, who sought his arbitration of their conflicts. The succession of synods and assizes, which went round the calendar, was broken only by occasional hunting forays in the vast game preserves that were Henry's pride, or by the loosing of falcons beside English streams. When they came to hall at night, three dishes sufficed for their evening meal. If young Henry had been capable of benefiting by his tutelage, he might have learned the elements of statecraft and caught some vision of his kingly role, for great Henry, freed for an interval from the threats and thwartings of the past decade, now gave England the stoutest fabric and the most ordered government in the western world.

But the elder king's providence was lost upon his son. To the prince the shallowness of the procedure to engage him in kingcraft seemed obvious, for not one tittle of authority had been relinquished to him. Though equipped and rehearsed for the part, he still had no kingly role, no tasks of his own, no realm, no subjects — only a crown, a trumpery seal, regal trappings, and a stipend inadequate for the grandiose pretensions to which the heir of the Plantagenets and the son-in-law of the King of France had been bred. His favorite academy was not the sober and practical one of synod and assize in Britain, but the romantic court of Poitiers, or Paris with its swarms of young men always imagining a new thing; his favorite companions not those legists and men of affairs in London and Rouen, but the impecunious gallants bred on Arthurian romance and Ovidian sophistries in the entourage of the Countess of Champagne.

The deepest bitterness of the young king was rooted in the fact that, after the peace of Montlouis, while he was held in leash, Henry had sent Geoffrey and Richard off to their own prospective provinces with some show of administrative authority. The Count of Poitou had found an outlet for his hardier genius in the substantial business of subduing the feudal anarchy that was perennial in Aquitaine and that had latterly found occasion, in the embarrassment of the elder king, to flare up with unwonted fury.[19] In the south the chief feudatories were individually too strong to be held in a common vassalage. Each sought to get a regional control, and all were restive under the oppressive stewardship of their duchess' foreign consorts. With the job of reducing these barons, Richard proceeded with a savagery and success worthy of the Conqueror himself. One after another the rebel strongholds fell into his hands, and his reprisals spread terror and desolation in the land. He took the fortresses of his enemies, razed their castles, burned their towns, uprooted their orchards and vineyards, sowed their fields with salt, ordered the hands of his captives cut off and their eyes gouged out, and dishonored the women of his hostages with a very sovereign severity.[20] No person, no property was safe from roving bands of *routiers* who lent their aid without scruple to the highest bidder on either side, and in the intervals of unemployment made their livelihood by pillaging the countryside.[21] Geoffroi de Vigeois reports that the people of the Limousin, despoiled of all means of living, were obliged to join the brigands to get a share of their own provisions. Husbandry came to a standstill and the four horsemen stalked the land. The queen's provinces were desolated from end to end. Though Henry never dealt so harshly with conquered foes, this effective work of crushing anarchy was something he could appreciate in a scion of his house. When Richard's resources were not enough for the mercenaries and the siege engines required, the elder king subsidized his son's enterprise.

Before the first breath of spring, the fever to get abroad and rejoin his boon companions took possession of the young king. Richard's reports on his exploits at the Easter meeting of the brothers in Winchester inflamed his zeal. He sought leave to take up his residence in his own titular domains, and when Henry dared not loose him, as he had loosed his brothers, in those old centers of intrigue, the young king declared himself suspicious because Henry had received the homage of Richard and Geoffrey at Montlouis, but had excluded him from this rite.[22] Had this been a plot to deny him his portion by excluding him from the king's allegiance? Was he not, as the Capets had warned him, a captive in his father's palaces? He was sick with suspicion. He railed at the dullness of routine, his meager revenues, his diminished household, his shadow role.

When practical pretexts for getting abroad failed to move the elder king, the prince sought leave to make a Lenten pilgrimage to Saint James of Compostella.[23] Henry saw the youth was frantic to rejoin the malcontents who in the rebellion had put the whole Angevin empire in jeopardy. The elder king had his suspicions too. The young king proved incurably Poitevin and was perhaps at the very moment in the service of the queen. In her school for cavaliers his heir had learned to love the spring not for its summons to pious pilgrimage, but because, as the trouvère Bertran de Born put it, when Lent was over, knights took to the road and the ground trembled with the quake of tournaments. The centers where the flower of chivalry forgathered were the rendezvous of those old enemies who "found more profit in turmoil than in peace." Somehow the elder king stifled the project of pilgrimage, but, as a sop to the young king's discontent, he gave him leave to visit Paris with Marguerite and promised that he should later lend his aid to Richard in his warfare in Poitou.[24] At the same time he kept his hand on the prince's revenues to limit the young man's enterprise.

After a brief stay in Paris, the prince, foot-loose and sour, took his way through Flanders and poured out his spleen to his cousin Philip, whom he found in Arras.[25] The season of tournaments was at hand and heralds were proclaiming the rendezvous and the champions of the lists. Meanwhile the young king, prince among cavaliers, had not the wherewithal to muster his *mesnie* and lead his knights upon the field. Philip of Flanders wiped out this shame at great expense. The heir of Britain was brilliantly equipped by his old associate in the rebellion, and little time was needed to gather again some of those *preux chevaliers* who had fared ill since their banishment by the elder king. The queen's champion and the prince's master-at-arms, Guillaume le Maréchal, flew to his summons. There ensued through the spring a succession of tournaments that revived chivalry from its recent languishment — such splendid affairs as gave some luster at last to the young king's vain titles. Not only rival champions vied with each other in the lists, but squadrons of cavaliers of Normandy, Brittany, Flanders, and the Île de France met each other in heroic contests on the fields. The royal entertainments, the taxes for damage to the countryside, staggered the imagination of prudent men.[26]

When Saint John's day put a term to tournaments, the young king again visited Paris and then journeyed down to Poitou to give that promised aid to Richard, who was still struggling with his barons in the deep south. The young king had no idea of employing himself strenuously to increase the prowess of the Count of Poitou, of whom he was already outrageously jealous. But among Queen Eleanor's fiefs he found again many of his whilom familiars, the portionless "younger sons of younger brothers" whom the elder king had once sent flying from his household, together with sundry outlaws from Anjou and barons from France who had been ruined in the late rebellion. With these the young king found himself a hero, a patron, a prince indeed. These faithful friends courted his magnanimity, nursed his jealousy and wounded pride, awakened dozing suspicions of Angevin treachery. In Poitiers, where the sun lay warm on old roofs and walls, Britain seemed, as it had seemed to the queen, far away on the foggy edges of the world.

In that safe place sedition grew so fast and became so open that the deacon Adam Chirchedune, whom the elder king had set, in guise of vice-chancellor, to keep an eye on the doings of the young king, was on the point of dispatching letters of warning to Henry in Britain; but he was discovered by counterspies with the letters on his person.[27] He was dragged for judgment before the tribunal of the young king and his followers, and the fury of that council at the treachery of the elder king was without bounds. Some held that Henry's agent should be put to death, others that he ought to be flayed alive. The Bishop of Poitiers, interposing, plead Adam's immunity as clerk, so the most drastic suggestions could not be carried out. The young king gravely considered what might be the utmost penalty he could exact from his father's servant for such betrayal. Gathering himself together after a long silence, he said,

"Take him and bind his hands behind his back and have him flogged naked in the squares and outskirts of Poitiers and follow him with a crier that all may know his perfidy. Then take him to Normandy and imprison him in Argentan, and flog him in the public squares of all the towns through which you pass." [28]

Not since Louis Capet, in the ardor of his youth, had come down from Paris to hack off the hands of the queen's rebellious vassals and send their heirs to exile, had Poitiers seen such spectacles in its streets. When Henry had his servant brought to him from Argentan more dead than alive, he suffered an Angevin fury. But he knew beyond peradventure that the rebellion had been reborn.

In the early summer of 1177 Henry was sojourning in Woodstock when a flood of disquieting news reached him from overseas to add to his anxiety over the errantry of the young king. Henry received "unwelcome tidings" from his heir.[29] It is very possible that these concerned the removal of Marguerite from Argentan to Paris to bring forth her first born, not in Anjou or Normandy, but in the city of the Capets. He presently likewise heard that, in spite of the price he had paid for it, his appeal for divorce had failed in the *curia*; and he was warned that a papal legate was hastening from Rome, at the instance of the Capets, to lay an interdict on all his lands unless he speedily celebrated the marriage of Alais and Richard in accordance with the terms of Montmirail.[30]

Henry, who had been at such pains to restore his relations with the church after the Becket tragedy, saw a dire shape in these portents. How was he to contrive simultaneously to keep peace with the church, make sure of the dowry of Alais, so indispensable to his frontiers in Touraine and Poitou, and prevent nevertheless her marriage to the Count of Poitou? It seemed to the Angevin of prime urgency to get Alais's dowry in hand in order to confront the legate with a *fait accompli*, which would shift his own position from that of the aggressor party to that of the aggrieved. With his foot on the soil of Berry, Henry might seem to be merely vindicating long deferred claims to the property against the dilatory Capets; while the legate would be in the inferior position of showing reason why the King of England should withdraw, instead of forbidding him to proceed. The urgency of the situation in Berry was aggravated by the fact that Raoul of Déols, the chief magnate of the province and seigneur of the stronghold of Châteauroux, had lately died (1176), leaving as his sole heir a daughter three years old. It was obviously necessary for Henry to get this marriage prize into his possession as hostage for his demands.

With his baffling program in mind, Henry got together a considerable army, and with this at his back to give weight to his dialectic, he crossed early in September to Normandy. He was later than he meant to be because the outbreak of an old wound from a horse's kick had detained him for a month in Winchester.[31] In Rouen he was met by Richard and the young king, and he found the fulminous legate already beating at the gates with threats of interdict. As always in a dilemma, Henry labored to postpone conclusions. He now asked only for a parley with his overlord with a view to a reasonable settlement of the issues between them.

This interview took place near Ivry on the borders of Normandy late in September.[32] With Louis, besides the legate who had journeyed from Rome to bring the Angevin to justice, were the highest magnates of France — Guillaume, Archbishop of Reims, Philip of Flanders, Thibault of Blois, and others. Louis spoke in his own behalf with deep emotion, charging Henry with a long chapter of unjust encroachments on his domain reaching back for years, but declaring the matter in Berry the most unmitigated affront in that unhappy history. He acknowledged that, because of creeping age and waning strength, he could not with arms vindicate his rights, but he did not therefore renounce them. Appealing to heaven with flowing tears, he charged the heir that had been vouchsafed him and the vassals of his realm to enforce his just claims at a future time. So saying he drew back among his kinsmen.[33]

The moment had come for bringing the wily Angevin to book. But it so befell that the legate had come to the parley consumed by another matter in which the good offices of both kings were required. He had been charged to bear down on the calamitous tidings from Jerusalem that were pouring in flood into the western world and upon a violent upsurge of heresy nearer home in the County of Toulouse. These matters captured the foreground of the parley to the disparagement of the original program. There was never any difficulty in persuading Louis to subscribe to a crusade; and Henry grasped in the project a blessed meed of time for the completion of his own particular designs. What resulted from the conference at Ivry was not the chastisement of the Angevin, but a commitment of the two kings to a joint crusade, the articles for which were hastily stipulated. In the light of this vast project the matter in Berry seemed paltry, thwarting the larger enterprise. Louis agreed to submit his grievance to arbitration; and Henry said he would, after the dowry had been completely resigned to him, look to the promised marriage.[34]

These issues quieted for a time, Henry hastened from the proximity of the legate. He went down to Berry to make all fast in that quarter. He had previously assigned to the vagabond young king the job of securing by force of arms the orphaned heiress of Déols;[35] but since the profits of any such expedition would inevitably enrich the Count of Poitou, the young king was suspected of not having employed his utmost energies on that mission. He had indeed taken the chief fortress of Châteauroux, but only to find the little countess had been spirited away toward the French frontier. The elder king now speedily possessed himself of the infant heiress and took her in custody.[36] He then went southward into Aquitaine to survey the enterprises of his son Richard against his rebel barons. On this journey he ran, by Angevin good fortune, into a very profitable business. Finding the Count of La Marche in difficulties for money to go upon crusade, he purchased his important fief at a handsome bargain. Its situation on the borders of Berry and Poitou made it the most desirable of acquisitions for the defense of Alais's dowry.[37]

For the Nativity in 1177, in order to signalize his successes on all fronts, Henry convened a court of unusual splendor in Angers.[38] There were no local Christmas courts in other feudal centers of the Angevin empire where the *preux chevaliers* could assemble beyond the surveillance of the king. His eldest three sons and his vassals gathered about him in an imposing display of power, peace, and amity. No such concourse of knights was remembered by living men, save only for the coronation of Henry himself and for the crowning of the young king.

✤

From the Capetian point of view the peace of Montlouis had been disquieting. All the odds in the long rivalry seemed in the hands of the crafty Angevin. Henry had recovered his losses and appeased his rebel sons; the nobles who had supported them beheld their castles in ruins for their pains. Not only Louis's chief vassal, the Countess of Poitou, but his own younger daughter were prisoners in Britain. Louis in his sixth decade, in an age when men were old at fifty, felt his grasp on life relaxing. In the latter seventies of the century he began to put his house in order for his "migration from this world." At home he could lay his burdens down gladly, for his heir, Philip Dieu-Donné, had reached the age for knightly exercise. Upon him and his generation would devolve the vindication of the Capets. According to the custom of the royal house, which Henry had already imitated in England and the Countess of Poitou in Aquitaine, Louis planned the consecration of his only son as his successor. He chose for the date of the coronation the Assumption of the Virgin (August 15, 1179) and summoned the magnates of his realm and his remotest vassals to be present on that day in the royal cathedral of Reims.

Louis and the prince with their retinue set out accordingly for the episcopal city, and broke their journey for rest in Compiègne.[39] Here Philip was given leave to hunt with his *mesnie* in the vast forest of the province and for that purpose was given a mettlesome horse, as befitted his rising dignities. The dogs, at once starting a boar, led the huntsmen deep into the wood. For a long time Philip followed the windings of the forest, attended, as he supposed, by his escort. Near sundown he found himself alone in the midst of a vast solitude. The baying of the dogs, the call of the horns had ceased. Unable to take his bearings, the frightened prince gave rein to his horse, but the beast only carried him hither and thither into deeper fastnesses and the haunts of wild creatures. He hallooed, but only the sound of his own voice answered him in the evening stillness. He crossed himself, called upon God, the Blessed Virgin, Saint Denis. At dusk after long meanderings he came upon a little clearing, and there, in the glare of an oast, he beheld a grimy fellow with a hatchet suspended from his neck, busy with his charcoal burning, who looked up at the sound of the youth's approach as if he saw an apparition in the parting of the trees. Philip controlled his fright and addressed him courteously. Surprised beyond measure by the prince's story, the yokel dropped his bellows and led Dieu-Donné quickly by a short path back to the royal lodging. Louis, who had dispatched all the huntsmen to beat the brush with hue and cry, was found beside himself with anxiety.

As a result of fright and exposure, Philip fell into a fever and became so ill that the coronation was out of the question on the day fixed for it, and the physicians even despaired of his life. Louis labored in a panic of woe and dread. For three successive nights the king beheld a vision of Saint Thomas of Canterbury,[40] who admonished him to go to the shrine in Britain to make supplication for his son's recovery. Louis's barons warned him against putting himself at the mercy of "another king" on foreign soil, especially since there was no time to seek safe-conduct; but nothing shook his resolution. Fortifying himself with the name and habit of a pilgrim, and subduing that dread of the sea he had acquired on his return from crusade, he set sail from Wissant by the route Thomas had taken to his martyrdom, and drew up duly under the white cliffs.[41]

Henry, apprised of his imminent arrival, rode all night under a moon in eclipse to meet his overlord in Dover, whither a suitable company of bishops and barons had been hastily summoned to form an escort. Thomas' successor in the See of Canterbury and the king greeted Louis with every mark of sympathy and deference, and the cortege brought him without delay to the shrine. As soon as he arrived in the holy place, the King of the Franks laid a cup brimming with gold upon the tomb and pledged the monks of

Canterbury one hundred tuns of champagne and burgundy annually, together with perpetual freedom from tolls in the Île de France. The author of the *Saga* reports that he even gave to the sanctuary a glowing carbuncle which he highly prized and which Thomas had once desired for the altar of his church.[42]

Louis made a strictly pious business of his one journey to England. So inward was he on this expedition that he scarcely looked over the hedges of the Dover road to survey the rich lands of the Angevin king, which in the time of the rebellion he had rashly pledged to Philip of Flanders. It would be interesting to know what the two kings may have talked about as they traveled together, once they had exhausted the topic of the sick prince. Of Saint Thomas? Of Henry's recent scourgings at the shrine? Of the queen in Salisbury Tower? Of the late rebellion? Of the Princess Alais? There was of course the matter of a new crusade brewing in Europe in consequence of the fearful tidings that continued to arrive from Jerusalem. We do not know what their discourse could have been. Within four days Louis had recrossed to Wissant. Upon his return he found the prince had awakened refreshed from the coma of his fever.

The coronation was set again, this time for All Saints. It was an occasion not less splendid than that which had marked the consecration of the young king in London. Henry did not attend because, as Diceto declares, he wished, as a king himself, to avoid doing homage to Dieu-Donné. But his sons were there to support their rank as vassals. The young king, as Seneschal of France, preceded the prince, carrying the crown. Richard and Geoffrey brought the homage of their provinces, and Philip of Flanders bore in the procession the great sword of Charlemagne.[43]

※

Louis, most pious and Christian King of the Franks, a prince of many virtues and immortal memory, laid aside the burden of the flesh, and his spirit fled to the skies to enter upon its eternal reward with the elect princes.

William of Tyre, II, 45

Louis himself was unable to attend the rite that meant so much to him.[44] The trip to Canterbury had exhausted him; and after that journey, to leave no stone unturned, he had gone to Saint Denis to petition in that holy place the patron saint of France. There in the autumn dampness he caught cold, was attacked by chills, and then suffered a stroke that hampered speech and movement. Thereafter he drifted through the next nine months, a patient valetudinarian, to his last rest. With the shadow of death upon him, he ordered all he had of gold and silver, gems, precious clothing, and royal ornaments, brought to his presence. By the advice of the Archbishop of Paris and the Abbés of Saint Germain and of Saint Genevieve, he looked them over and assigned them to the poor.[45] In September 1180, in his city of Paris, he "paid the debt to nature."[46] The Chronicle of Auxerre relates that he died in the abbey of Notre Dame.[47] At his own request he was taken for burial to the Cistercian abbey of Barbieux, which he had endowed, a tranquil spot upon the Seine. There Adele of Champagne provided a noble tomb for him with a place beside it for herself.[48]

Contemporaries of the king praise his virtues. Says Map, "Because he was gentle in manner and kindhearted, unaffectedly simple toward men of any rank, he seemed to some lacking in force; yet he was the strictest judge, and even when it cost him tears, he meted justice with even hand to meek and arrogant alike."[49] Newburgh adds, "Louis Capet was a man of warm devotion to God and of extraordinary lenity to his subordinates; a devout respecter of the holy orders. He was however a little more credulous than befits a king, and prone to listen to advice that was unworthy of him."[50] Giraldus, eager to testify to Louis's superiority to the Angevin, lauds his piety, his frequent fasts, his restraint and moderation. The king shares the chronicler's praise for the Capetian dynasty in general, to which he imputes justice and morality, leniency and affability. He notes that the Capetians do not, like some princes he could mention, swear by the eyes, the feet, the teeth, the throat of God, and that their device is not bears, leopards, lions, but the lily.[51]

Louis lay in the chapel of his abbey of Notre Dame, shriven, anointed, redolent of spices, garbed not in the splendor of a feudal king, but in the seemly wrappings of a cenobite.[52] He had put away his bauble scepter for all eternity and clasped on his breast the abbatial cross of Notre Dame. The eyes, so long in quest of inwardness, were now shuttered finally on the false shows of this world, on temporal thrones and powers and principalities. A great sigh had escaped his lips and left him eased forever. Fifty-nine strokes the bells of Paris tolled for his years in the century.

Eleanor was fifty-seven, and she had been in durance for six years.

19 ✚

The Christmas Court

AFTER THE JUST CAPETIAN fell asleep at the end of his long reign of forty-two years, the Angevin enjoyed a brief peace unchallenged by the malice of the Franks. Perhaps at no time in Henry's reign had he such untrammeled opportunity as now to give substance to his spacious vision of the kingly office. To review the activities in which he engaged at this time is to ask what he might have achieved in a lifetime, if, free from the Capetian enmity and the disorders of his own household, he had been able to devote his whole insight and energy to replacing the crumbling pillars of the feudal world with a more enduring structure.

His was the task (though it was not given to him to finish it) of converting an uncentralized society with diverse local law, custom, tradition, dialect, into a well-functioning organism. He had the vision, the experience, the energy for comprehensive plan and effective execution. To regularize, to build, and to infuse the functions of government with life and movement was the work of his predilection.

Tirelessly he journeyed from end to end of his far-spread provinces, carrying government with him to the remotest quarters, inspecting every detail of feudal life, learning from contact with every type of person. He himself overlooked his garrisoned castles, the operations of his stewards and his seneschals. Traveling with his justiciars from place to place, he established more equitable justice which reached subjects of every estate. He systemized taxes and instituted new forms of military levies designed to create an army answerable directly to the king and less convenient for employment in local insurrections.

In seeking counsel the king went beyond the circle of those privileged nobles whose interests since his advent had been inimical to his own. He surrounded himself with sober men in any guise, lay or clerical, valuing ability, learning, trustworthiness, above prestige of rank.[1] The demand and the rewards for men of talent led every burgher, as Diceto tells, to strive for the education of his son, to whom public life offered unprecedented opportunity. There thus grew up a confident and prosperous *bourgeoisie*, men skilled in professions and competent in trade.

The heirs of privilege in his time accuse Henry of parsimony. It is true that sycophants found little to gratify them in the king's generosity. His gifts were not the usual prizes of chivalry bestowed for personal valor or to win attachment. He did not give, as nobles of his day were wont to do, for display or to beget a following; yet he was careful to reward the humblest service and to requite his servants for unexpected losses in executing his behests.[2] His gifts to religious foundations, it was said, did not fulfill the traditions of his house; yet his contributions to "religion" were large in the aggregate, especially those to support Templars and Hospitallers on crusade and to equip individuals for their pilgrimage. His endowments of houses of religion and seats of learning, such as Grammont, Bec, and Fontevrault, make a long list, but one unmarked with ostentation. In time of famine in Anjou, he opened his provincial treasury of grain and wine for the support of a whole population until a new harvest and vintage.[3]

His largest expenditures were secular and of practical benefit to the general economy: the reconstruction of ancient capital cities on ampler sites, with better access and more salubrious disposal of huddled industries; the building of roads, bridges, and levees for flood control; the improvement of markets and fairs; the repair of strongholds overlooking uneasy frontiers. His revenues, though uneven from year to year, were more stable and abundant than those of earlier times; but the expenses of his roving government with frequent crossings of the Channel, his diplomatic missions moving ceaselessly over the face of Europe, the conflicts for which he hired mercenaries, the numerous and extravagant households that he maintained, were a heavy drain on his treasury. On his perpetual journeyings, he must have been gratified by evidences of an expanding economy, a growing population and rising prosperity; and in these signs he must have found wherewith to assuage the disquietude that haunted him.

❧

The young Plantagenets, though for a time less exposed to the machinations of the Franks, had not been reclaimed from the "demon of Anjou" by the solemn oaths exchanged at Montlouis. Richard, given license to suppress the anarchy surviving the rebellion in Aquitaine, pursued his course with such success that he, rather than his brother, seemed to all the world the virtual heir of Angevin supremacy.

In the meantime the elder prince, that young man with the highest pretensions in Europe, filled his days of ennui with counterfeit exploits and spurious renown. Rootless, without the spur of necessary strivings, he led his dazzling puppet show of knights errant over the jousting fields of Normandy and the Île de France. Under his patronage the noble pastime of chivalry became a profession that gathered to itself the foot-loose and restless younger generation: heirs waiting for their patrimonies, the cadets of noble houses, obscure young men of bravery and brawn eager to gamble on luck in a joust to escape their destined misery. For a time the stir and the flying fame of the tournaments absorbed the young king, gave vent to his turbu-lence. But the ironic contrast between the mimic king of England and the conquering hero of Aquitaine deceived no one. It ended by provoking a desperate rancor in the younger Henry that no pageant could divert, nor any palliation of the elder king disguise or assuage.

By the spring of 1182 the strife in Aquitaine had reached such a pitch of ferocity that Henry could no longer leave the situation to the Count of Poitou's unaided operations. The barons of the south, perennially in local con-federation against each other, were finally brought to a common ground by their enmity toward Richard. But they found among themselves no accept-able leader and they lacked the means to finance an army of resistance against the effective mercenaries in the pay of the Angevins. In the young king they saw a man cut to their very pattern: the prince of cavaliers, rich, prodigal, with a following of elect knights, and with a grievance they knew how to inflame.

The demagogue of the conspiracy against the Count of Poitou was Bertran de Born,[4] seigneur of the castle of Hautefort near Périgueux and its thousand souls. He was in every way extravagant, an epitome of the violent contrasts that made the peculiar genius of the south country. Poet and warrior, cynic and romantic, hot-headed and cold-blooded, he gloried above all things in the spectacle and excitement of warfare, where prizes went to the reckless and the bold. He had a rich stake in the barons' conflict, for Hautefort was on the program of Richard's operations. Bertran's instrument for rousing and fusing the movement for revolt was the troubadour's topical song, the *sirventés*. He spilled out his fiery and provocative rhymes as from an inex-haustible horn, and his jongleur, Papiol, sounded them far and wide in the river valleys of the Lot and the Dordogne, and in the high places of the Limousin.

I care not for Monday nor Tuesday
Nor for weeks nor months nor years,
Nor do I cease in April and March
Seeing to it that harm may come
To those who do me wrong.

. . . . .

Peace does not comfort me,
I am in accord with war,
Nor do I hold or believe
Any other religion.[5]

The bucklers of cavaliers with their glints of blue and white, their banners unfurled to the breeze, their polished helmets, tents and pavilions spread upon the plain, the thunder of horses charging, splintered lances, shields hacked and broken, the debris of the battle field — these were the trouba-dour's delight.

Papiol easily found the ear of the young king and into it poured martial music, the purport of which was unmistakable. Why should he, the eldest of the Plantagenets, alone lack a particular domain? [6] Without much subtilty, the firebrand troubadour offered the castles of the Limousin, the barons of Aquitaine to his banners, the lordship of Poitou to the quasi-lord of Normandy. Bertran threw out impudent lampoons designed to sting the young king's pride and fix his resolution. The Duke of Normandy, the heir of England, "is lord of little land." The prince may have a fine title, but he has neither wealth, nor power, nor security, and his living is but a Norman carter's tax. "As for me, I prefer a little land with honor to an empire with dishonor." "I should not care to be Lord of Toledo, if I could not stay there with confidence." [7]

In the summer of 1182, the succession of tournaments for a time suspended, the young king moved about in Poitou and Aquitaine. Ostensibly he was lending a hand, at the instance of the elder king, in restoring peace in the provinces, where towns, castles, and granges were aflame with the sullen fires of war. But he could be employed only languidly to support the Count of Poitou. His ardors for the moment seemed not military but pious. In making pilgrimages to the shrines of the Limousin, he beheld the ruin of the countryside and was moved by the miseries of the people, who found no sanctuary, even in the churches, for the goods they tried to save from fire and pillage. On the pilgrim routes, the stinging music of Papiol everywhere reached his ears. He was in Limoges for the feast of Saint Martial, and on the saint's day, in the city where Richard had been consecrated Duke of Aquitaine, he presented to the famous abbey a mantle of green brocade embroidered with the legend *Henricus Rex*, perhaps the one he had worn at his own coronation.[8] In these weeks he was honeycombed with indecision, and in the labyrinthine maze of mind and will, pride met honor; temptation, compunction; jealousy of his brother, fealty to the king.

The Count of Poitou was in the meantime by no means unaware of the disaffection of the young king and of his connivance with the barons of the south. Bertran's *sirventés* reached his ears, too. He acted with Angevin bravado. Without taking counsel of anyone but himself, he took measures to fortify his borders against treachery. In that critical wedge of land where the inheritances of the Plantagenet princes converged on the marches of Maine, Poitou, and Brittany, Henry held in his own hands the three formidable castles of Chinon, Loudun, and Mirebeau (those with which he had sought to endow John in 1177). Encroaching upon this neutral ground, Richard hastily built a new strong castle at Clairvaux.[9] Again Papiol's song was heard:

Between Poitiers and Île Bouchard, between Mirebeau, Loudun, and Chinon, at Clairvaux, someone has built a beautiful fortress in the very center of the plain.

I should not like to have the young king know of it or get sight of it, for it would scarcely please him. But I fear nevertheless that he will see it from Mateflon, for from there it shows white on the horizon.[10]

Henry himself was in the queen's provinces through the summer, trying to moderate the strife, to beat out the fires that struggled up from the ash and rubble of desolated towns; observing meanwhile with deepening uneasiness the bitterness between his sons. But in the midst of his pacific operations a new crisis diverted him to Normandy. He went there hastily in August to offer asylum to his daughter Matilda and her lord, Henry the Lion, Duke of Saxony, with their children, expelled from Germany by the malice of the Emperor Barbarossa, who had decreed their exile for a period of seven years and had distributed their four duchies to his partisans.[11] The downfall of the duke, through a series of unfortunate events, was a heavy blow to Angevin prestige, for Henry of Saxony had been a striking figure in the destinies of the Empire, the kind of man the king could appreciate, a pillar of enlightenment, rich, powerful, a builder of cities, a patron of the church, a crusader whose exploits beyond the seas had spread his fame through Christendom. The duke and duchess were accompanied in their exile by some two hundred German magnates of their following. Henry barely anticipated the arrival of this army of noble guests in Rouen, where he threw open his castles and his bailiwicks for their reception. The size of the retinue however was sufficient to outreach even a royal hospitality. Henry lodged Matilda and her children in the castle of Argentan. The Duke of Saxony, already an illustrious pilgrim, was counseled to employ the leisure of his exile in visiting the shrine of Saint James of Compostella. As for the magnates, Henry rewarded them liberally for their fidelity to the Saxon cause and bade them Godspeed upon their homeward way.

The young king, who might be involved in heaven knew what occupation in Poitou, was summoned to Rouen to greet the exiles. But when he arrived, he was discovered to be full of his own affairs. He was miserably unhappy, sick with pique and suspicion, desperate with discontent. He responded to none of the indulgences that usually beguiled him from his spleen. He had reached a decision, it seemed, from which nothing could dislodge him. Let the king give him his inheritance, or at least Normandy, or at the very least Anjou. He required a capital seat where he and his young queen could hold their own court without let or hindrance; and soldiers of his own; and revenues sufficient for the maintenance of a royal household. He no longer offered himself to the world as a butt for vagabond jongleurs.

When Henry tried to postpone him to a later time, he flew in a Poitevin rage to Paris and poured out his wrongs before the sympathetic Capets. Shortly he came back with a new string to his harp. He was now sad rather than angry. He would accept banishment. Disprized and dispossessed of his inheritance, he would take the cross. Never again would he submit to his puppet role as King of England. In Palestine, where valor made a man, he could find exercise. He had a calling at last. What matter where it led? And — he went on — if the king should contravene his vows, he would end his miserable life with his own hand. The beautiful prince raged like Absalom.[12]

Not for the first time Henry faced the specter of crusade. It was a nightmare that not only the young Plantagenets but all the aggrieved scions of feudal houses had learned to conjure up as a last resort against parental tyranny. But what might be expected with the crowned heir of the Plantagenets on that freebooter's highway, or in confederation with factions in Jerusalem where the Angevin dynasty was plainly tottering to its fall? On balance it seemed better to pay the living for a seditious following for the young king in Europe. Henry dipped into his treasure to appease the prince. He promised him £100 Angevin a day with £10 additional for Marguerite, agreed to give him residence in Argentan (with sensible Matilda of Saxony) and to maintain one hundred soldiers for his service for a year. For this limited and recoverable grant, the young king solemnly pledged himself to remain in the king's allegiance and to make no additional demands.[13]

As Advent approached Henry was impatient to cross to England, but the young king's desperation and the disorders in the queen's provinces kept him abroad. He deemed it politic to hold in Normandy a Christmas court that should signally reaffirm the prestige of the Angevins; an occasion for the young king to exploit his newly won ascendancy; for bringing his sons to a fraternal amity in the eyes of the world; for hunting the barons out of their aeries on both sides of the Loire and bringing their intrigues to light. Philip Augustus was holding his first plenary court in Paris, and Henry had no idea of leaving his sons and his feudatories free to resort to the palace on the Seine.

For rendezvous Henry chose the city of Caen,[14] with its newly rebuilt castle of the Norman exchequer, its massive great hall, and its formidable dungeons; Caen with its century-old memorials of William the Conqueror and Matilda of Flanders, its evidences, in flourishing markets and ample hostelries, of strength and prosperity. All baronial courts were forbidden in the provinces. Nobles and prelates were summoned to renew their homage in presence of a cloud of witnesses.[15]

In the short and lowering days of late December 1182, one thousand knights from Aix to Finisterre, from the Rhine to the Garonne, from Saint Gilles to Cologne, clattered over the cobbles past the Abbaye-aux-Dames and the Abbaye-aux-Hommes to their lord's hall, where cheer and plenty defied the dreary mizzle of the Norman winter. To the foyer of their forebears came the young Plantagenets. As chatelaine, in lieu of the imprisoned queen, shone Marguerite in the flower of her youth, and the Duchess of Saxony, in the pride of her young matronly beauty. With Matilda came her lord, Henry the Lion, lately returned from his pilgrimage, their children, their household, imposing as befitted the lords of sixty-seven castles and forty towns in Germany; Count Geoffrey with his proud wrangling Bretons; Count Richard, accompanied by kinsmen and vassels of the absent queen; the young king, resplendent in the recent spoils of Rouen, trailing those gallants whose exploits on the jousting fields were the talk of the world. Bishops and nobles, *dames choisies*, the toasts of the troubadours, thronged the king's great hall. There shone vair and gris and ermine, wrought leather and brocade, linen from the looms of Tripoli, gold work of Cologne. In the streets the bleariest-eyed yokel in Normandy might stare at horses from Lombardy and Spain caparisoned with oriental silks and mounted by the fabled knights of war, tournament, crusade, tossing their plumes, spreading their pennants, and, in bursts of pale sunlight, flashing the armor of Blaye and Limoges, Damascus and Toledo. The hostelries and the burghers' houses in Caen overflowed with menials and with the factions that had brought axes to grind at the great assize. Guillaume le Maréchal, alone among the *preux chevaliers*, did not arrive in the train of the young king.

✧

Foul cup, evil drink.
(*Mauvais vase, mauvais boire.*)
Guillaume le Maréchal, III, 65–66

The court at Caen might have been what the chroniclers declare it — the most splendid ever seen in Normandy, even by ancients who remembered the days of Henry Beauclerc, but for the rancor and intrigue that were rife among the princes and their followings. Unhappily, the design of Henry to engage the young king in delusions of grandeur was contravened by a special malice that put the prince out of humor with his role. Though recently appeased with the outward trappings of a king, he arrived in Caen in a mood that no regal display could conceal. Everyone, and especially those lordlings who looked to a Christmas largess, saw that he was by no means his genial and convivial self. He was gloomy, testy, inaccessible, short of speech; he stood off from his intimates, shunned praises of the marshal's exploits, avoided the circle of the gay young queen. His spleen gave substance to the scandal that spread among the thousand elect knights and the ladies who had been bred in the courts of love. From the great hall of the castle to the dingiest pothouse in the town, it was noised abroad that Guillaume, the trusted marshal, master of the young king's household, had dared to lift his eyes Poitiers-fashion to the young Queen Marguerite.

Honest Guillaume did not hide himself from the vengeance to which these reports exposed him, nor did he suffer in silence as the *Tractatus de Amore* recommends. He came straight to Caen and made a scene at the Christmas court. He demanded of the elder king his vassal's right to wipe out the calumny in ordeal by combat. In the presence of all and sundry, he challenged the felons, who out of jealousy for his prowess in the lists had maligned him and aspersed the young queen, to come forth and defend themselves in a three days' tournament. Where all could hear him, he offered, even with the forefinger of his right hand cut off, to fight three successive champions for three successive days without respite: the reward for victory, the simple vindication of his honor; the penalty for failure, to be hanged for the crime in the presence of the company. The slanderers dared not declare themselves, much less take issue with the redoubtable marshal upon the field of honor: but the affair poisoned the atmosphere and shed a gloom upon conviviality. Guillaume, the beau ideal of the cavalier, scorning to argue his innocence when combat was denied him, left the assembly more in grief than dudgeon, to seek redress at the shrine of the three Magi in Cologne.[16]

At the Christmas court the prince was otherwise beset. Bertran de Born was one of the noble guests in the following of the Count of Poitou. The pacification, even temporary, of the young king, was not at all what the Seigneur of Hautefort had sought to achieve by taunting the prince as "lord of little land." The troubadour made good use of the king's vast convocation in Caen to undo what Henry had lately accomplished in Rouen with deep misgiving and much expense. Papiol renewed his lampoons in the bailiwicks of the barons of Aquitaine, and music spread their scorching epigrams abroad on the wings of the wind. A certain young king was "the prince of cravens." "It ill beseems a crowned king to live upon a dole and spend but a Norman carter's tax."[17]

Bertran employed his gifts to embroil all the Plantagenets with the Count of Poitou. His jongleur voiced the wish that Geoffrey, Count of Brittany, were Duke of Normandy, for he was "un courtois" and would know how to vindicate his rights. Bertran tried to engage the Duchess of Saxony, and is said to have followed her to Argentan after the Christmas court. With the softer music of the courts of love, he praised her fresh and delicate beauty, her welcoming grace, the liveliness of her talk.[18] But Matilda, whose education had followed the sensible traditions of her grandmother, Matilda Empress, rather than those of her mother in the court of Poitiers, was apparently not amused. Thereupon Bertran distilled sour grapes in his comments on the comfortless boredom and the frugal fare of Henry's castles. "I should feel less than myself in a cheerless palace," he declared. "A court without largess is but a barons' warren."[19]

It was with Bertran's taunts in his ears and with suspicions of Guillaume le

Maréchal hot upon his heart that the young king met the Count of Poitou at the Christmas court. There needed only a stave from one of the *sirventés* sung by a careless squire to set them off: "Between Poitiers and Île Bouchard someone has built a beautiful fortress in the middle of the plain." The young king flew straight to his father with demands for a summary redress of his grievances. But the king, who had lately soothed his transports in Rouen, was now found to be in a contrary disposition. Giraldus relates that for a time Henry let the strife among his sons take its course to prevent their uniting against himself, as in the late rebellion.[20] To the young king's surprise, his father met him with something less than cordiality.

"I gave Richard the right," said the king, "to confiscate the lands of barons who made war upon him."

"But he was attacking high barons who have long been my vassals. I have a right to give aid to my own men," cried the prince.

"Then do so," replied the king, "I do not hinder you." [21]

It was another insinuation that the eldest son might do worse than imitate his junior's hardihood. The heir of England flew into a passion. Unless he were freed once and for all from interference with his affairs and given the powers belonging to his titles, he would renounce the empty honors that only made him ridiculous. He would take the cross and seek a more fitting fortune under some alien prince.

Map relates that the young king never earned any wrath from his father that he could not allay with his first tears, and desired nothing that he could not procure with a few blandishments.[22] The elder king was moved by the outburst. In the threat of crusade he recognized the voice of Philip of Flanders and certain French barons. He resolved again to propitiate his heir. He summoned Richard and Geoffrey to offer homage to the eldest born. For Geoffrey, who had already done homage to his brother for Brittany, a renewal was but an easy gesture. But Richard, who jointly with Henry had done homage to the King of France for his own provinces, revolted. Since when had he been Henry's vassal, and for what? Were not he and his brother of the same stock, alike illustrious? Let Henry attend to his own glittering affairs north of the Loire and keep his men out of Poitou. A demand for feudal submission to the Duke of Normandy aroused Richard's liveliest suspicions.[23]

After this outbreak neither the prodigal liberality of the king, nor all the good offices of the Duchess of Saxony, nor the entreaties of the magnates, availed to persuade the young king and the Count of Poitou to sit down together at the bountiful table of their father. As the quarrel spread to the rival vassalages, the reunion in Caen to affirm the unity of the Plantagenets became an imbroglio that signalized for the whole malignant world the fractures in the structure of the Angevin empire.

Aroused at last to the need of once more conciliating the young king, Henry abridged his Christmas court and before the first of January drew off his sons from the corroding atmosphere of intrigue and counterplot in Caen to the capital of Maine. In Le Mans, by dint of threats and promises, he brought Richard to acknowledge, in the presence of certain of Henry's vassals, his aggressions against Anjou. The young king, mollified again by the elder king's indulgence, then eased his rancor and his conscience. Of his own free will, as Benedict relates, and with his hands upon the Gospels, he swore, in the presence of many witnesses, that he would remain all his life long his father's liege man and show him honor and service due. Furthermore, he confessed that, provoked by the fortification of Clairvaux, he had conspired with the barons of Poitou against his brother, but declared that, if the king would take Clairvaux into his own custody, he would be reconciled with Richard. A few days later, in Angers, Richard, in the presence of Angevin barons, was constrained to repeat the homage of Le Mans; but his concessions were so qualified and so ungracious that, when he withdrew "uttering nothing but curses," the young king declined to receive them, and the brothers were more estranged than ever.[24]

20 ✠

War Was in His Heart

Do you not know that it is our inheritance from remote times that no one of us loves another, but that always, brother against brother, and son against father, we try our utmost to injure one another?

Geoffrey of Brittany[1]

IN THE MEANTIME, Geoffrey had been dispatched to report the new "accord" to the barons of Aquitaine and to disperse the forces they had mustered on the marches near Mirebeau awaiting the expected arrival of the young king to lead them. But the seigneurs of the Limousin were not prepared to dissolve their movement for liberation from the Count of Poitou on the report of an "accord" between the brothers Plantagenet. They had already given too many hostages to the fortunes of war, and they strongly suspected the oaths of fealty exchanged in Maine and Anjou. Whatever Geoffrey's intentions may have been when he quitted Angers, on the marches of Poitou he betrayed his mission. Instead of fulfilling the mandate of the king, he joined the rebels with a horde of mercenaries already rallied in Brittany, ravaged everything he could reach in Poitou, and pushed on as fast as he could to the Limousin to make juncture with the enemies of his house.[2] These he found abundantly among the victims of Richard's tyranny; among vassals from Maine and Anjou, resurgent from the last rebellion; among French barons streaming from Burgundy and the Île de France. Frugal Dieu-Donné, more interested in injury to the elder king than in assistance to any of his sons, sent down his "infernal legions," a rabble of recently disbanded *routiers*, who knew how to support themselves without his pay by rapine in the land. From the four quarters the mutineers gathered to the banners, as they supposed, of the young king.

Richard, well apprised of the inpouring of insurgents from every direction, set forth from the borders of Poitou with a force of mercenaries in furious pursuit of Geoffrey and the barons, who had gathered under the leadership of Count Aymar of Limoges near Mirebeau. He drove them before him to the Limousin and, but for the foundering of his horses and the exhaustion of his men, he would have captured those seigneurs upon whom the uprising chiefly depended.[3]

When it was learned in Angers that Geoffrey had betrayed his mission, the young king was sent after him to call off the insurrection. Some instinct of clairvoyance led him before setting out to send the young queen "for safety" to Paris,[4] and to recall Guillaume le Maréchal from exile. He then went southward to find the rebels organizing their positions in Limoges under Count Aymar and Geoffrey of Brittany. As soon as the young king arrived, one castle after another was opened to him.[5]

The chroniclers who record the ensuing events in most detail charge the young king with treason and perfidy. But might it have been indecision rather than wanton falseness that marked his now incredible behavior? There are evidences that, even in the midst of fatal vacillations, compunction stirred in the devious windings of his mind. Inconstancy had already involved him so deeply that he found no way to withdraw from a situation that left him, in any direction, hopelessly compromised. He was torn between affection for his father and jealous hatred for Richard, between his recent sacred pledges to the king and his previous oaths to the barons. In his school of chivalry and his role of patron, he had never learned to withstand appeals to his magnanimity, and his habit of ingratiation left him always the victim of the last advocate and led him to justify himself first to one faction, then to the other. Since he found no position to which he could retreat, he played for time to put off the tragic decision, the fateful end of which no man could foresee. In this course he fell at first into the strange role of mediator. In playing this part, the chroniclers find him disingenuous, maneuvering for time in which the rebels could gather their resources.[6]

Henry himself arrived before Limoges late in February with a small force of mercenaries.[7] After his efforts in Angers to pacify the young king, he now appeared in the defense of Richard who, deprived of his normal levies by the defection of his barons, stood starkly in peril of losing not merely his patrimony but his very life. The conflict, grown beyond the scope of original plans, had become nothing less than a fratricidal war between the young king and the Count of Poitou for the succession to the Angevin empire, a ghastly struggle in which Henry was obliged to take a living share, abetting first one and then the other of his furious sons.[8] The king's movements, in which he exposed himself freely to foul play, reveal that he still kept confidence in feudal pledges, in the efficacy of negotiation, the potency of law. He came into the Limousin near the beginning of Lent, seeking parley with the renegades.

The river Vienne, flowing through the midst of Limoges, divided it into two separate bourgs, the Château and the Cité. In the Cité was the cathedral of Saint Étienne with the bishop's domain; in the Château, the abbey of Saint Martial with the richest treasury of the Limousin and the castle of the counts.[9] Into the strongly fortified Château Count Aymar brought the insurgent barons. The elder king established his camp in the more open Cité. Six weeks before in Angers the brothers Plantagenet had sworn to keep the peace among themselves and to preserve their allegiance to the king their father.[10] To his dismay Henry now learned that his sudden defense of Richard had driven the young king to join the insurgents in the castle.

Upon the king's approach to Limoges with his mercenaries, the young king, from the stronghold of the rebels, appealed to his father to seek a negotiated peace with the barons. Under this reassurance, Henry, with a small escort, advanced to the Château to treat with them. To the horror and astonishment of his following, an arrow, launched from the barbicans, sang in the air and its head lodged in the king's tunic, striking his coat of mail. At this untoward reception, under a pledge of truce, Henry withdrew with Richard to the nearby castle of Aix for greater security.[11]

There in the evening the young king visited him to explain that the arrow was unauthorized, the random shot of a panic-stricken burgher keeping the watch upon the wall. Here the rebellion might have ended with another burst of tears and a renewal of indulgence; but a fatal madness possessed the prince. "War," quotes Map, "was in his heart." [12] He came into his father's presence armed cap-a-pie, as if against the suspicion of treachery. Invited to lay off his trappings and dine with the king, he refused to disarm or to break bread. The elder king, deeply hurt by the attack upon his person and the failure of the old affectionate appeals, rejected the prince's excuses for his castellans and sent him off in dudgeon.

Henry did, however, make a second attempt to negotiate with the rebels, himself going again to the Château as a rendezvous. Again, as he approached, an arrow sped from the barbican seeking out the king. By a mere chance his horse, rearing at that very moment, received the shaft in its neck and so prevented its striking the king's breast.

After this second felony, the young king went once more to his father, protesting again his innocence of evil intention. He even declared that, unless the barons accepted the king's offer for peace, he would utterly abandon them. To dispel suspicion of treachery, he gave into his father's custody his horse and arms. For some days he remained quietly with the elder king, keeping his company and dipping from the same dish at table. In the meantime Henry had cut off the young man's stipends, which might be used to pay the clamorous *routiers* in the Château. He knew how certainly want begets humility. He could afford to wait for that eventuality. But the barons' financiers were not so near their wits' end as the elder king supposed. The chroniclers declare that the young king's peaceful sojourn with his father during Lent was designed merely to give the rebels the respite they needed. In this interval they made their exit from Limoges to ravage the countryside. Pouring out from the Château, they spread desolation as far as Angoulême. Thenceforth the pious Limousin, traversed by its immemorial pilgrim routes, enriched with famous shrines, witnessed a general sacrilege. Under the leadership of Geoffrey of Brittany, the brigands looted the shrine of Saint Leonard, that patron of the earliest crusaders. They pillaged Saint Martin in Brive, dispersed the monks, held some for ransom at "eighteen *sols* a pair." [13] They visited the monastery of Saint Étienne de Muret in Grammont. Here in the abbey which the elder king had nobly endowed and where he had designated a place for his own burial, the pillagers weighed up as bullion the altar vessels, even a precious golden dove which Henry had dedicated as a repository for the sacred host.[14]

At some stage in these events the young king returned from his father's side to the Château, ostensibly to try again to make peace with the rebels. Failing in this, or perhaps having tried only languidly, he went off to Dorat, as if wishing to escape the whole situation. During these impious forays, which Geoffrey led without a qualm, the young king wavered in a turmoil of emotion between a mood of abandonment to the sacrilege and one of pious revulsion. He was now half of a mind to yield anything for peace, now resolute for the bitter end. On one day he would lead a band of *routiers*; on the next he might be found, quiet and withdrawn, among the monks of Uzerche, absorbed in reading the life of their patron, Saint Yrieix.[15] The rebellion, as exemplified by the fickle prince, hung by a hair.

As the conflict proceeded, Peter of Blois exerted his epistolary talents to restrain the young king:

> You make yourself an enemy of God and Justice and a transgressor of all laws if you do not obey your father to whom you owe all that you are. . . For who provides for your material existence? Your father. Who educated you? Your father. Who bred you to arms? Your father. Who put himself aside to make you king? Your father. Who labored in every way that you might possess all things in peace? Your father. You can accuse him of nothing but an excess of grace, devotion, munificence, and prodigal liberality. . . We cannot conceal our grief that you pursue your father and give over his lands, which you ought to keep from bloodshed, to rapine and plunder. Wherefore have you become a leader of mercenaries, and wherefore do you consort with the lost and excommunicate? In what has your father, to whom you owe gratitude, offended you? Never has he shown himself overmastering . . . but as a most serviceable administrator of your affairs. He lives not for himself, but for you. Yours is his power, his knowledge, his action, his wealth — all he has. Where is your filial affection? Where is your reverence? Where is the law of nature? Where your fear of God? [16]

When Henry recalled the young king from Dorat to account for the continuance of the pillaging, he returned, not to his father, but to the Château, and there, taking his vow solemnly on the body of Saint Martial, he swore to take the cross, knowing full well that the elder king's concern over this act would extinguish his recriminations. On the vigils of Easter he visited his father again. He blamed Geoffrey for the horrible desolation of

the Limousin. Then he made known his vow and his resolution. The king
was confounded. On his knees and with tears Henry besought the prince
to retract the rash vow taken without the royal leave. But the young king
was fixed by an irrevocable oath sworn on the holiest of relics. He explained
that he had that day taken communion, and it had been revealed to him in
the sacred host that he ought long ago to have assumed the cross. He declared
gravely that this purpose had been for some time in his mind, but he had
waited to reveal it because he hoped that he might set out at a happier
moment with his father's blessing, without which he could not expect to
prosper.[17] The young man's sadness smote the king. Was it indeed pure
piety that had moved him to this course? Had rancor or poverty perhaps
anything to do with his decision? The young king declared that he had
dedicated himself of his own free will for the remission of his sins, and that,
if obstacles were laid in his way, he would end his wretched life with his
own hand. After a deep silence Henry spoke.

"God's will and yours be done. And I myself, with God's help, will so
provide you that no one of whom I have heard shall have gone to Jerusalem
with such abundant resource." [18]

The hearts of the two kings melted to each other. The young king, in
gratitude, promised to bring hostages from the Château to sue for peace.
When brought, these proved, however, to be only a few burghers, and when
Henry sent to collect others that were promised, his envoys were set upon,
wounded, cast into the moat.[19]

⚜

During Lent Henry forbore to disturb the Truce of God. He remained
piously quiet and collected, hoping the lack of resource would presently
bring a collapse of the rebellion. But the continuance of the sacrilegious
pillaging and the failure of the young king to end the ravages obliged him
to act. Before Easter he invested the Château.[20]

The burghers of the citadel, confused by the situation in which the king
and his vicegerent sons were at war with one another, fell under the direction
of their own Count Aymar. Under his compulsion they razed whatever en-
cumbered the circuit of their bastion, destroying churches, dwellings, towers,
even the house of Saint Valerie and the orchards of Saint Martial. Consternation spread within the walls. The monks, carrying the magnificent golden
casket containing the head of Saint Martial, the most precious relic of the
Limousin, went in procession about the ambit of the barbicans, invoking
divine protection. The women meanwhile spun a hempen strand with which
they encircled the outposts of the citadel. This they then cut into candle
wicks and hastily dedicated them in their churches, calling upon all the
venerable saints of the Limousin, and especially their patron Saint Martial,

to defend them from the perils of a siege. A sodden winter rain washed the ruins of the bourg, droned through broken roofs, and cascaded in the gutters of the narrow streets.[21]

Inside the Château the waiting through Lent for Henry's attack had consumed the resources of the rebels in spite of the ravaging of the holy soil of the Limousin. The *routiers*, who were paid for fighting, not for waiting, were vexed by the delay. They were practical bargainers and, as excommunicates, without scruple. Under the leadership of two experienced brigands, Sancius and Curburan,[22] they threatened to leave the Château and apply to the elder king for a better wage. At length they became imperious. Sancius was a capable executive. "Why lose a righteous cause," he argued, "for want of funds, when the treasure of Saint Martial, fabulously rich from the pilgrim traffic, reposes within the citadel?" The abbé of the monastery, misdoubting some such issue, had withdrawn to the Souterraine, but the rebels found a means of dealing with his deputies. The young king "borrowed" 20,000 sols from the abbey treasury, giving warrant with the hitherto worthless seal which he had acquired upon his coronation. When this sum was speedily exhausted, looting began, and monks and burghers and outlying peasants yielded what they had. At last the holiest sanctuary of the abbey itself was violated. With Geoffrey of Brittany in the lead, the brigands drove out the monks and weighed up the gold and silver vessels of the altar where countless pilgrims had come to bring tribute and seek the blessing of the apostle martyr of Aquitaine.[23]

In spite of his crusader's vow and his protestations to his father, the young king appeared to feel an obligation to help sustain the clamorous troops in the Château. His double-dealing with the king must have grown out of their altercations over the stakes of Richard in the struggle. At any rate, during the siege of the citadel, the prince went far southward with Guillaume le Maréchal and the Count of Tonnerre (one of the rebel barons) and scaled the sequestered heights of Rocamadour in quest of treasure.[24] Here they took their toll from that holy shrine where pilgrims had long flocked to see the great sword of Roland. Finding there the Abbés of Dalon and Obazine, they exacted tribute also from them. The *Histoire de Longuedoc* reports that this expedition was a blind to cover a juncture with the Duke of Burgundy and Raymond of Toulouse, who were advancing with armed forces to join the rebels.[25]

Returning northward toward Brive from the raid on Rocamadour with Guillaume and the Count of Tonnerre in the burning heat of June, the young king felt himself out of sorts and therefore, before the day was spent, turned in for rest at the dwelling of one Étienne Fabri in the little bourg of Martel.[26] There he fell into a fever. His condition occasioning some alarm, the Abbé of Dalon and the Bishop of Agen went to his bedside. These men of God, while ministering to his needs, obtained from the prince a salutary confession of his sins. They learned that the sick young man desired to see the king his father, to ask his forgiveness, and engage him, if need were, to fulfill his testament. While messengers went to fetch the king, the Count of Tonnerre diverted the townsfolk from alarm by entertaining them with a tournament.

The messengers found Henry encamped upon the Vienne, at no great distance from Limoges. At tidings of the gravity of the young man's illness, the king prepared to go to him at once with every kind of succor. But he was warned against visiting his favorite son's bedside. There might be treachery in the summons. Let the king remember the attacks upon his person before the Château. Let him remember that the prince was desperate and pressed by desperate men; that only his own royal person stood between the mad and fickle prince and the highest seat in Europe. Let him consider what disorders would ensue upon any mischance in the Limousin. No. Let the king send messengers to the prince; physicians; a present of gold; but let him forbear to visit him.[27] Upon these counsels, Henry drew from his finger a ring familiar to the prince, set with a precious sapphire that had belonged to the treasury of Henry Beauclerc,[28] and gave it to the Bishop of Agen, who had come as emissary from Martel. With it he sent assurances of help and comfortable words. When the sick prince should be recovered, the evils that estranged them might be healed. The young king was to give heed to his physicians and command the King of England for his needs.

Returning to the house in Martel, the bishop and his escort found the young king laboring in a fever with a presentiment of death. He seized and kissed the token of the elder king's forgiveness. Bidding his attendants to bear witness, he called upon the mercy of God and the help of the Virgin and the saints, and especially of Saint Martial. He then adjured them to bear his last petitions to the king: that, first of all, he should show grace and mercy to the queen, his mother, held now so long in captivity; that he should provide for the needs of the young Queen Marguerite, a pensioner in exile in the French court; that he should requite those of his *mesnie* whom, by reason of his calamity, he could not repay for their loyalty.[29] Then he asked that they lay his crusader's cloak upon his breast and permit him to die with his cross upon his shoulder. Turning to Guillaume, who stood by, he said,

"Maréchal, you have always been true and loyal to me. I bequeath to you my cross and beg you to bear it for me to the Holy Sepulcher. You shall redeem my pledge to God."[30]

When his spiritual counselors had again heard his confession, the young king ordered a halter to be brought and put upon his neck. Dragged thus naked from his bed, he prostrated himself before them on a bed of ashes and had bare stones laid under his head and feet. Lying there, he supplicated all the saints whose shrines the rebels had despoiled to have regard for his salvation. He then gave directions for his burial, which, after the practice of the times, distributed his relics: his eyes, brain, and entrails should rest beside the grave site of the elder king in the ravaged monastery of Grammont; his body should rest with those of the Dukes of Normandy in Notre Dame of Rouen. In accordance with custom, his clothes and trappings were brought, and these he renounced and ordered laid aside for charity — all but the token ring. The monks standing by to sustain him with wholesome admonitions, noted the sapphire on his finger. Said one of them,

"You ought to renounce all earthly impediments, so that you may go unencumbered from the sorry shipwreck of this world as naked as you came."

The prince, says the chronicler, replied courteously that he no longer felt desire for any earthly thing. The monk called attention to the ring.

"You ought to put it off," he said, "to be free from insidious snares."

"I do not keep the ring," replied the prince, "by reason of desire to possess it for itself, nor by reason of levity; but only so that, before the tribunal of the Supreme Judge, it may be an open proof that my father has restored me to the fullness of his grace."

However, he consented to give it up, if so advised. But when the monk bent to remove it, to the astonishment of all, it refused to come. This the bystanders judged an awesome token of Henry's forgiveness and of divine clemency.[31]

The hot June day drew to the ninth hour. The Bishop of Agen administered extreme unction. Thereupon the young king sank to unconsciousness, but rallied briefly to reiterate his requests and commend his soul to God. In the obscure little town of Martel in the Limousin, in the heart of the queen's domains, the scion of the Plantagenets yielded up the ghost. Henry was but twenty-eight, young in years, as Newburgh says, but full of time when measured by the experiences of his life.[32]

The following day the Prior of Vigeois, who relates most of these details, climbed with a few awe-struck villagers to a little eminence above his town to see the cortege of the young king pass by on its way northward from Limoges. The day, he says, was clear and serene. The king's bier was followed by a forlorn and tattered remnant of his valiants, Aymar of Limoges, Geoffrey of Lusignan, inveterate haters of the house of Poitou, by Guillaume le Maréchal, and others. All were destitute. At Uzerche they paused at daybreak for a mass for the repose of the young king's soul. The abbé himself supplied the wax lights for the requiem. The prince's horse had gone for the expenses in Martel. A throng of peasants and villagers, starting from their burrows upon rumor of this august matter in their midst, crowded the streets in expectation of wonder and largess. But when an alms was taken among the young king's followers, only a dozen deniers were found, and these the chaplain swept into his wallet to buy bread for the cortege. One of the pallbearers sold his shoes for breakfast, and the others were glad to appease their hunger with the simple charity of the monks.

On the same day the procession reached the first burial site in Grammont. The Bishop of Limoges, pointing to the despoiled sanctuary, declared the young king excommunicate and threatened to hold his body for ransom. But softer counsels prevailed on intimation that the elder king had guaranteed to make good the spoliation. The requiem was sung by the ravaged monks, and the funeral relics were deposited where the elder king had planned to lie. At Grammont many of the escort fell away, not daring to approach more nearly to the King of England.

�֎

I charge you not with grief, but with excess of grief.
Peter of Blois, letter to Henry

Bernard Rossot, a monk of Grammont, was dispatched from Limoges to inform Henry of the calamity that had befallen his house. He found the king retired from the heat of the midafternoon in a villager's house at Mas, and accosted him alone. Recognizing the monk, the king greeted him and was greeted again.

"What news?" the king asked quietly.

With lowered countenance Bernard replied, "It is not good." [33]

No other words were necessary. The king dismissed those who had gathered for the tidings, and, alone with the monk in the little village room, he heard the story of the sordid tragedy, the lively compunction of the young man dying, his supplications, his plea for forgiveness, his testament, his want and desolation, the meanness of his obsequies. Alone the king mourned like David for Absalom.

Presently Guillaume arrived from the requiem in Grammont, the only one of the young king's *mesnie* who dared to face the king. Before receiving him, Henry had so possessed himself that no one could guess from his countenance with what sentiments he remembered the young king. [34] He listened to Guillaume's story, his son's dying request, the bestowal of his crusader's cross and cloak, the absolution of his sins, and when it was ended he said only,

"God grant him salvation."

At length Guillaume broke the silence. "Sire, what would you have me do?"

"Conduct your lord's body to Rouen," replied the king.

"Alas, Sire, that I may not do," replied Guillaume, "for I am hostage to one Sancius, the *routier*, for a debt of 100 marks Angevin owed by my lord the young king."

At sight of his son's royal seal upon the warrant, the king was for a long moment silent. It was a very large sum. He thought of the treasure he had poured out to suppress the young king's rebellion — even his jeweled coronation sword — of the fortunes he had expended on the prince's households, his coronation, his tournaments. When Sancius came to redeem his claim, he half sighed, half groaned,

"So be it. I agree. My son has cost me many a heavy sum. Would God that he could ever cost me more." [35]

Thereupon he would have committed the young king's body to the marshal. It was true he had been estranged from Guillaume and had gladly sped him from the prince's household at Christmas time. But it was nevertheless to the marshal that he had committed the keeping of his son in the days of his tutelage, and among all the gallants of his train, honest Guillaume alone had been loyal to his young lord through thick and thin, and brave enough to stand up to the consequences of his loyalty. It would have been fitting that the young king should pass through Normandy with his master-at-arms, who had bred him to all chivalric arts and given him the accolade; with the friend who in place of kindred had assisted the last flutterings of his spirit in the flesh; but this boon was denied by Guillaume's obligation to the remnant of the young king's following. Before dismissing the marshal, Henry bestowed upon him horses and livery and the wherewithal to accomplish his pilgrimage with the young king's cross to the Holy Sepulcher. [36]

⚜

At the same time Henry dispatched the Archdeacon of Wells to England to report to the queen the death of her eldest son. When this clerk came into her presence, he found her in strict confinement, dragging out her years in bitterness of heart, but he was surprised to learn that she had not been cut off by the stones of her prison nor by her remoteness from the scene from the tragedy that had overtaken the Plantagenets. She explained that she had been apprised of the calamity in a dream before any vulgar rumor reached her. She had not even needed an interpreter of her vision, for she was, as the archdeacon says, not only clairvoyant, but a woman of acute understanding. She told him that the young king had appeared to her in her sleep with more than mortal joy and serenity of countenance, wearing two crowns, one superimposed upon the other. The nether one shone with an incomparable brightness; the other by contrast seemed dimly effulgent. What, she asked, could be signified by a crown, which has neither end nor beginning, but eternity; and what by the ineffable glow save eternal felicity? The duller crown, it seemed to her, signified the young king's earthly sovereignty, now dimmed and eclipsed by the glory of his immortal state. "Eye hath not seen, nor ear heard," she reminded herself and the archdeacon, "neither have entered into the heart of man, the things which God hath prepared for them that love Him." [37]

✤

When, in the *Inferno*, Dante and Virgil reach the eighth circle of Hell, they come upon one of the figures in the tragedy of the young king.[38]

"I saw," recounts the poet, "and cannot shake off the sight, a headless body moving in procession as others moved with mournful steps. This body held its severed head by the hair, as one would bear a lantern. The eyes were turned upon us and a voice moaned, 'Alas.' . . . When the body came to the end of the bridge, it held the head at arm's length so its words could reach us. 'Behold the horror of my punishment, you, who living, visit the dead. Is aught else so dreadful? Report this in the upper air. I am Bertran de Born, who gave evil counsel to the young king. I set the son against his father. Achitophel was not more false when he roused Absalom against his father David. Because I have sundered those bound by ties of blood, I carry my head dissevered from my body. Behold the retribution.' "

In Dante's time Bertran had been in Malebolge for a century. But so long as he lived in this world, Henry dealt with him more mercifully. The biographer of the troubadours relates that the king restored to him his castle of Hautefort, and this he was moved to do as requital for a matchless elegy which the poet composed on the heir of the Plantagenets.[39] This lament remains as one of the classics of that brilliant, short-lived school of troubadour poetry. None of it can be brought whole into any other language, for either its substance, its lyric mood, its strophic pattern, or its multiple rhymes escapes in the process. In this "plaint" (*planh*) Bertran mourns a loss that leaves him to finish his days without solace, choked with pain and grief. He laments the beauty of the young king, his graciousness and liberality, the ordered magnificence of his household where cheer and hospitality reigned and good company and entertainment were ever found. Death in taking his dear lord has slain the noblest cavalier that ever lived.

21 ✢

Henry Revokes His Lands

THE UNTIMELY DEATH of the young king altered all the complicated dynastic schemes set in being at Montmirail in 1169, when the queen's resolution to leave Henry's palaces and install her second son as Count of Poitou had forced Henry to assign to his other sons their respective inheritances. For nearly twenty years the king had struggled and connived to offset the untoward consequences of the treaty which had balked his enterprise and twice driven him to defend his empire and his life.

In spite of the young king's intransigence, the deepest paternal affection in Henry was spent upon his heir. The prince had not belied his destiny. He had shone with kingly aspect, a royal distinction of person and bearing, an irresistible charm. His weakness and inconstancy had not seemed incurable vices so long as the king could keep control of his powers. With the young man's untimely death everything was changed. Richard, already invested with the dukedom of Aquitaine and the county of Poitou, suddenly became also, against every expectation, the presumptive Duke of Normandy, Count of Maine and Anjou, and heir of England. As chief of the Plantagenet princes, Richard would obviously present sterner resistance to management than the young king had offered. He was no puppet warrior of the lists, but seasoned in the field; and he was freer from interference in his own estates, not only because of their outlying situation and their special temper, but because of his tenure from the queen. The "hammer" rather than the "shield" grasped the heritage of the Conqueror; the queen's heir and favorite son touched the crown.

Henry's first concern in the changed situation was to retract the disastrous provisions of Montmirail and set up a new balance among his sons that should curb them all and relieve him from the insecure position into which their rivalries had forced him. Without regard for the habits and expectations those settlements at Montmirail had bred in the princes and their vassals, he undertook to revoke the entire Plantagenet empire and redistribute the prospective inheritances, with sharper definitions of his own claims to supervise the whole. His first care was to diminish the lion's share that seemed destined to fall to Richard; and at his expense, to make a provision for lack-land John, now a youth of seventeen pushing his way to a place in the sun. Geoffrey, as consort of its heiress, still held Brittany, but seemed doomed to be a residual legatee of any convenient loppings elsewhere that would satisfy his greed.

The king summoned his three sons to Angers to receive their portions.[1] As a preliminary measure, in anticipation of possible vehement resistance on their part, he took key fortresses into custody and manned them with garrisons of his own. To prepare the eaglets for acceptance of his dispositions, he constrained them to make peace with each other and with him as their liege lord. He then called upon Richard to cede Poitou and Aquitaine, not to Geoffrey, as second son, but to John, who, it now appeared, had crossed the Channel expressly that he might do homage to the heir of England for these lands.

It was transparent that Richard was being invited to assume the role of that gilded vagrant, that impecunious grandee, the young king; and it was very plain that whoever was highest placed in the Plantagenet hegemony was destined to find himself least endowed with independence and wherewithal. Nothing could have been more inacceptable to the Count of Poitou than to exchange the opulent southern provinces in which he had been bred, with their salubrious climate, lively culture, vast pleasure grounds, and matchless high places remote from the scrutiny of London and Rouen, for the counties of the young king north of the Loire. As for England, Richard viewed that island as a living space for merchants and yokels, a mine for revenue, but scarcely as a residence for the scion of Poitevin seigneurs. Pressed to make the exchange, he employed the Angevin tactics of delay. Having secured a time in which to make up his mind, he took French leave of Angers. Mounting his horse at sundown, he absconded to Poitou. From a safe distance he informed Henry that under no circumstances would he yield a furrow of his lands to anyone.[2]

No such profound alterations in the disposition of the Plantagenet empire could ignore the Countess of Poitou. Though she had been for a long time quiescent, she was still queen of feudal chess. The proposals to endow John with Poitou and Aquitaine brought Eleanor from the long obscurity of her confinement to take her place again in the councils of the dynasty. The eaglets were summoned to her presence in Windsor. Even the jealous princes realized the suicidal madness of their strife, for they laid down their arms and gathered in London to storm it out in argument. In 1179, under pressure from Henry, Eleanor had "ceded" her provinces to Richard, and this forced cession, in which the Count of Poitou had concurred, had estranged her from her favorite son; now the Count of Poitou became her ally in resisting Henry's new disposals.[3]

At the time of the Windsor court the queen was sixty-two, but she did not there appear as a superannuated dowager recalling a superseded scheme of things. The untoward Poitevin stood squarely in the way of Henry's plans for a new order. She refused her consent to the endowment of John, who emerged at Windsor as the king's new darling. The walls of her prison had certainly not shut out of her ears the rumors of Henry's purpose to reserve the Princess Alais for himself, or to wed her to John. In her resistance, the queen was championed by her elder sons, and the rectitude of her feudal decisions earned for her the support of Archbishop Baldwin of Canterbury and other magnates who shared the councils. No one could doubt that Philip Augustus would abet his vassal, the Countess of Poitou, in dispositions so well calculated to thwart the Angevin. The most that Henry could do was to force Richard to restore the provinces to the queen herself, and this he did by threatening to lead Eleanor with an army with banners into her own territories.

Since Henry could by no subtilty get ultimate control of the lands below the Loire, the Windsor conclave was not a triumph for the king. However, he sent Geoffrey, who was unlikely to connive with Richard, as *custos* to Normandy. The Count of Poitou, the "third nestling" of the queen, returned to Poitiers, with his wings merely somewhat clipped. His dismissal was safe for the moment, for Henry had already taken the chief fortresses in custody and set a watch upon his heir.

Geoffrey had not obtained his morsel at Windsor. He had reached for Henry's own patrimony of Anjou, as widening the frontiers of Brittany, for which province he was nominally vassal of Philip of France; and naturally Philip had supported his aspirations. The issue drew the two young men together. Geoffrey, as *custos* of Normandy, was presently in Paris living like a blood brother with his overlord in the palace on the Seine, privy to the counsels of the prime enemy of his house. But before conspiracy could reach its object, Geoffrey, by sheer fortuity, was removed from the scene, carried off, as some report, by a fever, or, according to others, killed by a fall from his horse in the melee of a tournament.[4] Philip in a frenzied display of grief was scarcely restrained from leaping into the tomb of his bosom friend, who was buried with circumstance in Notre Dame.[5] The Countess Marie of Champagne, who, since the days of the queen's court in Poitiers, cherished an affectionate interest in her Angevin half brothers, was present at his requiem and signalized her grief by establishing a mass for the repose of his soul.

Of all that fruitful progeny of the Poitevin, which had so filled the Capets with dismay, only two remained: Richard, the queen's champion, and John, whom Henry had fashioned with indulgent foresight as the instrument of his new dispensation.

✤

If the death of the young king had profoundly disturbed the Plantagenets, it had brought to dust and ashes the Capet's long-term plan to compensate for the lost provinces of Poitou and Aquitaine through the marriage alliance of Marguerite with the heir of the prosperous Angevins. With an unseemly haste, Philip Augustus sought to square the fortunes of his house with the new Plantagenet regime, for the tragedy in the Limousin had undeniably left the Capets in an anomalous position with reference to it. Unhappily for them, both the French and the Angevin dowers of the widowed Marguerite were securely in Henry's hands: the first of these, that strategic frontier between the Epte and the Andelle, known as the Norman Vexin; the second, the revenues from certain Norman and Angevin cities bestowed upon her by the King of England as her marriage portion.

The Franks demanded both the retrocession of the Vexin and the continuation of Marguerite's perquisites in the "honors" of her Angevin dower. On this issue the Franks held that Henry had frequently sworn that, if the young king should predecease him without heirs,[6] these dowers should revert unconditionally to the young queen. Philip's second demand was more embarrassing to Henry than the first. He required that his sister Alais, who was still strictly guarded in Winchester and still unwed,[7] should speedily be married to the Count of Poitou. In the matter of Alais, the Franks maintained that Henry had agreed that the Capetian princess should be wedded to the prospective heir of England and thus step into the place of the widowed Marguerite.[8] To them the heir of England now meant no other than the Count of Poitou.

The Frankish nuncios harried Henry with these demands wherever he went in Normandy and Anjou in his efforts to reëstablish a balance between his jealous and defiant sons. For a time the king put off these emissaries with legal verbiage. For twenty years since Montmirail, he had contrived, in spite of all processes, to keep the coveted Vexin in his hands as the indispensable protection of Rouen. No one had forgotten with what unseasonable haste he had snatched its fortress castles from the custody of the Templars under Louis's very nose, while the latter was absorbed in his own hasty marriage with Adele of Champagne in 1162. To Philip's nuncios Henry went into history to prove that the Vexin had belonged to Normandy by ancient right; and declared that Louis, recognizing this fact, had quitclaimed it forever on the marriage of Marguerite to the young king. For the time he evaded the matter of the Angevin revenues, making decision contingent upon a prior settlement of other matters.

When it came to the affair of Alais, it was plain that Henry had no intention of fortifying the Count of Poitou with a Frankish alliance that would enable him, as the young king had done, to fly for refuge to Paris and foment rebellions there whenever an uncomfortable issue arose at home.

But Henry's evasions in this matter led the Franks to credit the rumor that the king meant to dispossess Richard as his heir in England and renounce the Plantagenet eaglets as the illegitimate brood of a consanguineous marriage.[9] Gervase relates that Richard, in his anxiety to certify himself by this marriage as heir of England, sought the good office of the church to obtain his bride.

When the wearing process of uncertainty had produced some effect, Henry consented to a parley. An immemorial elm spread its branches over a vast circuit on the mooted boundary of the Vexin between Gisors and Trie, providing a familiar landmark for rendezvous.[10] Here for generations it had been the custom for the French kings and the Norman dukes to negotiate their differences. Under its bare limbs the two kings with their escorts drew up on Saint Nicholas' day, December 6, 1183.

❧

It had already become apparent that the youth who had put on the crown of the Capets was harried by no such doubts and scruples as had darkened the counsels and balked the enterprise of Louis VII. There was a tougher fiber in Philip Augustus, inherited doubtless from the house of Champagne, a house which had never been famous for its retiring character. A contemporary [11] describes the scion of the Capets as a prince of well-composed figure, elegant in bearing and comely in person, with a lively expression and high color; a hearty eater and drinker, prone to self-indulgence, generous to friends, mean with enemies, a man of practical skills, punctilious in religious observance, foresighted, persistent, swift and keen in judgment, fearful of treacherous designs against his life, easily excited and as easily appeased; a prince severe with barons in any way hostile to his rule and ready to foment discord among them; yet one who never slew captives in dungeons nor harbored more than transient enmities; a ruler who often heeded the advice of common men, made himself a scourge to the presumptuous, was a defender of the church and a sustainer of the poor. The new king's mind was solid, with all that connotes in lack of more sprightly qualities. His education left him literal, dogmatic, precise, without the liveliness, humor, and grace that characterized the least of the Plantagenets.

At sixteen, while his barons were gathering for a council, he was once observed sitting apart from company, gnawing a hazel shoot with an abstracted air. One of his suite remarked that he would give a good horse to know of what the king was thinking. "I was wondering," said Philip, "if it might ever please God to grant that I, or some heir of mine, should restore this kingdom to the state in which Charlemagne had it." [12] This was a daydream that opened to his fancy, among other things, the prospect of recovering those portions of the Carolingian empire that had slipped into the possession of the Angevins. A longheaded plan, simple and unoriginal, unfolded in his mind for realizing his dream: to divide the resources of his adversary and to unite his enemies. But at eighteen he was not yet quite a match for Henry under the Gisors elm.

Henry, though nominally defendant in the case, took the initiative in the parley, as had been his wont in dealing with the Capets. He came to Gisors completely documented and produced his own plan for a settlement. His proposals disconcerted the Franks, for their imaginations were in no wise prepared for the extravagant turn Henry gave to the situation.

He renewed the historical argument on the Vexin, but declared himself willing to compensate the Franks for its loss by endowing Marguerite with £2750 in money of Anjou, to be paid annually in Paris during her life.[13] As for the Angevin dower of the young queen, he declared himself unable, by reason of a legal obstacle, to comply with the French demands. He had, he said — and could prove it in court — bestowed the "honors" of Marguerite upon Queen Eleanor in lieu of the latter's dower when she had relinquished her provinces to Richard in 1179. In fact, to give substance to his claims, he summoned the queen from her sequestration in England to make a six months' progress in company with reliable Matilda through the lands of the Angevin dower.[14]

When they came to the matter of Alais, Henry promised that, if she were not forthwith wedded to the Count of Poitou, she should shortly be married to John. The intrusion of lack-land John into these negotiations bred lively suspicions in the war of nerves. Did this mean that John was designated by this alliance as heir of England, or of Poitou, or of both? Richard's alarm was increased when Henry proffered his own homage to Philip for all the continental domains of the Plantagenets.[15] It was said that Henry had absented himself from Philip's coronation because, as king himself, and more than peer of the Capetian king, he had not wished to give homage to his stripling overlord. But in offering that homage now, he publicly revoked into his own hands all the provinces he had long ago assigned to his sons. At last he had wiped out the last vestiges of that fatal treaty of Montmirail. He was master again in his own house. His sons, like fractious horses recovered from the field, were stabled again in the royal mews, dependent upon the royal bounty.

✤

Above the darkening destiny of the Angevin house in Europe there presently loomed the more pervasive shadow of its eclipse in the Orient.[16] While the royal dynasty in Jerusalem, revived for two generations by the infusion of western blood and valor, had again been crumbling to decay, the Moslems had been rallying their forces. Powerful new leaders had arisen among them, and the final collapse of the Latin Kingdom threatened. Baldwin IV of Jerusalem, own cousin of Henry Fitz-Empress, was smitten with leprosy,[17] and in 1183 was forced by reason of his blindness to resign the throne to his nephew, Baldwin V, a child of five. Since the boy king of Jerusalem was Henry's kinsman, a scion of the same root in Anjou, sole legatee of King Foulques, what was more inevitable than an appeal to Henry for the leadership, the men, the revenue, to recoup the fortunes of that noble lineage in the East? It seemed clear in Jerusalem that Henry himself, or at the very least one of his sons, should lay aside all earthly concerns and take up the unavoidable burden of warfare in Palestine. In the spring of 1185, Heraclius, the Patriarch of Jerusalem, to whom even the King of the Holy City owed homage, himself undertook the embassy to the West to lay the whole matter in Henry's hands, to offer him the Kingdom of Jerusalem, with the keys to the city, to bid him bring quickly men and arms and treasure to salvage the Latin Kingdom overseas from the imminent vengeance of the infidel. Heraclius could not conceive a more urgent mission for a Christian king than the rescue of the holy places from the doom that menaced them.[18]

Henry was in the north of England when the arrival of Heraclius was announced. Leaving his own concerns, he bore southward and met the Patriarch near Reading, whither magnates had flocked from all quarters to lay eyes on the keeper of the holy places. The king heard gravely of the disasters of the house of Anjou overseas and of the impending calamities of his fellow Christians in the East. But this was not the first time he had parried entreaties for the relief of Jerusalem. He had more than once withstood the obvious appeals to conscience and responsibility by equipping proxies for crusade and subsidizing the orders protecting the holy shrines. As for himself, he had gradually divined something chimerical in the movement to reverse history in Palestine, gaining his convictions from the eyewitness testimony of many a battered paladin returning from beyond the seas: from Louis his overlord and Eleanor his queen, from Henry the Lion and the Counts of Flanders and Champagne, as well as from many lesser but equally credible deponents. He had by no means forgotten that Louis had lost not merely his armies, his queen and her provinces overseas, but had come within an ell of losing his kingdom at home by going forth to battle with the paynim; nor that Conrad had suffered irreparable loss of men and treasure in the same enterprise; nor that the astute Philip of Flanders, after inspecting the situation on the spot more recently, had declined the glory of remaining abroad to buttress the throne of Jerusalem. To Henry crusading had never seemed a business to exchange for the solid certainties of forging an empire in the West. In the course of time he had evolved a repertory of excuses for not going on crusade proof against legatine missions and the representations of the Pope himself. But never before had any solicitation been so direct, so urgent, as this.

To the crusading generation the Patriarch of Jerusalem was hardly less august than the Pope of Rome, and it was a wonderful sight to behold him on his knees, with tears and lamentations, before the Angevin, who seemed clearly marked by heaven to uphold the tents of Christendom. The patriarch moved the assembly to groans and tears. He brought in his hands as gifts to Henry memorials of Christ's birth, passion, resurrection; keys of the Tower of David and of the Holy Sepulcher; and the banner of the Holy Cross. Heraclius laid the whole weight of saving the holy shrines on the king's shoulders. The magnates, who were certain to bear the heat and burden of the day, pressed about to hear the king's words. But from the proffered keys of Jerusalem and the banner of the Holy Cross, Henry drew back.[19] He was inexpressibly honored, gravely concerned. He would certainly engage to find subsidies for the holy war; and champions to engage the paynim. But as for himself, he could not set out for Jerusalem, leaving his own realm to its fate.[20] He had things to say about the depredations that the most Christian King of the Franks could be expected to commit on his continental possessions, if he were to journey to the Orient.

The patriarch, accustomed to the homage of temporal kings, was profoundly amazed by these paltry evasions. He turned speedily from entreaty to admonition.[21]

"You will accomplish nothing, O King, by this decision, for you will neither win your own salvation nor save the heritage of Christ. What we seek is a leader rather than resource."

If anyone could have saved Henry from his errors and his vices, Giraldus Cambrensis would have been his rescuer. On the first occasion he could find, that excellent young man put forth his influence for the patriarch. Addressing Henry apart, he said,

"Sire, you should feel honored that you have been chosen above all kings of earth by the patriarch."

Henry's reply was so sharp that Giraldus did not mistake his mood as one of veiled jocularity, nor hope any longer for his conversion.

"If the patriarch or any others come to us, they seek their own advantage rather than ours . . . The clergy may well call us to arms and peril, since they will parry no blows on the battlefield, nor take on themselves any burdens they can avoid." [22]

When he could in no wise move the king, Heraclius begged that Henry would send one of his sons at least, so that the Angevin race should not perish in the East and all the toils and martyrdoms of three generations should not be forfeit to the infidel. John threw himself at his father's feet and begged to be sent upon that brilliant mission. But Henry was obdurate.

He would send treasure, but no scion of his race.[23] Finding no succor for his beleaguered state, Heraclius sped back to Jerusalem and there shortly died, as it was said, of chagrin at the incredible failure of his embassy.[24]

Again in 1187 the most appalling tidings of disaster in Palestine reached the Christian courts of Europe. The worst predictions of Heraclius were now realized.[25] Not only had most of the Christian citadels been lost, the flower of chivalry been slain, the Templars and Hospitallers made captive, but the very cross of redemption had fallen into the hands of the "infidel dogs" and it was doubtful whether the tomb of Christ could be defended from the resurgent Saracens.

A consternation greater than that which followed the fall of Edessa in the mid-century spread over Europe. Pope Lucius collapsed on learning of these things and closed his eyes upon a calamitous world, and Pope Urban shortly followed him.[26] King William of Sicily, the husband of Joanna Plantagenet, put on sackcloth and, withdrawing from mankind, mourned for days without respite. Cardinals everywhere vowed to eschew all luxury and go forth on foot as mendicants preaching a new crusade in the highways and byways of the western world. A fast of Lenten severity was imposed on Christians every Friday for five years, with abstinence from meat on Wednesdays and Saturdays as well.[27] New missions from the Orient hastened to Europe. To bring the urgency of action to kings and prelates, the Archbishop of Tyre crossed the Mediterranean and the Alps.

Just as this dignitary arrived with his devastating reports,[28] Henry and Philip Augustus were again drawing up their cohorts under the Gisors elm to treat of their ancient grievances — the custody of the Vexin and the still unwedded Alais. The archbishop had not come, like Heraclius, with proffers of honors to the house of Anjou. He had come to summon universal Christendom to Armageddon. Hearing of the forgathering of Christian princes on the frontiers of France, Normandy, and Flanders, he hastened to Gisors to make use of that convocation for the spreading of his tidings, and he was there most honorably received by the potentates of Gaul. Benedict of Peterborough records that he presented the situation of the holy places so vividly and preached the word of God with such remarkable ardor that the conversion of all the congregated princes was achieved within a week. This was clearly seen to be a miracle. Those who had arrived as enemies parted as allies. To the astonishment of many, Henry and Philip sank their differences,[29] which now seemed puny and unworthy, in the Truce of God, and gave and received the kiss of peace. Philip and Richard, the Counts of Flanders and of Blois, and all the valiant young men in their prime talked of nothing but preparations for a new movement to the East. Decisions were taken and oaths exchanged. Red crosses were bestowed upon the Franks, white upon the English, green among the Flemings.[30] Henry himself, Philip, Richard, the

Count of Flanders, and the most noble bishops and barons took the ensign upon their shoulders.[31] Thereupon an image of the cross was seen to hover in the fair spring sky above the Gisors elm,[32] and the vast concourse was seized with an inexpressible transport of joy. A wooden rood was planted on the place of dedication, and the spot was named Holy Field (Saint Champ). It appeared that the ardors of Urban at Clermont, of Bernard of Clairvaux at Vézelay, had been surpassed and heaven and earth were joined in one wide resolution.

Henry's sudden espousal of a general crusade for the recovery and defense of the holy places was a public astonishment, for it reversed the considered policy of his whole career. Was he overborne by the universal *élan* at Gisors, as long before the sober Emperor Conrad had been overborne by the fervors of Bernard of Clairvaux and the popular clamor these evoked at Speyer? There are other possibilities. A crusade in 1187 might have turned to the advantage of the Angevin. A common cause outside the scope of dynastic wars, embraced with zeal by all the princes of Europe, a common cause which should moreover redound to the glory of the house of Anjou, might well allay the internecine strife and the disaffection spreading broadcast from the Channel to the Pyrenees; might engage for a restoring interval the restless energies and displace the rancors of Henry's headstrong, now foot-loose, heir; would put off those infernal reckonings under the Gisors elm. If no conspirators were left behind in Europe, a grand crusade would retard, and might deflect, the forces of sedition besetting the king on every hand.

As a matter of fact, in spite of the enthusiasm, the bare prospect of crusade, as now forecast, was not one to enlist the whole heart and soul of Philip Augustus. Though desirous of sharing a campaign in the East, he had a particular objection to leading the Franks on an expedition under the inevitable leadership of the English king, his vassal, to obtain for Henry or one of his sons the overlordship of Jerusalem. In the face of this objection, the plight of the holy places moved him only very slightly.

Meantime the portionless Richard, former Count of Poitou, heir apparent to the throne of England, pretender to Normandy, was looking for the likeliest place to hang his bonnet, plumed with the gorgeous but inexpensive roadside broom. Would this be Rouen or Paris? Which of his frugal overlords should he prefer? Like that other gentleman adventurer, his brother Henry, he had taken the cross (before the convocation at Gisors) without consulting the king his father.[33] While waiting to choose his course more clearly as events unfolded, he cast about for a high commission in the campaign overseas.

From the negotiations at Gisors these three went about their separate businesses, the issues that had brought them together still unresolved. Henry adjourned to Le Mans with a strong ecclesiastical following ardent for crusade. He and his prelates arranged for levies of men and treasure and drew up a prospectus for the ordering of the campaign obviously designed to avert from it the catastrophes into which the guileless reasoning of Abbé Bernard had betrayed the second crusade. For instance, the new expedition was not to be regarded as the penance of any particular king, nor as an incidental means of delivering Europe from every species of malefactor and the gross overpopulation in the mendicant orders of society. Indeed, no tatterdemalion recruits were to be admitted for the sake of their own salvation; every man's array must be whole and seemly. It was further enacted that no one pledged to crusade should swear profanely or play at dice, though later by amendment princes and the higher orders of the clergy were freed from these restrictions. After the ensuing Easter no one was to wear gris, beaver, sable, or scarlet, or indulge in more than two dishes at table. There were positively to be no Amazons. No one was to take any woman with him, unless haply some laundress, who, following on foot, should give no occasion for suspicion.[34] Says Ambrose, "Forgotten were the dances, the singing of lays and ballads, sweet converse, and every earthly joy."

When he had settled his affairs in Anjou, Henry crossed early in 1188 to do likewise in Britain. On both sides of the Channel he levied income and personal property taxes that drew cries of anguish from Jews and Christians, lay and clerical.[35] However, the treasure realized in the Saladin tithe assured a formidable campaign against the Moslem foe and one in which all the other princes of the West would of necessity be auxiliary.

Henry's preparations were proceeding prosperously when, with the impact of a thunderclap, reports reached him in June that his ally, Philip Augustus, in contravention of his pilgrim's vow to observe the Truce of God, had struck into Berry, which belonged, by Angevin reckonings, to Queen Eleanor's estates, but by Capetian divinations, to the dower of the unhappy Alais. Philip had taken Châteauroux and other castles and had finally been held up in his raid only by the strong fortress of Loches on the Loire.[36]

It now began to appear more or less confusedly to Henry's contemporaries that a shift in Capet–Plantagenet relations was taking place. Had Henry at last passed the frontier of disaster toward which, especially since his alienation from the Countess of Poitou, he had been tending? Chroniclers, accustomed for three decades to see the initiative with the Angevins, were perplexed as it passed by degrees to the Capets; they were slow to envisage Henry, the arbiter of Europe, with powerful allies in Germany, Sicily, Castile, the king to whom, as it was believed, had been offered the crown of the Holy Roman Empire, the keys of Jerusalem, in a defensive role. The *preux chevaliers*, as they mustered their contingents for crusade, were filled with misgivings by evidences of change. They withheld their counsels and drew back to lines of expediency.[37]

Since the apparently gratuitous attack from his fellow crusader was very surprising to Henry, he at once sent Archbishop Baldwin of Canterbury and other prelates to learn why the King of France had broken the Truce of God, and to demand a restoration of his strongholds. When these ambassadors returned without satisfaction, Henry sent John to the French king. It was then learned that the acts of Philip were neither more nor less than reprisals for the aggressions of Richard, former Count of Poitou, in Toulouse, whose count was Philip's vassal.

Richard, leaving the great assembly addressed by the Archbishop of Tyre, had accompanied his father to Le Mans and had then gone southward to impose the Truce of God in Poitou, where the old enemies of the ducal house were, as usual, in revolt.[38] Thence he had indeed proceeded to Toulouse to take vengeance for alleged attacks upon certain Poitevin merchants and pilgrims passing through that county on their return from Galicia. In this business he had gone to the length of taking eighteen castles and the town of Cahors from the Count of Toulouse. Count Raymond had thereupon appealed to his overlord, the French king, and Philip had taken Châteauroux to avenge his vassal.[39]

It was obvious that this outbreak must not only seriously disturb the preparations for crusade, but rekindle all the enmities the crusade was intended to avert. Henry hastily levied recruits in England and Wales and in July crossed from Portsea to Barfleur to take a firm stand. His last stage before embarking was Salisbury, which may have been the stronghold to which the queen was remanded after her ungrateful performance at Windsor. If in the customary pandemonium of his departure, he found time to bid Eleanor farewell, his words were the last she heard from his lips. He was setting out for Jerusalem. This time she would not be one of the vast concourse below the Towers of David and of Tancred, nor hear the trampling of the horses, the clash of arms, the shouts of "Saint George," "Dix nous aide," "Monjoie," "Saint Denis," nor to see the marshaling of the thousand banners, to hail her Lord or one of her sons to the throne of King David and King Foulques in that new Jerusalem she had seen rising white and glistening in the mid-century. She would not be there! In a fortress of Britain she would be as remote from all that stir of the new generation as Louis, asleep in his sequestered tomb by the Seine.

22 ✠

The Fallen Elm of Gisors

WHEN HENRY LEFT ENGLAND for crusade he was fifty-five, tending toward obesity, his ruddy hair close cropped and somewhat gray. One of his legs, which were bandy from life in the saddle, was lame from a horse's kick sustained some years before. His gray choleric eyes still flashed fire, his angers rose as hot as ever. He was still quick, urgent, indefatigable. But his face bore the inscription of malaise, of disappointment, hopes deferred, blows parried, of dogged resolution and endurance against heavy odds. The chroniclers say he was aged beyond his years, worn with his ceaseless exertions.[1] His clothes were rich and befitting, but carelessly worn. His hands moved restlessly. On his rough hairy finger the precious ring of Henry Beauclerc which had gone as token to the young king was replaced by a signet engraved with the Plantagenet leopard, which he sometimes made shift to use as a seal.

A favorable wind furrowed the Channel as he set sail, but before noon a fierce gale arose, bringing a violent thunderstorm and a shower of hailstones "the size of doves' eggs."[2] In storm he had come with Eleanor from Barfleur to take England from the house of Blois. In storm he had brought to harbor the captive queen and the ladies of her famous court. In a tempest he had set forth to suppress the rebellion of his sons. And now in a tumult the island faded from his wake, blotted out in a fury of wind and rain. His whole life had been like the crossings, a struggle with the intractable elements of gale and tide.

Henry had resolved to put an end to those recurrent skirmishes at Gisors by which Philip Augustus contrived at untimely moments to stir up disaffection. God's Eyes! If Philip could not keep the peace with his vassal, the Duke of Normandy, then let him face war with his peer, the King of England! Feeling himself at the moment the hero of the church and the elect champion of the Christian world, Henry was arrogant. In August the Kings of England and France again drew up their cohorts on the banks of the Epte near Gisors. The elm, now in full leaf, spread its vaulted tent of shade over the place of parley. Henry's retinue occupied the cool side, while Philip's forces, advancing to their rendezvous, were exposed to the withering summer glare in the open fields. The King of England, ensconced in the shade, awaited the explanations of the culprit who had broken the Truce of God. But Philip had not journeyed to Gisors in the August heat to explain anything to his vassal. Instead he demanded the retrocession of the Vexin and the marriage of the unfortunate Alais. Only when these demands had been met, he affirmed, would he enter on the matter of Châteauroux. The King of England rejected all these claims severally and *in toto* and waited in the shade for other proposals.

The comfortable repose of the English under the elm exasperated the French, who were sweltering in the open. The situation passed to taunts. French wags challenged some elderly worthies of Henry's following to settle differences in single combat with elect champions of France. They made fun of Henry's Welsh contingent, whereupon one of those savage fellows let fly an arrow at the French. At this violation of immunity for parley, the French rushed headlong upon the English with such frenzy that the latter took shelter behind the barbicans of the nearby castle of Gisors. When the French found the English out of reach, they turned with fury on the elm spreading its shade over the ancient meeting place of the Kings of France and the Dukes of Normandy. With ax and sword they fell upon its monstrous trunk.[3] An end to parley between the Capets and the Plantagenets! An end to treachery! An end to ignominious chafferings! The knights of Philip's retinue who had taken the cross, awestruck, saw the gigantic landmark of the Vexin crash to the ground, and they took it for an evil omen. Philip of Flanders and Thibault of Blois ungirt their swords and vowed never to use them again against Christians until they should have returned from Palestine.[4]

In the midst of these untoward events, as if in judgment on the impious bickerings of Christian kings, came fresh news of sacrilege in Jerusalem. Henry received a letter from the Master of the Temple in the ravaged city with a report as straight as words could make it of the catastrophes.

> To his most beloved Lord Henry. . . Health in Him who gives health to kings. Be it known to you that Jerusalem, with the Tower of David, has been surrendered to the enemies of Christ. Thereupon Saladin ordered the cross to be taken down from the Temple of our Lord and had it carried about the city for two days in public view and beaten with sticks. After this he ordered the Temple of our Lord to be cleaned inside and out with rose water from top to bottom, and his laws in regard to it to be promulgated in four different places with wondrous acclamations.[5]

At the fall of the tree, Henry, who had always been careful to violate no feudal rights, renounced his vassal's allegiance to the King of France and challenged Philip to war. He entered the French domain and ravaged the royal city of Mantes and the region round about. By the Splendors of God! He would have something even more precious than the Vexin to barter for the return of Châteauroux! These gestures brought Philip to a conciliatory mood, but nothing was accomplished to heal the breach when the kings met at Châtillon in October. After this encounter Henry observed with alarm that some of his *routiers* melted away at promise of a higher wage. The impossibility of trusting his continental vassals had obliged him to hire mercenaries at heavy cost. His treasure touched bottom, for the Saladin tithe, by this time in the hands of the Templars, had dried the source of revenue.

In November the kings met again at Bonmoulins,[6] still farther from the mutilated stump of Gisors, farther within the frontiers of Normandy. A considerable escort on both sides gathered in a wide circle about the place of parley, the knights of the kings' banners and their bishops pressing as closely as they could to see and hear. It was soon evident that Philip had made progress with his diplomacy since the impasse at Châtillon a month before. To Henry's dismay, Richard arrived at this conference in company with the King of France. One of those sudden suspicions to which the Angevins were subject leapt to Henry's mind. However, he concealed his anxiety and spoke casually.

"Where do you come from, Richard?"

"Beau Sire, I happened to fall in with the King of France upon the road," replied the heir of England. "It seemed too pointed, since I was so near, to avoid him. It is in the interests of peace to treat him with courtesy."

"Very well," returned the king, "but be careful that it so turns out."

This time Philip launched the parley. He renewed his moldy demands for the return of the Vexin, for the speedy marriage of his sister Alais. But this time there was a great deal more. The daughter of Louis Capet should marry no undistinguished vagrant nourished on promises and contingencies. Philip demanded that Henry at once cede to the whilom Count of Poitou his former estates, together with Touraine, Maine, and Anjou, and that the vassals of these provinces should at once do homage to the Duke of Normandy and heir of Engand.

Suddenly Henry saw himself again in the old entanglement in which he had been involved with the young king!

"So this is what you bespeak from me," he said. "Indeed, I perceive that you are interested in my son's preferment; but you ask what I am not prepared to yield."[7]

An impassable chasm yawned between the kings who had vowed to unite upon crusade. Perusing the inalterable refusal written in Henry's every lineament, Richard stood forth in the midst of the astonished crowd as one driven by desperation to an unnatural act.

"I now see as plain as day," he said, "what heretofore has been to me incredible."

Thereupon he ungirt his sword and, throwing himself upon his knees before the French king, he openly, in the presence of the king his father and the lords and bishops of his realm and the nobles of France, did homage to Philip Augustus for all the continental domains to which he claimed inheritance, by this act assuming the vassalage Henry had recently renounced at Gisors; and Philip received him as his liege man for all these possessions.[8]

The bystanders were astounded. Those who desired war were elated; those who desired peace deeply downcast. Among them it was said, in explanation of Richard's perfidy, that Henry had plotted to disinherit him altogether and make John his heir, and it was for this the English king had obtained Philip's consent under the elm to marry Alais to whichever son he, Henry, might elect. Others said that Philip had seduced the heir of England with false promises; others still that the old unquenchable Poitevin rebellion had broken out again. "From the devil they came; to the devil they will go." Henry's vassals murmured. Had they staked their fortunes wisely on the king? The great circle of witnesses dissolved in a babel of conjecture and prediction.

The French king and his liege man, the Count of Poitou, left Bonmoulins together, the latter slipping away softly to avoid detention.[9]

"Alas," groaned Henry when he learned that Richard had escaped, "I might have expected it. My sons will never give me peace. They will ruin both me and themselves. They have always injured me."[10]

He was reënacting, he saw swiftly, the very episodes of the drama of the young king. He remembered the latter's flight from Alençon in 1173, in the same fever of madness, to the same sanctuary. And again this time he could not keep his son's pace in flight. He dispatched Guillaume le Maréchal in pursuit. It was noon when Guillaume reached Amboise, where Richard had lodged the previous night and whence, the marshal learned, he had sent out two hundred letters summoning to his banners the king's vassals, Normans, Angevins, and Poitevins.

Turning back from a fruitless pursuit, Guillaume rejoined Henry in Tours, and there the king learned the full measure of his son's revolt. He turned southward in a desperate effort to invoke a parley with the renegade. But he was too ill to endure that furious course in the saddle. He turned back, weary and depressed, to Saumur for the feast of the Nativity. The court was somber and depleted; a few bishops, a very few *fideles*; of his family, only John. A great part of his baronage held aloof, uncertain where their interests lay. Many had plainly defected.[11]

In the meantime Henry learned that in Paris Philip Augustus and Richard held a joint Christmas court with unusual cheer. They were closer than brothers. In high spirits they rode together in public as elect crusaders, dined in the palace from the same dish, slept in the same bed, shared all their counsels, were locked like David and Jonathan in indissoluble amity. They no longer, out of pride or shame, withheld their mutual confidences in the affair of Alais. The Capet princess was the paramour of the English king, and she had superseded both the incomparable Clifford and the Countess of

Poitou. If the child of this impious union had lived, the king would have disinherited his rightful heirs for a new brood. Now doubtless he plotted to wed Alais to John and raise them to the throne. It was for this he had contrived at Gisors. Such scandals were rife in Paris.[12]

Through Lent the king lay sick of an old wound in his native city of Le Mans.[13] Toward the feast of Saint John, which marked the beginning of the open season for war, he sent an embassy to Philip Augustus and did indeed secure a renewal of conference at La Ferté-Bernard in Normandy. But the issues were no longer negotiable. The question of Alais was not even discussed. And why should Richard chaffer for what he already held? The King of France and the Count of Poitou played upon the theme of John. The King of England, they affirmed, meant to aggrandize him. John, they held, must go upon crusade.[14]

The church with her maternal eye upon the afflictions of Jerusalem could only view the schism in the ranks of her defenders with fearful agitation. While her Christian princes rent each other for their local concerns, the "patrimony of Christ" was swallowed by the infidel. Pope Urban, as well as Lucius, had died from shock over the fate of Jerusalem. Clement, who had girt on the sword of Saint Peter, dispatched his cardinal legate to enforce a peace between the kings vowed to rescue the holy places. At La Ferté-Bernard, John of Agnani charged Philip and Richard, on pain of excommunication, to abate their demands upon the King of England. The King of France and the Count of Poitou were contumacious. Richard jostled the cardinal rudely. Philip advised him to stick to his own concerns, which were certainly not interfering between a vassal and his overlord. He charged the cardinal of having "smelt the sterling" of the English king.

It was plain that the young men who flaunted the Pope of Rome and the puissant King of England sought not peace but war. Henry was conscious, as he fell back on Le Mans, that his adversaries no longer feared him. They saw that life had battered him; that the old energy with which he met challenge to his will had begun to ebb. As all hope for appeal to filial ties vanished, he drew back to the foyer of the Angevins, to the city of his nativity, the home of his father, Geoffrey the Fair. No doubt he recalled, as he passed over the familiar sun-drenched countryside, his exultant ride down from Paris in 1151, when "full of engin," he and the Duke of Normandy had plotted the Angevin alliance with the unhappy Queen of France; when they had laughed at the evil predictions of the withered little Abbé of Clairvaux; when Geoffrey, having laved the hot dust of the road from his body in the cold streams of the Loir, turned in at a wayside castle, and there, in the prime of his life, sickened and died.

Henry's barons no longer gave him counsel. They too were uneasy with misgivings. Their number had dwindled notably. With the king, as he journeyed to Maine, went Geoffrey the Chancellor, his eldest natural son, and John, the youngest of the Plantagenets — all those between, dead or alive, were false — and Guillaume le Maréchal. They had not proceeded far when their progress became a retreat. Philip and Richard, following hard upon his rear, possessed themselves of Henry's strongholds, one after another, as soon as he had passed them by: [15] La Ferté-Bernard, Montfort, Beaumont, Ballin, and the lesser castles of Trôo, Montoire, Château-du-Loir. It became plain that the renegades were hunting down the person of the king. Quickening his pace, Henry drew into Le Mans, which, through the quiet weeks of Lent, he had strengthened against attack. The church of Saint Julian being rebuilt after a recent fire,[16] the gray castle of his forebears, familiar from his childhood, rose reassuringly on the mount. Under his orders his men razed certain suburbs, cleared the moats, closed the bridges and the gates.

On June 11 a deep fog enshrouded the mount and the valleys of the Sarthe and its tributary Huisne.[17] It was impossible to get the bearings of the approaching forces or to measure their strength. Guillaume le Maréchal, pushing up the Huisne with a few reconnoiterers, learned that an army of French was creeping under cover of the mist along the river whose streams separated it from Le Mans, not more distant than an arrow's drive. Richard well knew the fords, the avenues of access to and retreat from the old capital of the Angevins, which he had explored from childhood. He was now bringing the Capets to its weakest gate. The reconnoiterers took counsel whether or not to tell the king, and it is significant of their despair that they decided nothing could be gained by dealing him that blow.

"What a pity," said Geoffrey of Brûlon to the marshal, "that Emenidus had not such a messenger as you. You would have been useful to him." It was an allusion in the midst of ruin to the romance of Alexander in which Henry and his barons had delighted in the prosperous days before the queen had spread the vogue of the Arthurian romance. Even now the knights laughed.[18]

Issuing from the south gate, Henry ordered his men to break the bridge over the Huisne, drive spiles in the ancient fords, scatter sharp stones in the bed of the stream. During this proceeding the fog lifted and he himself beheld the pavilions in which the French had passed the night spread along the edge of the wood where he was accustomed to hunt, only a few yards from the river. At this sight Henry turned to Guillaume as to one who should wake him from a nightmare and permitted himself to be led back within the walls. There they stayed all night, watching and waiting. The next morning they heard mass at daybreak. A strong feudal instinct possessed the king. He could not believe they would attack his person. He disarmed his body-guard and with his son John went forth in his "cotte de linge." It was well that they had set the day ahead with early mass, for there along the Huisne the French, sounding the stream with their lances, had found an abandoned ford and were crossing below the spiles pell-mell for the south gate. Cries rose in the city.[19]

"Here, here! Now God help the marshal!"

A melee began in which Guillaume took a heavy toll of Poitevin barons pressing on the gate. In the meantime Stephen of Tours, Henry's seneschal, fired the suburbs on the eastern slope of the mount to destroy cover for the besiegers. But a veering wind sucked the flame along the wall. It rose with billows of smoke and roaring leapt the ramparts, catching eagerly in many places at once. The denizens of the *faubourg* fled in panic from their blazing thatches. Passing through the quarter to stay the fire, the king and Guillaume came upon a woman weeping bitterly as she dragged her household gear into the street. The marshal, "always piteous by nature," as became a *preux chevalier* nurtured in the court of Poitiers, himself dismounted to help the woman. He seized a feather bed smoldering on the under side, and the smudge, penetrating his helmet, forced him to take it off. While thus delayed, the fire pressed on their heels. Seeing the quarter of his capital seething with flame, Henry challenged heaven.

"Christ," he cried, "why should I honor Thee, who takest from me all I hold most dear on earth, who sufferest me to be thus shamefully beset by that stripling traitor." [20]

With his household rallied by Guillaume, he left the north gate and took the road at a gallop for Fresnay, pausing only to destroy bridges and block fords in his wake.[21]

The French meantime from their pavilions on the Huisne waited for the fire to do its work. Inside the walls the citizens toiled, not comprehending the strife, to defend their blazing roofs. Their count, who had sworn never to desert the city of his predilection; the king, who in a lifetime of conflict had never turned his back upon a challenge to his power, had fired the mount and taken to the road, the Count of Poitou and his train in hot pursuit. The intolerable feuds of the Angevins! From the devil they came; to the devil they might go! [22]

Turning for a last look at the mount reeking against the brazen June sky, Henry vented his bitterness.

"The city I have loved best on earth, the city where I was born and bred, where my father lies buried, where is the body of Saint Julian, this, O God, to the increase of my shame, Thou has reft from me. I will requite as best I can. I will assuredly rob Thee of the thing Thou prizest most in me, my soul." [23]

Out of a cloud of dust behind their flight there came galloping knights with Richard in the lead. Guillaume fell back from the king's rear, turned upon them, and interposed his lance. The startled Count of Poitou faced his old master-at-arms.

"By the feet of God, Maréchal," he cried, "do not kill me. I wear no hauberk."

"May the devil kill you, for I will not," shouted the marshal, at the same moment driving his lance into the count's horse so that it fell and Richard plunged to the ground. By this feat Guillaume saved the king from capture, perhaps from death. At night Henry reached Fresnay, fifteen kilometers from Le Mans, so worn with fatigue and chagrin that he refused to undress, but lay with Geoffrey the Chancellor's cloak upon him. Somewhere in the melee John had disappeared.

A major part of Henry's following, supposing he would take the same course, struck northward from Le Mans to Alençon in the heart of Normandy, where both succor and a means of flight were more secure. Thither Guillaume and Geoffrey the Chancellor went to bring them back with all possible recruits. They were two weeks evading the ambush of the French along the roads Henry had been expected to follow from Maine. In the meantime, struggling painfully, the English king made his way with a handful of his men to his invincible treasure castle of Chinon in Anjou, and there he lay suffering from an old sore freshly envenomed by the killing ride from Le Mans. There he heard disquieting rumors. In the fortress of Chinon they made a little pretense of gaiety to cheer the king when Guillaume returned from Normandy. But the feint was apparent.

"Maréchal," said Henry, "did you hear, as you passed over the road, that the King of France has taken my city of Tours?"

"Sire, the bold Capetian does you much injury. It is even so."

Hard upon this confirmation of bad news came an embassy from Philip Augustus in the persons of Philip of Flanders and that spokesman of the house of Champagne, the Archbishop of Reims, to summon the King of England to an interview near Tours. Henry's counselors urged him to make an attempt to retrieve his lands. Dismissing all but the knights of his banner, he journeyed painfully to Columbières and there lodged with the Templars.

"Maréchal," he said, on reaching his hostel, "a cruel pain, beginning in my heel, has spread through my feet and legs. My whole body is on fire."

Guillaume saw indeed that the king's countenance flushed and darkened. They stretched him on a bed to await the conference.

The next day the King of the Franks summoned the Plantagenet king to appear before him. He heard that Henry, his vassal, was very ill, had eaten nothing, could neither stand nor sit. But Richard assured Philip that the king was at his old tricks, plying a ruse. Stung by the taunt from his son, Henry rose from his bed with a supreme effort.

"Only end this thing," he cried, "I will yield anything to get away. But one day, I swear, if I live, I will recover my lands."

When he appeared at the parley, even Philip was moved by his aspect. Less brutal than Richard, he begged a folded cloak and invited Henry to sit upon it. But the king scorned his pity. He would, as had always been his custom at parley, keep his horse.[24] He desired to know what they wanted of him, and why they had cut off his lands. He then learned that he had been summoned, not to treat of peace, but to hear a sentence pronounced upon him. He must first renew his homage to the King of France, which he had renounced by the fallen elm of Gisors. He must cede Poitou, Normandy, Maine, Anjou, and Touraine to Richard and call upon his barons on both sides of the Channel to swear homage to his son for all the possessions the latter claimed. He must pay Philip a heavy indemnity for his expense in the conquest of Berry in which he had taken from Henry the castle of Châteauroux. Philip and the Count of Poitou would hold all the castles they had lately seized, or if the King of England preferred, the Norman Vexin, as surety for the performance of these acts. As for Alais, Henry would commit her at once to five knights of Richard's choosing, so that the count might have his bride upon his return from crusade. Ah yes, they had all been going to Jerusalem! Where was John? [25]

There was a silence during which all bent upon Henry's answer to this call for his abdication. Suddenly a clap of thunder leapt from the clear sky. For whom this omen — the victors or the vanquished? Still in silence the kings fell apart, when a second clap, louder than the first, startled the company. Henry reeled and but for the support of his men, would have fallen from his horse. He murmured acceptance of the terms, asking only that a written list of all those who had deserted him should be prepared. When Richard advanced to receive from his father the kiss of peace, Henry breathed fiercely in his ear,

"May God not let me die, until I have avenged myself on you as you deserve." [26]

❧

No friend hath death.
(Mort n'a ami.)
        Guillaume le Maréchal, III, 114

Though worn with pain and utterly depressed by his losses, Henry had not accepted the idea of ultimate defeat. He was surprised beyond measure at the sweeping and relentless conditions imposed upon him. It was the climax of his woe that his own son had compassed the first humiliation he had ever known. They bore him back to Chinon in a litter and on the way he cursed the day he had been born, called upon heaven to curse his sons and

EFFIGIES FROM THE TOMBS OF HENRY II, ELEANOR, AND
RICHARD AT FONTEVRAULT, AND OF JOHN AT WORCESTER
CATHEDRAL

APSE OF TWELFTH-CENTURY CHURCH IN
TALMONT

ENTRANCE TO CASTLE OF ANGERS

himself.[27] The Archbishop of Canterbury and the Bishop of Hereford, who accompanied him, besought him in vain to retract his dreadful words. But when he reached his stronghold above the Vienne and looked down upon the busyness of the town, the tranquil windings of the river and the bridge he had built leading down to Poitou, he was seized with compunction. He asked to be taken to the fortress chapel and there yielded a confession, was absolved, and received communion.

But no medicine could be found for the malady that possessed his body. Groaning he awaited the list of those who had deserted him, which Roger Malchael had stayed behind to obtain in Tours. When Roger unfolded the parchment to read, his breath failed.

"Sire, may Christ help me," he faltered, "for the first name that is written here is the name of Count John, your son." [28]

The king's countenance flushed.

"Is it true that John, whom I loved beyond all my sons, and for whose gain I have suffered all this misery, has forsaken me?"

The unnatural prognostication of the fresco of eaglets in the palace of Winchester had been fulfilled. Henry turned his face to the wall.

"It is enough," he said, "no need to read the others. Let the rest go as it will. I care no more for myself nor for aught in this world." [29]

His muttering then grew incoherent, but the bystanders gathered scraps of his thought.

"Shame, shame," he muttered, "shame on a conquered king."

It was the son of his youth, no scion of the disastrous Poitevin, who administered the small human comforts at the last. It was Geoffrey the Chancellor who propped the king's head upon his breast and fanned from his face the flies that swarmed and buzzed in the July heat; who, when moments of consciousness returned, soothed him with words of affection; who strained his senses to gather his father's dying thoughts.

"Dearest son," whispered Henry, "whatever a son could show of filial faith and gratitude, you have shown. God grant that I may requite you as the best of fathers should. In all my fortunes you have shown yourself a son with natural affection."

"Your health and prosperity," returned the chancellor, "are all I ask, and if God will preserve these, I shall desire nothing more."

It was to Geoffrey that Henry gave as token the Plantagenet signet ring with the leopard upon it which he wore as he started for Jerusalem.[30]

Henry died in his Angevin treasure castle, but as at the death of William the Conqueror in Rouen, no suitable regalia for his burial could be found. His retainers had rifled his personal apparel. Some trappings were levied here and there, a sword, a cloak, a makeshift scepter. For crown a fillet of gold embroidery from some woman's gear was bound upon his brow. In Chinon the first night his household kept his wake. The place in Grammont which he had once designated for his burial he had renounced after the death of the young king.[31] There were disorders and disaffections in Le Mans, which was the necropolis of his Angevin forebears. They made shift to bury the king in the nearby abbey of nuns in Fontevrault. It was the place where fourteen years before he had tried to immure the seditious queen. As in the case of the young king, when the poor gathered at the bridge for the funeral alms, none was forthcoming. The nuns came out processionally to meet the cortege of their patron, kept a wake for him all night, and received his body honorably in their choir.[32]

To Fontevrault the Count of Poitou came for the entombment of the king. Like Henry himself at the death of the young king, Richard so controlled himself that none could say with what emotion he gazed upon the dead. Kneeling courteously, he remained before the bier for the space of a paternoster. At that moment, to the horror of the bystanders, blood burst from the nostrils of the king and oozed to the floor.[33] It was as if from another world the dead king renewed the curse he had uttered on the road from Tours. But unperturbed by the maledictions of a ghost, the Count of Poitou sped from the burial in the crypt of the nuns and hastened away to the treasure castle of Chinon.

> *I was Henry the King. To me*
> *Divers realms were subject.*
> *I was duke and count of many provinces.*
> *Eight feet of ground is now enough for me*
> *Whom many kingdoms failed to satisfy.*
> *Who reads these lines, let him reflect*
> *Upon the narrowness of death,*
> *And in my case behold*
> *The image of our mortal lot.*
> *This scanty tomb doth now suffice*
> *For whom the earth was not enough.*[34]

23 ✠

The Lion Heart is King

The eagle of the broken pledge shall rejoice in her third nestling.
Geoffrey of Monmouth, *Prophecies of Merlin*, Book VII, 3

She is called the "eagle" because she spread her wings over two realms, the French
and the English; the "broken pledge" signifies that she was disjoined from the French
king by reason of consanguinity, and from the English king by her imprisonment,
which lasted sixteen years. By her "third nestling" is signified Richard, her third son.
Ralph of Diceto, II, 67

HENRY DIED ON THE SIXTH OF JULY 1189. Guillaume le Maréchal, who had been
in charge of his household in the last days, accompanied his body to Fontevrault, and there, before the obsequies, fronted the heir to the throne whom
he had unhorsed on the road from Le Mans to Fresnay two weeks before.
He did not, in the circumstances, expect to be made chancellor of England
nor seneschal of Poitou. But, as a soldier of fortune, Guillaume had always
taken his luck as he found it. He could at least reflect that loyalty to the
dead king had not been treason to the latter's rebel son. Fidelity was something to barter for in the feudal world and might commend itself to the next
Plantagenet, who knew the stuff of which Guillaume was made and would
at once have need of men whom he could trust. Moreover, the marshal had
something to say. But when the two met in the crypt of Fontevrault,
Guillaume waited for the heir to speak.

"Maréchal," said the Count of Poitou, "you tried to kill me, and would
have done it, if my arm had not turned aside your lance."

"Fair Sire," replied Guillaume, "I had no intention of killing you, nor
did I make any attempt to do so. If I can drive my lance aright when armed,
I can surely do it when unarmed, as I then was, and it would have been as easy
for me to strike you as to strike your horse. If I killed your horse, I do not
think I did wrong, nor do I repent."

"Maréchal," said the count, "I pardon you and hold no enmity."

"I thank you, fair sweet Sire," rejoined Guillaume, "but I did by no means
desire your death."

It was the kind of reconciliation that *preux chevaliers* bred in the queen's
court in Poitiers might be expected to make. Bygones were bygones.

"Maréchal," the count went on, "go forward with my Sheriff Piepart to look after my lands and my affairs in England until I come. Tomorrow I will myself bury the dead with the honors due so high a man."

Guillaume lingered valet-wise on one foot hesitating. He was thirty-five. The days of tournament were over. He had fulfilled in Palestine his crusader's vow as proxy for the young king. It was time for him to settle down. In all the bestowal of rewards with which Richard was certain to inaugurate the new regime, was there no recompense for a knight who could be trusted with a Plantagenet's high business? He gently reminded his new patron that the king who lay dead beside them had promised to reward his sterling fidelity with the young and exceedingly rich Countess of Pembroke and Striguil. The Count of Poitou had already offered this matchless prize to Baldwin of Béthune, who had ridden with him into Le Mans, but bethinking him that this was no time to cross his liege man, he revoked his promise to Baldwin then and there and bestowed the lady with her excellent fiefs upon Guillaume.[1]

Two decades and many arduous undertakings had measured Guillaume's ascent from penury to magnificence. Twenty years before, as Patrick of Salisbury's landless nephew, he had in his first knightly exploit rescued Queen Eleanor from the ambush of the Lusignans on a highway in Poitou; and her graciousness and liberality had opened to him the palace of Poitiers in the days of its utmost splendor. He had then risen to the status of equerry to her sons, again to that of master-at-arms, tutor, mentor, tournament champion of the young king; had become the right arm of the elder king in his last days. He had known and served all the Plantagenets honorably, laying each in turn under some bond of gratitude. In the confused feuds of the reigning house, he had found himself tossed from side to side, but never in treason to his knightly vows. And now he came at last in his prime to the mighty dignities of Pembroke and Striguil. The girl bride, "the beautiful, the good, the wise lady of high birth," found Guillaume kind. The story of their long devotion, related in Guillaume's biography, is one of the most affecting domestic chapters in feudal history.

Guillaume sped with Piepart through Maine and Normandy to take ship at Dieppe,[2] pausing only to certify his possession of some of his heiress' estates in the neighborhood of the port. In their haste to catch a ship, both suffered injuries in the crash of a landing stage, and Guillaume alone succeeded in making the crossing. With all haste he made for Winchester to break the bars of the queen's prison and restore her to the world. To his great surprise he found her at liberty upon her own recognizance, her gates wide open to the English summer. "Could any be so uncivil or so obdurate as not to bend him to that lady's wishes?" Cavalcades of magnates were already moving over the highways of Britain to proffer homage in her court.[3] No one, not even De Glanville, the keeper of the Plantagenet hostages and marriage prizes, the custodian of the queen, had dared to hold her one day in captivity when the death of Henry was certified. Times had changed. Guillaume found her welcoming (*avenante*) as in the old days in Poitiers and, in spite of the catastrophic events abroad, "happier than she had been."[4]

Queen Eleanor was now about sixty-eight, a ripe age for the twelfth century. For fifteen years of her precious prime she had been restrained from that share in the fashioning of her era to which her feudal fortunes entitled her. Her years of grace had been squandered. Yet she came from her retirement not as one who had set her face against her day, but as one furnished with richer understanding and prepared to meet the issues of the hour. It had been impossible to keep her out of commerce with her world. She had had her occasional traffic with bishops and barons and with emissaries from her sons, with whom she had never lost her authority. Even in utmost penury she had known the ministrations of chaplains and clerks, of keepers and serving folk. She emerged with no diminution of her energy or insight, but with a political sagacity and prudence that had not characterized her earlier days. It was as if, in her captivity, she had nourished her spirits at night on Boethius' *Consolation of Philosophy* and listened by day, not only to the echoes of the greater world, but to the little voices of little men that penetrated the fine chinks of her prison.

Guillaume was a rude chronicler, but the queen read current history from his garbled tale as from an open book, plucking from his blunt and succinct words the salient facts and deciding at the same time what must be done. While Richard was delayed abroad to accept the homage of Henry's doubtful vassals, to make his castles safe, and to receive the glaive and banners of Normandy in Rouen, Eleanor at once assumed the regency in England. Gathering a retinue with that sudden urgency to which Henry's vassals were accustomed, she proceeded at once with the marshal to London. There she convened at Westminster all the nobles and prelates within reach of her summons and took from all, under the witness of the Archbishop of Canterbury, oaths of allegiance to the new king. No one questioned the authority of the aging woman suddenly brought from her long seclusion to set her own seal upon affairs of state. During her brief stay in London, among other duties, she assisted in the distribution of the valuable marriage prizes that had been accumulating in the custody of the Plantagenets, and so cemented the allegiance of strong young men.[5] Only the Princess Alais was kept in reserve and under strict surveillance. Here Guillaume received the young Countess of Pembroke. He had no leisure to woo her according to the *Tractatus de Amore*. In view of the urgency of the times, he was advised not to dally. He borrowed decent clothes from a friend, wed the countess without delay, and then retired, as his biographer relates, to a "quiet and pleasant place" in Surrey to nurse his recent injury during his honeymoon.[6]

From London Eleanor made progresses to other centers. She convened her assemblies, as the chronicler says, "wherever she pleased," received the oaths of homage to her son, and transacted the business of court and chancellery, setting her own seal upon her sovereign acts. She appeared without hindrance in the royal castles,[7] not as agent or emissary, but as their undisputed mistress. Rome was arrested at her gates. She expelled a papal legate for presuming to set foot on English soil without her warrant and safe-conduct.[8] Never had her mandates been more authoritative.

The queen's statesmanship in this period was neither subtle nor roundabout. Her measures were timely and practical. She made a plain ingenuous bid for popularity and addressed herself with perspicacity to those who bore grievances under Henry's dispensation. She knew that Richard, bred for another destiny, was neither known nor loved in Britain. Though born in Oxford, he had since his infancy made two brief visits to the island, and then his first thought had been to put the Channel between himself and Southampton as soon as possible. He knew neither the language nor the visage of the domain which a series of fatalities had brought to his inheritance. Richard, as *preux chevalier*, might be the beau ideal of Poitiers, but the islanders, less exposed to the utter refinements of chivalry, were not to be overborne by his merely sumptuary aspect. The castellans and burghers of Britain had somehow to be bewitched into forgetting that they had recently been at large expense of life, limb, and treasure to extinguish the seditions of this splendid fire brand Count of Poitou.

In this difficult situation the queen knew exactly what to do. Her long confinement had taught her, as Hoveden says, "how hateful prisons are," and that it is "a most delightful refreshment to the spirits to be liberated therefrom." The English dungeons teemed with subjects awaiting the justice that Henry's confusions on the Continent had long delayed, and especially with trespassers against his oppressive forest laws.[9] "For the good of Henry's soul," Eleanor opened the keeps where these culprits languished and loosed scores of obscure creatures to praise in scattered towns and hamlets the clemency of the new regime.

She gave clerks likewise a reason to rejoice. For his sudden journeyings Henry had stabled relays of horses in the abbeys, where the burden of maintaining them was an intolerable nuisance and expense to the abbots and the chapters. The queen delivered the orders from this imposition and thenceforth cowled personages, riding to and fro upon their multifarious business, proclaimed in priory and town and chapter house a new, more spacious time. Meanwhile she did not neglect preparations for a magnificent coronation. "Such as I see you, thus I deem you," was a proverb in Poitou. Nothing so puts a populace in good humor as to pay for a splendid demonstration. The queen well knew the value of effects.

So competently had Eleanor managed that when, on the 20th of August, Richard landed in Southampton, England was joyful at his advent,[10] hoping by all the good auguries of the month just past for an amendment of their affairs. Whom Henry had dispossessed, says Hoveden, Richard had restored; whom Henry had banished, Richard had recalled; whom Henry had imprisoned, Richard had set free; whom Henry had afflicted with penalties, Richard had sent away rejoicing.[11]

✤

Little time was gone by ere he had himself crowned at London. There did I see great gifts given, and I saw such abundance of meats set forth that none might keep tally thereof; nor ever in my life have I seen a court served in nobler fashion. And I saw vessels of great price in that hall so fair, and tables saw I so close pressed together that they could in no wise be numbered.

Ambrose, *L'Estoire de la guerre sainte*, p. 13

For the first time since the Conqueror the succession was undisputed. Against the coming of the king, London streets, so long without royal display, were cleaned and sweetened with the strewing of fresh rushes. House fronts were hung with tapestries, garlands, and green boughs, and in window embrasures burghers set their holy images. In cellars and kitchens butchers, bakers, and vintners, and guilds of citizens, each with special perquisites, vied in making ready the prodigious coronation feast.[12] The crowning was set for Sunday, September 3, marked on the calendar as an "Egyptian" or unlucky day; [13] but time pressed and the Plantagenets were less superstitious than the folk of the time.[14]

The coronation ceremony still in use in Britain was already, in Richard's day, traditional. Then as now it presented that twofold dramatic allegory, prefiguring in act and symbol not only the already historic relation of the king to the people who accepted him, but also that mystical relation between the state and the church, the king and the primate, that even the martyrdom of Becket had not dissolved. No one but the Archbishop of Canterbury could crown and consecrate the king accepted by the people; but the primate might not touch the crown before the king had himself taken it from the altar and placed it in the hands of the archbishop, who only then, and with the assistance of two nobles, placed it upon the royal head. In the ceremony echoed the salvos, "saving the dignity of our order," "saving the honor of the king."

Richard, moving amidst all the colors of the estates and the orders and the symbols of temporal and eternal efficacy that pricked through the clouds of incense and the fluttering glow of tapers, appeared on this day less august as heir of all the Angevin empire than as the soldier of Christ destined to lead the forces of Christendom to the rescue of the holy shrines. The white cross of his dedication outburned the gold and gems of the royal regalia. Many of that host in Westminster were signed with the same emblem. The *Te Deum* that swelled in the vaults of the abbey were presently, if prayers were fulfilled, to resound in the citadel of Jerusalem.

❧

The King then put up for sale everything he had, castles, vills, and estates.

Hoveden

In spite of the ingratiating exertions of Queen Eleanor in her son's behalf, the British were not long in discovering that, so far as the newly arrived Count of Poitou was concerned, his coming to England had as its main object the gathering of a massy additional weight of sterling for crusade. Henry had already in the preceding year collected in Britain an abundant Saladin tithe, but this, regrettably for Richard, had been entrusted to the custody of the Templars. Coeur-de-Lion, however, found means of reaping harvests from fields already gleaned. Men of consequence, holding employment under Henry, redeemed their offices with ransom. The chancellor recovered his seal with £3000. De Glanville, the incorruptible keeper of Henry's prisoners, including the queen, was so ruined by exactions that he was obliged to take the cross to compass his necessities.[15] Nobles and prelates who had been overborne by the popular enthusiasm to go upon crusade found they could buy immunity, and their compositions, says Devizes, "rolled like nuts into the exchequer." Jews were plundered. Public offices were sold. Bishops learned that fortunes accumulating in their sees could be profitably invested in lands and rents, and many a manor, many a castle with its honors, passed into the hands of prelates.

In the carnival of speculation, the Bishop of Durham, an elderly relative of the royal house, purchased the secular title of Earl of Northumberland to add to his ecclesiastical dignities. "Behold," exclaimed Richard, "how out of an old bishop I have made a new earl." "I would sell London itself," declared the king, "if I could find a purchaser." [16] Men whose memories reached back to Stephen's reign saw Henry's lifelong efforts to bring the great castles under royal control squandered in a few months, and the land committed again to such anarchy as had prevailed in those unhappy days.

While these transactions were going forward at a lively pace, Richard assembled in Dover and other southern ports all the seaworthy ships to be found from Hull to Bristol, for he had given up the overland route to Palestine for which Henry had procured safe-conduct from the King of Hungary and the sublime Comneni.[17] Perhaps Eleanor, remembering the perils and fatigues of that route, the crafty Greeks, the unspeakable Turks, and the wintry landscapes of Paphlagonia, dissuaded him. Also, with the queen's counsel, he planned for the safety of the Angevin empire during his absence, and for the firm observance of the Truce of God.

The policies of the Plantagenets were directed less toward outright benefits for their subjects than toward the appeasement or repression of possible troublemakers. Many of these were disposed of by the simple expedient of forcing them into the crusade.[18] The queen's gravest anxiety at this time in which Richard was exposing his life to peril was the matter of the succession. The Plantagenet race had dwindled and the long dalliance with the Princess Alais had left Richard at thirty-five without direct heirs.

In the meantime, until Richard could secure the future of his dynasty, there were three possible aspirants to the crown, and not one of these satisfied the queen. Among them, her grandson, Arthur of Brittany, the three-year-old son of Geoffrey Plantagenet, had, in a strict view of legitimacy, the highest claim; but he was without a powerful following, even abroad, and his house was, for reasons not fully understood, detested by the ruling Plantagenets. He was still a child. There would be time and occasion to deal with him.

The second was Geoffrey,[19] Henry's bastard son and his last chancellor, designated by the elder king on his deathbed as Archbishop of York. He had preferred no claims to recognition as of the royal line, and had promptly resigned his chancellor's seal upon the death of Henry. But he was bold, ambitious, unprovided, and determined to establish himself in the general distribution of the Plantagenet spoils. He had once, in the company of his familiars, set the lid of a golden bowl upon his head and called out with deprecating laughter, "Is not this skull fit to wear a crown?"[20] The law of legitimacy was stern, but Geoffrey was a man to rise in some hour of feudal anarchy, as had the bastard Conqueror. He was now beyond thirty-five, unapt by every gift of nature, and by his nurture, for ecclesiastical preferment. But Richard and the queen, who might in other circumstances have prevented his elevation to the great See of York, actually promoted it, because his taking of orders rendered him ineligible for royal roles.[21]

The third was lack-land John. John, since the first general alarm for the Holy Land, had sought royal leave to go upon crusade, but Henry had refused to offer the last of the eaglets to the perils overseas. Richard had no desire to have his broilsome cadet go with him to Palestine. For his renunciation of the crusader's vow, Lackland was contented with brilliant prospects nearer home. The Plantagenets appeased his lust for prestige with such enormous grants of land as seemed to fortify him against any rival claims to the succession. A chain of towns and fortresses running lengthwise through the midst of the island, together with estates in Cornwall, entrenched John in strategic strongholds and supplied him with a royal revenue.[22]

Such reckless distribution of the castles that Henry had struggled to bring into the king's hands gave rise to unsettling rumors and to murmurings of indignation among the magnates. It was said that Richard planned to abandon Britain to the youngest Plantagenet and content himself with the Angevin domains upon the Continent;[23] that he would himself mount the throne of his great-grandfather, Foulques of Jerusalem; that he was prey to a secret malady and would not survive the hardships of crusade;[24] that he had had a premonition that, as a soldier of the cross, he would redeem with his life his crime of patricide.

In providing for the administration of the affairs of Britain, the Plantagenets followed the simple "hungry falcon" theories laid down long before for Henry's guidance by Matilda Empress — to place relatively obscure men in seats of responsibility where their ambitions, their dependence upon bounty, and their gratitude, in various combinations, could be expected to keep them vigilant and honest.

The elevation of William Longchamp, the chancellor, to the bishopric of Ely made him that coveted instrument, a business manager for royalty that might be expected in his character of prelate to keep the peace with ecclesiastical interests. Ely could, says Newburgh, "use both hands as right hands." He was a "hungry falcon" with a fanatical zeal for his king and such pride of office as only a parvenu could feel. He was especially relied upon to hold John in check. His physical limitations were calculated to keep him out of intrigue. Though it is not necessary to accept Giraldus' malicious description of him as malformed, low-browed, hirsute, and generally repulsive, he was by no means commanding — small of stature, lame, stammering.[25] His usefulness was his Argus-eyed vigilance where he felt the king's interest concerned. He could be counted on to be ruthless with the king's enemies. To the chancellor were added several justiciars, some of the old regime, some younger men, among these the dependable Guillaume le Maréchal, now Earlelect of Pembroke. In the meantime important sees were filled.[26]

At the heart of the structure the queen reigned supreme. Restored not only to her own dower, but to those of two predecessors as well, she lacked no resource to give effect to her will.[27] As regent she trusted no testimony regarding events. The Countess of Poitou forgot that she was growing old and, like Henry in his prime, she bustled about with hastily mustered escorts and examined the state of the realm with her own ear and eye, and gave orders for the righting of grievances and the discipline of recreants. She was in her native role at last; and no sovereign in Europe had had a more varied experience with men and affairs than she.

✤

Richard's fleet comprised great ships with broadsides well protected, manned with stout crews well able to defend them. On board he put abundance of gold and silver, rich furs, utensils, precious vestments, arms of all sorts, supplies of bacon, wine, cheese, flour, biscuit, pepper, cumin, wax, electuaries, various drinks, spiced meats, and syrups.

Guillaume le Maréchal, III, 124

While admirals looked to the lading of the ships, Richard hurried abroad to set affairs in order in his continental domains and to gather new resources for the expedition overseas,[28] and held his Christmas court in Bures.[29] Queen Eleanor followed him in February with the Princess Alais; and since Eleanor can hardly have desired that young woman's company at the gatherings of magnates among whom she showed herself with restored prestige as mistress of the Norman castles, it was probably at this time that Alais became the prisoner of the Plantagenets in the fortress of Rouen. From Bures Eleanor went with Richard to Anjou to put her urgent or restraining hand on the affairs of that region, woefully confused since the untoward death of Henry.

For the first time in years the queen escaped the fog and darkness of the English winter and breathed freely the delicious air of mild familiar lands. While Richard made a circuit of the counties of Poitou, she appears to have remained in Chinon or the neighborhood, where numerous charters bearing her seal attest her presence.[30] From the lofty heights of the treasure castle, where Henry had wrestled with death, she could look down upon the bridge, the road, the river valley, toward the abbey where the king slept quietly in the choir of the nuns, in that very refuge where he had designed to immure her as abbess. In one of her charters, "for the repose of Henry's soul," she made a grant to Fontevrault.

After finishing a round of his provinces, Richard kept a rendezvous with Philip Augustus at Gisors to arrange details for the final muster of western Christendom for crusade. Here, in spite of the urgency of military matters, Philip insisted on raising the harassing question of Alais and harping upon her injuries. If Richard should not survive the hazards of the holy war, what then became of all the glittering promises made to that princess? The King of the Franks desired to see his sister married forthwith; or, if the Plantagenets were resolved to repudiate their reiterated vows, then at least he looked to see Alais returned to her kin, together with her marriage portion. The site where once the Gisors elm had spread its great branches over a place of truce and concord had become a spot marked for conflict. Richard did not succeed in pacifying Philip, but he circumvented him. Since the compact of Christian sovereigns forbade women to accompany the crusade, Coeur-de-Lion put the Capetian off with promises to fulfill his engagement on his return from Palestine; and in order that he might find his bride safe in that day, he held it best to keep her still in custody, together with her dower. In spite of the transparency of the subterfuge, the King of the Franks could not press the issue with the great movement of troops afoot all over Europe.

✤

Had ye but seen the host when forth it came! The earth trembled with its coming.
                                                                    Ambrose

Richard's contingents for the holy war were mustered in Tours,[31] where
he had first taken the cross without his father's knowledge [32] and whither he
now returned to receive his staff and scrip. The ovation to the king, dedicated
at the very outset of his reign to his heroic mission, passed all bounds. The
city could hardly contain the armies, to say nothing of the folk gathered to
bid farewell to the soldiers of Christ. They came from every side, says the
chronicler, "as thick as drops of rain." Tears flowed freely in the streets as men
signed with the cross broke from the embraces of their kindred and, turning
from the groans and cheers of their beloved, took place, each under his own
knight's banners, and set their faces for Jerusalem. Though the chroniclers
are silent, the queen must have been there to bedew her "third nestling" with
pious tears. "Saint Leonard" and "Saint George" and "Dix nous aide." To the
strains of that crusaders' song, "Wood of the Cross," the host was lost to
sight on the route for Vézelay.

24 ✢

The Sicilian Interlude

Satan, jealous of the auspicious beginning of the crusade of Christian princes, sowed discord among them.

Guillaume de Nangis

THE HOST THAT GATHERED on the slopes of Vézelay in the early days of July 1190, "when the rose was sweetly blowing," [1] was no such penitential throng as had swarmed under Louis's banners at the summons of Abbé Bernard in the mid-century. There were, for the time being, few mendicants, no paroled convicts, no Amazons, no curious travelers, no devouring camp followers in this new stirring of the Christian world. This was cleanly a military enterprise, its armies better calculated to frighten Saladin and the kings of Babylon than any that had heretofore pitched its countless tents on the hillsides of Burgundy. On the 30th of June the English fleet raised its sails in the harbor of Dover, taking off for Mediterranean ports.

The chronicler, reviewing the grand muster, concluded that it was the devil that stirred up enmities between the Kings of the Franks and the English before they left Vézelay. If these rancors were indeed the work of Satan, the betrayer of mankind never had more golden opportunity to ply his malice. In the last months of preparation Philip's enthusiasm for the holy war had declined. He had recently lost his queen, Isabelle of Hainaut,[2] and her death gave him new anxieties over her inheritance in the Low Countries for the son she had bequeathed to him. The Carolingian dreams that he had confessed to his vassalage at the outset of his reign had so far not materialized. But grosser afflictions than these brought his spirits down. He was consumed by a venomous jealousy of his vassal and brother-in-arms, the King of England.

In Vézelay Richard, without having done anything to merit his peculiar fortunes, was the observed of all observers. He was ten years older than his liege lord; his exploits as a warrior were already legendary, his treasure past reckoning, his trappings magnificent. He was more prepossessing, too, more commanding in presence, more eloquent, more openhanded with his bounty. The knights, even those of the Frankish banners, sought his counsel on practical details of the journeys and the campaigns that lay ahead, and these colloquies left Philip gnawing a reed on the edge of the field. Why should the King of the English, assuming a divine election, undertake the direction of the holy war, which the two kings had publicly sworn to share and share alike? Not far below the surface of the royal intercourse rankled the insult to the Capets in the matter of the disprized Alais, now Queen Eleanor's prisoner in the fortress of Rouen and the topic of unseemly talk among those familiar with the courts of kings. The interests that before the death of Henry had made Coeur-de-Lion and Philip bedfellows and trencher-mates in Paris had dissolved with Henry's death, and Richard himself had become the irreconcilable Angevin enemy of the Capets. The chronicler saw the work of the devil in these strange mutations.

From Vézelay the armies of the Franks and the English proceeded to-gether as far as Lyon en route for the final gathering of the fleets in Sicily. All along the way the folk came out to speed with gifts and cheers that vast host signed with the cross whose destination was the holy place of Zion. Women brought jugs of drinking water to the roadsides and lifted up their babes to the pilgrim-soldiers for a laying on of hands. Shouts went up as mothers and wives caught last glimpses of their own in the ranks that flowed like a river through Burgundy.

From Lyon, to facilitate the provisioning of so vast a host, the kings parted company. Philip, who had inherited his father's horror of the sea, went overland as far as possible.[3] Richard proceeded to Marseille to embark with his fleet.[4] There he learned that the ships he had forwarded from Dover and other Channel ports, together with the squadrons recruited in continental harbors, were still laboring with adverse winds off the Pillars of Hercules.[5] Impatient of delay, he decided not to await his transports. Having dispatched the rank and file of his armies by various routes, he himself hired some solid Pisan boats, and, setting sail with an elect company, he made the most of opportunity to visit the famed Italian shores.[6] From his galley, *Piombone*, he dropped in at points of interest; then pursued his journey for a day or two by land; then caught his ship again at some remoter port. He took the time it needs to appreciate the Bay of Naples, Vesuvius with its white plume, Amalfi, Salerno, and the islands. But presently, having learned that the winds delaying his ships had enabled Philip Augustus to reach Messina ahead of him, he diverted his vessels to Sicilian ports and made haste to cross the Faro lest the King of the Franks should take advantage of his earlier arrival. The suspicion was well grounded, but it came too late. When, amidst the press of painted sails and the blare of trumpets, Coeur-de-Lion's lead ship emerged in the harbor of Messina, and the king himself stepped forth from the silken canopy that sheltered him, the populace gathered on the shores acclaimed him as a sovereign non pareil;[7] but the actual custodians of the island to his surprise directed him to pitch his tents outside the walls of the city,[8] for the King of the Franks had already established himself in the palace of Count

Tancred; and Tancred had recently, and without benefit of any suffrage, seated himself upon the throne of Sicily.

✤

Until the autumn of 1189, Sicily had been the happy and prosperous realm of that good and liberal King William, who in 1174 had made Joanna Plantagenet his queen. William had been signed with the cross and his resources in men and ships and especially in treasure, were immense. His untimely death in the previous November [9] had deprived the crusade of one of its richest and most ardent leaders. The widowed Joanna, still young and regally dowered, kept her residence in the palace of Palermo, and Coeur-de-Lion, in the circumstances, had expected a hearty reception in the island. But the situation he found upon landing was so unexpected and so urgent that he was compelled to divert his energies from the crusade for the time being and employ them in the interests of Joanna.

King William, who had deceased without issue, had made a liberal provision for his queen; but he had designated as his heir his aunt Constance, who in 1186 had been married to Henry Hohenstaufen, the heir of Frederick Barbarossa and of the Holy Roman Empire. But Henry was in Germany at the time of the landings in Sicily, engrossed by the confusions attending his succession to his father. Taking advantage of the emperor's preoccupations on the other side of the Alps, Tancred, Count of Lecce, the bastard nephew of the late King William, seized what seemed a good chance to usurp the Sicilian throne and the vast properties of his uncle. He was well known, on the spot, preferred by the islanders to a foreign overlord, and he was thus entrenched for a firm stand. The marshaling of the crusaders in Sicily at this juncture of affairs was, from his point of view, embarrassing. As a measure of precaution he was detaining Queen Joanna in Palermo. The approach of Coeur-de-Lion's incomparable army would have made him more uneasy than he was, if he had not already divined that he could count upon a certain support from Philip Augustus. Hence the King of the Franks was installed in Tancred's palace in Messina when Coeur-de-Lion made his resplendent landing on the Sicilian shores.

Richard's first act, after mastering the main features of his sister's situation, was to issue a peremptory demand upon Tancred to render up the captive Joanna, together with her dower, which was very handsome indeed.[10] With the forces of the famous Plantagenet king encamped upon the island, Tancred could not be arrogant. He therefore sent the young queen from Palermo to Messina with her widow's portion, her bed and its furniture, and a decent sum for her expenses. But he retained the rich revenues with which William had endowed her; and he also forgot to include with the shipment the valuable legacy which William in his testament had bequeathed to the late

King Henry Plantagenet, for whom he had always cherished the highest admiration, a legacy Richard now claimed by inheritance.[11]

Coeur-de-Lion went out to sea to meet Joanna and bring her into Messina with the honors due a queen. He had perhaps not seen his sister since he had escorted her through Poitou, when, as a maiden of eleven, she had journeyed from Normandy to Saint Gilles on her way to her marriage and her coronation. Even then the Sicilian envoys sent to negotiate the alliance had been charmed with her distinction of mind and the grace of her bearing. As a child she had been bred in Fontevrault [12] and polished occasionally in the court of Poitiers. Joanna was now twenty-five, spirited, accomplished, beautiful, like all the daughters of Henry Plantagenet and Queen Eleanor. Her lot, as marriage prize, had deposited her, like her sisters, beyond the borders of the Ahgevin world, but in one of the richest regional cultures of her time; for Sicily lay on the crossway where the Mediterranean civilizations of Greek and Saracen enriched the more somber heritage of northern Europe, and William and his forebears had been hospitable to both. In this realm of luxury and light, Joanna had rooted and bloomed; and kin and homeland, even native dialect, had grown strange to her.

The queen's arrival brought an access of splendor to the establishment of Richard, which was not unremarked, if Benedict may be believed, even by the King of the Franks. A sudden inspiration attaching to his Carolingian dream seemed for a moment to take shape in Philip's mind. Observers, says Benedict, thought they noticed a sudden unaccountable warmth between the crusading kings after the arrival of the lovely young widow of William. When the King of the Franks went ceremoniously to greet Joanna in the hospice where (for want of a palace) she was lodged, Philip's countenance "glowed with a joyful expectation." But the conjecture must have been some Frank's wishful surmise, since nothing ever came of it. In the course of a few days, Richard seized the priory of La Bಬniare on the mainland of Calabria for the queen's residence, and so put Scylla and Charybdis between Philip and Joanna.[13]

In the meantime, Coeur-de-Lion sent messages anew to Tancred specifying what additional properties belonging to his sister were to be dispatched to Messina. Among the articles especially coveted were a gilded table more than twelve feet long, a golden chair, and a dinner service of twenty-four gold and silver plates and cups.[14]

While Tancred was hesitating over the next step he ought to take to protect his prospects, he appears to have received some suggestions from Philip that encouraged him. It was revealed to him that he might, to further his own larger purposes, play upon a certain hostility that kept cropping up between the kings destined for crusade. Acting intuitively on this line, he sent Philip some handsome presents.[15] To Richard he had offered not so much as an egg.[16] The zigzag behavior of Tancred at this time betrays an ingenious improvisation of plan as events unfolded. He now invited Coeur-de-Lion on a pilgrimage to see Mount Etna and some especially venerated shrines in the vicinity.[17] At Taormina, on the way back, Tancred displayed confidentially letters which he alleged he had lately received from Philip with the latter's seal dangling from them in which the King of the English was painted as a troth breacher on whom no reliance could be placed, and in which the writer offered to aid Tancred if the latter should see fit to repel Richard's unreasonable demands with reference to the properties of the Queen of Sicily.

Tancred's openness in thus exposing to him the black heart of Philip Augustus so moved Coeur-de-Lion that he made up his mind at once to regard the usurper of Sicily as a friend. Though stickling for Joanna's furniture and plate, he mitigated some of his other demands; and since he had now had an opportunity to talk with Joanna, he agreed, in return for valuable considerations in movables, and without much regard for the Hohenstaufens in Germany, to recognize Tancred's claim to Sicily.[18] But so that the kingdom might not pass out of the orbit of Plantagenet interests and presently become a prey to the predatory Hohenstaufen, he improvised an alliance on the spot. He agreed to affiance Tancred's infant daughter to his own child nephew, Arthur of Brittany, whom he promised to recognize as his heir in default of issue of his own.[19] As token of an enduring compact, he then offered to Tancred Excalibur,[20] the priceless sword of fabled King Arthur, which some recent archaeological researches of the late King Henry were said to have unearthed in Glastonbury.[21] Altogether these manifestations of good will were much more than Tancred had expected.[22]

When Richard returned to Messina and fronted Philip with the evidence of his perfidy, the King of the Franks denounced the letters to Tancred as forgeries gotten up by collusion to discredit him. From this beginning he worked himself up to a fever of indignation by reciting the whole chronicle of his wrongs at the hands of the Plantagenets. Richard, he maintained, was fabricating excuses to quarrel with him so that he might find a pretext for repudiating the Princess Alais. "Let the King of the English know this for certain," he cried, "if he puts aside my sister Alais and marries another woman, I will be the enemy of him and his, as long as ever I live!" [23]

This attack upon his honor roused Richard's Angevin choler and incited him to review publicly the history of that hapless woman, which heretofore, although it had been whispered in courtly closets and been no secret to anyone, had not been thus openly proclaimed by any of the principals. Coeur-de-Lion affirmed that Alais had been his father's mistress and that she had borne him a child and that it was for this reason that he had forborne to marry her.[24] This deposition having been certified by credible witnesses "after much exchange of language," the bishops and barons all agreed that Richard should be freed from his intolerable compact; but they also held that he must restore the dower lands to Philip with the injured Alais and offer a financial compensation to the princess for the final extinction of hopes so fair. Richard consented to accept his penalties in the judgment, but only after his return from crusade. For the time being, Alais remained in the tower of Rouen and her dower in the custody of the Plantagenets.

These events had delayed the main body of the crusading armies in Sicily beyond any hope of reaching Palestine before spring. Several contingents of Franks and English, impatient of delay and viewing with alarm the fruitless exhaustion of the resource for which they had pawned their estates, went forward to Syria to fulfill their vows before the gales of winter should break upon the sea; and presently tidings that many of these had already been cut down by heat, fever, famine, dissension among factions, and the onslaught of the paynim, reached the kings, still harbored, late in December, in Messina.[25]

⚜

Philip of Flanders, arriving in Messina in November on his way to Palestine, had arbitrated the case of Alais and secured the delivery of Richard from his compact. It fell to him, as high vassal of the French crown and kinsman of the English king both by birth and marriage, to end the quarrels that threatened to dismember the army destined for the recovery of Jerusalem.[26] But it was not hidden from the magnates that in this matter the Count of Flanders had been employed as advocate of the Plantagenets; nor was the reason dark why he had been in such a hurry to accomplish his mission. The news circulated before Advent that Queen Eleanor herself, loaded with business, had already crossed the Alps on her way to Sicily; and that she was bringing in her train the Princess of Navarre.[27] Philip of Flanders was not merely the envoy of the queen; he was her harbinger and had been of her escort as she labored over the mountain passes and descended to the Lombard plain.

Some months previously Eleanor had established herself in one of the Angevin lookouts on a crossroads in Poitou; but she had not resigned herself to the repose or the aimless luxury which her new-found freedom invited, or her age excused. The question of the succession continued to harass her, and the one acceptable solution was to see to it that Richard secured his dynasty with issue of his own. Her plans must extinguish Alais once for all, nullify the claims of all pretenders, and render Richard's naïve disposal of his inheritance to Arthur of Brittany and the heirs of Tancred completely null and void. Hers was the straightforward plan of providing her son with a wife worthy of her calling, who should produce an incontestable heir for the Angevin empire.[28] In these matters of policy she had obviously been in close touch with Coeur-de-Lion.

Among the princesses of Europe few were entitled by their birth to look so high; and fewer still were those not disqualified by consanguinity. The lady summoned to the throne of the Plantagenets was Berengaria, daughter of Sancho the Wise, King of Navarre, who was herself a notable exemplar of all the graces of the courts of love, one born to the familiar culture of the south. Her brother was a famous jouster, a fellow cavalier of Coeur-de-Lion in the lists. Richard is said to have paid court in Pamplona to Berengaria, according to the rules of the *Tractatus*, on the occasion of a tournament that had brought together the best champions on both sides of the Pyrenees.[29] Says Devizes, the king (then Count of Poitou) had at that time greatly admired the accomplishments of her mind as well as the attractions of her person. This chronicler adds, of his own observation, that she seemed "more accomplished than beautiful," but he was perhaps influenced by the comments of the Franks and the Burgundians in Messina. Ambrose, who also saw her in Sicily, describes her as "a prudent maid, a gentle lady, virtuous and fair, neither false nor double-tongued." [30]

Not even the queen's age nor the dangers of a wintry journey over the mountain passes daunted her in giving effect to her plans.[31] The Alps were after all less formidable than the wilderness of peaks in Paphlagonia. Her escort brought her and the princess through the gorges and then into the not less hostile plain, where the crusading hosts, like locusts swarming, had left not even the leaves upon the trees; and then they skirted regions under interdict; bartered for safe-conduct with little potentates at war with one another; avoided the ambush of those freebooters that lay in wait for travelers whose ransoms were worth while;[32] at Lodi, south of Milan, by accident of travel, she encountered Henry of Hohenstaufen on his way to Rome for his coronation as Holy Roman Emperor. What passed between them is not recorded, but the interview must have taxed even the queen's matchless aplomb, for Henry had by no means given his consent to Richard's disposal of his pretensions in Sicily to Tancred. In the course of time, the queen's escort made its way to Pisa, to Naples, and finally to Brindisi.

Richard sent a stout ship under command of a Sicilian admiral to bring the queen's party from Brindisi to Reggio; and he himself crossed the Faro to welcome the travelers with the highest honors; to present to the queen her daughter Joanna who, in the long years since her childhood, had grown strange to her own mother; and to receive from Eleanor's hand the Princess of Navarre.

⚜

Queen Eleanor, a matchless woman, beautiful and chaste, powerful and modest, meek and eloquent, which is rarely to be met with in a woman; who was sufficiently

advanced in years to have two husbands and two sons crowned kings, still indefatigable for every undertaking, whose power was the admiration of her age, came to
Pisa . . . there to await the king's pleasure, together with the King of Navarre's
ambassadors and the damsel. Many know what I wish none of us had known. The
same queen, in the time of her former husband, went to Jerusalem. Let none speak
more thereof; I also know well. Be silent.

Richard of Devizes

This dark passage from the chronicler makes clear at least that the queen's
sagacity and authority were recognized by her contemporaries; also that,
wherever crusaders forgathered, she was a legend — still, among the Franks
and Teutons, the topic of trouvères' ballads and minnesingers' songs. In
Messina Devizes had evidently heard again the moldy anecdotes of Antioch,
which the Franks in half a century had not ceased to circulate to her disparagement. Her sensational arrival in Sicily on the eve of a new crusade
gave the stories fresh pertinence and revived their vogue.

Philip Augustus did not await the arrival of the queen in Messina. He
had been appalled by the necessity of squandering the winter in Sicily and
by the melting away of his treasure; and he was impatient to get on with
the holy war and have done with the Saracens. Although in April the sea
was still unsettled, he took advantage of a favoring wind and set sail for
Acre on the morning of the very Thursday that Queen Eleanor and Berengaria arrived in Messina. So there was nothing to mar the harmony of the
four brief days vouchsafed the Plantagenets on the island. Richard, now in
possession of the Sicilian plate and furniture, entertained the royal ladies
sumptuously in the quarters he had thrown up for himself outside the city
walls. Since Eleanor and Berengaria had been unable to get over the Alps
before the beginning of Lent, the marriage of the king and the princess
could not be celebrated in Eleanor's presence; and the disquieting state of
affairs both in Britain and in Palestine forbade a longer sojourn. It was
therefore decided to make a peremptory exception to the ruling about wom-
en's going on crusade, and to provide a transport on which Berengaria
could travel to the East; and in order that the princess might not be dismayed
and scandalized in that company of warriors, she was committed to the
custody of the widowed Queen of Sicily. Joanna and Berengaria developed a
warm attachment in Messina and subsequently lived for a year or two "as
doves in cage." [83]

In the course of those crowded hours in Sicily, the queen and her clerks
reported to the king on the progress of the hungry-falcon statecraft in Britain:
on John's efforts to get control of matters in England, of his collusions with
Geoffrey of York, and of the clashes these had produced with the chancellor.
As for Ely, the queen admitted she was herself dismayed at the whirlwind
speed and thoroughness with which he had proceeded to relieve his asso-

ciates in the administration of all their responsibilities and gather these into his own hands. There was ever so much more sap in the little Norman than even she had suspected. A legatine commission made Ely's intolerable control supreme in every quarter. To get the resulting confusions in hand, it was obviously necessary for Eleanor as regent to confer with the Pope in Rome.[34]

Richard himself set her back on her way to Gaul.[35] She was escorted by the Archbishop of Rouen, whose crusader's vows were commuted in Messina, Gilbert de Vascoeil, and other magnates; and with her she carried a sheaf of letters patent and other enabling mandates for the rectification of the government and the control of all disturbers of the Truce of God. She arrived in Rome on Easter Sunday,[36] the very day when Hyacinthus Bobo, now a man of eighty, was consecrated as Pope Celestine III.[37] She had known Hyacinthus as archdeacon in the difficult days of Becket's intransigency, and she was able to remind him that he had fared well in those times through the favor of Henry Plantagenet.

The queen found Celestine well disposed and had no great difficulty in getting the understandings and the manifestoes she required. The Pope was induced to consent, against the opposition of the suffragans of York, to the election of Geoffrey the Bastard to the See of York, where his orders would put him out of any possibility of reaching for the crown.[38] Celestine also conferred a super-legateship on the Archbishop of Rouen that could be brought to light to curb William of Ely in case the energetic little chancellor should get altogether out of hand. With these contrivances, Eleanor, as great Henry would have said, had the regency in her pocket.

The queen stayed only long enough in Rome to arrange with money-lenders for her forward journey.[39] She had no time, as on the occasion of her previous visit with Louis Capet in 1148, to make a grand tour of the shrines. It is possible that she was urgently eager to leave Rome in her wake; for it happened by sheer coincidence of travel that she passed through the city at the very moment Henry of Hohenstaufen and Constance, whom William of Sicily had designated as his lawful heirs, arrived at the portals of the Lateran to be consecrated as Emperor and Empress of the Holy Roman Empire, and, thus panoplied, to move into Apulia and Calabria to wrest their heritage from Tancred. From Rome she struck across to Aqua Pendente. Having escaped disastrous encounters with the Hohenstaufen in the holy city, the queen made haste to put the barrier of the Alps behind her. Thence her journey took on a more leisurely character as she followed the advancing spring as far as Bourges. In a little time she had taken up her post of observation in the castle of Rouen.

25 ✚

Things Done Overseas

The wind was high, and lofty were the waves. . .
Swift as the swallow flieth, so sped the ship with bended mast.

Ambrose

ON THE DAY FOLLOWING ELEANOR'S DEPARTURE from Messina, Richard forwarded the Princess of Navarre and the Queen of Sicily on a large dromon, less swift than a galley, but more commodious for their baggage and attendance, which are described as considerable.[1] With two escort ships under command of the most reliable navigators, the dromon climbed the lofty waves that tossed their whitecaps eastward from the island.

Some days later in Holy Week, the king marshaled his fleet of some hundred and fifty vessels or more and ranged them in the harbor.[2] During the stay in Sicily the boats had been beached, repaired, and dewormed and now tugged at their moorings for the take-off. The ships were of every type — busses, galleys, dromons of many sizes and various speeds — some crowded with men and horses, others laden to their brims with fodder and provisions, and all the equipment for warfare: siege engines, stagings, and the excellent round sling stones for the mangonels,[3] which had been selected on the shores of Sicily. At Richard's clarion call, oar and sail strained, and the fleet bounded forward for "God's unhappy country." The king, in the prow of the foremost galley, rallied his host. By day the trumpet of the royal ship, by night its lantern, kept the squadrons more or less together.[4] At last Richard pressed his admirals, for news had reached him that the contingents that had gone ahead were by no means enough to deal with the Saracens; and he had only a moderate confidence in what Philip Augustus might undertake overseas in the circumstance.

Though the transit from Messina to Acre usually required about three weeks, Coeur-de-Lion's passage among the Mediterranean islands took twice that time. In spite of horn and lantern, the adverse winds of early spring drove the squadrons of the fleet apart, some to shelter in one harbor, some in another. In rounding up the stragglers, the king drew into Crete and Rhodes and finally came to Cyprus, where he found some of his missing vessels wrecked. It was here, after days of anxious reconnaissance, he found the royal ladies stranded in their dromon where the storms had washed them up, and so spent with peril and distress that they rued ever having left the comfortable shores of Sicily.[5]

Isaac, the Emperor of Cyprus, was of the family of the sublime Comneni [6] and, having that ingrained distrust of western crusaders that characterized his imperial house, he had not, according to Richard's mariners, offered the vaunted Greek hospitality to the distressed voyagers shipwrecked on his shores. When Richard learned of this intolerable offense, the repulse of his ships and the exposure of the royal ladies to the terrors of the sea, he did not hesitate. He postponed for the time being his progress toward Acre and went ashore in force to deal with Isaac and his "base rabble of Greeks and Armenians."

The operation of bringing Isaac to his knees consumed two or three weeks, but it was a signal success and very profitable. The pusillanimous Greeks took to the hills; the emperor and his daughter were taken prisoner; the little girl ("on whom her father's life hung") was turned over to Berengaria for reëducation;[7] and the booty was so rich that it went far to recoup the exhaustion of treasure in Sicily. The prosperous island was seen moreover to offer a granary for feeding the famished Christians manning the trenches outside the walls of Acre. The danger of inviting the hostility of the imperial Comneni at the moment seemed hardly worth consideration.

In the lovely city of Limassol, after the conquest of the island, it was decided to celebrate the royal marriage and crown the Princess of Navarre.[8] Lent was over; bishops and chaplains were of the company; and it was doubtless felt that appropriate ceremonies in the camp at Acre might be difficult and would in any case seem an unwarranted affront to Philip Augustus, whose emotions with regard to Alais had by no means subsided. There was a three-day festival for these events, for which the flowery Cyprian spring and the Bay of Limassol, with the fleet busy refitting itself upon the waters, made a gorgeous setting. The chroniclers do not say what was worn by the Princess of Navarre for her bridal and her coronation; but the *Itinerarium* describes the marvelous figure cut by the bridegroom in that week. His prancing charger, says the chronicler, was of Spanish breed. The king bounded into his saddle, which glittered with gold spangles interspersed with red, while on the hinder part of the trappings two small golden lions affronted each other, poised on their forelegs and reaching forth as if to devour. The king's feet were adorned with golden spurs, and he was clad in a rose-colored cotte, worked with rows of silver crescents that sparkled like the sun. He was girt with a proven sword, its handle gold, its scabbard clasped with silver. On his head he wore a scarlet bonnet wrought by hand with birds and beasts of various shape, sewed in with orphrey work. He carried his staff, and his matchless bearing afforded the highest gratification to all who saw him.[9]

In Cyprus, in time for the nuptials, the first emissary from the Holy Land arrived to greet the King of England and advise him on the course he ought to take for the rescue of the holy places overseas.[10] This personage loomed out of Coeur-de-Lion's Poitevin past. He was that Guy of Lusignan who had been banished from the Limousin twenty years before for his attempt to capture Queen Eleanor by ambush as she passed over one of her highways in Poitou. The blood of Earl Patrick of Salisbury, her bodyguard, was on his sword. But Guy was now translated from his condition as outlaw; he was King of Jerusalem.[11]

For more than two generations the Latin Kingdom had been the Promised Land for the disprized cavaliers of western Europe — for exiles, malcontents, dispossessed heirs, the younger sons of younger brothers, for whom the cloister offered no allurement. The history of the four Latin fiefs furnished abundant records of European buccaneers who had redeemed their sunken fortunes in that eastern world of sudden chance and change. In spite of the infusions of western blood, the dynasty of the Latin Kingdom tended persistently to decay. The royal line, bolstered for a few years by Foulques of Anjou, speedily dwindled again after his untimely death. The hazards of warfare, intrigue, heat, Oriental diseases, to which Occidentals were especially prone, bore heavily upon the men, so that great fiefs fell with unnatural incidence into the helpless hands of women.

An ambitious cavalier from the West, brave, personable, the bearer of a good name, by being on hand at the propitious moment, could rescue a countess or a queen from the burdens thrust upon her, and crown himself with fortune and a fame that spread back to Europe. So had Eleanor's footloose uncle, Raymond of Antioch, made himself a peer of the Latin Kingdom; and so had that even more famous adventurer, Renauld of Châtillon. Prudent men, like Henry the Lion of Saxony, Henry the Liberal of Champagne, and Philip of Flanders, having surveyed such prospects, renounced them for their more solid patrimonies at home. But for men like Guy, whose tenures were uneasy, the Latin Kingdom was indeed the Promised Land.

The ups and downs of Guy on his way to fame and fortune make in themselves a chronicle of violent adventures tied up with the calamities of the Latin Kingdom. He was a very giant of derring-do, a man of unmeasured energy and of a reckless valor that commended him for the hazardous enterprises on the frontiers of pagandom. Baldwin, the leper King of Jerusalem, had chosen him as a second husband for his sister Sibylle (who was certain to be his heir), not as in all respects an ideal king, but as the best prop offering at the moment to support the royal interests against a powerful party of barons, who had other aspirants in view. The barons, for their part, described Guy with uncompromising words as "softheaded and inadequate" (*simplex et insufficiens*), lacking in judgment, a fool acting on the counsel of other fools.[12]

On the death of Baldwin and the frail little son of Sibylle who briefly succeeded him, Guy, by reason of his marriage, stepped up to the throne of Jerusalem, and the great barons, though he was not their choice, were forced to accept him as their overlord.[13] For six years he had discharged his royal obligation with his naked sword, fighting on every front wherever he found an enemy. He had spent more than a year as Saladin's prisoner, been paroled on his oath to leave the Levant, and had lived to take up arms once more against the Saracens. With the forces he could muster, he had recklessly undertaken the siege of Acre before the arrival of the fresh hosts of crusaders from the West.

Late in the summer of 1190, some nine months before the advent of Philip Augustus, while Guy was laying siege to Acre, fate took a hand in the destinies of the Latin Kingdom. Queen Sibylle, who was sharing her lord's hardships in the camp before the beleaguered city, sickened and died, and her two young daughters with her, leaving Guy but a figurehead diademed with the crown of Jerusalem. The legal succession fell to Sibylle's younger half sister Isabelle, who was already married to Humphrey de Toron, one of the baronial party opposed to Guy. But Humphrey, who had been born and bred in Syria, was not disposed to risk his fortunes for the tottering crown of Jerusalem. He took surreptitious leave of the baronial assembly that threatened to make him king, fled to Jerusalem, and offered his allegiance to King Guy. This knavery of Humphrey's of course gave Isabelle, as well as the barons, grounds for malice toward him, and they resolved to get rid of him and furnish the heiress with a new husband worthy to be king.

The likeliest cavalier at hand for the vacant role was a relatively new arrival in the field of politics in Syria — Conrad, Marquis of Montferrat. This corsair had swooped down upon the Holy Land from the direction of Byzantium, where his services for a few years in behalf of the Comneni had brought him into a series of uncomfortable dilemmas that finally indicated the wisdom of departure for other fields of knightly enterprise.[14] The marquis was highly connected,[15] a seasoned warrior and strategist, schooled in the crafts of state by his experiences in Byzantium. He was furthermore related, through the house of Maurienne, with the Capets; and his elder brother William had been the first husband of Queen Sibylle and father of the child king Baldwin, who had reigned so briefly. When, after the calamitous battle of Hittin in 1187, Saladin had almost completely blockaded the Christians from succor by sea, Conrad, by a bold coup, had succeeded in occupying Tyre, which still held as the last free port of entry for the crusaders on the Mediterranean shore. By lineage and by merit Conrad seemed to the barons cast by destiny for the role of King of Jerusalem.

The large company of English magnates, who, faring ahead of Philip Augustus and Coeur-de-Lion from Sicily, arrived in Syria in the early autumn of 1190, were at once confronted by the barons' proposal to separate Humphrey from Isabelle.[16] The Archbishop of Canterbury and the Bishop of Salisbury, who were of their number, protested stoutly, taking a strong stand upon the canons. But the Bishop of Beauvais, who was a Capet,[17] discovered a touch of consanguinity between the principals. To him it seemed a matter of exigency to undo the marriage. Thereupon Isabelle was at once united to the marquis. As for Conrad, he did not raise the question of dissociating himself from either of two former wives abandoned in the backward areas of his rovings.[18]

This coup, with its threat to Guy's crown, had the effect of splitting the Christian hosts dedicated to the rescue of the holy places into two irreconcilable camps, and obliged newcomers, as they arrived in companies from the West, to assume the colors of one camp or the other.[19] The vanguards of the Franks, Thibault of Blois, the Bishop of Beauvais, and others, lined up with Conrad; so also did Barbarossa's son, the Duke of Burgundy, and the remnants of the emperor's Teutonic knights, and Leopold of Austria. Some magnates, compelled by their dependence upon bounty, favored one side or the other, or both by turns, as the exigencies of their condition required.

Philip Augustus, who arrived in the midst of these events, was now seen by Guy to be gliding, as if moved by the mysterious hand of destiny, into the camps of Conrad;[20] and he was, as if divinely commissioned to direct proceedings, taking charge of operations intended to break the long stalemate before Acre. He even sent messengers to Cyprus with peremptory demands that Coeur-de-Lion leave all secondary campaigns en route, get forward with all his forces, and lend his aid in the final overthrow of Saladin.

When these backgrounds of politics and history had been reviewed by King Richard and King Guy in Cyprus, a common Poitevin descent counted more than the ancient enmities that had sundered them. They easily came to terms. Guy's *de facto* state as King of Jerusalem, his openness, his bravery in the face of odds, made him seem for the moment a valuable ally. The developments in the Latin Kingdom described by Guy brought the two kings very close together and speeded their departure from Cyprus.

✤

Great was the joyance and the night was clear.
                                        Ambrose

It was a Saturday evening early in June when the hard-pressed veterans of the assault on Acre, worn with combat, stricken with famine and disease, looked to the west and saw their desperate valor justified. Lifting their eyes, they saw the level sun reflected from a thousand bucklers, the sea white with the foam of oars, and such a flock of painted sails as had not been afloat in eastern waters since Agamemnon drew up to the shores of Troy. The ships of Coeur-de-Lion, laden with men, horses, food, engines, the treasure of Sicily and Cyprus, were banking oars and slackening sail. On the devices of the pennants streaming from the mastheads, the soldiers of Christ read the roster of the great lords coming to their relief; and somewhere in the midst of that incomparable host approached the already fabled champion dedicated from the day of his crowning to the rescue of the holy places. There were no distracting episodes, for the queens, as usual, had been dispatched ahead with their Cyprian handmaiden and were already ashore to witness the coming of the king.

When Coeur-de-Lion stood forth upon his landing stage, he was the quickening soul of the whole crusading enterprise. In him were blended all those strangely incongruous stirrings, grand and grandiose, that toughened the crusader's sinews and melted his heart. No figure in the whole world was at the moment so suffused in glamor. The crowds upon the shore went wild with jubilation. Processions gathered to the music of drums and timbrels, horns and flutes. After the long drought, wine spilled in abundance in the streets of the port. So many tapers burned that Saladin, watching the arrival from the citadel with intelligent alarm, was persuaded that the "Christian dogs" had put the whole valley to the torch.[21]

Without delay Coeur-de-Lion's forces were disposed in the arc thrown about the citadel where the Saracens were entrenched. Says the *Itinerarium*, nearly every man of renown in the Christian world, baron or prelate, besides thousands of foot soldiers, ranged themselves in order,[22] each company with its own siege towers and mangonels named in contempt of Saladin.[23] The eleventh-hour arrival of the King of England, with enough additional force to compel a surrender, made the fall of the city certain; but all the battalions that had borne the heat and burden of the protracted siege foresaw that the glory of routing Saladin would redound to the latest comer. For a time, however, the Franks, Burgundians, Teutons, and some of Conrad's forces, eager to claim their guerdon and their spoils, wrought together with a fury.

At the outset of the fresh attack, Richard fell victim to the quartan fever raging in the camp, and fear of his death smote the armies with dread.[24] But he had himself wrapped in a silken quilt and borne in a litter to posts whence, in the intervals of his ague, he could direct the operation of the petaries and rally the crews of the siege towers,[25] battering rams, and scaling ladders which were being deluged with Greek fire and burning pitch from the ramparts of the citadel — rivers of abominable stench and livid flame that, says the chronicler, "consumed both flint and steel." Day and night without ceasing, darts, arrows, and sling stones rained on the beleaguered city. The pressures of blockade and assault were at last made effectual, so that, after a little more than a month of carnage, Saladin's satraps, on the 12th of July, raised the white flag.

The victorious allies now stormed into Acre, each "nation" driving pell-mell to take possession of a favorable quarter and a share of the credit and the spoils. The Franks set up their bailiwick in the establishment of the Templars. The standard of Coeur-de-Lion went up over the palace of the kings.[26] The knights of Leopold of Austria, though sweating as freely as others with victory, were, in the melee, shouldered out of a first-class rallying place of their own; so someone of the duke's following ran up his pennant beside that of the English king on the battlements of the palace. An unnamed partisan of Richard's dragged this proud banner down and cast it disdainfully into the filth and debris of the moat. The insult to the Duke of Austria was later imputed to the arrogance of Coeur-de-Lion, who was seen in all his doings to brook no rival to his supremacy. The incident gave substance to envious murmurings; and many factions among the Christian hosts took up the cause and shared the umbrage of Duke Leopold and vowed vengeance upon the haughty Plantagenet.[27]

The capture of Acre was the first signal victory of the Christians since the occupation of Tyre. Its fame flew over western Europe; and from Damascus to Cairo a panic spread among the Saracens, so that, even beyond the Jordan, Moslem women stilled their babies with the threat that "Melek Ric" would get them.[28]

✤

It was certainly not the fear of God nor any stirring of penitence that inspired them; but pride and vainglory directed all their enterprise.

Pope Celestine III

Apart from Saladin, the person least moved to celebrate the arrival of Coeur-de-Lion in Syria was his brother-in-arms, the King of the Franks. Before Richard's arrival Philip Augustus, freed from the overweening presence of his vassal, had enjoyed an hour of prestige. He had been welcomed as the liberator of the Holy Land and the harbinger of more relief to come. But when Richard came ashore with his glitter and fanfare, all was changed again.

In spite of the pledges of the two kings at Vézelay to share and share alike, Philip's resources were conspicuously inferior, and they melted like wax under the necessity of supporting knights and prelates whose substance had been wasted in the long journey overseas. Without his bounty, some of the lesser ranks were driven into the bosom of Islam for the sake of food. Many went home.[29] The extremes of the Syrian climate distressed the king. The trenches about Acre were anything but salubrious. In their pestilential foxholes, through the deluge of spring rains and the broiling summer heat, men of all ranks, afflicted with plague and vermin, died like flies. Philip could not sleep for the din of drums and tom-toms by which the wakeful hosts sought to drive off the swarms of mosquitoes and sand flies that made the night more awful than the day.[30] The steady stream of corpses to the burial pits in the rear made him think seriously of all he was risking for his people and his infant heir by putting his own life in jeopardy. In the midst of his nightmares he too fell ill, and was horrified to lose his hair and the nails of his fingers and toes.[31] Everything suggested the wisdom of his going home and leaving the holy war to him who would in any case contrive to claim the palm.[32]

An incidental calamity in the siege of Acre brought Philip's manifold misgivings to a head. His high vassal, Philip of Flanders, lost his life in the early days of the siege, in the flower of his age.[33] He died without direct heirs, leaving his rich estates in the Low Countries exposed to the villainy of the crafty and the strong. In this connection Philip thought inevitably of the Plantagenets. He soon commuted his suspicions to certainties, and from them he wove the tissue of a plot to betray and undo him. The lands of Philip of Flanders were contiguous to Gisors and the Vexin. Richard had cunningly retained these dower lands of the Capetian princess in his own hands; and the Princess Alais herself was the prisoner of the Countess of Poitou in the tower of Rouen. Nothing was plainer to Philip Augustus than that the Plantagenets were conspiring to violate the compact of Messina, swallow the Vexin and enrich themselves, heaven only knew to what extent, at his expense. Nothing was clearer than his duty to go home.[34]

The French king's anxiety to quit the holy war was hard to conceal. It became public ten days after the fall of Acre. The most exalted among his following, his cousin, Philip of Dreux, the Bishop of Beauvais, and the Duke of Burgundy, together with other high magnates, waited upon Richard in his palace to make Philip's resolution known. The Capetians of the party were all endowed with the valued gift of tears. Coming into Coeur-de-Lion's presence, these heroes of crusade with one accord burst into such floods of weeping that they could not find words to give shape to their utterance.[35] Richard's intuition helped them out.

"Give over tears," he said, "for I know what you have come to say. Your lord, the King of France, wants to go home, and you have come to get my consent to this breach of our compact as brothers-in-arms."

The Franks hung their heads in anguish. "Sire," said their spokesman, "you have divined what is in our minds. We are compelled to ask your consent, for our lord king will surely die if he does not quickly leave this land." They then itemized the king's symptoms and described the alarming alteration of his mien.

Richard, who was still laboring with his intermittent fever, expressed his feelings with a touch of irony.

"It will be an everlasting shame to the Franks," he said, "if your king should return leaving unfinished the task for which he came. It is my belief that he ought not to go; but of course, if his life is in the balance, let him do as his advisers see fit." [36]

When these oblique reproaches were brought to Philip Augustus, a quarrel ensued between the two kings. Employing attack as the best defense, Philip launched a demand for half the spoils of Cyprus,[37] in accordance with the compact of Vézelay. Coeur-de-Lion riposted with a demand for half the spoils of Flanders.[38] This made Philip certain that the Plantagenets had treacherous designs upon the heritage of the Count of Flanders. Vituperations on both sides rose so high that the magnates, says the chronicler, had great difficulty in preserving any semblance of brotherly accord before the rank and file.

⚜

The resolution of Philip Augustus to return to his own lands precipitated a fresh contention over the kingship of Jerusalem. Conrad was undisposed to speed his strongest partisan on his homeward way before the matter was concluded; and Richard by now so needed Conrad's support in the holy war that, in spite of his sympathy with Guy, his mood was somewhat conciliatory. The assembly of magnates met in Acre a few days after the angry colloquy of the two kings. Each contestant argued his own case. Guy was in possession of the crown and he had, as he declared, "done nothing to forfeit it." [39] Conrad possessed the heiress and a stout following, and he had greater talents as an orator. After two days of dialectic, the assembly reached one of those just and equitable compromises that settle nothing. Guy should keep the crown and the title for his lifetime, with one half the revenues of the kingdom and the lordship of certain cities; Conrad and his heirs should succeed, and in the meantime should enjoy the revenues and lordship of certain other cities.[40]

Philip Augustus committed his troops, under command of the Duke of Burgundy, to Richard's campaigns, and Conrad, who was sharply disappointed by the ambiguous outcome of the debate over the kingship, grudgingly promised the collaboration of his forces. The Frankish armies to be left behind were a doubtful blessing, because, although the man power was desperately needed, the support of the host was contingent upon Saladin's paying the ransom for the Moslem captives taken in the fall of Acre, a payment which failed to materialize. In the end, in order to make an example of the wages of perfidy, Richard felt obliged to massacre some five thousand of these hapless wretches in view of the Saracens and to undertake the support of the Franks with irredeemable loans.[41]

It cannot be supposed that, in all the circumstances, Richard was easy in his mind over the departure of Philip Augustus. Before the King of the Franks took off, Coeur-de-Lion, in the presence of credible witnesses, both barons and bishops, required him to make an oath of fidelity, as one crusading king to another. With his hands on the Gospels and the holiest of relics, Philip swore that he would strictly maintain the Truce of God, and that he would not only do no injury to the realm of his brother-in-arms, but that he would protect, as if they were his own, all the lands and properties of the Plantagenets from injury by any traitors whomsoever.[42]

Ten days later, on July 31, Philip Augustus left Acre [43] with two or three galleys, which the English chroniclers declare were generously lent by Coeur-de-Lion, but which the French say were provided by the Genoese. With eagerness he cast the sand of Syria from his feet and went off reviling the inequities of fortune. As he sailed away with Conrad for the port of Tyre, he itemized his injuries and reviewed every prospect that Richard's enemies had been able to suggest for a condign revenge.

He visited Tyre and Antioch, put in for a little time in Rhodes, and, passing among the islands infested with Barbary pirates off the coast of Rumania, he made port in Corfu.[44] Here he spent some time while his envoys sought safe-conduct from Tancred of Sicily. Early in October he landed in Otranto and journeyed thence to Rome. Pope Celestine entertained him for a week, in the course of which he judged the king by reason of his plague — the marks of which were plainly visible — quit of his crusader's vows, and bestowed upon him the cross and palm, with his benediction.[45]

During these days Philip opened his heart to the pontiff and the cardinals. He disclosed that he had left Palestine in terror of his life because of the intrigues of Coeur-de-Lion. He lived in constant fear of poison or the dagger and was forced to keep a bodyguard about him. The King of England coveted Flanders, and no one could guess with what guile he would despoil the Franks. He recited the injuries of the Capetian princess at the hands of the Plantagenets. Finally, he held it only just that Celestine should give him a dispensation to right his wrongs by incursions in Normandy as soon as he could get home.[46]

This eyewitness survey of the holy war and the Plantagenet's part in it must have shocked Celestine. However, he held the King of the Franks to his crusader's vow not to injure his fellow pilgrim during the latter's absence overseas, and forbade him, on pain of anathema, to seek redress by force of arms. The same vow, he made sure, would protect Flanders from Coeur-de-Lion. As for the matter of Alais, Celestine had probably reviewed her history thoroughly with Queen Eleanor in Rome and no doubt thought it best not to foment discord on that issue at the moment.

From Rome Philip passed northward and had a conference with Henry Hohenstaufen, the Holy Roman Emperor, who was in Italy settling those scores with Tancred that had prevented his joining the crusade. For Henry, Philip reviewed again the chronicle of the holy war. Here his accounts fell upon more sympathetic ears, for the head of the Hohenstaufen was related to the Duke of Austria and, through him, to the Emperor of Cyprus. The wanton dragging down of Leopold's banner in Acre, Richard embellishing himself with Isaac's treasure and disporting himself before the Christian hosts on Isaac's Arab stallion, Isaac himself in durance, the Cypriote princess the captive plaything of the English queen — these made telling incidents, and their exposure warmed the intercourse of the emperor and the king and forged a bond between them. Hoveden, reporting the interview, asserts that Henry vowed that, if Coeur-de-Lion should pass through his territories on his return from crusade, he would lay hands upon him.[47]

Thence Philip crossed the Alps, traversed Maurienne, and reached Paris shortly before Christmas in 1191.[48] From Paris rumors spread about the perfidy of Coeur-de-Lion in the Land of Promise, his insolence to his allies, his luxury and pride.[49] These of course very soon reached London and Rouen and gave Queen Eleanor a deep anxiety which greatly aggravated the troubles she was already having with the regency in Britain.

※

There were heroic episodes in the warfare between paynim and crusader after Philip Augustus sailed away: brilliant and costly battles in which the noblest blood of Christian and Saracen flowed freely in the arid sands; prodigies of valor, martyrdoms that never won their meed of glory in this world. But the cause that had aroused such ardors and drawn such treasure of men and gold from Europe in the early summer of 1190 now languished in the late summer of 1191.[50] Only about one fourth of those who had set out ever returned home. They had been consumed by disease, the sword, starvation, or intolerable labor. "Blessed," quotes the chronicler, "are the dead who die in the Lord."

As Philip turned his prows westward, Coeur-de-Lion took stock of the remainder of that mighty host that had gone out from Vézelay with flags flying and the fervor of the *Lignum Crucis* on the lips of every highhearted pilgrim soldier. Conrad, in dudgeon over the denial of his kingship, held aloof in Tyre with chief barons of the Latin Kingdom and offered a rallying post for all the malcontents in the divers forces left to Richard's banners. When besought to join forces with Coeur-de-Lion, he declared openly that he was not such a fool as to place himself in the service of the English king. Like Philip Augustus, he lived in dread of secret plots.[51]

The Franks and Burgundians bequeathed to Richard under the compact of Vézelay and left under command of the Duke of Burgundy were little disposed to support any triumph of the English king, though they needed

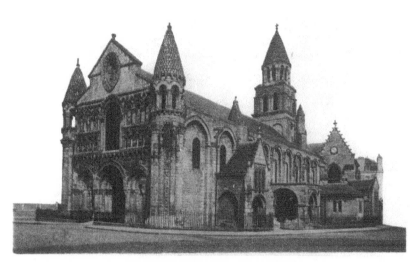

NOTRE-DAME LA GRANDE, POITIERS

NUNS' KITCHEN, ABBEY OF FONTEVRAULT

SAINT PIERRE DE MONS, NEAR BÉLIN

MURAL IN THE TEMPLE CHURCH, LONDON, SHOWING STEPHEN, HENRY II, HENRY THE YOUNG KING, RICHARD, AND JOHN

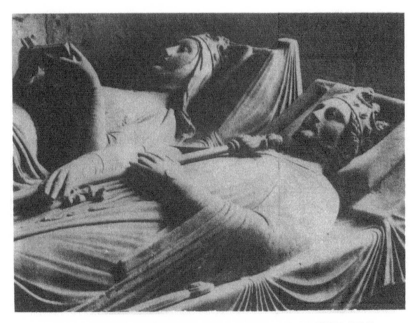

TOMB EFFIGIES OF ELEANOR AND RICHARD AT FONTEVRAULT

his subsidy to carry on at all.[52] Many of the more prescient among these had
already folded their tents and taken passage home without ever a sight of
Jerusalem. Even the Templars and the Hospitallers were divided, and the
Italian merchant princes abetted one faction or the other as their own interests
decreed.

Left thus with only a fraction of the Christian forces, yet by his very
presence challenged to action, Richard was reduced to limited objectives,
risky exploits, and sudden forays against the Saracens. With stout fighting
he took coastal towns southward from Acre, but never succeeded in gathering
a united host to push inland to Jerusalem. Twice the Christian armies came
within a few leagues of the Holy City; and once Richard, as sole guerdon for
his valor, caught sight from the high ground of Emmaus of the clustered
domes and towered walls of Zion. Says the *Itinerarium*, the army now rejoiced that they should soon set their eyes on the Lord's sepulcher; and all
began to brighten up their armor, their helmets, and their swords, so that not
a single spot should spoil their brightness.[53] But, explains Bernard the Treasurer,[54] the Franks under the Duke of Burgundy, begrudging the English
king the glory of entering the gates, demurred, and the vision, like mirage
in the desert, dissolved into thin air. With tears and lamentations the soldiers
of Christ, denied at the eleventh hour the boon for which they had suffered
their hardships and their losses and put their lives in danger, turned away
from that glorious prospect and set their faces toward sunset and the sea.
"God," says the chronicler, "did not yet judge them worthy of the higher
bounties of His grace."

✤

In times of stress the barons of the Latin Kingdom, who had learned to
live with danger and gamble for time in their unremitting struggles with the
Saracens, found ways of bargaining with Saladin even while war was in
progress. Conrad, after the conclave in Acre had denied him the kingship,
employed all his Byzantine experience in the wiles of diplomacy to secure
agreements with Saladin that might bring profit to himself or discomfiture
to Richard.[55] Threatened with this snare, Coeur-de-Lion found that he too
had a knack for politics. And Saladin, as keen in strategy as in warfare, did
all he could in parley with one or the other to rive them apart in order to
devour them separately. Encouraged by the departure of Philip Augustus for
his own lands, Saladin produced a competition between Conrad and Richard
for prior settlement with him.

In the course of these negotiations, Richard conceived a brilliant plan
by which at one stroke to end the holy war with credit, extinguish forever
the pretensions of Conrad, and reëstablish the Angevins on the throne of
Jerusalem. Since Saladin, after the successes of the Christians at Acre, was

extravagantly eager to see Coeur-de-Lion set sail in the wake of Philip Augustus, it was not difficult to open parley.

Coeur-de-Lion, without, as it subsequently appeared, having sufficiently warmed up his project beforehand with his own following, made a generous proposal to Saladin: nothing less than that he should bestow his widowed sister Joanna in marriage upon the Moslem Saphadin, the valorous brother of Saladin himself. The pair, according to the plan, were to receive the titles of King and Queen of Jerusalem and obtain Palestine and the shrine city as their dower; and the Christians were to recover the sacred rood and have free access forever to the holy places. In a burst of enthusiasm, Richard went through the ceremony of dubbing Saphadin in the western manner and offered to have him baptized. To this alliance Saladin, who asked only to see the Christians turning homeward, interposed no obstacle.

But an Arab chronicler relates that Joanna Plantagenet, when the plan was broached to her, entered into a genuine Angevin passion, which she justified on religious grounds, and called all the clergy to witness in her behalf. The throne of Jerusalem might be a high seat and one upon which her great-grandfather Foulques of Anjou and his descendants had sat; but the crusading queen declared that she would not be brought, even for the peace of Christendom, to mount the throne with one of the very paynim she had journeyed to Palestine to defy. For his part, Saphadin, though he submitted to be dubbed, rejected the rites of baptism and the sumptuary restrictions of Christianity.[56]

At this crisis in the negotiations Richard visited the splendid tent of Saphadin, where he was entertained with gifts, refreshments, and an exhibition of Oriental dancing women. When they finally came to business, Richard said nothing about Joanna's indignation, but related that he had struck an unexpected snag in the attitude of his clergy. He meant, however, to take the matter over their heads to the Pope, who could act with sovereign authority in the marrying of widows; and if by any chance he should fail to get the Pope's consent to his sister's bestowal in marriage, he declared he would engage to give Saphadin instead his niece Eleanor, the "pearl of Brittany," who, being a maiden, was disposable by himself without clerical interference. But since this compact seemed rather vaguely contingent, the Saracens dallied with it no further.

The intricacy of this diplomacy, with the frequent necessity of acting on the low ground of expediency rather than on the high plateau of principle, was not clear to the limited understanding of the populace; wherefore the news that Richard was trafficking with the infidel brought him no honor even in his own following. In Tyre, in Acre, in Rome, in Gaul, the story circulated that he, who had been the first of Christian princes to take the cross, had sought to make terms with the despoiler of Jerusalem, the wanton profaner of the holy rood; and the farther from the scene the rumor flew, the more dreadfully it resounded in the ears of Christendom.[57]

Through the winter of 1192 Richard lingered on, hoping against hope for some favorable turn of fortune. He had sent urgent messages to the Abbé of Clairvaux and to the magnates of influence who could still be moved by the afflictions of the Christians overseas, beseeching them to send new levies and the subsidies needed to sustain them in the field. His treasury touched bottom.[58] Joanna's Sicilian dower had gone with the rest.[59] As these harassments increased, a new disquietude took possession of his mind and paralyzed his will. Early in 1192 envoys reached him with secret messages from Ely the Chancellor,[60] reporting the burgeoning of seditious plots in Britain, involving Philip Augustus and Prince John; describing disorders in the regency in Britain; and imploring him, as he valued his crown, to give over the conquest of the Saracens and come home on the wings of the wind.[61] Through Lent many other messengers arrived, each more pressing than the last.

With mind divided and uneasy, Coeur-de-Lion marked time through the winter in Ascalon. He himself wrought with the masons relaying the ashlar of its toppled walls.[62] In April there arrived another embassy. This time John of Alençon came directly from Queen Eleanor with letters of the utmost urgency. As regent she reported Philip Augustus' attempts, in contravention of his vows in Acre and in defiance of papal prohibitions, to invade Normandy, to recover Alais and her dower, and to seduce John. The queen warned Coeur-de-Lion that John was pillaging the exchequer, seizing royal domains, demanding oaths of allegiance from the English barons, and intriguing with Philip to repudiate the Countess of Gloucester and marry Alais himself as a step toward grasping the crown. Eleanor had employed her energies heart and soul to promote the crusade; but she now implored Richard to abandon every other project and return with all speed to his own estates.

In the spring a fresh attack of fever brought Coeur-de-Lion to the very point of death. His physicians whispered to his anxious familiars that few recovered from the semitertian, and the rumor spread that the King of the English was about to "migrate from this world." These tidings, with reports of the quandary in Richard's mind and the division among his counselors whether he should go or stay, were discussed in Tyre and encouraged Conrad to press again the issue of the kingship. The barons of the marquis's following and the forces of the Duke of Burgundy refused allegiance to Guy of Lusignan, and there was now no means of sustaining him. The decision, submitted to the bishops and the barons who would have to carry on if Richard were to depart, went strongly in favor of Conrad.[63] Guy for the forfeit of his crown was contented with a little kingdom of his own in Cyprus, which he colonized with refugees from the strife and havoc on the mainland.[64]

The young Count of Champagne was sent to Tyre to confirm the judgment of the magnates. When the news of Conrad's triumph spread, the streets of the city were hung with banners and the flowery garlands of the early spring, and the place resounded with joyful noises in every quarter of the city and the port.[65] The people borrowed money for robes and display, and the garrisons polished their rusty arms, sharpened their swords, rubbed their lances, and gave rein to their rejoicing with tournaments. But the jubilation was hardly stilled when the music of tabor and flute rose again suddenly in the mournful rhythm of ululation, and the city was thrown into a panic. Conrad, returning to his palace from a convivial dinner with the Bishop of Beauvais, was set upon as he passed the Change by a pair of villains and foully slain in the street. The assassins accosted him from opposite sides of the narrow passage and, while one proffered him a message, the other drove a poniard into his back. The marquis was borne still living to a church and then to his palace, but he breathed only long enough to adjure his young wife Isabelle to protect the Kingdom of Jerusalem from imposters, and to commend his soul to God.

One of the murderers was killed on the spot; the other, who took sanctuary in a church, confessed himself under torture a disciple of the "Old Man of the Mountain," of the secret cult of the "Assassins," [66] and declared that he had been employed for six months in Christian disguise as a servant in Christian houses in Tyre, in order to find an opportunity to kill the marquis. Only on this very day, at the climax of Conrad's triumph, had he found a chance to fulfill his mission.[67]

Employed by whom? The instigator of the murder has never been certainly identified. So many persons might have profited by the death of Conrad that the circumstantial evidence pointed in no one direction. The question was asked on every hand, and it was variously answered. The partisans of Conrad openly charged Richard with thus ridding himself of a hated rival,[68] and reminded the world that Conrad had himself foretold the villainy; and certain Arab annalists upheld this view. The King of the English denounced the slander and called to witness the assassin, who stuck to his original testimony that he and his accomplice were avenging the private grievance of the Old Man of the Mountain, whose ships had been seized by Conrad in the port of Tyre and whose appeal for redress had been ignored.[69] One Moslem chronicler [70] declares that Saladin himself procured the murder.

✤

It was May when flower and leaf are renewed.
Ambrose

The affairs of the Latin Kingdom were again thrown into utter confusion. The crown of Jerusalem once more became a hollow symbol grasped in the frail hands of a woman. The Franks on the spot urged the taking of Tyre for Philip Augustus. But the young queen refused to yield it up.[71] And to whom should it be yielded? With consternation the barons of all factions cast about for a likely third husband for Isabelle. In the canvass of possibilities, one eligible was found in Henry, Count of Champagne. As nephew of both Richard and Philip Augustus, he offered some promise of reuniting the Christians in Syria and Palestine. He was in the flower of his age, a noble cavalier bred in the famous court of the Countess Marie of Champagne, personable, one whose valor in the holy war had been many times displayed.

Envoys hastened to bring him back from Acre, whither fortunately he had set out too early to have been implicated in the assassination of the marquis. It proved not difficult to persuade the count to turn back to Tyre, for, says the *Itinerarium*, there is no trouble in persuading a willing man.[72] The chroniclers suggest that he was very fain, for the young widow was "altogether fair and lovely, whiter than any pearl." So they robed Isabelle in bridal dress instead of widow's weeds and, within a bare week from the murder of the marquis, she was united to Count Henry. In a fortnight Tyre had celebrated the election of two kings to the throne of Jerusalem and mourned the death of one. "Then," says the chronicler, describing the advent of Henry, "had ye seen a noble welcoming, processions ranged in order, all the streets bedecked with tapestries, in every window censers filled with incense."[73] Clerks escorted the new king to the minster, exposed the relics, and offered for his adoration a fragment of the Holy Cross. And so with honors they brought him to the palace and there ordered a banquet to be served.

✤

O Jerusalem, now art thou indeed helpless. Who will protect thee when Richard is away?
Ambrose

The Christian factions in the Holy Land were thus by fortuitous events reunited under one leadership. But the forces for crusade had been dissipated, and Islam gathered new levies to drive the Christians, both the lords of the fiefs of the Latin Kingdom and the new arrivals, with all their baggage and their works into the Mediterranean where other empires had been engulfed before. In these circumstances dalliance with Saladin became more popular.

Through the summer, as Richard's anxieties increased and his fever sapped his strength, Saladin successively whittled down the demands of the Christians for a truce: first, from a retrocession of all they once possessed to half of their former possessions together with the Holy Cross; then to mere holding of existing conquests and the privilege of visiting the Holy Sepulcher and exercising their religion there.[74] At length they came to terms on the extreme of Saladin's demands.[75] Neither enemy should lift sword against the other; the coast towns taken by the Christians should remain *in statu quo*, except Ascalon, which, after the Christians' winter labor to restore it, had to be razed. Henry of Champagne as "King of Jerusalem" should command the remnant of the Christian army, but without injury to Saladin. For the time being Henry and Saladin were proclaimed allies against the upsurge of any foe. Thereupon Saladin provided Henry with a royal aba and turban so that he might not seem a pariah among the Oriental satraps.

As for the cross, Saladin, although he pronounced it "an offense to God," kept it against the exigencies of diplomacy in the future; and subsequently, according to Bohaddin, when the fear of the crusaders had abated, remitted it to the Emperor of Byzantium for a prodigious sum in gold.[76]

After the agreement, Saladin, hoping, as his chronicler explains, to hasten the departure of the Christians from the Orient, graciously permitted little bands of pilgrims, unarmed and under reliable guides, to visit Jerusalem. The Bishop of Salisbury took a party, which made a tour of the shrines.[77] As humble pilgrims they refused the luxury of lodgment in Saladin's palace, but they accepted the privilege he offered them of adoring the rood. Richard's jongleur Ambrose went with a less distinguished group and relates that they visited the Sepulcher, Calvary, the Tomb of the Virgin, and other sacred places; that their tears ran as they saw how Christians had been employed as slaves to reinforce the Moslem defenses of Jerusalem, and how the shrines were polluted by the offenses and the neglect of the infidels. They visited the prison chamber where Christ awaited the crucifixion, but did not linger long because some fellow pilgrims who had pushed their explorations a bit too far had been slain in the gloom of neighboring crypts.[78]

Richard was of course invited by Saladin to pay a visit to Jerusalem with the honors due a king, but the noble mind of Coeur-de-Lion would not consent to receive from the courtesy of the infidel what he could not obtain by the gift of God.[79] After all, he had borne witness to a truce, not a renunciation. "If the ram draws back," says the Poitevin proverb, "it is only to strike the harder." The king, though worn with fever and disturbed by a grand malaise, was still Plantagenet. He turned away from the domes of Jerusalem and set his face toward home. With the gesture of oblation he registered his vow: "O Holy Land, I commend thee to God, and if His heavenly grace grants me so long to live, I hope, I pledge, to come one day to succor thee." [80]

26 ✤

Shipwreck and Disguise

IT WAS NIGHTFALL ON OCTOBER 9, 1192,[1] that Coeur-de-Lion gave orders to his mariners to spread the canvas of his one galley in the port of Acre. The queens with their household and their Cyprian captive had been dispatched ahead on the day of Saint Michael, more than a week earlier, in a slow but stout and commodious dromon. They followed the open sea route and were duly reported in Sicily, and subsequently in Rome.[2]

There was no concealing the departure of the King of England from Syria. The city that had hailed his arrival with unmeasured joy was plunged in gloom as his galley was seen in the harbor preparing to take off. Then, says Ambrose,[3] the people went about weeping softly and praying for him, and retelling all his deeds of prowess, of valor, and largess. But Coeur-de-Lion kept the day and hour of his departure, the course of his voyage, and the make-up of his following obscure, for he had been warned that powers and principalities lay in wait to make sure that he should never reach his own lands. There were few allies that he could trust, many enemies that he must fear. For safe-conduct he appealed to the Templars, those guardians of pilgrims and their travel routes.

"Master," he said, "I know very well that few love me; and if I go to sea, and my enemies know that I have done so, I can find no port where I shall not be killed or taken. Therefore, I pray you, lend me some of your knights and men-at-arms, who will go with me, and when we are far from here, they will conduct me as a brother Templar to my own country."[4]

It was with a band of Templars and men disguised as Templars that the king left the port of Acre, commending himself to the Truce of God. The ship was well armed and provisioned; but one chronicler at least declares that, in spite of precautions, a knave slipped aboard whose business it was to betray the king to his enemies.[5]

All that first autumnal night the king and his company scudded over the dark waters under a heaven bright with stars and took their bearings from the sky.[6] The ship, avoiding the open sea, took its secret course among the islands where, although the passage was more dangerous, it was easier to elude pursuit and to take refuge in secluded ports. The waters they chose were the profitable hunting grounds of those Greek and Barbary pirates that throve on the lonely ships of pilgrims and merchants as they made their way through the confined and ill-charted passages.[7]

The galley first made port in Cyprus, and then within about a month from its sailing from Acre, it came to Corfu,[8] where Philip Augustus had also landed on his return from Syria the year before. In the meantime the king's ship had passed through that mariners' limbo in which Queen Eleanor and Louis Capet had been adrift in the custody of corsairs at the end of the second crusade, a region whose perils and alarms had certainly figured in the nursery mythology of Coeur-de-Lion's earliest years.

In Corfu and the nearby islands were outposts of the Sicilian admiral Marguerite that offered harborage and supplies for the vessels bent on those infested waters, together with agents to provide for exchange and safe-conducts.[9] Here the pilgrims touched a zone of safety and a means of reaching the only attainable sanctuaries, the protection of Tancred and the Pope, or the more distant security of ports on the shores of Provence.

Subsequently a traveler who made port safely in another vessel identified the king's galley "en route from Corfu to Brindisi." [10] From this point there is confusion in the accounts of the king's journey. For Richard never reached Brindisi. The most credible account of his course is related in the chronicle of Coggeshall and purports to be the story of Anselm the Chaplain, who shared the perils and hardships of the king on his eventful progress.[11] This account states that from Corfu Richard set out not for Brindisi, but for Marseille, and that his galley, after six weeks' travail on the wintry sea, had come within three days' sailing of the destined port. Putting in for reconnoiter, perhaps at Pisa, where he was on good terms with the shippers,[12] he learned that Raymond of Toulouse and his allies, eager to avenge the ruthless justice Richard had imposed upon them in 1190, had ambushed every useful port of the seaboard on which he wished to land. According to one report, the king now considered a passage by open sea through the Pillars of Hercules, but was dissuaded by the violence of the weather as winter drew on. In spite of the unfavorable condition of the waters and the bitterness of turning back when he had almost attained his goal, he resolved to reverse his sails and set his prow again for Corfu. Since no safe course was open to him, he probably trusted to surprise, disguise, and Plantagenet luck to strike boldly but secretly through the territories of his Teutonic enemies. Perhaps he had a hope that, with good fortune, he could cross some land bridge touching the Adriatic into the territories of his brother-in-law, the Duke of Saxony. He may even have had from the duke some assurance of succor.

So the galley turned back over the tempestuous seas to Corfu. In the neighborhood of this island, according to Anselm's account, the king's galley was approached by two high-beaked Rumanian pirate ships. Perhaps by this time Richard's galley had suffered sea damage. At any rate, Hoveden declares that the king hired the pirate vessels for two hundred marks of silver.[13] Richard embarked on one of these, keeping with him a score of his closest associates, among them Baldwin of Béthune, Philip, his clerk, Anselm the Chaplain, and certain Templars.

Skirting the east coast of the Adriatic, the ships, now numbering two or three, put in on the Rumanian coast near Ragusa, but some circumstance, probably the inhospitality of the hinterland, forced them again to sea. According to the account in Hoveden, the ships were driven by gales of unusual fury on the coast of Istria at the head of the Adriatic, and there they were broken or foundered near the shore.[14] The passengers of the king's ship, and possibly some other survivors, were cast up on the land in territories held by vassals of Count Leopold of Austria.

At once the king sent a messenger to the castle of the local Count Mainerd [15] requesting safe-conduct under the Truce of God for a company of shipwrecked travelers. The king, says Anselm, on his return journey had bought three very precious rubies from a certain Pisan for nine hundred bezants (about $2700). While on board ship he wore one of these set in a golden ring. This ring he now sent by the agency of his messenger as a gift to the lord of the castle. When the messenger was closely questioned by the count as to who those were that sought safe-conduct, he replied that they were pilgrims returning from the Holy Land.[16] The count then asked their names.

"One of them," replied the messenger, "is Baldwin of Béthune and another is one Hugo, a merchant, and it is he who sends you this ring."

The count examined the token closely for some time as if turning over various things in his mind. At length he spoke.

"His name is not Hugo but King Richard. I had sworn that I would arrest all pilgrims coming from those parts and that I would accept no 'gifts' from them. However, because of the preciousness of this token and the high condition of him who thus honors me, I return the gift and give your lord freedom to proceed."

When the messenger reported this interview to the "pilgrims," they were mightily disturbed. They contrived somehow to obtain horses, left the village in the middle of the night, and were for a little time at large in the territories of Count Mainerd. The count's magnanimity, as the fugitives suspected, was less than it seemed, for he at once sent spies to his brother, Frederick of Betestowe, through whose land the travelers would have to pass, advising him that the king would soon be ripe for capture, and giving him the time which he had not had himself to prepare the necessary forces.

As soon as Frederick was apprised that the fugitives had entered his confines or were about to do so, he summoned one of his most trusted men, a certain Roger, a native of the Norman city of Argentan, who had been in his service for twenty years. He directed Roger to search all the hospices in the vicinity where pilgrims were wont to lodge, to see if he might trace the king either by his foreign speech or some other indications, and promised him, if he succeeded, half of the city where they were as his reward. Roger, after a diligent search, at last found where the king was staying. For some time Richard denied his identity, but at last he confessed who he was and put himself at Roger's mercy, invoking the Truce of God. To the king's astonishment, Roger, instead of taking him captive, burst into tears over his plight, pressed a superb horse upon him, and besought him to flee for his life. Anselm imputes Roger's sudden change of front to the Norman blood in his veins; but possibly the heroic character of the king, his chivalric bearing, some of the Plantagenet eloquence, and the sacred Truce of God had to do with the matter. Returning to Frederick, Roger reported that the rumors that the king was at hand were false and that the suspected characters were Baldwin of Béthune and some of his companions.[17]

In their extremity the fugitives employed a ruse they must have previously rehearsed and so saved the king from capture. Baldwin drew attention to himself as a person of consequence, and the men of Frederick, who had not relied altogether upon the Norman Roger for their espionage, seized him with several of his following, probably supposing they held the king.[18] At Freisach, a little farther inland, six more men were taken. Baldwin's impersonation of Coeur-de-Lion enabled the latter to get away with a small escort of serviceable young men, among them William de l'Étang and a boy who understood German. The king kept his disguise as a merchant traveling with his colporteurs and in these roles, by extraordinary luck, they reached a village, Ganina, on the Danube in the neighborhood of Vienna and found lodgings in a squalid tavern. The Angevins knew how to press horses to the utmost and to keep the saddle day and night, but this dash must have exceeded all previous exploits. The distance from the coast to Vienna is nearly two hundred miles as the crow flies, and the king and his men covered three quarters of those leagues in three days of posting without stopping for food or rest.

Coeur-de-Lion was not yet fully recovered from the tertian fever that had stricken him in Syria, and the exertions and privations of his flight brought even his matchless endurance to an end. He fell at once upon his tavern bed and plunged into a fathomless sleep. In the meantime his interpreter went out to forage for provisions. Needing coin of the country, he sought out an exchange, and making the most of opportunity to get a supply for future needs, he poured out a fine, telltale stream of the golden bezants current in Syria. The abundant gold and the imperiousness of the young man, who doubtless betrayed the utmost haste to be off, excited remark, and he was detained by citizens and sharply questioned. Asked who he was, the youth replied that he was the courier of a certain very rich merchant who would be coming to the town in a few days. When he had thrown his inquisitors off the scent, he flew back to the tavern, roused the king from his stupor, and besought him to take to the road again with all haste. But Coeur-de-Lion was unequal to the effort and could not be persuaded. In spite of the filth and squalor of the place and the danger to his person, he kept to his bed for several days, and the youth in the meantime was obliged more than once to go to the public markets for their necessities.[19]

On the 21st of December, which was a feast day, he appeared in the market with the king's gloves bearing royal insignia thrust carelessly into his belt. His haste and lavishness in buying luxuries for his sick and weary king drew attention. The youth was reported to public officials, who arrested him, tortured him, and threatened to cut out his tongue unless he yielded to questioning and told the truth.

Advent was at hand and Leopold of Austria had convened his Christmas court in Vienna. The youth's story was made known to the duke, who lost no time in ordering the king's hospice surrounded. Richard, roused by the hubbub outside his quarters,[20] discovered that all escape was cut off. He once more, and on the spur of the moment, improvised a new disguise, such as the house afforded. He fled to the kitchen and drew on a scullion's smock. Taking his place by the hearth and slumping in the attitude of a stupid fellow, he busied himself with the spit on which some spatchcocks were roasting for his dinner.[21] In Templar's disguise, with beard and staff, the Count of Poitou might pass unsuspected, for Templars were usually men of condition; he might even act the part of the wealthy merchant; but the old smock and the scullion's role betrayed him. There were men in Vienna who had seen him in Acre and knew his every lineament.

Anselm relates that when Richard heard the guttural German tumult outside the tavern, he felt a strong repugnance to yielding himself to that barbaric rabble. He demanded that Duke Leopold himself be summoned and declared that he would give himself up to no other. One of the chroniclers relates that Leopold, avid for his quarry and eager to witness the humiliation of the proud Plantagenet, hastened to the tavern. The surrender was made with due chivalric rites as befitted the dignity of the king, and Coeur-de-Lion was led away with the duke's escort to the castle. At first received honorably in custody, he was presently put under guard of men-at-arms who stood about him day and night with drawn swords.[22]

27 ✠

Eleanor Queen of England

FROM THE TIME OF RICHARD'S ACCESSION and her own release from captivity, and notwithstanding the marriage and crowning of Berengaria in Limassol, the Countess of Poitou styled herself, and was addressed by others, as "Eleanor, by the grace of God, Queen of England."

As the perils grew that threatened the Angevin empire, she rose with a majesty that amazed her contemporaries. The fruit of her early disciplines in Henry's school of feudal statecraft had matured in Salisbury Tower. In her long restraint, with only philosophy for her exercise, she had, it seemed, accumulated wisdom and somehow kept pace with the progress of history. In those years she had gained from her narrow windows a long-range view of Angevin destiny. She had attained Henry's capacity for bold maneuver, but she was more folk-wise than he, more sensitive to popular drifts, and more ingenious in taking advantage of these. Her sagacity, her decisiveness, her adroitness and dispatch, her vigilance, her multifarious activities, her sudden and wearisome journeyings, were the marvel of her age. Her acts in the crises of Angevin history that confronted her reveal a core of sound policy governed by a prudence and farsighted vision that had not characterized the conduct of her prime. From the time of her release her foremost place among the magnates of the realm was never questioned.

Earlier and more clearly than her associates she divined that the crusade, which had stirred the emotions and engrossed the thoughts of every rank in the feudal world, was not the most critical concern of the Plantagenets. Her memory was long, and she saw looming beyond the horizons of the holy war, dangers that threatened, near the end of her days, to disrupt the proud empire that Henry Plantagenet had built out of the mosaic pieces of western Europe; and unlike her familiars, she saw the chief menace to that structure not in the wars with Saladin, nor in the tangle of affairs in Britain, nor in the turbulence in Poitou, but in the single-eyed design of Louis Capet's heir.

She had had an unexampled opportunity of knowing the quality of the pride that underlay the patience and humility of the pious Louis and the caution and pertinacity of Philip Augustus. She did not, like Richard, underestimate either the capacity or the resolute malice of the younger Capet, dedicated from his birth to the prime object of wiping out the grievances his house had suffered from the Plantagenets in half a century; to the object of redressing that balance of power his dynasty had lost through her own withdrawal from the citadel of the Franks in 1152; of rectifying those gradual encroachments of Henry in Brittany, Normandy, Auvergne, Berry and Toulouse; of avenging the scorching insults flung at the Capets in the dismissal of the young Queen Marguerite and the betrayal of Alais and the withholding of the Capetian dowers.

In the third quarter of the century, when time and destiny were hers, the Angevin empire had seemed strong enough to counter any rancors of the puny and spineless Capets. But within the dozen and more years of her imprisonment the position of the Plantagenets vis-à-vis the Capets had deteriorated, more through the strange fortuity of events than through failure of design. Henry — so many years her junior — had vanished from the scene. Of the five sons with whom she had fortified the empire, only two remained, glorious Richard and graceless John. As long as Richard remained childless, the succession was insecure, and certain, if Richard were to meet an untimely end upon crusade, to provoke an internecine strife and offer the Capets their long-awaited opportunity to divide and conquer. Of the daughters given as hostages for foreign alliances, two remained. Joanna, widowed, and impoverished by Richard's crusade, no longer offered prestige nor support to the royal house; and Eleanor, married in 1170 to the King of Castile, had been rooted in the world beyond the Pyrenees and swallowed up in peninsular affairs. Matilda was dead, and her widowed husband, in perennial conflict with the Holy Roman Emperors, merely complicated the continental problems of the Plantagenets. In the oncoming generation among her grandsons of the houses of Saxony and Brittany, Queen Eleanor recognized another brood of fierce eaglets, like those of the Winchester fresco, tearing at the heart of empire and continuing the fratricidal strife that had divided her own sons.

She could see the Capets and the Plantagenets, whose names both she had borne, coming to grips for the possession of her world, the whole Continent of Europe from the lower Alps to the western sea, from the Channel to the Pyrenees. It was to be a conflict stripped of all pretense of feudal loyalties. No longer could crusaders' vows or oaths of feudal allegiance in a common cause conceal, nor could papal anathema prevent, the fateful and inextinguishable enmity between the two royal houses. In the struggle that mounted she saw the insecurity of the Plantagenet succession her matter of first concern.

Until Richard should have secured his own succession, John loomed as the second defense of empire; but the youngest Plantagenet was by no means ideal as a pretender to the Angevin domains, and no one knew this more certainly than the queen. Eleanor during her captivity had not been bemused by the resort of her three elder sons to the court of the Capets, each one in

turn there to be transformed into an enemy of his own house, an agent for
its ruin. She remembered the young king provided in Paris with an army
and a seal of state to usurp Henry's empire; Richard in company with
Philip Augustus hounding the elder king through his estates to his death
in Chinon; Geoffrey of Brittany, Philip's trencher-mate in Paris, cut off in
the midst of intrigue against his own race and entombed in Notre Dame.
These events, in which she had certainly borne a share, now composed themselves with stark clarity into a preview of disaster. John too had learned the
way to Paris. The youngest eaglet gave Eleanor a terrible anxiety. Should
he be appeased or be driven by rebuffs to follow his elder brothers into the
camp of the archenemy?

The prince who had been born too late for his proper share in the splendid inheritance of the Angevins had been called John Lackland in his infancy.
As a child he had seen himself the object of a tender solicitude to the king
his father, who had tried to endow him with a realm in Ireland; to carve
him a little estate by abridging his brothers' domains where they converged
at the heart of the Angevin inheritance; to gain for him by marriage the
Province of Maurienne; and at last to deprive Richard in his favor by giving
him Poitou and transferring to him the alliance with Alais of France. But
nothing materialized; everywhere the finer luster of his brothers' lots made
his portion paltry. And when the death of two elder brothers gave room in
the empire, he still had no solid domain, while one sole brother inherited the
whole. Yet was not he a Plantagenet, born of the same root, with the blood
of the Conqueror purple in his veins, and of the Angevins, and of the
Poitevins?

Given his character, the youngest of the Plantagenets was just near enough
the throne to be tempted to override the obstacles and suppress the scruples
that separated him from it. Giraldus Cambrensis had measured John's abil-
ities with those of his brother Geoffrey, with no disparagement of John. In
wit he was the nimblest of all the brothers and of a lightning suddenness
of action, unrestrained by disturbing afterthoughts or any twinge of conscience. His perfidy had already been fully displayed in his heartless desertion
of his father in his last days, and it now shone forth in his shameless bargaining with the regency to keep him loyal to his absent brother. The cynical
impudence of John, his slick agility in changing front, were preternatural,
as if he were indeed the posterity of that celebrated demon ancestress of the
Plantagenets, who was seen at one moment kneeling piously at mass as
Countess of Anjou and, at the next, when the host was elevated, vaulting out
of the window in the guise of a witch.[1]

Richard's handsome grants to John before his departure for Syria were
designed to satisfy Lackland's ambitions in Britain and to keep him out of the
preferred continental domains and out of the best opportunities of collusion

with the Capets; but they gave him a position of great wealth and power and contributed to the presumption that he would be Richard's heir at least in England, a presumption strengthened during the crusade by the popular belief that Coeur-de-Lion was destined not to return to his island kingdom. So great was the dread of John's maneuvers among those who had Richard's interests at heart, that the prince was put under oath to forego the occupation of his English castles and remain abroad for a period of three years while Richard was overseas.

Queen Eleanor, having in project her journey to Sicily, had not dared to leave John foot-loose upon the Continent, free to range with Richard's malcontent vassals, to come at the tower of Rouen, or to proceed to the court of France. She therefore, as the lesser of two evils, procured his release from his oath of exile and sped him to Britain, where the magnates were expected to keep him in check.

While the queen was making her momentous journey to Sicily, John made good use of his time in Britain. "He perambulated the kingdom," says Devizes,[2] and made himself known, as Richard never was known, to the people of the island, people of every rank. He showed himself, like the young king, liberal and affable, magnificent and generous in hospitality. By pressure and by intrigue he possessed himself of several of his forbidden castles, took up his residence now in one, now in another, set up a quasi-royal court with its officers and household, maintained his own justice, and enjoyed large revenues. Wherever he went, and upon all occasions, he stimulated the belief that Richard would not return and that he was the certain heir of England. Says the chronicler, "It lacked nothing but that he should be hailed as king."

The magnates of the regency were cautiously reluctant to withstand John's aggressions and his arrant exploitation of himself.[3] Doubt about the ultimate plans of Coeur-de-Lion clouded their counsels. So far the king had held no steady course. At Henry's death he had swept out most of the old servants of government. Then he had altered his purposes in Sicily and might do so again. Moreover, under the influence of rumors spread by John, many of them believed that the latter might soon be king,[4] and they were wary of opposing a prospective monarch who would certainly know how to wreak his vengeance. The situation commended a policy of temporizing with the youngest Plantagenet. Prudence suggested easing the prince's tether, but without giving him irrecoverable rope. Only Ely the Chancellor in the interest of Richard ventured to resist him publicly; but Ely's unpopular operations in other fields had so far isolated him from his fellow magnates that he became a target for John rather than a bulwark against him.

Since Henry's death, John, in considering his interests under the new regime, had kept an open mind as to whether those interests would be more profitably served by maintaining good relations with Richard, or by collusion with Philip Augustus; and he was not long in discovering that this judicial attitude put him in a good position to bargain with either party. But the news of Richard's compact with Tancred, designating Arthur of Brittany as the king's heir, precipitated John's decision about where his interests lay. When by secret means he learned that Ely was engaged in Richard's behalf in confirming that compact in Scotland, his course was no longer dark to him.[5] He indulged in a livid Angevin rage and then set himself to procure the downfall of the presumptuous chancellor. In this project of injuring Ely, the prince made good use of the chancellor's unpopularity to insure his own prestige.

There seems no doubt of Ely's loyalty to the king. But his arrogant assumption of authority over his colleagues, his exactions of tax and tithe, his pompous exploitation of his dignity as legate and chancellor, had won him a cordial detestation in every quarter. Baldwin, the Archbishop of Canterbury, had recently died on crusade, and the prelates of Britain were fearful that Ely might make his mastery complete by slipping adroitly into the primacy.[6]

The church was further outraged at the moment by a fortuitous incident in which Ely's excess of zeal undid him. Geoffrey, elect of York, like John, had been under oath to remain abroad for three years during Richard's absence. But he had recently, in consequence of Eleanor's negotiations in Rome, received his pallium, and he was ambitious to assume the administration of his diocese, the revenues of which during the vacancy were flowing into the coffers of the chancellor. Making John's release from his oath a warrant for disregarding his own, Geoffrey landed in Dover against Ely's injunctions, to take possession of his see. Thereupon Ely ordered his arrest, and his overzealous minions subjected Geoffrey, newly invested with his holy orders, to gross indignities.[7]

The anxiety of bishops and barons alike to do nothing compromising in uncertain times had heretofore condemned the regency to impotency in dealing with the chancellor. But the case of Geoffrey, which aroused widespread popular indignation, offered an actionable cause. In this they were glad, however, to employ John as their figurehead and as a potential scapegoat in the event that Richard should support his insufferable chancellor. In these commotions, John, fearing neither chancellor nor legate overmuch, nor his brother either, appeared before the people as the righteous instrument of the bishops and the champion of the popular discontent, and in this role he presently found admirable ways of advancing his own interests.

The prince, the bishops, and the justiciars met in Reading, where they took council together and found due warrant for acting against Ely.[8] Here was produced that super-mandate obtained by the queen and the Archbishop of Rouen in Rome, a manifesto authorizing the regency to check the chancellor if matters came to extremity and to accept Rouen's counsel as supreme. They summoned the chancellor, who was at Windsor, to hear their complaints, and this he promised to do. But when his outriders discovered that the bishops and barons were headed by John and accompanied by some armed knights and a force of Welsh soldiery, Ely made excuse that he was sick and retired to the security of the Tower of London.[9]

In the meantime Geoffrey and his partisans had already roused the citizenry of the capital over the outrage of his treatment in the dungeon of Dover. When the Reading council pursuing the chancellor reached London, it was night and the city gates, by Ely's orders, were closed against them. Certain custodians, however, fearing to bar the gates in the face of the king's brother and the assembled magnates, let them come inside where excited streams of burghers were pouring into the dark streets with lanterns to learn what was afoot.

The next day in a public gathering under the very shadow of the Tower, in presence of ten thousand Londoners, the chancellor was called to account for his administration.[10] Up to this moment Ely had felt himself so panoplied with civil and ecclesiastical authority as to be beyond the reach of rabbles. The consolidation of the regency into a party of opposition armed with a super-mandate, together with the popular uprising, overwhelmed him with astonishment and panic. Facing that hostile throng almost alone, the chancellor answered the charges against him with a show of boldness, reaffirming his loyalty to the king. Then before the whole gathering he hurled defiance at John. He warned the magnates publicly above all things to beware of the youngest Plantagenet, who was beyond any doubt bent upon usurping his brother's crown while that brother was signed with the cross and absent upon crusade. However, when he fronted John and the magnates, says Devizes, "he was as pale as one who treads upon a snake with his bare feet."

Two days later an assembly at Saint Paul's decreed the chancellor's banishment from Britain and placed at the head of the government the Archbishop of Rouen under the mandate which he and the queen had forethoughtfully procured in Rome the previous spring. In the new dispensation, John fared well. His valor and forthrightness in defying the chancellor buttressed the courage of the new regency. The prince was made chief justiciar and recognized as heir of Britain. But the magnates at the same time drew in his rope a little. John surrendered the custody of his castles for the time being, though continuing to enjoy large revenues. The members of the reconstituted government then pledged their oaths anew to the absent king. The Bishop of Ely, thrown into utter panic by his reverses, escaped from Britain ignominiously, as if in fear of his life, in the disguise of a woman.[11] In the meantime the people, who had witnessed these movements and exerted their pressures upon them, had learned a useful lesson in how to be rid of tyrants; and they had taken the measure of John's brilliant audacity.

⚜

Sometime after her return from Sicily, Eleanor stationed herself in Rouen at the very center of the agitations that raged about her. With the expulsion of Ely late in October, the confusions that had disordered Britain leapt the Channel and brought to her palace gates dilemmas so grave that her right hand hardly dared to know what her left hand was doing. She now had the firebrand Bishop of Ely in her own bailiwick, and he was by no means extinguished. Once on the safe side of the water, he quickly recovered his aplomb, and although he had been excommunicated at Reading, he erected himself again to his full stature as chancellor and legate. The queen was faced with the immediate dilemma of trying to keep the injured chancellor from the camp of the enemy in Paris without at the same time obstructing the operations of the regency to keep him out of Britain. However, as if moved by a law of nature, the offended prelate took the way of all those who bore grievances against the Angevins straight to the seat of the Capets. In Paris, says Benedict, he paid the bishop of that city to receive him processionally with all the honors due the dignities he had once possessed.[12] In addition to this comfort, whether by arrangement or by chance, the deposed chancellor seems to have encountered two cardinals arriving from Celestine [13] and to have received from them the renewal of his legateship, with which he was presently seen to be fortified.

The queen was of course wary of cardinals. It was spread abroad that the new arrivals had come to reëstablish the peace between the Bishops of Ely and Rouen and thus clarify the somewhat ambiguous policy of Rome toward the regency. But since it was Eleanor's acute desire not to precipitate anew the crisis between the one-time chancellor and the regency, even to have it resolved by arbitration, she had no mind to negotiate with emissaries bringing a cool and dispassionate justice from Rome. In the back of her mind too was an uneasy misgiving lest the cardinals, who had sojourned in Paris on their way, might have some undisclosed mission for the Capets and might, if once they set foot in Normandy, raise questions about Gisors and the unhappy prisoner in the tower of Rouen.[14]

The cardinals, remarks Devizes dryly, appeared to suppose that Normandy was a province of the French domain, for they had not taken the precaution to obtain from the queen letters of safe-conduct for the passage of the frontier. Since the days of Becket's appeals to Rome and his fulminations against the Angevins, Henry had made it peculiarly difficult for alien prelates to rove about Normandy. Accordingly, when the Cardinals Jordan and Octavian drew up their cohorts before the castle of Gisors with the intention of traveling thence to Rouen on their mission, they found the drawbridge raised and the seneschal on hand to explain about the indispensable letters of safe-conduct. This functionary cited Richard's right as a crusader to protection from the penetration of his territory by any foreign agents whomsoever without royal letters patent.[15]

Since the legates were in possession of Celestine's letters patent, arguments ensued. As the cardinals scanned the sheer walls of the fortress, the moat, the raised drawbridge, and the firm portcullis, their dignity "rose and swelled with rage."[16] They threatened to employ that spiritual weapon that overleaps barriers of water, stone, and oak. But "they did not plead with boys," observes the chronicler. The garrisons with swords, the burghers with drawn fists, made countermovements of menacing import. The cardinals thereupon withdrew their cavalcade, "rejoicing," as the records say, because "it is meet for the servants of the Lord to suffer contumely from His adversaries."

In the course of her days the queen had learned how to deal with the fulminations of ecclesiastics hurled forth to impede the operation of civil powers, and she had even found ways of turning them to profit. She knew how to appreciate the value of anathema in certain circumstances without overrating its efficacy in others. But the tempest of fulminations that now descended on the domains of the Plantagenets brought all her experience into play. A sulphurous pall settled over both sides of the Channel as Advent approached, and in this murky atmosphere it was difficult to plot an undeviating course.

The cardinals excommunicated the Seneschal of Normandy and his garrison and put the whole province under interdict, but without touching the person of the queen. In the meantime Ely, fortified by his new legateship and disregarding his own excommunication at Reading, excommunicated the regency in England severally and by name, saving only John and one lone justiciar who had remained at least neutral in the late upheavals. As if caught up in the spirit of the time, Geoffrey of York, for interests of his own, excommunicated his suffragan, the Bishop of Durham.[17] Since it was unlawful to eat or drink with excommunicates, to buy from them or sell to them, or to have any commerce with them, the effect of these operations was confusing and not all fulminations could be duly honored. It became a nice question as to who had prior and superior rights to excommunicate whom. The cross fire of blast and counterblast, and the defiance of resolute sinners cut off from grace, made it difficult, even for bishops and barons, to decide with which of their confreres they might sit down and dine.[18]

The flaw of the system was of course that the fulmination, to have its intended effect, had to completely overawe the miscreant. Thus groups were more likely than individuals to defy a sentence. In this instance the regency disregarded the operations of the excommunicate Ely with respect to themselves and, instead of succumbing, put the chancellor's own diocese under interdict and confiscated all his properties. Thus, with Christmas at hand in 1191, whole provinces were cut off from sacraments. There was no communion, no marriage, no lighting of altars, no ringing of bells, no ritual for the burial of the dead, who lay in fields awaiting the return of their parishes to the mercies of salvation.[19]

In the midst of the confusions produced by the cardinals in Normandy, Ely entered the province, doubtless to intercede with Eleanor for a return to England. Here, although provided with his new legateship, he found himself, to his deep chagrin, regarded as excommunicate, and so turned back from an interview that might have proved difficult for Eleanor in her unsteady role as custodian of such peace as prevailed. It can thus be seen how, in her dilemmas, the queen let excommunications in one way or another serve her ends. In the case of Ely, she respected fulminations and so avoided a painful session with him; but in the case of the cardinals she resisted their ban by appealing to Celestine, who promptly lifted it.[20] For the moment she did not interfere with the interdict upon the diocese of Ely, but later, in 1192, having visited the diocese and seen with her own eyes the miseries of the people denied the sacraments even for burial, she demanded and obtained from the Archbishop of Rouen the removal of the ban. "To meet her there," says the chronicler, "there came out of hamlets and manors, wherever she passed, men, women, and children, a piteous company, their feet bare, their clothes unwashed, their hair unshorn. Their flowing tears spoke for them." [21]

※

The queen, having just weathered these thunderblasts and averted interference with her affairs, was holding her modest Christmas court in Bures near Rouen [22] when news reached her that Philip Augustus, returning from his brief expedition overseas, blessed by the Pope with cross and palm, had been welcomed processionally in Paris and had convened his Christmas court in Fontainebleau.[23]

With Philip came a feast of news for a news-hungry world, which was now regaled with the choicest morsels. The tidings were firsthand, vouched for by the heroic King of the Franks, who had been in the thick of things in Palestine. The eager world learned for certain that it was only the valor of the Franks that had brought down the banners of Saladin from the ramparts of Acre; [24] heard that Philip's devastating malady had issued from a poison cup; [25] that he had left the Holy Land in fear of his life because of the treachery of his sworn allies. The king and his following detailed the impious bickerings of Coeur-de-Lion with Saladin.[26] As Philip mounted the stairs of his indignation, incidents multiplied and wonders grew. The Flanders affair . . . the infamous matter of Alais. . . Did not such violations of the oaths of Vézelay, sworn on the evangels and the relics of Saint Mary Magdalene, call for redress? Philip went straightway to Saint Denis and thanked God publicly for having so far delivered him from the perils that threatened his health, his life. Even in his own city of Paris he went about with armed guards and carried a bludgeon himself to protect him from the long arms of assassins.[27] In the meantime he directed his engineers to perfect the fortifications he had ordered built in divers places during his absence. The armorers of Paris kept their forges roaring day and night.[28] The King of the Franks counted his serviceable knights. It was manifest that he was about to execute in summary fashion a justice too long delayed. Normandy first.[29]

These astonishing eruptions in the Île de France greatly disquieted Queen Eleanor in Bures, but without suggesting major movements. She strengthened border castles, issued directions to seneschals, looked to the manning of garrisons, and then waited for eventualities. She had not long to wait. On the 20th of January Philip Augustus, having requested an interview, met the Seneschal of Normandy between Gisors and Trie, near the old trysting place by the stricken elm where Henry had so often contrived to put Louis Capet off with promises and excuses.[30] Philip offered for the seneschal's inspection the written compact of Messina with authentic seals attaching to it, and demanded the delivery of his sister Alais and the surrender of Gisors, Aumale, and Eu without evasion or delay. The seneschal, who was not taken by surprise, repeated the refusal he had offered to the cardinals and stood upon it in the face of threats. Unable to breach the gates of Gisors with menaces, Philip returned to the Île and raised an armed force to give effect unilaterally to the worthless compact of the Plantagenets.

While the queen was anxiously scanning the frontiers of Normandy for signs of action, the most alarming news came from the opposite direction, that is, from Britain. She was credibly warned that her son John had assembled a force of mercenaries, which he had gathered in his domains, and that he was about to lift sail in Southampton for Channel ports. He was on his way, she learned, to join Philip Augustus, to offer homage to the King of the Franks as his overlord, to open the stubborn gates of Normandy, take to himself the disprized prisoner of Rouen, and thereupon receive investiture as Duke of Normandy.[31] By these stark reckonings, the King of England counted no more among the living. The objective of John was fully disclosed. The catastrophe of the Plantagenets rose before the vision of the queen, with every role personified. She was left alone to defend the Angevins, the Poitevins, the heritage of Coeur-de-Lion against a rising tide of malice and of power.

With a dispatch that must have reminded her escort of Henry's embarkations, the queen put forth upon the wintry Channel and landed in Portsmouth on February 11, before John could get the wind in his sails.[32] She sought no arguments with her son, but went straight to the magnates,[33] who, if they dared, could shut off the prince's revenues and so impede his crossings. The barons were dispersed upon their eyres and evidently hardly interfering with the muster of the forces in Southampton. They must have been convinced by the rumors sedulously spread from Paris that Richard would return no more and to have believed that John was merely taking precaution to secure his heritage, which they themselves had recognized.

The queen speedily convened councils in Windsor, Oxford, London, and Winchester. It required an energetic dialectic and tears shed in many palaces to bring the slumbering magnates to their senses; but finally the bishops and barons awoke and pinned their faith to Eleanor and not to John. In her representations they at last found courage to threaten the prince with seizure of all his estates in England. Thereupon his foreign campaign collapsed and he retired sullenly to Wallingford.

As if John were not problem enough, nuncios from the exiled chancellor now took the occasion of the London assembly and its embarrassment with John to announce that Ely, armed with his new legateship, had landed the previous day in Dover and lodged in the castle there.[34] These harbingers saluted the queen courteously, but they filled the assembly with alarm. If the magnates were indeed to prevent Ely from return, they desired the concurrence of John in a decision that threatened to embroil them with Rome. Yet John at the moment they held under discipline. When a delegation from the magnates waited on the prince in Wallingford, they found him prepared to make good use of his lucky situation. His words were brief, but they fell like a thunderclap.

"The chancellor," he declared, "fears the threats of none of you, nor of all of you together; nor will he beg your suffrance if only he may succeed to have me for his friend. He has promised to give me £700 of silver within a week, if I shall have interposed between you and him. You see, I am in want of money. To the wise a word is sufficient." [35]

The prince had no mind to labor his case, but promptly withdrew, so that the magnates who had recently cut off his revenues might of their own insight come to their senses. In view of the circumstances, it seemed "expedient" to the magnates to propitiate the prince, and the money was found in the king's exchequer to outbid the bribe of Ely. Anything was better than to complicate affairs in England by restoring the chancellor. At least they had got rid of him. Having bought John's support with a good price, says the chronicler, "the queen writes, the clergy write, the people write: all with one voice admonish the chancellor to bolt, to cross the Channel without delay — unless he has a mind to take his meals under the custody of an armed guard."

All the Plantagenets were quick to learn, and John was by no means the least astute among the brothers. The king's absence provided him with useful lessons in the political chess play of his time, taught him to move the pieces on the board, king and bishop, knight and castle, and the humbler pawns, but not to capture the queen.

For the rest, the year 1192 passed drearily. Philip's incursions in Normandy were for the most part checked not only by the collapse of John's support, but by the refusal of his own barons to violate the Truce of God. The valorous knights of Britain were overseas with the king. In England, castles and great houses were closed or grimly manned for the defense of towns.[36] The anxious messages in which the regency besought the king to return from Palestine were long in transit and uncertain of effect upon the champion of Christendom, immersed in bitter warfare with the enemies of Christ. Tidings of disaster, disturbing rumors, but meager good news came from that distant field of conflict. During the winter, life itself was frozen: in the towns a little stir of merchants; the passage of cowled figures in twos and threes; on the manors only the diurnal toil of husbandman and shepherd. From remote clearings rang the forester's ax; in lonely places smoke uprose from the maltster's oast, the charcoal burner's kiln. Interdict lay for a long time on the diocese of Ely. Elsewhere prayers were said daily for the king's return.

28 ✠

The Ransom

Eleanor, by the wrath of God, Queen of England.
Letter of Eleanor to Pope Celestine III

AS THE YEAR 1192 DREW TOWARD AUTUMN, it was generally known in Europe that the King of England purposed to celebrate his Christmas court in his own estates. Late in the fall the first companies of pilgrims thronging home from the Holy Land for Advent, and others gathering in Normandy to welcome the king's arrival,[1] spread along the thoroughfares, in ports and market towns, their eyewitness accounts of the many chaptered enterprise in Palestine. These palmers recounted, along with the king's imperishable deeds of valor, the occasions in which Coeur-de-Lion had incurred the enmity of the greatest princes in Christendom — the King of the Franks and his high vassals, the Holy Roman Emperor, the powerful house of Montferrat, the Duke of Austria, and the Byzantine Comneni, bound to all the others by ties of blood. New companies of crusaders reaching their homelands just before Christmas were astonished that Richard, who had certainly sailed before them from Acre, had not preceded them home. There had been unwonted gales and many shipwrecks on the Mediterranean, but credible witnesses reported having seen the very galley in which the king had embarked in Palestine nearing the friendly harbor of Brindisi. As December came on and the king had not joined even his household in Italy, an alarming suspicion spread — and this on the lips of his enemies was converted to a certainty — that Coeur-de-Lion had encountered some calamity and would never reappear. The blithe and arrogant behavior of Philip Augustus in this period, and his good rapport with John, gave weight to dark hints of secret collusion and foul play.

Within the borders of Normandy a tense expectancy prevailed, fraught with conjecture and misgiving. By the queen's order the border castles were strongly held, the walls and fortifications of the towns strengthened and repaired. In England, where Eleanor held her Christmas court, an intolerable apprehension quenched all festivity. On the frontiers an armed truce, sustained by papal menace to France, held Philip Augustus in check. Paris too was quick with expectancy, but of a more sprightly quality. However, Advent passed on both sides of the Channel without news or incident. Berengaria

and Joanna still abode in Rome.[2] The champion of Christendom, signed
with the cross, journeying home from crusade, was six weeks overdue and
had not been heard from in any port.

On the 28th of December, a year and a day from Philip Augustus' return
from the holy war, it suddenly became known in what general region Richard
had celebrated Christmas. The ominous dearth of news broke in a flood. On
that day Philip received in Paris a marvelous letter from his illustrious friend,
the Holy Roman Emperor; and at once the world was filled with rumors
that brought every Christian alive stock still in his tracks.

> Henry by the grace of God, Emperor of the Romans and ever august, to his
> beloved and special friend Philip, the illustrious King of the Franks, health and
> sincere love and affection. Inasmuch as our imperial highness does not doubt that
> your royal mightiness will be delighted at all things in which the omnipotence of the
> Creator has honored and exalted ourselves and the Roman Empire, we have thought
> proper to inform your nobleness by means of these presents that while the enemy of
> our empire and the disturber of your kingdom, Richard, King of England, was
> crossing the sea for the purpose of returning to his dominions, it so happened that
> the winds brought him, the ship being wrecked on board of which he was, to the
> region of Istria, at a place which lies between Aquileia and Venice, where, by the
> sanction of God, the king, having suffered shipwreck, escaped, together with a few
> others. A faithful subject of ours, the Count Maynard of Gortze, and the people of
> that district, hearing that he was in our territory and calling to mind the treason and
> treachery and accumulated mischief he was guilty of in the Land of Promise, pursued
> him with the intention of making him prisoner. However, the king taking flight,
> they captured eight knights of his retinue. Shortly after, the king proceeded to a
> borough in the archbishopric of Salzburg, which is called Frisi, where Frederic de
> Botestowe took six of his knights, the king hastening on by night, with only three
> attendants, in the direction of Austria. The roads however, being watched, and
> guards being set on every side, our dearly beloved cousin Leopold, Duke of Austria,
> captured the king so often mentioned, in an humble house in a village in the vicinity
> of Vienna. Inasmuch as he is now in our power, and has always done his utmost for
> your annoyance and disturbance, what we have above stated we have thought proper
> to notify to your nobleness, knowing that the same is well pleasing to your kindly
> affection for us, and will afford most abundant joy to your own feelings. Given at
> Creutz, on the fifth day before the calends of January.[3]

The destination of the letter put every advantage of time in the hands
of the Franks. But the queen's service of information had been alert. It was
not long before Eleanor and the magnates in England received a precise
copy of the emperor's ingratiating letter to the King of the Franks, neatly
furled in a message from the Archbishop of Rouen, who broke the tidings
with as many steadying precepts from Scripture as he could bring to bear
upon a situation so anomalous.

Instantly, as though animated by a single nerve, the subjects of the king
converged from far and near upon the crisis. The first matters were to find
out where Richard was held captive and to reach the ear and conscience

of Henry Hohenstaufen. Savary, Bishop of Bath, a kinsman of the emperor, went straight from England to the imperial high place;[4] William of Ely, the exiled chancellor, made his way from the court of France, where he had taken refuge; Hubert, Bishop of Salisbury, who met the news in Italy on his way home from crusade, changed his course: all these pressed into Germany by various routes, following rumor from town to town.[5] The queen's emissaries, the Abbots of Boxley and Pontrobert, explored Swabia and Bavaria.[6] It was perhaps at this time that the tale of Blondel, imperishably a part of the saga of Coeur-de-Lion, first took shape upon some German highway: the story that the trouvère Blondel, himself in quest of his lord, lodged below the craggy tower of Durrenstein, there heard Richard singing from his prison one of the poet's two-part songs, capped the couplet, and so, engaging the king in bandying stave for stave, made certain of his whereabouts and established communication between him and his rescuers.[7]

As for Queen Eleanor, whose responsibilites held her to her post, she set herself to correspondence in her son's behalf with the Pope and with prelates everywhere, reminding them with abundant scriptural citation of the pious mission of Coeur-de-Lion, and admonishing them in the most vigorous language to employ all the resources of Rome against the impious captors of the king.[8] But her principal travail in the first weeks of her calamity was the circumvention of Philip Augustus and that incorrigible renegade, her youngest son.[9]

These two colleagues, with their heads together, acted on the cold presumption that, so far as their plans were concerned, Richard was as good as dead. No sooner had the news of the king's capture spread than John, as if playing a role he had rehearsed, fled to Normandy, declared himself the king's heir, and boldly demanded the adherence of the Norman barons. Knowing how well guarded was the fortress of Rouen where Alais was still the queen's prisoner, he convened as many barons as he could in Alençon.[10] But gaining nothing substantial from these hardheaded feudal lords, he proceeded to Paris. Warmed by the counsels of Philip Augustus, the youngest Plantagenet assumed his brother's role in the French court, proffered his homage as Duke of Normandy to Philip,[11] engaged to set aside the Countess Isabelle of Gloucester, whom he had married three years before, and take to wife the Princess Alais. He further agreed to confirm to Philip the Norman Vexin and all the other fruits of the French king's aggressions, since his return from crusade, upon the lands of Richard.[12]

Having justified himself by these negotiations with the Plantagenet "king," Philip seized time by the forelock, threw papal menace to the winds, and fell upon the Vexin, that gateway to Rouen and the sea. Gisors, the chief castle of the Capetian princesses' dower land, for whose possession Henry Fitz-Empress had fought and plotted through all his reign, yielded, through the treachery of its keeper, to the King of the Franks. From Gisors Philip moved without hindrance upon the capital of Normandy. He addressed himself to the seneschal of that fortress as lord of the province by virtue of the homage of John, demanded the instant delivery of his sister Alais and immediate possession of the city.[13] The Earl of Leicester, who commanded the garrison, was however less impressed by the tales that were afloat than the custodian of Gisors had been. He declared that he had received no official notification of a change in the succession, nor any order from King Richard to deliver up the prisoner; and he stood stoutly upon his words. Nevertheless, he offered Philip the hospitality of the castle, to which his claims as overlord entitled him, if he cared to cross the drawbridge. A sharp suspicion crossed the king's mind that he might find himself a counter valent for the precious prisoner in Austria. Having been overconfident, Philip had not come with force enough to take the fortress. In a rage he withdrew his troops, smashing his own siege engines and voiding his wine casks in the Seine. He would, he swore, revisit the city with a rod of iron.[14]

While these matters were proceeding in Normandy, John returned to England in a mood of elation. With the aid of Philip he had recruited a troop of mercenaries with which, as soon as Lent should be over, to man his castles and put down resistance. He swaggered in his role as king-elect. He went to London and filled the ears of the queen with all the rumors current in Paris concerning the dire fate of Coeur-de-Lion, laboring to persuade her that Richard would be seen no more. He made ready to receive the allegiance of the magnates and to take over the royal castles.

Eleanor, in painful quandary over the destinies of her two sons, acted with the strictest caution and moderation. She did not drive the scapegrace into open defiance of her authority. She forbore to provoke open strife by arresting him as a traitor or dispossessing him of all resource. Her measures were defensive, but so punctual that they anticipated John's treasonous plots. Through the vigilance of the magnates, the precursors of the prince's Flemish mercenaries were arrested in England during Lent, and the queen had time, between Good Friday and Easter, to close the Channel ports and man the coasts toward Flanders with a hastily mustered home guard armed with anything they could find to fend off invasion, even the tools of their yeomans' labor on the land. The coast so bristled with burghers and plowmen that the seafaring *routiers*, when they had surveyed the situation, gave up the expedition.[15] All the while Eleanor maintained a sharp oversight of the royal castles and their keepers, and from time to time she exacted new oaths of allegiance from the bishops and barons of the realm. Through Lent, in an anguish of uncertainty, she played for time.

❧

About the middle of March the Abbots of Boxley and Pontrobert made contact with the captive king near Ochsenfurt in Bavaria,[16] as he was en route with an imperial escort from Würzburg to strongholds on the Rhine. With him, and high in his graces, rode Ely, the exiled chancellor, who had been the first to reach him, and by whose agency, it was said, Coeur-de-Lion was being transferred from remote to more accessible fortresses.

After his capture near Vienna, Richard had been imprisoned incommunicado under the closest guard by day and night in the castle of Durrenstein on its lofty crag above the Danube.[17] Early in January, at the emperor's behest, he had been brought up the river to Ratisbon and then moved again to Würzburg. In these places, in a series of debates, Henry of Hohenstaufen and Leopold of Austria had concluded agreements upon the conditions of his custody. As suzerain, the emperor laid claim to the royal captive; but Leopold, who had taken him, and who had scores of his own to settle, held him for a price; and it required some fierce haggling to adjudicate these claims.

For Henry Hohenstaufen, Richard was a prize without peer in all the world. He was not merely the author of all the "accumulated mischiefs" alluded to in the Christmas letter to the King of the Franks, but he was the very hostage of hostages to secure the emperor against a flood of present troubles in which he was involved with Rome and his own feudatories. For Henry was engaged, somewhat as Henry Fitz-Empress had been in the case of Becket, in a complicated struggle over that question, irresolvable by dialectic, of the limits of ghostly and temporal authority. He was also, like Philip Augustus, consumed by a Carolingian dream of expanding empire. Richard, the figurehead of Christian warfare in Palestine, the protégé of Rome, was an inestimable pawn in these circumstances. Furthermore, the Hohenstaufen's inconclusive struggles with Rome had brought him into dangerous collision with many of his own bishops, whose enormous land tenures and strong armies in Germany made their opposition formidable And his most powerful secular vassal, Henry the Lion of Saxony, who was Richard's brother-in-law, out of ancient rancor toward the imperial house, had failed to support his campaigns in Italy and taken every opportunity to foment revolt among the magnates of the Empire. Now "by divine grace" — as the Christmas letter explained — Henry had in hand the most useful instrument in the world to wrest justice from his enemies.

In Würzburg in the middle of February, Henry of Hohenstaufen and Count Leopold concluded their previous debates over the disposition of their prize and imposed their terms upon their captive. Richard was to be the emperor's prisoner, as was meet.[18] To put the champion of the warfare in Palestine to death would have been to unite the enemies of the emperor all over Christendom, and to waste the real worth of the hostage. The King of

England, they concluded, should be redeemable, but at a price that would bring Plantagenet arrogance to the dust: 100,000 marks of silver with two hundred hostages as surety for the payment, these to be chosen from among the first magnates of England and Normandy or their heirs; [19] the Emperor of Cyprus to be released from the silver chains in which Richard had left him languishing, and the handmaid of Berengaria restored to the emperor her father; Eleanor, "the pearl of Brittany" (child sister of Arthur of Brittany), who had recently been offered to Saphadin as a substitute for Joanna, to be affianced to the son of Leopold. The redemption would be heavy, but let it not be thought the price was mere "ransom"; it was, in the case of the emperor, indemnification for injuries suffered; in Leopold's case, dower for the marriage of his son. [20]

When the Abbots of Boxley and Pontrobert met the king, his chancellor, and his escort at Ochsenfurt, Richard was in fine fettle and by no means cast down by his hapless state. "It was," says Hoveden, "the admiration of all how boldly, how courteously, how becomingly he behaved." He had lost no inch of his regal stature, nor any grain of his aplomb. He was in excellent spirits, sanguine about his fate at the hands of the emperor, who, he believed, in spite of his imperial crown, would prove but a gosling in diplomacy. The Hohenstaufen had shown himself very angry at Ratisbon, at first refusing to look upon his victim, but Plantagenet *courtoisie* and dialectic had presently availed to temper his emotions. [21] The matter of the ransom weighed not too heavily upon the king's mind. According to his observation, sterling always renewed itself; and *preux chevaliers* expected ransoms in the give-and-take of combat and must meet fortune as they found it, gallantly. From Ely he heard the lurid chronicle of John's inconstancy with vexation, but not alarm. "My brother John," said he, "is not the man to subjugate a country, if there is one person able to make the slightest resistance to his attempts." But his wrath flared hotly against his archenemy, the King of the Franks. When encountered at Ochsenfurt, the king was on his way to the emperor's Easter court in Speyer, and heartily glad to have left behind the barbaric crudity, the squalor and monotony of the Danubian fortresses for the amenities of more civilized surroundings near the Rhine. [22]

The Easter court in Speyer, to which the whole company repaired, was an august affair, and it brought forth prodigies of diplomacy. In presence of the Holy Roman Emperor was convened an imposing array of vassals, lay and clerical. Before this tribunal Richard was brought to defend himself against the charges preferred and to receive the semblance of a judicial sentence for his accumulated mischiefs: the recognition of Tancred of Sicily to the prejudice of the rights of the Empress Constance, an act that had involved the Hohenstaufen in extensive wars to recover her inheritance; the "treason and treachery" of his conduct in the Land of Promise; his insults to

Leopold of Austria; his outrages against the house of Montferrat; his violence to the Emperor of Cyprus; the jeopardies to which he had exposed the King of the Franks. Coeur-de-Lion was to be made to feel in the marrow of his bones the might and dignity of the Holy Roman Empire, which he had presumed to flout, and to learn the deference that Christian kings owed to its potentate.

A little company of Richard's vassals and familiars had been able to reach Speyer from various directions to stand with the king: Savary of Bath and Hubert of Salisbury; Ely the Chancellor; the Abbots of Boxley and Pontrobert; the Norman chaplain, William of Saint Mary l'Église. For the trial the emperor was armed with righteous indignation and a bill of particulars; Richard only with suavity.[23] The king relied upon no spokesman in his little entourage, but stood forth valiantly in his own behalf before the charges of the emperor and met them all with such reason and restraint, such grace and candor, and gave such a simple and guileless account of himself in Sicily and Palestine that the emperor's vassals were visibly moved and the imperial tremendousness seemed somehow ill judged and out of place.[24] The crusading king appeared as shining as his legend, the very exemplar of all *preux chevaliers*. He, the injurious one, contrived to make himself the injured, persecuted for righteousness' sake. Henry Hohenstaufen, becoming aware of the sentiment of admiration for the captive among his hostile feudatories, tempered his invective. When the eloquence subsided and Coeur-de-Lion knelt courteously before the emperor, a concordant murmur of applause went the rounds and many of the assistants, especially the bishops, wept with joy. The emperor passed by degrees from awfulness to moderation and then to leniency. At last, according to Newburgh, he seemed moved not only by pity but reverence. He burst into tears, of which he too had the gift, came down from his high seat, lifted the captive from his posture of humility, and handed him to the dais. Richard's success was, in a sense, a triumph for the school of manners in Poitiers. On Maundy Thursday, William of Saint Mary l'Église left for England with the terms of the ransom in his wallet.

Throughout the week Richard was the guest of the emperor and enjoyed, with a certain relaxation of custody, the amenities of the palace city on the Rhine. But suddenly he was transferred to the strong and isolated mountain castle of Trifels on the borders of Swabia.[25] This was an imperial dungeon from which political prisoners rarely returned to the light of day. Here he was again guarded day and night and sequestered from intercourse with his cautioners.

It appears to have been at about this time that Henry Hohenstaufen was thrown into misgivings about his agreements with his prisoner in Speyer by an embassy from Philip Augustus,[26] whose grievances had been more or less lumped with all the others in the imperial indictment. The details of the intercourse between the emperor and the King of the Franks was of that confidential kind not usually preserved for history by the chroniclers. But it seems probable from subsequent events that Philip, whose campaigns in Normandy, after his first rebuff in Rouen, seemed more hopeful, was both alarmed and taken aback when the compact of Speyer for the release of the prisoner became known. He evidently had not dreamed that the emperor would think of arranging for the disposal of the captive without his own knowledge and consent. How otherwise could he construe the warmth of Henry's Christmas letter and his protestations more than a year before in Italy? In all the premises, Philip too had a stake in the prize. The long and short of it was that the King of the Franks bespoke a partner's consideration in the lucky fortunes of war and would go as far as he could to make justice profitable for the emperor.[27]

The most important concern of Henry Hohenstaufen at the moment was not the affair of Coeur-de-Lion: it was to resolve his formidable conflict with his own disaffected feudatories, among them the Bishops of Mainz and Cologne and the powerful Dukes of Louvain, Lemberg, and Saxony. This group charged him with having exiled the Bishop of Liége, who was the brother of the Duke of Louvain, and having then procured his murder in France. It is probable that Philip Augustus, who was seeking a means of gratifying the emperor, offered to support him against this coalition — at a price — and to procure for him the mediation of the Archbishop of Reims. A meeting was proposed for the King of the Franks and the emperor for Saint John's day, June 24, at Vaucouleurs.

The possibility of collusion with Philip, when viewed in all its aspects, was fraught with risks for Henry Hohenstaufen, but it also offered more benefits than the latter had counted on. The contract with the English magnates for the king's release had, to be sure, been signed, sealed, and dispatched; but Henry, whose pursuit of empire had dried up his revenues, cast about for some way of taking advantage, even if somewhat tardily, of the French king's helpfulness. It occurred to him that a competition between the magnates of the Plantagenet empire on the one hand, and the King of the Franks and the heir of England on the other, might pour a refreshing flood into his treasury. Furthermore, he saw himself confirmed, by this turn in the wheel of fortune, in that imperial role he coveted as supreme arbiter and judge between Christian potentates. And thereupon he fell into a quandary about which suppliant would in the long run prove the more valuable ally.

✤

No prisoner can tell his honest thought
Unless he speaks as one who suffers wrong;
But for his comfort he may make a song.
My friends are many, but their gifts are naught.

Shame will be theirs, if, for my ransom, here
   I lie another year.

    .   .   .   .   .

They know this well who now are rich and strong
  Young gentlemen of Anjou and Touraine,
  That far from them, on hostile bonds I strain.
They loved me much, but have not loved me long.
Their plains will see no more fair lists arrayed,
  While I lie here betrayed.

Richard Coeur-de-Lion, *Sirventés* [28]

Before setting out for England with commission to collect the hostages, the indefatigable William of Ely induced the emperor to move his captive from Trifels to Hagenau, where the imperial court passed the lovely weeks of Pentecost. Here, for greater accessibility, as it was said, Richard seems to have spent the months of April and May without suspecting the new value set upon his head by the offers of Philip Augustus. Within the limits of a strict surveillance, he appears to have enjoyed many of the privileges of a royal guest. It was doubtless in this interval that the emperor and the king, poets both, discovered each other's talents for balladry and matched troubadours' rondels with minnesingers' songs. In his unwonted leisure, Coeur-de-Lion burnished the poetic gifts that were his Poitevin heritage.

He employed his favorite lyric form, the *sirventés*, that vehicle of irony which he had learned from no less a master than Bertran de Born. With it, lately in Palestine, he had exchanged taunts with that fire-eating Capetian versifier, the Bishop of Beauvais.[29] He used it now in the interests of speeding up the ransom, and he addressed himself, among others, to his dear sister, the Countess of Champagne, in whose school he had been taught. It is difficult in English, with its relatively meager stock of rhymes and its weight of consonants, to render completely the disarming grace of this reproach to fair-weather friends, the suave cadence, the delicate strophic scheme that embodies his appeal to the countess and, through her, to his familiars in hall, in tournament and war. In this sally the king shows himself no paltry descendant of Guillaume, the troubadour Count of Poitou.[30]

From Hagenau, Coeur-de-Lion dispatched a flood of letters in his own behalf to abbots, earls, barons, clerks, and freeholders, bespeaking their efforts for his release and promising them his "grateful thanks." Of course he wrote to the queen.[31] Without so much as mentioning Berengaria, he addresses her as "Eleanor, by the grace of God, Queen of England," his "much-beloved mother." He writes cheerfully of the consideration he meets in the court of Hagenau and of the delightful amenities of the company and the entertainment. He expects soon to be home. The ransom is of course a difficulty, but one he seems to feel sure his loyal subjects will be prepared to meet, as one of those occasional setbacks inevitably encountered in the operations of the brave. He mentions the sum required, and admonishes the queen and the justiciars themselves to set a high example of liberality and to see to it that the clergy bear their share in rounding out the sum, even to the weighing of their altar vessels if necessary. He lays upon the queen the special care of keeping the whole collection under her own seal against the day of reckoning. He then hints obscurely at some advantages likely to arise from his present predicament and declares that he would not, for any consideration, have missed the ultimate benefits to accrue from his intercourse with the emperor. He explains about the hostages and advises the regency that William of Ely, his chancellor, will presently arrive in Britain to assemble them for transportation to the Empire. As a precaution against a possible day of reckoning in the tribunals of France, he addressed the chief of the Assassins in the fastnesses of Syria, bespeaking a deposition from the Old Man of the Mountain that should clear him of the charges of having procured the murder of Conrad of Montferrat.[32] By his admiral, Stephen of Turnham, the king sent to England the armor he had worn upon crusade, that the exhibition of this poor empty scaffolding in which he had defied the enemies of Christ might stir the liberality of his faithful subjects.[33]

It is said that in all these weeks not a shadow sullied the brow of Coeur-de-Lion, even when he looked out from the narrow slits of his fortress chamber in Trifels. He amused himself by wrestling with the stalwarts set to guard him and made them comically tipsy with the Rhenish vintages supplied for his own table. The heavy role of count, crusader, king, rolled off in these secret hours and left him to the spontaneous delights provided for the baser portion of mankind.[34]

⚜

That which the palmerworm hath left hath the locust eaten; and that which the locust hath left hath the cankerworm eaten; and that which the cankerworm hath left hath the caterpillar eaten.

Joel 1:4

Richard's messages from Hagenau, though they assuaged the queen's long anguish of dread, could not wholly restore her peace of mind. The weight of the ransom must appall the subjects of the king, following as it did the requisitions of Henry Fitz-Empress and Coeur-de-Lion for the grand crusade. And where, after the exodus of *preux chevaliers* to Palestine, were the hostages to be found? However, the queen put her shoulder to the wheel of her ungrateful task without delay.[35] With her, for the collection of the ransom, she associated the Archbishop of Rouen and the Bishop of Salisbury, the latter recently nominated by the king for the vacant See of Canterbury, the Earls of Arundel and Warenne, and, as a nerve to reach all the substantial burghers of London, the mayor of that newly ratified commune.[36]

The levy was pressed in every quarter with no distinction between layman and clerk, burgher and rustic. Every privileged subject held his peace in the hope of being passed by. No one could say, declares Newburgh, "Behold I am only So-and-So or Such-and-Such. Pray let me be excused." [37] The barons were taxed a fourth of a year's income, and lesser persons by a descending scale. The churches and abbeys measured up by weight their treasure "accumulated since olden time," gold and silver vessels, candelabra, the very crosses on their altars. Reliquaries were shorn of their cabochons, basins scraped of their jewels. The Cistercians, those humble brethren of Saint Bernard, possessing no corruptible treasure of this world, sheared their flocks and gave a year's crop of wool. [38]

Peter of Blois wrote to his old school friend, the Bishop of Mainz (who was no friend of the emperor), that the Germans, "those children of perdition, were levying a treasure that would not be drawn from the royal exchequer, but from the patrimony of Christ, the pitiful substance of the poor, the tears of widows, the pittance of monks and nuns, the dowries of maidens, the substance of scholars, the spoils of the church." [39] It is the chronicler Newburgh who, in describing the conscription of property, cites the prophet Joel. [40] The ravages of the caterpillar left no live shoot upon the vine. As the sluggish tithes flowed in, they were sealed with the queen's own seal and kept for safety in the cathedral of Saint Paul.

It was certainly no mitigation of the difficulty of gathering the hostages that the exiled and sometime excommunicated Bishop of Ely was sent with royal mandate to read off their roster and herd them for transportation to the Rhine. [41] With many valuable bishops and barons still abroad, the roll had to be made up partly of prospective heirs to great estates, some of them mere children. Not since Henry Fitz-Empress had banished the kin of Becket from the shores of England had such groanings gone up from sundered families. This draft was as grievous as that conscription of Eleanor's vassals which Louis Capet long before, in the green days of his statecraft, had mustered for banishment in the public square of Poitiers.

Even Ely, whose tact was never sufficient, realized that his sweet triumph over the regency's sentence of exile might render his mission difficult. He did not approach the shore of Britain as a reinstated chancellor with an army and banners, but came unostentatiously as a simple bishop, a humble instrument of grace, rendering his due service to his captive king. The citizens of London, however, refused to deal with him in any guise, and he dared not show himself in that newly constituted commune. In these spring days Philip Augustus was making his incursions in Normandy. The queen, desperate over the course of events and the dangers of delay, met Ely with some of the magnates at Saint Albans and with him threshed out the horrible business of the roster. In the course of the arrangements, she held out stoutly against including any of the children of Henry of Saxony, who since their mother's death (with the exception of the two elder sons) had grown up in the courts of the Plantagenets. History bears no detailed records of these interviews, nor of the even more lamentable appeals that must have followed; but there can be no doubt that they were a heavy strain upon the tact and fortitude of the queen, who bore the brunt.[42]

The recruiting of the hostages naturally gave a certain impetus to the raising of the ransom, since the more sterling in the coffers in Saint Paul's, the fewer the number of the hostages required. But even so the collection dragged. The first campaign having yielded far less than the sum required, the queen sent gleaners into the field. A second levy was made, and then a third. In this most difficult of all enterprises, Eleanor did not spare herself. She sent agents abroad to stimulate the sluggish flow of treasure from the lukewarm barons of Anjou and Aquitaine, and from the rich abbeys along the pilgrim route from Saint Martin's of Tours to the shrines of the paladins near Bordeaux. From the abbey of Saint Martial in Limoges, which had had the honor of investing the reigning duke now captive, she extracted the sum of one hundred marks of silver.[43] But the labor as a whole progressed at a snail's pace, and every delay was a succor to the king's enemies.

In the intervals of her sudden journeyings, her multifarious interviews, and her eagle-eyed oversight of Philip Augustus and John, she found time to address the Pope with urgent correspondence. In her salutation she styles herself "Eleanor, by the wrath of God, Queen of England." She may have employed clerks to put her ideas into impeccable Latin, but the sentiments bear the marks of authenticity.

> What afflicts the church and excites the murmur of the people and diminishes their esteem for you, is that, in spite of the tears and lamentations of whole provinces, you have not sent a single nuncio. Often for matters of little importance your cardinals have been sent to remote parts with sovereign powers, but in this desperate and deplorable affair, you have not sent so much as a single subdeacon or even an acolyte.
>
> The kings and princes of the earth have conspired against my son, the anointed of the Lord. One keeps him in chains while another ravages his lands; one holds him by the heels while the other flays him. And while this goes on, the sword of Saint Peter reposes in its scabbard. Three times you have promised to send legates and they have not been sent. In fact, they have rather been leashed than sent [*potius ligati quam legati*]. If my son were in prosperity, we should have seen them running at his call, for they well know the munificence of his recompense. Is this the meaning of your promises to me at Châteauroux,[44] made with so many protestations of friendship and good faith? Alas! I know today that the promises of your cardinals are nothing but vain words. Trees are not known by their leaves, nor even by their blossoms, but by their fruits. In this wise we have known your cardinals.

The queen then lifts before the eyes of Celestine the specter that was forever haunting Aquitaine and that had tempted Henry in the days of his trials with Becket: the threat of schism.

Recall when Frederick of Germany, the author and promoter of the great schism, gave his allegiance to that apostate Octavian against the rightful Pope, Alexander, and the Kings of France and England were beset by legates now for one, now for the other, how King Henry, my husband and the father of this king, grieving to see the tunic of Christ longer divided, was first to give allegiance to Alexander, and how he with prudent counsels brought the King of the Franks to a similar allegiance, and thus the ship of Saint Peter, threatened with certain shipwreck, was brought to a safe harbor . . . But I declare to you that the day foretold by the Apostle is not far distant. The fateful moment is at hand when the tunic of Christ shall be rent again, when the bonds of Saint Peter shall be broken, the catholic unity dissolved.

The letters are long; there is much more to the same general effect, delivered in language searing and forthright.[45]

It is only fair to pause for a reasonable sympathy for the Pope in the situation in which he found himself. He had instantly, upon receiving news of the capture, excommunicated the Duke of Austria for the violation of Richard's immunity as a pilgrim from the Holy Land;[46] he had threatened the King of the Franks with an interdict if he should trespass upon the territories of the captive king; and he had menaced the English with interdict if they should fail to raise the ransom.[47] But the church was in difficulty with Henry of Hohenstaufen in Italy, and Celestine doubted how far he might proceed against a Holy Roman Emperor who, besides trespassing on papal territories, unleashed agents who displayed a terrible ferocity toward papal emissaries, plucking their beards and cutting their throats with unexampled *Schrecklichkeit*.[48] Perhaps half the lands in Germany were ecclesiastica. property, and the Pope did not feel sure of the outcome of the issues between the emperor and some of the latter's ecclesiastical feudatories. Perhaps also he did not forget with how firm a besom the queen had recently swept from her frontiers his nuncios when she had not wished to deal with them. With all the concern in the world for "the Lord's anointed," Celestine was obliged to act in the framework of the total situation.

Sometime in June Coeur-de-Lion's employment with the arts of poesy and letter writing and his harmless bouts with his jailers were interrupted by an invitation to make a journey down the Rhine to Worms,[49] whither, with the advancing season, Henry of Hohenstaufen presently arrived with his *mesnie*. In the weeks of Pentecost the emperor had had time to revolve in his mind the fearful but tempting prospects unfolded by Philip Augustus; and he had concluded, before meeting Philip in Vaucouleurs,[50] to review in Worms the findings of the imperial court four months before in Speyer with respect to the prisoner.

In Worms on the Rhine the imperial court sat impressively in plenary session for five days. With Richard were the Bishops of Ely and Salisbury, one of his justiciars lately arrived, and Baldwin of Béthune, that noble comrade of crusade whose impersonation of the king had saved him from capture

on the seacoast of Istria. How much of the detail of the interchange between
Philip Augustus and the emperor transpired to Richard and his company is
not clear, for its purport became manifest to Richard, as Hoveden explains,
"indirectly"; but it was enough to fill them with consternation. The force of
the bribe from France was now felt in the emperor's demand for an increase
in the ransom, which was then and there raised by one half, and the roster
of the hostages adjusted upward accordingly. The biographer of Guillaume
le Maréchal cites Baldwin of Béthune as the most liberal of all the contribu-
tors to the sum for the king's release.[51] This occasion may have stimulated
his generosity. The new compact was sworn to "on the soul of the emperor"
and witnessed by the attendant magnates.

To fix the limits of the ransom unequivocally was of critical importance
certainly; but more important still it appeared to Coeur-de-Lion to prevent
the meeting of Philip and the emperor, as a result of which he seemed very
likely to be sold into a Capetian dungeon with small hope of looking out
again upon the jocund river valleys of Poitou and Aquitaine. To settle ancient
scores with Philip Augustus would require something more than ransom.

In this crisis Coeur-de-Lion had recourse to his brother-in-law, Henry the
Lion of Saxony, whose role in securing the king's release is somewhat
shadowy in the chronicles.[52] Richard had already enlisted the sympathy of
the disaffected vassals of the emperor by his candid defense of himself in
Speyer. But nowhere had the skill and celerity of Plantagenet diplomacy
shown more brilliantly than it now appeared in Worms. For the king succeeded not only in bringing about the concord between Henry of Hohenstaufen and his hostile feudatories, which Philip had only promised to essay
in Vaucouleurs, but also in laying the grounds for a peace between the emperor and Henry the Lion, which was a little later confirmed by the marriage
of Henry's son and heir to Constance of Hohenstaufen, the cousin of the
emperor and the most valuable marriage prize in his bestowal.

The double accord, brought to pass by Coeur-de-Lion, proved a major
setback for Philip Augustus: the reconciliation of the emperor and his feudatories brought down the Frankish bargaining power; and the settlement with
Henry of Saxony offered the King of the Franks a new and smarting injury.
In the course of the spring, fired by a considerable success in Normandy,
Philip had cast about for allies with whom to build up a coalition against
the Plantagenets. John, as an ally, had proved not much better than a reed,
because, since the dispersal of his Flemish mercenaries from the shores of
England by the queen's home guard, the regency had prevented his leaving
the island and intercepted all communications with him. In looking about
for new allies, Philip chose Canute, the King of Denmark, whose sea dogs
might be induced, like the Danes of old, to harry the coasts of Britain. To
cement the bond, Philip proposed to end his widowhood by marrying the

king's sister, Ingeborg. Although King Canute did not commit himself on the matter of attacking England, he dispatched to France the Princess Ingeborg, described by the Frankish chronicler Rigord as a maiden "of great beauty and innocence," [53] with a noble suite and a boatload of presents and equipment. Philip met her processionally in Arras and conveyed her in state to Amiens, where she was duly married [54] and crowned Queen of France by Philip's uncle, the Archbishop of Reims.

But even in the midst of the marriage and crowning of Ingeborg, Philip found himself confused by a disturbing afterthought. Awkwardly late he saw how much better it would have been in the circumstances to ingratiate the Holy Roman Emperor by offering a queen's crown to the latter's cousin Constance.[55] Upon inquiry he found that the emperor would favor the alliance and arrangements were made accordingly. So, on the day after his marriage to Ingeborg, Philip dismissed that lady on grounds of consanguinity, gave her leave to return to her brother's court, and sent her household home to Denmark. Preparations were on foot for the more auspicious marriage, when it was suddenly discovered that Constance, thoroughly alarmed at the course events were taking, and not wishing to risk the fate of Ingeborg even for the crown of France, had secretly, with her mother's connivance, married the son of Henry the Lion of Saxony.

The emperor, though he expressed chagrin at the miscarriage of plans to which he had agreed, declared himself unable to undo a marriage in all respects canonical. Ingeborg, instead of going home, took refuge in a convent of nuns at Soissons to weather the tragedy and await an appeal to Rome; [56] and Philip Augustus, to fill the measure of his injuries, presently found himself excommunicated for the repudiation of the Danish princess, and the Danes, if there should be any virtue in them, thrown into the camp of the English. The circumstances were so singular that some chroniclers attributed the whole affair to sorcery. If so, it was certainly an operation of the demon of Anjou. When the outcome of the deliberations in Worms became known, Philip found a way to warn John to beware, "for the devil was unloosed." [57]

During the summer the emperor sent his emissaries to Britain to supervise the collection of the ransom and the assembly of the hostages, which, with the dismaying additions agreed to in Worms, dragged through harvest to the end of autumn. The round figure was not completed by the last month of the year, but such a weight of silver had been amassed in London that the emperor decided to wait no longer to possess it. On the 20th of December he wrote to the queen and the magnates as follows:

> Henry, by the grace of God, emperor of the Romans, and ever august, to his dearly beloved friends, the archbishops, earls, barons, knights, and all the faithful subjects of Richard, illustrious King of England, his favor and every blessing. We have thought proper to intimate to all and every of you that we have appointed a certain day for the liberation of our dearly beloved friend, your lord Richard, the

illustrious King of the English, being the second day of the week next ensuing after the expiration of three weeks from the day of the nativity of our Lord, at Speyer, or else at Worms; and we have appointed seven days after that as the day of his coronation as King of Provence, which we have promised to him; and this you are to consider certain and undoubted. For it is our purpose and our will to exalt and most highly honor your aforesaid lord, as being our special friend. Given at Thealluse, on the vigil of Saint Thomas the Apostle.[58]

At the same time Coeur-de-Lion expressly summoned Queen Eleanor and the Archbishop of Rouen to attend him in Speyer and to bring the ransom under their own personal escort and supervision, since the English were responsible for the whole sum of it until it reached the frontiers of Germany. For the festive occasion indicated at the end of the emperor's letter, Richard bespoke his royal regalia and a fitting retinue.

✤

Lord, now lettest thou thy servant depart in peace,
According to thy word.
Luke 2:29, prescribed for reading at Complin on Candlemas day

In the dead of winter the queen, accompanied by earls and bishops, many of them destined as hostages, and the youthful heirs of great estates, together with the retinue for Richard's crowning as King of Provence, the armed guard for the coffered ransom, and the royal household of chaplains, clerks, stewards, and serving folk, took ship upon the Channel and, journeying thence by river and by road, arrived in the valley of the Rhine for the appointed day in January.[59] The queen's *mesnie* from Britain must have been impressive in any case, but especially so in view of the program of ceremonies indicated in the emperor's letter; and it must have been animated by a wide range of emotions. Eleanor and the magnates who were not upon the roster of the hostages were certainly in joyful expectation of a triumph at last over their long afflictions. But they had no sooner arrived in Germany than they became sensible of a chill more than that which blows off the Rhine in January. In the brief interval since the emperor had invited them to the festivities with which he had determined to celebrate the release of his prisoner, something had upset his resolution to go through with the affair.[60] He had in the meantime discovered circumstances that altered the case, and he could not, without further deliberations, keep to the precise day he had proposed for the delivery of his captive.

What Henry of Hohenstaufen alleged in Speyer as reasons for his procrastinations is not told in the chronicles. Nor can it be known certainly that Eleanor and Coeur-de-Lion were admitted at all to the first conference. But the emperor's demur was enough to throw the friends of the captive into panic and awaken very accurate suspicions of what was afoot. The queen, after all she had endured, was for a fortnight tossed in a new abyss of dread and despair. After two fruitless days in which the bishops and barons of the German court labored with the emperor in behalf of the prisoner, the court was adjourned for more than two weeks to convene again at Mainz on Candlemas. It may be presumed that the atmosphere of Speyer had been vitiated by the developments and that the English claimed a change of venue and the privilege of being heard under ecclesiastical auspices in the friendly episcopal city with its gates open to the Rhine and somewhat nearer to the sea.

In Mainz for two days more, beginning on Candlemas (February 2), the emperor labored with his feudatories. Various issues, it seemed, were involved, and when these had been reviewed, Henry behaved toward the English with amazing candor and simplicity. The crucial fact emerged that Philip Augustus and John had recently made a new proposal with respect to the prisoner, which, as emperor and divinely ordained arbiter among Christian princes, he felt he could not ignore. In short, the King of the Franks and the heir of England offered to reward the emperor with 100,000 marks of silver if the latter would hold the captive in custody until Michaelmas next ensuing, by which season they hoped they would have secured their own justice for the accumulated mischiefs they had suffered.[61] This was, of course, but a promise as contrasted with the solid English sterling already sewed up in the English sacks and deposited in Germany, but it was an arresting offer from which the emperor was apparently not bound to deduct a liberal percentage for the compensation of the Duke of Austria. It might be expected to yield more in the end than the contract with Richard in Worms, although this had been sworn to "on the soul of the emperor" and sealed in the name of the Holy Trinity. Of the sum now proposed, Philip engaged to furnish 50,000 marks and John an equal sum. There was no doubt about the bona fide character of the offer, for the emperor with disarming objectiveness displayed the documents in court with Philip Augustus' familiar biscuit seal dangling from the parchment.[62]

The new offer was not in actual amount in excess of the ransom gathered by the English, but the offer itself provided the emperor with an instrument for pressing Coeur-de-Lion to new concessions. Henry Hohenstaufen had no idea of emerging from his lucky situation without having secured either of his suppliants as his ally. If he flouted the French, their alliance was lost in his conflict with his feudatories; and the English would certainly not have been ingratiated by his humiliation of their king and the exaction of the ransom and the hostages. He could therefore not let the English go without some substantial guarantees of future friendship. What he contemplated was that Richard Plantagenet should acknowledge his vassalage to the Hohenstaufen, a homage in any case meet from a mere king-duke-count to the Holy Roman Emperor. This proposal left the English aghast. In the face of it, the ransom was a mere item in a perennial tribute.[63]

The disclosures provoked a violent remonstrance among the emperor's feudatories, who threatened to revoke the peace they had agreed to in Worms under the good offices of the captive and to resume their former hostility. No nuncio came from Rome at Eleanor's solicitation, but protests against the king's captivity were produced from the Abbé of Cluny and other prelates of wide authority. Though surrounded by his ablest magnates, Coeur-de-Lion stood forth in the hall of Mainz as his own advocate. The Angevin choler that now and then possessed Henry Fitz-Empress flashed from his countenance. He employed in his own defense the rich and sinewy martial eloquence that was the gift of his house. "He had," says the *Itinerarium*, "the eloquence of Nestor, the prudence of Ulysses." [64] He called upon the ecclesiastical feudatories of the Empire to vindicate the sanctity of oath, to recognize the inviolability of the Christian warrior vowed to crusade. It is related that he brought forth a letter from the Old Man of the Mountain himself vindicating him from all charge of having procured the death of Conrad of Montferrat,[65] and he cleared himself once more from the other indictments brought against him by his adversaries. His words excited universal admiration, and as at Worms, there were exclamations of applause from the assistants.

But in the horrible dilemma that still faced the English it was the queen who resolved the conflict. She had nothing but a choice between evil alternatives. She chose the one that was remediable. On her advice Richard, having brought his oratory to a finish, doffed his royal bonnet and laid it courteously in the hands of the emperor, signifying thereby that he renounced his allegiance to the perfidious Capets and transferred it to the Hohenstaufen.[66] The effect of this gesture on the English is not related. But a warmth of feeling sprang up in the hall of Mainz. The bishop of the city, in whose palace or chapter house the conclave perhaps occurred, gave words to the public sentiment. The Bishop of Cologne supported him. All wept.[67] Henry of Hohenstaufen condescended grandly; the captive's fetters were unloosed; the ransom was conveyed; the hostages were given over, among them the Archbishop of Rouen, who had been the queen's stay in so many crises, her protector on so many journeyings; and the queen herself, worn with labor and anguish, fell weeping into the arms of Coeur-de-Lion. She was, as she had written to Pope Celestine, "worn to a skeleton, a mere thing of skin and bones, the sap consumed in her veins, tears all but dried in the fountains of her eyes." All the bystanders let their tears flow at the spectacle of this aged woman, the most astute and venerable sovereign in Europe, still at seventy-two a figure of significance in the counsels of men, raining her tears on the bosom of her glorious son. There may have been in that concourse some patriarchal bishops who remembered her as the young Queen of France getting herself and her baggage wains over the Rhine in this very city of Mainz a half century before on her way to the Holy Land, for she too had been signed with the cross; and for the younger generation the mere sight of her would evoke the airs of troubadours' and minnesingers' songs that had kept her name alive in all the intervening time with malice or with praise.

Nothing more is heard of the crowning of Richard as King of Provence. Candlemas, the day of the *nunc dimittis*, had been desecrated. The Plantagenets, with the emperor's safe-conduct in their wallets, felt no eagerness to turn back to Speyer for any further ceremonies. The queen and her son accepted the invitation of the Bishop of Cologne to spend the end of the week in the capital of his diocese on their way down the Rhine to the sea. In Cologne the prelate did his best with sumptuous banquets and valley wines and every distraction offered by the splendors of his city to divert the minds of the English from their hardships and misfortunes. When the royal guests visited his cathedral of Saint Peter to hear mass, the bishop himself, entering the choir like a mere precentor, chanted, instead of the introit for the day, the other that begins, "Now I know that the Lord hath sent his angel and snatched me from the hand of Herod." [68]

From Cologne the leisurely progress of Richard and the queen among the emperor's feudatories had almost the nature of a triumph, and the good fruits of Coeur-de-Lion's graciousness among them was later seen. Everywhere with his affability and his impulsive liberality, the king won the friendship of doubtful barons whose fiefs abutted the domains of the Franks, the Flemings, and the emperor. It is related that after Richard had passed out of Swabia, Henry Hohenstaufen, stimulated anew by pressures from Philip Augustus, repented him of having so lightly delivered his captive and sent followers to pursue and overtake him; and that Philip coöperated in this plan by placing ships in the Channel to intercept the royal party. [69]

However this may have been, the king and queen avoided all these traps and came at last to Antwerp to the castle of the Duke of Louvain, where they were honorably entertained. Here Richard's admiral, Stephen of Turnham, received the travelers on the famous ship *Trenchemer*. On March fourth the royal smack, making out from the estuary of the Scheldt, brought them to the port of Sweyne. [70] Hoveden relates that they made their way among the islands by day with the skillful pilot of *Trenchemer*, and by night, for greater comfort and security, they lay upon a great galley that came out from Rye. On March twelfth, [71] at about the ninth hour of the day, [72] the ships bore into the harbor of Sandwich. Richard had been freed in Mainz seven weeks before upon an Egyptian day; [73] but as the vessels rode into Sandwich, the sun stood a man's height above the horizon and shone with such ruddy effulgence that Kentish men driving their oxen in the furrow, and the coast guard looking toward Flanders, and the wherry men on the Thames, and the watch on the city walls, took it for a good omen and, speaking one to another, said that it betokened the coming of the Lion Heart and was a good augury for spring.

29 ✢

Captive and Betrayer

The news of the coming of the king, so long and desperately awaited, flew faster
than the north wind.
          William of Newburgh

IT WAS SIX YEARS SINCE the potentates of Europe had taken the cross for the
rescue of Zion; four years since the tumultuous departure of the armies from
Vézelay. The great emprise for which they had gone forth was nevertheless
far from attainment. Saladin still held Jerusalem; the true cross and the holy
places remained in his custody; and the fabulous treasure of the West had
vanished into the East as if swallowed by the sea. There was a notable contrast between the glorious stir and elation of Richard's departure from Dover
in 1190 and his unceremonious return to Sandwich in 1194. No procession
greeted Coeur-de-Lion and the queen on their landing. No army with music
and banners followed them along the Dover road. The veteran foot soldiers
who had survived the crusade had already returned and scattered to their
homelands. The bishops and barons who should have come to meet the
Plantagenets were also dispersed, some of them as hostages in Germany, some
in the siege of English fortresses. The land was smoldering in various regions
with a sullen civil strife maintained by the partisans of John in the castles he
held by gift of the king. The youngest Plantagenet was not on hand to greet
his brother. Upon the certainty of Richard's release from captivity, he had
betaken himself to the shelter of the French court.[1]

Coeur-de-Lion on crusade had not made himself famous for tact. It was
notorious that his brashness and candor had frequently proved expensive to
Plantagenet interests. Queen Eleanor, though spent with recent anxieties and
feeling the burden of her declining years, remained at his elbow in Britain to
explain, admonish, interpret, to curb that Angevin abruptness and impatience
that, when Richard was left to unguided impulse, raised up fatal enemies in
his wake. More familiar than the king with the tissue of intrigue and contrivance that had made the history of the regency, and also more aware of
the temper of the islanders, she was still at the heart of policy. Hers was the
mission on the one hand of composing the disorders of the public mind, of
regilding the hero of the holy war in the sight of those who had equipped his
luckless armies and paid his ransom; and on the other, of opening the some-

what disregardful eyes of her son to the inestimable worth of Britain as a bulwark of his threatened continental provinces. She led Coeur-de-Lion first to the great shrines.[2]

Together from the landing in Sandwich they went to Canterbury to pay reverence to Saint Thomas and to honor the establishment that had contributed so greatly to the king's deliverance. The news of the arrival flew from that sanctuary like the wind, confuting the dismal rumors lately spread abroad by John. The pause in Canterbury gave London time to deck itself with spring garlands for the advent. In the capital Richard was heralded as the champion of the holy war, "the anointed of the Lord," the hero betrayed by his Christian allies in the midst of his pious enterprise and ransomed by the sacrifice of his people. He was, says Diceto, "hailed with joy upon the Strand." Processions of citizens led him to Saint Paul's, and the bells rang out tumultuously in the valley of the Thames. Certain German magnates in London at the time to overlook details of the balance still due upon the ransom remarked with surprise the popular joy and especially the thronging, prosperous city, which they had been led to believe reduced to misery by the exactions of the emperor;[3] they declared the Hohenstaufen would have held out for a much larger sum if they had not been overborne by the representations of the English.

Before addressing themselves to the reduction of John's castles, Richard and Eleanor took their thank offerings to the shrine of the protomartyr of Britain in Saint Albans. Thence they went straight to the center of sedition in Nottingham.[4] The mere rumor of the king's coming was as potent as Joshua's horn before the walls of Jericho. So thoroughly had John convinced his followers that Richard counted no more among the living, that the first reports of his approach were suspected as a ruse.[5] But when agents came at Richard's invitation to take testimony with their own eyes, they were as amazed as if confronted with a ghost. Panic spread among the garrison and the castle fell with only a gesture of resistance. Tickhill, besieged simultaneously by the Bishop of Durham, followed suit. In Cornwall the keeper of Saint Michael's Mount fell dead of fright when he learned that the king himself was leading his soldiers.[6] The other strongholds surrendered one after another, and the magnates charged with the various besieging operations converged on Nottingham. A fortnight had sufficed to recover the castles in the king's control. The end of Lent was near, and, while waiting for the magnates to assemble from their triumphs for an Easter court, the Plantagenets took advantage of the respite for a spring holiday.

⚜

King Richard hearing of the pranks
Of Robin Hood and his men,
He much admired, and more desired,
To see both him and them.

Ballad of Robin Hood [7]

Richard's itinerary shows that the king's party spent the week end of April second in Clipston Palace on the edge of Sherwood Forest in that region where place names still memorialize the exploits of Robin and his merry men.[8] This fact and Richard's known relish for histrionics and disguise give warrant for surmising that some figment of reality underlies the famous old English ballad that relates the encounter of the stouthearted robber outlaw and the prince of chivalry, who was his overlord. Furthermore, the relaxation of the forest laws and the royal leniency to trespassers with which Eleanor had marked the opening of her son's regime would have given happy auspices for the ballad's episodes.

Coeur-de-Lion, who knew little enough of his native England, had never visited Sherwood Forest, the vast hunting preserve of Henry Beauclerc and Henry Fitz-Empress, with its miles of dark cover, rich with game, its routes marked by lodges and hamlets in tiny clearings, the umbrageous domain as well of Robin and his outlaw band. No hunting forest of Angevin predilection on the Continent, not Chinon nor the Talmont nor the reserves near Rouen, outrivaled this spacious haunt of stag and wild boar.

The ballad relates, as every school child knows, that Richard, eager to form his own ideas of the famous outlaw who pillaged sumptuous prelates to succor the poor, disguised himself as an abbot and rode into Sherwood, with a "clerical" retinue, and was promptly halted by Robin and his men.

He took the king's horse by the head:
"Abbot," says he, "abide;
I am bound to rue such knaves as you,
That live in pomp and pride."

In a dialogue that follows, Richard discovers that Robin, while summary with prelates, is a loyal liege man to his king; and Robin, for his part, agrees to exempt the "abbot," who represents himself as a messenger on royal business.

Then Robin set his horn to his mouth,
And a loud blast he did blow,
Till a hundred and ten of Robin's men
Came marching all of a row. . . .

So then they all to dinner went
Upon a carpet green;
Black, yellow, red, finely mingled,
Most curious to be seen.

Venison and fowls were plenty there,
With fish out of the river;
King Richard swore, on sea or shore,
He neer was feasted better.

In good brown ale the "abbot" toasts the king, and then all ride to hunt in Sherwood. When at length the disguise is thrown off, Richard leads the outlaw to London to be made a peer. The ballad may indeed bring down the wind some echo of a dramatic interlude with which the Plantagenets entertained their household on holiday and celebrated the approach of Easter by acts of royal condescension.

❧

The Easter court, which William of Scotland joined on the confines of the forest, progressed from Nottingham to Northampton.[9] It was a plenary session to consider the state of the world and to take stock of the Plantagenet's mission in it. Papal letters testified to the continued perils in Palestine and admonished all Christians to give heed to first things first. But events in the foreground obscured the distant horizon overseas. Nothing could conceal the fact that the mounting conflict of the Capets and the Plantagenets eclipsed the vision of recapturing Zion. England, which had long resisted the proposal to supply men as well as tithes for continental wars, now faced the certainty of new burdens merely to defend the transmarine provinces of her Angevin king.

Resources were the nub of discourse in Northampton.[10] The levies for the ransom were still incomplete, and Henry's Saladin tithe and Richard's procurements for crusade had preceded the ransom. These vast sums had vanished like dew without bringing the hoped-for consummations to the islanders. Royal and episcopal treasuries had been drained, and the orders had paid their tribute in kind. The prospect of reaping a new harvest seemed grim. But, as if with a divining rod, the Plantagenets discovered new sources of wealth. They came forward with a perfectly simple scheme for refreshing the treasury. Richard retracted the offices he had sold upon his accession and sold them again to the highest bidders. Ely, restored to favor by his exertions for the king's deliverance, bought his chancellorship a second time. Sheriffdoms brought good prices, and other holdings in proportion to their emoluments. The captives taken in John's castles were sorted out according to their worth and yielded a valuable sum in ransoms. Presently, on the grounds of affording martial training to the youth of Britain, Coeur-de-Lion licensed tournaments,[11] which the English had previously denounced as foolish and extravagant, and took a fee from every knight who entered the lists. These income and amusement taxes and indemnities made it possible for the Plantagenets to consider strategy again in a spacious way.

Among the barons and clergy there lingered misgivings about the nature and extent of the concessions the Plantagenets had made to the Holy Roman Emperor, and especially about that desperate measure advanced by the queen at the last moment to secure her son's deliverance — Coeur-de-Lion's proffer of fealty to the Hohenstaufen. To wipe out misunderstandings that might arise anywhere in the feudal world in consequence of that display of submission, the bishops and nobles in Northampton resolved upon a rededication of the king, a reaffirmation of his untrammeled sovereign state, and a new definition of their own vassalage.

The magnates gathered in the old capital of Winchester on the octave of Easter and reënacted features of the original coronation.[12] The king, refreshed with baths and spiritual purgations at Saint Swithin's, the next day issued from his chambers in royal regalia and, covered by a silken canopy and escorted by nobles and clergy bearing the symbols of earthly power and heavenly grace, made his progress to the altar, where his crown was placed on his head by the Archbishop of Canterbury. Again he made his royal offering and sat enthroned during the mass.

Eleanor, "by the grace of God, Queen of England," surveyed the triumphant spectacle from a dais reared for her service in the north transept of the minster. Hoveden relates that she was encompassed, as in the sumptuous days of the courts of love, by a host of noble beauties, the valuable marriage prizes of the Plantagenets.[13] But Alais had been set aside, and Berengaria, crowned and dowered as Queen of England in Limassol, bore no share in that illustrious pageant. Among the royal ladies Eleanor reigned supreme.

Now, as at the time of assuming the crown of Britain, the king was impatient to cross the Channel. From Portsmouth, early in May, Richard set sail [14] in the face of tempests and was driven back; but on the ninth, followed by one hundred ships and accompanied by the queen, he made off for the port of Barfleur.[15] The motley sails of the fleet bent to the wind, their prows breasted the swells, and the coast of England shrank quickly away in a shroud of mist. The eyes of the Plantagenets strained for the shores of Normandy. The queen was going home at last from the kingdom that had been her prison. In the tumult of taking off, the king did not guess that he too weighed anchor for the last time in an English harbor.

⚜

The Plantagenets, revolving elements of strategy betimes, landed in Barfleur in the second week of May. Thence they went to examine the exchequer in Caen and the news in Bayeux.[16] Their progress was everywhere a triumph. Processions of burghers and clerks and country folk and a rabble of suppliants led them from stage to stage with dance and song. The crowds that lined the wayside to hail their duke, who had survived the rumors of his vanquishment and death, were so great, declares the biographer of Guillaume le Maréchal, that no one could have tossed an apple in the air without hitting someone's head. Thus escorted, the king and queen arrived at the house of John of Alençon in Lisieux to pass the night.

Here they received a visit perhaps not very surprising to them and one for which they were prepared.[17] In the merciful half light of evening, Lackland arrived at the archdeacon's gate on foot, in a state, says the chronicler, "of abject penitence." He begged to see the queen his mother that he might beseech her good graces to bring him to a reconciliation with the king.[18] He had been having a tough time as liege man of Philip Augustus. The loss of his castles and his revenues had brought him to utter misery, and for his needs he had found no suitable relief in the courts of Paris. Richard had guessed that the impoverished culprit could not long delay his appearance.

In view of all Lackland's perfidies, the king's greeting of his downcast cadet reads like a role that had been rehearsed. The Plantagenets, it seems, had already resolved, as the first step in their strategy, to retrieve John and thus to seize the dilemma of the succession by the horns. Lackland might have no virtue with which to bless himself, but he, rather than Arthur of Brittany, could at any rate be counted on to fight for his whole Plantagenet patrimony on both sides of the Channel; and of the two he was by far the more dangerous instrument to leave in the hands of the Capets.

"John mistakes me if he is afraid," said Richard. "Bring him in. After all, he is my brother. Of course he has been foolish, but I won't reproach him now. The ones I want to settle with are those who seduced him."

When John fell at his feet in a flood of penitential tears, Richard raised him gently.

"Don't be afraid of me, John. You are young [he was twenty-nine] and you have been the victim of bad advice. Your counselors shall pay for this. Come, get up, and have something to eat."[19]

Richard had become the patriarch of the Angevins. His words echoed great Henry's cockerings of the young king. Although John had abundantly fulfilled the evil augury of the fresco in Winchester, he dandled the crown. A fresh salmon which had just been brought as a gift for the king was cooked instead for Lackland, who dried his penitential tears and ate his supper under the consoling warmth of maternal solicitude and the relief of his brother's absolution. The colloquy over the salmon must have lasted far into the night, and there in all probability the question of the succession was settled among them before they slept in the house of their vassal; for from the time of this reconciliation John's views of his personal interests persuaded him that loyalty to his own house offered him the fairest future prospects, and thenceforth for some time he was proof against the efforts of the Capets to suborn him. Although he did not at once recover his castles, his wallet was replenished and he was given a troop of knights and sent to prove his contrition by relieving Richard's garrison at Evreux, sorely beset by the forces of Philip Augustus, and this he did.

✤

When Richard arrived in Normandy, Philip's campaign for the conquest of Angevin provinces was well advanced. Both pride and interest led the King of the Franks to strike toward Rouen for the delivery of Alais. But in the midst of sharp operations on the Norman frontier, he also made forays at the narrow waist of the Plantagenet domain in Berry to recover the portion of his sister's dowry that was there in dispute; and on the guardian castles of the Loire in an effort to sever the queen's provinces from Anjou and Touraine; and in the south he reawoke the anarchy upon which the Capets had played in Henry's last wars with the young king. The *sirventés* of Bertran de Born revived in Poitou the native rebels' hope of throwing off the Angevin yoke and gaining freedom to settle their own feuds in their own summary way.

The frontiers of Normandy were safeguarded not by formidable barriers of terrain, but by a series of strong fortifications commanding the roads and river routes. During Richard's captivity, Philip had secured Gisors through the treachery of its castellan and had thus opened the way to Rouen on the right bank of the Seine, and he was, when Richard reached Lisieux, blockading Verneuil, the key to the left bank; and he already held a crest of border castles spearheading between Gisors and Verneuil upon the capital of Normandy itself. Verneuil, under siege since the 10th of May, if lost, would put Rouen and the whole course of the lower Seine in jeopardy.

Richard arrived in Normandy at the eleventh hour, but his whole being stirred at the prospect of coming at last to grips with the archconspirator against his life and empire and of wreaking his own vengeance on the traitor. Without mercy for human endurance nor for horseflesh, he pressed on from his meeting with John in Lisieux, covering the leagues to Verneuil in three prodigious stages. On the 28th of May he came in sight of the plateau above the Eure, where the fortresses set there long before by Henry Beauclerc were holding out desperately against the French blockade.

Philip had not the same ardor to meet in combat the prince of chivalry whom he had wronged beyond the hope of mercy. He knew that he too was worth a ransom. A sound instinct warned him not to expose his person on the marches. On hearing of Richard's approach he put some leagues between himself and the frontier, abandoning engines and supplies in the field. On the 28th the garrison of Verneuil opened its gates to Richard. The Normans defending the fortress, who had been exposed not only to assault but to bribes and treachery and the rumors of the king's death, "embraced each other," says the chronicler, "with tears of joy," for they knew that if the Franks could not take Verneuil, Normandy was redeemed. From Verneuil Richard passed swiftly to the relief of Vaudreuil, near the tip of Philip's penetration toward Rouen.

Then, "swift as a Balearic sling," [20] the king turned southward to the valley of the Loire to recover the castles surrendered by John during the captivity, and the strongholds of Loches and Châteaudun, which he himself had yielded under duress. Moving with incredible speed, Coeur-de-Lion overtook the intercepting forces of Philip near Fréteval and drove them back so sharply that their withdrawal became a rout. [21] Again the Capetian showed no desire to meet his foe on the field of battle. [22] Near Vendome he was forced to abandon not only his engines but his chapel and his treasury. While Guillaume le Maréchal engaged the Frankish rear and gathered in abundant loot, Richard and Mercadier pursued Philip himself in headlong flight toward the marches of the Île. Dieu-Donné, cut off from his forces and with his archenemy at his heels, turned into a side road and took sanctuary in a church, so that Richard lost wind of him and rode by furiously, only to find, when he had galloped leagues beyond the turning, that he had missed his quarry far in the rear. Among the spoils gathered in by Guillaume in the backward areas of the rout were the charters of the particular Breton, Angevin, and Poitevin barons who had pledged their allegiance to the Franks. The capture, while it gave abundant evidence of John's recent collusions with Philip and revealed the Plantagenets' domains honeycombed with treason, also unmasked the traitors singly and severally for vengeance. [23]

Thence Richard turned to Aquitaine. The absence of Eleanor from her provinces since 1192 had left her vassals, in spite of the rigors of her seneschals, a measure of freedom for their seditious plans. For the time being they forgot their internecine feuds to combine against Richard, whose ferocity before crusade they vividly remembered. The Count of Angoulême, whose vast domains cut across the ducal highway between Bordeaux and Poitiers, and the great seigneur, Geoffroi de Rançon, whose castles marked the valley of the Charente, merged their rancors against Coeur-de-Lion and trusted to widespread confusions to right their own grievances. Raymond of Toulouse, the weather vane, bestirred himself to settle old scores with the house of Poitou. And all these smoldering hostilities were blown into flame by the rousing *sirventés* of Bertran de Born and Philip's timely proffers of assistance.

When Richard came to Poitou, he came home, and this time he came to finish what he had left undone on leaving for crusade. He and Mercadier knew the fortresses of the rebels inside and out, their sites and their defenses, every access, every cranny. Coeur-de-Lion had learned his first lessons in the use of military engines in assaults on their ramparts and had sharpened his sword time and again on their barred gates. In the month of July he fell upon the traitor strongholds with a fury and spread desolation far and wide. Within three weeks he wrote to the Archbishop of Canterbury:

"Know that, by the grace of God, who in all things has consideration of the right, we have taken . . . all the castles and the whole territory of Geoffroi de Rançon, as well as the city of Angoulême and all the territories of the viscount. The city and the borough of Angoulême we took in a single evening; and we have taken full three hundred knights and forty thousand armed men." [24]

The foremost cavalier of Europe had emerged from captivity with no diminution of his valor. In the first contest for the great stakes, Coeur-de-Lion had won every round and driven his foe within his own borders. It was ten weeks since he had left England. Says Diceto, "From Verneuil to the Pyrenees not a rebel showed himself to the King of the English." [25]

But the conflict was nowhere decisive nor could any conclusion be foreseen. New excursions and reprisals devastated the marches. The razing and burning of strongholds continued in many localities as the tide ebbed and flowed. In the chronicles that record events in Normandy, where Philip made his strongest thrusts, place names crowd the pages as great border castles fell, were recovered, and fell again.

Both church and vassalage viewed with dire dismay the progress of a catastrophic struggle that had already wasted the mighty effort of crusade and threatened to prevent its resumption. The turbulent first years of Richard's reign and the colossal perfidies that had issued from events had brought the feudal lords of the Angevin domains a dangerous insecurity. The plots hatched during Coeur-de-Lion's captivity betokened an early onset of something more unsettling than the perennial struggle for local advantage or the rectification of frontiers. Richard's spectacular recovery of prestige in his first campaigns restored a temporary outward confidence among his liege men, but the times invited anarchy and imposed a fear on those among them who understood the unresolved personal rancor that divided the kings. Uncertainty about the outcome of a renewed struggle gave occasion for intrigue. Insecurity bred treason and treason insecurity. While Richard's successes were still resounding, clergy and march barons on both sides sought by every means to allay the strife. They urged mediation and arbitration, the purchase of disputed march properties, indemnities, the old expedient of uniting scions of the rival dynasties by marriage.

These pressures by the magnates brought the kings or their representatives together at various stages for a series of *pourparlers*. But the "truces" were illusory, for, as one chronicler relates, they merely provided respites for the reaping of harvests and the recuperation of forces on both sides. The atmosphere in which they were invoked reminded the Dean of Saint Paul's of Egypt's darkness in the days of Pharaoh.[26] Now here, now there, the conflict raged anew, and many march barons changed their allegiance as they changed their coats.

✤

In all the fortunes of war Eleanor shared with Richard the burden of policy. Though the chroniclers have little to say of her special activities during this period, her whereabouts is known and events occurring within her purview bear the mark of her Poitevin ingenuity. She appears to have left purely military affairs to her competent son and devoted herself to matters that belonged more properly to her natural sphere. She took up her station, as she had so often done for Henry, at a crossway near the heart of the Angevin empire whither access was convenient from all directions and whence she could bend her eye and ear over a wide circuit and root out sedition within her radius. The court of Poitiers had long since dispersed. It had never revived as a center of civility after Henry's purge of 1174. The pomps of chivalry were effaced by war. The queen began to realize her age. She needed release from the distractions of a great chatelaine; comfort rather than pomp, escape from trivialities, freedom to come and go. She set up her unostentatious chancellery in Fontevrault. Here she could barricade herself in the inviolable cloisters from the rabble of hangers-on that swarmed wherever she fixed her residence, deny herself to troublesome visitors, have rest when she needed it, and all this without losing grasp of what was afoot in the provinces.

The domain of the abbey, where the river Vienne wound in sunny shallows through cultivated fields and vineyards, or darkened in the shade of woodlands, had a mellow and tranquil charm. It was familiar. Within its walls her younger children had been secluded from the too stimulating air of the Poitevin court in those gorgeous days when the Countess of Champagne had presided over it. The Princesses Eleanor and Joanna and lack-land John had been nurtured there for their high royal callings. In the nuns' choir in the crypt, great Henry, with his rough hands folded on his breast, slept amidst the sweet odors of sanctity. There was plenty of agreeable society (although perhaps too prone to reminiscence) among the superfluity of royal ladies washed up in this refuge from the corners of feudal creation; and there was abundance of news to be had from those hooded brethren who plied the thoroughfares north, south, east, and west, and from the assorted wayfarers who beat a perpetual tattoo upon the gates. No site could have been more admirable as a listening post. Fronting the disorders in Anjou and the intrigues in Brittany, the queen could keep the eye in the back of her head upon Poitou.

In the comparative quiet of the abbey Eleanor seems to have given her attention to unraveling the matrimonial perplexities of the Plantagenets in the best interest of the dynasty and of a peace, which she had come above all to desire. The problems, which were very individual, centered especially in Berengaria, the widowed Joanna, and Alais Capet, the latter still awaiting justice long delayed in the tower of Rouen.

The relations of the Plantagenets to Berengaria are not made clear in the chronicles. The associations of Richard and the Princess of Navarre were occasional and of brief duration; yet whenever the royal court assembled the younger queen seems to have enjoyed the respect due to her. The position of Eleanor left but a small office for Berengaria in the palaces of the Plantagenets, eager as they had been to fetch her from Navarre, and richly as they had endowed her. Her failure to provide Richard with an heir left her without a role in destiny. However, Richard was in any case too restless and too incessantly at war for life in residential seats. Even more vagrant than Henry, he lived in the saddle and on the field in ceaseless movement and activity. Though reared in the Countess of Champagne's school of manners in Poitiers and bred to its punctilious observances, he was no captive in the courts of love. His vassals complained that, in order to build castles, he had forgotten gallantry and forsaken courts and tournaments.[27] His delights were in hardy exercise; his "parloir" his barracks; his poetry, not the languishments of Ventadour, but the rousing *sirventés* of Bertran de Born. It is also possible that Berengaria, who had been gently bred, had had enough of shipwreck and *chevauchée* in the course of her pilgrimage to the Holy Land to desire again the life of a camp follower. Though apparently upon fair terms with Eleanor, who had certainly usurped her function, she seems to have kept mainly to her own dower properties in Maine, but without establishing a court of resort for herself or Richard.[28]

The widowhood of the Queen of Sicily, as Joanna continued to style herself, renewed her status as a Plantagenet marriage prize. Her defiance of Richard's projects to dispose of her upon crusade suggests she knew her value. Before the death of King William, Joanna had known only luxury and ease, but afterward a kind of persistent adversity stalked the young queen. Her rich dower had been squandered on the expedition to the Holy Land, so that glory was all the treasure she brought back to endow her lineage. And then, on her way home from Palestine, fate moving injuriously and under her very eyes snatched away a rich but unperceived possibility of recovery.

Berengaria and Joanna returning from Acre had been accompanied not only by their little Cyprian handmaiden, but by a niece of Guy of Lusignan, who had been placed in their custody for a visit to the fiefs of her forebears in Poitou. The party had landed in Calabria shortly before the capture of Coeur-de-Lion and had remained in papal territory under the escort of one of Richard's admirals and the protection of Pope Celestine through the first anxious months of the captivity, not daring to stir for fear of the king's enemies, especially the Hohenstaufen. In the spring of 1193, under escort of a cardinal and with papal safe-conduct, they had ventured to Genoa and Marseille. Richard, returning from crusade at the end of 1192, had turned back from the port of Marseille through fear of Raymond of Toulouse. But the house of Toulouse had the dismaying habit of favoring the Capets or the Plantagenets as best suited their own transient interests, and Count Raymond had, at the time of the queens' arrival at his borders, altered his role as enemy of the Plantagenets. He even sent his son and heir to meet the royal ladies in his port of Saint Gilles and to convoy them in safety across his county to Poitou.[29]

When Raymond the younger greeted the travelers in Saint Gilles, he chanced for the moment to be married to Beatrix, the heiress of Béziers. But as soon as he laid eyes on the beautiful Bourguigne of Lusignan in the custody of the queens and considered her preciousness as a marriage prize, he directed a summary charge of consanguinity against Beatrix, designated a decent allowance for her maintenance, and relegated her to a nunnery. In the meantime, in defiance of threats of excommunication, he attached Bourguigne before she could come to the end of her journey.[30]

This marriage, executed so peremptorily, offered alarm to the Plantagenets. The union of the heir of Toulouse, who was Philip Capet's cousin, with one of the most broilsome houses of Poitou was a menace that could not be tolerated. The marriage of Raymond to the demoiselle of Lusignan, like two or three of his previous matrimonial exploits, was very brief. Though the chroniclers have nothing to say upon the circumstance of its dissolution, it is hard not to see in it the remedial operation of Eleanor. There appeared in the mercurial nature of Raymond and the fluidity of his policies a chance not only to undo the dangerous misalliance and to reëndow Joanna, but at the same time to settle that matter, now two generations in dispute, of the queen's own claims to the inheritance of Toulouse, for which she had embroiled each of her royal spouses in turn.

At Epiphany in 1195 Raymond succeeded to his patrimony. Though still excommunicate for his repudiation of Beatrix, he was presently seen mounting another rung in the ladder of his ascendant career. He repudiated Bourguigne, as he had cast off Beatrix, and contracted a marriage with Joanna Plantagenet.[31] The frontiers of Toulouse and Queen Eleanor's provinces, so long uneasy and a prey to Capetian intrigue, were brought by its terms to peace and security. There was one hazard in this otherwise prosperous affair, for Raymond was not only the cousin of Philip Augustus, but he had lately been his friend and ally; and who does not know that a weathercock turns his face to every wind that blows? The Plantagenets checked Raymond's supine surrender to the wind by taking a precise agreement from him to dower Joanna in Toulouse and make that province the heritage of her issue.

The case of Alais, which touched the Capets even more nearly than the situation in Toulouse, called for the most cautious forethought. The plight of the princess was one of the many disastrous fruits of the treaty of Montmirail by which the magnates a quarter of a century before had striven to compose the dangerous rivalry of the royal houses. Little could Louis Capet have dreamed, when he committed this one of his "frightening superfluity of daughters" to the Plantagenets as a bride for the Count of Poitou, what vicissitudes she would suffer in the court of his Angevin vassal. It was twenty-four years since she had been delivered to Henry Fitz-Empress for nurture in the palaces of her destiny, and she was now thirty-three and still unwed in a court whence the daughters of Henry and Eleanor had been sped to their matrimonial callings at the age of eleven or twelve. Since Henry had disposed of the embarrassment of Marguerite's Angevin dowers by securing her marriage to King Bela of Hungary,[32] Alais had lived in Britain or under surveillance on the Continent without personal ties with the Capets. Denied the marriage contracted at Montmirail, she had become a mere hostage employed to enforce all sorts of terms not stipulated in her bond. Her youth had been wasted, her fame sullied, and, at the end of her sordid experiences, she had fallen at last under the justice of a queen not likely to acquit her of treasonous intrigue. The wheel of fortune to which she and Eleanor had been bound by their relationships had made a complete revolution. As Eleanor once had been, so now was she, a prisoner without hope.

In the gyrations of her fortunes, the value of Alais, even as a hostage, had diminished. The treachery of Philip and John during the captivity had given the Plantagenets the best of reasons for delay in the execution of the compact of Messina; but now that John had been reattached to his own house by the strong bonds of self-interest, the princess had become not only a chattel of little worth, but an encumbrance to the Plantagenets, a perennial theme for scandal, and an indictment of a king's honor in keeping his sworn engagements. The clergy and the nobles were alike urgent for a settlement of her case. Negotiations began for her restoration to the Capets with Gisors and the Norman Vexin in the late summer of 1195.

During the period of Philip's incursions in Normandy, the princess had been removed from the tower of Rouen and held in Caen and other Norman strongholds safe from rescue. Her long duress and all her proud pretensions ended when, late in August, she was brought as a counter for bargaining in one of the recurrent "truces." Near Verneuil on the frontier, the captive, outcast from the house of her adoption and strange to her own kin, was thrust over the marches of her native land. Her history, so obscure in its details, was certainly filled with unrecorded drama. Her annals, if some clerk had set them down, would be precious as illuminating many a dark corridor in the domestic palaces of the Plantagenets.[33]

Philip contracted no throne for his recovered sister. He bestowed her promptly on his vassal, Guillaume de Ponthieu,[34] to whom she was at once married in the city of Mantes. Thus at last she got an honorable name of her own and passed from the palaces and fortresses of the Plantagenets into the release of comparative obscurity. Her marriage to Guillaume was, however, an affair of strategy, for his lands made a little wedge that prevented Richard and Baldwin of Flanders from striking a common frontier on the lower Somme, near its entrance to the Channel. To this extent Alais, even after her deliverance, remained an instrument that could now and then be usefully employed, but henceforth by the Capets.

30 ✢

The Treasure of Châlus

SOME CHRONICLERS COMMENT upon a mood of blandness that possessed Richard after those first triumphs on the Continent had restored his security and prestige; after his reconciliation with John and his settlement of the compact of Messina. Perhaps the change on which they comment betokened a new ripening phase, which, if time had been his, might presently have revealed more of the sobriety and amplitude of the Angevin genius. He had been, according to Giraldus, a debonair young man, not so much pricked by the ardors of youth as submissive to its desires, more prone to luxury and ease than to hardening disciplines, to self-indulgences than to virtuous effort. In former times he had now and then been subject to onsets of compunction,[1] but now a genuine catharsis was observed, accompanied by good works and significant reforms. His amenable humor was attributed by some to the sobering effects of his disasters on crusade and gratitude for his deliverance; by others to the operation of clerics on a mind and conscience made tender by an illness that overcame him at Easter time in 1195. But more reasonable it seems to ascribe the lenity the chroniclers remark to the king's release at last from the entanglements that had heretofore boggled all his movements toward realizing his destiny. Against heavy odds he had recovered Angevin prestige and comparative security.

He began now to restore to religious foundations the vessels he had exacted from them for ransom. He fed the poor from the royal treasury through a period of drought.[2] He went to mass every day and, unlike King Henry, who stirred about and scribbled during the offices,[3] he remained reverently quiet from Secret to Communion. At table, says Coggeshall, he was mild and affable with his familiars, subduing his harsher moods with jests and games.[4] Like Henry he heard the rebukes of the clergy without losing his Angevin temper. He even enjoyed in the evenings, when darkness had cut off his perambulations, to draw out the hermits and interpreters of visions who pressed their way to his presence and to parry reproaches hidden in their oracular discourse with pungent retort. To covert insinuation, he replied with a caustic humor that revived the memory of Henry's ways of dealing with presumption. To this frame perhaps belongs the incident with which Hoveden spices his chronicle.[5]

On such an occasion the hardy evangelist Foulques de Neuilly brought the medicine of his evangels to the king. In the presence of a group, the preacher, with something of the valor of Daniel at Belshazzar's feast, delivered his blast.

"I warn thee, O King, on behalf of almighty God, to marry at once thy three most shameless daughters."

"Thou liest," said Richard, "for thou well knowest I have no daughters whomsoever."

"Beyond a doubt," replied the priest, "I do not lie, for thou hast three most shameless daughters, whose names are Pride, Avarice, and Sensuality."

"Give ear," retorted Richard, including the circle of bystanders, "to this hypocrite who warns me to marry my shameless daughters. Bear witness, I give my daughter Pride to the Knights Templars, my daughter Avarice to the Cistercians, my daughter Sensuality to the prelates of the church."

⚜

The treaty of Louviers,[6] January 1196, which finally confirmed the compact of Messina and defined the new borders between the Vexin and Normandy, though it briefly pacified the Capets could not delude Coeur-de-Lion with visions of false security. The sacrifice of the strategic Vexin had opened a dangerous gap in his Norman frontiers, and events pointed to Normandy as the field of ultimate decision for the historic enmity between the rival dynasties and the culmination for good or ill of Philip's Carolingian dream. Not only had the ring of outworks on the old marches, built and strengthened by four generations of his forebears, been penetrated by the restoration of the Vexin to the Capets; but the fortresses that remained had been outmoded by new engines of assault. In spite of its arc of guardian castles, Rouen itself was exposed. Philip, at the height of his predatory exploits, had pitched his tents but twelve miles from the capital of the Norman dukes. Richard resolved to establish an impenetrable barrier against future excursions of the Capets in this direction.

On the right bank of the Seine, Coeur-de-Lion fixed his mind upon a peerless height for a fortress that should surpass anything yet seen in Europe, a very mountain of defiance to obstruct the valley of the Seine by river and by road. Two thirds of the distance, as the crow flies, from Paris to the sea, the river described a deep loop, washing the chalky cliffs of an abrupt eminence that offered a panoramic survey of the whole region to its remote horizons. This height, the "Rock of Andelys," had not escaped the appraising eye of Philip, but it loomed a few leagues beyond his reach.

The Angevin genius for building stirred mightily in Coeur-de-Lion as he reconnoitered this matchless site. From the days of his earliest memory he had prowled about the massy ancient piles reared by Foulques the Black, William the Conqueror, Henry Beauclerc, Geoffrey the Fair, and Henry

Fitz-Empress on the heights of Loches, Falaise, Chinon, and many another dominating lookout. In the Latin Kingdom he had explored with amazement and delight the newest military construction of the Templars and Hospitallers at least in Margab and Acre, Ramleh and Ascalon. For a time the heir of the Angevins fell under the spell of his architect's dream, and everything else was vexation until it could be realized.[7]

Though the site lay in the episcopal domain of the Archbishop of Rouen, neither the prelate's remonstrances nor the interdict he laid on Normandy for its seizure delayed the king's project. In defiance even of an ill-omened "shower of blood" that was said to have rained upon his masons, Richard pushed the work forward.[8] His skillful engineers altered the face of nature, rerouting nearby streams tributary to the Seine, and taking advantage of the precipitousness of the cliffs, so that the Rock was not only marooned by waterways but islanded aloft in the air. Only one narrow and easily defensible ridge linked it with the plateau of which it was the crown. On Andelys Richard laid out his masterpiece and overlooked the laying of its stones. Its complicated outer defenses, the unconquerable strength of its walls, its gigantic bastions, its intricate communications, and, above all, its unassailable site were designed to mock the puny engines of the Franks and deride their petty maneuvers in the river valley. Richard drove his builders with all his Angevin energy, and the work filled every respite of his warfare for three years and more.

"Behold," exclaimed the architect king to his amazed liege men at the end of 1196, "how fair my daughter has grown in a single year."

With raillery he named the pile *Château Gaillard*. Saucy Castle, or Petulant Castle, it has been called, though the English hardly renders the mocking challenge of the French.[9]

Philip surveyed the mass of Gaillard looming on his path with a dismay that was not concealed by his defiant bluster.

"If its walls were made of solid iron," he cried, "yet would I take them."

And over the ramparts Richard shouted back, "By the throat of God, if its walls were made of butter, yet would I hold them." [10]

The Rock became the seat of Richard's councils and of such court as he maintained. Here he convened his magnates, barons and bishops, castellans and seneschals; here he received the emissaries of other potentates. Within its dungeons he gathered the prisoners he took in war. No doubt jongleurs bandied *sirventés* in the hall, but conversation certainly did not turn upon the *Tractatus de Amore*. The talk at Gaillard was of battles and hostages, taxes and levies, of ransom, of the famine and hard times that war had brought to the provinces of the Angevins, and, more than all, of the persistent treachery and menace of the Franks. As the castle uplifted its mass against the sky, Plantagenet policy with respect to this menace took shape and became manifest. It was seen that Richard's experience in the Holy Roman Empire had given him insight into the political strategy that underlies an ultimate resort to arms between two powerful enemies. Whereas once his pride and confidence had led him to spurn and offend his potential allies, he now was seen to cultivate friends near and far and to appreciate their uses.[11]

Two fortuitous events outside his own domains presently gave him opportunity to employ the weapons of diplomacy: the death of Henry of Hohenstaufen before the prime of his age, and the succession of Innocent III to the papal throne. The Holy Roman Emperor had remained excommunicate[12] until the moment of his deathbed repentance for his violation of the Truce of God in holding Richard captive. His sudden death in Messina[13] in September 1197 left only the infant son of Constance of Sicily as heir to the Empire. Important German magnates rejected this child, for whom a long regency would have multiplied disorders. The emperor's brother, Philip of Swabia, was unacceptable to the great lords of the church. Those German magnates whom Coeur-de-Lion had so impressed during his captivity summoned Richard himself to counsel the choice for the imperial crown, perhaps to assume it himself.[14]

It was said that the same destiny had once beckoned Henry to cross the Alps of Maurienne and descend to the Lombard plain, but that his domestic embarrassments with his sons, or perhaps the sound Angevin instinct that warned him to reach for those gains only that were certainly attainable, had restrained him from adding the knotty dilemmas of the Empire to his problems at home. At any rate, he had contented himself with the consolidation of his Angevin provinces and the addition of such marginal lands as chance placed at his mercy. The experiences of Richard and Eleanor in Speyer and Mainz had made them wary. As Henry was said to have done before him, Richard now renounced the honors proffered him. A ripening judgment rose to curb the sudden impulse that in the first years of his reign had led him to seize fortune recklessly without regard for consequence. But in order not to sacrifice imperial prospects unconditionally, Coeur-de-Lion proposed for the emperor's crown his nephew, Otto of Brunswick, a son of Matilda Plantagenet and Henry the Lion of Saxony. Otto had grown up for the greater part of his life in Plantagenet courts because of the long exile of his father and the early death of his mother in 1189.[15] He was a valiant and personable knight in his early twenties, in good odor with the church, and he had recently had some administrative training under Eleanor's supervision as bailiff in Poitou.[16] Otto's destiny was arranged at Gaillard and thence, resplendent with trappings and retinue, the young man proceeded to Speyer. In January 1198 he was married to the infant daughter of the Duke of Louvain, who had befriended Richard in his captivity. On the following day in Aachen, with a bride beside him who was too small to wear her crown, he put on the imperial diadem and was acclaimed by this powerful party of German magnates as the Holy Roman Emperor.[17]

In 1198 the aged Pope Celestine, whose supineness Eleanor had so bitterly berated during the captivity, was succeeded by the young and energetic Innocent III; and the new successor to Saint Peter made it at once apparent that the church would not regard as an inevitable and perennial curse the strife among the potentates of Europe that postponed from month to month and year to year the promised succor of the Latin Kingdom in Palestine. In the papal survey, when once the compact of Messina, which the church had endorsed, had been given effect, Richard's record was much fairer than Philip Augustus' had been. The Plantagenets did not let it be forgotten that Philip had violated the Truce of God by invading the lands of his fellow crusader and by contributing to the captivity; that he had suborned John and spread false rumors with evil intent. Furthermore, Philip was not only under interdict for his stubborn resistance in the matter of the Princess Ingeborg, who still abode with the nuns of Soissons while Danish emissaries labored at the *curia* for her restoration to the throne of France, but he had contracted an unblessed union with a German heiress, Agnes of Méranie, who with her "bastards" flourished in his palaces with all the semblance of legitimacy.

As the century drew toward its close, Gaillard overlooked the valley of the Seine saucily indeed. It was the most impregnable fortress on the Continent, and the alliances issuing from it were seen to forge a ring about the French domain. Philip saw his potential allies drawn one by one into the camp of the enemy: John Plantagenet, the Danes, the Counts of Flanders and Boulogne, the barons palatinate of the Rhine, the Count of Toulouse. The Rock was properly dreaded in the Île as breeding disaster for the Franks.[18]

※

Stir not the embers with the sword.
　　　　　Hoveden

While in the latter nineties the Plantagenets' fortification of their boundaries progressed, the warfare on the marches of Normandy and other frontiers proceeded without much regard for the seasonal truces contrived by prelates and castellans to bring about a permanent accord. The restoration of the Princess Alais and the Norman Vexin by the treaty of Louviers (1196) had for a brief time seemed to anxious vassals to mark a cessation of the interminable struggle. But, in spite of the treaties, the Vexin remained the indispensable defense of either king against the other, and so a perennial bone of contention between the rival dynasties.

Confronted by the menace of the Rock, Philip could not regard the treaty of Louviers as definitive. His suspicions were further aroused by Richard's issuing a levy for the mustering of troops in England. He weighed measures to secure the advantages he had gained through the restoration of the Vexin, and considered how he might extend its boundary northward to the Channel on the borders of the region held by Count Guillaume de Ponthieu, to whom he had assigned his sister Alais as a marriage prize. The Plantagenets had recovered Aumale, which protected Rouen from short-range attack from the north and east. Philip made a sudden onset on Aumale. Richard, though unprepared for assault in that quarter, set forth from Gaillard with boldness and all speed. With Guillaume le Maréchal and Mercadier commanding detachments of his forces, he drove Philip in a rout out of the Norman Vexin into the French domain. Through the gateway of Gisors the French king's flight was so precipitate that the bridge over the Epte gave way, twenty of his knights weighted by their armor were drowned, and Philip himself plunged into the stream and was narrowly rescued from death. Richard wrote exultantly to the Bishop of Durham: "The King of the Franks had river water for his drink that day, and nearly a hundred knights were captured." [19]

At this defeat, involving the loss of many of his serviceable barons and much booty, Philip returned to Paris with a deep foreboding. The disaster of being expelled from the Vexin was so signal that, after taking counsel of his magnates, he resolved, in spite of his offenses against the church, to solicit the good offices of Rome.

The church, appalled by the new outbreaks, had already set about its own measures to bring order to Christendom. Philip's appeal to Rome of course opened the painful necessity of arbitrating the long-standing case of Ingeborg, whose agents were still clamoring for justice in the *curia*. Innocent, prevented from intervention in person, sent his legate. Cardinal Peter of Capua arrived in France about Christmas time in 1197 and, after a brief sojourn in the capital of the Capets, procured a parley of the kings at a place on the Seine between Gaillard and Vernon.

The Plantagenets, after their recent triumphs, were supercilious about a truce. Since the cardinal arrived at the rendezvous from Paris, they professed to suspect the legate of being bought with Frankish gold. Peter was, says the biographer of Guillaume le Maréchal, "one who had been to school and learned to turn matters inside out." [20] However, Coeur-de-Lion, when sounded on his demands, declared that he wanted nothing that was not his own; only that his enemy should get out of the lands he held by hereditary right. He even said that, if Philip would retire to his own frontiers and stay there, he would make no claims for the recent damage to his Norman castles. The cardinal professed to find these terms stiff for the Franks. He took the view that Philip could hardly be expected to relinquish the ground it had cost him so much to gain. He explained to the King of the English the meaning of compromise. At this the famous Angevin choler rose in Coeur-de-Lion.

"What!" he burst forth, "you ask me to leave my castles and my lands in his possession? Not while I breathe."

At this point Peter tried to divert Coeur-de-Lion's thoughts to the jeopardy to which Jerusalem was exposed by the royal quarrel. This was a mistake in judgment. The vials of Richard's wrath were broken by the mention of the Holy Land.

"If the King of the Franks had left my lands in peace," he cried, "if I had not been forced to come home on his account, all Palestine would have been delivered from the infidel. But he betrayed me. By his counsel I was held in captivity, so that he could have a chance meanwhile to despoil me of my heritage. But God willing, he will not prosper in his scheming." The chronicler reports that Richard "panted with anger like a wounded boar." [21]

At length, however, through the mediation of magnates desperate for peace, a ground was found for negotiation. For the sake of a new crusade, Richard at length agreed to a truce for five years, during which Philip might hold "in gage" the moot castles which were at the time in his possession; but the *chatellanies* (the surrounding tributary lands) should be held of Richard. This left the final situation as complex as ever; but Coeur-de-Lion's counselors helped him to see that in five years' time the castles, without their lands, would become as worthless as girdled trees that could be lopped off at will. Hence at length he agreed.

All might have proceeded without catastrophe from this point if the un-lucky cardinal had not brought forward a demand for the release of Philip's cousin, the Bishop of Beauvais, whom Mercadier had dragged to Gaillard with other Frankish prisoners in the recent campaigns. This prelate, derisively known among the Normans as the "chanter of Beauvais" and described as more apt for fighting than for prayer, had been one of the most dogged of Richard's enemies in Palestine, and he was worth a precious ransom from the Franks.[22]

"It is against the canons," said the legate, "to hold in captivity one con-secrated by the church."

"What! I hold a clerk in chains? Never!" cried Coeur-de-Lion.

"Sire, do not evade," returned the cardinal. "The Bishop of Beauvais is entitled to the protection of Rome."

This challenge produced a remarkable example of Plantagenet eloquence lit up by fury.

"By my head," shouted Richard, "a consecrated man indeed! Better call him desecrated. It was not in the guise of a bishop that I took him, but as a knight with his armor all laced on. If this is what you came here for, Sir Advocate, you have missed your calling. I swear if you were not the bearer of a message, Rome would not save you from a drubbing to take back as souvenir. Does the Pope suppose I am a fool? I know very well that Rome only mocked me when, though I was in the service of God, I was made captive. I besought the Pope's aid and he could not take the trouble to help me. And now he asks me to give up a brigand, a firebrand, who has done nothing but ravage my lands by night and day. Leave this place, Sir Traitor, liar, swindler, suborner, and take care not to be found on my path again."

The cardinal hardly waited for the collection of his paraphernalia. He took to his mount and rode without stopping to Paris. When he related his amazed impressions of the King of the English in the Capetian city, the magnates exchanged knowing smiles. "King Richard," they said, "is no leveret. He is not easily cowed. He intends to avenge his losses." [23] Perhaps elders among them recalled great Henry's outbursts at the legates who presumed to bring him to terms with Becket.

On no condition could Peter of Capua be induced to return to personal negotiations with the Plantagenet king. In February Philip and Richard met again under the auspices of the Archbishop of Reims, who took over the unfinished business of Innocent's legate. Philip with his company came to the trysting place on the Seine between the Rock and Vernon, and kept his saddle, according to the custom of parley in the open. But Richard arrived with his delegation from Gaillard in a barge and did not land. He had resolved that there should be no setting for any acts of homage nor for the kiss of peace. With the clean stream of the Seine flowing between them, the kings came to terms for a final negotiation. In that last interview Coeur-de-Lion dealt as master toward his overlord, but he assented to certain tentative agreements to be confirmed at later interviews.[24]

The King of the English demanded that the King of the Franks restore all the land he had taken; that he give up the presentation of the archbishopric of Tours, through which he had been able to meddle in the affairs of Touraine; that he end his opposition to the election of Otto as Emperor of the Romans and give him his support. Gisors, where once the vast elm had marked the place of parley betwen the Capetian kings and the Norman dukes, remained the fatal crux of the situation. For three successive years the call to arms and the ravaging of fruitful fields had added famine and disease to the miseries of northern Europe. Prelates, desperate for peace, and hoping at least for a postponement of crisis, resorted to the traditional scheme for deferring conclusions on that moot landmark. They invoked the old compromise, a marriage of the rival houses, but with Gisors this time as dowry for a Plantagenet bride. A previous scheme to marry Eleanor of Brittany to the son of Philip had been dropped after the exclusion of Arthur as Richard's heir; and now a new alliance was discussed. It was proposed that Richard affiance one of his nieces, a daughter of his sister, Queen Eleanor of Castile, to the scion of the Capets.[25]

✤

There's not a penny in Chinon.
(Savies qu'a Chinon non a argent ni denier.)

Sirventés addressed by Coeur-de-Lion to the Count of Auvergne in 1199 [26]

When the terms of Louviers had been defined but not ratified, Richard turned his back on the Seine and the Rock and the French frontiers to make a *chevauchée* long delayed by his entanglements with Philip Augustus to more distant quarters of his realm. He was in fine fettle, for he had given to Christendom a fresh exhibition of valor and success. With his own arm he had vindicated his ancestral rights and reëstablished the prestige he had lost in captivity. His most pressing anxiety at the time was over the failure of his treasury. He had drained the coffers of England and Normandy in his mighty building projects, in the support of mercenaries, and in "gifts" to restore powerful but wavering march barons to his allegiance.

Attending to various incidental matters en route, he made his way to the treasure castle of Chinon and there spent some days in early March of 1199. Here, or at Fontevrault, he certainly held conferences with Queen Eleanor in her bailiwick; for he learned a great deal about the unrest in Maine, Anjou, Brittany, and Touraine, where many barons kept in agitation by the house of Brittany and incited by Philip were spotted with treason and only awaited a favorable moment for revolt. Below the Loire those perennial firebrands, Aymar of Limoges and Adémar of Angoulême, had covertly thrown off their allegiance to the house of Poitou and appealed to the protection of the King of the Franks. In Chinon Richard verified the fact that the Angevin treasury had little to yield for his financial necessities.

While Coeur-de-Lion was giving ear to these depressing matters and attending meantime to the wearisome details of feudal business that had accumulated, affixing his seal each day to a multitude of tiresome charters, he had, it seemed, a providential stroke of luck. Some unknown courier brought him news of a treasure-trove that had recently been unearthed in the Limousin.[27] A poor husbandman laboring in a field in one of the lesser *chatellanies* of Count Aymar of Limoges, had accidentally turned up from the ground a massy golden treasure. The precious object seemed to represent a king seated at a table in company with his family. Its origin and significance were unknown, but it had probably been buried in the soil of the Limousin from times of Roman antiquity.

Was the treasure miraculously designed to replenish the empty chests of Chinon? At any rate, Aymar deserved to suffer its loss for his treachery. Richard at once demanded possession of the trove from his vassal. With Richard and Mercadier on his borders, Aymar chose the better part of valor and offered half of the treasure to his overlord. Richard's reply was to appear, in spite of Lent, with a force of *routiers* before the little castle of Châlus where the treasure was believed to be hidden.

The castle was no first-class fortress, but it stood on a defensible rise of ground. It was unmanned save for two or three armed knights, probably stationed there to drive off robbers; and it was otherwise peopled by about two score laborers and householders belonging to the fief.[28] Such a paltry outfit offered no difficulties to Coeur-de-Lion. Having refused the garrison's belated offers of capitulation, Richard surrounded the place and set sappers at the foundations of the protecting walls. Driven to bay, the motley garrison strove with such weapons as they could contrive to defend their lord's castle from the *routiers*. From their battlements they rolled down stones on their besiegers and from the vents in the barbicans exhausted their supply of arrows. In the meantime they sent to Count Aymar for relief, and he in turn appealed to Paris.

The siege was brief.[29] On the 25th of March after supper, Richard returned in the early twilight from his lodgings to the precincts of the castle. In company with Mercadier, he went about the circuit of the fortifications to examine the work of the sappers. With a shield, but carelessly, he protected himself from the random arrows that fell here and there about him. Suddenly in the dusk a shaft from a strong bow sang in the air and struck him in the shoulder. The heavy missile entered his flesh below his nape and near his spine. It proved to be one from his own armory which some sharpshooter had retrieved from a cleft where it had lodged in one of the barbicans. It went so deep that its head could not be withdrawn.

Without uttering a sound in evidence of surprise or pain, Coeur-de-Lion mounted his horse and rode to his hospice under cover of the falling night, so only his intimates knew what had occurred. His lodgings were at once cleared of all save four of his familiars, for fear of spreading alarm among the *routiers*. Then the king was laid upon his couch. In vain his companions tried to draw out the head of the arrow by main force. The remnant of the shaft gave way, but the barb remained embedded. Mercadier then summoned a "surgeon" from amongst his following, and he, by the glimmer of a lantern, gashed the flesh, to lay bare the missile. In a ghastly operation the leaden barb was dug from the king's shoulder. His companions dressed his wounds with unguents and poultices; but fatal mischief had been done and the assistants soon saw that their medicaments would be vain.[30]

Richard, with lively presentiment, sent for Queen Eleanor whom he had left in Lenten retreat at Fontevrault some days previously. She at once dispatched the Abbess Matilda northward to break the news to Berengaria and to summon John, both of whom were in Maine, but not together. With the Abbé of Turpenay [31] for comfort and escort, she set out on her journey of more than one hundred miles. She must have traveled day and night, possibly part of the way by river, for she reached her son's hospice as if borne by the wind.[32]

Coeur-de-Lion was already beyond the reach of his physicians and her own agonized ministrations. Only the offices of his chaplain, Milo, who had accompanied him on crusade [33] and attended other illnesses, any longer availed. But the king had time to pour into his mother's ears his last testament. Their covenant to recognize John as the heir was reiterated and some personal gifts to Otto were designated, together with such small sums as Richard could commend to charity for the repose of his soul. In his last hours he manifested the magnanimity and compunction that had at other times impressed the chroniclers. It is said indeed that he condemned the surrendered garrison of Châlus to be hanged, but this order is perhaps to be attributed to Mercadier or others of his following. Hoveden relates that when all Coeur-de-Lion's testamentary affairs had been arranged, he ordered his slayer to be brought to his presence. This felon proved to be an obscure youth of the Limousin whose name is variously recorded.[34] Haled in chains into the chamber where the king lay, he was placed at the foot of the royal couch, where he stood terrified but with a desperate bravado. From his story it appeared that on the fatal day he had manned the barbican from dawn to dusk, launching from the shelter of a huge frying pan employed as shield whatever enemy missiles he could pluck from clefts in the walls. The shot that fatally wounded the king with his own arrow gave the youth, in spite of his chains, the character of avenger for the impious Lenten assault on Châlus, and this realization perhaps moved Richard to his last act of chivalry.

"Why," said the king, "did you wish to injure me?"

"Because," replied the youth, "you slew my father and my brother. Do with me as you will. I do not repent me of the vengeance I have taken."

"Go hence in peace," said Coeur-de-Lion. "I forgive you my death and will exact no revenge. By my bounty behold the light of day." [35]

Thereupon, to the edification of the whole company, the king ordered the young man unshackled and dismissed him, not only with his pardon but with a gift in token of the fullness of his mercy. The chroniclers, however, add a feudal footnote to the incident. They relate that the youth was later flayed alive; by one account, on order of Mercadier; by another, at the command of Joanna Plantagenet.[36]

When all else had been done, Richard made a salutary confession to Milo, his chaplain, in the course of which he avowed that he had indeed betrayed his father in his last days to the King of the Franks, that archenemy of his house, and asked that, as evidence of his belated penitence, he be laid to rest at Henry's feet in the crypt of the nuns at Fontevrault. He admitted that, upon the advice of his spiritual counselors, he had abstained from the sacrament because of his hatred of Philip Augustus; but now he put hate away.[37] He had stormed Châlus in the holy season of Lent, and for this impiety he made atonement. In his final dispositions he bestowed his lion's heart on Rouen, where the body of the young king already lay in the necropolis of the Norman dukes. No relic was bequeathed to England, the land of his nativity; and Poitou won only foul remains in token of its betrayals.[38] In his last hours his thoughts went back to the Rock, whither he sent messengers with his seal to seek out Guillaume le Maréchal and the Archbishop of Canterbury with instructions from himself and the stricken queen. On the 6th of April Abbé Milo gave him absolution and communion, and when his ghost passed in the gathering darkness, the man of God bathed his brow with balm and closed his eyes upon the world, its golden treasures, the advent of spring, and the destiny of the Plantagenets.[39]

Martel, where the young king had breathed his last, lay hardly a hundred miles away in the same deep heart of the Limousin. As she gazed upon the noble figure of Coeur-de-Lion, Queen Eleanor must have recalled the vision of that other fair young man that had visited her in her prison at the time of his passing, wearing his double crown. It must have cut her like a sword thrust that, of all the Winchester eaglets, only John remained — John, the fondling of Henry Fitz-Empress, the fiercest, the most ungovernable of all the brood; that he who had been Lackland now grasped the inheritance of all his elder brothers.

Richard was forty-two and he died childless save for one bastard son known as Philippe of Cognac, who was about fifteen at the time of his father's death.[40] As for the fatal treasure of Châlus, no more is heard of it. From the court of Ventadour, where for three generations poets had never ceased to sing, Gaucelm Faidit launched his *planh* for Coeur-de-Lion. But poetic ardor had waned in the Limousin. Gaucelm jangles the conventional coins of the troubadour, but fails to give his lament the note of personal grief that runs through Bertran de Born's elegy for the young king.

"Ah God," exclaims Faidit, "the valiant King of the English is no more. . . Of all *preux chevaliers* he was the first. . . A thousand years shall never see his peer, so openhanded, noble, brave, and generous. . . Men that love truth will say not Charlemagne nor Arthur outmatched his valorous deeds." [41]

While Richard was in captivity, Eleanor, writing to the Pope in his behalf, reminded Celestine of her previous losses. "My posterity," she wrote, "has been snatched from me. . . The young king and the Count of Brittany sleep in the dust. Their unhappy mother is forced to live on, ceaselessly tormented by their memory." Of Richard in duress she moaned, "I have lost the staff of my age, the light of my eyes."

These words, recalled in her final loss, go nearer to the heart than the clichés of the poet.

31 ✠

Lackland's Portion

Now the clamor of war resounds not only in the high places, but in the remote corners of the realm. The people are filled with dismay. Fear creeps into the towns and villages. No place is safe, neither the bourg as refuge nor the open country as a way of escape. Men know not whether it is safer to flee or to stay.[1]

Magna Vita Sancti Hugonis, 282

NEAR THE END OF LENT IN 1199, Hugh, Bishop of Lincoln, was in the neighborhood of Le Mans on episcopal business. Incidentally he was bending his way to Angers to replace the absent bishop of that city in the services of Palm Sunday. Hugh was traveling with his wonted simplicity, mounted on a horse bare of housings, with his baggage, which was trussed up in hides and coarse blankets, tied behind his saddle, his outfit an unspoken sermon of rebuke to the clerks who rode with him on well-trapped hackneys, their more abundant goods laden on sumpter beasts that followed after.[2] As he jogged along he was surprised to fall in with the little retinue of the Abbess Matilda of Fontevrault, still abroad on her mission from Queen Eleanor to Berengaria, and she put into his ear the dreadful secret tidings that had been entrusted to her.[3]

Hugh, like Saint Bernard, whose disciple he was, had been a mentor of kings, and he was near to the Plantagenets. Henry Fitz-Empress had loved him like a brother for his disarming guilelessness, and it was known that he could disenthrall Coeur-de-Lion from his passions by his fearless refusal to be cowed by anger; so Hugh had long been a boon to harassed liege men of the Angevins. Revolving the purport of Matilda's tidings with anxious mind, the bishop resumed his journey with his clerks. Two or three days later he was accosted by Gilbert de Laci, a citizen of Saumur, with news of Richard's death and the plans for his burial next day at Fontevrault.[4]

By this time, in spite of efforts to keep the matter secret, the king's cortege from Châlus had published the calamity, and rumors flying their mysterious course faster than horses' hoofs could carry them spread consternation far and wide. In market and tavern, churchyard and hall, men huddled together whispering their dread. Who would now be strong enough to hold the heartland of the Angevin empire, divided as it was among the adherents of Arthur of Brittany and Philip Augustus and the brothers Plantagenet? Few doubted the authority of Eleanor, but the queen was old.

How could she, who had just lost the staff of her age, meet her adversaries? Many castellans drew into their strongholds and victualed them for siege. There was a sudden holiday for brigands, and little men lay low in their burrows waiting to see.

The clerks of Hugh of Lincoln urged him to take shelter from the dangers of the highway; but instead the bishop, forsaking the duties awaiting him in Angers, took a by-route through a dark forest to visit Berengaria, who, he learned, was lodged in the castle of Beaufort, possibly on her way to Châlus or Fontevrault.[5] He found the young queen mourning her loss inconsolably. Hugh celebrated mass at Beaufort and then, having sustained Berengaria with words of wisdom and devotion, he traveled on the same day to Saumur, where he passed the night in Gilbert de Laci's house.

The next day, Palm Sunday, he reached Fontevrault just in time to meet the cortege of Coeur-de-Lion as it arrived from Châlus in the precincts of the abbey. Here crowds were already swarming from a wide radius — Cardinal Peter of Capua whom Richard had charged never to cross his path again, seneschals of neighboring provinces, clergy, relatives, suppliants made anxious by a change of regime.[6] Berengaria and Matilda of Perche, the daughter of Matilda Plantagenet, had joined Queen Eleanor. It was the most cherished privilege of Bishop Hugh to perform offices for the dead. With the Bishops of Agen, Poitiers, and Angers, Milo the Chaplain, the Abbé of Turpenay, and other prelates who had gathered, Hugh assisted with the rites. Because of his ancient ties with the Plantagenets, he remained to console the bereaved for three more days during which, with mass and psalmody, he commended to eternal felicity not only the two Angevin kings entombed together in the crypt, but all the faithful souls asleep in Christ in the shelter of the abbey.

John Plantagenet did not arrive in time for the obsequies. He had latterly been at odds with Richard, who, lacking funds himself, had shortened his cadet's allowances. The news of Richard's calamity found John in Brittany, conniving, as some believed, to draw his nephew Arthur of Brittany into some new design with himself and Philip Augustus against Coeur-de-Lion. But when the sudden disaster in Châlus cut across his plans, he dropped his affair with Arthur, whatever it may have been, and "incautiously," as the *Magna Vita* states, "let his nephew slip from his grasp," while he himself made haste to secure the Angevin treasure and stronghold in Chinon.

In the meantime Hugh of Lincoln, on his way home from Fontevrault after the three days' mourning, passed by Chinon. John, aware of the advantage of being seen in the company of that man of good repute, besought the bishop to join his household and retinue and continue the good offices he had rendered to the Plantagenets who were no more.[7]

The bishop was by no means happy over the prospect of the new regime. For one thing, as a good Cistercian, Hugh clung to the idea that Eleanor's marriage to Henry had been adulterous and that nothing excellent could be expected from any of the "spurious" Angevin brood. John was now thirty-two and Hugh had known him from childhood, the cleverest, the most in-tractable, and certainly the slipperiest of the Plantagenet eaglets; the deserter of his father in his last days, betrayer of his brother in his captivity, ruthless, sudden, guided by no steady purpose, a shameless troth-breacher. He turned back with the prince in no very optimistic hope, even in this moment of solemnity, of subduing John's levity, his irreverence, his vainglory, of im-buing him with a sense of royal obligation. Without consenting to join the prince's household, he retraced his steps with him to Fontevrault for a con-ference with Queen Eleanor. In the days of this sojourn John gave the mourners a preview of his sovereign role.

The heir of the Plantagenets arrived out of season at the portals of the abbey. However, being now master of events and impatient, he beat upon the gates importunately. The clamor brought two nuns to the grill. In re-sponse to his imperious demands, they replied, with voices decently sub-dued, that it was permitted to no mortal to visit the crypt or the enclosures of the abbey out of hours while the abbess was away. "Having thus spoken," says the chronicler, "these prudent virgins restrained the knocking prince out-side, and having carefully locked the door, returned to their cloister." [8]

In the few days that John and the bishop spent together at Fontevrault, Hugh labored to awaken in the heir some traces of Angevin greatness. His precepts were monitory. He exposed the vices that beset men in high place — hypocrisy, vainglory, superstition, arrogance, impiety. For a time John, aware of a want of cordiality among those over whom he had been called to rule, sought to ingratiate himself. He took Hugh's lectures with a show of meek-ness; he listened to advice, promised good works, and proffered an alms from the newly found resources of Chinon. To all these protestations the bishop replied that he would let good works, if they were accomplished, speak for themselves.

The bishop and the prince were together one morning in the narthex of the chapel, and there Hugh drew John's attention to sculptures depicting the Last Judgment, where the wicked kings of earth were being consigned by fiends to eternal fire; but John, no whit appalled, turned to the opposite wall, where righteous kings were being led by joyful angels to everlasting felicity.

"You ought," said John, "to have shown me this scene, for it is the example of these kings that I intend to follow, and it is the fellowship of these that I expect to attain."

Since Easter was upon them, Hugh stayed over to celebrate for the con-siderable congregation still assembled about the abbey. The bishop got his paschal theme from the incident in the narthex. With the heir of the

Plantagenets compelled to sit before him under the eyes of the assembly, he preached an exhaustive sermon, thoroughly documented with scriptural citation, on the character of good and evil kings, a sermon that drew tears of unction from those on whose ears it fell. The congregation, well pleased with the timeliness of Hugh's discourse, listened with patient approbation long past the time for benediction. But John's temper, worn thin by the week's constraints, showed itself in new exhibitions of levity.

Three times during the sermon, he sent messages to the pulpit calling upon Hugh to put a term to his observations, and reminding him that it was high time to break the Lenten fast. When his suggestions were ignored, he scandalized the worshipers by jangling the coins he had brought for the offering. At this wanton disturbance, Hugh addressed the prince directly.

"What are you doing there?" he asked. And John, as if he intended to provoke that very question, replied,

"I am considering these gold pieces and thinking that, if I had had them a few days ago, I should not have given them to you, but swept them into my own wallet."

Hugh, says the chronicler, "blushed for the impiety."

"Cast them into the dish," said the bishop, "and leave the sanctuary."

The congregation dispersed with dismayed commentary. It was remembered that it had been John's custom, since "the age of reason," to refuse communion.[9]

⚜

In Normandy, too, the advent of John was received with a temperate enthusiasm, even by the liege men of the Plantagenets. Guillaume le Maréchal, to whom Richard had sent his seal a few days before his death, was in his lodgings not far from Rouen when the fatal tidings came. He had taken off his shoes for bed when the messenger from Châlus arrived at his door. Filled with foreboding, Guillaume dressed again and hastened to the hospice of the Archbishop of Canterbury.

"Ah," groaned Hubert Walter, "the king is dead! What hope is left to us? There is no one in sight that can defend the kingdom. I foresee the French will overrun us."

"We must," said Guillaume, "make all haste to choose his successor."

"In my opinion," declared the archbishop, "we ought to choose Arthur."

"Ah Sire," rejoined the marshal, "that would not do. Arthur is in the hands of evil counselors, and he is stormy and stiff-necked. He hates the English, and if we put him at our head, we shall suffer for it. . . John as the heir stands nearer to the king his father than this boy."

"Maréchal," replied the archbishop, "it shall be as you say, but I warn you that you will regret this more than any decision you ever made."

"Perhaps," groaned Guillaume, "but still I believe it best." [10]

Thereupon messengers were sent to England to prepare the islanders to receive their king. No one in England wanted Arthur, a youth and an alien in the custody of counselors whose stakes were on the Continent; but it took the best arts of faithful Guillaume and other justiciars who had sustained the regency to pave the way for John. A council of magnates met in protest in Nottingham to review John's perfidies and his banishment from Britain during the captivity. However, for want of a more acceptable heir, they consented in the end to accept the youngest Plantagenet upon condition of solemn commitments at the time of coronation.[11]

⚜

At the end of Richard's reign Queen Eleanor, who had survived so many kings, was seventy-seven. How could she, burdened with years, prevail against the avalanche of calamity that now threatened her from every side? Again, as during the crusade and the captivity, the inexorable movement for the dismemberment of the Angevin empire took on momentum. The advance had seemed to be checked by Plantagenet valor and contrivance after the return of Coeur-de-Lion; but now once more the ground trembled under her feet and she saw the fateful oncoming advanced by a score of years and threatening to come within the compass of her "life-days in the world."

She had supported many crises with the Angevins, but none so desperate as this. On the accession of Coeur-de-Lion she had been obliged to ingratiate a son scarcely known to his subjects, but nevertheless the unquestioned heir and a resplendent figure for exploitation. Now she was summoned to support one whose claim to the empire was in question and whose infamy was notorious, and known to no one more certainly than to herself. Yet John, of all that royal brood of eaglets she had brought to the dynasty, was the only one of her posterity whose interests would lead him to oppose the partition of the empire she had helped to build. Berengaria had failed; Otto's destiny was cast in the Holy Roman Empire; Arthur of Brittany could only be Philip's instrument for the dismemberment. And nothing was more certain than that Philip would seize his moment. Indeed, he had already seized it.

On Easter, while Hugh of Lincoln was detaining his congregation to hear the fate of evil kings, the Bretons, under their Countess Constance, and many barons of Maine and Anjou under the leadership of a powerful Angevin baron, Guillaume des Roches, took possession, in the name of Arthur of Brittany, of Angers,[12] hardly ten leagues from Fontevrault; and thereupon Le Mans yielded to the same coalition,[13] which proclaimed the boy Arthur, on grounds of primogeniture, the rightful heir not only of Brittany, but of the Angevin domains. Moreover, while this confederation occupied the capital cities of Maine and Anjou, the barons of the Limousin, roused by Richard's recent campaign against the Count of Limoges, were spreading sedition in the south. And the heart of the general revolt was seen to be Philip Augustus, who, on learning of Richard's death, hastened down the Loire valley to Tours, whence, as from the center of a spider's web, he could find commerce with the "traitors" and direct all movements toward the realization of his Carolingian dream.

For Queen Eleanor in her travail and bereavement, there was no respite for fatigue or grief. In the midst of requiems she gathered her counsels and in these she did not spare herself. Mercadier had accompanied the king's cortege from Châlus. He at once drew his *routiers* from their operations in the Limousin. With these forces, and under the escort of that tough old campaigner of Henry Fitz-Empress and Coeur-de-Lion, Eleanor went herself to the recovery of Angers. At her approach Constance and Arthur and the ringleaders fell back upon Le Mans, while the *routiers* ravaged the capital of Anjou and took from the citizenry a throng of prisoners.

In the meantime John with another force went northward from the region of Fontevrault to secure Le Mans. There the insurgents were too hastily rallied to withstand the seasoned troops of the Plantagenets, even within the fortifications of the mount. John, when he had forced the gates, took a terrible vengeance upon the traitors. The old capital of Maine reeked as it had reeked thirteen years before when Henry in his last battle fled from its walls. What was not burned was razed, and many of the citizens were taken captive. But Arthur and Constance, who had escaped from Eleanor at Angers, eluded John also in Le Mans.

The sagacious Plantagenets had long been seeking to secure the person of Arthur, if only to keep him from the "protective" custody of Philip Augustus. They had no sooner brought John back to the bosom of his own dynasty by agreeing among themselves on his succession than, for John's sake, they began efforts to win control of Arthur. Twice they had bungled. Three years before his death, Richard had made a strong move to gain custody of the young count, so that he might rear him in his own court to a proper view of his destiny. At this time he had summoned Constance to Normandy to do homage for herself and the boy, who until then had been in her tutelage. On her way from Nantes to Rouen a curious incident cut her journey short. As she moved along the marches, Ranulf of Chester, the husband that Henry Fitz-Empress had bestowed upon her to keep her within the Plantagenet confederation,[14] arrested her, for reasons not related, and shut her up in his castle of Saint James de Beuvron in Normandy near the Breton frontier, with the consequence that Arthur was not remanded by the Bretons to the Norman court.[15]

This Bluebeard proceeding, the significance of which is itself obscure, had however a sequel that affected the destiny of Arthur; for Constance was presently separated from Ranulf of Chester and married Guy, a younger brother of the Count of Thouars.[16] The huge fief of the family of Thouars lay on the marches of Brittany and Poitou, a bridge between the two provinces; and the counts were bound by ancient ties of relationship and feudal service to the house of Poitou. The marriage of Guy and Constance occurred at about the time of Richard's death, and the sudden alliance gave new anxiety to the Plantagenets, since it pointed to possible new understandings between Philip Augustus in connivance with the Bretons and Queen Eleanor's rebel vassals in the Limousin, and to a new guardianship for Arthur. It was perhaps in some connection with this disturbing alliance that John was found, at the time of Richard's death, in the company of Arthur in Le Mans. But the sudden emergency of his own succession led him, as the *Magna Vita* observes, "incautiously" to allow his nephew for a second time to escape the custody of the Plantagenets.

In the taking of Le Mans, in spite of his triumphs, John failed to get possession of his nephew, who now eluded the Plantagenets for the third time. In the night by stealth Constance and Guy, with the help of the Count of Thouars, spirited the lad away to Tours, where Philip, who was conveniently waiting there, took him into his protection and at once sent him to the greater security of Paris.[17] The boy was now thirteen and fit for knightly exercise. Philip established him in his palace, where, as boon fellow of his own son and heir, who was about the same age, Arthur made what he could of dialectic under the best of tutors. Like any loyal Frank, he made his pilgrimage to Saint Denis, besought the suffrage of that patron saint, and as token of his piety and devotion, offered a silken mantle upon the altar.[18] In Paris the Count of Brittany was bred to delusions of grandeur. He learned to regard himself as the incontestable heir not only of Brittany, but of Maine, Anjou, Touraine . . . of Poitou, when his grandmother Queen Eleanor should be dead or dispossessed. England and Normandy floated more distantly in his vision.

✤

Eleanor, turning back from the rout of the Bretons in Angers, at once set forth again from her headquarters in the abbey, this time to secure her own provinces from the anarchy that Richard's last campaigns in the Limousin had reawakened and that his death had unloosed. She had the makings of an escort among those gathered about her in Fontevrault, and to these she added recruits along the way. With an imposing retinue of bishops and nobles, she moved majestically into her own estates. Avoiding the region of Richard's last exploits, she cleared a wide swath through her domains from Poitiers to Bordeaux and the frontiers of Spain. Henry Plantagenet himself could hardly have covered more ground nor accomplished more objects in the same space of time.

On this journey she did not exploit John as her heir, as she had once paraded Richard, for her vassals were weary of Angevins. She went through her provinces as duchess of her own domains, showing herself a paragon of largess and magnanimity on the highways and in the towns where feasts and fairs drew gatherings of the people. Wherever she arrived came those who had supplications to make, old grievances to redress, claims to adjudicate. With whatever pangs of secret dread, she paid out, like jewels plucked from her coronet, domains and tithes and privileges that once enriched her inheritance, buying therewith the support of seigneurs and abbés who flocked to her presence as fast as their hackneys could bring them, each eager to grasp his portion while the treasure was abundant. In these barters she laid hands on some of the properties with which the Plantagenets had dowered the futile Berengaria; and when she could, she traded mere estates for strongholds; thus she exchanged even the favorite hunting grounds of the Counts of Poitou and the Angevin kings in the Talmont for assets more practical.

However, her most striking success was popular. As at the time of Richard's accession, a sound instinct advised her to appeal for the suffrage she needed to the nascent third estate. In that earlier crisis, "knowing how irksome it is to be a prisoner," she had emptied dungeons and relaxed laws that Henry had let fall oppressively on common folk. Now, with like prescience, she addressed herself to the aspirations of that *bourgeoisie* rising in wealth and power in all the larger centers. She turned her eyes on those agglomerations of merchants and artisans that in her lifetime had settled haphazardly outside the episcopal walled towns that marked the main thoroughfares of trade and pilgrimage, those huddled urban populations distinct from clerks, yet free from serfdom on baronial soil. To those anomalous folk, troublesome by their very nature to prelate and seigneur, she showed her favor. In the course of a journey that lasted from late April to mid-July, she visited Loudun and Poitiers, Niort, Andelly, La Rochelle, Saintes, Saint Jean d'Angély, Bordeaux, and many other populous places, and presently at least five of these received from their duchess their charters as communes.[19] Did she understand that these new associations of the burghers at the crossroads of travel were presently to impose law on the ancient brigandage and anarchy of the elder estates?

On this good-will tour[20] the duchess did not of course overlook the religious foundations of the south. Among others she visited the Grande-Sauve near Bordeaux. There she was shown a deed of privilege that recalled old times. It was fixed with the seal of Thomas Becket the Chancellor and it revived the memory of the sanguine days when she and Henry had made their first *chevauchée* through her patrimonial estates. In commemoration of those days, she indited a new letter patent to the monastery.

> Eleanor, by the grace of God, Queen of England, Duchess of Normandy and Guienne, Countess of Anjou, to the archbishops, bishops, abbés, salutation. The late King Henry, our very dear husband of gracious memory, and we ourselves long ago took the monastery of the Grande-Sauve under our special protection. But that Henry, as well as our son Richard, who succeeded him, having both since died, and God having left us still in the world, we have been obliged, in order to provide for the needs of our people and the welfare of our lands, to visit Gascony. We have been brought in the course of our journey to this monastery . . . and we have seen that it is a holy place. For this reason we have commended both ourselves and the souls of those kings to the prayers of this community; and that our visit may not have been unserviceable, we hereby confirm the ancient privileges of this foundation.[21]

When she had reassured and tranquilized her own domains, the queen set forth directly on the most difficult part of her whole mission, this time to Tours. Here in the city whose castle and bourg belonged to the heritage of Anjou, her painful necessity brought her face to face with her unspeakable overlord, Philip Augustus, Dieu-Donné, scion of Louis Capet, the betrayer of Coeur-de-Lion, the suborner of John, the custodian of her grandson, Arthur of Brittany. Eleanor saw clearly that the odious thing she had determined upon would have to be done, and somehow she got through with it. In Tours the old queen rendered her homage in person to Philip for all her patrimony south of the Loire. This legal act, however painful, was indispensable to her design, for it had the merit of excluding John explicitly from any present claim to her inheritance. However, for the sake of the future, as soon as the ordeal of homage had passed, she had a new document prepared in which she designated her "very dear son John" as her heir in Poitou and Aquitaine, but withheld to herself sole sovereignty over her provinces for the days of her life. Thus ended any possibility of Arthur of Brittany's laying claim to Poitou in prejudice of John, no matter what might occur in the Angevin domains north of the Loire.[22] In the interests of the Angevin empire, the queen had made in three months of summer heat a progress of more than a thousand miles.

Having by these acts regulated the prospects of her posterity, she closed her chancellery on the Vienne for the time being and hastened before the end of July to rejoin John in Rouen; for her dearest hope was still unrealized — the consummation of that compact made before Richard's death for the marriage of her granddaughter of Castile to the heir of Philip. To this alliance she especially looked as a means of checking for a blessed interval the aggressions of the Capets.

⚜

In Rouen as autumn approached the remnants of the Plantagenets forgathered with their magnates to review events and coördinate their enterprise. But here domestic matters upset the routine of chancelleries. The court
was distracted by the disasters of Joanna. The remarriage of the former Queen
of Sicily, which had retrieved Toulouse for the Plantagenets, had been ill
starred, and her prosperity had rapidly declined.

Joanna had rejoined Eleanor in Niort, in the course of the queen's recent
Poitevin tour, in a state of desperation. Her story was that, while Count
Raymond was off on the edges of creation in warfare with some of his vassals,
she had been called upon herself to suppress revolt in another quarter of the
south. She had had good lessons in military strategy on crusade, but here in
a corner of Toulouse she had fallen victim to a treachery that no science and
no valor could forestall. Some of Raymond's own knights had betrayed her
to the very castellans upon whom she had brought her siege engines to bear,
had provided them with victuals and men, and then, as a climax of perfidy,
had set fire to her bivouac. Joanna had escaped by the skin of her teeth. She
had been on her way to bespeak redress from Coeur-de-Lion, when, hearing
of the calamity at Châlus, she had turned aside to find the queen in Niort.
From Niort Eleanor had sent her to recuperate in care of the nuns in Fontevrault.

Joanna now arrived in Rouen to make her affairs a matter of consideration
in the counsels of the Plantagenets.[23] Especially, since Raymond had not provided for her needs, she required a living allowance from the royal exchequer.
When she arrived she was in an advanced state of pregnancy, sick, worn with
fatigue and desperation, convinced that her days were numbered. She insisted on making her will, designating the small gifts at her disposal to the
abbey that had been her nursery and her refuge, for the maintenance of the
nuns' kitchen that had been built through the liberality of Queen Eleanor.

Then, to the consternation of the pious persons at her bedside, she demanded to be made a nun of Fontevrault so that she might put off vainglory
and end her days in the trappings of poverty and humility. Her demand was
of course irregular, but majesty was imperious. Joanna so persisted that a
messenger was sent to Fontevrault to fetch the abbess for consultation. When
it was realized that Matilda might not arrive in time to receive the postulant,
Joanna summoned the Archbishop of Canterbury, who was in the court, and
entreated him to consecrate her to the order. Hubert Walter was, like all the
others, edified by the aspirations of Joanna and moved by the anguish of
Queen Eleanor, but he demurred from presuming upon the functions of
Matilda, who might at any time arrive. In reasoning with the Countess of
Toulouse, he kept as far as possible to generalities, explaining that there was
nothing in the canons to provide for the admission of one spouse to a religious
order while the other lived, and nothing to cover the case of her unborn

child. But Joanna was not to be thwarted by obscurations of the law. She insisted with so much zeal and fervor that she wore down the canonists who were obviously not to be given much time for dialectic. A conference was called of nuns and clerks and all agreed that such conviction of vocation was inspired by heaven. With the consent of this council, the archbishop offered the countess to God and the order, in the presence of Queen Eleanor and many pious witnesses. There was just time. In September 1199 Joanna, aged thirty-four, closed her eyes upon the world.[24] A few minutes after her death, she was delivered of a son, who survived long enough to receive baptism. She had already in 1197 borne Count Raymond a son and heir;[25] but the adherence of Toulouse, for which such efforts had been made, again became, through the inconstancy of Raymond, uncertain and tenuous.

Queen, crusader, countess, nun. If Joanna's career had ended early, it had nevertheless offered a vast gamut of experience and had been characterized at every stage by Plantagenet gallantry. The ending of the Sicilian court, the squandering of her rich substance on crusade, the marriage of Toulouse, brought her swiftly, in a nun's garb, to the narrow gate. To worldlings her progress was, in fortune, downward in a swift decline; but to the ministrants who closed her eyes, a swift ascent to glory. Coeur-de-Lion, whom Joanna had idolized, was only five months dead. When the old queen counted her brood again in Rouen, only two of all the ten remained — John at her side, and Eleanor in faraway Castile.

32 ✢

Blanche and Isabella

FOR THE REALIZATION of Philip Augustus' aspirations in the west, the death of Coeur-de-Lion had been premature. The Capetian was not quite ready for a new onslaught on the Plantagenets when the necessity to support Arthur of Brittany's succession confronted him. He had expected more time for the ripening of his plans; time for Arthur to reach his majority and become himself a champion to rally the Bretons; time to secure a more solid adherence among the vassals of the Angevin domains. However, he seized the occasion, while the Plantagenets were establishing John's succession, to ravage the frontiers of Normandy and to take into his custody castles belonging to Arthur on the marches of Anjou. In these operations his zeal for conquest at last aroused the apprehensions of many Angevins who had at first collaborated with him. These barons reflected sagely that they had not abandoned the Plantagenets to be swallowed body and bones by the Capets. Guillaume des Roches, the Angevin who, as surety for Arthur, had at first abetted Philip, protested the manning of certain of Arthur's castles with Frankish garrisons as going beyond the articles of agreement; and Philip in reply advised Guillaume that he would do as he thought best with castles secured by Frankish arms. The answer expressed one of those failures of perception that now and then blurred the clear vision of Dieu-Donné. The Angevin magnates thereupon put their heads together, consulted their own interests in the dynastic confusions that prevailed, and waited for events to point their course.

John, presumably escorting his sister's cortege from Rouen to Fontevrault, took shrewd occasion to pass by Le Mans while the barons were in their doubtful state of mind. In the ruins of that city or nearby, the new king achieved a contact with Guillaume des Roches, as the chroniclers declare, by dint of bribes and promises.[1] Arthur, in the temporary custody of Constance, was in the neighborhood. In the interview John persuaded Guillaume to renounce Philip Augustus and return to the allegiance of the Plantagenets, and he induced him, as earnest of honest intentions, to transfer the Count of Brittany from the "protection" of Philip to his own custody. The plot was hardly hatched when Constance and the brothers Thouars got wind of it, and they, absconding with Arthur in the night, remanded him to Paris. Again, but by the barest margin, the Count of Brittany slipped from his uncle's grasp.[2] For his "treachery" in facilitating the boy's escape, John dismissed Count Amaury of Thouars from the stewardship of Chinon and so from a long loyalty to the house of Poitou.

It was in these altered circumstances that Philip and John met soon after Christmas for reconsideration of the truce, involving the marriage of Louis of France to a princess of Castile, that had been broken off by Richard's death. The recent events in Anjou made Philip a little less arrogant than when the matter of this compact had been broached in August. He relinquished his claims in the name of Arthur to Maine and Anjou and agreed that the Count of Brittany should do homage to John for Brittany alone; but he refused under any terms to surrender custody of the youth. John, on his side, renewed King Richard's agreement to yield up the Norman Vexin, besides the County of Evreux in Normandy proper, and to pay a sum of 30,000 marks of silver. These latter concessions were granted not as an empty forfeit, but as a dower for a princess of Castile, who was by the articles affianced to the heir of the Capets.[3]

The agreement was no sooner reaffirmed than Queen Eleanor, whose *mesnie* must have been already mounted, herself set forth on the long pilgrim route to Spain to fetch a granddaughter for the throne of France. This was a mission she could entrust to no one. As she moved with her escort past ford and bridge and town, she must have reviewed in memory the cavalcade of five hundred *preux chevaliers*, the best of France, whom Louis the Fat had sent down to Bordeaux more than sixty years before to lead her to the Capetian throne. The queen's procession moved rapidly, for Eleanor felt the urgency of clinching the bargain with the Capets.

Her route [4] obliged her to pass through the fief of the brothers Lusignan and over the stretch of road where a quarter of a century before scions of the same broilsome house had waylaid her for a boon; whence Guy of Lusignan, having slain her bodyguard, was exiled to his glorious fate in Palestine; and where Guillaume le Maréchal had won his first knightly laurels in her rescue. The same brigandly tribe, led by Hugues le Brun, cut off her passage now and held her for the forfeit of the County of La Marche, which Henry Fitz-Empress had long ago acquired in a hard bargain with the Lusignans.[5] The affair of La Marche was one of the grievances the queen had overlooked in the course of her good-will tour. The county was wide and rich and it lay dangerously on her highway from Poitiers to Bordeaux. To surrender it was to yield a border rallying place for enemies in adjoining provinces. As was her wont when confronted with dilemma, she took the course, however painful, that was remediable. She understood the irony of ransom and the folly of opposing brigandage with dialectic, so she yielded up the county for the freedom to proceed;[6] but she marked the brothers Lusignan in her archives for future reference. Beyond the ambush she made her way with incredible speed through Gascony and over the Pyrenees, and arrived in mid-January in the opulent courts of Castile.

Queen Eleanor had to go back years to conjure up the memory of her namesake daughter, though she may possibly have laid eyes on her once or twice in an interval of more than three decades. In the midst of administering her own Poitevin court in the gay seventies of the century, the queen had herself accompanied her daughter to Bordeaux, where the envoys of Alfonso of Castile had received the younger Eleanor and led her off to Spain for her brilliant betrothal in Tarragona and her splendid marriage in Burgos.[7] Though the little damsel went from the court of Poitiers in the days of its prime, she was perhaps too young to have been polished to the luster of a *dame choisie*; yet some believe that she carried over the Pyrenees as part of her bridal furnishings those Arthurian tales that had so enthralled her mother's court.[8] In going to Castile she had gone to one of the fountainheads of those refined rituals which the Countess of Champagne had sought to impose in Poitou. The troubadour Ramón Vidal has preserved a fleeting glimpse of the Princess Eleanor Plantagenet as queen in the elegant court of Alfonso VIII.

> *And when the King had summoned to his court*
> *Many a knight, rich baron, and jongleur,*
> *And the company had assembled,*
> *Then came Queen Leonore*
> *Modestly clad in a mantle of rich stuff,*
> *Red, with a silver border wrought*
> *With golden lions.*
> *She bows to the King*
> *And near him takes her seat.*[9]

The Plantagenets gave their daughters in marriage prudently, and the lot of Eleanor, like that of Joanna in Sicily, had been rosy and prosperous. Now in middle age the Queen of Castile was gracious, pious, learned, wise, still beautiful, the patroness alike of prelates, grandees, and troubadours. Eleanor found in Burgos and Toledo the full flowering of those civilized customs so rudely broken off in Poitiers by Henry's invasion of her palace and her own long captivity. The Spanish days and nights were too short for all the history that had piled up in the epos of the Plantagenets.

Eleven children eventually blessed the house of Castile, and six or eight of them were on hand to greet the venerable grandmother whose vicissitudes had certainly made the substance of their nursery wonder tales. Several comely girls, three of them of marriageable age, confronted the judges who had come to select a queen for France. Among them, if Eleanor had only had the happiness to know it, there were, in spite of Abbé Bernard's certainty that the Angevins would return to Satan whence they came, two princesses destined to become the mothers of saints.[10] Though this ultimate glory was veiled from her, the old queen had the clairvoyance to choose one of these for France. Berengaria, the eldest of the three, being already betrothed to the heir of León, was not available.[11]

A late Spanish chronicle [12] reports that the next two, Urraca and Blanche, were adorned with royal splendor and brought before the queen and the envoys for performance and audition. Both were beautiful, well taught, distinguished in manner, in every way meet to be queens. But it was generally supposed that Urraca would be chosen on grounds of seniority, and for this reason she was somewhat more richly accoutered and more exploited in the court. However, Eleanor, who, as everyone admitted, was a shrewd judge of people (*admirabilis astuciae*), found some undeclared reason for preferring Blanche as a queen for the Capets. Since French history confirms the soundness of her judgment, she cannot be accused of rancor in her choice. The envoys, put to it to justify their curious preference to the Spaniards, explained that the name of Urraca was bound to seem harsh and alien to the Franks, but that Blanche would roll easily in the *langue d'oïl* spoken in the Île. Thereupon Urraca was assuaged by betrothal to the heir of Portugal, and Blanche was made ready for her surprising destiny.

Easter was at hand and the marriage designed to compose the enmity between the Capets and the Plantagenets was set for the end of Lent. At this season the roads of Galicia swarmed with pilgrims, horse and foot, thronging to Saint James of Compostella, and Eleanor's thoughts must have turned with them to the shrine where her father lay in his palmer's grave before the altar. But she was already behind time and there was no possibility of joining their procession. Breasting the tide of pilgrims flowing westward, she pressed forward toward the storied pass of Roncevaux and soon brought her convoy down to the Gascon plains. In Bordeaux, safe within the moats and bastions of her own citadel, she rested from the fatigues of her journey, and her *mesnie* celebrated Easter with the Bordelais. Here from the galleries of the Ombrière, she could point out to Blanche the low hills of Larmont on the far side of the Garonne, where the magnates of France had pitched their gilded tents when they had come so long ago to fetch Eleanor herself for the throne of France.

While resting in Bordeaux and tutoring her grandchild betimes for the destiny to which she had been called, the queen suffered an untimely loss that the Plantagenets were much to rue. The joy and solemnity of Easter were broken by cries of alarm in the streets, and out of the sudden melee in the public square there rose the news that Mercadier, the captain of the *routiers*, was slain in some personal quarrel.[13] He had come from a vacation in his castle of Périgord to pay his respects to his liege lady, and probably to guard her *mesnie* as it ventured again into the valley of the Charente among the craggy lairs of seditious vassals. The devotion of this old campaigner went far back to Henry's time, and his loss left Eleanor with more than a sense of personal bereavement. Mercadier had been, since Richard's death, the best strategist devoted to her cause, a disciplined and capable commander of the *routiers* upon whom now,. since the good faith of so many vassals was in question, the Plantagenets more and more relied.

After this calamity the queen somehow reached the blessed haven of Fontevrault. But here her strength failed and she was unable to finish her journey to Normandy. Blanche, in custody of the Archbishop of Bordeaux, was dispatched to John, who entertained her with her escort at Gaillard until the Capets could be satisfied of Plantagenet good faith and affirm their acceptance of the princess that Eleanor had fetched from beyond the Pyrenees. The articles of the marriage were quickly certified. Philip, who at the moment was at odds with Rome over his private concerns, was awkwardly restrained from attending the marriage of his heir and the Princess of Castile, but he provided handsomely for the entertainment. The town of Piramor, just inside Normandy and so outside the bounds of interdict, was chosen as offering both fit ecclesiastical setting and a field for tournaments. The Archbishop of Bordeaux, who was untouched by the fulminations of Rome, performed the rites, and when these were over, the young cavaliers of Normandy and France vied in *belles passes d'armes* upon the lists. Arthur of Brittany, a youth of fourteen, still in the wardship of Philip and not yet knighted, disported himself upon the field before the pavilions of the royal spouses and the *dames choisies*. On the same day, with the French king's consent, he did homage to John for Brittany.[14]

Soon after the event, Bishop Hugh of Lincoln, on one of his episcopal peregrinations, passed through Paris. Philip Augustus was restrained by his alienation from the church from paying his respects to Hugh, but in his royal stead, Prince Louis and the Count of Brittany called upon the bishop in the house where he was lodged. Hugh embraced them both joyfully, and then, as his custom was with princes, bestowed upon each appropriate advice. Louis Capet, says the chronicler, received his admonitions deferentially, as his grandfather would have done; but Count Arthur manifested a deep rancor that burned in his breast when Hugh counseled him to keep peace and friendship with the King of England. Louis then besought Hugh to visit the young wife he had taken from the Plantagenets, because, as he explained, she had for days been cast down by "some recent occurrence" and the anxious bridegroom could hit upon nothing to raise her spirits. Such missions were precious to Hugh. He dealt so tenderly with the little bride that she "put off the sorrow that had oppressed her and put on a more cheerful countenance."[15] Had she too, when she had dismounted in the parvis royal by the ancient olive tree and ascended the long flight of hollow stairs leading to the palace of the Capets, felt dismay as she fronted her solemn spouse and as her memory flew back to sunny southern towns and the familiar children of her native palaces?

❧

King John was doomed by some mysterious judgment of heaven to make enemies of all his friends and to gather the withes for his own chastisement.
Philippide, VI, 155

When John was crowned King of England, Isabelle of Gloucester, to whom he had been married twelve years before at the time of Richard's accession, had not been crowned with him. The childless marriage, which had been arranged by Henry to secure for Lackland Isabelle's rich estates, had grown odious to both spouses; yet no English prelates had been found to dissolve it on grounds of consanguinity, inasmuch as a papal dispensation had been required to authorize it in the first place. John at thirty-three, like Richard at his accession, lacked an heir. That the Count of Brittany's claim to inheritance would soon be pressed anew was made certain by the fact that his mother Constance was now known to be a leper who could not long survive. A second marriage for John became a matter of first urgency for the Plantagenets. When the matter was pressed in these circumstances, prelates were found on the Continent to dissolve the union with Isabelle, who, for her part, made no resistance to their edict.[16]

Eleanor had no doubt revolved this concern of her dynasty in the course of her match-making journey to Spain. In northern Europe there was still a dearth of eligible princesses free from consanguinity or from suspicious alliances. In recent years the Plantagenets had turned southward to seek new relations. Henry had looked afield in the marriage of his two younger daughters to Mediterranean outposts; and Eleanor had gone to Navarre for Berengaria. Queen Eleanor, an important part of whose business it was to tutor and dispense marriage prizes, had certainly in the course of her journey, and with John's requirements in mind, reviewed the roster of Galician princesses; and since little Urraca of Castile, whose name had failed to please the Franks, had been forthwith affianced to the heir of Portugal, Eleanor had certainly made notes on the desirable princesses of that house, if they had not indeed passed in review before her.

After the peace had been concluded by the marriage of Louis Capet and Blanche of Castile, John, secure for a time in his relations with Philip Augustus, turned away from the Rock of Andelys to look after disorders in more distant quarters. But first he made a visit to Eleanor, who was still ill at Fontevrault. He had no sooner come to conclusions with her than he sent an embassy of bishops and knights to Galicia to bespeak one of the

Portuguese paragons for the crown of England. This cavalcade set forth to cross the Pyrenees in July 1200.[17]

While the envoys were on their way, John warily visited Poitou with the object of getting the queen's vassals in hand before the return of his embassy. The first important stage of his progress took him to the castle of the Lusignans. The brothers of that numerous tribe, appeased by their possession of the County of La Marche as a consequence of their ambush of Queen Eleanor, and impatient for royal confirmation of it, were now eager to make peace with the house of Poitou and even undertook to mediate a truce between John and the Counts of Limoges and Angoulême, with whom Richard had been at war in his last days; and these latter, having been comprehended in the general peace between John and Philip, were now prepared for reconciliation.[18] Hugues le Brun of Lusignan, who had so featly become Count of La Marche, had ties with Angoulême, for he was affianced to the heiress of Count Adémar. The grand accord at Lusignan, where all the parties gathered, was the occasion of a fete in the hospitable tradition of Poitou. Isabella of Angoulême, as Hugues's betrothed, was the *dame choisie* of the entertainments, a fair young marriage prize without a peer in all the Poitevin domains.

John, who was at the hour in a matrimonial humor, was violently attracted by the excellent beauty of Isabella, and various considerations arose in his mind as he surveyed her charms.[19] It at once occurred to him that her marriage to Hugues le Brun must at all hazards be averted, since it would link two of the most powerful houses in Poitou in a potential alliance against the Plantagenets; and that Hugues, in view of the rape of La Marche, was getting altogether more than his deserts. Briefly he rued having sent envoys to Portugal. Without sleeping much over the project that boiled up and took shape in his brain, he sought a parley with the Count of Angoulême, of which Isabella was the object. Before the count's lustful and astonished eyes, he hung up visions of a much more ambitious destiny for Isabella than that offered by Hugues le Brun. It was agreed, however, because of the certain wrath and known violence of the brothers Lusignan, to postpone execution to another more propitious time and place, and meantime to disarm their vengeance.

The far-reaching tribe of Lusignans, as old-time vassals of the Poitevins and the Plantagenets, held widely dispersed estates in England and Normandy, as well as in Poitou. John found pretexts for sending the brothers off on scattered missions to remote quarters, while Isabella, in the interval of their absence, made a prenuptial visit to her own home in Angoulême to prepare for her marriage to Hugues le Brun.

While the Lusignans were occupied abroad and Isabella was snugly in retirement, John went forward with his own itinerary, which took him by way of Bordeaux to Agen, where he arranged for the interest of Joanna's son in the properties of Toulouse.[20] Somewhere on the way his *mesnie* unobtrusively picked up the Archbishop of Bordeaux. On the 23rd of August, a little more than a month from the visit to Lusignan, he arrived without fanfare in Angoulême. On the following day, a Sunday, on the date and in the place originally agreed upon for Isabella's marriage to Hugues le Brun, Archbishop Hélie of Bordeaux married the demoiselle to the King of England.[21] News of this master stroke of policy, which suddenly reshuffled the alliances of the south, took swift wing along the roads and river courses of Poitou. John hastened with his bride to the safety of Chinon. The envoys from Portugal, returning from their mission beyond the Pyrenees with encouraging tidings from the king of that country, encountered the report on their way northward from Bordeaux.

There were contemporary annalists who saw evil portents in this coup for the King of the English. The biographer of Guillaume le Maréchal goes so far as to say that it was the cause of the war in which John lost his lands;[22] but the exhilaration of his exploit, the sweet vengeance on the Lusignans, the charms of Isabella, bemused John, and the ramparts of Chinon sheltered him for a time from acute anxiety. From Chinon it is probable that he convoyed Isabella to Fontevrault for a visit to the queen, who was too old and sick to stir abroad in such unsettled times. Isabella had not at first appeared in the horoscope that Eleanor had cast for John, but her shadow must have crossed it before the marriage in Angoulême, for the Gascon Archbishop of Bordeaux would hardly, without the old queen's consent, have taken a step upsetting the alliances among her vassals and disposing of her richest marriage prize. The interval of six weeks between the fete at Lusignan and the bridal in Angoulême had given plenty of time to get her suffrage, if not her joyful assent. As evidence of her good will in the face of a *fait accompli*, she at once dowered Isabella with two of the best cities in her gift, Niort and Saintes.

While news of the marriage of the King of England reverberated in the capitals of Europe, John hastily put things in order in the region of the Loire. The treasure castle of Chinon he placed in charge of Guillaume des Roches, whose recent defection from Philip Augustus made him especially reliable. He took the precaution of placing in the custody of his own bailiffs various properties belonging to the brothers Lusignan. To thwart treachery and break incipient conspiracy among his own following, he shifted the castellans in many of his fortresses.

In the meantime, with a stout escort, but no abject haste, he himself escorted Isabella across Normandy, taking the occasion to examine his garrisons on the way. In the first week in October he crossed to Portsmouth. On the eighth of the month, Isabella was crowned in Westminster, and John appeared with her wearing his royal diadem.

In England the issue of the Lusignans burned less hotly, and the sovereigns lingered in the comparative tranquillity of the island to attend to accumulated business. For eight months John, in the constant company of Isabella, made wide circuits of the realm, receiving in his principal cities the homage of his vassals, adjusting grievances, descending with vengeance on nodding functionaries, looking sharply after harvest and shearing, the gleaning of tithes and revenues. The magnates of England thought they saw in the king some of the Angevin energy and dispatch that had characterized Henry Fitz-Empress; an overlord who, unlike Richard, had been bred in England, learned its speech, willingly stayed among its people. For a time John's diligence disarmed those who at his coronation had demurred over his ungovernable folly and his treason. The king and queen convened their Christmas court in Guildford, and at Easter made their pilgrimage to the shrine of Becket, where they were nobly entertained by the archbishop and wore their crowns in the presence of their magnates.[23]

33 ✠

Mirebeau

WHILE THE SOVEREIGNS TARRIED in Britain, Queen Eleanor kept her watch on the frontiers of Anjou and scanned with rising dread the horizons where the Lusignans were stirring. They had of course appealed to Philip Augustus as their super-overlord for the redress of their wrongs, and were marshaling their partisans in Poitou and concocting heaven knew what conspiracies with the faithless vassals of the Plantagenets. Constance of Brittany neared her end, and her death would signal new uprisings. The queen added her urgency to that of the Norman barons, beseeching John with ever increasing stress, to return for the defense of the empire with all he could command of insular resource. While waiting for his coming, she did everything she could to stay the tide of defections in the valley of the Loire and to recover some of the friends that John had alienated. She writes to her son of her diplomatic triumph with the Count of Thouars, whom John had relieved of the wardship of Chinon. The letter provides a glimpse of the situation she surveyed.

> I want to tell you, my very dear son, that I summoned our cousin Amaury of Thouars to visit me during my illness, and the pleasure of his visit did me good, for he alone of your Poitevin barons has wrought us no injury nor seized unjustly any of your lands. I made him see how wrong and shameful it was for him to stand by and let other barons rend your heritage asunder, and he has promised to do everything he can to bring back to your obedience the lands and castles that some of his friends have seized.[1]

Soon after Pentecost John and Isabella at last arrived in Barfleur and went straightway to the Rock.[2] Presently there was observed a pantomime engaging the two kings that the chroniclers were at a loss to explain, for it corresponded to none of the realities. The puzzling shadow play did not, however, encourage them to believe that a genuine peace was in prospect. Hoveden reports that for three days Philip Augustus was the "guest" of John and Isabella near the island of Andelys. The King of the Franks appeared amazingly affable toward the Plantagenets considering the fact that he had already welcomed the appeal of the Lusignans and promised them redress. The annalist, recording the bare fact of the parley, says only that "the kings came to a full agreement, no one but themselves being aware of what passed between them."

A few days later John and Isabella with a noble escort made a visit to Paris and there, to the infinite amazement of those not privileged to share the royal counsels, they were "honorably entertained" through most of July in the palace of the Capets on the Seine.[3] Philip, cut off from the solace of Christian society by his altercations with Rome, vacated his royal residence for the Plantagenets and himself retired to Fontainebleau. In Paris the Franks showered the English with rich presents — horses, armor, stuffs — and all but drowned them with champagne. Through a succession of fetes the young brides, Blanche of Castile and Isabella of Angoulême, vied as the *dames choisies*. The Frankish chronicler noted, with bilious eye, the curious show of mutual esteem between the kings. He remarks sourly that, though the royal cellars yielded up the best vintages of the Île, the English thirst for beer blunted their appreciation of the finer flavors. It is not said whether Arthur of Brittany shared the reunions in Paris. Constance was very near her end, down in Brittany, and the uncertainty of his destiny brooded like a sultry cloud over those midsummer days.

⚜

Philip Augustus had not been ready when Richard died to seize his opportunity for undoing the Plantagenets; but he intended not to be caught again if fortune should favor him a second time. But even now in the summer of 1201 he was unprepared for the impending succession of Arthur to Brittany. From the time of his abandonment of crusade, the King of the Franks had traveled unchecked a long way on the path of the transgressor; but justice had at length caught up with him. Pope Celestine III, in the matter of the captivity, had not taken the extreme measures against him demanded by Queen Eleanor in her famous correspondence with the pontiff. But Pope Innocent III proved more downright. With a long career and a new crusade in prospect, he undertook at once to purge the courts of Europe of the moldy scandals that divided Christian princes and balked the enterprise of Rome. What finally brought Philip up short in his evil courses and trammeled his freedom to avenge himself on the Plantagenets was the wretched affair of the Danish Princess Ingeborg.[4]

In the twelfth century women were not yet persons; but Ingeborg gave unmistakable evidence of personality. It did not occur to her valorous soul to go home to Denmark when, on the day after her marriage, Philip gave her leave to do so. She planted her foot firmly on the Île and, grasping with one hand, as it were, the door knocker of sanctuary and with the other the irised crown of France, she cried out incessantly to heaven and holy church to avenge her wrongs. From the shelter of the nuns of Beaurepaire in Soissons, she dispatched envoys to Rome, paying out her bridal finery and her gems to compass the expense; and in these embassies she was abetted in the *curia* by the Danes, who also had contingents for crusade. Philip's comparatively easy experience with Celestine had tempted him to flout the mandates of Rome in those matters he regarded as affecting his political rather than his ecclesiastical concerns. In 1199, under the auspices of his uncle of Champagne, the Archbishop of Reims, he had had his marriage with Ingeborg "annulled," and thereupon had rested the crown of France on Agnes of Méranie. And thenceforward, without regard for the outcries of the Danes or the fulminations of Rome, he had stood obstinately for Agnes and the "bastards" she had borne him. The stiff-necked behavior of Philip Augustus offered not only an unwholesome spectacle, but a dangerous example of disobedience to the kings and emperors of Christendom, who, by self-evident law, received their glaives from the church universal in the first place.

In the interest of justice to the Danes, Pope Innocent sent legates to France, but nothing was accomplished by argument, in which the weapons of dialectic collided with futile violence. In October 1199 Innocent issued a fiat. Philip was to restore Ingeborg, and was given an interval of grace in which to make up his mind, at the expiration of which interdict was threatened. To papal envoys bringing this decree, Philip closed his palace gates, declaring that he had himself appealed to Rome for inquiry into the legality of his marriage to Agnes, which had been sanctioned by no less an authority than the Archbishop of Reims, and that he could take no steps before hearing from his envoys. Thereupon the legate, as a warning, darkened the altars of Dijon where the inquiry had been held. When the period assigned for repentance had passed, and results were seen to be negative, the interdict fell.[5] Thenceforth, wherever Philip Augustus appeared, the sacraments were withheld, the altars were darkened, the crucifix veiled, and the king became a singular figure bearing publicly the mark of the transgressor. The sentence of Rome had the effect moreover of alienating many of Philip's prelates and of giving pious nobles an excuse for something less than zealous service. It hampered him at every turn; preventing him from attending the marriage of his own son and heir to Blanche of Castile, and from having it celebrated, as it ought to have been, within the boundaries of the Île. It balked him likewise in his enterprise with the Plantagenets.

Through Lent and Pentecost and the early days of summer, Philip bore up under the hardships of interdict. His entanglement with the Danes had become a *cause célèbre* in the *curia*, where it was pursued without respect for his involvement with the Plantagenets. Perhaps he would have persisted longer in his obstinate defiance, if his affair with the Angevins had not been ripening too fast. Under the pressure of hastening events, Philip himself sought an inquiry in September 1200, and a little ground was gained when Agnes, in all her innocence, was presented to the council in her own behalf. The prelates concluded, however, that before Rome could look into her personal distresses, Philip would have to get back to fundamentals by first restoring Ingeborg and placing Agnes for the time being in the position of compromise. Then, after rehearsing the whole course of events, the council might be expected, if evidence warranted it, to proceed step by step in canonical sequence to compose the disorders of the royal house and find justice or mercy for Agnes.

There was only one thing for Philip to do. He agreed to recognize Ingeborg publicly as the lawful Queen of France. Thereupon the interdict was lifted, altars burst into light, bells rang. But in spite of the decree, Ingeborg did not accompany Philip on his return to Paris. He shut her up with her royal dignities, incommunicado, in the castle of Étampes; and while she was in durance, Agnes bore him another child whom he honored with the name of Philip.

Neither the Danes nor the legates who had sat in judgment had expected Ingeborg to wear her crown in the seclusion of Étampes, and it was presently obvious that the matter could not rest. In March 1201 a new council was convened in Soissons, that famous arena for ecclesiastical tournaments. Philip and Ingeborg were brought face to face in the course of the proceedings, and at the end of days of dialectic, the king a second time agreed to acknowledge her. On this occasion he rode from the court through the streets of the city with Ingeborg pillioned on the saddle behind him, as evidence to all the world of his honest intentions this time with respect to her.

In July, while the King and Queen of England and their *mesnie* were happily beguiled in Paris, detained from mischief's way, Philip held aloof in Fontainebleau,[6] and there fate relieved him of his long impasse with Rome. In the middle of the month, Agnes of Méranie, "overcome with chagrin, entered the way of all flesh."[7] The Plantagenets had just left his palace in Paris when on September 4 Constance closed her eyes in Brittany. The time was very ripe to deal with John. But one matter remained to perplex Philip's imperial plans. His dynasty was not soundly fortified with posterity. Louis Capet was its sole bulwark. Had he not seen the abundant offspring of Henry Fitz-Empress rapt one by one away? He determined to require that Rome declare legitimate the children of Agnes of Méranie. Until this boon was secure, Philip forbore to break the five-year truce with John.

Throughout the autumn, while this last affair of Philip's was in abeyance in Rome, no outward disturbance in the Angevin domains marked the passing of Constance and the recognition of Arthur, who was still the

French king's ward, as Count of Brittany. John and Isabella, presently joined by Berengaria, passed the vintage in Chinon in a round of palatine festivities with their vassals that bore no indication of hostility. The old queen appeared to nod in her dotage in Fontevrault. The Lusignans ventured no breach of the peace on the marches of Poitou. At last, sometime in March 1202, Rome, deeming Philip's chastisement adequate and salutary, put upon his infants the stamp of authentic royalty.[8] On April 28 Dieu-Donné struck at the Plantagenets in behalf of the brothers Lusignan.

When he was ready the King of the Franks cited the King of England to come to his overlord's court in Paris to answer for his accumulated mischiefs: to wit, his failure on his accession to do homage to the King of France for Normandy, and for his injuries to the Count of Eu, who was Raoul de Lusignan, with estates on the Norman marches only a few leagues from Rouen. Philip offered John safe-conduct to Paris, but gave him no assurances that, in case of adverse judgment, he could freely travel back. This appeared to the Plantagenet too much like an invitation to a beheading. He sent word that, as King of England and the peer of other kings, he could not be summoned to the seat of justice in Paris. Philip replied that he was summoning his vassal, the Duke of Normandy, and it was no concern of his if the Duke of Normandy chanced also to be King of England.[9] To this legal thundering John replied that he would meet the King of France for parley on the frontiers of Normandy, as had been the ancient custom of their forebears, and suggested a rendezvous between Boutavant and Tillières.

When Philip arrived at the trysting place, the King of England was not there. The reinforcements for which he had appealed to England had not come; his continental forces were scattered in the garrisoning of strategic strongholds in the west; many of his own barons were not to be relied upon; and Mercadier, who knew how to raise *routiers* out of the earth by sowing dragons' teeth and how to hurl them wherever danger threatened, had been murdered in Bordeaux.

Philip Augustus had come to the rendezvous with a strong force at his back. John's failure to appear gave him an excuse to declare the truce between them broken, and his possession of the Vexin enabled him to fall with sudden fury on the marches of Normandy. By-passing only the strongly fortified castles of Aumale and Gournay, he cut a wide swath from Boutavant toward Eu, burning and razing as he went, until finally he pitched his tents before Arques, not a half dozen leagues from Rouen. When he had anchored the northern end of his line on Eu, he wheeled about and attacked the by-passed castles. He set up a siege before Arques and at Gournay flooded out the garrison by cutting the dam of a reservoir that fed its moats.

His success resounded. This was not like fighting Coeur-de-Lion. Dieu-

Donné had groped through the devious corridors of John's mind during the captivity and he knew his way through that dungeon in the dark. He was not overawed by the strategy of this last of the eaglet brood. But his ardor led him to act too precipitately. When he had washed Gournay into the river Epte, he took possession of its meadows, long famous as a jousting field, and there he knighted Arthur of Brittany and in the presence of his magnates received that youth's homage not only for Brittany, but for Maine, Anjou, Touraine; for Poitou also, when the old queen should be dispossessed. Further, he affianced to Arthur the five-year-old daughter of Agnes of Méranie. In a mood of elation he provided the young count who was to be his son-in-law with a household of two hundred elect knights and sent him forth to take possession of the properties with which he had been endowed. The "Hope of Britain," girt with his clean maiden sword, hastened down the valley of the Loire to take over his inheritance.[10]

Flushed with pride in his sudden accession of honors and the grandeur of his mission, the young count led his knights to Tours to await the arrival of reinforcements from Brittany and the development of strategic plans. To Tours, where all roads met for the crossing of the Loire, the brothers Lusignan with a small force of their partisans came to join him with news and advice. They reported that Queen Eleanor, having caught the echo of distant rumblings in Normandy, had seemed suddenly to remember that the abbey of Fontevrault was not a fortress, in spite of the enclosures with which she had provided it. She had bestirred herself and set out with a meager escort for the greater security of Poitiers.

Her journey obliged her to pass through that border region where, a half dozen times in her life, she had been ambushed and waylaid for forfeits. This time, proceeding with special caution, she had stopped on her way at the march castle of Mirebeau. The Lusignans urged a movement on that stronghold. The Frankish knights were cautious. They counseled waiting for the contingents from Brittany before taking on this diversionary scheme. But the Lusignans pressed their argument. The old Duchess of Aquitaine would be a hostage nonpareil. For her ransom they could, without the cost of strife, wrest from John every concession they required. They would thus capture the very ark of the Plantagenet confederacy. The queen's mind, reaching beyond the memory of most men living, had become a chronicle, an archive encompassing the history of more than three score years and ten; and it was common knowledge that it was from her that John (and his vassals as well) drew their counsels. Never again would she be so exposed; the distance was short; the duchess' *mesnie* was weak; the risks were small, the stakes high. The Lusignans bared their breasts.[11] They would lead the expedition through roads over which they could find their way at midnight. And so, with some misgivings, the Count of Brittany and the Frankish knights put themselves under governance of the brothers Lusignan and set forth from Tours for Mirebeau.

✢

The castle of Mirebeau in which Eleanor had taken refuge was an old landmark near the marches of Anjou and Poitou, a walled citadel and keep encircled by a small walled town. The forces of Arthur very soon battered down the gates and took possession of the bourg. Eleanor and her escort in the meantime moved into the keep and tower and lowered the portcullis. Since her assailants wished to take her alive, the preposterous young count opened parley with his grandmother, demanding her surrender. He even offered, if she would first assent to the disposals which Philip Augustus had recently made of her inheritance, to permit her to proceed on her way. Eleanor, who had found a means of sending word of her plight to Guillaume des Roches in Chinon, and to John, who was a good hundred miles away in Maine, spun out negotiations, weaving and unraveling her web, like Penelope, to drag out time.

Meanwhile the Franks and the Poitevins, confident of their quarry, devoted themselves to making the town secure against assault. They walled up all the gates save one, which they kept free to receive their supplies and the expected contingent from Brittany. When nightfall came, and the queen had not yet surrendered, Arthur's army bivouacked in the houses and streets of the town. It was the last of July and, the night being warm, they laid aside their armor and their vestments and fell into the fathomless sleep of soldiers.

John was in the neighborhood of Le Mans when news of the brilliant coup of the Lusignans reached his ear. He had apparently been scouting the marches and recruiting forces, and so was prepared to move without delay. The poet Guillaume le Breton tells the story for the Franks with a few details not found in the barer chroniclers. He relates that the night was magnificent. The great constellations of the Wain and the Herdsman wheeled in the heavens, and the midsummer moon poured light upon the roads, the fords, the bridges, as John's men took them at breakneck speed. Before dawn the king had reached the neighborhood of Mirebeau.[12]

With him were Guillaume de Braose and other liege men, and Guillaume des Roches, who, as warden of Chinon, had probably joined him with some forces along the road. These men looked with proper dread upon the possible consequences of the night's work, whatever its issue might be. Especially they feared for Arthur if he should be exposed to the fury of John. They too had high stakes in the boy, for if he were lost, they themselves were no more than corn between the millstones of the two kings. Besides, many of their own baronial colleagues were among the forces of

Arthur in the town. They stopped short of the walls of Mirebeau for parley. The poet reports the substance of their interview.

Said Guillaume des Roches to the king, "We will overcome your enemies this night, if you will swear that you will put no one of your captives to death, that you will receive your nephew in peace, that you will leave all those who are his partisans on this side of the Loire until a truce shall have been made between you."

"To this I agree," said John. "I swear that if I do otherwise, you and these nobles here present may leave my homage, and thenceforth no one of you shall hold me for a king."

It was further agreed that Arthur, if taken, should be given into the custody of Guillaume de Braose, who, as an intimate of John, must have been, among the barons, a candidate of compromise.[13]

Then John's men crept furtively upon the town, "the armed upon the unarmed." Light was breaking, and inside the walls Hugues de Lusignan with some of his men were dispatching an early breakfast of pigeon pie, while most of the force lay still half dressed and snoring in the streets. No trumpet sounded the attack. Guillaume des Roches and the *routiers* burst in at the one free gate and thus shut off all hope of escape. A wild melee ensued as men drunk with sleep roused themselves in dead-end streets and doorways, a hand-to-hand encounter in which John himself gave his nephew a show of knightly exercise. Not a man of Brittany's force escaped. Guillaume de Braose, who himself took Arthur, brought his captive to the king — Count of Brittany, Maine, Anjou . . . Lord of Touraine . . . Count of Poitou indeed!

The captives were almost too many to handle. The Lusignans and their partisans, among them many of the noblest Frankish and Poitevin seigneurs, including even some of the queen's relatives, were put in chains and, as a special mark of shame, were bound to ox wains, their faces turned disgracefully to the carts' tails, and thus they were paraded for the next few days through their own countryside to the crossing of the Loire. There were far too many prisoners for the dungeons of the marches, so there was no question of John's keeping the oath he had made with respect to his captives. Convoying the most precious of his prizes, the king went forward as quickly as possible to the fortresses of Normandy, and among these he distributed the prisoners secretly so that rescuers would be baffled, not knowing where any particular person might be hidden.

Hugues le Brun he consigned to a special tower under special custody in Caen. Many of the others he sent to England where, in the next few months, some were starved and some were blinded and a few in the course of time escaped. Among those who went to captivity in England was Arthur's sister, the "pearl of Brittany." What had happened to her was a mystery to the Franks for years.[14] Treaties made more than a decade later were based upon the contingency of her survival. About August 10 John placed his capital prize in the grim castle of Falaise, whose dungeons had since the time of William the Conqueror engulfed generations of Angevin captives in oblivion. He cleared out other prisoners from the fortress to prevent any contacts and placed there the "Hope of Brittany" under the sole responsibility of his chamberlain, Hubert de Burgh.

34 ✤

The Hope of Brittany

A crooked thing is ruined and fit only to ruin everything else.
(Chose tournée est corrumpue et propre à tout faire tourner par suite.)
Guillaume le Maréchal, III, 170

PHILIP AUGUSTUS RECEIVED THE NEWS from Mirebeau while his forces were engaged in the siege of Arques, the capture of which was to be the climax of his exploits in Normandy, for its fall was to uncover the ramparts of Rouen itself. The monk who brought the disastrous tidings from the west trembled for his life as he approached the king.[1] To Philip the news was incredible from end to end. The folly of the hothead Lusignans! The simplicity of Arthur! The stupidity of the Frankish mentors of the count! The demonic fleetness of the Plantagenets! The Count of Brittany, the instrument of all the Frankish imperial plans, dungeoned in the rock of Falaise! Elect barons of France to the number of more than two hundred in Angevin fortresses beyond hope of rescue! And all this for the prize of the superannuated queen, who might have been left, at eighty years of age, to sleep herself away in her dotage. And that crafty beldame, the root of all evil, for whom so many pawns had been wasted, had moved triumphantly, like a queen in chess, within the safety of her own bourne! No such irretrievable disaster had marked the whole struggle of the rival dynasties. The flower of chivalry was in chains. The Carolingian dream, a week before so rosy and so palpable, retreated to the horizon and faded to mirage. Overdepressed in defeat, as oversanguine in victory, the King of the Franks ordered the catapults and mangonels he had brought to the siege of Arques dismantled, and retired to seclusion to put his mind in order and recast his shattered plans. His only gesture for the moment was to send forces down the Loire valley to Tours, where they despoiled the royal portion of the city. Thereupon John sent his *routiers* to burn the ecclesiastical portion in a bootless reprisal; so that rich and beautiful city, with its noble monuments, was, like Angers and Le Mans, reduced to desolation, and its citizens turned away from the ruthless Plantagenet and his Angevin furies.

After Mirebeau, Guillaume des Roches followed John some way into Normandy, hoping to mitigate the ferocity of the king's lust for vengeance on the captives whom the barons had taken under his own leadership and under the king's oath. When he found John implacable, he turned from him, as from a crooked one impossible to deal with and fit only to ruin all those with whom he treated. He sacrificed the custody of Chinon to his honor with his peers and drew to himself the other seigneurs who were dismayed by the king's faithlessness and inhumanity. Among these was Amaury of Thouars, who had seen his younger brother Raoul tied to an ox cart on his way to Normandy. And now barons of the western provinces, many of whom had relatives or friends among the captives, withdrew in numbers from John's allegiance, says the chronicler, and joined the forces of resistance.[2]

By the middle of October these had gathered strength to seize Angers, whose citizens had first acclaimed Arthur of Brittany as Coeur-de-Lion's heir for the Angevin provinces; and at the end of the month they came very near to bringing off a coup that would have forced John to negotiate for the release of Arthur himself. The agents of Guillaume des Roches marooned Isabella of Angoulême in Chinon, where John had left her for safety, and it was only by sheer good fortune that the queen succeeded in rejoining the king in Le Mans under the adroit escort of one of his knights, Jean of Préaux. Thenceforth the huntsman's art in the Angevin provinces became the pursuit of hostages. In reprisal for the threat to Isabella, John's forces, under the ferocious *routier* Louvrecaire, carried off the wives and daughters of his enemies. Then, says the chronicler, from day to day miseries were multiplied in Maine, Poitou, Anjou, and Brittany, as vills, castles, towns were looted and burned, and the ravagers spared neither age, nor sex, nor condition.

King John had reason to fear Guillaume des Roches who, besides being an excellent strategist and a fearless knight, had served on both sides of the conflict and had recently been privy to his own counsels and knew too much about the poverty of his resource in men and treasure and the deviousness of his contrivings. The autumnal maneuvers of the barons under Guillaume brought the king back from Normandy to secure the marches of Anjou. Through November he kept cautiously to the strong fortifications of Saumur and Chinon, whence he could survey events both north and south of the Loire. His presence was enough to dissuade the barons from overt acts. But his castles were surrounded by enemies he had made at Mirebeau, and the emptiness of his treasury forbade his taking strong measures to repress the growing sedition. His stark necessities were revealed in November, and the barons were astounded at the recklessness with which he met his crisis. After having secured custody of their castles and taken hostages for their good faith, he freed for ransom two of his richest prizes and most irreconcilable foes, the brothers Hugues le Brun and Raoul of Eu, who speedily, notwithstanding their pledges, joined the baronial party.[3]

In the meantime not much transpired regarding the fate of the Count of Brittany, and lack of news bred dark rumors.[4] As fall wore to winter and horrors seeped like ooze from the dungeons of certain of the captives, the barons dared no longer postpone efforts for their release, even at the peril of exposing Arthur or other individual prisoners to extreme hazards. They decided, in spite of the risk of reprisal on some of the prisoners, to bring pressures to bear on John. Around Christmas time Philip Augustus in their name called upon the Plantagenet king to account for the well-being of his nephew.

The impatience of Philip Augustus to grasp the prize of his Carolingian forebears had exposed the Count of Brittany to the utmost danger. The youth,[5] who had been bred on the bitter rancors of Constance and inflated by all he had learned in Paris concerning his pretensions, had been thrust at Mirebeau upon the open field between the two kings at feud and had become himself the object of the direst intrigue on either side. The moot titles with which Philip had endowed him marked him for the Plantagenets as the dupe and tool of the Capet's imperial plans and so a fit prey for vengeance. For the Franks, he was the indispensable counter in all negotiations to squeeze and harry John into acceptance of Capetian claims. For many of the barons of the western provinces, the young count, malleable, still innocent of the perfidies that had made both kings infamous to their vassals, seemed a more hopeful overlord than either Capet or Plantagenet; and to many his claims to the inheritance of Coeur-de-Lion appeared more just than John's. To have custody of Arthur rose to prime importance.

John's sudden success at Mirebeau found him unprepared to profit by his victory. Plantagenet luck had put the stakes in his hand; but the barons observed no perspicacious plan to end the feud that weekly consumed the fairest provinces of Christendom. Instead of directing the course of affairs, the king merely improvised, ransacking each event as it occurred for his advantage, and taking meantime such occasions as he could to slake his thirst for vengeance.

The prisoners from Mirebeau were hardly disposed in their dungeons when some of Arthur's own household sought a rendezvous with John to secure the count's release, but nothing came of it.[6] Barons tried to intercede for the youth "for fear he would disappear." Some of John's own vassals offered their homage to Philip Augustus for the duration of Arthur's imprisonment. But none of these tactics produced the desired result. However, Philip's summons to John in December to account for Arthur found the King of the English ill at ease.

At the end of January he made a visit to Falaise for a parley with his nephew, who had now had six months to reflect upon his position as Count of Maine, Anjou, and so forth. By this time John appears to have been seized with the idea of reattaching his captive to the destinies of his own house. But his overtures failed. He found in the youth a stouthearted Plantagenet infused with the Scotch blood of his mother and the wild strain of Brittany.

When offered reinstatement in his inheritance on condition of homage and obedience, the count became possessed of the Angevin demon. He replied with a vehemence that ill became a captive with three iron rings on his feet that there could be no peace until John rendered up to him not only Brittany, of which there could be no question, but Maine, Anjou, Touraine . . . Poitou . . . England . . . everything of which Richard was possessed or of which he was heir on the day of his death.[7]

The stiff-necked intractability of the youth after six months of imprisonment infuriated John. But his fury was half fear. Had this preposterous boy some assurance of rescue that he dared be so bold? Were some of his own barons in collusion with the heir of Brittany? The moth of suspicion began to prey upon the mind of the king and gradually spread its work of corruption. He who knows not whom to suspect, says the Poitevin proverb, ends by suspecting everyone. The prisoner became too hot to hold, far too precious to deliver. John revolved schemes for disposing of the torment of his anxiety. His counselors, says Coggeshall, persuaded him that no peace could stand while Arthur lived as a potential menace, and urged that he put an end to intrigue that was certain to continue interminably in behalf of the count by having the youth blinded and so maimed as to render him forever unfit to be a royal figurehead.

From the fierce interview John remanded Arthur to his dungeon. Leaving Falaise for Rouen, he ordered three sergeants to the prison fortress to carry out the mutilations. But only one, reports the chronicler, kept his stomach for his dastardly assignment; and this one raised such an outcry from Arthur that Hubert de Burgh himself intervened, and the young count, limp with terror and exhaustion, was left to his custody alone. Hubert, when taxed for preventing the crime, asserted that he had done it to save John from the consequences of an act which the king himself would disavow when his passion was spent; that the repercussions among the barons would break the loyalty of men still attached to him, so that he would presently be unable to man his castles with faithful knights.

However, there had been too much smoke to conceal the fire that had been kindled in the castle of Falaise, and something had to be done to obscure the situation. It was given out that Arthur had pined away of chagrin in his captivity. His knell was rung in the town and his garments were distributed to the lazar house.[8] But this report, spreading from the fortress, produced such fierce resentment against John that presently a second rumor followed the first, to the effect that Arthur was not really dead, but had recovered from a desperate illness and was still in custody.

The incident, as it turned out, taught John a helpful lesson. He discovered how to turn the anxiety that had tormented him upon his enemies. He observed the value of mystery. He neither denied nor affirmed, and the confusion of rumors respecting Arthur paralyzed the enterprises of the latter's partisans. If he were dead, should they support a "regency" of Guy of Thouars for the infant daughter of Constance of Brittany? Or go over to Philip Augustus? Or cleave to John? If he were not dead, to stir might be to procure his death or invite reprisal upon captive barons. They could only wait and see. To the Plantagenet who knew his "matter of Brittany," there was something sardonic in the disappearance of the "Hope of Brittany," who, like his legendary namesake, appeared to have cast Excalibur away and betaken himself to Avalon. The doubts gave John time to wait on fortune. In the next weeks various stories were current among the Bretons. Their count had been slain at the behest of the king by one Peter of Malendroit; he had been secretly buried in the abbey of Saint André de Gouffern in the diocese of Sées; John with his own arm had pushed him off a cliff at Cherbourg and drowned him in the sea.[9]

Soon after the failure of the plot in Falaise, John, perhaps suspecting that the loyalty of Hubert de Burgh would not go so far as to dispose of Arthur, caused his prisoner to be removed to Rouen,[10] where through Lent he made his own chief residence. On the eighth of March the king gave the tower of Rouen with its garrison into the custody of Robert de Vieuxpont, who thus became the surety for Arthur;[11] and on the thirty-first he made a very considerable grant to Robert — the two castles of Appleby and Brough in Westmoreland with all the bailiffry of that district — and ordered these properties to be delivered to two servants of Robert, who were authorized to take them at once in his name.[12]

On Wednesday of Easter week (April 2) John betook himself to Molineaux, a fortified manor a few miles down the river from Rouen, to which he was wont to retire frequently from the commotions of the capital. With him were his loyal Norman baron, Guillaume de Braose, and three of his justiciars from England, Geoffrey Fitz-Peter, William Briwere, and Reginald of Cornhull, perhaps others. Guillaume le Breton relates that at about this juncture in the affairs of Arthur, Guillaume de Braose appeared before John and his barons and publicly disclaimed further responsibility for the captive he had taken at Mirebeau.

"I know not," said Guillaume, "what fate awaits your nephew, whose faithful guardian I have been. I return him to your hands in good health and sound in all his members. Put him, I pray you, in some other happier custody. The burden of my own affairs bids me resign."[13]

The king's associates at Molineaux can hardly have been unaware of the agitation of John's mind during the rendezvous, nor uncertain about the root of it. But what occurred in the next days of Holy Week was of such import that knowledge was dangerous. They disclosed nothing, and the chroniclers of events in Normandy dared not set down in their annals any of the circumstances that may have come to their hearing. However, in spite of the strictest secrecy, almost at once new and sinister reports spread from Rouen. All that subsequently emerged in the chronicles was the fact that, after the eve of Good Friday, the young count was seen no more by any man with a tongue in his head or the ability to scrawl a message to the world. Says Matthew Paris, "It was not safe to write of him even when he was dead." The tongues of suspicion wagged, however, and certainly those who talked had access to testimony whispered from ear to ear. The reports accused the Plantagenet king of foul play, of the impious crime of murdering with his own hand his nephew, a youth tender of sinew and unarmed, and of committing this dreadful sin on the eve of Good Friday in Rouen.

The most circumstantial account that has been found came to knowledge after the events of 1203 had become history. In the annals of the abbey of Margam in far-off Wales, a monk set down in the chronicles of his monastery the story as he had heard it perhaps considerably after the occurrence, from some source now suspected of being Guillaume de Braose or Hubert de Burgh, or some of their followings.[14] The annal is succinct: "On the day before Good Friday, after dinner, when he was drunk with wine and filled with the devil, he [John] killed him [Arthur] with his own hand and tied a heavy stone to his body and cast it into the Seine, whence it was dragged up in the nets of fishermen and, having been brought to shore, was identified and secretly buried in Notre-Dame des Prés, a priory of Bec, for fear of the tyrant." [15]

The *Philippide*, in which the French king's chaplain celebrates the reign of Philip Augustus, presents the more detailed story that circulated among the Franks, who were more than eager to fix the blackest of crimes upon John himself. The poet, it seems, heard much the same story as that transcribed at Margam. He relates that on the eve of Good Friday in the middle of the night, John sailed up the channel of the Seine in a small boat and, coming to Rouen, drew up at a haven whence, when the tide had somewhat ebbed, he could have access to a postern of the tower in which Arthur was imprisoned. He ordered his nephew to be brought down and, himself standing in the high stern, dragged his victim into the boat and at once made off. Deaf to the wild supplications of the youth, John seized him by the forelock and dispatched him with his sword and then cast his body, weighted with a great stone, into the Seine. The poet omits the tale of the recovery of the body by the fishermen and of its burial at Notre-Dame des Prés.

Within two weeks of Easter Queen Eleanor and the magnates in her region received in Poitou a messenger from John bearing an oral communication too confidential to be committed to writing, together with a letter which survives. The letter proceeded from Falaise under date of April 16 and was attested by Guillaume de Braose. It conveyed to Eleanor in cryptic language the certain knowledge that her grandson, the "Hope of Brittany," would no more darken the horizon of the Plantagenets:

> The King . . . to the Lady Queen his mother, the Lord Archbishop of Bordeaux, Robert of Turnham, Seneschal of Poitou, Martin Algais, Seneschal of Gascony and Périgord, Briscius, Seneschal of Anjou, Hubert de Burgh, Chamberlain, brother Peter of Vernolio, William Mangot, and William Cocus, greeting. We send to you brother John of Valernt, who has seen what is going forward with us, and who will be able to apprise you of our situation. Put faith in him respecting those things whereof he will inform you. Nevertheless, the grace of God is even more with us than he can tell you; and concerning the mission which we have made to you, rely upon what the same John shall tell you thereof. And we command you, R. de Turnham, not to distribute the money we have transmitted to you, unless in the presence of our mother and William Cocus. Witness Guillaume de Braose, at Falaise, on the 16th of April.[16]

Philip Augustus' summons in the name of the Bretons to produce Arthur, accompanied by "ferocious threats" from the barons themselves, made it clear to John that the value of his mystery would be limited. The report that Arthur had really perished must have spread soon after Easter, to judge by the stirrings among them. The strength and cohesion of the baronial revolt had increased from week to week in the preceding months and turned inevitably to Philip for support. John's victory at Mirebeau now drove him to defense. He had all the hostages and all the mystery, but these in the issue availed him little. The captives were too dangerous for release, even for the huge ransoms they were worth, yet to keep them increased the fury of hostility; and the mysterious rumors exposed him to revulsions that spread among his own followers. His forces were scattered for defense against the treachery he suspected everywhere. Because he could not trust his vassals, the king had to rely more and more on hired *routiers*, and these mercenaries had lost their experienced leadership when Mercadier was murdered in Bordeaux. The royal revenue, shallow at his accession, had dwindled through the loss of the Vexin and the defection of the baronage.[17] He was forced now to negotiate with the great moneylenders of the Continent. He sent magnates to England for levies of men as well as for tithes; he appealed to his nephew Otto, the Holy Roman Emperor, and sent envoys to Innocent in Rome. In the meantime he concentrated what he could of military strength in Anjou in order to prevent his enemies from cutting off Queen Eleanor in Poitou.

✤

> The French king will destroy the royal race of England as an ox crops the grass at its roots.
>
> *Magna Vita Sancti Hugonis*, 332

John was too late. In his victory at Mirebeau the sacredness of the feudal oath, abjured in so many previous instances, vanished entirely, and with it the solidity that law gives to societies. The empire caved in less from outward pressure than from inner corruption. Anarchy supervened and those individuals saved themselves who could. Defections even in Normandy came fast in the wake of the rumors that spread after Easter. The hammers of war merely finished the work.

On the ninth of April Guillaume des Roches took, almost without a blow, the Angevin castle of Beaufort only a few miles from Fontevrault, where the figures of great Henry and Coeur-de-Lion slept with their crowns on their heads and their scepters in their hands. With this stronghold protecting his right flank, Philip proceeded cautiously down the Loire by boat and took possession of the strategic castle of Saumur, a short distance from Angers. Then, finding the garrison of Chinon offering a stiffening resistance, he struck suddenly northward through Maine and Anjou by way of Beaumont and Alençon. A line of castles covering main routes from the fortresses of the lower Loire to Rouen fell like ripe fruit into his hands. Through the spring and summer Sées, Conches, Le Mans, Falaise, Domfront, Coutances, Bayeux, Lisieux, Caen, Avranches, surrendered one after another, some through defection, some through John's failure to provide for their defense.[18] In the course of these disasters John sent his noblest magnates, Hubert Walter of Canterbury, Guillaume le Maréchal, and the Earl of Leicester to the French king to negotiate a truce. But Philip, as always in a time of rising fortunes, made catastrophic claims and the envoys came away unable either to accept the terms or to enforce better ones.[19] Now the denizens of Normandy were subjected to the spectacle that had outraged the western provinces. Captive knights, this time of John's allegiance, bound to their mounts, their faces turned to their horses' tails, were paraded over the roads of the Vexin on their way to the dungeons of the Franks. Heaven, said the chronicler, was imposing retribution at last for the crimes of the Plantagenets.

Philip's triumphant course was halted briefly at Vaudreuil, where only a deep loop of the river and twelve miles of road separated him from Rouen. Here a stout resistance was expected, for Vaudreuil was manned by English defenders. But this bastion of the lower Seine yielded without assault. In August, looking backward toward Paris from this vantage point, Philip cast up his eyes at the cliffs of Château Gaillard, which Coeur-de-Lion had sworn to defend even if its walls were made of butter. The huge bastion hewn in the rock and molded to its contours with heaviest masonry loomed disdainfully upon its height.

Elated as usual by success, Philip took the measure of Gaillard with deliberation.[20] No engines could breach the ramparts of the Rock, which he had sworn nevertheless to take even if its walls were made of iron. The situation of the fortress with all its encircling outworks seemed proof against anything but earthquake. But here was the citadel of Normandy, the true barrier between Paris and Rouen, the lower Seine, the sea. It was worth a king's ransom and had cost Coeur-de-Lion not much less. The King of the Franks set about the difficult business of blockade. He directed his engineers to destroy the outworks that secured access and controlled the waters. They breached the stockade of spiles driven to obstruct the traffic of the river below the fort, demolished the bridges that connected the Rock with the isles of the Seine and the left bank of the river. Pioneers working like ants threw up embankments to isolate the fortress from the landward side. In the fall days Philip set up his vigil below Andelys, prepared, if need were, to outsit the seasons. In the course of the autumn one of his maneuvers drove the dwellers in the town of Petit Andelys into the keep for protection and gave the beleaguered garrison five hundred extra mouths to feed from their irreplaceable stores. These wretched villagers, driven out again by the exigencies of the garrison, were obliged to winter, starving and defenseless, in crannies of the Rock, and many of these hapless refugees were kindred of the defenders of the castle. While Philip's six months' campaign gathered momentum, where was John that he let his Norman fortresses fall one by one into the hands of his enemy? What was he waiting for?

As 1203 drew to its close, the Plantagenet horizons were altogether dark. While the castles of his Angevin inheritance fell to bribes and threats and assaults, John kept closer and closer to Rouen and the port of Barfleur. He made a few onsets to divert Philip from the valley of the Seine and to recoup his losses in the west by a movement at the heart of old military operations in Falaise and Argentan, and by ravaging the borders of Brittany; but Philip let these affairs take their course and kept his eye steadfastly upon the Rock.

When his diversionary maneuvers failed of their object, the Plantagenet took to fitful movements in Normandy controlled by no apparent plan. Even his intimates were sometimes at a loss to account for his flittings,[21] or to guess what projects infused him with energy. Like a fugitive with hounds on his trail, he moved furtively from place to place, traveling at unexpected hours, before daybreak, after sundown, over secondary roads, to obscure destinations, changing suddenly his routes and schedules, so that his comings and goings were matters of secret or surprise. Castellans with whom he had lodged for the night woke to find the king had departed without farewell while they thought him still asleep, and was already seven leagues on his way. He shifted his treasure, his charters, his hostages from place to place and changed his castellans with the suddenness of doom. Messenger followed messenger, the second to overlook the first; and his communications were set in codes and signs or cryptic language. Though John was irreligious, he was superstitious, and some of his counselors could account for his devious courses only by suspecting he had resorted to fortunetellers and astrologers.[22] Others guessed him haunted by the specter of Arthur and fear of reprisal for the doom of that young man; by fear of the ancient law, an eye for an eye and a tooth for a tooth. When his soberer intimates tried to find a method in his confused operations and besought him to consider some solid means for checking the progress of the Franks, he affected a debonair self-confidence that drove his followers to desperation.

"Let me alone," he said. "Let me alone. When the time comes, I will shortly recover all I have lost." [23]

At last in December when little remained but Rouen and the beleaguered Rock and the Norman fringes of the Channel, John bestirred himself; but even his own men were doubtful whether his sudden resolution indicated a genuine purpose to defend his heritage, or merely veiled a flight from the dismal military situation and the treachery that had engulfed him on the Continent. Accompanied by Queen Isabella and a few of his associates, Guillaume le Maréchal, Guillaume de Braose, Robert de Vieuxpont, and others, he sailed from Barfleur. From Portsmouth he set about a tour of his master castles, and visited Winchester and the Tower of London on pretext of obtaining men and money to recover the Angevin empire from the marauding Capets and the faithless baronage.[24]

But the English, without ignoring the perils of his situation, had suffered enough for the unprosperous Plantagenets, whose proverbial Angevin luck seemed, with Henry's death, to have forsaken them. They reviewed the crusade, the ransom, the cost of fortifying and defending the continental empire of their kings, the pressure of new levies to redeem Lackland's vanishing fortunes and his debts. The seeds of Runnymede and Magna Carta were burgeoning in their minds. What had their poured-out treasure of men and gold profited them? Why pour more into the fathomless pit of his calamities? They had had enough of John's faithlessness, his capriciousness, his tall talk, his reckless passions. The horrible betrayal of the captives in Corfe Castle on their own shores, without regard for the feudal custom respecting hostages, had spread abroad; and the sinister rumors regarding Arthur's disappearance led all sorts of men to look askance at John. Clergy and other pious folk did not overlook his persistent rejection of communion nor his cynical disregard for other holy sacraments. Tongues were emboldened to voice their discontent by the vast numbers of the king's enemies. Even the English barons with estates in Normandy, when all was weighed in the balance, had a better prospect of prosperity as vassals of Philip Capet than of John, since Philip at least kept war from his own borders and managed his affairs more thriftily. As John prolonged his stay in Britain for months, many desired to know why the Duke of Normandy did not go with those transmarine forces, whose business it was, to the defense of his marches and his sorely beset castellans, instead of living softly with Isabella in strongholds safely remote from the catastrophe.

35 ✣
The Queen Goes Home

This is the worm that dieth not, the memory of things past.
Bernard of Clairvaux, *De Consideratione*

IN THOSE DAYS WHEN the foreshadow of some new order in the world was dimly taking shape in the minds of men, and the appeal to "ancient custom" was giving place to new sanctions, the Britons took account of the worsening of their lot since the steady, if heavy, hand of Henry Fitz-Empress had been withdrawn. What demon had entered into the race of the Angevins? The prestige of Queen Eleanor suffered in the general distrust of transmarine ties. She had doubled the Angevin empire for Henry and enriched his house with a brilliant posterity; and when he had gone, she had defended his empire with a political sagacity that had brought the highest magnates to her counsels and earned for her the trust and confidence of popes and emperors and kings. But now she became an object of calumny. Clerks, like Giraldus Cambrensis, with rancors of their own to appease, asked to know what could be expected of the brood of the "eagle of the broken pledge," of the Poitevin who had renounced the pious King of the Franks for the Angevin king and abandoned one crown for another. Hugh of Lincoln, that disciple of Saint Bernard, held that her marriage with Henry was "adulterous" and the Angevin eaglets "spurious."[1] Although throughout her long history as Queen of England, no breath of scandal had touched her good fame, the old legends the Franks had used in the mid-century to discredit her — legends discreetly suppressed in Henry's day — were brought out of limbo and refurbished and bequeathed to balladeers, who used them to season broadsides and chapbooks down to the seventeenth century. The impossible story of Eleanor's murder of Rosamond Clifford got its vogue and passed into folklore, and has never ceased to serve to her disparagement as theme for opera, romance, and poetry.

After Mirebeau Eleanor had withdrawn from the habitations of kings to her own ancestral provinces, to places familiar before she had dwelt with Louis Capet or Henry Plantagenet. She left the roar of hopeless war behind. She could no longer lead armies in the field, collect ransoms, scale mountain barriers, or deal with magnates or envoys in the interest of empire. In Poitiers she was safe among the loyal citizens of her own capital. Like Henry at the last, she was obliged to put off vainglory and echo his words, "Let all things go as they will. I care no more for aught of this world."

The eternal aspect of her earth, unchanged by all the ravages of conflict, must have renewed its patient poetry and solace. Beyond the rivers that moated the ancient high place of the Poitevin counts the land ebbed away, nursing on its bosom here a hamlet, there a mill, yonder a priory. The immemorial toil of ox and colon went forward in the field, and the tireless magpie skimmed the furrow. The chestnuts bloomed again. In the busy commune all about the palace were heard the creak of wheels, the slithering of horses' hoofs upon the cobblestones, the drumming of hammers, the rasp of the stonecutter's adz, the voices of housewives, and the cries of children; and over all the other sounds the dissolving resonance of bells — the bells of Saint Pierre, Saint Radigonde, Saint Porchaire, and Notre-Dame la Grande, proclaiming the office and the calendar of the everlasting church.

The great assembly hall where the duchess once held her courts of love is now used as an antechamber to justice and is known as the "hall of lost footsteps" (*la salle des pas perdus*). Already in the queen's day it thronged with ghosts, some of whose footfalls had died away in the long past: the ribald, philandering, musical troubadour, her grandfather, with his huge laughter and his inimitable travesties; the gay Countess of Châtellerault; her father, fire-eating Guillaume le Toulousain, of the gorgeous appetite and the reckless imbroglios; Louis Capet, young, wilted with the summer heat, and plainly dazed by his confusing role as king, bridegroom, count of the Poitevins; the lovely Countesses of Champagne and Flanders ushering in the areopagus of the courts of love, the marriage prizes of the south; André the Chaplain with his choir of poets and his corps of clerks polishing the peerless *Tractatus de Amore*; the troubadours of the Limousin and the valleys of Provence — Ventadour, Rudel, Vidal, and many more; Guillaume le Maréchal, brave and loyal, leading in her sons triumphant from the jousting fields, the beautiful young king, gallant Coeur-de-Lion, the clever Count of Brittany, with their households of *preux chevaliers*, their hair smoothed down with sweet-smelling unguents and their nostrils shaven; Marguerite and Alais of France, Constance of Brittany, Joanna of Sicily, and Eleanor of Castile; Thomas Becket, with the tall figure and the burning eyes . . . Thomas the Chancellor . . . Thomas Becket, Archbishop of Canterbury . . . Saint Thomas . . . Thomas Martyr! The grim figure of Henry Fitz-Empress on the threshold of her palace hall; the awful ghost of Falaise and Rouen, his spectral eyes still stricken with a horror that was mortal; the ghastly Channel crossings to and from the foggy island on the edges of the world. Salisbury Tower. This is the worm that dieth not, the memory of things past.

Tableaux from remoter times must have taken semblance and fled away, dismembered and recombined, strange interminglings of feudal palaces at the crossroads of Christendom, and of personages that made the century glow. Paris, the Île de la Cité moored like a barge in the Seine, teeming with students and clamorous with bells, stirred now by the love songs, now by the fulminations of Abélard, now by the subtle discourse of Abbé Bernard . . . Saint Bernard, "that well of flowing doctrine"; wise and temperate Abbé Suger; the Counts of Champagne; Petronilla and the one-eyed Count of Vermandois; nights on the Danube below Durrenstein; Byzantium crowned by the domes of Sancta Sophia set between the sweet and bitter waters of the West and East; sleek and crafty Manuel and his dowdy German empress, who had not learned, even in Byzantium, how to lay on her fards . . . The horrible geography of Paphlagonia, the unspeakable Turks; Antioch the glorious, the lilies of the field, the latter rains; Jerusalem, the Holy Sepulcher, the tottering dynasty of the Latin Kingdom, the stony pilgrim roads of Palestine . . . the pirates of Barbary, Pope Eugenius in Tusculum.

"This life," says the chronicler, "is but a journey and a warfare."[2] In the day of every man's pilgrimage to holy shrines, the metaphor had special meaning. The duchess' long road, beset with every kind of accident and every sort of weather, had brought her home at last, but in a night of storm. Had she chosen the saints of her devotion, her route and destination, or had she been driven by the press of throngs and the waywardness of storm to unforeseen harborages, to havens not even on the map? Had Fate been capricious, or had she?

Above the Loire the masonry of Henry's empire, which she had helped to build and fortify, slid down under the blows of Philip Capet, Dieu-Donné, whom, according to Giraldus, heaven had sent in answer to the prayers of Louis and the Cistercian brotherhood to be "a hammer to the King of the English"; and not an Angevin stirred among the smoking rubble of its towns to retrieve the inheritance of his forebears. Only the echo of crashing ramparts reached her as one fortress after another from Rouen to Saint Michael-in-Peril-of-the-Sea fell to the son of Louis Capet. She did not live to hear of Bouvines or Runnymede; perhaps even the news of the surrender of Gaillard fell on deaf ears. But it was as if the messenger reporting the loss of that master fortress of the Angevins brought her summons too. On the sixth of March the castle hung out its white flag. Barely three weeks later the queen "passed from the world," "as a candle in the sconce goeth out when the wind striketh it." She was in her eighty-third year. Chroniclers are not even agreed about the place in which she died. The chronicle of Saint Aubin of Angers declares she ended her days in her own capital; but others say she was taken at the last to Fontevrault, where she put on the garb of a nun before closing her eyes.[3]

In the terror and dismay that swept over the heritage of Henry, her death was hardly noticed. The nuns of Fontevrault, who knew her through many stages of her journey, gave her a paragraph in their necrology:

> She enhanced the grandeur of her birth by the honesty of her life, the purity of her morals, the flower of her virtues; and in the conduct of her blameless life, she surpassed almost all the queens of the world.

Matthew Paris ventures to say, "In this year the noble Queen Eleanor, a woman of admirable beauty and intelligence, died in Fontevrault."

But among the discreet chroniclers, whose records were subject to review by the clerks of various kings, the inscription is noncommittal and meagerly informative about Eleanor of Aquitaine and the four kings. Scanning a dozen entries yields no more than this: Anno 1204. In this year died Eleanor, Duchess of Aquitaine, who was divorced from the French king by reason of consanguinity, and then married Henry Fitz-Empress, and was the mother of Richard, called the Lion-Heart, and of John, who in turn succeeded him.

The queen's cortege brought her at any rate to Fontevrault, and her tomb was erected in the crypt. The nunnery had become, as Merlin was believed to have prophesied, the necropolis of the Angevins. The tombs, all crowned with effigies, were disturbed during the French Revolution, but were subsequently replaced in the choir in new array, all of them damaged in detail by the ravages of time and war. The queen now reposes between Henry Fitz-Empress and Richard Coeur-de-Lion, whose scepters and crowned heads are epitaph enough. Nearby rest Joanna and Isabella of Angoulême. Here Eleanor lies serene, the play of a smile in her whole expression, in her hand a small volume, which one of her apologists has said need not be regarded as a missal. Tranquil, collected, engaged with her book, the queen seems to have found at last, beyond the wrath of kings and the ruin of the Angevin empire, that domain of peace and order to which her vast journeyings amongst the high places of feudal Christendom had never brought her. The highhearted Plantagenets are marble still. The dusty sunlight falls softly where they sleep.

1204: In hoc anno obiit Alianor.

NOTES

NOTES

NOTES TO CHAPTER 1: THE RICH DOWER

1. *Ch St D*, 195.
2. Sug, *Vie L. VI*, 127; *Ch Eg*, 432.
3. G de V, *HGF* XII, 435.
4. Sug, *Vie L. VI*, 128.
5. Sug, *Vie L. VI*, 58–59.
6. Sug, *Vie L. VI*, 121–22.
7. Sug, *Vie L. VI*, 128.
8. *Ch M*, 83.
9. G de V, *HGF* XII, 435.
10. R of Dic, II, 292.
11. *PL* 141:823.
12. *Ch Eg*, 373.
13. Wm of M, II, 510.
14. G de V, *HGF* XII, 434–35.
15. *G le M*, III, 28.
16. Sug, *Vie L. VI*, 129.
17. *Ch M*, 83–84.
18. Sug, *Vie L. VI*, 129.
19. *Ch T*, 134.
20. OV, IV, 182.
21. Sug, *Vie L. VI*, 129.

NOTES TO CHAPTER 2: O PARIS!

1. For the configuration of Paris, see Halphen, 5–100; Poëte, chap. IX.
2. Guy de Bazoches, *Éloge de Paris*, tr. Helen Waddell.
3. J de V, cited Rashdall, II, 691.
4. G le B, *Gestis P.A.*, 82.
5. Berthaud, 55.
6. Pierre de la Celle, *PL* 202:519.
7. J of S, *PL* 199:113.
8. Stephen of Paris, 89.
9. Ab, *Hist Cal*, 15.
10. Héloïse to Abélard, *PL* 178:185.
11. Sug, *Vie L. VII*, 150.
12. Richard, II, 67, citing Lair, *Bibl. de l'école des Chartres*, XXXIV (1873), 591.
13. Sug, *Vie L. VII*, 151.
14. Ab, *Hist Cal*, 11.
15. Ab, *Sic et Non*, 1339ff.
16. Bern, *Vita Prima*, 305.
17. Bern, *Vita Prima*, 246.
18. Bern, *Vita Prima*, 327; *Vita Tertia*, 527.
19. Bern, *Epist*, 386.
20. Bern, *Epist*, 540; Berengarius of Poitiers, *PL* 178:1861.
21. Bern, *Epist*, 281.
22. Bern, *Vita Secunda*, 505.
23. Adapted from Bern, *Epist*, 257–259 (epistle cxiii).
24. Bern, *Epist*, 286.
25. *Ch M*, 87; *Hist Fr*, 116.
26. Sigebert, appen., 331.
27. *Hist Fr*, 116.
28. *Hist Fr*, 116.
29. Bern, *Epist*, 385.
30. Gervaise, *Hist Suger*, III, 94.
31. Bern, *Epist*, 191.
32. Panofsky, 64–67.
33. Gervaise, *Hist Suger*, III, 98.
34. Gervaise, *Hist Suger*, III, 96.
35. Frag. *Vita S. Bernardi*, *PL* 185:332, 527.

NOTES TO CHAPTER 3: VIA CRUCIS

1. G de N, 25.
2. O of F, 530.
3. Wm of T (ed. Babcock and Krey), II, 143. Unless otherwise indicated, this edition of Wm of T is cited throughout the notes.
4. Wm of T, II, 77ff; *Ch M*, 88.
5. *Gst L. VII*, 224; Wm of T, II, 179.
6. O of D, 1207.
7. O of D, 1206.
8. G de St D, *Vita Sugerii*, *HGF* XII, 108.
9. *Ch Eg*, 146.
10. O of D, 1207; *Ch St D*, 199; *HGRL VII*, 126.
11. Mich, *Hist of Crusades*, I, 360.
12. Wm of N, I, 82, 66.
13. Gervaise, *Hist Suger*, III, 118; De Larrey, *Hist d'Éléonor de Guyenne* (ed. 1691), 37; see OV, II, 494, for a similar tale.

That the Khevsouris, a nomadic people of the Caucasus, preserve traditions of the Second Crusade is suggested not only by their custom of wearing medieval chain armor in tournaments and duels, but by the existence among them today of a song, "The Frankish men, they have a Queen, Eleanor, Eleanor." Cf. George and Helen Papashvily, *Anything Can Happen* (New York: Harper, 1945), p. 120.

14. Bern, *Vita Prima*, 381.

15. O of D, 1206.
16. J of S, *Hist Pont*, 53.
17. Bern, *Epist*, 654.
18. Bern, *Epist*, 566.
19. Wm of N, I, 66.
20. Nicetas, 404.

NOTES TO CHAPTER 4: FEAR THE GREEKS

1. O of D, 1211.
2. O of D, 1223.
3. "Bouche de Lion," B le T, 79.
4. O of D, 1221.
5. O of D, 1222.
6. On the splendors of Byzantium, see Chalandon, *Les Comnène*; Diehl, *La Société Byzantine*, 23ff; F of C, 28; O of D, bks. IV and V; Runciman, 185ff; Wm of T, II, 450.
7. O of D, 1221.
8. Runciman, 186.
9. R of Clari, 102ff.

10. Panofsky, 115.
11. O of D, 1222–23.
12. Louis to Suger, *HGF*, XVI, 11.
13. O of D, 1229–30; Wm of T, II, 168.
14. O of F, 537.
15. O of D, 1235.
16. O of D, 1236–37; Wm of T, II, 168–176; *Gst L. VII*, 220.
17. O of D, 1239.
18. G de N, 31.
19. O of D, 1243.
20. O of D, 1244.

NOTES TO CHAPTER 5: ANTIOCH THE GLORIOUS

1. Wm of T, II, 179.
2. O of D, 1246.
3. On Antioch, see F of C, 41–42; Wm of T, I, 199ff.
4. Wm of T, II, 80.
5. Wm of T, II, 179.
6. Wm of T, II, 180.
7. J de V, 175–177.
8. J de V, 175–177.
9. J of S, *Hist Pont*, 53.

10. *Gst L. VII*, 225.
11. Wm of T, II, 180.
12. J of S, *Hist Pont*, 53; Wm of N, I, 32–33.
13. Minstrel of Reims, 259.
14. Wm of N, I, 32; Sug, *Vie L. VII*, 163.
15. Bern, *Epist*, 394.
16. Sug, *Epist*, 509.
17. Wm of T, II, 180–81.
18. J of S, *Hist Pont*, 53.
19. G of C, I, 149.

NOTES TO CHAPTER 6: JERUSALEM

1. Edward Henry Richards in the *New York Times*, January 2, 1938.
2. B le T, Mich II, 568.
3. On Jerusalem, see Abel, *L'État de Jerusalem*; Wm of T, I, 339ff.
4. Wm of T, II, 182.
5. *Ch St D*, Mich II, 485; Wm of T, II, 181.
6. Hugh of Sens to Suger, 712.
7. Wm of T, II, 184.
8. Wm of T, II, 187–194; *Gst L. VII*, 227. An Arab chronicler (Mich, *Bibl des Crois*, IV, 94) reports circumstantially that the Emir of

Damascus bribed the King of Jerusalem (with spurious coin) to retire.
9. Sug, *Epist*, 509.
10. Wm of T (ed. P. Paris), II, 150, n. 4.
11. G de N, 34; BG, 232; Poole, Intro. to J of S, *Hist Pont*, xxviii; Louis to Suger, *HGF* XV, 513–14, 518.
12. J of S, *Hist Pont*, 51–53.
13. Gervaise, *Hist Suger*, III, 349.
14. O of F, 538.
15. Bern, *De Consid* (ed. Lewis), bk. II, chap. i, pp. 37–38.
16. *Gst L. VII*, I, 222; Wm of T, II, 177.

NOTES TO CHAPTER 7: THE QUEEN AND THE DUKE

1. R of C, 13; R of Dic, I, 291.
2. Suger to Louis, *Epist*, 509.
3. *Ch St D*, 201.
4. Wm of T, II, 181.

5. Chartrou, 72; R of T, 162; *Ch Eg*, 147.
6. Chartrou, 83.
7. *Ch T*, 136.
8. Chartrou, 66, n. 6.

9. Wm of N, I, 70.
10. Bern, *Epist*, 575.
11. Gir Camb, *DPI*, 309.
12. *Ch Eg*, 147; Chartrou, 69; R of T, 162.
13. Geof. of Clairvaux, *Vita Bernardi*, cited Chartrou, 74.
14. Wm of N, I, 93.
15. Gir Camb, *DPI*, 300; WM, *De Nug Cur*, 297.
16. Wm of N, I, 93.
17. For definition and history of the Vexin, which continued to embitter relations between Capets and Plantagenets, cf. Landon, *Itin Rich*

I, appen. H; and Powicke, *Loss of Normandy*, 128, n. 2.
18. R of T, 162.
19. R of T, 163.
20. *Ch T*, 135; Richard, II, 104ff; G de N, 36; G de V, *HGF* XII, 438.
21. *HGRL VII*, 127.
22. Bouchet, *Annales d'Aquitaine*, 141.
23. *Ch T*, 135. Some accounts differ regarding details of place.
24. Wm of N, I, 93; *Ch T*, 135–36.
25. BG, 231.

NOTES TO CHAPTER 8: THE COUNTESS AND THE POET

1. G of C, I, 149.
2. R of T, 165.
3. Richard, II, 113.
4. Richard, II, 115.
5. R of Dic, I, 291–92; *Archives d'Anjou*, I, 6; Rashdall, vol. II, pt. i, p. 148; Hilarius, 15, 18, and *passim*.
6. G of C, I, 125; Norgate, *Eng. under Angevin Kings*, I, 375.
7. Waddell, *Wandering Scholars*, 99.
8. WM, *De Nug Cur*, 278.
9. Richard, II, 118.

10. On Ventadour, see Appel, Berry, Carducci, Hill and Bergin.
11. Raynouard, III, 84.
12. R of Dic, I, 296.
13. Gir Camb, *DPI*, 155.
14. Wm of N, I, 90; R of Hov, I, 213.
15. WM, *De Nug Cur*, 298.
16. On Henry, see WM, *De Nug Cur*, 71, 298, 302–03; P of B, *Epist*, PL 207:66; Gir Camb, *DPI*, 160, 213; *Magna Vita*, *passim*; *HGF* XVI, 518.
17. Vais, III, 87.
18. Niño, 34–36.

NOTES TO CHAPTER 9: THE SECOND CROWN

1. R of T, 182.
2. R of Dic, I, 299.
3. On the coronation, see G of C, I, 159; R of T, 182; Wm of N, I, 101.
4. G of C, I, 160.
5. Loomis, *Tristram and Ysolt*, 274; Wm FS, 2–3; G of T, 425–26.
6. Wm FS, 8, 11.
7. G of C, I, 161.
8. Wm of N, I, 103ff.
9. WM, *De Nug Cur*, 298; P of B, *Epist*, PL 207:121.
10. Hall, appen., 244.
11. WM, *De Nug Cur*, 234.
12. G of C, I, 160.
13. Icelandic Life of Becket, I, 29; J of S, *Life of Becket*, 302; Wm of C, 3; EG, 359.
14. Wm FS, 17.
15. Wm FS, 24.
16. Wm of C, 5; EG, 363.
17. P of B, *Epist*, PL 207:47.
18. Icelandic Life of Becket, I, 107.
19. Wm FS, 19; Eyton, 40; Ramsay, *Revenues*, I, 82.

20. Wm FS, 19.
21. P of B, *Epist*, PL 207:198.
22. Loomis, "Bleheris and the Tristram Story."
23. Loomis, *Tristram and Ysolt*, Intro., xi.
24. Gir Camb, *De Rebus*, 119.
25. Gir Camb, *DPI*, 126; *Spec Ec*, 47.
26. Tamizey de Larroque in *Revue d'Aquitaine* (1864), 102, cited De Villepreux, *Éléonore de Guyenne*.
27. B de Ste M, *Roman de Troie*, vv. 13431–13470.
28. Philippe de Thaün, *Le Bestiaire de*, ed. Emmanuel Walberg (Lund, 1900) Intro., xviii.
29. Lachmann and Haupt, *Des Minnesangs Frühling*.
30. J of S, *Polycraticus*, PL 199:402–406.
31. WM, *De Nug Cur*, 186.
32. Cf. Bernard's *Tractatus de Cantu*, PL 182:1121.
33. Wm FS, 2ff.
34. Eyton, 42–43, and *passim*.
35. R of T, 189.

NOTES TO CHAPTER 10: FORGING THE EMPIRE

1. Wm of N, I, 112; Stubbs, *Hist Intros*, 96.
2. On Henry's building enterprises, see Norgate, *Eng. under Angevin Kings*, II, 196; Ramsay, *Angevin Empire*, 255, *Revenues*, I, 77; Powicke, *Loss of Normandy*, 276; R of T, 196, 209.
3. "Nombre effrayant de princesses," *HGF* XVI 1.
4. R of T, 196–97; R of Hov, I, 218.
5. Wm FS, 29.
6. G of C, I, 166; R of T, 197; R of Dic, I, 302–03.
7. Eyton, 42.
8. R of T, 198.
9. R of T, 201; Wm of N, I, 123–25.
10. Ramsay, *Revenues*, I, 75.
11. R of T, 207.
12. R of Dic, I, 303.
13. G of C, I, 167–68; *HGRL VII*, 128–29.
14. R of Hov, I, 218.
15. R of Dic, I, 303.
16. Wm of N, I, 159.
17. R of Hov, I, 218.

NOTES TO CHAPTER 11: KING AND ARCHBISHOP

1. G of C, I, 168–69.
2. Wm of C, 4–6.
3. R of T, 184.
4. Icelandic Life of Becket, I, 121.
5. HB, 181; Wm of C, 7; J of S, *Life of Becket*, 305.
6. Anon, *Life of Becket*, 13.
7. HB, 187–88.
8. HB, 228.
9. Wm of C, 10; HB, 208.
10. HB, 250.
11. EG, 376.
12. EG, 376; J of S, *Life of Becket*, 306.
13. Wm of C, 12; HB, 185.
14. Icelandic Life of Becket, I, 141.
15. Icelandic Life of Becket, I, 147; R of Hov, I, 220; R 67, IV, 201.
16. Ramsay, *Revenues*, I, 81.
17. G of C, I, 176; R of Hov, I, 221; EG, 379.
18. EG, 388.
19. R of Hov, I, 224; G of C, I, 182; EG, 390; HB, 296.
20. Wm FS, 50.
21. R of Hov and EG give the sum as £500.
22. Icelandic Life of Becket, I, 191; Wm of C, 30; HB, 298.
23. Wm FS, 57–58.
24. EG, 395.
25. Icelandic Life of Becket, I, 223.
26. HB, 310.
27. Anon, *Life of Becket*, 51–52.
28. A of T, 333.
29. Wm FS, 67.
30. G of C, I, 186.
31. G of C, I, 189ff.
32. HB, 332, and Anon, *Life of Becket*, 58, give Compiègne as the meeting place. EG, 401, gives Soissons.

NOTES TO CHAPTER 12: BECKET IN EXILE

1. EG, 388.
2. Wm FS, 70.
3. G of C, I, 190ff; HB, 335ff; A of T, 337.
4. HB, 232–33.
5. A of T, 338.
6. R of T, 215.
7. Wm of N, I, 142; Wm FS, 75; HB, 359.
8. BG, 232.
9. G le B, *Vie de P.A.*, 191.
10. Gir Camb, *DPI*, 292.
11. Gir Camb, *DPI*, 290.
12. Ch St D, 207.
13. Alexander, *Epist*, R 67, IV, 421.
14. R of Dic, I, 329; G of C, I, 196.
15. Wm FS, 76; HB, 357.
16. G of C, I, 204.
17. Becket, *Epist*, V, 266ff.
18. R of Hov, I, 241; G of C, I, 200; HB, 404.
19. J of S, *Epist*, R 67, V, 382.
20. R of Hov, I, 238; Becket to Alexander, *Epist*, V, 386; Becket to his suffragans, *Epist*, V, 292.
21. J of S, *Epist*, VI, 417.
22. J of S, *Epist*, VI, 68.
23. Guernes, p. 136, stanza 807.
24. Ramsay, *Angevin Empire*, 93.
25. Becket, *Epist*, VI, 270.

NOTES TO CHAPTER 13: MONTMIRAIL AND CANTERBURY

1. Wm of C, 52.
2. Eyton, 112.
3. G of C, I, 207.
4. Wm of C, 73–74.

5. R of T, 240; J of S, *Epist*, R 67, VI, 507.

6. Alais was born in 1160 (R of Dic, I, 303).

7. R of T, 228.

8. Gir Camb, *DPI*, 157; Richard, II, 154, 189.

9. G de V, *HGF* XII, 442; Eyton, 137.

10. G of C, I, 208; HB, 418.

11. HB, 423.

12. A of T, 347.

13. Wm FS, 97.

14. R of Dic, I, 335; HB, 441.

15. Eyton, 127.

16. Becket, *Epist*, VII, 73.

17. Becket to Guillaume de Sens, *Epist*, VII, 165.

18. Gir Camb, *DPI*, 288, imputes other words to the prince.

19. R of Dic, I, 335–337.

20. G of C, I, 213.

21. Wm FS, 111.

22. HB, 444.

23. R of Hov, II, 3; G of C, I, 216; Wm of C, 77.

24. Eyton, 137.

25. Eyton, 139.

26. R of T, 245.

27. Wm FS, 103.

28. Becket, *Epist*, VI, 603.

29. G of C, I, 219; B of P, *Gesta Henrici*, I, 5. Unless otherwise indicated, all references to B of P designate the *Gesta Henrici*.

30. Wm of C, 368; Polydore Vergil, 215–16.

31. Wm FS, 104.

32. Becket, *Epist*, VII, 326.

33. Becket, *Epist*, VII, 332.

34. Wm FS, 116.

35. Henry to Becket, *Epist*, VII, 400.

36. Wm FS, 116–17.

37. Icelandic Life of Becket, I, 491.

38. G of C, I, 222; Wm of C, 89.

39. Wm FS, 119.

40. Wm FS, 122.

41. Wm of C, 123; HB, 489.

42. Wm FS, 128.

43. EG, 429; Wm of C, 122.

44. Wm FS, 129. See Icelandic Life of Becket, I, 503, for other details of the interview.

45. Wm FS, 142–149.

46. B of P, I, 14.

47. R of Dic, I, 345; Alexander, *Epist*, R 67, VII, 438.

NOTES TO CHAPTER 14: THE FLOWER OF THE WORLD

1. Thomas Percy, *Reliques of Ancient English Poetry*, 3 vols. (London, 1857), II, 156–57.

2. Gir Camb, *DPI*, 165.

3. RN, 168.

4. See Heltzel, *Fair Rosamond*, for an interesting and scholarly study of the Rosamond story.

5. Hearne, III, 730; Eyton, 62.

6. Hearne, III, 730.

7. Gir Camb, *DPI*, 165.

8. B of P, II, 231.

9. Hearne, III, 748.

10. R Hig, VIII, 54.

11. R of T, 229.

12. R of T, 236; *Ch Eg* (St. Aubin), 41.

13. *G le M*, III, 25; G of C, I, 205; R of Hov, I, 273.

14. Richard, II, 151.

15. G de V, *HGF* XII, 442.

NOTES TO CHAPTER 15: THE COURT OF POITIERS

1. Richard, II, 141; Dufour, 251ff.

2. Markham, 311.

3. Richard, II, 148–181 *passim*.

4. The custom may be studied in the history of various fiefs. Cf. Imbart, *Les Vicomtes de Thouars*.

5. For facts other than literary about Marie, see D'Arbois de Jubainville, *Hist ducs et comtes de champagne*. The clue to the presence of Marie in the court of Poitiers is the fact that André the Chaplain mentions her specifically as taking part with Eleanor in 1174 in judgments under the rules of the *Tractatus*. In 1174 Eleanor's court was in Poitiers and she was there present. For a somewhat fuller presentation of the backgrounds for this chapter, see Kelly, "Eleanor of Aquitaine and her Courts of Love," *Speculum*, XII, 3.

6. Bernard, *Epist*, 575.

7. Andreas (ed. Parry), 31. Unless otherwise indicated, Parry's edition of Andreas is cited throughout the notes.

8. For translation, see Parry.

9. Nostredame, *Les Vies des Poètes Provençaux*, 83.

10. Andreas, 175.

11. Nykl, chap. VII.

12. Loomis, *Tristram and Ysolt*, Intro., viii–ix.
13. Andreas, 174.
14. Andreas, 170.
15. Andreas, 172.
16. Andreas, 171; Vais, III, 226.
17. For another identification of Marie, cf. Holmes, 189.
18. G de V, *HGF* XII, 450.
19. Andreas, 176.
20. Richard, II, 161.
21. Andreas, 167–68.

22. Andreas, 184.
23. Andreas, 106, 175.
24. "Holi Meidenhed," cited Power, 441.
25. Words and music as rendered at meeting of Mediaeval Academy, April 23, 1942; adapted from Guido Adler, *Handbuch der Musikgeschichte*, 2 vols. (Berlin, 1930), II, 190. See also Carl Appel, *Die Singweisen Bernarts von Ventadorn* (Halle, 1934), 36.
26. Gir Camb, *DPI*, 301, 309.

NOTES TO CHAPTER 16: HENRY AND HIS SONS

1. WM, *De Nug Cur*, 281.
2. *Magna Vita*, 204.
3. WM, *De Nug Cur*, 382.
4. R of Dic, I, 431. For the all but incredible story of Agnes Capet, see L. du Sommerard, *Anne Comnène et Agnès de France* (Paris, 1907).
5. R of Hov, II, 21.
6. Wm of N, I, 163.
7. R of Dic, I, 350.
8. R of Hov, II, 34; G of C, I, 237.
9. Gir Camb, *DPI*, 295.
10. Gir Camb, *DPI*, 301.
11. G of C, I, 242–43.
12. Gir Camb, *DPI*, 173ff; G of C, I, 304; Wm of N, I, 233; R of T, 305; WM, *De Nug Cur*, 178; R of Dic, I, 428; G of T, 447.
13. R of T, 253.
14. Coulton, *Med Pan*, 236.
15. G de V, *HGF* XVIII, 216.
16. R of T, 305.
17. Wm of N, I, 234.

18. Gir Camb, *DPI*, 246; G of C, I, 304; *Itin*, 143, 144; Amb, 19; *Ch T*, 144; G of T, 448.
19. R of C, 97.
20. *Ch T*, 141.
21. Gir Camb, *DPI*, 177.
22. *G le M*, III, 15 and *passim*.
23. Langlois, 115.
24. *G le M*, III, 62.
25. *G le M*, III, 22.
26. *G le M*, III, 45.
27. B of P, I, 226.
28. R of Hov, II, 18.
29. R of Hov, II, 25.
30. Gir Camb, *DPI*, 156; R of Dic, I, 348.
31. R of Dic, I, 351.
32. R 67, VII, 514.
33. G of C, I, 238; B of P, I, 31; Wm of N, I, 165.
34. R of Hov, II, 35.
35. R 67, VII, 514ff.

NOTES TO CHAPTER 17: SEDITION

1. R of Hov, II, 45; G de V, *HGF* XII, 443; B of P, I, 37.
2. R of Dic, I, 353–355; B of P, I, 41.
3. Vais, III, 167ff.
4. G de V, *HGF* XII, 443.
5. R of Dic, I, 371; R of T, 257.
6. Wm of N, I, 170; R of T, 256; R of Dic, I, 355.
7. R of Hov, II, 40–46; G of C, I, 242–43; B of P, I, 41; R of C, 17.
8. R of Hov, II, 41.
9. Wm of N, I, 170.
10. B of P, I, 43.
11. R of Hov, II, 46–47; B of P, I, 44.
12. *G le M*, III, 93.
13. R of Dic, I, 372.
14. R of Dic, I, 382.

15. R of Hov, II, 49; R of Dic, I, 373.
16. Gir Camb, *DPI*, 163; G of C, I, 245ff; Wm of N, I, 169ff.
17. R of Hov, II, 52; B of P, I, 46, 59.
18. R le P, Addenda, 419; R of T, 256.
19. *HGF* XVI, 629.
20. G of C, I, 242.
21. Richard, II, 170 (n. 2) suggests that Eleanor's betrayers were the Poitevins, Guillaume Maingot, Porteclie de Mauzé, Foulques de Matha, and perhaps Hervé le Panetier, since these presently received valuable grants from Henry.
22. R of Hov, II, 82–83; B of P, I, **99**.
23. R of Hov, II, 61; R of Dic, I, 382.
24. R of Dic, I, 382.
25. G de V, *HGF* XII, 443.

26. Gir Camb, *DPl*, 164; R of Hov, II, 61; B of P, I, 72.
27. G of C, I, 248.
28. JF, 367; Wm of N, I, 194–95.
29. JF, 371; R of Hov, II, 63; Wm of N, I, 189–90.
30. G of C, I, 249ff; Wm of N, I, 190; R of Hov, II, 65.
31. R of Hov, II, 65.
32. R of Dic, I, 351.
33. R of Dic, I, 394; R of Hov, II, 67; B of P, I, 77–78; Wm of N, I, 196.
34. R of Dic, I, 79.

NOTES TO CHAPTER 18: POOR PRISONER

1. G of C, I, 256–57.
2. Gir Camb, *DPl*, 232.
3. Gir Camb, *DPl*, 306.
4. A dependency of Anjou, but part of the diocese of Poitiers (Richard, II, 205).
5. It was, says a chronicler, an establishment to which rich old ladies betook themselves.
6. Eyton, 197, 252, 293, and *passim*.
7. G of C, I, 256.
8. B of P, I, 313.
9. B of P, I, 305; G of C, I, 326.
10. B of P, I, 162.
11. R of Hov, II, 100.
12. R of Dic, I, 397.
13. R of Hov, II, 143.
14. R Hig, VIII, 60–61; RN, 168; R of Hov, III, 99; *Ch Mx*, I, 256.
15. R of Dic, I, 399, 404.
16. B of P, I, 82.
17. B of P, I, 91.
18. B of P, I, 138ff; R of Dic, I, 414, 416, 419.
19. B of P, I, 131ff; R of Dic, I, 414.
20. B of P. I, 292.
21. The Lateran Council of 1179 decreed excommunication for *routiers* and all who favored them (B of P, I, 228–29).
22. B of P, I, 79, 82–83.
23. B of P, I, 114.
24. B of P, I, 115.
25. *G le M*, III, 36.
26. R of Dic, I, 428.
27. B of P, I, 122–23; R of Hov, II, 94.
28. B of P, I, 123.
29. B of P, I, 177; R of Hov, II, 136.
30. B of P, I, 190.
31. B of P, I, 182.·
32. B of P, I, 190.
33. Gir Camb, *DPl*, 226.
34. B of P, I, 191ff.
35. B of P, I, 132, 194.
36. B of P, I, 195–96.
37. R of Dic, I, 425; B of P, I, 197; R of Hov, II, 147.
38. B of P, I, 198; R of Hov, II, 150.
39. B of P, I, 240; R of T, 282–83, 287; Rig, 12.
40. B of P, I, 240.
41. B of P, I, 240; R of Dic, I, 433; G of C, I, 293.
42. Icelandic Life of Becket, I, 477–479.
43. B of P, I, 242; R of Dic, I, 438–39.
44. R of Hov, II, 194; B of P, I, 243.
45. R of Dic, II, 7.
46. B of P, I, 243, 250; R of Hov, II, 197; G of C, I, 295.
47. *Hist Epis Autissiodorensium*, 305.
48. BG, 233.
49. WM, *De Nug Cur*, 276.
50. Wm of N, I, 223.
51. Gir Camb, *DPl*, 134, 318, 321.
52. G le B, *Vie de P.A.*, 194.

NOTES TO CHAPTER 19: THE CHRISTMAS COURT

1. R of Dic, I, 434–45.
2. WM, *De Nug Cur*, 303.
3. R of Dic, I, 406–07.
4. Raynouard, V, 76; Clédat, *Rôle Hist de B de B*; Thomas, *B de B, Poésies Complètes*; Stimming, *B von B*, 1–52 ("Lebensbeschreibung").
5. Thomas, *B de B*, "Poésies politiques," poem xlvi; Stimming, *B von B*, poem iii, vv. 25–29, 21–22; translation by U. T. Holmes.
6. B of P, I, 292.
7. Clédat, 44.
8. G de V, *HGF* XVIII, 212; *Ch St M*, 60.
9. R of Dic, II, 18; B of P, I, 292ff.
10. Thomas, *B de B*, "Poésies politiques," poem iii; Stimming, *B von B*, poem v, vv. 33–40. Mateflon is in Anjou.
11. R of T, 303; B of P, I, 288–89.
12. B of P, I, 291–92.
13. B of P, I, 289.
14. R of T, 304.
15. R of Hov, II, 273.
16. *G le M*, III, 70–74.
17. Clédat, 44.

18. Thomas, *B de B*, "Poésies amoureuses," poem vii, vv. 17–21.

19. Thomas, *B de B*, "Poésies politiques," poem v, vv. 43–45. Cf. also Joscelin of Salisbury's strictures on the "bad beer of Argentan, abhorrent to gentle folks" (Eyton, 123).

20. Gir Camb, *DPI*, Intro., xxvii.

21. *G le M*, III, 76.

22. WM, *De Nug Cur*, 180.

23. G of C, I, 303.

24. B of P, I, 291; R of Hov, II, 273–74; G of C, I, 303.

NOTES TO CHAPTER 20: WAR WAS IN HIS HEART

1. Gir Camb, *DPI*, 302.

2. R of Hov, II, 275.

3. G de V, *HGF* XVIII, 213.

4. B of P, I, 296.

5. B of P, I, 292.

6. R of Hov, II, 276.

7. G of C, I, 304.

8. B of P, I, 293.

9. G de V, *HGF* XVIII, 216.

10. R of Hov, II, 274ff.

11. G de V, *HGF* XVIII, 213.

12. WM, *De Nug Cur*, 180.

13. G de V, *HGF* XVIII, 214–15; B of P, I, 296–97.

14. G de V (Bonnélye ed.), 7.

15. G de V, *HGF* XVIII, 212, reports the elder Henry as going to St. Yrieix; Bonnélye's edition, p. 153, speaks of Henry, "the brother" of Richard, which seems more probable.

16. P of B, *Epist*, PL 207:110.

17. B of P, I, 296–298.

18. R of Hov, II, 277.

19. B of P, I, 296–302.

20. G de V, *HGF* XVIII, 215.

21. G de V, *HGF* XVIII, 215–16.

22. G de V, *HGF* XVIII, 214.

23. B of P, I, 299; *Ch St M*, 190–91.

24. R of Hov, II, 278.

25. Vais, III, 195.

26. G de V, *HGF* XVIII, 217–18.

27. G de V, *HGF* XVIII, 217–18; B of P, I, 300; Wm of N, I, 234.

28. G de V, *HGF* XVIII, 217–18.

29. G de V, *HGF* XVIII, 220; R of T, 306.

30. *G le M*, III, 81.

31. Thomas Agnellus, 266.

32. B of P, I, 301; G de V, *HGF* XVIII, 218; Wm of N, I, 233; G of C, I, 305; R of T, 305.

33. G de V, *HGF* XVIII, 218.

34. *G le M*, III, 82.

35. *G le M*, III, 83.

36. *G le M*, III, 84.

37. Thomas Agnellus, 272–73.

38. Dante, *Inferno*, Canto XXVIII, vv. 118–123, 127–142. (My translation.)

39. Hill and Bergin, Poem 57, p. 85.

NOTES TO CHAPTER 21: HENRY REVOKES HIS LANDS

1. B of P, I, 304–05.

2. B of P, I, 311.

3. R of Hov, II, 5; G de V, *HGF* XII, 442.

4. B of P, I, 350; Gir Camb, *DPI*, 176.

5. R of Dic, II, 41.

6. The child born to the young king and Marguerite in 1177 died in three days. They had no other children.

7. G of C, I, 337.

8. *Ch St D*, 368.

9. *Ch Mx*, I, 256.

10. R of Dic, II, 40.

11. *Ch T*, 304.

12. Gir Camb, *DPI*, 293–94.

13. B of P, I, 306, 344.

14. Pipe Rolls, 26 Henry II, 135. For suggestion that Eleanor went to Aquitaine, see *ibid.*, 206, 215.

15. R of Hov, II, 284; B of P, I, 306.

16. Wm of N, I, 240–271.

17. Wm of T, II, 398.

18. Gir Camb, *DPI*, 202–206.

19. R of Dic, II, 33.

20. *Flores Hist*, II, 96.

21. Brompton, 735.

22. Butler, 88.

23. R of Hov, II, 304; B of P, I, 338.

24. Gir Camb, *DPI*, 67.

25. *Flores Hist*, II, 74.

26. R of Hov, II, 305; B of P, II, 14.

27. B of P, II, 19.

28. Cf. Wm of T, I, 25, n. 24.

29. *Itin*, 32.

30. R of Hov, II, 335.

31. B of P, II, 58.

32. Amb, 12; G of C, I, 406.

33. R of Dic, II, 50; G of C, I, 389; *Itin*, 32.

34. R of Hov, II, 335.

35. G of C, I, 422; B of P, II, 33.

36. Vais, III, 207.

37. G of C, I, 435.

38. B of P, II, 33; R of Hov, II, 339ff.

39. R of Hov, II, 343.

NOTES TO CHAPTER 22: THE FALLEN ELM OF GISORS

1. Wm of N, I, 249.
2. G of C, I, 433.
3. G le B, *Vie de P.A.*, 202; B of P, II, 59; R of Hov, II, 345.
4. B of P, II, 49.
5. R of Hov, II, 346.
6. R of Hov, II, 354; G of C, I, 435.
7. *G le M*, III, 97.
8. B of P, II, 50; R of Hov, II, 355; R of Dic, II, 58; *Ch St D*, 368; Gir Camb, *DPI*, 254.
9. G of C, I, 436.
10. *G le M*, III, 97.
11. B of P, II, 60; Wm of N, I, 277; Gir Camb, *DPI*, 254.
12. Gir Camb, *DPI*, 232.
13. *G le M*, III, 99.
14. B of P, II, 66; R of Hov, II, 363.
15. R of Dic, II, 62.
16. R of Hov, II, 289.
17. R of Dic, II, 63.
18. Cf. Meyer, *G le M*, III, 103, n. 4.
19. *G le M*, III, 104ff; Gir Camb, *DPI*, 283; R of Hov, II, 363; R of Dic, II, 63.
20. Gir Camb, *DPI*, 256.
21. B of P, II, 67; G of C, I, 447.
22. Gir Camb, *DPI*, 301.
23. Gir Camb, *DPI*, 283.
24. *G le M*, III, 111-113.
25. B of P, II, 72.
26. Gir Camb, *DPI*, 296.
27. Gir Camb, *DPI*, 297; R of Hov, II, 366; *Flores Hist*, II, 102.
28. *G le M*, III, 114.
29. Gir Camb, *DPI*, 295.
30. Gir Camb, *Vita Galfredi*, 370-372.
31. R of Hov, II, 367; G of C, I, 449; B of P, II, 71.
32. G of C, I, 450.
33. B of P, II, 71; Gir Camb, *Vita Galfredi*, 372, *DPI*, 305.
34. R of Dic, II, 65.

NOTES TO CHAPTER 23: THE LION HEART IS KING

1. *G le M*, III, 118-19.
2. *G le M*, III, 121.
3. R of Dic, II, 67, 68; G of C, I, 443; Ingulph's Chronicle (Bn, 275) says a rumor of Henry's death reached England before he died.
4. MP, II, 4.
5. R of Hov, III, 7.
6. *G le M*, III, 122.
7. B of P, II, 74; R of Dic, II, 67.
8. R of Dic, II, 72.
9. R of Hov, III, 4.
10. R of Hov, III, 5.
11. R of Hov, III, 6.
12. R of Hov, III, 12; B of P, II, 83.
13. On "Egyptian days" and the manner of reckoning them, see R. T. Hampson, *Mediaeval Kalendarium, or Dates, Charters, and Customs of the Middle Ages*, 2 vols. (London: 1841), II, 107.
14. The Pipe Rolls for Richard I show large expense for Eleanor, Alais, Isabel of Pembroke, and others, for the coronation.
15. Wm of N, I, 302-03; R of D, 385.
16. Wm of N, I, 304-306.
17. R of Dic, II, 51ff.
18. Stubbs, *Hist Intros*, 207.
19. On Eleanor's dislike of Geoffrey the Chancellor, see Stubbs, *Hist Intros*, 268.
20. Gir Camb, *Vita Galfredi*, 379.
21. Stubbs, *Hist Intros*, 234.
22. Wm of N, I, 301.
23. Wm of N, I, 306; R of D, 385.
24. Wm of N, I, 306.
25. Gir Camb, *Vita Galfredi*, 420.
26. Wm of N, I, 300.
27. B of P, II, 99.
28. R of Hov, III, 28.
29. B of P, II, 105.
30. Richard, II, 268.
31. *Itin*, 147; R of Hov, III, 36.
32. *Itin*, 32.

NOTES TO CHAPTER 24: THE SICILIAN INTERLUDE

1. Amb, 15; B of P, II, 111.
2. R of Dic, II, 77.
3. R of D, 393.
4. R of Dic, II, 65.
5. B of P, II, 114ff.
6. R of Hov, III, 39ff; *Itin*, 152.
7. *Itin*, 156.
8. Wm of N, I, 324.
9. B of P, II, 101.
10. R of Dic, II, 85.
11. R of D, 395.
12. Vais, III, 248.
13. B of P, II, 126ff; R of Hov, III, 56.
14. R of D, 395-96; B of P, II, 132-33.

15. Amb, 23.
16. *Itin*, 167.
17. B of P, II, 158; *Itin*, 170–71.
18. R of Dic, II, 85.
19. B of P, II, 133.
20. P de L, II, 49; Gir Camb, *DPI*, 126.
21. R of Hov, III, 97; B of P, II, 159.
22. Rig, 91–92.
23. R of Hov, III, 99.
24. B of P, II, 160; *Ch Mx*, I, 256; Gir Camb, *DPI*, 282.
25. *Itin*, I, 171.
26. R of D, 395ff; R of Hov, III, 99.
27. B le T, 177; R of Dic, II, 86; R of Hov, III, 95.
28. Wm of N, I, 346.

29. Amb, 26.
30. R of D, 402; Wm of N, I, 346; Amb, 33.
31. B of P, II, 157; Landon, *Itin Rich I*, 47.
32. R of Dic, II, 86; R of D, 175. For Eleanor's encounter with Henry Hohenstaufen at Lodi, see Landon, *Itin Rich I*, 45.
33. P de L, II, 49.
34. R of Hov, III, 100; B of P, II, 161; R of Dic, II, 86; *Itin*, 176; Landon, *Itin Rich I*, 66; G of C, I, 512.
35. R of Dic, II, 81.
36. R of Hov, III, 100.
37. B of P, II, 161.
38. Richard II, 276; Stubbs, *Hist Intros*, 224.
39. Landon, *Itin Rich I*, 192.

NOTES TO CHAPTER 25: THINGS DONE OVERSEAS

1. R of Hov, III, 105; *Itin*, 176.
2. R of D, 405.
3. R of Hov, III, 72.
4. *Itin*, 178.
5. B le T, 179.
6. Stubbs, *Hist Intros*, 312, note.
7. R of Hov, III, 111.
8. B of P, II, 166; R of Hov, III, 110; *Itin*, 196.
9. *Itin*, 197.
10. R of Hov, III, 108, note; *Itin*, 195; Landon, *Itin Rich I*, 49.
11. La Monte, 29–43.
12. B le T, 19.
13. B le T, 47; *Itin*, 59; Wm of T, II, 493.
14. G de N, 63.
15. Ramsay, *Angevin Empire*, 326.
16. *Itin*, 97; B le T, 173.
17. *Itin*, 67.
18. *Itin*, 122; Amb, 62.
19. B of P, II, 171; Wm of N, I, 349.
20. Wm of N, I, 353–355.
21. *Itin*, 212.
22. *Itin*, 218ff.
23. Amb, 70.
24. *Itin*, 220.
25. *Itin*, 225.
26. *Itin*, 234.
27. G of C, I, 514.
28. B le T, 195; *Itin*, 279.
29. B of P, II, 181; Wm of N, I, 360, 373–375.
30. *Itin*, 254.
31. G le B, *Philippide*, 108.
32. Wm of N, I, 358; *Itin*, 236.
33. Wm of N, I, 357.

34. R of Dic, II, 95.
35. B of P, II, 182ff.
36. R of Hov, III, 123–24; B of P, II, 182.
37. Wm of N, I, 354.
38. B of P, II, 171; R of Hov, III, 114.
39. R of Hov, III, 124.
40. B of P, II, 184.
41. *Itin*, 239; B of P, II, 184; Wm of N, I, 357.
42. R of Hov, III, 125–127.
43. Rig, 105.
44. B of P, II, 204.
45. Wm of N, I, 358.
46. B of P, II, 229; R of Hov, III, 166.
47. R of Hov, III, 167.
48. B of P, II, 235.
49. R of Dic, II, 104.
50. Wm of N, I, 376.
51. *Itin*, 341; R of D, 450.
52. Wm of N, I, 363.
53. *Itin*, 305.
54. B le T, 190–91.
55. *Itin*, 336.
56. Bohaddin, 334–338.
57. *Itin*, 296.
58. R of D, 443.
59. B le T, 175.
60. R of D, 418.
61. *Itin*, 351, 358.
62. B of P, II, 192.
63. *Itin*, 333–335.
64. B le T, 199.
65. *Itin*, 338.
66. On the Assassins, see *Itin*, 339.
67. Wm of N, I, 363; B le T, 203; G de N, 76.

68. Ansbertus, in R of Hov, III, cxliii.
69. B le T, 201.
70. Alatir (Mich IV, 339n).
71. *Itin*, 342.
72. *Itin*, 348.
73. *Itin*, 348.
74. Bohaddin, 346.

75. Wm of N, I, 378; Stubbs, *Hist Intros*, 362ff.
76. Bohaddin, 347n.
77. Wm of N, I, 378.
78. *Itin*, 436.
79. R of D, 454.
80. *Itin*, 442.

NOTES TO CHAPTER 26: SHIPWRECK AND DISGUISE

1. R of Hov, III, 185.
2. Wm of N, I, 382; R of Dic, II, 106.
3. Amb, 159; *Itin*, 441.
4. B le T, 209.
5. B le T, 211.
6. *Itin*, 442.
7. R of Hov, III, 185.
8. R of Dic, II, 106.
9. R of C, 53.
10. R of Hov, III, 194.
11. R of C, 53–60.
12. Richard had used Pisan ships on his outward journey, and Pisans had supported him in the East.

13. R of Hov, III, 185.
14. Wm of N, I, 382.
15. Rig, 109–10.
16. R of C, 54.
17. R of C, 55.
18. At an earlier stage Baldwin seems to have impersonated Richard near Ragusa. For Richard's disguise, see R of Hov, III, 185.
19. R of C, 55–56; R of Hov, III, 186.
20. R of C, 56.
21. B le T, 213–14. Otto of St. Blaise, p. 543, says Richard was betrayed by a precious ring he forgot to remove.
22. R of C, 56.

NOTES TO CHAPTER 27: ELEANOR QUEEN OF ENGLAND

1. Gir Camb, *DPI*, 301.
2. R of D, 406.
3. R of D, 406.
4. R of D, 406.
5. Wm of N, I, 336.
6. Stubbs, *Hist Intros*, 227.
7. Gir Camb, *Vita Galfredi*, 382, 387–393; B of P, II, 211; Wm of N, I, 340.
8. B of P, II, 212.
9. Wm of N, I, 342ff; R of Hov, III, 144.
10. B of P, II, 213.
11. Gir Camb, *Vita Galfredi*, 410–11; B of P, II, 215.
12. B of P, II, 221.
13. R of D, 419.
14. B of P, II, 246.
15. B of P, II, 247; R of D, 419.
16. R of D, 420.
17. B of P, II, 225.
18. B of P, II, 223.

19. R of D, 419.
20. R of D, 420.
21. R of D, 431–32.
22. G of C, I, 514; R of Hov, III, 179.
23. B of P, II, 235; *Flores Hist*, II, 107.
24. G le B, *Philippide*, 108.
25. Wm of N, I, 266–67.
26. Rig, 105.
27. B le T, 204; Wm of N, I, 366.
28. R of D, 431.
29. R of Hov, III, 187.
30. B of P, II, 236.
31. B of P, II, 236.
32. B of P, II, 237.
33. R of D, 432; B of P, II, 236.
34. Gir Camb, *Vita Galfredi*, 413; R of Hov, III, 188.
35. R of D, 434.
36. R of D, 406.

NOTES TO CHAPTER 28: THE RANSOM

1. G of C, I, 514; R of Hov, III, 194.
2. R of Hov, III, 228.
3. R of Hov, III, 195.
4. R of Hov, III, 195–96.
5. Wm of N, I, 388.
6. R of Hov, III, 198.
7. Minstrel of Reims, 275.

8. Richard, II, 282.
9. Wm of N, I, 384; G le M, III, 128.
10. R of Hov, III, 204.
11. G of C, I, 514–15.
12. R of C, 61–62.
13. B of P, II, 236.
14. R of Hov, III, 207.

15. G of C, I, 514-15.
16. R of Hov, III, 198.
17. Ansbertus, in R of Hov, III, cxl.
18. Wm of N, I, 286-87.
19. Ansbertus, in R of Hov, III, cxli-cxlii. Stubbs, *Hist Intros*, 249, estimates that £100,000 sterling was more than twice as much as the whole revenue of the country accounted for in the last exchequer of Henry II. Ramsay, *Revenues*, I, 211, concludes that the ransom was equal to three years' average revenues in the time of Henry II.
20. R of Hov, III, 215-16.
21. R of Hov, III, 199.
22. R of Dic, II, 106-07.
23. *Flores Hist*, II, 108.
24. R of Hov, III, 199; Wm of N, I, 388.
25. R of Dic, II, 106-07.
26. G of C, I, 516.
27. Wm of N, I, 389.
28. The original poem may be found in Raynouard, IV, 183. Translation is by Henry Adams in *Mont-Saint-Michel and Chartres* (Boston: Houghton Mifflin Company, 1904), p. 222, and is quoted by permission of the publisher.
29. *Itin*, 67.
30. Coeur-de-Lion addresses himself particularly to those on whom he had at his crowning bestowed valuable marriage prizes.
31. R of Hov, III, 208-09.
32. R of Dic, II, 127.
33. R of Hov (Bohn ed.) II, 288. The passage is omitted in the Rolls.
34. R of C, 58.
35. R of Hov, III, 210.
36. Caen, the seat of the Norman exchequer, contributed more than London to the ransom (Davis, *Eng. under the Angevins*, 335).
37. Wm of N, I, 399.
38. R of Dic, II, 110; Annals of Margam, 22.

39. P of B, *Epist*, *PL* 207:431.
40. Wm of N, I, 400.
41. Gir Camb, *Vita Galfredi*, 415.
42. R of Hov, III, 212.
43. *Ch St M*, 192.
44. The castle of Bourges. The allusion is to Henry's support of Alexander against Octavian (cf. Hugo Pictaviensis, *Vezelaicensis Monasterii*, *HGF* XIX, 278n).
45. *Fd*, I, 72-78.
46. O of St B, 540.
47. R of Hov, IV, 31.
48. Rig, 137-38.
49. R of Hov, III, 212-214.
50. Wm of N, I, 398.
51. *G le M*, III, 133.
52. Landon, *Itin Rich I*, 77.
53. Rig, 112-13.
54. Wm of N, I, 368-370.
55. R of Hov, III, 225; Wm of N, I, 385-86.
56. R of Dic, II, 111.
57. R of Hov, III, 216.
58. R of Hov, III, 227.
59. Landon, *Itin Rich I*, 82-83; Pipe Rolls, 6 Richard I, Intro., xiv; R of Dic, II, 112.
60. R of Hov, III, 229-233.
61. Wm of N, I, 402.
62. R of Hov, III, 232.
63. R of Hov, III, 202; Landon, *Itin Rich I*, 83.
64. *Itin*, 143.
65. *Flores Hist*, II, 109.
66. R of Hov, III, 202.
67. R of Hov, III, 233.
68. R of Hov, III, 235; R of Dic, II, 114.
69. Wm of N, I, 404.
70. Wm of N, I, 404.
71. R of Dic, II, 114; G of C, I, 524.
72. R of Hov, III, 235; R of C, 62-63.
73. R of Hov, III, 233; Annals of Burton, 190.

NOTES TO CHAPTER 29: CAPTIVE AND BETRAYER

1. *G le M*, III, 134.
2. *Flores Hist*, II, 109.
3. R of Dic, II, 114; Wm of N, I, 406.
4. G of C, I, 524.
5. R of Hov, III, 238; Wm of N, I, 407.
6. R of Hov, III, 238.
7. *English and Scottish Popular Ballads*, edited from the collection of Francis James Child by Helen Child Sargent and George Lyman Kittredge (Boston: Houghton Mifflin Co., 1904).

8. Landon, *Itin Rich I*, 87; R of Hov, III, 240, 243.
9. Wm of N, I, 408.
10. R of Hov, III, 242.
11. R of Dic, II, 120; R of Hov, III, 268.
12. *G le M*, III, 136; G of C, I, 525; R of Hov, III, 247-48.
13. R of Hov, III, 248.
14. G of C, I, 527.
15. R of Hov, III, 251.
16. *G le M*, III, 136.

17. R of Dic, II, 114; *Flores Hist*, II, 110.
18. R of Hov, III, 134.
19. *G le M*, III, 134–137.
20. R of Hov, III, 252.
21. R of Dic, II, 117.
22. R of Hov, III, 301.
23. R of Hov, III, 256; R of Dic, II, 117.
24. R of Hov, III, 257.
25. R of Dic, II, 119.
26. R of Dic, II, 120.
27. Cf. Richard's *sirventés* to the Count of Auvergne in Le Roux de Lincy, *Chants historiques*, 65.
28. Gir Camb, *De Rebus*, 153.
29. Richard, II, 292.
30. Vais, III, 219–240.
31. Vais, III, 219–240; Annals of Winchester, 250.
32. *Ch St D*, 362.
33. R of Hov, III, 303; Landon, *Itin Rich I*, 227–229.
34. Rig, 121–22.

NOTES TO CHAPTER 30: THE TREASURE OF CHÂLUS

1. B of P, II, 146.
2. R of Hov, III, 290.
3. RN, 169; R of C, 97.
4. R of C, 92.
5. R of Hov, IV, 76.
6. R of Hov, IV, 3.
7. For Richard's other building in Normandy, see Powicke, *Loss of Normandy*, 168, 281.
8. *Flores Hist*, II, 118.
9. G le B, *Vie de P.A.*, 223.
10. Gir Camb, *DPI*, 290.
11. *Flores Hist*, II, 116.
12. R of Hov, IV, 31.
13. C. T. Lewis, 200.
14. R of Hov, IV, 37.
15. Matilda died July 13, 1189, a few days after the death of Henry II (R of Dic, II, 65).
16. Richard, II, 300.
17. *Flores Hist*, II, 117.
18. G le B, *Philippide*, 164.
19. R of Hov, IV, 56ff; *Flores Hist*, II, 119.
20. *G le M*, III, 152.
21. *G le M*, III, 156.
22. The Bishop of Beauvais, says De Larrey (1691 ed., p. 205), was the ambassador Philip Augustus had sent to Henry of Hohenstaufen to urge Richard's retention in captivity.
23. *G le M*, III, 156.
24. R of Hov, IV, 80–81.
25. There had been other marriage projects: Alais Capet to John; Philip's daughter Marie to Arthur of Brittany; Philip's son to Marie of Limoges (*Ch St M*, 137); Eleanor of Brittany to Louis Capet (R of Hov, III, 303).
26. Le Roux de Lincy, *Chants historiques*.
27. R of C, 94; Rig, 145. For a conjecture on the nature of the trove, see Richard, II, 322n.
28. G de V (Bonnélye ed.), 183.
29. G of C, I, 592, names the castle Nantrum; R of C, 94; R of Hov, IV, 82ff.
30. R of C, 95–96; R of Hov, IV, 83; G of C, I, 573; R of Dic, II, 166; R of W, I, 282–83.
31. On the Abbé of Turpenay, see Imbert, *Les Vicomtes de Thouars*.
32. R of C, 96; Landon, *Itin Rich I*, 144.
33. R of C, 98.
34. R of Dic, II, 116, calls him Pierre Basile; R of Hov, IV, 83, gives Bertran de Gurdun; G of C, I, 593, names him John Sabroz.
35. R of Hov, IV, 83.
36. By Mercadier, R of Hov, IV, 84; by Joanna, Annals of Winchester, 71.
37. R of C, 96.
38. R of W, I, 283; *Flores Hist*, II, 94.
39. R of C, 98.
40. On Philippe of Cognac, see Richard, II, 330; R of Hov, IV, 97.
41. Le Roux de Lincy, *Chants historiques*.

NOTES TO CHAPTER 31: LACKLAND'S PORTION

1. On the disorders, see R of C, 98; *Ch Eg*, 52; *Magna Vita*, 284.
2. *Magna Vita*, 113.
3. *Magna Vita*, 282–83.
4. *Magna Vita*, 284.
5. *Magna Vita*, 286.
6. Richard, II, 332–33, lists Peter of Capua, the Bishop of Agen, the Treasurer of the church of Angers, R. de Turnham, Berengaria, and Matilda of Perche.
7. *Magna Vita*, 286–87.
8. *Magna Vita*, 288.
9. *Magna Vita*, 290–93.
10. *G le M*, III, 159.
11. On legitimacy of the succession, see for John's case, R of Dic, II, 166, and *G le M*, III, 160; for Arthur's case, R of Hov, IV, 87, and G le B, *Philippide*, 149.
12. Addenda to *Ch Eg*, *HGF* XVIII, 325; *Ch T*, 145–46; R of W, I, 286.

13. R of C, 99–100; R of Hov, IV, 86.

14. Ranulf as hereditary viscount of the Avranchin made connection between Normandy and Brittany (Ramsay, *Angevin Empire*, 350).

15. R of Hov, IV, 7.

16. *Ch française des rois de France*, 762, n. 9; Richard II, 362; R of Hov, IV, 97.

17. G le B, *Philippide*, 131, and *Vie de P.A.*, 219–20.

18. Rig, 146; *Ch St M*, 295.

19. On the character of communes developing

in the time, see Henri Pirenne, *Mediaeval Cities*, tr. F. D. Halsey (Princeton, 1925). Guibert de Nogent (from the ecclesiastical view) calls them "pestilential communes."

20. Richard, II, 335ff.

21. Cirot de la Ville, *Hist de la Grande-Sauve*, II, 141.

22. Rig, 146; *Fd*, I, 113.

23. Vais, III, 246ff.

24. R of Hov, IV, 96.

25. Raymond, born in 1197 in Beaucaire (Vais, III, 243; R of Hov, IV, 21).

NOTES TO CHAPTER 32: BLANCHE AND ISABELLA

1. R of W, I, 289; W of C, II, 150.

2. R of Hov, IV, 87, 97.

3. R of Hov, IV, 107.

4. Richard, II, 335ff.

5. Cf. above, p. 154.

6. André des Trois Fontaines, 762.

7. Mariana, chap. XI.

8. Entwistle, 32ff.

9. In Appel, *Prov Chrest*, 27.

10. Blanche of Castile, mother of Saint Louis of France; Berengaria, mother of Saint Ferdinand of Spain.

11. Mariana, chap. XI.

12. Niño, 36ff.

13. R of Hov, IV, 114; *Ch St M*, 67.

14. R of Hov, IV, 115; R of Dic, II, 168; Rig, 153.

15. *Magna Vita*, 305.

16. R of Dic, II, 166–67; R of Hov, IV, 119; *G le M*, III, 161.

17. R of Dic, II, 170; Richard, II, 373.

18. R of Hov, IV, 119.

19. R of Hov, IV, 119.

20. R of Hov, IV, 124.

21. R of Hov, IV, 120; *G le M*, III, 162; *Ch T*, 146.

22. R of C, 135.

23. *Flores Hist*, II, 123; R of Dic, II, 172; R of Hov, IV, 139.

NOTES TO CHAPTER 33: MIREBEAU

1. *Fd*, I, 122.

2. *Flores Hist*, II, 123.

3. R of Hov, IV, 164; Rig, 154.

4. R of Hov, IV, 112ff; Rig, 112, 153, 155; *Ch Eg*, 51.

5. The interdict held from March 19, 1200, to September 7, 1200.

6. *Ch française des rois de France*, 760.

7. Rig, 155. Agnes died at Passy, July 19 or 20.

8. *Ch Brit*, 330; G le B, *Vie de P.A.*, 221.

9. R of C, 136.

10. Rig, 156; G le B, *Philippide*, 159; *Flores Hist*, II, 124–25.

11. G le B, *Philippide*, 165; R of C, 137; *Ch Eg*, 51; *Ch T*, 146; *Flores Hist*, II, 125.

12. G le B, *Philippide*, 162ff; R of C, 137.

13. G le B, *Philippide*, 167–68.

14. Hardy, *Rot Lit Pat*, Intro.; *Ch L*, 12, and *passim*; *Ch Nor*, I, 117.

NOTES TO CHAPTER 34: THE HOPE OF BRITTANY

1. *G le M*, III, 165.

2. *G le M*, III, 171–72.

3. R of C, 139.

4. *Ch Eg*, 52–53.

5. Arthur was born March 29, 1187 (R of Dic, II, 48).

6. Hardy, *Rot Lit Pat*, p. x.

7. *Flores Hist*, II, 125; R of W, I, 315.

8. R of C, 140–41.

9. R of C, 141; *Ch L*, 12.

10. G le B, *Philippide*, 170.

11. Hardy, *Rot Lit Pat*, 26.

12. Hardy, *Rot Lit Pat*, apud March 31.

13. G le B, *Philippide*, 170.

14. Powicke, *Loss of Normandy*, 468.

15. Annals of Margam, 27.

16. Hardy, *Rot Lit Pat*, 28f. Richard (II, 424–25) suggests the connection of this letter with the murder of Arthur; and Powicke (*Loss of Normandy*, 476) concurs.

17. *G le M*, III, 172.

18. Rig, 165; G le B, *Vie de P.A.*, 235–36.

19. *G le M*, III, 172, 176–77.
20. G le B, *Philippide*, 176, and *Vie de P.A.*, 226.
21. *G le M*, III, 172, 174, 175.

22. R of W, I, 317.
23. MP, I, 96–97.
24. R of C, 144.

NOTES TO CHAPTER 35: THE QUEEN GOES HOME

1. *Magna Vita*, 332; Gir Camb, *DPI*, 159, 300.
2. R of Hov, II, 13.
3. *Ch Eg* alone gives Poitiers as the place of her death. Peter of Blois (431–434) states that she died in the abbey of Fontevrault, where she had been received for penance at the end of her life, and that she there put on the monastic habit. So also *Ch St M*.

BIBLIOGRAPHY

Most of the twelfth-century sources are to be found in one or several of the following collections. Each collection is identified below by an abbreviation. In order to indicate the text that has been cited, the appropriate abbreviation for the collection from which it derives is then placed after each special source in the bibliography. The abbreviations that precede items are those used in the notes to identify particular sources frequently cited. In a number of cases, recent editions of medieval works are substituted for original texts as being more accessible.

Proper names offer difficulty for the bibliography as well as for the text, since the chroniclers offer them in English or French or Latin, often with many variants, and no scheme for regularizing them seems free from serious disadvantages. Certain names, in whichever language, have come through frequent use to identify individuals or places that would seem strange under other designations. Whatever are assumed to be familiar titles are therefore retained.

COLLECTIONS

Bn — Bohn, H. G., *Bohn's Antiquarian Library*, 44 vols. (London, 1847–1913).

R — *Chronicles and Memorials of Great Britain and Ireland during the Middle Ages*, Rolls Series, 198 vols. (London, 1858–1899).

HGF — Delisle, Léopold, ed., *Recueil des historiens des Gaules et de la France*, 24 vols. (Paris, 1869–1880).

Guiz — Guizot, F. P. G., *Collection des Mémoires relatifs à l'histoire de France, depuis la fondation de la monarchie française jusqu'au 13ᵉ siècle*, 32 vols. (Paris, 1823–1836).

Mich — Michaud, Joseph, *Bibliothèque des croisades*, 4 vols. (Paris, 1829).

PL — Migne, J. P., *Patrologiae Latinae, Cursus Completus a Tertulliano ad Innocentium III*, 221 vols. (Paris, 1844–1864).

HC — *Recueil des historiens des croisades*, Auteurs occidentaux (5 vols.; Paris, 1844–1895), et auteurs orientaux (5 vols.; Paris, 1872–1906), par les soins de l'Académie Impériale des Inscriptions et Belles-Lettres.

Fd — Rymer, Thomas, and Sanderson, Robert, *Foedera, Conventiones, et cujuscunque generis Acta Publica*, 20 vols. (London, 1704–1735).

INDIVIDUAL WORKS

Ab — Abaelardus, Petrus, *Opera Omnia* (*PL* 178).
   Epistolae (*PL* 178:113ff).
   Historia Calamitatum. See Bellows.
   Sic et Non (*PL* 178:1329ff).
   Abel, F. M., *L'État de la Cité de Jerusalem au XIIᵉ siècle*, in Publication of the Council of the Pro-Jerusalem Society (1920–1922).
   Adams, Henry, *Mont-Saint-Michel and Chartres* (Boston: Houghton Mifflin Co., 1904).

A of T — Alan of Tewkesbury, *Life of Becket*, J. C. Robertson, ed. (R 67, II).

Amb — Ambrose, *L'Estoire de la guerre sainte. See* Stone.

Andreas   Andreas Capellanus, *De Amore. See* Pagès, Parry.
André des Trois Fontaines, *Ex Chronico* (*HGF* XVIII).
Anonyme de Béthune, Chronique d'un (*HGF* XXIV²).
Anonymous, *Life of Becket*, J. C. Robertson, ed. (R 67, IV).
Ansbertus, *Historia de Expeditione Frederici Imperatoris*, J. Dobrowsky, ed. (Prague, 1887). Also in Hoveden (R 51), III, appendix 2.
Appel, Carl, *Bernard von Ventadour, seine Lieder* (Halle, 1915).
   Provenzalische Chrestomathie (Leipsic, 1912).
Baudri de Bourgueil, *Les Oeuvres poétiques*, Phyllis Abrams, ed. (Paris, 1926).
Becket, Thomas, *Thomás Saga Erkibyskups; A Life of Archbishop Thomas Becket in Icelandic* (Icelandic Life of Becket), M. Eiríkr Magnússon, ed. and tr., 2 vols. (R 65).
   Epistles and Known Letters of (R 67, V, VI, ed. J. C. Robertson; VII, ed. J. B. Sheppard).
Bellows, H. A., ed. and tr., *Peter Abélard's "Historia Calamitatum"* (St. Paul, 1922).

B of P   Benedict of Peterborough, *Gesta Regis Henrici Secundi* (Chronicle of the reigns of Henry II and Richard I, 1169–1192), William Stubbs, ed., 2 vols. (R 49). Modern scholars doubt that Benedict wrote the chronicle that has borne his name; but since his name occurs in the title to the text cited here, B of P is used to designate references to that text. Unless otherwise noted, B of P references are to the *Gesta*.
   The Passion and Miracle of . . . Becket, J. C. Robertson, ed. (R 67, II).

B de Ste M   Benoît de Sainte-Maure, *Chronique des ducs de Normandie*, F. Michel, ed. (Paris, 1938).
   Le Roman de Troie, L. Constans, ed. (Paris, 1904).
Berengarius Scholasticus (of Poitiers), *Apologia pro Petro Abaelardo* (*PL* 178:1857ff).
Bermondsey, Annals of, H. R. Luard, ed. (R 36, III).

Bern   Bernard of Clairvaux, *Opera Omnia* (*PL* 182–185 *bis*).
   De Consideratione. See Lewis, George.
   Epistolae (*PL* 182).
   Vita Prima, 7 pts., by Guillelmus, Ernaldus, Galfredus, and Herbert (*PL* 185:225ff).
   Vita Secunda, by Alanus (*PL* 185:469ff).
   Vita Tertia, fragments by Galfredus Clarae-Vallensis (*PL* 185:523ff).

B le T   Bernard le Trésorier, *Continuation de l'histoire des croisades de Guillaume de Tyr* (Guiz XIX).

BG   Bernardus Guido, *Ex Libro* (*HGF* XII).
Berry, André, ed. and tr., *Florilège des troubadours* (Paris: Firmin-Didot, 1930).
Berthaud, Auguste, *Gilbert de la Porrée* (Poitiers, 1892).
Bohaddin, *Suite de la troisième croisade*, M. Reinaud, ed. (Mich IV, 302ff).
Boissonnade, Prosper, *Histoire de Poitou* (Paris, 1926).
Borenius, Tancred, *St. Thomas Becket in Art* (London: Methuen and Co., 1932).
Bouchet, Jean, *Les Annales d'Aquitaine* (Poitiers, 1644).
Brittain, Fred, *The Medieval Latin and Romance Lyric* (Cambridge University Press, 1937).

Bromton, Jean, *Chronique* (Mich II, 732ff).

Burton, Annals of, H. R. Luard, ed. (R 36, I).

Butler, H. E., *Giraldus Cambrensis, Autobiography* (*De Rebus a Se Gestis*), (London: Jonathan Cape, 1937).

Cambridge Medieval History, J. B. Bury, general editor, 8 vols. (New York, 1911–1936).

Carducci, Giosuè, "Un Poeta d'amore nel secolo XII," in *Opere*, 20 vols. (Bologna, 1889–1909), vol. VIII (1893): *Studi letterari*.

Chalandon, Ferdinand, *Les Comnène, Études sur l'empire byzantin au XI' et au XII' siècles* (Paris, 1912).

Chartrou, Josèphe (Mme Josèphe [Chartrou] Charbonnel), *L'Anjou de 1109 à 1151, Foulque de Jerusalem et Geoffroi Plantagenet* (Paris [1928]).

Chevalier, Ulysse, *Répertoire des sources historiques du moyen âge, bio-bibliographie*, 2 pts. in 3 vols. (Paris, 1877–1888).

    Topo-Bibliographie (Paris, 1894–1903).

Ch Brit   (Ex) *Chronico Britannico* (*HGF* XVIII).

    (Ex) *Chronico Britannico Altero* (*HGF* XVIII).

Ch Eg   *Chroniques des églises d'Anjou*, P. Marchegay and E. Mabille, eds. (Paris, 1869).

Ch L   *Chronicle of Lanercost*, Joseph Stevenson, ed. (Edinburgh, 1839).

Ch M   (Ex) *Chronico Mauriniacensi* (*HGF* XII).

Ch Mx   *Chronicle of Meaux*, E. A. Bond, ed., 3 vols. (R 43).

Ch Nor   *Chroniques de Normandie*, Francisque Michel ed. (Rouen, 1839).

Ch St D   *Chronique de St. Denis* (*HGF* XIII; Mich II) = *Suite des grandes chroniques de France*.

    Chronique française des rois de France (*HGF* XXIV ') = *Anonyme de Béthune*.

Ch St M   *Chronique de St. Martial*, H. Duplès-Agier, ed. (Paris, 1874).

Ch T   *Chronique de Touraine*, A. Salmon, ed. (Tours, 1894).

Cinnamos, Jean, *Histoire de* (Mich III, 434ff).

Cirot de la Ville, *Histoire de l'abbaye et congrégation de Notre-Dame de la Grande-Sauve*, 2 vols. (Bordeaux, 1845).

Clédat, Léon, *Du rôle historique de Bertrand de Born* (Paris, 1879).

Coulton, G. G., *Life in the Middle Ages*, 4 vols. (2nd ed.; New York: The Macmillan Co., 1930).

    Mediaeval Panorama (New York: The Macmillan Co., 1938).

D'Arbois de Jubainville, M. H., *L'Histoire des ducs et des comtes de Champagne* (Paris, 1860).

Davis, H. W. C., *England under the Normans and Angevins, 1066–1272* (London, 1921).

Dawes, E. A. S., *The Alexiad of the Princess Anna Comnena* (London, 1928).

Dawson, C. H., *Mediaeval Religion* (New York: Sheed and Ward, 1934).

De Larrey, Isaac, *Histoire d'Éléonor de Guyenne* (Rotterdam, 1691, and London, 1788).

Demimuid, Maurizio, *Jean de Salisbury* (Paris, 1873).

De Montfaucon, Bernard, *Les Monumens de la monarchie françoise*, 5 vols. (Paris, 1729–1733), vol. II: *La Conquête de l'Angleterre . . . jusqu'à Jean II.*

De Villepreux, L., *Éléonore de Guyenne* (Paris, 1862).

Dickinson, John, *The Statesman's Book* (New York, 1927). Portions of John of Salisbury's *Polycraticus.*

Diehl, Charles, *La Société byzantine à l'époque des Comnènes* (Paris, 1929.

Diener, Bertha, *Imperial Byzantium*, tr. Eden and Cedar Paul (Boston: Little, Brown and Co., 1938).

Dufour, J. M., *De l'ancien Poitou et de sa capitale* (Poitiers, 1826).

Eales, S. J., *J. Mabillon's Life and Works of St. Bernard, Abbot of Clairvaux*, edited with additional notes (London, 1889).

EG   Edward Grim, *Life of Becket*, J. C. Robertson, ed. (R 67, II).

Entwistle, W. J., *The Arthurian Legend in the Literatures of the Spanish Peninsula* (London, 1925).

Eyton, R. W., *Court, Household, and Itinerary of King Henry II* (London, 1878).

Flores Historiarum ("Matthew of Westminster"), H. R. Luard, ed., 3 vols. (R 95).

F of C   Fulcher of Chartres, *Chronicle of the First Crusade* (*Historia hierosolymitana*), M. E. McGinty, ed. and tr. (Philadelphia: University of Pennsylvania Press, 1941).

Gaillard, A., *Deux Paroisses de l'ancien temps* (Bordeaux, 1909).

G of M   Geoffrey of Monmouth, *Historia regum Britanniæ*, Acton Griscom and R. E. Jones, eds. and trs. (London, 1929).

G de V   Geoffroi de Vigeois, *Chronique* (*HGF* XII and XVIII).

Geoffroy, Prieur de Vigeois, La Chronique de, F. Bonnélye, ed. and tr. (Tulle, 1864).

Gervaise, F. A., *Histoire de Suger*, 3 vols. (Nevers, 1721).

G of C   Gervase of Canterbury, *Opera Historica*, William Stubbs, ed. 2 vols. (R 73).

G of T   Gervase of Tillbury, *Otia Imperialia*, Joseph Stevenson, ed. (R 66).

Gst L. VII   *Gestes de Louis VII* (Mich I, 212ff).

Gir Camb   Giraldus Cambrensis, *Itinerarium Kambriae*, J. F. Dimock, ed. (R 21, VI).

DPI   *De Principis Instructione*, G. F. Warner, ed. (R 21, VIII).

De Rebus a Se Gestis. See Butler.

Speculum Ecclesiae, J. S. Brewer, ed. (R 21, IV).

De vita Galfredi, J. S. Brewer, ed. (R 21, IV).

Great Roll of the Pipe for the First Year of the Reign of Richard I. (*1189–90*), J. Hunter, ed. (London, 1844).

Green, M. A. E., *Lives of the Princesses of England from the Norman Conquest*, 6 vols. (London, 1857).

Gross, Charles, *The Sources and Literature of English History* (London, 1900).

Grousset, René, *Histoire des Croisades*, 3 vols. (Paris: Plon, 1935).

Guernes de Pont-Sainte-Maxence, *La Vie de Saint Thomas le martyr*, E. Walberg, ed. (Lund, 1922).

G le B   Guillaume le Breton, *La Philippide* (Guiz XII).

Vie de Philippe Auguste (Guiz XI).

De Gestis Philippe-Auguste (*HGF* XVII).

G le M   *Guillaume le Maréchal, L'Histoire de*, Paul Meyer, ed. and tr., 3 vols. (Paris, 1891–1901).

G de N   Guillaume de Nangis, *Chronique* (Guiz XIII).

G de St D   Guillaume de St. Denis, *Vita Sugerii* (*PL* 186; also *HGF* XII).

Hall, Hubert, *Court Life under the Plantagenets* (London, 1901).

Halphen, Louis, *Paris sous les premiers Capétiens* (Paris, 1909).

Hardy, T. D., ed., *Rotuli Litterarum Patentium in Turri Londinensi Asservati* (London: Commission on the Public Records of the Kingdom, 1835).

Harvey, John H., *The Plantagenets, 1154–1485* (London: B. T. Batsford, 1948).

Haskins, C. H., *The Renaissance of the Twelfth Century* (Cambridge: Harvard University Press, 1927).

    The Rise of Universities (New York, 1923).

    Studies in Mediaeval Culture (Oxford: Clarendon Press, 1929).

Hearne, Thomas, *Guilielmus Neubrigensis, Historia Rerum Anglicorum*, 3 vols. (Oxford, 1719).

Heltzel, V. B., *Fair Rosamond* (Evanston: Northwestern University, Studies in the Humanities, no. 16, 1947).

H of H   Henry of Huntingdon, *Historia Anglorum*, Thomas Arnold, ed. (R 74).

HB   Herbert Bosham, *Life of Becket*, J. C. Robertson, ed. (R 67, III).

Hilarius, *Versus et Ludi*, J. J. Champollion-Figeac, ed. (Paris, 1938).

Hill, R. T., and Bergin, T. G., *Anthology of the Provençal Troubadours* (New Haven: Yale University Press, 1941).

(Ex) *Historia Episcoparum Autissiodorensium* (*HGF* XII).

Hist Fr   *Historia Francorum* (*HGF* XII).

HGRL VII   *Historia Gloriosi Regis Ludovici VII* (*HGF* XII).

Holmes, U. T., *A History of Old French Literature, from the Origins to 1300* (New York: F. S. Crofts and Co., 1937).

Hucher, Eugène, *Études sur l'histoire et les monuments de la Sarthe* (Le Mans, 1856).

Hugh of Sens to Suger, *Epistolae* (*HGF* XV).

Hutton, W. H., *Philip Augustus* (New York, 1896).

    Thomas Becket, Archbishop of Canterbury (rev. ed.; Cambridge University Press, 1926).

Imbert, Hugues, *Notice sur les Vicomtes de Thouars* (Thouars, 1864).

Itin   *Itinerarium Peregrinorum et Gesta Regis Ricardi* ("Vinsauf"), William Stubbs, ed. (R 38, I).

J de V   *Jacques de Vitry, Histoire de Jérusalem* (Mich I, 168ff).

J of S   John of Salisbury, *Epistolae* (R 67, V, VI; also *PL* 199).

    Historiae Pontificalis Quae Supersunt. See Poole.

    Life of Becket, J. C. Robertson, ed. (R 67, II).

    Polycraticus (*PL* 199:385ff). See also Dickinson, Pike.

JF   Jordan Fantosme, *Metrical Chronicle*, Richard Howlett, ed. (R 82, III).

Kiessmann, Rudolph, *Untersuchen über die Bedeutung Eleanorens von Poitou für die Litterature ihrer Zeit* (Bernberg, 1901).

Kirby, T. A., *Chaucer's Troilus, A Study in Courtly Love* (Louisiana State University Press, 1940).

Lachmann, Karl, and Haupt, Moriz, *Des Minnesangs Frühling* (Leipsic, 1875).

La Monte, J. L., *Feudal Monarchy in the Latin Kingdom of Jerusalem 1100–1291* (Cambridge: Mediaeval Academy of America, 1932).

Landon, Lionel, *The Itinerary of King Richard I* (London: printed for Pipe Roll Society by J. W. Ruddock and Sons, 1935).

Langlois, C. V., *La Vie en France au moyen âge* (Paris, 1926).

Le Roux de Lincy, A. J. V., *Recueil de chants historiques français depuis le XII⁰ jusqu'au XVIII⁰ siècle*, 2 vols. (Paris, 1841–42).

Lewis, Charlton T., *A History of Germany from the Earliest Times* (New York, 1885).

Lewis, C. S., *The Allegory of Love* (Oxford: Clarendon Press, 1936).

Lewis, George, tr., *Saint Bernard, On Consideration* (Oxford, 1908).

Loomis, R. S., "The Arthurian Legend before 1139," *The Romanic Review* (February 1941).

    "Bleheris and the Tristram Story," *Modern Language Notes*, vol. XXXIX, no. 6.

    The Romance of Tristram and Ysolt by Thomas of Britain, tr. from Old French and Old Norse (rev. ed.; New York: Columbia University Press, 1931).

    "Tristram and the House of Anjou," *Modern Language Review*, XVII (January 1922).

Louis VII to Suger, *Epistolae* (*HGF* XV, XVI).

Luchaire, Achille, *Histoire des institutions monarchiques de la France*, 2 vols. (Paris, 1891).

Lyttelton, Lord George, *The History of the Life of King Henry the Second*, 4 vols. (London, 1767–1771).

McCabe, Joseph, *Peter Abélard* (New York, 1901).

McNeal, E. H., tr., *Robert de Clari, The Conquest of Constantinople* (New York: Columbia University Press, 1936).

Magna Vita Sancti Hugonis Episcopi Lincolniensis, J. F. Dimock, ed. (R 37).

Mariana, Juan de, *Historia de España* (Madrid, 1780).

Margan (Margam), Annals of, H. R. Luard, ed. (R 36, I).

Markham, V. R. *Romanesque France* (New York, 1929).

MP   Matthew Paris, *Historia Anglorum, sive, ut vulgo dicitur, Historia Minor, 1067–1253*, Sir Frederick Madden, ed., 3 vols. (R 44).

Michaud, Joseph, *A History of the Crusades*, W. Robson, tr., 3 vols. (New York, 1881).

Minstrel of Reims, *Chronicle of Reims. See* Stone.

Molinier, Auguste, *Les sources de l'histoire de France des origines aux guerres d'Italie*, 6 vols. (Paris, 1901–1906).

    Vie de Louis le Gros par Suger, suivie de l'histoire du roi Louis VII (Paris, 1887).

Morey, C. R., *Mediaeval Art* (New York: W. W. Norton and Co., 1942).

Munro, D. C., *The Kingdom of the Crusaders* (New York: D. Appleton-Century Co., 1935).

Nicetas Choniate, *Histoire de* (Mich III, 402ff).

Niño, Don Pedro, *Sumario de los Reyes de España*, in *Colección de las crónicas de Castilla* (Madrid, 1782), vol III, pt. 1.

Nitze, W. A., and Dargan, E. P., *A History of French Literature* (3rd ed.; New York, 1938).

Norgate, Kate, *England under the Angevin Kings*, 2 vols. (London and New York, 1887).

　　John Lackland (New York, 1902).

　　Richard the Lion Heart (London, 1924).

Nostredame, Jehan de, *Les Vies des plus célèbres et anciens poètes provençaux*, Camille Chabaneau and Joseph Anglade, eds. (Paris, 1913).

Nykl, A. R., *Hispano-Arabic Poetry and its Relations with the Old Provençal Troubadours* (Baltimore: J. H. Furst and Co., 1946), esp. chap. VII.

O of D　　Odonis de Diogolo (Odo of Duilio), *De Ludovici VII Francorum Regis, Profectione in Orientem* (*PL* 185 *bis*: 1205).

OV　　Ordericus Vitalis, *The Ecclesiastical History of England and Normandy*, Thomas Forester, ed. and tr., 4 vols. (London, 1853). (Bn)

O of F　　Otto of Freising, *Des Gestes de l'empereur Frédéric Ier* (Mich II, 528ff).

O of St B　　Otto of St. Blaise, *Chronique* (Mich II, 540ff).

Pagès, Amadeu, ed., *Andreas Capellanus, De Amore* (Castelló de la Plana, 1930).

Panofsky, Erwin, ed. and tr., *Abbot Suger, on the Abbey Church of Saint-Denis and its Art Treasures* (*De Administratione and De Consecratione*) (Princeton: Princeton University Press, 1946).

Parry, J. J., ed. and tr., *The Art of Courtly Love* (*De Amore*) *by Andreas Capellanus* (New York: Columbia University Press, 1941). Unless otherwise indicated, this edition of Andreas is cited throughout the notes.

P of B　　Peter of Blois, *Opera Omnia* (*PL* 207).

Petrus de Ebulo (Pietro da Eboli), *Liber ad Honorem Augusti*, G. B. Siragusa, ed. (Rome, 1906), with Part II, which contains reproductions of miniatures of the period.

Pierre de la Celle, *Epistolae* (*HGF* XII, 398ff).

P de L　　Pierre de Langtoft, *Chronicle*, Thomas Wright, ed., 2 vols. (R 47).

Pike, J. B., *Frivolities of Courtiers and Footprints of Philosophers* (Minneapolis: University of Minnesota Press, 1938). Portions of John of Salisbury's *Polycraticus*.

Pirenne, Henri, *Economic and Social History of Mediaeval Europe*, tr. I. E. Clegg (New York: Harcourt Brace and Co., 1937).

Poëte, Marcel, *L'Enfance de Paris* (Paris, 1908).

Polydore Vergil, *Anglicae Historiae* (Basle, 1557).

Poole, R. L., *Illustrations of the History of Medieval Thought and Learning* (2nd ed., rev.; New York, 1920).

　　John of Salisbury's *Historiae Pontificalis Quae Supersunt* (Oxford: Clarendon Press, 1927).

Porter, A. K., *Mediaeval Architecture, its Origins and Development*, 2 vols. (New York, 1909).

　　Romanesque Sculpture of the Pilgrimage Roads, 10 vols. with plates (Boston, 1923).

Potthast, August, *Bibliotheca Historica Medii Aevi*, 2 vols. (Berlin, 1896).

Power, Eileen, *Mediaeval English Nunneries* (Cambridge University Press, 1922).

Powicke, F. M., *The Christian Life in the Middle Ages* (Oxford: Clarendon Press, 1935).

    The Loss of Normandy (Manchester University Press, 1913).

R of C   Ralph of Coggeshall, *Chronicon Anglicanum*, Joseph Stevenson, ed. (R 66).

R of Dic   Ralph of Diceto, *Opera Historica*, William Stubbs, ed., 2 vols. (R 68).

RN   Ralph Niger, *Chronica*, Robert Anstruther, ed. (Caxton Society, 1851).

Ramsay, Sir J. H., *The Angevin Empire* (Oxford University Press, 1903).

    A History of Revenues of the Kings of England, 1066–1399, 2 vols. (Oxford: Clarendon Press, 1925).

R Hig   Ranulf Higden, *Polychronicon*, 9 vols.: I–II, Churchill Babington, ed.; III–IX, J. R. Lumby, ed. (R 41).

Rashdall, Hastings, *The Universities of Europe in the Middle Ages*, 2 vols. in 3 (Oxford: Clarendon Press, 1895).

Raynouard, F. J. M., *Choix des poésies originales des troubadours*, 6 vols. (Paris, 1816–1821).

Reese, Gustave, *Music in the Middle Ages* (New York: W. W. Norton and Co., 1940).

Richard, Alfred, *Histoire des ducs et des comtes de Poitou, 778–1204*, 2 vols. (Paris, 1903).

R of D   Richard of Devizes, *Chronicle*, Richard Howlett, ed. (R 82, III).

R le P   Richard le Poitevin, *Ex Chronico* (*HGF* XII).

Rig   Rigord, *Vie de Philippe Auguste* (Guiz XI).

R of Clari   Robert of Clari, *The History of Them that Took Constantinople. See Stone.*

R of T   Robert of Torigni (Robert de Monte), *Chronicle*, Richard Howlett, ed. (R 82, IV).

Robinson, J. A., "Peter of Blois," in *Somerset Historical Essays* (London, 1921).

R of Hov   Roger of Hoveden, *Chronica*, William Stubbs, ed., 4 vols. (R 51).

R of W   Roger of Wendover, *Flores Historiarum*, H. G. Hewlett, ed., 3 vols. (R 84).

Rorimer, J. J., *The Cloisters* (New York: The Metropolitan Museum of Art, 1938).

Runciman, Steven, *Byzantine Civilisation* (London, 1936), esp. chap. viii.

Sigebert, Appendix (*HGF* XII).

Smith, C. E., *Papal Enforcement of Some Mediaeval Marriage Laws* (Baton Rouge: Louisiana State University Press, 1940).

Stenton, F. M., *Norman London*, Essay with translation of William Fitz-Stephen's description by H. E. Butler and a map of London under Henry II by M. B. Honeybourne, annotated by E. J. Davis (London: G. Bell and Sons, 1934).

Stephen of Paris, *Fragmentum Historicum de Ludovico VII* (*HGF* XII).

Stimming, Albert, *Bertran von Born* (Halle: Romanische Bibliothek, 1892).

Stone, E. N., tr., *Three Old French Chronicles of the Crusades*: Ambrose, *L'Estoire de la guerre sainte*; Robert of Cleri, *L'Estoire de chiaus qui conquisent Constantinople*; Minstrel de Reims, *La Chronique de Reims* (Seattle: University of Washington, 1939).

Stothard, C. A., *The Monumental Effigies of Great Britain*, J. Hewitt, ed. (new ed.; London, 1876).

Stubbs, William, *Historical Introductions to the Rolls Series*, Arthur Hassell, ed. (London, 1902).

    Lectures on Mediaeval and Modern History (Oxford, 1887).

Sug   Suger, *De Administratione and De Consecratione*. See Panofsky.

    Epistolae (HGF XV).

    Vie de Louis le Gros and *Vie de Louis VII*. See Molinier.

Suite des grandes chroniques de France = *Chronique de St. Denis*, q.v.

Thomas Agnellus, *De Morte et Sepultura Henrici Regis Angliae Junioris*, Joseph Stevenson, ed. (R 66).

Thomas, Antoine, *Bertran de Born,, Poésies Complètes* (Toulouse, 1888).

Timbs, John, *Curiosities of London* (London, 1868).

Turner, T. H., *Some Account of Domestic Architecture in England, from the Norman Conquest to the 13th Century*, 3 vols. (Oxford, 1851–1859).

Vac   Vacandard, Elphège, *Vie de Saint Bernard, Abbé de Clairvaux*, 2 vols. (Paris, 1927).

Vais   Vaissete, Joseph, *Abrégé de l'histoire générale de Longuedoc*, 5 vols. (Paris, 1799).

Waddell, Helen, *Mediaeval Latin Lyrics* (New York: R. R. Smith, Inc., 1929).

    The Wandering Scholars (New York: Houghton Mifflin, 1927).

W of C   Walter of Coventry, *Historical Collections*, William Stubbs, ed., 2 vols. (R 58).

WM   Walter Map, *De Nugis Curialium* (*Courtiers' Trifles*), Frederick Tupper and M. B. Ogle, eds. and trs. (London, 1924).

Waverley, Annals of, H. R. Luard, ed. (R 36, II).

Webb, C. C. J., *John of Salisbury* (Oxford: Clarendon Press, 1932).

Wm of C William of Canterbury, *Life of Becket*, J. C. Robertson, ed. (R 67, I).

Wm FS   William Fitz-Stephen, Life of Becket, J. C. Robertson, ed. (R 67, III).

Wm of M William of Malmesbury, *De Regum Gestis Anglorum*, William Stubbs, ed., 2 vols. (R 90).

Wm of N William of Newburgh, *Historia Rerum Anglicarum*, Richard Howlett, ed. (R 82, I, II).

Wm of T William of Tyre, *A History of Deeds Done Beyond the Sea*, E. A. Babcock and A. C. Krey, eds. and trs., 2 vols. (New York: Columbia University Press, 1943). Unless otherwise indicated, this edition of Wm of T is cited throughout the notes.

    Guillaume de Tyr et ses Continuateurs, Paulin Paris, ed., 2 vols. (Paris, 1879–80).

Winchester, Annals of, H. R. Luard, ed. (R 36, II).

Wright, J. K., *The Geographical Lore of the Time of the Crusades* (New York: American Geographical Society, 1925).

INDEX

Abélard, Peter: women and, 14; attacked for heresies, 15–17; trial of, 18–19; mentioned, 74, 79, 87, 108, 162, 386

Acre: council at, 67, 274; siege of, 269, 270–272, 273; Richard sails from, 283

Adalia, *see* Satalia

Adelaide of Louvain, Queen of England, 101

Adele of Champagne, Queen of France, 110–11, 126, 127, 140, 160, 202, 227

Adémar, Count of Angoulême, 326, 341, 362

Agen, Bishop of, 218, 219, 220, 346

Agnes, Abbess of Maillezais, 7

Agnes of Maurienne, Queen of France, 14, 26

Agnes of Méranie, 337, 367, 370

Agnes Capet, 169

Agret (Eleanor's brother), 6

Alais Capet, Princess of France: affianced to Richard, 136; and Eleanor, 159, 323, 385; and Henry, 184, 192–93, 197, 226, 229, 234, 239–40; and Philip, 227, 237, 238, 244, 279, 297, 303; Eleanor's prisoner at Rouen, 255, 258, 273, 275, 289, 294, 302, 331; and Richard, 136, 192, 228, 261–62; release of, 331–32, 337, 338

Alexander III, Pope: and Henry, 117, 190, 312; and Becket affair, 119, 122–23, 125, 128, 129, 132, 134, 137, 139, 141

Alexius, Emperor of Byzantium, 44

Alfonso VIII, King of Castile, 289, 358

Alix (Capet), Countess of Blois, 74, 80, 126, 159

Alix of Maurienne, 159

Alphonse-Jourdain of Toulouse, 34

Amaria (Eleanor's maid), 191

Amaury, Count of Thouars, 351, 357, 365, 375

Amazons: on second crusade, 35, 38–39, 41, 47–48, 50, 56, 72, 169; banned from third crusade, 234, 257

Ambrose: quoted, 170, 234, 251, 256, 263, 266, 270, 281; cited, 282, 283

André the Chaplain (Andreas Capellanus): quoted, 157; at Eleanor's court, 162–164, 385; and courts of love, 163, 164; at Marie's court, 183. See also *Tractatus de Amore*

Angers: Eleanor in, 83–84, 151; Henry's courts in, 129, 199, 225; Arthur and, 349–50, 375

Angers, Bishop of, 346

Angevins: characteristics of, 75; demon ancestress of, 125–26, 170, 290

Angoulême, 327

Anjou, county of: strategic importance of, 75, 104–05; famine in, 204; rebellious barons of, 213, 341, 349; Richard in, 255; John ravages, 375

Anor (Eleanor's mother), 6

Anselm the Chaplain: with Richard, 284, 285; cited, 285, 286, 287

Antioch: in danger, 30; Eleanor and, 31, 52–61, 386; crusaders in, Ch. 5

Aquitaine, duchy of: strategic importance of, 2; description of, 4–5; Eleanor and Louis in, 78–79; heirs at Eleanor's court, 159; rebellious barons of, 176, 199, 205, 213, 326

Archimbaud de Bourbon, 51

Argentan, castle of: repaired, 105; Henry's Christmas court at, 135, 154; young king and, 193, 197, 208

Aristotle, 12, 13

Arnold of Brescia, 18

Arnulf, Bishop of Lisieux, 149

Arques: siege of, 369, 374

Arthur, Count of Brittany: as Plantagenet heir, 253, 262, 292, 324, 340, 349; affianced, 261; and John, 346, 350, 351, 356–57, 360, 376–77, Ch. 34 *passim*, 382; and Philip, 349–50, 356, 366, 370; in Paris, 351, 357; and Eleanor, 353, 370–372, 385; capture and imprisonment, 372, 373, 374, 376, 378; rumors and legends of death, 377–78, 379, 380; mentioned, 305, 345, 383

Arthur, King, 100, 163, 175, 261, 344; Excalibur, 261, 378

Arundel, Earl of, 309

Ascalon, 279

"Assassins," 280, 309

Aumale, 181, 297, 338

Auvergne, Count of, 341

Auvergne, province of, 146, 147, 179

Auxerre, chronicle of: cited, 202

Avranches, 108, 177–78, 381

Aymar, Count of Limoges, 213, 214, 217, 220, 341, 342, 350, 362

Baldwin I, King of Jerusalem, 65

Baldwin II, King of Jerusalem, 66

Baldwin III, King of Jerusalem, 61, 65, 75, 136

Baldwin IV, leper King of Jerusalem, 230, 268

Baldwin V, boy King of Jerusalem, 230

Baldwin of Béthune, 248, 285, 286, 312, 313

Baldwin of Boulogne, 54

Baldwin, Archbishop of Canterbury, 226, 235, 245, 249, 270, 292

Baldwin, Count of Flanders, 332, 337

Ballad of Fair Rosamond: quoted, 150

Ballad of Robin Hood: quoted, 320–21, 322

Barbary pirates, 275, 283–84, 386

Barbieux, abbey of, 202

Barcelona, Count of, 109

Barfleur, 91

Bayeux, Bishop of, 141

Beatrix of Béziers, 330

Beaugency, castle of, 79–80

Beauvais, Bishop of, 270, 273, 280, 308, 339

Bec, abbey of, 109, 204, 379

Becket, Thomas, Archbishop of Canterbury: student in Paris, 13, 18; described, 96; as chancellor, 96–98, 106–108, 109; and Eleanor, 97–98, 107, 320, 385; and Thibault, 96, 113; becomes archbishop, 114, 115–16; and young king, 115, 116, 117, 130, 139, 146, 147, 148, 172; breach with Henry, 117–122, 126, 128, 129, 132, 139, 141; and Constitutions of Clarendon, 118, 119, 120, 121, 122, 128, 129, 131, 138; and Alexander III, 119, 122, 128, 132, 134, 149; and Louis, 107, 123, 124–25, 137, 138, 140, 141, 144, 200–01; excommunicates Henry's men, 131, 142–43, 146; meets Henry, 137–38, 140–41, 144–146; returns to England, 146–47; murder of, 148–49, 153, 167, 169, 176, Henry's penances for, 177–78, 184–85

Bela, King of Hungary, 252, 331

Belin, xii, 6

Benedict of Peterborough: quoted, 174; cited, 212, 232, 260, 294

Benoît de Sainte-Maure: quoted, 100–01

Berengaria, Princess of Castile, 359

Berengaria, Queen of England (orig. Princess of Navarre): and Eleanor, 262, 263, 264, 349, 352, 361; and Richard, 267, 288, 323, 329, 342, 345, 346; on third crusade, 266, 267, 271, 283; in Rome, 300–01

Berenger of Poitiers, 18

Berkhampstead, manor of, 117, 120

Berlai, Geraud, 76, 78

Bermondsey, 93, 94, 98

Bernard, Abbé of Clairvaux: and Abélard, 16, 17, 18–19, 74; and Eleanor, 19, 20, 21, 23, 27–28, 59, 61, 66, 79, 386; and Guillaume X, 19–20; and Louis, 23–24, 26, 79; and

Suger, 24–25; and crusade, 32, 33–34, 35, 36, 37–38, 41, 47, 50, 55, 65, 72, 131; and Conrad of Hohenstaufen, 35, 36, 37, 46; and Angevins, 76, 78, 167, 170, 358; death of, 90; quoted, 15, 20–21, 24, 33, 37–38, 61, 161; cited, 102, 384

Bernard of Cluny: quoted, 64

Bernard of Ventadour, 85–87, 94, 101, 167, 329, 344, 385

Bernard the Treasurer: cited, 277

Berry, county of, 105, 136, 192, 197–98, 199, 234, 244, 289, 325

Bertrade, Queen of France, 1

Bertran de Born, Seigneur of Hautefort: and young king, 171, 205–207, 210–11, 223; cited, 195; sirventés of, 308, 325, 326, 329; quoted, 205, 206–07, 211; Dante on, 223

Béthizy, 1, 2, 8

Blanche of Castile, Queen of France, 359, 360, 361, 366, 367

Blaquernae, palace of, 42, 43

Blois, house of, 77, 80, 82, 87, 89, 105, 126, 236

Blondel, 302

Bobo, Hyacinthus, see Celestine III

Boethius, 249

Bohaddin: cited, 282

Bohemund I, Prince of Antioch, 41, 46, 52

Bohemund II, Prince of Antioch, 30–31, 40

Bonmoulins, 238–39

Bordeaux, 3, 4, 5, 7, 57, 89, 357, 358, 359, 363, 369

Bosham, Herbert: cited, 144–45

Bouchet, Jean: cited, 80

Boukoleon, palace of, 42, 43

Boulogne, Count of, 181, 182, 337

Bourges: Eleanor and Louis crowned at, 21; Christmas court at, 32, 33; Alais' dowry, 192

Bourguigne of Lusignan, 330

Boxley, Abbot of, 302, 304, 305, 306

Briscius, Seneschal of Anjou, 380

Brittany: Henry and, 104–05, 126, 176, 289; Arthur and, 351, 357, 360, 370; John and, 375, 382

Briwere, William, 378

Brough, castle of, 378

Bures, Christmas courts at: Henry's, 147, 148; Richard's, 255; Eleanor's, 296–97

Burgundy, Duke of (Barbarossa's son), 218, 270, 273, 274, 276, 277, 279

Byzantium: crusaders in, 35, 41, 46, 48; described, 42–45; Eleanor and, 42–45, 58, 386; Agnes Capet goes to, 169

Caen: Norman exchequer in, 105, 323; Henry's Christmas court at, 208–212; Eleanor in, 141, 142

Caerleon on Usk, 100, 163

Caesarea Philippi, 55, 67

Calabria, 70, 260, 265, 329

Canterbury: shrine of Becket at, 18, 169, 193, 320; and Becket, 96, 121, 122, 140, 147; and Henry, 113–14, 115, 126, 129, 139, 184–85; rivalry with York, 190; Louis's pilgrimage to, 200–01

Canute, King of Denmark, 313–14

Celestine III, Pope (Hyacinthus Bobo): at Abélard's trial, 18; and Eleanor, 265, 275, 296, 302, 366; quoted, 272; and Philip, 275; and Richard, 294, 295; letters from Eleanor, quoted, 300, 311–12, 317, 344; succeeded, 337; and Ingeborg affair, 366, 367

Châlus, castle of: treasure of, 341, 344; siege of, 342; Richard killed at, 342, 343, 354

Champagne, house of: Eleanor and, 22, 159, 386; and Louis, 23, 111, 126; attacks Plantagenets, 111, 181; characteristics of, 228

Chansons de geste, see Literature

Charente river, 8, 326, 359

Charlemagne, 5, 7, 100, 201, 228, 344

Chartres, Bishop of, 18

Chartres, cathedral of, xi, 12, 16, 25

Château Gaillard (Rock of Andelys): Richard builds, 334–35; Richard's court at, 336, 338, 344; Philip and, 337, 381–82; John's court at, 360, 365; fall of, 386

Châteauroux, 198, 199, 234, 235, 244, 311

Châtellerault, Countess of, 6, 8, 109, 157, 385

Châtellerault, house of, 55, 159

Chaumont, castle of, 111, 145

Chichester, Bishop of, 125

Chinon, Angevin treasure castle: strategic importance of, 104, 105, 179, 206; Henry at, 130, 132, 180, 243, 244–246, 290; Eleanor at, 255; Richard at, 341; John at, 346, 363, 369, 375

Chirchedune, Adam, 196–97

Chrétien de Troyes, 163, 183

Clairvaux: abbey of, 17, 25, 127; castle of, 206, 212

Clarendon, 95, 118, 172

Clarendon, Constitutions of, see Becket

Clement III, Pope, 240

Clement of Alexandria: quoted, 10

Clifford, Rosamond: affair with Henry II, 150–51, 192, 193, 239; death of, 151; Eleanor and, 150–51, 153, 384

Clifford, Walter de, of Bredelais, 151

Cluny, Abbé of, 317

Cluny, abbey of, 5, 25, 26

Cocus, William, 380

Coggeshall, chronicle of: cited, 284, 333, 377

Cologne, 210, 318

Cologne, Bishop of, 307, 317, 318

Comneni (Greek royal family), 40, 43, 45, 252, 267, 269, 300

Compiègne, 124, 125, 200

Conrad III (Hohenstaufen), King of Germany and Holy Roman Emperor: enemy of Pope, 35, 70; and Bernard, 36, 233; on second crusade, 37, 41, 45, 46, 47, 48, 49, 52, 65, 67, 68, 230; and Manuel, 46, 47

Conrad, Marquis of Montferrat: and kingship of Jerusalem, 269, 270, 274, 276, 277, 279; murder of, 280, 309, 317

Constance of Antioch, 31

Constance, Countess of Brittany: affianced to Geoffrey Plantagenet, 136, 187; at Eleanor's court, 159; Henry banishes, 184; and Arthur, 349–50, 356, 376; marriages of, 350, 351; a leper, 361, 365, 366; death of, 368; and Eleanor, 385

Constance, Queen of Sicily, Holy Roman Empress, 259, 265, 305, 313, 314, 336

Constance of Spain, Queen of France, 90, 106, 108, 110, 111

Constantinople, see Byzantium

Corfu, 275, 284

Courts of love: in England, 101; Poitiers, 163, 165–167; Provence, 163; Marie's, 183

Crusade, first, 6, 32, 35, 38, 41, 46, 52, 57, 109, 233

Crusade, second, Chs. 3–6

Crusade, third, Chs. 24–25

Curburan (*routier*), 218

Cyprus, 266, 268, 270, 274, 284

Cyprus, princess of, 267, 271, 276, 283, 305, 329

Damascus, siege of, 67–68

Dante: quoted, 223

Déols, heiress of, 198, 199

Devizes, see Richard of Devizes

Diceto, see Ralph of Diceto

Dover, castle of, 181, 298

Durham, Bishop of, 252, 295, 320, 338

Durrenstein, castle of, 302, 304, 386

Edessa, fall of, 29, 30, 31, 32, 48

Eleanor of Aquitaine, Queen of France and Queen of England: as marriage prize, 1–2, 4, 61; described, 5–6, 77, 158, 170–71,

263–64, 317; and her children, 28, 74, 87, 94, 103, 106, 126, 152, 153, 158–59, 253, 355, 361; on second crusade, 33, 34, 35, 37, 38–39, 42–45, 47–48, 49, 50, 52–60, 61–63, 66, 69, 386; part in Henry's government, 83–85, 103, 109, 110, 114, 128–29, 142, 144, 152; poetry about, 100–01, 189; court at Poitiers, 134–35, 153, 155, Ch. 15, 384–85; capture and imprisonment, 183–84, 190–91, 193, 199, 202, 225–26, 235, 248–49; release from captivity, 248–250; as Richard's regent, 249–251, 253–54, Ch. 27, 300, 309–312, 345–46, 350, 351–353, 365; trip to Sicily, 262–265; trip to Germany, 315–318; trip to Spain, 357–360; last years, 384–386; death of, 386–87; tomb at Fontevrault, 387. *See also* Louis VII; Henry II; Richard I; John Lackland

Eleanor (Plantagenet), Queen of Castile, 103, 159, 289, 328, 340, 355, 358, 385

Eleanor, "pearl of Brittany," 278, 305, 340, 372–73

Emma of Anjou, 165, 184, 192

English Channel, ports of, 141, 142, 148, 258, 297, 303

Eugenius III, Pope: and second crusade, 32, 33, 34, 35, 36–37, 41, 55, 72, 73; and Holy Roman Emperor, 35, 46; and Eleanor and Louis, 70–71, 79; and Eleanor, 74, 386

Eustace of Blois, 76, 83, 87

Eye, manor of, 117, 120

Faidit, Gaucelm: quoted, 344

Falaise: Henry's Christmas court at, 110; Easter court at, 115; Arthur imprisoned in, 373, 374, 377, 379–80

Fitz-Peter, Geoffrey, 378

Fitz-Stephen, Thomas, 131, 191

Fitz-Stephen, William: cited, 98, 102

Flanders, 274, 275, 303

Fontainebleau, 296, 366, 368

Fontevrault, abbey of: Henry and, 190, 204; tombs at, 246, 255, 387; Eleanor at, 328–29, 342, 347, 351, 360, 361, 363, 369, 370, 386, 387; Richard and, 343; Joanna and, 354–55

Foulques V, King of Jerusalem (orig. Count of Anjou), 65, 66, 67, 68, 75, 84, 173, 230, 235, 254, 268, 278

Foulques de Neuilly, 333–34

Foulques, Patriarch of Jerusalem, 31, 61, 65, 67

Foulques the Black, Count of Anjou, 170, 173, 334

Frederick I (Barbarossa), King of Germany and Holy Roman Emperor, 36, 47, 207, 259, 312

Frederick of Betestowe, 285–86, 301

Fréteval, 144–45

Garonne river, 4, 5

Geoffrey IV (the Fair), Count of Anjou, 2, 75–78, 84, 88, 105, 106, 240, 334

Geoffrey of Anjou (Henry II's brother), 80, 83, 91, 104, 105

Geoffrey, Archbishop of Bordeaux, 8, 79, 80

Geoffrey Plantagenet, Count of Brittany: birth, 103; affianced, 136; at Eleanor's court, 159; described, 170, 173–74; in revolt against Henry, 176, 213–14, 216, 218; and terms of Montlouis, 187, 194; and Philip, 201, 226, 290; at Caen, 209, 210; quoted, 213; Henry's plans for, 224–25; killed, 226; and Eleanor, 344, 385

Geoffrey of Brûlon: quoted, 241

Geoffrey of Lusignan, 220

Geoffrey of Monmouth: quoted, 100, 247

Geoffrey de Rancon (the Poitevin), 33, 39, 49, 50, 59

Geoffrey of Thouars, 39

Geoffrey (the Chancellor), Archbishop of York: Henry II's natural son, 152, 241, 253; with Henry, 243, 245; and John, 264; elected to York, 265; and Ely, 292, 293, 295

Geoffroi de Rançon, Sieur of Taillebourg, 8, 326, 327

Geoffroi de Vigeois: quoted, 165, 171; cited, 195, 220

Gervase of Canterbury: cited, 63, 191, 228; quoted, 92, 170–71

Gestes de Louis VII: quoted, 37

Gilbert de Laci, 345, 346

Giraldus Cambrensis: cited, 77, 152, 173, 192–93, 211, 254, 290, 333, 384, 386; quoted, 127, 150, 168, 170, 173, 202; and Henry, 231; mentioned, 100, 103

Gisors: elm of, 182, 228–29, 232, 236–37, 244; parleys at, 133, 255; castle of, 294–95, 297, 302–03, 325, 331, 338, 340

Glanville, Ranulf de, 185, 191, 248, 252

Gloucester, Countess of, 279

Gloucester, Earl of, 172

Glyme river, 95, 151, 152

Godfrey of Bouillon, 44, 52, 100

Godstow, nunnery of, 151, 152, 192

Golden Legend: quoted, 15

Gournay, 369, 370

Grammont, monastery of, 204, 216, 220, 221, 246

Grande-Sauve monastery, 352–53
Guillaume de Braose, 371, 372, 378, 379, 380, 383
Guillaume le Breton: quoted, 361, 378; cited, 371, 372, 379
Guillaume le Maréchal: and Eleanor, 154, 249, 257, 385; and young king, 171, 175, 196, 214, 218, 219, 220, 221–22; and Marguerite, 209–10; and Henry, 239, 241, 242–43; and Richard, 242–43, 247–48, 326, 339, 344, 348; marriage of, 248, 249; as justiciar, 254; and John, 348–49, 381, 383
Guillaume le Maréchal: quoted, 171, 193, 209, 244, 254–55, 338, 374; cited, 174, 313, 324, 363
Guillaume Plantagenet, 87, 90, 92, 103
Guillaume V (le Grand), Count of Poitou, 5, 30, 153, 159, 183
Guillaume IX (le Troubadour), Count of Poitou: disastrous crusade of, 6, 32, 38, 41, 46, 109; characterized, 170; mentioned, 5, 8, 79, 153, 157, 159, 308, 385
Guillaume X (le Toulousain), Count of Poitou: death of, 1, 2, 3, 4, 8; and Bernard, 19, 79; and Count of Anjou, 75; born, 109; Eleanor and, 385
Guillaume de Ponthieu, 332, 338
Guillaume des Roches, 349, 356, 363, 371, 372, 374–75, 381
Guillaume, Archbishop of Sens, 126, 137, 139, 140
Guy de Bazoches: quoted, 10
Guy de Lusignan, King of Jerusalem and Cyprus: career of, 268–69, 274, 279–80; and Eleanor, 357
Guy of Thouars, 351, 378

Hagenau, 308, 309
Hautefort, castle of, 205, 223
Hélie, Archbishop of Bordeaux, 360, 363, 380
Héloïse, 14, 74, 87
Henry (Plantagenet), the young king: birth of, 94, 103; marriage of, 106, 111; Henry and, 106, 111, 114, 135, 153, 171–72, 176, 177, 179–80, 187–88, 199, 207–08, 211, 212, 216–17, 219, 221–22, 224, 239; and Eleanor, 110, 141, 159, 222–23, 290, 344, 385; coronation of, 130, 142–144; second coronation, 170; and Louis, 135, 172, 180–81; described, 171, 172, 173, 175–76, 204–05, 209, 214; rebels, 177, 180–182, 184, 186, 187, 195–197, 214, 215, 218; death of, 218–221, 223, 344. See also Becket; Marguerite; Bertran de Born
Henry I (Beauclerc), King of England, 30,

84, 88, 93, 101, 209, 219, 236, 321, 325, 334
Henry II, King of England: as Angevin heir, 75–76, 78, 88–89; described, 76, 89, 92, 99, 169, 170, 236; marries Eleanor, 77, 81, 82, 83; and Louis, 83, 105, 108–09, 110, 111, 134–137, 140, 144, 177, 187, 200–01; Channel crossings, 83, 91–92, 141, 184, 236; early years with Eleanor, 83, 86, 87–88, 94, 97–98, 103, 110, 111, 112, 116; and Matilda Empress, 88; becomes king, 91, 92; consolidates empire, 94–95, Ch. 10, 113–14, 126, 169, 203–04; and Alexander III, 128, 129, 134, 312; and papal legates, 132–33, 139, 177–78, 190, 294; breach with Eleanor, 134–35, 137, 139, 144, 150–51, 153–54, 169, 176, 180, 182–83, 188, 189–191, 222, 225–26, 235; and sons, 135–137, Ch. 16, 191–92; revolts of sons, Ch. 17, 193–199, Chs. 19–20, 224–229, 238–246; and Rosamond Clifford, 150–51, 152, 192; and Philip, 140, 213, 228–29, 234–35, 236–37, 238, 240–41, 243–44; plans for crusade, 229–235, 236, 237; death of, 243, 244–246, 247; influence on Eleanor, 250, 288, 384; tomb at Fontevrault, 255, 328, 343, 381. See also Becket; Henry, the young king; Richard; John
Henry VI (Hohenstaufen), King of Germany and Sicily and Holy Roman Emperor: and Sicily, 259, 261; and Eleanor, 263, 265, 314–15; and Philip, 275–76, 301, 306–07, 312; and Richard, 302, 304–306, 312, 315, 316–17, 318, 320, 323; and Pope Celestine, 312; death of, 336
Henry of Blois, Bishop of Winchester, 115, 120
Henry (the Liberal), Count of Champagne: at Vézelay, 34; and Marie Capet, 106, 126, 160; mentioned, 83, 268
Henry, Count of Champagne and King of Jerusalem, 281, 282
Henry, son of Thierry of Flanders, 55, 66, 68
Henry of Huntingdon: quoted, 92
Henry (the Lion), Duke of Saxony, 207, 209, 230, 268, 304, 311, 313, 336
Heraclius, Patriarch of Jerusalem, 230–232
Hittin, battle of, 269
Hohenstaufen, see Conrad III; Henry VI
Holy Field (Saint Champ), 233
Holy Land: pilgrimages to, 34–35, 69. See also Jerusalem
Hospitallers, 204, 232, 277, 335
Hoveden, see Roger of Hoveden
Hubert de Burgh, 373, 377, 378, 379, 380

Hugh, Bishop of Lincoln, 151–52, 168, 345, 346, 347–48, 349, 360, 384

Hugues le Brun of Lusignan, Count of La Marche, 357, 362, 363, 372, 375

Huguezon, Cardinal, 190, 192

Huisne river, 241, 242

Humphrey de Toron, 269, 270

Île Bouchard, 206, 211

Île de France, 17, 25, 31, 76, 82, 105, 124, 134, 192, 196, 297

Ingeborg, Princess of Denmark and Queen of France, 314, 337, 338, 366–368

Innocent II, Pope, 2, 15, 21, 26

Innocent III, Pope, 336, 337, 338, 366–67, 380

Ireland, 176, 191

Isaac, Emperor of Cyprus, 267, 276, 305, 306

Isabel, Countess of Flanders, 164, 183, 385

Isabella of Angoulême, Queen of England (John's second wife), 362–63, 364, 365–66, 369, 375, 383, 387

Isabelle, Countess of Gloucester (John's first wife), 191–92, 302, 361

Isabelle of Hainaut, Queen of France, 257

Isabelle, Queen of Jerusalem, 269, 270, 280, 281

Itinerarium: cited, 267, 271, 277, 281; quoted, 317

Ivry: parley at, 198

Jerusalem, Latin Kingdom of: threatened, 29–30, 198, 230, 232, 237, 319, 322; Holy Sepulcher, 29, 30, 64, 65, 237, 281, 282; lords of, 30–31, 66, 230–31, 268–270, 274, 280, 281; described, 64–65; Louis and crusaders in, 64–69; Eleanor and, 66, 69, 386; Richard and crusaders in, 268–282, 300

Joanna (Plantagenet), Queen of Sicily and Countess of Toulouse: born, 103; and William of Sicily, 132, 190; and Eleanor, 159, 263, 289, 328, 385; and Henry, 184; and Sicilian crisis, 259, 260, 261; and Berengaria, 264; on crusade, 266, 271, 278, 279, 283, 301, 329–30; and Raymond of Toulouse, 330; death of, 354–55; tomb, 387

John (Lackland), King of England: birth of, 103, 152, 153; and Eleanor, 159, 226, 289–91, 297–98, 303, 324, 344, 349, 353, 355, 361, 363, 365, 370, 379–80, 387; and Henry, 170, 176, 179, 184, 188, 191–92, 224–25, 226, 229, 231–32, 239, 241, 243, 245, 290; and Philip, 235, 279, 292, 300, 302–03, 313, 314, 316, 356–57, 360, 365–66, 368–70, 380–382; intrigues during crusade, 264,

279, 292, 297–299, 302; and Richard, 253, 290–91, 298, 305, 319, 324–25, 337, 343, 346, 357; becomes king, 347–48, 349; marriages of, 361–364; barons revolt against, 374–75, 376, 380–81, 383. *See also* Longchamp; Arthur of Brittany

John of Alençon, 279, 324

John of Oxford, 131, 132, 146

John of Salisbury: scholar in Paris, 13; cited, 60, 62, 70–71, 80, 101, 102; quoted, 97, 113; and Eleanor, 98; and Becket, 121, 132

Jordan, Cardinal, 294–95

Joscelin, Count of Edessa, 29, 54

Kiss of peace, 42, 78, 82, 115, 140, 141, 145, 146, 149, 232, 244

Knights Templars, *see* Templars

La Marche, county of, 357, 362

Langres, Bishop of, 32, 34, 41

Langue d'oïl, 14, 359

Langue d'oc, 33, 56, 58, 86

Laodicea, 48

Latin Kingdom, *see* Jerusalem

Leicester, Earl of, 122, 303, 381

Le Mans, 172, 241, 349–50

Leopold, Duke of Austria, 270, 272, 276, 285, 287, 300, 301, 304, 306, 312, 316

Limassol, 267, 288, 323

Limoges, 4, 5, 7, 79, 155–56, 179, 206, 214–218

Limoges, Bishop of, 165, 221

Limousin, 154, 165, 195, 206, 213, 341, 344

Lisieux, Bishop of, 34, 37, 75

Literature: discussed, 99–103; *chansons de geste*, 5, 30, 99, 100; dramatic spectacles, 102; fabliaux, 102; *lai*, 102, 165; minnesingers, 98, 101; miracle plays, 102; Eleanor and poets, 100–01, 161; *planh*, 223, 344; romances, 87, 99, 100, 102, 165, 174, 175, 194, 241, 358; *sirventés*, 205, 206, 211, 307–08, 325, 326, 329, 335, 341

Loir river, 78

Loire river, 5, 325

London: Henry and Eleanor in, 92–94, 114; described, 93–94; Becket in, 97–98, 147; Eleanor's influence in, 98–103; Windsor court, 225–26; Eleanor in, 249, 303; Richard in, 251–52; Ely and John in, 293

London, Bishop of, 94, 139, 141, 142, 146

Longchamp, William, Bishop of Ely and Chancellor of England: as chancellor, 254, 264–65, 292, 322; and John, 254, 291, 292, 293, 295, 298; intrigues on Continent, 294,

295, 296; and Richard, 302, 304, 305, 306, 309, 310, 312

Loudun, castle of, 104, 179, 206

Louis VI (the Fat), King of France, 1, 2, 3, 8, 10, 15, 24, 66, 75, 90, 357

Louis VII, King of France: as Capetian heir, 2–3, 130; described, 3, 13, 51, 168–69, 202; and Eleanor, 3–4, 7–8, 15, 21, 22, 24, 26, 34, 50, 56, 58, 59, 60–62, 69–71, 73–74, 78–80, 82, 153, 384, 385, 387; and Vitry, 23, 24, 26, 29, 58; and crusade, Chs. 3–6, 73, 230, 257, 284; career of, 82–83, 84, 90, 105–06, 111, 126, 134; marriages of, 90, 110–11; and daughters, 106, 108, 110, 126, 136, 144, 159, 160, 170, 192, 331; and Philip, 127, 198, 199–201, 386; and revolt against Henry, 180–82, 186, 187, 188, 197; death of, 201–02. See also Becket; Bernard of Clairvaux; Henry II; Suger

Louis, Prince of France (later Louis VIII), 340, 357, 360, 361

Louvain, Duke of, 307, 318, 336

Louviers, treaty of, 334, 337, 341

Lucius III, Pope, 232, 240

Lusignan brothers, 154, 362, 365, 369, 370–372, 374

Magna Vita Sancti Hugonis: quoted, 345, 346, 380; cited, 351

Mainerd (Maynard), Count of Gortze, 285, 301

Maine, county of: in Angevin heritage, 75, 78, 135, 224; rebellious barons of, 341, 349–50; John ravages, 375

Mainz, 316–17, 336

Mainz, Bishop of, 307, 310

Malchael, Roger, 245

Manuel I Comnenus, Emperor of Byzantium: and Conrad, 37, 46, 47; and crusaders, 40–45, 52, 69, 169, 386; and Turks, 41, 45

Map, Walter: cited, 77, 94, 101, 211; quoted, 95, 102, 103, 124, 202, 215

Margam, abbey of: chronicle quoted, 379

Marguerite (Capet), the young queen: and young king, 106, 108, 111, 136, 142, 144, 170, 193, 208, 219; and Eleanor, 108, 142, 158–59, 229, 285; and Becket, 117, 172; and Henry, 184, 192, 227, 229, 289; in Paris, 196, 197, 214; at Caen, 209–10; and Bela of Hungary, 331

Marie (Capet), Countess of Champagne: born, 28; and Henry, 76, 82; and Louis, 80; and Henry of Champagne, 106, 126; and Richard, 161, 173, 308; at Eleanor's court, 160–61, 164, 183, 192, 194, 328, 358, 385;

and André, 162–164; and court of love, 163–64; subsequent career of, 183; and Geoffrey Plantagenet, 226; and Henry of Jerusalem, 281

Marie de France, 165, 184, 192

Marshall, John, 119, 120, 121

Martel, 218, 219, 220, 344

Matilda, Abbess of Fontevrault, 342, 345, 354

Matilda Empress: and Henry, 75, 77, 88, 91, 113, 114, 192, 254; court at Rouen, 84, 161; and Eleanor, 88; "hungry falcon" politics of, 88, 174, 254, 264; and Stephen, 92

Matilda (Plantagenet), Duchess of Saxony: born, 103; and Eleanor, 110, 191, 229; and Henry the Lion, 129, 134; and Henry, 207, 208; at Caen, 209, 210, 211; dead, 289; and Otto of Brunswick, 336; and Matilda of Perche, 346

Maubergeonne, tower of, 8, 81

Mayenne river, 84, 105

Maurienne, Count of, 49, 50, 136, 179

Maurienne, infant of, 179, 184, 191

Melisende, Queen of Jerusalem, 65, 66, 67

Mercadier: and Richard, 326, 338, 339, 341, 342, 343; and Eleanor, 350; murder of, 359–60, 369, 380

Messina: Richard in, 258–265; compact of, 262, 273, 297, 331, 334, 337; Eleanor in, 264–65

Metz, 37–38

Milo (Richard's chaplain), 343, 344, 346

Minstrel of Reims: quoted, 60; cited, 62

Mirebeau, castle of: strategic importance of, 104, 179, 206; attempted capture of Eleanor at, 370–372, 376, 380, 384

Monte Cassino, annals of: cited, 69

Montlouis, peace of, 187–88, 193, 194, 195, 199, 204

Montmartre, 140, 145

Montmirail: Henry and Louis at, 134–137; Henry and Becket at, 137–139; treaty of, 140, 167, 169, 187, 191–92, 197, 224, 229, 331

Mont-Saint-Michel, 108–09

Mont-Saint-Michel, Abbé of: cited, 135, 171

Mount Silpius, 52, 53, 58

Music, 44, 52, 65, 102, 165, 167

Nevers, Bishop of, 141, 142

Nevers, Count of, 3, 18

Nicetas: quoted, 38–39

Normandy, duchy of: Henry and, 76, 83, 104, 177, 207; Louis and, 83, 108–09, 144;

Philip and, 297, 299, 307, 310, 313, 356, 369, 381; Richard and, 326, 327, 337, 341
Northampton: Becket's trial at, 119–122; Richard's Easter court at, 322–23
Nostredame: cited, 163
Nottingham, 320, 349

Odo of Duilio: cited, 38, 42; quoted, 48, 53; mentioned, 36, 50, 59, 66
"Old Man of the Mountain," 280, 309, 317
Ombrière, palace of, 4, 7, 57, 359
Otto IV of Brunswick, Holy Roman Emperor, 336–37, 340, 343, 349, 380
Otto of Freising: quoted, 48; cited, 72
Otto of Ostia, 132, 133
Ovid, 5, 99, 161, 162, 163, 194
Oxford, castle of, 103, 151, 152, 153

Palestine, see Jerusalem
Paphlagonia: massacre at, 49, 50, 55, 72; mountains of, 50, 52, 252, 386
Papiol (jongleur), 205, 206–07, 210
Paris: described, Ch. 2; Merovingian palace in, 9, 10, 45, 74, 108; scholars of, 12, 130; Eleanor in, 8–9, 10, 13–14, 31, 71–72, 73–74, 158, 386; Louis and, 31, 71–72, 84; compared with London, 93; Becket in, 107–08, 141; Philip in, 127, 276, 297, 338, 366; Arthur in, 351, 356
Paris, Matthew: quoted, 379, 387
Patrick, Earl of Salisbury, 154, 248, 268
Pembroke and Striguil, Countess of, 248, 249
Peter of Blois: cited, 14, 99, 172; quoted, 98, 216, 221, 310
Peter of Capua, Cardinal, 338–340, 346
Petit Andelys, 382
Petronilla (Eleanor's sister), 6, 22–23, 27, 386
Philip II (Augustus), King of France: birth of, 127; coronation of, 199–200, 201; campaigns against Angevins, 213, 234, 241, 297, 299, 302–03, 310, 325–26, 337–38, 356, 380–382, 386; and Geoffrey Plantagenet, 226; as king, 227, 238; described, 228; and crusade, 232–33, 257–262, 264, 270, 272–276, 296–97; and Richard, 201, 235, 239–40, 244, 255, 257–58, 273–74, 275, 290, 326, 335, 338–340, 343; and Celestine III, 275, 312; and Henry VI, 275–76, 301, 306–07, 312, 316, 318; and Eleanor, 276, 288–89, 353; and Ingeborg, 313–14, 366–368; and son, 360. See also Alais; Henry II; Louis
Philip Capet (Louis VII's brother), 2, 29, 110
Philip of Dreux, 273
Philip, Count of Flanders: and young king,
171, 184, 185, 196, 211; revolts against Henry, 177, 181, 182, 183; at siege of Rouen, 186, 187; at Ivry, 198; and Philip, 201; on crusade, 230, 232–33, 237, 243, 262; death of, 273
Philip of Swabia, 336
Philippa of Toulouse, Countess of Poitou, 6, 15, 109
Philippe of Cognac, 344
Philippe de Thaün: quoted, 101
Piepart, Sheriff, 247, 248
Pierre de la Celle, 191
Pierre de la Châtre, 21, 22, 27
Pillars of Hercules, 57, 258, 284
Pipe Rolls: cited, 110, 191, 192
Piramor, 360
Plantagenets: succession, 106; characteristics and legends of, 75, 126, 170, 290; signet ring of, 236, 245
Plato, 12, 13
Poitevins, 4, 14, 54, 56, 79, 170–71
Poitiers: Eleanor in, 8, 79, 81, 83, 134, 135, Ch. 15, 384; as sedition center, 15, 176, 179; Henry's Christmas court in, 153; royal children in, 158–59; as court of love, 163–167; young king in, 176; Henry in, 183; decline of, 328; school of manners of, 329; mentioned, 183, 194, 211, 248, 310
Poitiers, Bishop of, 197, 346
Poitou, county of: and crusade, 36, 37, 40, 58, 62; as cultural center, 5, 99; Richard in, 326–27; John in, 362; mentioned, 2, 3, 7, 83, 154, 155, 197, 206, 225, 244, 255, 325, 365, 370, 375
Pontrobert, Abbot of, 302, 304, 305, 306
Provence, King of, 315, 318
"Pullani," the, 57, 61

Ralph of Diceto: cited, 133, 182, 193, 201, 203; quoted, 247, 320, 327
Ranulf de Broc, 126, 131
Ranulf of Chester, 350, 351
Raoul of Caen: quoted, 13
Raoul of Déols, 198
Raoul de Faye, 183
Raoul de Lusignan, Count of Eu, 369, 375
Raoul, Count of Vermandois, 3, 22–23, 82
Raymond V, Count of Toulouse, 109, 179, 218, 235, 284, 326
Raymond VI, Count of Toulouse, 330, 354
Raymond of Toulouse, Prince of Antioch: background of, 30, 31, 53–54, 109, 268; enemy of Comneni, 40; and second crusade, 54–55, 58, 59, 60, 66, 68; and Eleanor, 30, 52, 56, 58–59, 60, 61, 62–63

Raynouard: quoted, 85
Reims, 2, 12, 17, 29, 130, 156, 200
Reims, Archbishop of, 17, 80, 198, 243, 307, 314, 340, 367
Richard I (Coeur-de-Lion), King of England: birth of, 103; and Henry, 106, 114; and Eleanor, 135, 153, 155–56, 159, 160, 167, 173, 224, 250, 252–53, 255, 256, 262–265, 276, 279, 301–02, 308–09, 315, 317–18, 319–20, 323, 328, 341, 342–344, 346, 385, 387; and Louis, 135–36, 141, 180; described, 170, 173, 257, 267, 333–34; and Henry, 176, 187–88, 194–95, 198, 204, 205, 206, 209, 213, 214, 224–25, 226, 229, 238–39, 241, 242–244, 246; and crusade, 232–33, 252, 255–56, Chs. 24–25; becomes king, 249, 250, 251–254; and Sicilian crisis, 259–262; marriage of, 267; and Saladin, 277–78, 281–82; capture of, Ch. 26; hostage of Henry VI, Ch. 27; as poet, 307–08; in England, 319–323; campaigns in France, 325–327; builds Gaillard, 334–35; death of, 341–344; tomb at Fontevrault, 343, 346, 381, 387. See also John Lackland; Philip II
Richard of Devizes: cited, 153, 263, 294; quoted, 252, 263–64, 291, 293
Richard of Ilchester, 131, 142
Richard le Poitevin: quoted, 189
Rigord: quoted, 181; cited, 314
Robert, Count of Dreux 68, 73, 83
Robert of Newburgh, 108
Robert of Turnham, Seneschal of Poitou, 380
Robert de Vieuxpont, 378, 383
Rock of Andelys, see Château Gaillard
Robin Hood, 320–322
Roger of Hoveden: quoted, 131, 250, 252, 305, 333–34, 337; cited, 151, 251, 276, 285, 313, 318, 323, 343, 365
Roger of Sicily, 69, 70
Roger, Archbishop of York, 121, 122, 132, 134, 141, 143, 146, 147
Roland, 100, 218
Romances, see Literature
Rome (as papal city), 71, 128, 265, 275
Rouen: Matilda Empress' court at, 84, 161; Henry and Eleanor in, 88–89, 110; capital of Norman dukes, 89; Henry in, 91, 181; Eleanor in, 158; young king in, 176, 181; siege of, 186–87; "old Rouvel," 187; tower of, 262, 273, 291, 294, 331; Alais imprisoned at, 329
Rouen, Archbishop of: and Becket, 146; and Henry, 149; and Eleanor, 182–83, 190; and Richard, 335; mentioned, 80, 141, 265, 292–93, 296, 301, 309, 315, 317

Routiers, 157, 174, 195, 213, 215, 216, 218, 238, 303, 341, 342, 350, 360, 369, 372, 374, 380
Runnymede, 383, 386

Saga (Icelandic life of Becket): cited, 201
Saint Aubin (Angers), chronicle of: cited, 386
Saint Denis, abbey of, 24–26, 27, 44, 65, 201, 351
Saint Étienne de Muret, abbey of (Grammont), 216
Saint Hilaire, Abbé of, 156
Saint James of Compostella, shrine of, 1, 90, 207, 359
Saint Jean d'Angély, 79, 352
Saint Martial, abbey of (Limoges), 155, 214, 217–18, 311
Saint Valerie (Limoges), 155–56, 217
Saladin, 62, 237, 257, 269, 271, 272, 274, 277–78, 280, 281–82, 288, 296, 319
Saladin tithe, 234, 238, 252, 322
Salimbene: cited, 171
Salisbury: tower, 184; mentioned, 235
Salisbury, Bishop of, 139, 141, 146, 147. See also Walter
Sancho the Wise, King of Navarre, 263
Sancius (routier), 218, 221, 222
Saphadin (Saladin's brother), 278, 305
Satalia, 50, 51, 55, 59
Savary, Bishop of Bath, 302, 306
Scotland, 292
Sens, 16, 25, 122–23, 124, 125
Sens, Archbishop of, 17, 79
Sherwood Forest, 321, 322
Sibylle, Queen of Jerusalem, 268, 269
Sicily, 258, 260, 266, 283, 291, 306
Sirventés, see Literature
Soissons, 16, 314, 337, 366, 368
Southampton, 184, 251, 297, 298
Spain: Louis in, 90; Eleanor visits, 357–59; mentioned, 174, 209, 351
Speyer: Easter court at, 305–06; mentioned, 36, 46, 307, 315, 316, 336
Stephen of Blois, King of England, 4, 83, 84, 88, 91, 92, 93, 94, 96, 106, 116, 252
Stephen of Turnham, 309, 318
Striguil, Countess of, see Pembroke
Swabia, 302
Suger, Abbé: and Louis, 3, 8, 15, 45, 68–69; quoted, 24, 62, 68–69; and Bernard, 24–25; and abbey of Saint Denis, 25–27; and crusade, 32–33, 38, 42, 47; good work of, 73; death of, 72, 82; mentioned, 1, 53, 71, 386
Sybille, Countess of Flanders, 34, 66
Syria, 52, 58, 93, 262, 270, 275, 283

Talmont, 15, 83, 352

Tancred of Sicily, 46, 52, 259, 260–61, 265, 275, 276, 284, 292, 305

Templars, Knights: escort Louis into Jerusalem, 65; new halls in Paris, 107; and Becket, 121; Henry and, 111, 204, 243; Richard and, 283, 285, 287; mentioned, 54, 61, 64, 67, 68, 108, 232, 238, 272, 277, 335

Tetburge, Abbess of Ronceray, 84

Theodoric, of Flanders, 55, 66, 68

Thibault, Count of Blois: ambushes Eleanor, 80–81; and Alix Capet, 106, 126; crusade vow, 237; mentioned, 83, 111, 135, 181, 198, 270

Thibault, Archbishop of Canterbury: guardian of Eleanor, 98; and Becket, 96, 120; career of, 113; mentioned, 91, 92, 114

Thibault, Count of Champagne: mentor of Louis VII, 3, 82, 111, 168; lands restored, 27; at Vézelay, 34; mentioned, 22, 23, 59, 61, **79, 84**

Thierry, Count of Flanders, 51, 55, 68

Thierry Galeran: and Louis, 36, 61, 74, 78; and Eleanor, 59, 61, 71; mentioned, 66

Thomas of Erceldoune: cited, 87

Tiberias (town), 67

Tonnerre, Count of, 218, 219

Torigny: cited, 83

Toulouse: Eleanor claims, 15, 109, 330; heresy in, 198; mentioned, 235, 289, 354, 355, 363

Touraine, 181, 197, 238, 244, 340, 341

Tournaments, 174–75, 195, 196, 204–05

Tours, 239, 243, 256, 340, 350, 353, 370, 374

Tours, chronicle of: cited, 80–81

Tower of David (Jerusalem), 64, 65, 231, 235, 237

Tower of London, 93, 186, 293, 383

Tractatus De Amore (André): quoted, 157; discussed, 162–164; mentioned, 167, 184, 210, 249, 263, 335, 385

Trifels, castle of, 306

Tripoli, 43, 54, 61, 66, 68, 209

Tripoli, Count of, 65, 67

Tristram, story of, 86, 87, 100, 165; quoted, 134

Troubadours: on crusade, 39; conventions of, 85–86, 99; mentioned, 5, 163, 385

Truce of God: during crusades, 37, 76, 253, 283, 285, 286, 299, 336, 337; between Henry and young king, 217; between Henry and Philip, 232, 234, 235, 236; Richard's, 265; between Philip and Richard, 275

Turpenay, Abbé of, 246, 342

Tusculum, 14, 70, 74, 82, 386

Tyre, 62, 181, 269, 272, 275, 276, 278, 280, 281

Tyre, Archbishop of, 232, 235

Urban III, Pope, 232, 233, 240

Urraca of Castile, 359, 361

Vaucouleurs, 307, 312, 313

Vaudreuil, 326, 381

Venice, 11, 57, 301

Ventadour, Countess of, 85

Vermandois, Count of, 23, 27, 386

Verneuil, 182, 325, 326, 327, 331

Vexin, the: Henry's campaigns in, 91; Marguerite's dower, 106, 111; mentioned, 22, 78, 105, 192, 227, 228, 237, 244, 273, 302, 331, 334, 337, 338, 357, 369, 380, 381

Vézelay: crusade council at, 33; bull of, 37, 38, 39; church of, 131; mentioned, 35, 38, 50, 146, 233, 256, 257, 258, 272, 274, 297, 319

Vidal, Ramón: quoted, 358; mentioned, 385

Vienne river, 105, 130, 214, 219, 245, 328, 353

Vitalis (priest), 142

Viterbo, 32

Vitry, 23, 24, 26, 55, **58**

Vivian, 139, 140, 141

Wace, 100

Wales, 126, 151, 235, 379

Wallingford, 95, 114, 298

Walter, Hubert, Archbishop of Canterbury: as Bishop of Salisbury on third crusade, 270, 282, 302, 306, 309, 312; and Richard's death, 344, 348–49; and Joanna Plantagenet, 354; mentioned, 323, 327, 381

Warenne, Earl of, 309

Wells, Archdeacon of, 222

Westminster Abbey, 92, 143, 156, 252, 364

Westminster, court of, 93, 98, 103, 117, 143, 185, 249

White Ship, the, 30, 92, 184

William, Earl of Salisbury, 152

William, King of Scotland, 76, 181, 185, 187, 322

William, King of Sicily, 132, 190, 232, 259, 260, 265, 329

William of Malmesbury: quoted, 170

William of Newburgh: cited, 34, 77, 186–87, 220, 306; quoted, 171, 202, 254, 310, 319

William of Pavia, 132, 133

William of Saint Mary l'Église, 306

William of Tyre: cited, 31, 54, 60, 62, 67, 68; quoted, 65, 72, 201

William the Conqueror, 84, 88, 121, 188, 195, 208, 245, 251, 253, 290, 334, 373

Winchester, palace of: Henry's fresco in, 170, 289, 324; Easter court at, 190; mentioned, 92, 95, 114, 115, 146, 147, 189, 191, 192, 195, 198, 227, 248, 298, 323, 383

Windsor Castle, 235, 292, 298

Woodstock, palace of, 95, 151, 152, 192, 197

Worcester, Bishop of, 142, 144

Worms, 312, 313, 314, 315, 317

Harvard University Press is a member of Green Press Initiative (greenpressinitiative.org), a nonprofit organization working to help publishers and printers increase their use of recycled paper and decrease their use of fiber derived from endangered forests. This book was printed on 100% recycled paper containing 50% post-consumer waste and processed chlorine free.